CELEBRATING Z YEARS

ZAGAT SURVEY

Back in 1979, we never imagined that an idea born during a wine-fueled dinner with friends would take us on an adventure that's lasted three decades – and counting.

The idea – that the collective opinions of avid consumers can be more accurate than the judgments of an individual critic – led to a hobby involving friends rating NYC restaurants. And that hobby grew into Zagat Survey, which today has over 350,000 participants worldwide weighing in on everything from airlines, bars, dining and golf to hotels, movies, shopping, tourist attractions and more.

By giving consumers a voice, we – and our surveyors – had unwittingly joined a revolution whose concepts (user-generated content, social networking) were largely unknown 30 years ago. However, those concepts caught fire with the rise of the Internet and have since transformed not only restaurant criticism but also virtually every aspect of the media, and we feel lucky to have been at the start of it all.

And that wasn't the only revolution we happily stumbled into. Our first survey was published as a revolution began to reshape the culinary landscape. Thanks to a host of converging trends – the declining supremacy of old-school formal restaurants; the growing sophistication of diners; the availability of ever-more diverse cuisines and techniques; the improved range and quality of ingredients; the rise of chefs as rock stars – dining out has never been better or more exciting, and we've been privileged to witness its progress through the eyes of our surveyors. And it's still going strong.

As we celebrate Zagat's 30th year, we'd like to thank everyone who has participated in our surveys. We've enjoyed hearing and sharing your frank opinions and look forward to doing so for many years to come. As we always say, our guides and online content are really "yours."

We'd also like to express our gratitude by supporting **Action Against Hunger,** an organization that works to meet the needs of the hungry in over 40 countries. To find out more, visit www.zagat.com/action.

Nina and Tim

Nina and Tim Zagat

ZAGAT®
CELEBRATING 30 YEARS

Texas
Restaurants
2009

LOCAL EDITORS
Claudia Alarcón, Mike Riccetti, Julia Celeste Rosenfeld and Kay Winzenried

STAFF EDITOR
Michelle Golden

Published and distributed by
Zagat Survey, LLC
4 Columbus Circle
New York, NY 10019
T: 212.977.6000
E: texas@zagat.com
www.zagat.com

ACKNOWLEDGMENTS

We thank Teresa Byrne-Dodge, Valerie Jarvie and Steven Shukow, as well as the following members of our staff: Caitlin Eichelberger (assistant editor), Aleksandra Shander (editorial assistant), Brian Albert, Sean Beachell, Maryanne Bertollo, Jane Chang, Sandy Cheng, Reni Chin, Larry Cohn, Alison Flick, Jeff Freier, Andrew Gelardi, Justin Hartung, Roy Jacob, Garth Johnston, Ashunta Joseph, Cynthia Kilian, Natalie Lebert, Mike Liao, Dave Makulec, Andre Pilette, Kimberly Rosado, Becky Ruthenburg, Jacqueline Wasilczyk, Sharon Yates, Anna Zappia and Kyle Zolner.

The reviews in this guide are based on public opinion surveys. The ratings reflect the average scores given by the survey participants who voted on each establishment. The text is based on quotes from, or paraphrasings of, the surveyors' comments. Phone numbers, addresses and other factual data were correct to the best of our knowledge when published in this guide.

Contents

Ratings & Symbols

Zagat Top Spot	Name	Symbols	Cuisine	Zagat Ratings			
				FOOD	DECOR	SERVICE	COST

Area, Address & Contact

Z Tim & Nina's ◑ *BBQ*

∇ 23 | 9 | 13 | $15

Downtown | 1000 E. Salinas St. (Cecilia St.) |
210-555-1234 | www.zagat.com

Review, surveyor comments in quotes

"Deep in the heart of" Downtown, this "quirky winner" may be short on decor, but it's staffed by "hardworking folks" serving a "veggie version" of Texas BBQ, including a "to-die-for beet brisket sandwich" – though insiders insist it's the "outrageously delicious chicken-fried cabbage" that's "the lone star of the menu"; P.S. remember the "à la mode" for your parsnip-tofu cream pie.

Ratings

Food, Decor and **Service** are rated on the Zagat 0 to 30 scale.

0	–	9	poor to fair
10	–	15	fair to good
16	–	19	good to very good
20	–	25	very good to excellent
26	–	30	extraordinary to perfection
∇			low response | less reliable

Cost

Our surveyors' benchmark estimate of the price of a dinner with one drink and tip. Lunch is usually 25 to 30% less. For **newcomers** or survey **write-ins** listed without ratings, the price range is shown as follows:

I	$25 and below	E	$41 to $65
M	$26 to $40	VE	$66 or more

Symbols

Z	highest ratings, popularity and importance
◑	serves after 11 PM
S	closed on Sunday
M	closed on Monday
⊄	no credit cards accepted

About This Survey

This **2009 Texas Restaurants Survey** is an update reflecting significant developments since our last Survey was published. It covers 1,600 restaurants in the state, including 107 important additions. We've also indicated new addresses, phone numbers, chef changes and other major alterations to bring this guide up to the minute.

WHO PARTICIPATED: Input from 5,039 avid local diners forms the basis for the ratings and reviews in this guide (their comments are shown in quotation marks within the reviews). Collectively they bring roughly 1,050,000 annual meals' worth of experience to this Survey. We sincerely thank these participants – this book is really "theirs."

HELPFUL LISTS: Our top lists can help you find exactly the right place for any occasion. See Austin (pages 11–16), Dallas/Ft. Worth (pages 84–90), Houston (pages 191–198) and San Antonio (pages 295–300). We've also provided 127 handy indexes.

OUR EDITORS: Special thanks go to our local editors, Claudia Alarcón, a contributor to various Austin-area publications; Mike Riccetti, author of *Houston Dining on the Cheap*; Julia Celeste Rosenfeld, the dining writer for *San Antonio Magazine*; and Kay Winzenried, a culinary/wine travel consultant and freelance writer.

ABOUT ZAGAT: This marks our 30th year reporting on the shared experiences of consumers like you. What started in 1979 as a hobby has come a long way. Today we have over 350,000 surveyors and now cover airlines, bars, dining, entertaining, fast food, golf, hotels, movies, music, resorts, shopping, spas, theater and tourist attractions in over 100 countries.

INTERACTIVE: Up-to-the-minute news about restaurant openings plus menus, photos and more are free on **ZAGAT.com** and the award-winning **ZAGAT.mobi** (for web-enabled mobile devices). They also enable reserving at thousands of places with just one click.

VOTE AND COMMENT: We invite you to join any of our surveys at **ZAGAT.com.** There you can rate and review establishments year-round. In exchange for doing so, you'll receive a free copy of the resulting guide when published.

AVAILABILITY: Zagat guides are available in all major bookstores as well as on **ZAGAT.com.** You can also access our content when on the go via **ZAGAT.mobi** and **ZAGAT TO GO** (for smartphones).

FEEDBACK: There is always room for improvement, thus we invite your comments about any aspect of our performance. Did we miss anything? Just contact us at **texas@zagat.com.**

New York, NY
March 4, 2009

Nina and Tim

Nina and Tim Zagat

What's New

The restaurant industry in Texas – like just about everywhere else – has taken a hit from the country's current financial turmoil. But with restaurateurs increasingly looking to cater to a more value-focused public, diners can find a glimmer of a silver lining in the economic storm clouds. And there's no shortage of new openings to keep things interesting.

AUSTIN RESHUFFLES: Though it's home to one of the state's most varied and vibrant dining scenes, Austin hasn't been immune to the effects of tough economic times. Long-standing favorites like Cibo, Mars and Stortini closed their doors, while many others are adjusting prices or adding specials – such as happy hours and two-for-one dinners – to remain competitive. At press time, Doña Emilia's changed its name to **Latin Café Austin,** and is now serving a pared-down South American menu with equally pared-down prices, while tony **Aquarelle** offers half-price appetizers on its bar menu. Also catering to those pinching their pennies are the new spate of refurbished trailers dishing up interesting edibles – like **Lulu B's** Vietnamese street snacks and **Torchy's** offbeat tacos – at modest prices. Likewise, casual wine bars serving inventive small plates are flourishing with the additions of **Grove, Mulberry, Taste Select Wines** and **Uncorked,** attracting Austinites seeking a sip and a nibble for less than the cost of a full meal. Meanwhile, entrepreneurs continue to open ambitious new restaurants apace, as evidenced by noteworthy destinations like **Olivia, Parkside** and the spectacularly revamped **Paggi House.** Up next: perennial Japanese favorite **Uchi** will spawn a satellite in Central Austin, and chef Larry McGuire of **Lambert's** fame is readying two SoCo spots – **Perla's Seafood & Oyster Bar** and **La Condesa,** a modern Mexican outfit.

DALLAS AND FT. WORTH DELIVER: Economic upheavals haven't derailed plans for the much-anticipated relighting of Dallas' Reunion Tower orb and the arrival of Wolfgang Puck's latest – the revolving fine-dining venue **Five-Sixty** – which will serve his Asian-inflected cooking from its perch 560 feet above street level starting in early 2009. Also on the horizon: **Hully & Mo,** the Uptown taproom from Dallas Stars hockey legends Brett Hull and Mike Modano, and Stephan Pyles' Downtown tapas haunt, **Samar.** Megadevelopment projects like Victory Park and Watters Creek – all planned during the commercial real-estate boom – continue to flourish. Although national chains like **The Cheesecake Factory** are critical components of these projects, home-grown entries like soba house **Tei An** and upscale Southerner **Screen Door** – both at the new One Arts Plaza complex – are staking out their share of the territory. Similarly, in Ft. Worth: an outpost of the quirky **Tillman's Roadhouse** is slated for the Seventh Street development near the Arts District next summer. Meanwhile, the sushi tsunami continues with newcomer **Sushi Axiom** plus forthcoming expansions for **Shinsei** and **Yutaka.** And health-conscious diners are finding solace south of the Trinity River at **Bolsa,** a hip, organic cafe, and **Spiral Diner,** a vegan transplant from Ft. Worth. But while sushi and sustainability were big buzzwords in early 2008, many diners this year are retreating to familiar favorites, hence the pizza craze at **Brix, Fireside Pies** and **Grimaldi's.**

HOUSTON HOLDS STEADY: Hurricane Ike, which blew ashore mid-September, had a significant effect on Houston's restaurant

economy, ushering in a number closures, most notably the historic Brennan's, a Vieux Carré–like landmark since 1967. Struggling eateries like Rouge and Café Malay also closed in the storm's aftermath, while popular mainstay **Ruggles Grill** remains temporarily shuttered due to structural damage. Still, new restaurants outnumbered the losses. **Voice,** one of the year's most eagerly awaited arrivals, made a splash in Downtown's Hotel Icon with chef Michael Kramer's innovative American cooking, while the modern British **Feast** rewards intrepid diners with the likes of pork cheeks and black pudding. The Heights area – once a restaurant wasteland – continued to heat up with ambitious efforts from Robert Gadsby (ex **Noé**) and Scott Tycer (**Gravitas**), who opened New Americans **Bedford** and **Textile,** respectively. Meanwhile, Lower Westheimer near Montrose has blossomed into a late-night nexus with Cajun **BB's,** the recently relocated Greek **One's A Meal** and burger haven **Little Bigs** (from the folks at **Reef**) joining **Katz's Deli** to offer eats into the wee hours, something that's long been missing in the city.

SAN ANTONIO SHIFTS GEARS: Despite the many decades of Tex-Mex domination, this year San Antonio saw the arrival of several sophisticated new Europeans like **Luca,** serving wood-fired pizzas and boutique wines, and **Tre Trattoria,** where chef Jason Dady (**Bin 555**) turns out artisanal charcuterie and rustic Italian dishes. Joining them soon is **Il Sogno** from chef Andrew Weissman, bringing Roman cooking to the revitalized Pearl Brewery complex. Continuing the city's northward expansion, several inner-circle institutions have headed to the outer stretch of Loop 1604 to follow the housing growth. Damien Watel built his own complex in Stone Oak to accommodate **Ciel** and **Ciao2** – offshoots of existing hot spots **Bistro Vatel** and **Ciao Lavanderia** in Olmos Park. **Frederick's** Asian-French fusion in Alamo Heights begat **Frederick's Bistro** near Shavano Park, while chef Scott Cohen opened the doors at **Brasserie Pavil,** which warms suburban souls with its Parisian vibe and cooking. In both the outer reaches of the city and Downtown, bargain prix fixe deals popped up in venues like the **Grill at Leon Springs** and **Bistro Thyme II,** but the question remains: will the area's influx of midrange national chains like **Maggiano's Little Italy** and **Mimi's Café** deal a strong blow to independents struggling for a share of shrinking diner wallets? Indeed, there have already been closings across the price spectrum, from the upscale Café Paladar to the more affordable Eclipse Café. And though generations were weaned on tortillas at Karam's Mexican Dining Room, it shut its doors last summer. Nevertheless, San Antonio's robust tourist and convention traffic, relatively healthy business climate and love of a good time keep many tables filled.

THE BOTTOM LINE: Though Dallas diners spend an average of $34.61 per meal – about equal to the national average of $34.03 – tabs are cheaper in Austin ($26.74), Houston ($29.10) and San Antonio ($27.33). Perhaps that's why Texans eat out so often, especially Houstonites, leading the country with 4.2 restaurant meals out per week.

Austin, TX
Dallas, TX
Houston, TX
San Antonio, TX
March 4, 2009

Claudia Alarcón
Kay Winzenried
Mike Riccetti
Julia Celeste Rosenfeld

AUSTIN
AND THE
HILL COUNTRY

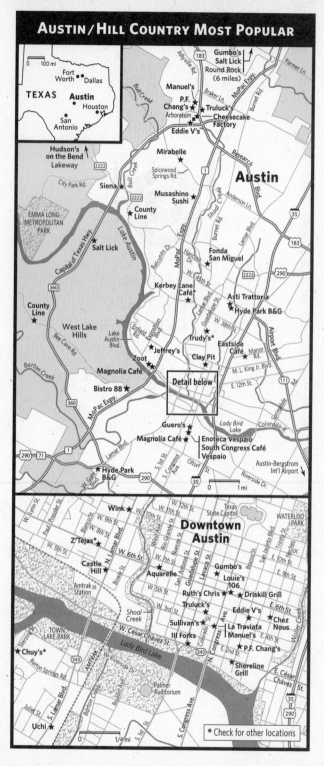

AUSTIN/HILL COUNTRY MOST POPULAR

TEXAS

Fort Worth • • Dallas

Austin •
Houston •

San Antonio •

Gumbo's
Salt Lick
Round Rock
(6 miles)

Manuel's ★

P.F. Chang's ★
Arboretum ★ ★ Truluck's

★ ★ Cheesecake Factory

Eddie V's ★

Mirabelle ★

Hudson's
on the Bend
Lakeway

Austin

Spicewood
Springs Rd.

Siena ★

County Line ★

Musashino Sushi ★

EMMA LONG METROPOLITAN PARK

Salt Lick ★

Fonda San Miguel ★

Kerbey Lane Café ★

Asti Trattoria ★
Hyde Park B&G ★

County Line ★

West Lake Hills

Trudy's ★

Eastside Café ★

Jeffrey's ★

Clay Pit ★

Zoot ★

Magnolia Café ★

Bistro 88 ★

Detail below

Guero's ★

Magnolia Café ★ — Enoteca Vespaio
South Congress Café
Vespaio

Hyde Park B&G ★

Austin-Bergstrom
Int'l Airport →

Wink ★

Texas State Capitol

Downtown Austin

WATERLOO PARK

Z'Tejas ★

Castle Hill ★

Gumbo's ★

Louie's 106 ★

Aquarelle ★

Amtrak Station

Ruth's Chris ★ ★ Driskill Grill

Truluck's ★

Eddie V's ★

La Traviata
Manuel's ★

TOWN LAKE PARK

Sullivan's ★

Chez Nous ★

III Forks ★

★ P.F. Chang's

Chuy's ★

Shoreline Grill ★

Palmer Auditorium

Uchi ★

***** Check for other locations**

Most Popular

1. Vespaio | *Italian*
2. Eddie V's | *Seafood/Steak*
3. Chuy's | *Tex-Mex*
4. Uchi | *Japanese*
5. Salt Lick | *BBQ*
6. Fonda San Miguel | *Mexican*
7. Wink | *American*
8. Driskill Grill | *American*
9. Hudson's on the Bend | *Amer.*
10. Clay Pit | *Indian*
11. Z'Tejas | *Southwestern*
12. Chez Nous | *French*
13. Jeffrey's | *American/Continental*
14. Trudy's | *Tex-Mex*
15. Kerbey Ln. Café | *Eclectic*
16. Aquarelle | *French*
17. P.F. Chang's | *Chinese*
18. County Line | *BBQ*
19. Siena | *Italian*
20. Hyde Park B&G | *American*
21. Guero's | *Mexican*
22. III Forks | *Steak*
23. Truluck's* | *Seafood*
24. Asti Trattoria | *Italian*
25. Eastside Café* | *Amer./Eclectic*
26. Gumbo's | *Cajun/Creole*
27. Mirabelle* | *American*
28. Manuel's | *Mexican*
29. Cheesecake Factory | *American*
30. Enoteca Vespaio* | *Italian*
31. Louie's 106 | *Mediterranean*
32. Musashino* | *Japanese*
33. La Traviata | *Italian*
34. Magnolia Café* | *American*
35. Shoreline Grill | *Continental*
36. South Congress Café* | *SW*
37. Bistro 88 | *Asian/European*
38. Zoot | *American*
39. Ruth's Chris | *Steak*
40. Sullivan's | *Steak*

It's obvious that many of the above restaurants are among the Austin area's most expensive, but if popularity were calibrated to price, we suspect that a number of other restaurants would join their ranks. Thus, we have added two lists comprising 40 Best Buys on page 16.

KEY NEWCOMERS

Our editors' take on the year's top arrivals. See page 70 for a full list.

Cissi's Mkt. | *Deli*

Fion Bistro | *American*

Grove | *American*

Maria Maria | *Mexican*

Olivia | *French/Italian*

Paggi House | *American*

Parkside | *American*

Sazón | *Mexican*

Steiner Ranch | *Steak*

Taste Select Wines | *American*

Uncorked | *Eclectic*

Wine Cellar | *American*

* Indicates a tie with restaurant above

Top Food Ratings

Excludes places with low votes.

28 Uchi | *Japanese*
Hudson's on the Bend | *American*
Vespaio | *Italian*

27 Wink | *American*
TRIO | *American*
Cooper's | *BBQ*
Musashino | *Japanese*
Aquarelle | *French*

26 Fonda San Miguel | *Mexican*
Driskill Grill | *American*
Eddie V's | *Seafood/Steak*
Zoot | *American*
Kreuz Mkt. | *BBQ*
Jeffrey's | *American/Continental*
Café Josie | *Caribbean*

25 Enoteca Vespaio | *Italian*
Tacodeli | *Mexican*
Louie Mueller | *BBQ*
Chez Nous | *French*
Ruth's Chris | *Steak*

Bistro 88 | *Asian/European*
Mirabelle | *American*
Roy's | *Hawaiian*
Siena | *Italian*
Starlite | *American*
III Forks | *Steak*

24 Gumbo's | *Cajun/Creole*
Jasper's | *American*
Eastside Café | *Amer./Eclectic*
Roaring Fork | *Southwestern*
Salt Lick | *BBQ*
Southside Mkt. | *BBQ*
Shoreline Grill | *Continental*
Louie's 106 | *Mediterranean*
Fleming's | *Steak*
Sullivan's | *Steak*
Asti Trattoria | *Italian*
Din Ho | *Chinese*
Judges' Hill | *American*
La Traviata | *Italian*

BY CUISINE

AMERICAN (NEW)

28 Hudson's on the Bend
27 Wink
TRIO
26 Driskill Grill
Zoot

AMERICAN (TRAD.)

23 Houston's
22 1886 Café
21 Magnolia Café
Dirty Martin's
Hyde Park B&G

BARBECUE

27 Cooper's
26 Kreuz Mkt.
25 Louie Mueller
24 Salt Lick
Southside Mkt.

ITALIAN

28 Vespaio
25 Enoteca Vespaio
24 Asti Trattoria
La Traviata
23 Taverna Pizzeria

MEXICAN

26 Fonda San Miguel
25 Tacodeli
22 El Chile
Manuel's
21 Curra's Grill

SEAFOOD

26 Eddie V's
23 Pappadeaux
Truluck's
Finn & Porter
21 McCormick & Schmick's

SOUTHWESTERN

24 Roaring Fork
23 Ranch 616
22 South Congress Café
Z'Tejas
19 Cool River Cafe

STEAKHOUSES

26 Eddie V's
25 Ruth's Chris
III Forks
24 Fleming's
Sullivan's

TEX-MEX

21	Chuy's
20	Trudy's
19	Vivo
18	Matt's El Rancho
	Hula Hut

BY SPECIAL FEATURE

BREAKFAST

24	Judges' Hill
22	1886 Café
21	Magnolia Café
	Curra's Grill
	Taco Xpress

BRUNCH

26	Fonda San Miguel
25	Enoteca Vespaio
24	Eastside Café
	Judges' Hill
23	Green Pastures

BUSINESS DINING

28	Uchi
	Hudson's on the Bend
27	Musashino
	Aquarelle
24	Jasper's

CHILD-FRIENDLY

24	Eastside Café
	Salt Lick
	Din Ho
23	Hilltop Café
	Ruby's

MEET FOR A DRINK

28	Vespaio
27	TRIO
26	Eddie V's
25	Starlite
24	Jasper's

OFFBEAT

23	Ranch 616
	Hut's
21	Magnolia Café
	Taco Xpress
	Chuy's

PEOPLE-WATCHING

25	Chez Nous
23	Home Slice
22	1886 Café

	Z'Tejas
21	Frank & Angie's

POWER SCENES

27	TRIO
26	Driskill Grill
	Eddie V's
25	Ruth's Chris
24	Jasper's

QUICK BITES

27	Cooper's
26	Kreuz Mkt.
25	Louie Mueller
24	Southside Mkt.
23	Home Slice

QUIET CONVERSATION

27	Aquarelle
26	Driskill Grill
	Zoot
	Jeffrey's
25	Chez Nous

SINGLES SCENES

26	Eddie V's
24	Sullivan's
23	Finn & Porter
22	South Congress Café
21	Chuy's

TRENDY

28	Uchi
	Vespaio
27	Wink
	TRIO
26	Eddie V's

WINNING WINE LISTS

28	Hudson's on the Bend
	Vespaio
27	Wink
	Aquarelle
26	Driskill Grill

BY LOCATION

ARBORETUM

26	Eddie V's
23	Truluck's
22	Carrabba's
	P.F. Chang's
	Z'Tejas

CAMPUS/ WEST CAMPUS

24	Judges' Hill
23	Fino
21	Dirty Martin's
	Madam Mam's
20	Kerbey Ln. Café

CHERRYWOOD/ EAST AUSTIN

24	Eastside Café
22	El Chile
21	Hoover's
19	Vivo

CLARKSVILLE/ OLD WEST AUSTIN

27	Wink
26	Zoot
	Jeffrey's
	Café Josie
22	Z'Tejas

DOWNTOWN

27	TRIO
	Aquarelle
26	Driskill Grill
	Eddie V's
25	Chez Nous

NW AUSTIN/NW HILLS

27	Musashino
25	Tacodeli
	Mirabelle
	Siena
24	Jasper's

SOUTH CONGRESS (SOCO)

28	Vespaio
25	Enoteca Vespaio
23	Home Slice
22	South Congress Café
21	Magnolia Café

WAREHOUSE DISTRICT

25	Starlite
24	Sullivan's
23	Truluck's
22	Kenichi
21	219 West

WEST LAKE HILLS

25	Bistro 88
21	Las Palomas
20	County Line
	Thai Kitchen
19	Suzi's

ZILKER

28	Uchi
21	Chuy's
19	Shady Grove
18	Green Mesquite
17	Romeo's

Top Decor Ratings

27	Fonda San Miguel	Hudson's on the Bend
	Siena	III Forks
	Driskill Grill	Eddie V's
26	Uchi	Fino
		Oasis
25	Jasper's	Belmont
	Judges' Hill	TRIO
	Green Pastures	1886 Café
24	Shoreline Grill	Roy's
	Aquarelle	Fleming's
	Roaring Fork	

OUTDOORS

Fino	NoRTH
Grove	Shady Grove
Jasper's	Shoreline Grill
Joe DiMaggio's	Trattoria Lisina
Moonshine	TRIO

ROMANCE

Aquarelle	Sagra
Bess	Shoreline Grill
Carmelo's	Siena
Chez Nous	Starlite
Driskill Grill	Zoot

ROOMS

Aquarelle	Joe DiMaggio's
Belmont	Judges' Hill
Bess	Ranch 616
Driskill Grill	Siena
Fonda San Miguel	Woodland

VIEWS

County Line	Salt Lick
Eddie V's	Shoreline Grill
Hilltop Café	Trattoria Lisina
Hula Hut	TRIO
Oasis	Z'Tejas

Top Service Ratings

26 Hudson's on the Bend	**24** Vespaio
Driskill Grill	Fonda San Miguel
Jeffrey's	Green Pastures
Wink	III Forks
TRIO	Shoreline Grill
25 Uchi	Louie's 106
Zoot*	Jasper's
Eddie V's	Mirabelle
Ruth's Chris	
Aquarelle	**23** Roaring Fork
	Sullivan's

Best Buys

In order of Bang for the Buck rating.

1. Tacodeli	11. Home Slice
2. Taco Xpress	12. Kreuz Mkt.
3. Dirty Martin's	13. Golden Wok
4. Hut's	14. Magnolia Café
5. Player's	15. Shady Grove
6. Texas Chili	16. Kerbey Ln. Café
7. Mangieri's	17. Pei Wei
8. Meyer's	18. Chuy's
9. Ruby's BBQ	19. El Sol y La Luna
10. Frank & Angie's	20. Iron Works

OTHER GOOD VALUES

Alborz	Gypsy Italian Bistro
Chez Nous	Hoover's
Din Ho	Korea House
El Azteca	Oaxacan Tamaleo
El Chile	Opal Divine's
El Mesón	Quality Seafood
Elsi's	Sunflower
Evangeline Café	Ventana
Flip Happy Crepes	Whip-In Parlour
Gene's	Zax Pints

Austin and the Hill Country

	FOOD	DECOR	SERVICE	COST

Abuelo's *Mexican*
19 | 21 | 19 | $21

Southwest Austin | Barton Creek Square Mall | 2901 Capital of Texas Hwy. (MoPac Expwy.) | 512-306-0857 | www.abuelos.com

A "cut above" is how fans sum up this "better-than-typical chain Mexican" offering a few "unique items" along with the standards; some say the service is "hit-or-miss", but their "atmosphere is nicer than most" examples of the genre, with many branches boasting "interesting artwork" "for your viewing pleasure."

Alborz *Persian*
21 | 13 | 18 | $19

Northwest Austin | Shoal Creek Plaza | 3300 W. Anderson Ln. (MoPac Expwy.) | 512-420-2222 | www.alborzpersiancuisine.com

The "authentic menu" of "delightfully different" Persian cuisine "with a focus on wonderfully spiced vegetable dishes" is "nicely served" by a "friendly staff" at this "relaxing spot" in Northwest Austin; perhaps the ambiance "isn't great" due to the "strip-mall location", but many "enjoy" the "tantalizing" scenery offered by the "occasional belly dancer" (Friday and Saturday evenings).

Andiamo Ⓢ *Italian*
- | - | - | M

North Austin | 2521 Rutland Dr. (Burnet Rd.) | 512-719-3377 | www.andiamoitaliano.com

Hidden away in a North Austin strip mall, this midpriced Italian eatery serves from an ample menu featuring classics like linguini with clam sauce as well as house creations like salmon-wrapped scallops, all at fair prices; lace curtains, white linens and pastel walls create a quaint atmosphere, while a doting staff adds an equally homey touch.

Aquarelle Ⓜ *French*
27 | 24 | 25 | $58

Downtown | 606 Rio Grande St. (6th St.) | 512-479-8117 | www.aquarellerestaurant.com

"Set in a lovely cottage", this "family-run" Downtown "oasis" is consistently called "the best French restaurant in town" thanks to its "impressive wine list" and "excellent", "creatively prepared and presented food"; add in service that most find "near-perfect" (a few dissenters say "arrogant") and an "upscale, enchanting" vibe, and you've got what may be "hands down the most romantic setting" for "special occasions"; N.B. the adjacent wine bar offers drinks and more affordable bites.

Artz Rib House *BBQ*
21 | 10 | 18 | $18

South Lamar | 2330 S. Lamar Blvd. (Bluebonnet Ln.) | 512-442-8283 | www.artzribhouse.com

"Authentic slow-smoked" meats and "lipsmacking" ribs please the masses at this "quintessential" South Lamar BBQ joint; "never mind the decor" that feels a bit "like a run-down shack" because fair prices, "cold beverages" and "live local music" make for an "enjoyable", "low-key" night out nonetheless.

Asti Trattoria ☒ *Italian*

24 | 19 | 22 | $31

Hyde Park | 408C E. 43rd St. (bet. Ave. H & Duval St.) | 512-451-1218 | www.astiaustin.com

This "happening" Hyde Park "neighborhood trattoria" is "not your grandma's spaghetti and meatballs kind of place", but instead serves an "innovative" menu featuring "organic, locally grown produce" alongside a "fabuloso" wine list, all at a "fair" price; a team of "attentive but not overbearing servers" works the "tiny" room, which is done up in "minimalist", "modern" decor.

August E's *Steak*

▽ 27 | 23 | 24 | $50

Fredericksburg | 203 E. San Antonio St. (S. Llano St.) | 830-997-1585 | www.august-es.com

"Heavenly!" hail acolytes of this "upscale" Fredericksburg "gem" with "succulent steaks that melt in your mouth" and a wine list that's "fantastic"; art on the walls and cream-colored leather seating creates a "lovely" ambiance, which is enhanced by "added touches" like servers who know "the proper way to pamper and make you feel special."

Austin Land & Cattle Co. *Steak*

22 | 17 | 21 | $39

Downtown | 1205 N. Lamar Blvd. (bet. Shoal Creek Blvd. & 12th St.) | 512-472-1813 | www.austinlandandcattlecompany.com

Long "a favorite of politicians and lobbyists", this "authentic Texan steakhouse" strikes supporters as "the real McCoy" – and a "great local" alternative to "chain" restaurants – for its "savory" steaks, "consistent" side dishes (included in the "moderate prices") and "excellent" service; some surveyors find its Downtown location's "old Austin" atmosphere "dated, even by your parents standards", but most maintain it offers "more bang for the buck than the competitors."

Backstage Steakhouse Ⓜ *Steak*

▽ 26 | 18 | 22 | $33

Spicewood | 21814 Hwy. 71 W. (Crawford Rd.) | 512-264-2223 | www.backstagesteakhouseaustin.com

A Hill Country "gem" "in the little town of Spicewood", this "high-quality" Southwestern steakhouse serves "creative, impressive" eats in a "casual setting" manned by a "comfortable, relaxed" crew; regulars "come back for the warmth and the food", ensuring a "laid-back Texas atmosphere" in which "everyone knows everyone else"; P.S. on weekends "be sure to eat outside under the oak tree" and listen to the "cool" "live music."

Bellagio ☒ *Italian*

21 | 19 | 23 | $39

Jester Village | 6507 Jester Blvd. (Rte. 2222) | 512-346-8228 | www.bellagioitalianbistro.com

Located in an "off-the-beaten-path" shopping center, this "upscale" Jester Village trattoria is an "island of Italian bliss in a suburban sea", offering "always consistent" cuisine served by "very attentive" waiters; even detractors who decry the "cramped" dining room that "feels like a senior citizens' home" insist that the staff's "food and wine recommendations make up for the lack in ambiance."

FOOD DECOR SERVICE COST

Belmont, The *American* | 18 | 24 | 18 | $28 |

Downtown | 305 W. Sixth St. (Lavaca St.) | 512-457-0300 |
www.thebelmontaustin.com

"Frank Sinatra would love this place" swoon acolytes of the "retro-cool", "swanky" Downtown "hangout" featuring "rooftop views" and a "sumptuous Rat Pack vibe"; although the midpriced, classic American fare is "pretty good" and "service is knowledgeable", most say that dinner here is "not the main draw" – people come "for cocktails" and to "see and be seen."

Bess *Eclectic* | 17 | 23 | 18 | $32 |

Downtown | 500 W. Sixth St. (San Antonio St.) | 512-477-2377 |
www.bessbistro.com

Sandra Bullock's "basement bistro" is a "Downtown jewel" serving "solid" Eclectic "comfort food" in a "cozy", "dark" and "romantic" setting that's "surprisingly casual and unpretentious"; fans fawn over the "beautiful" decor and "friendly, helpful staff", though a few gripe that it's "a bit noisy", "overpriced" and "popular more because of the famous owner than the food"; P.S. "go at lunch to skip the wait."

Billy's on Burnet ● *American*   ▽ | 20 | 13 | 19 | $14 |

Rosedale | 2105 Hancock Dr. (Burnet Rd.) | 512-407-9305 |
www.billysonburnet.com

"Awesome burgers" plus "creative low-calorie/veggie options" and other affordable American classics are the mainstay at this "great neighborhood bar" and "family-friendly tavern" in Rosedale, where the "patio is full of jovial locals from all walks of life"; though there's "no decor to write home about", it's a "good gathering spot" and a "great place to watch a game" or to "bring your dog and sit outside."

Bistro 88 *Asian/European* | 25 | 20 | 23 | $41 |

West Lake Hills | 2712 Bee Caves Rd. (Edgegrove Dr.) | 512-328-8888 |
www.bistro88.com

"Superior presentation and quality" mark the "interesting" Asian-European fusion menu at this West Lake Hills Asian favorite, featuring a "well-thought-out" wine list; behind its "nondescript strip-center" facade lies an "elegant", "comfortable" interior, presided over by "quick yet personalized" service, so it's no wonder that, despite somewhat "expensive" tabs, most voters vow it's "absolutely wonderful . . . every time."

Blue Star Cafeteria *American* | 20 | 19 | 19 | $20 |

Rosedale | Rosedale Shopping Ctr. | 4800 Burnet Rd. (bet. 47th & 49th Sts.) | 512-454-7827 | www.bluestarcafeteria.com

This "nice neighborhood" eatery in Rosedale is "far from a cafeteria", since "you get table service" and "good affordable American "comfort food with a modern twist"; the staff is "competent" and "friendly", and the "retro" digs are "stylish", just know that the space is "usually crowded", meaning it can get "so loud at peak times that you can't even taste your food."

Brick Oven *Pizza*

| 19 | 14 | 18 | $17 |

Downtown | 1209 Red River St. (12th St.) | 512-477-7006
Great Hills | 10710 Research Blvd. (Braker Ln.) | 512-345-6181
Southwest Austin | 9911 Brodie Ln. (Slaughter Ln.) | 512-292-3939
www.brickovenrestaurant.com

Brick Oven on 35th *Pizza*

Brykerwoods | 1608 W. 35th St. (Glenview Ave.) | 512-453-4330 |
www.brickovenon35th.com

"Tasty pizzas straight from the brick oven" make for "heavenly smells" at this local chain known for its "crispy-crusted" creations; as for the rest of its "basic Italian" fare, most find it "satisfying" (if somewhat "unexciting"), though the "spotty" service has fewer fans.

Buster's Bar-B-Que Ⓜ *BBQ*

| ▽ 24 | 13 | 20 | $15 |

Bee Cave | 3927 R.R. 620 S. (Rte. 71) | 512-263-3999 |
www.bustersbeecavebbq.com

Set inside an "old VFW hall" in Bee Cave, this unpretentious joint serves "innovative BBQ dishes" and "some of the best brisket in Central Texas"; prices are cheap, while tables dressed in red-and-white checked oilcloth add to the "authentic atmosphere."

Café Josie Ⓢ Ⓜ *Caribbean*

| .26 | 20 | 23 | $34 |

Clarksville | Pecan Sq. | 1200 W. Sixth St. (Blanco Rd.) | 512-322-9226 |
www.cafejosie.com

This "locally owned" "hidden gem" in Clarksville serves up "wonderful Caribbean creations" including "some of the best-dressed fish in town" and a "reasonable, eclectic wine list"; add in its "relaxing, slow-paced" atmosphere and "intimate", "beautiful space", and you get a "sublime blend" of food and decor, further complemented by "very good service."

Cantina Laredo *Mexican*

| 21 | 20 | 20 | $23 |

Downtown | 201 W. Third St. (Colorado St.) | 512-542-9670 |
www.cantinalaredo.com
See review in Dallas/Ft. Worth Directory.

Carmelo's *Italian*

| 22 | 22 | 22 | $35 |

Downtown | 504 E. Fifth St. (Red River St.) | 512-477-7497 |
www.carmelosrestaurant.com

The "smell of roasting garlic pervades the air" at this "family-owned" West Houston and Downtown Austin midpriced duo where "exquisitely prepared" "old-school" Italian cookery is served by a "very attentive" staff; the "romantic ambiance" is enhanced by "soft lighting" and live accordion music on some nights, making them a prime choice for "special occasions", "business lunches", "date-night dinners" or "to share an evening with a friend – or several friends."

Carrabba's Italian Grill *Italian*

| 22 | 19 | 22 | $28 |

Arboretum | 6406 I-35 N. (bet. Koenig Ln. & Research Blvd.) |
512-419-1220
North Austin | 11590 Research Blvd. (Duval Rd.) | 512-345-8232
www.carrabbas.com
See review in Houston Directory.

	FOOD	DECOR	SERVICE	COST

Cedar Grove Steakhouse Ⓜ *Steak* | - | - | - | M |

Wimberley | 9595 R.R. 12 (R.R. 32) | 512-847-3113 |
www.cedargrovesteakhouse.com

Fans toast this "fun and quirky" Wimberley Steakhouse as "one of
the best, if not the best, in the Austin area" thanks to its "terrific
food", "laid-back" vibe, and limestone building and terraces that
scream 'Texas!'; the aged prime steaks are cut in-house to guarantee quality, and are matched with serious sides and wines from an
affordable, full-of-surprises list; N.B. open Thursdays–Sundays.

Cheesecake Factory *American* | 20 | 20 | 18 | $26 |

Arboretum | Arboretum Mall | 10000 Research Blvd.
(bet. Capital of Texas Hwy. & Great Hills Trail) | 512-241-0777 |
www.thecheesecakefactory.com

See review in Houston Directory.

Chez Nous Ⓜ *French* | 25 | 18 | 22 | $33 |

Downtown | 510 Neches St. (6th St.) | 512-473-2413 |
www.cheznousaustin.com

A "favorite" for over 25 years, this "tiny" Downtown French "keep-
sake", "run by true Parisians", offers "classic bistro food" and a
"cleverly selected" wine list at "awesome prices" (including a "wonderful prix fixe deal"); "friendly, casual" waiters with accents over-
see the "unpretentious" digs, where the decor may be "lacking", but
still, there's always a "very vibrant, cozy vibe."

Chez Zee American Bistro *American* | 21 | 20 | 20 | $26 |

Northwest Hills | 5406 Balcones Dr. (Rte. 2222) | 512-454-2666 |
www.chezzee.com

"Zee best combination of quality" eats, "fair prices" and "warm service" is how supporters sum up this "attractive" "haunt" in the
Northwest Hills, "a fun family place" that's "great for groups" of any
variety thanks to a "festive" feel and "reliable" New American menu;
it's especially "popular for brunch" on the weekends, but whenever
you go be sure to "save room for" the "marvelous desserts."

Ⓩ Chuy's *Tex-Mex* | 21 | 19 | 19 | $18 |

North Austin | 10520 N. Lamar Blvd. (Meadows Dr.) |
512-836-3218
North Austin | 11680 Research Blvd. (Duval Rd.) | 512-342-0011
Round Rock | 2320 I-35 N. (Old Settlers Blvd.) | 512-255-2211
South Austin | Shops at Arbor Trails | 4301 William Cannon
(MoPac Expwy.) | 512-899-2489
Zilker | 1728 Barton Springs Rd. (Lamar Blvd.) | 512-474-4452
www.chuys.com

"Gargantuan" plates of "tasty" Tex-Mex fare come with a side of
"kitsch" at this "lovable" "local" chain where "funky" "Elvis-
obsessed" decor and "awesome margaritas" add to the "playful" atmosphere; in spite of "interminable waits", "cheap" prices make it a
"favorite of university students", "singles" and "families" alike;
P.S. the Zilker branch in Austin was "the site of the Bush daughters'
underage drinking snafu."

NEW Cissi's Market *Deli*

| - | - | - | M |

SoCo | 1400 S. Congress Ave. (Gibson St.) | 512-225-0521 |
www.cissismarket.com

What started as a SoCo neighborhood market and gourmet deli has
evolved into this full-service wine bar featuring a seasonal menu of
French-tinged small plates set down in a bright, glass-walled modern building; despite its high-style makeover, it's still a popular all-
day stop for coffee, pastries and sandwiches on the go.

City Market 🗷🖘 *BBQ*

| ▽ 24 | 8 | 13 | $15 |

Luling | 633 E. Davis St. (Magnolia St.) | 830-875-9019

A true "landmark" that's considered "Luling's claim to fame", this
"BBQ mecca" is a "foodie wonderland" thanks to its "glorious sausage, ribs and brisket"; there's "no service" since you "order at the
counter", and the "old general store" environs aren't much to look
at, but still aficionados are willing to "fight any man who doesn't
think this is Texas' best BBQ."

Clay Pit: Contemporary Indian Cuisine *Indian*

| 23 | 20 | 19 | $25 |

Downtown | 1601 Guadalupe St. (16th St.) | 512-322-5131 |
www.claypit.com

"Traditional" Indian dishes are prepared with "modern" (some say
"Americanized") "twists" at these "upscale" eateries where the "extensive wine and cocktail list" and "friendly", if sometimes "haphazard" service makes for an "overall satisfying experience"; the
Addison branch features a waterwall and a dining room draped in
saris, while the separately owned Downtown Austin outpost is
housed in a "cool", "historic" building; the "reasonably priced lunch
buffet" reigns at both locations.

Cool River Cafe *Southwestern/Steak*

| 19 | 21 | 20 | $38 |

Northwest Austin | 4001 W. Parmer Ln. (Amherst Dr.) | 512-835-0010 |
www.coolrivercafe.com

"Part restaurant, part singles pickup joint", this upscale Southwestern
steakhouse chain is a "meat market in more ways than one" – thanks,
no doubt, to the presence of a "loud and hopping bar" with cigar
room, pool tables, live music (Thursday–Saturday) and "pretty people galore"; though "too pricey for everyday eating", the "great",
"original food" is "actually a highlight", as it's "creatively and well
prepared, while still managing to be hearty in size."

Cooper's Old Time Pit Bar-B-Que *BBQ*

| 27 | 11 | 17 | $17 |

Llano | 604 W. Young St. (Ashley Ave.) | 325-247-5713 |
www.coopersbbq.com

Look for the "smoke rising" and you'll know you're close to this
"huge" "BBQ heaven" in Llano, where "selecting your meat from the
outside pits" and eating at "picnic tables" is de rigueur; the food is
"awesome", its no-frills atmosphere "ain't fancy but it's the real
thing" and "cowboys and motorcycle dudes abound", so "get there
early if you don't like waiting in line."

	FOOD	DECOR	SERVICE	COST

NEW Corazón ⑤ *Mexican*
| - | - | - | I |

(fka Castle Hill)

Downtown | 1101 W. Fifth St. (Baylor St.) | 512-476-0728 |
www.corazonatcastlehill.com

Though the name has changed, much is the same at this revamp of
Downtown's Castle Hill where chef Michael Taddeo remains at the
helm, dishing out modern interpretations of interior Mexican fare
(think pork tenderloin in chipotle apple butter sauce); the inviting
space has been updated with paintings and crafts by local artists
and the addition of a copper-topped bar, while prices remain as gentle as they were before.

County Line, The *BBQ*
| 20 | 18 | 19 | $23 |

Northwest Hills | 5204 Rte. 2222 (Capital of Texas Hwy.) | 512-346-3664
West Lake Hills | 6500 W. Bee Caves Rd. (Knollwood Dr.) | 512-327-1742
www.countyline.com

See review in San Antonio Directory.

NEW Creek Road Café Ⓜ *American*
| - | - | - | M |

Dripping Springs | 301 Hwy. 290 W. (R.R. 12) | 512-858-9459 |
www.creekroadcafe.com

Dripping Springs arrives on the culinary map thanks to this ambitious entry featuring a seasonal New American menu and a short
but well-considered wine list; its casual yet romantic setup features
white tablecloths and soft lighting, with framed photographs of the
area lending the space a homey, small-town feel.

Crú Wine Bar *American*
| 20 | 23 | 21 | $34 |

Downtown | 238 W. Second St. (bet. Colorado & Lavaca Sts.) |
512-472-9463
NEW Northwest Austin | The Domain | 11410 Century Oaks Terrace
(bet. Domain Dr. & Frontage Rd.) | 512-339-9463
www.cruawinebar.com

See review in Dallas/Ft. Worth Directory.

NEW Cuatros *American*
| - | - | - | I |

Campus | 1004 24th St. (San Gabriel St.) | 512-243-6361 |
www.cuatrosaustin.com

This Campus area newcomer serves gussied-up American grub like
burgers and corn dogs plus beer and cocktails in a refurbished garage
exuding a laid-back Austin vibe; although the clientele is largely
comprised of UT students, the kids' menu is a draw for families,
while the dog-friendly patio (with water bowls and biscuits available) proves a pull for pet-lovers and Longhorns fans looking for a
cool place to watch the game on flat-screen TVs.

Curra's Grill *Mexican*
| 21 | 14 | 16 | $17 |

Travis Heights | 614 E. Oltorf St. (Eastside Dr.) | 512-444-0012 |
www.currasgrill.com

There's "none of that Tex-Mex Velveeta baloney" at this "lively"
"family" spot in Travis Heights that features "authentic" Mexican
dishes, including "many veg options", and a "large variety of margaritas" (the "creamy avocado" variety is "a must-have"), all at a "fan-

tastic value"; on the other hand, "decor is minimal – and not in a good way" – plus "service can be slow during peak hours."

Daily Grill *American* ▽ 24 | 25 | 26 | $30

Northwest Austin | The Domain | 11506 Century Oaks Terr. (bet. Braker Ln. & Burnet Rd.) | 512-836-4200 | www.dailygrill.com
"Simple" American food is "done extremely well" at this outpost of the California-based chain in Northwest Austin's Domain shopping center; the 1930s-inflected atmosphere has a "fancy" feel befitting the relatively upmarket tabs and "great service"; N.B. the happy hour with $2 appetizers equals "happiness."

Din Ho Chinese BBQ *Chinese* 24 | 9 | 12 | $15

North Austin | 8557 Research Blvd. (Fairfield Dr.) | 512-832-8788 | www.dinhochinesebbq.com
"The first thing you notice is the BBQ stand with hanging ducks, chickens and pork" at this "good, cheap and fast" North Austin eatery whose "authentic Cantonese-style cuisine" is "about as real Chinese as it gets deep in the heart of Texas"; it may not be much to look at, but the "large round tables with lazy Susans are great for large parties" – and best of all it "stays open late."

Dirty Martin's Kum-Bak Place *Burgers* 21 | 12 | 16 | $10

West Campus | 2808 Guadalupe St. (28th St.) | 512-477-3173 | www.dirtymartins.com
"An Austin classic" since 1926, this inexpensive Campus-area "joint" is the epitome of a "greasy spoon" with "heavenly burgers", "hand-mixed" vanilla cokes and "some of the best malts and shakes" in town hustled by a "friendly" counter staff; they've spiffed it up over the past few years, though it remains a "pre-game hangout" where "sports on the TVs" provides most of the atmosphere.

❷ Driskill Grill Ⓢ Ⓜ *American* 26 | 27 | 26 | $63

Downtown | Driskill Hotel | 604 Brazos St. (6th St.) | 512-391-7162 | www.driskillgrill.com
"A sure winner" swear supporters of this Downtown destination inside the historic Driskill Hotel that "rivals the best restaurants of NY" with "amazing" New American cuisine, an "excellent wine list" and "solicitous service" to boot; the interior is "luxuriously appointed in true Texas style" with "rich woods" and portraits of politicians lining the walls setting an "elegant" scene for one of the "best dining experiences in Austin", and one that's well "worth" the "expensive" prices.

Eastside Café *American/Eclectic* 24 | 21 | 22 | $26

Cherrywood | 2113 Manor Rd. (bet. Alamo & Coleto Sts.) | 512-476-5858 | www.eastsidecafeaustin.com
A "haven" for "wholesome" food, this Cherrywood "pioneer" "shows that healthy doesn't have to be boring" with an "amazing" menu of Eclectic–New American dishes featuring "fresh", organic produce and herbs harvested from their own gardens; it exudes a "homey" feel thanks to its "charming converted bungalow" setting, "friendly" staff" and "fair prices."

FOOD | DECOR | SERVICE | COST

☑ Eddie V's
Edgewater Grille *Seafood/Steak*

26	24	25	$49

Arboretum | 9400 Arboretum Blvd. (Capital of Texas Hwy.) | 512-342-2642
Downtown | 301 E. Fifth St. (San Jacinto Blvd.) | 512-472-1860
www.eddiev.com

Regulars "rave" about the "masterfully prepared" steaks and sea-food presented by "professional" servers at these "high-end", "high-energy" Austin-area surf 'n' turfers; the Downtown branch boasts "great" live jazz nightly, and both cultivate a "clubby" atmosphere with leather booths and lots of wood that appeals to the "political crowd", "over-40 types" and "sorority girls" alike.

1886 Café & Bakery *American*

22	24	21	$28

Downtown | Driskill Hotel | 604 Brazos St. (6th St.) | 512-391-7066 | www.driskillhotel.com

Enthusiasts attest this "lively and historic" Downtown destination "tucked into a corner" of the Driskill Hotel is "a must" for "classic" American cuisine with a "Texas twist", including "decadent" breakfasts, "civilized" lunches and "fantastic" pastries that sate any "sweet tooth"; though a few find it a little "pricey", insiders insist "it's worth a visit" even if just to gaze at the "palatial" "cattle baronesque" decor.

El Azteca ☒ *Tex-Mex*

▽	18	12	15	$15

East Austin | 2600 E. Seventh St. (Calles St.) | 512-477-4701 | www.elaztecaustin.com

For a true "mom-and-pop experience" or "one last Tex-Mex fix on the way to the airport", duck into this inexpensive, "small, family-owned" institution – "the only one of its kind in East Austin" – where "home-cooked flavors" abound (cabrito, or roasted goat, is a specialty) and "service is warm and friendly"; as for the "funky decor", think "Neo-Aztec warriors" and "virgin volcano sacrifice posters."

El Chile *Mexican*

22	17	17	$21

Cherrywood | 1809 Manor Rd. (Chicon St.) | 512-457-9900 | www.elchilecafe.com

"A standout among the plethora of Mexican restaurants in town", this small Cherrywood eatery serves "great drinks" and "superb, delicately prepared entrees" in a "cool, hip, fun" environment – and at "best-value" prices; critics complain that it gets "way too noisy" and say the staffers "try hard but are easily overwhelmed when it's crowded", yet all "enjoy" alfresco dining on the "nice deck" ("blankets are provided on cooler nights").

El Mercado *Tex-Mex*

15	14	16	$15

Allandale | 7414 Burnet Rd. (Richcreek Rd.) | 512-454-2500
Bouldin Creek | 1302 S. First St. (Gibson St.) | 512-447-7445
Downtown | 1702 Lavaca St. (17th St.) | 512-477-7689
www.elmercadorestaurant.com

Supporters of this "casual" local Tex-Mex chain favor its "reasonable" tabs, "large portions" and "good margaritas"; still, foes fault

the "unspectacular" eats, "unmemorable decor" and "sketchy service", recommending you "go for drinks but dine elsewhere" – though at the Allandale and Downtown branches you can do both via a "substantial appetizer buffet" that's "free during happy hour" with the purchase of an alcoholic beverage.

El Meson Taqueria 🅢 *Mexican*   ▽ 27 | 7 | 14 | $15

Southeast Austin | 5808 Burleson Rd. (Montopolis Dr.) | 512-416-0749

Intrepid eaters insist you "don't miss" this tiny, no-frills spot in Southeast Austin dishing out "delicious" "handmade" Mexican specialties like squash blossom quesadillas and boasting one of "the best breakfasts" around all at an "unbelievable price"; though it's "basically self service" (you pick up your order at the counter), all agree it's "worth the trip"; N.B. breakfast and lunch only.

Elsi's *Mexican/Salvadoran*   - | - | - | I

Brentwood | 6601 Burnet Rd. (Twin Oaks Dr.) | 512-454-0747 | www.elsisrestaurant.com

This colorful family-owned Brentwood eatery specializes in homey Mexican and Salvadoran staples – like pupusas and tacos ahogados – that keep devoted regulars coming back; tabs are cheap, especially during happy hour (3-7 PM) when domestic beers and margaritas are priced even lower.

El Sol y La Luna *Mexican*   19 | 13 | 18 | $15

SoCo | 1224 S. Congress Ave. (Academy Dr.) | 512-444-7770 | www.elsolylalunaaustin.com

First the "fresh, filling" fare (including "wonderful veggie" items) and then the check will "put a smile on your face" at this longtime SoCo Mexican eatery that predates the area's hipness; the decor "treads the line between funky and junky", but a "relaxed vibe", "live music" (weekends only) and a patio overlooking the "parade" of passersby add to the "fun atmosphere"; N.B. they plan to relocate to Sixth Street Downtown in 2009.

Enoteca Vespaio *Italian*   25 | 19 | 22 | $26

SoCo | 1610 S. Congress Ave. (Monroe St.) | 512-441-7672 | www.austinvespaio.com

"Fabulous" panini, 50 "well-priced" wines by the glass and an "amazing Sunday brunch" lure local foodies to this "more affordable" SoCo alternative to "big brother" Vespaio; with "knowledgeable servers", "casual" cafelike digs with a "nice small patio" and a "gourmet" take-out counter stocked with cheeses and housemade charcuterie, it's no wonder it's so "well-liked."

Estância Churrascaria *Brazilian/Steak*   ▽ 27 | 19 | 25 | $37

Southwest Austin | 4894 Hwy. 290 W. (bet. Brodie Ln. & Westgate Blvd.) | 512-892-1225 | www.estanciachurrascaria.com

"Beef lovers" bring a "hearty appetite" to this moderately priced Brazilian in Southwest Austin where "roving" "gaucho" waiters dole out an "expertly prepared" array of sirloin, ribs, pork and lamb that "just keeps coming and coming" until you cry uncle; as for the

"crowded" interior done up in an earthy style with exposed ceiling beams, most are "so busy eating", they "don't even notice."

European Bistro 🅼 *European* ▽ 24 | 20 | 21 | $30

Pflugerville | 111 E. Main St. (Railroad Ave.) | 512-835-1919 | www.european-bistro.com

"Well worth the drive" out of Austin, this bastion of European "bliss" "in a quaint jewel of a historic building" in Downtown Pflugerville offers a "unique menu" that "reflects a love for old-world cuisine" with its "wide variety of German, Hungarian, Russian", Czech and French dishes; the "tasty food" is both "delightful and authentic", but be sure to save "room for the housemade desserts."

Evangeline Café 🅢 *Cajun/Creole* ▽ 19 | 11 | 20 | $18

Southwest Austin | 8106 Brodie Ln. (bet. Alexandria & Eskew Drs.) | 512-282-2586 | www.evangelinecafe.com

"Friendly and homey", this Southwest Austin spot sports a "great" staff serving up "some of the best authentic Cajun-Creole" "vittles" "this side of the Mississippi"; the "casual atmosphere" really hops in the evenings when the tunes of "rousing bands" "go with the spicy food", adding to its status as a "really special place."

Finn & Porter *Seafood/Steak* 23 | 21 | 22 | $41

Downtown | Hilton Downtown | 500 E. Fourth St. (Neches St.) | 512-493-4900 | www.finnandporter.com

Ensconced within the Hilton hotel Downtown, this surf 'n' turfer features a "talented chef" who oversees everything from the "excellent steaks" to the "fabulous sushi" (complemented by a "good sake list"); the "gorgeous", "large dining room" can be "noisy", but it has a "cool", "big-city feel", and the two bars are a popular stop for cocktails.

Fino 🅢 *Mediterranean* 23 | 24 | 23 | $36

West Campus | 2905 San Gabriel St. (29th St.) | 512-474-2905 | www.finoaustin.com

"Inventive small plates", "exciting" wines and "fabulous" cocktails are the standouts on the "eclectic" midpriced Mediterranean menu at this West Campus "winner" (and sister to Asti) set in "stylish", "airy" digs and serviced by a "knowledgeable" staff; insiders insist that a seat on the "wonderful patio" is the "perfect ending to the workday."

🆕 Fion Bistro *American* - | - | - | I

Steiner Ranch | 2900 N. Quinlan Park Rd. (bet. Central Park & Steiner Ranch Blvd.) | 512-266-3466 | www.fionwinepub.com

Originally a wine and cheese shop, this Steiner Ranch entry now offers a full menu of upscale New American pub grub – like lamb sliders with mint pesto and home-cut fries – all at affordable prices; given its mind-boggling beer selection (over 500 brews) and cozy vibe, it's no wonder locals are already keeping it crowded.

First Chinese BBQ *Chinese* 25 | 9 | 12 | $15

North Austin | Chinatown Austin | 10901 N. Lamar Blvd. (Kramer Ln.) | 512-835-8889 | www.firstchinesebbq.com

See review in Dallas/Ft. Worth Directory.

	FOOD	DECOR	SERVICE	COST

Fleming's Prime Steakhouse & Wine Bar *Steak*
| 24 | 24 | 23 | $54 |

Downtown | 320 E. Second St. (bet. San Jacinto Blvd. & Trinity St.) | 512-457-1500 | www.flemingssteakhouse.com
See review in Houston Directory.

Flip Happy Crepes ⓈⓂ⊄ *French*
| - | - | - | I |

Zilker | 401 Jessie St. (Butler Rd.) | 512-552-9034 | www.fliphappycrepes.com

Operating out of a cutely refurbished Avion trailer in Zilker, Nessa Higgins and Andrea Dayboykin turn out toothsome homemade crêpes stuffed to the brim with savory and sweet fillings (like shredded pork with cheddar cheese or lemon curd with blueberries for dessert); although there's no indoor seating, the picnic area strung with Christmas lights and mismatched tables and chairs suits the steady stream of regulars just fine; N.B. breakfast and lunch only with evening hours in the spring.

Ⓩ Fonda San Miguel *Mexican*
| 26 | 27 | 24 | $37 |

Highland Park | 2330 W. North Loop Blvd. (Hancock Dr.) | 512-459-4121 | www.fondasanmiguel.com

"Nothing misses a beat" at this "long-running", "high-end" Highland Park "favorite" that's "truly a feast for the senses" with "lovingly prepared" Mexican cuisine "made from the best ingredients", "killer margaritas" and a "Sunday brunch that's not to be missed"; it's ranked No. 1 for Decor in Austin thanks to the "gorgeous, old-world" hacienda setting that's enhanced by a staff that "treats you like royalty."

Frank & Angie's *Pizza*
| 21 | 13 | 18 | $14 |

Downtown | 508 West Ave. (6th St.) | 512-472-3534 | www.hutsfrankandangies.com

"Austin ain't no pizza mecca", but this "fun *Lady and the Tramp*-style" Downtown "dive" "might just be the pie enthusiast's best bet"; its "great thin-crust" version is accompanied by "reasonably priced", "classic homestyle" dishes "named after famous Italians" and "served with a bit of nostalgic attitude", making it "great for a casual date" – especially for those "on a budget."

Gene's *Cajun/Soul Food*
| ▽ 25 | 6 | 17 | $14 |

East Austin | 1209 E. 11th St. (Wheeless St.) | 512-477-6600 | www.genesrestaurant.com

"You can't go wrong with a seafood po' boy" at this East Austin "find" turning out "authentic" Cajun dishes from a lineup of "comfort food" (like smothered pork chops and fried chicken) that "varies daily"; service is "friendly" and prices are cheap, though the "down-home" cafe-style setting has some customers clamoring for "takeout."

Golden Wok *Chinese*
| 22 | 19 | 19 | $17 |

North Austin | Tech Ridge Ctr. | 500 Canyon Ridge (I-35) | 512-228-3688 | www.golden-wok.com
See review in San Antonio Directory.

Gonzales Food Market ☒ *BBQ*

| - | - | - | I |

Gonzales | 311 St. Lawrence St. (St. James St.) | 830-672-3156 | www.gonzalesfoodmarket.com

The historic town of Gonzales is home to this no-frills, family-owned and -run BBQ mecca that started as a Downtown grocery store/meat market in 1959; these days, three pits can barely keep up with demand for its oak-smoked sausage, brisket, chicken and ribs (including a house-specialty lamb version); it's no wonder the small dining room is usually full of locals and visitors from around the country; N.B. save room for dessert.

Green Mesquite *BBQ*

| 18 | 13 | 17 | $16 |

Zilker | 1400 Barton Springs Rd. (Lamar Blvd.) | 512-479-0485 | www.greenmesquite.net

Specializing in "everything the cow and pig have to offer", this "Texas roadhouse BBQ joint" "conveniently" located just down the road from Zilker Park also offers "down-home flavors ranging from burgers to crispy catfish"; it's a "fun, boisterous" kind of place, with a "great patio" for anyone wanting "to listen to local music" (Thursday–Sunday); P.S. ask about the "all-you-can-eat special."

Green Pastures *Continental*

| 23 | 25 | 24 | $38 |

Bouldin Creek | 811 W. Live Oak St. (3rd St.) | 512-444-4747 | greenpasturesrestaurant.com

"A longtime favorite" for "weddings" and "celebrations", this "beautiful" Bouldin Creek destination is set in a "delightful", "rambling" 19th-century home with peacocks roaming free on the "peaceful grounds"; though a few find it "staid", most marvel at the "delicious" Continental cuisine and "thoughtful staff" and say the "cost is in line" with what they deem a "special" place that "stands alone in its class"; P.S. there's also an "excellent Sunday brunch."

NEW Grove wine bar | kitchen *American*

| - | - | - | M |

West Lake Hills | 6317 Bee Caves Rd. (Capital of Texas Hwy.) | 512-327-8822 | www.grovewinebar.com

West Lake oenophiles have a new option in this bustling wine bar pairing creative New American bites like panko-crusted crab cakes with affordable glasses and flights from a 100-bottle selection; its chic, Napa-inspired dining room flaunts an open vino storage system and looks out onto a large tiered patio that sits under a canopy of old oaks.

Guero's Taco Bar *Mexican*

| 20 | 18 | 17 | $19 |

SoCo | 1412 S. Congress Ave. (Elizabeth St.) | 512-447-7688 | www.guerostacobar.com

"Always crowded", this "loud and energetic" SoCo Mexican conjures up "the quintessential Austin experience" with "tourists", "under-35" locals and "the occasional celebrity" all chowing down on "killer tacos" and "fantastic" salsas in a "funky" converted feed store with a covered patio and local bands playing Wednesdays–Saturdays; margaritas "on the deck" help alleviate "long waits" on weekend nights as well as "surly" service from the "too cool" staff.

	FOOD	DECOR	SERVICE	COST

Gumbo's ⓈＳ Cajun/Creole
| 24 | 20 | 22 | $34 |

Downtown | Brown Bldg. | 710 Colorado St. (8th St.) | 512-480-8053 |
www.gumbosaustin.com

Round Rock | 901 Round Rock Ave. (Chisholm Trail) | 512-671-7925 |
www.gumbosroundrock.com Ⓜ

It "feels and tastes like New Orleans" at this "upscale" Downtown
Cajun-Creole, where visitors "enjoy the contrast between" the "elegant" interior and "the spice-a-thon on your plate"; not only is the
food "fantastic" and the service "refined", but the "cozy, intimate atmosphere" complete with "dim lighting" makes it quite the "romantic
hangout"; P.S. be sure to "visit the Round Rock location up north."

Gypsy Italian Bistro Ⓜ Italian
| - | - | - | M |

Bouldin Creek | 1025 Barton Springs Rd. (Dawson Rd.) | 512-499-0200 |
www.go2gypsy.com

Owned and operated by graduates from the Texas Culinary
Academy, this Bouldin Creek trattoria fuses old and new with
modern takes on traditional Northern Italian dishes – like lamb
chops with orzo pesto – served up in a cozy stone-accented setting;
though prices can feel high for the area, wallet-watchers find brunch
a less-expensive option.

Habana Cuban
| 21 | 15 | 15 | $23 |

Downtown | 709 E. Sixth St. (bet. East Ave. & Sabine St.) |
512-443-4252

South Austin | 2728 S. Congress Ave. (Cumberland Rd.) | 512-443-4253
www.habana.com

The "massive portions" of "great Cuban" fare will "make your taste
buds sing" at this "small" spot (and its South Austin offshoot) with
a "fun atmosphere" and tropical, earthy decor "off the beaten path"
Downtown; some say the staff can get "overwhelmed" at times, but
most predict you'll get "satisfaction for your dining dollar" – especially if you sample the "wonderful array of mojitos" and "really
good tres leches cake."

Hayashi Sushi & Grill Japanese
| - | - | - | M |

Cedar Park | 1335 E. Whitestone Blvd. (Rte. 183a) | 512-986-7176

Georgetown | 1019 W. University Ave. (I-35) | 512-868-9686
www.hayashigrill.com

Nouveau Japanese comes to the 'burbs via this midpriced duo whip-
ping up inventive dishes like sushi pizzas topped with seaweed and
fish, maki rolled with tropical fruits and a fine selection of sakes and
wines; both spots thrive in contemporary red-accented surroundings and offer happy-hour enticements during the week, but only
the Cedar Park outpost offers discounts on Sunday as well.

Hilltop Café Ⓜ Eclectic
| 23 | 20 | 20 | $29 |

Fredericksburg | 10661 Hwy. 87 N. (Rte. 648) | 830-997-8922 |
www.hilltopcafe.com

"In the middle of nowhere", this "wonderful find", an "old gas station"–
turned-cafe near Fredericksburg, is an "authentic Texas roadhouse
with urban eats" thanks to a menu on which "Cajun meets cowboy"

"meets Greek" – with "a punch of down-home thrown in"; the "funky", "casual" space is often full of "interesting characters", and "you never know when the cook (and owner) will leave his kitchen and start playing music", making for "a real Hill Country experience" that's "well worth the trip."

Hoffbrau Steakhouse 🗷 Ⓜ️ *Steak* | 16 | 11 | 19 | $22 |

Downtown | 613 W. Sixth St. (Nueces St.) | 512-472-0822 |
www.originalhoffbrausteaks.com

"It's all about nostalgia" at this "old-timey" Downtown steakhouse from 1934 that still holds strong with "decent" cuts of meat and salads served up "quickly" "on the cheap" to a motley crew of "politicians" and other assorted "regulars"; the location is "dilapidated" and decor is "nonexistent", but insiders insist "that's the charm" of this "beloved" "landmark."

Home Slice Pizza *Pizza* | 23 | 14 | 17 | $15 |

SoCo | 1415 S. Congress Ave. (bet. Elizabeth & Gibson Sts.) |
512-444-7437 | www.homeslicepizza.com

Fans of "authentic" "NY-style" pizza head to this "friendly" SoCo "hangout" where "hipsters" and "families" munch on "crispy crust" pies and sip "affordable wines" in a "funky", "noisy" setting; "if it's late and you're hungry, this is the place to go", since you can order slices "from the walk-up to-go window" until 3 AM on weekends.

Hoover's *Southern* | 21 | 10 | 17 | $18 |

Cherrywood | 2002 Manor Rd. (Alamo St.) | 512-479-5006
Northwest Austin | 13376 Research Blvd. (Anderson Mill Rd.) |
512-335-0300
www.hooverscooking.com

Get ready for "a belt-busting meal" of "excellent down-home Southern cooking" (including "better meatloaf than mother ever could have made") and "great soul food" – all "for a good price" – at this Cherrywood favorite near the University of Texas campus and its Northwest Austin sib; despite the "utilitarian", "cafeterialike atmosphere" and "friendly" but "often very busy" service, devotees declare it the place to go "when you need a comfort-food fix."

House.Wine. 🌑 *American* | – | – | – | M |

Fredericksburg | 327 E. Main St. (S. Lincoln St.) | 830-997-2665 |
www.intohousewine.com

Fredericksburg is home to this quirky newcomer boasting a well-appointed housewares and gift shop up front, and a comfy wine bar tucked away in back featuring over 200 selections accompanied by shareable New American plates; the knowledgeable staff keeps thing convivial at both the welcoming bar and the cozy low-lit dining area that's done up like someone's living room; N.B. there's also a patio for warm weather sipping.

Houston's *American* | 23 | 20 | 22 | $30 |

Northwest Austin | 2408 W. Anderson Ln. (Burnet Rd.) | 512-451-7333 |
www.hillstone.com
See review in Houston Directory.

ⓩ Hudson's on the Bend *American* | 28 | 24 | 26 | $56

Lakeway | 3509 Ranch Rd. 620 N. (Hudson Bend Rd.) | 512-266-1369 |
www.hudsonsonthebend.com

"Meat eaters" marvel at the "memorable" game choices – like venison,
bison and elk – that come "artfully prepared" at this Lakeway New
American set in a "quaint" old cottage with a "romantic patio" and
"five-star service" that's ranked No. 1 in Austin; in all, it's a "truly
unique" "treat" that surveyors swear is "easily worth" the 30 minute
drive from Downtown, not to mention the "splurge"-worthy prices.

Hula Hut *Tex-Mex* | 18 | 21 | 16 | $21

Old West Austin | 3825 Lake Austin Blvd. (Enfield Rd.) | 512-476-4852 |
www.hulahut.com

"Beautiful lake views" and a "good variety of margaritas" make this
"charmingly kitschy" "tiki hut"-esque spot an Old West "Austin
summertime must" for the "under-25" set; some say the "unique"
fare "isn't great", but others find it a "nice Polynesian twist on Tex-
Mex" food – plus, the fact that "you can arrive by boat" adds to the
"cool factor"; still, critics claim that the "unyielding crowds are intol-
erable", making the atmosphere "noisy" and service "erratic."

Hut's *Burgers* | 23 | 16 | 19 | $13

Downtown | 807 W. Sixth St. (West Ave.) | 512-472-0693 |
www.hutsfrankandangies.com

Proponents "pity the person who's never had a burger" from this
"legendary" "longtime favorite", a Downtown "hole-in-the-wall"
serving a "wide variety of tasty" patties along with "rich, thick
shakes and huge onion rings" in a "fun, relaxing environment" (think
"diner with checkered floors and a bunch of tables jammed in"); insider's tip: the two-for-one nights on Wednesdays "are the way to go."

Hyde Park Bar & Grill *American* | 21 | 18 | 19 | $20

Hyde Park | 4206 Duval St. (Park Blvd.) | 512-458-3168 ◑
Southwest Austin | 4527 W. Gate Blvd. (S. Lamar Blvd.) | 512-899-2700
www.hydeparkbarandgrill.com

Surveyors say this "cheery" Hyde Park "hangout" – a "favorite of old-
time Austinites" – "still does a fine job" with "simple" "all-American"
dishes that "aren't too expensive" set down by "pleasant" servers in
"comfy" quarters with local artwork on the walls; the newer outpost
on West Gate may "lack the funky ambiance of the original", but it
offers "more room" and "better parking" while maintaining the
same "home cooking'" and "legendary french fries."

NEW Imperia *Pan-Asian* | – | – | – | E

Warehouse District | 310 Colorado St. (bet. W. 3rd & 4th Sts.) |
512-472-6770 | www.imperia-austin.com

This über-trendy addition to the Warehouse District evokes an LA
nightspot with a stylish staff ferrying Pan-Asian small plates, sushi and
inventive cocktails in a posh chrome-and-onyx-decked space; though
high-end pricing comes with the territory, the weekday happy hour –
featuring $5 drinks, $5 appetizers and two-for-one sushi – is a good
way to live the experience without breaking the bank.

	FOOD	DECOR	SERVICE	COST

Iron Cactus *Tex-Mex*

18 | 19 | 18 | $25

NEW **Bee Cave** | 13420 Galleria Circle (Bee Cave Pkwy.) | 512-263-7636
Downtown | 606 Trinity St. (6th St.) | 512-472-9240
Great Hills | 10001 Stonelake Blvd. (Capital of Texas Hwy.) | 512-794-8778
www.ironcactus.com

The "well-priced" "Tex-Mex fare is "tasty" enough, but connoisseurs claim the real appeal" of this chainlet are the "70-plus tequila choices vying for your attention" and served up in a "mind-boggling array" of flights or in "specialty margaritas"; service varies by location, though all boast "comfortable" quarters that get a boost from patio seating.

Iron Works ☒ *BBQ*

22 | 15 | 13 | $15

Downtown | 100 Red River St. (Cesar Chavez St.) | 512-478-4855 | www.ironworksbbq.com

Set in a "historic" "restored ironworks factory" with "lovely creek-side seating" and an "awesome" Downtown location "right next to the Convention Center", this "great BBQ" place dishes out "huge portions" (including "ribs the size of Texas") in a "funky Western atmosphere"; you have to "order at the counter" from "indifferent", even "grumpy servers", but supporters swear that "just makes it taste better"; P.S. "there's no air-conditioning, so beware of the heat!"

☒ Jasper's *American*

24 | 25 | 24 | $42

Northwest Austin | The Domain | 11506 Century Oaks Terr. (bet. Braker Ln. & Burnet Rd.) | 512-834-4111 | www.kentrathbun.com

"Foodies rejoice" over this "lively" New American "standout" with branches in Austin, Plano and The Woodlands dishing up "inventively prepared" "comfort food" (the Maytag blue cheese chips are "worth the trip alone") courtesy of "incredible" chef-owner Kent Rathbun of Dallas' Abacus; the atmosphere is "casually elegant" with "modern" decor and patios that are "great for people-watching", so even if some feel it's "not a great value", it's a "winner" nonetheless; N.B. a San Antonio outpost will open in 2009.

☒ Jeffrey's *American/Continental*

26 | 22 | 26 | $53

Clarksville | 1204 W. Lynn St. (12th St.) | 512-477-5584 | www.jeffreysofaustin.com

"An old standard that hasn't lost a step", this Clarksville "wonder" "continues its great traditions" with "divine" Continental-New American cuisine and "wonderful wines" presented in "elegant", but "simple", flower-filled rooms that loyalists liken to "eating at a chef's home"; add in "solicitous" servers cherished by some as "the best staff in town", and it's no wonder it's often considered a "first choice" for "special occasions."

Joe DiMaggio's Italian Chophouse *Italian/Steak*

- | - | - | M

Northwest Austin | The Domain | 11410 Century Oaks Terr. (bet. Domain Dr. & Frontage Rd.) | 512-835-5633 | www.joedimaggiosrestaurant.com

Another addition to the burgeoning dining scene at The Domain in Northwest Austin, this swank chophouse serves a solid lineup

FOOD DECOR SERVICE COST

of steaks alongside pizzas and pastas in a 1940s-style setting decorated with memorabilia paying homage to the namesake Yankee legend; those seeking an expertly made cocktail can settle in at the ample bar area or sink into a seat in front of the fire pit on the lighted patio.

Judges' Hill Restaurant *American* | 24 | 25 | 21 | $46 |

West Campus | Mansion at Judges' Hill Hotel | 1900 Rio Grande St. (Martin Luther King Blvd.) | 512-495-1800 | www.judgeshillrestaurant.com

"An old, beautifully restored" West Campus mansion that's been turned into "an elegant inn" is the "lovely" setting of this "intimate dining room", "a well-kept secret" that's "great for cocktails and hors d'oeuvres", a "discreet power business dinner" or a "romantic meal"; though the "ambiance is old-world", the menu is New American, managing to "cover the basics" while also offering "unique food" that "doesn't lack creativity."

Katz's Deli & Bar ● *Deli* | 19 | 15 | 16 | $18 |

Downtown | 618 W. Sixth St. (Rio Grande St.) | 512-472-2037 | www.katzneverkloses.com

These 24/7 Austin and Houston-area delis are "all-night traditions" for "tastes of New York in the heart of Texas", offering "monstrous portions" at "reasonable prices" from an "extensive menu"; detractors declare that the "quality is variable", the "service is spotty" and the atmosphere is "nightmarishly kitschy", but they're always "really loud and busy on weekends", making them "fun places to people-watch."

Kenichi *Pan-Asian* | 22 | 22 | 19 | $43 |

Warehouse District | 419 Colorado St. (4th St.) | 512-320-8883 | www.kenichirestaurants.com

"The beautiful people love to eat" at this "swanky spot" in Austin's Warehouse District (and its newer Victory Park twin in Dallas) with "chic" "modern" decor and a Pan-Asian menu sporting a "great variety of sushi, rolls and sashimi" and "melt-in-your-mouth seafood" dishes, accompanied by a wide "range of sakes"; still, protesters pan the "pretentiously hip" vibe and certain staffers who are "more snobby than a Rockefeller at Tiffany's."

Kerbey Lane Café ● *Eclectic* | 20 | 14 | 16 | $15 |

Brykerwoods | 3704 Kerbey Ln. (35th St.) | 512-451-1436
Campus | 2606 Guadalupe St. (26th St.) | 512-477-5717
Northwest Austin | 13435 Research Blvd. (Anderson Mill Rd.) | 512-258-7757
South Lamar | 2700 S. Lamar Blvd. (Dickson Dr.) | 512-445-4451
www.kerbeylanecafe.com

"An eclectic clientele" savors the "Eclectic menu of fresh cooking" at this "home-grown" mini-chain of "24-hour heavens", the original "located in a charming midcentury bungalow" in Brykerwoods that boasts a "bohemian flavor"; regulars who revel in its "famously funky vibe" love having "breakfast any time of day"

("legendary pancakes"), though some say the "hippie-student" servers are a bit too "laid-back", "usually acting like you're interrupting their smoke break."

Kona Grill   *American*   20 | 21 | 18 | $27

Northwest Austin | The Domain | 11410 Century Oaks Terr. (bet. Domain Dr. & Frontage Rd.) | 512-835-5900 | www.konagrill.com
See review in Houston Directory.

Korea House   *Korean*   21 | 9 | 16 | $17

Northwest Austin | 2700 W. Anderson Ln. (Northcross Dr.) | 512-458-2477
This "authentic Korean hangout" in Northwest Austin serves "enjoyable" "traditional dishes" accompanied by "lots of interesting sides" (including "a wonderful range of fresh pickled vegetables"), as well as "good sushi"; the service is "attentive" and the prices are "great", making it "a fave for lunch", but "no-frills" decor "leaves much to be desired", so surveyors suggest sitting by the window and "looking out over the water feature in the courtyard."

Kreuz Market   🛇 *BBQ*   26 | 12 | 15 | $15

Lockhart | 619 N. Colorado St. (bet. Cemetery & Flores Sts.) | 512-398-2361 | www.kreuzmarket.com
"One of the greatest in the state" attest those "amazed" by this "German-style" BBQ "mecca" in Lockhart that's well "worth the drive" for "tender" smoked meats – like "standout" brisket and pork chops – served "right off the pit", without sauce, and tied up in butcher paper ("don't look for a fork", just unwrap and eat); no one minds the "huge rustic building" that "leaves much to be desired" or market-style service, since it's ultimately a "pure Texas" experience where "all that really matters is the meat."

Lambert's Downtown Barbecue   *BBQ*   23 | 21 | 21 | $29

Warehouse District | Schneider Brothers Bldg. | 401 W. Second St. (Guadalupe St.) | 512-494-1500 | www.lambertsaustin.com
Barbecue gets an "upscale" twist at Lou Lambert's "sophisticated" Warehouse District arrival turning out "delectable" oak-smoked and wood-grilled meats, "delicious" "nontraditional" sides and a "great Sunday brunch" all ferried to your table by a staff that "treats you like kin"; the setting in the "wonderfully restored" Schneider Brothers Building features "whitewashed brick walls" and "loud" live music Tuesday–Saturday confirming this "popular" destination is "as much about the scene" as the "awesome" food.

Las Palomas   🛇Ⓜ *Mexican*   21 | 14 | 19 | $22

West Lake Hills | West Woods Shopping Ctr. | 3201 Bee Caves Rd. (Old Walsh Tarlton) | 512-327-9889 | www.laspalomasrestaurant.com
"Tucked in the corner of a strip mall" in West Lake Hills is this "fabulous, sophisticated" little gem with an unexpectedly "excellent menu" of "authentic and delicious" Mexican fare "at reasonable prices"; an "inviting atmosphere" (including "nice patio seating") and "great service" from a staff that "always treats you like part of the family" are more reasons it's been a favorite since 1983.

Latin Café Austin S American

20 | 18 | 19 | I

(fka Doña Emilia's South American Bar & Grill)

Downtown | 101 San Jacinto Blvd. (Cesar Chavez St.) | 512-478-2520 |
www.donaemilias.com

"In a pretty setting" Downtown, this recently revamped eatery still
dishes out a "wonderful blend" of South American dishes – including "delicious Colombian fare" – albeit now at more modest prices;
the wine list is interesting, and the "novel drinks" make it "a fun
place for happy hour", plus there's "live music" on weekends.

La Traviata ☒ Italian

24 | 20 | 21 | $35

Downtown | 314 Congress Ave. (3rd St.) | 512-479-8131 |
www.latraviata.net

Downtowners are delighted by this "lovely" little midpriced trattoria offering "straightforward" Italian dishes like "heavenly"
pastas that really let the "fresh ingredients" shine; regulars recommend you "make reservations" because the "cozy" (some say
"cramped") "NYC-like setting" with whitewashed brick and red accents "fills up quickly."

Louie Mueller BBQ ☒ BBQ

25 | 10 | 14 | $16

Taylor | 206 W. Second St. (Talbot St.) | 512-352-6206 |
www.louiemuellerbarbeque.com

"There is a God and his name is Louie" proclaim proponents of this
decades-old Taylor BBQ institution famed for its "outstanding
brisket", "tender" ribs and "fantastic" sausages presented with
white bread on a "tray with butcher paper"; "barn"-like decor is
strictly "no-frills", but the "years of real smoke" on the walls "has to
count for something."

Louie's 106 Mediterranean

24 | 23 | 24 | $41

Downtown | Littlefield Bldg. | 106 E. Sixth St. (Congress Ave.) |
512-476-1998 | www.louies106.net

A "dependable" Downtown "favorite", this "lively" Mediterranean
features "fabulous tapas", a "reasonable wine list" and solid service all
coming together in a "lovely" space with marble floors and redwood
accents; regulars remark it works both for business lunches or a "romantic" meal and is "always popular" with "guests from out of town."

NEW Lulu B's Ⓜ⇗ Vietnamese

- | - | - | I

South Lamar | 2113 S. Lamar Blvd. (Oltorf St.) | 512-921-4828

Continuing the uniquely Austin trend of serving great food out of
trailers, this laid-back pit stop on South Lamar is quickly garnering
praise – and lots of loyal fans – for its inexpensive Vietnamese fare
prepared by sisters Laura Bayer and Christina Gustavson; though
the banh mi sandwiches and other street snacks prove a handy alternative to fast food, you can expect a wait during peak lunch
hours; N.B. seating is outdoors, with picnic tables under the trees.

Madam Mam's Thai

21 | 11 | 14 | $14

Campus | 2514 Guadalupe St. (Dean Keaton Pkwy.) |
512-472-8306

(continued)

Madam Mam's

Southwest Austin | 4514 W. Gate Blvd. (S. Lamar Blvd.) |
512-899-8525

www.madammam.com

This "budget"-friendly "Campus favorite" boasting the "best Thai food in town" and its West Gate offshoot offer the same "consistent authentic provincial dishes" from "spicy to subtle" with "crisp flavors" as "exotic and succulent as the entertainers at a Bangkok cabaret"; the newer location has better parking and a space featuring bright colors, Thai art and a beautiful rose garden, which stand in stark contrast with the original's "strip-mall" setup.

Madras Pavilion *Indian*

22 | **11** | **14** | **$17**

North Austin | Colonnade Shopping Ctr. | 9025 Research Blvd. (Burnet Rd.) | 512-719-5575 | www.madraspavilion.us

See review in Houston Directory.

Magnolia Café ☻ *American*

21 | **14** | **19** | **$16**

Old West Austin | 2304 Lake Austin Blvd. (Veterans Dr.) | 512-478-8645
SoCo | 1920 S. Congress Ave. (bet. Johanna & Mary Sts.) | 512-445-0000
www.cafemagnolia.com

"Peace, love" and pancakes abound at this "cheap", "funky" local "institution" with outposts in SoCo and Old West Austin dishing out "great breakfasts" served "any time of day" as well as an "eclectic" array of "hearty" "wholesome" American food with lots of choices for "vegetarians"; open 24/7, it's "always crowded" with a "diverse" crowd while the "artist and musician" staff provides proficient if sometimes "snobby" service.

Málaga Tapas & Bar ☻ *Spanish*

20 | **20** | **19** | **$31**

Warehouse District | 440 W. Second St. (bet. Guadalupe &
San Antonio Sts.) | 512-236-8020 | www.malagatapasbar.com

The destination for "moderately priced" tapas in the Warehouse District, this Spaniard eatery sports "something for everyone": its "informal, barlike setting" is "perfect" for everything from "mingling" during the "great happy hour" to "a light, casual meal", as diners "feel just as comfortable sitting alone with a glass of wine" from the "immense list" as they do "having a full-course dinner with a group"; still, surveyors are less smitten with the service.

Mandola's Italian Market *Italian*

22 | **18** | **15** | **$17**

North Central | 4700 W. Guadalupe St. (N. Lamar Blvd.) | 512-419-9700 |
www.mandolasmarket.com

Chowhounds hail this "charming" Italian market in North Central Austin stocked with breads, meats, cheeses, "amazing gelato" and assorted "gourmet products" and featuring a counter-service eatery offering "freshly made" pastas, panini and pizzas alongside a "great selection" of wines; the mood is one of "slightly organized chaos", but "if you can handle the wait to place your order", "you'll be rewarded with terrific food at a reasonable price"; P.S. there are also two small patios that make a "wonderful setting" for an alfresco meal.

	FOOD	DECOR	SERVICE	COST

Mangieri's Pizza Cafe Pizza | 22 | 16 | 20 | $15 |

Circle C | 5900 W. Slaughter Ln. (Escarpment Blvd.) | 512-301-0063 | www.mangieris.com

"Locals" "love" this counter-service Italian "hidden away" on a strip mall in Circle C for its "irresistible" "thin-crust" pizzas with "delicious" toppings and "good variety" of inexpensive pastas and salads; "it's a nice option when you don't feel like cooking", and though the casually rustic setting is well-suited for families, delivery and takeout are also available.

Manuel's Mexican | 22 | 20 | 19 | $24 |

Arboretum | 10201 Jollyville Rd. (Great Hills Trail) | 512-345-1042
Downtown | 310 Congress Ave. (bet. 3rd & 4th Sts.) | 512-472-7555
www.manuels.com

"Imaginative" Mexican fare is "prepared well" with "fresh ingredients" and served by an "attentive staff" at these "affordable" eateries; regulars report the Great Hills Arboretum outpost is famed for its tree-shaded patio (a "great place" to enjoy an "inventive margarita") while the Downtown location is more of a "see-and-be-seen place" that "can be a bit loud especially at lunch."

NEW Maria Maria La Cantina Mexican | - | - | - | E |

Warehouse District | 415 Colorado St. (bet. 4th & 5th Sts.) | 512-687-6800 | www.mariamarialacantina.com

This Warehouse District newcomer is the result of a partnership between Carlos Santana – yes, THE Carlos Santana – and renowned chef Roberto Santibañez (ex Fonda San Miguel), who interprets regional Mexican specialties with a modern twist; a large sculptural tree forms the centerpiece of the space, which is decorated in colorful original art and features a long, well-stocked bar that's often standing-room-only; N.B. it also plays host to bands and DJs on weekends.

Matt's El Rancho Tex-Mex | 18 | 17 | 19 | $19 |

South Lamar | 2613 S. Lamar Blvd. (bet. Bluebonnet Ln. & Manchaca Rd.) | 512-462-9333 | www.mattselrancho.com

A "local favorite with a loyal following" for more than half a century, this huge South Lamar "temple of Tex-Mex" still serves classic dishes from "1950s recipes", providing "a 'retro' experience" to "generations of regulars" in a "loud" but "comfortable setting" ideal for "families and large groups"; because it's "crowded and popular", though, "waits can be wicked" – especially "after Texas football."

McCormick & Schmick's Seafood | 21 | 21 | 20 | $41 |

Downtown | Frost Bank Tower | 401 Congress Ave. (4th St.) | 512-236-9600
Northwest Austin | The Domain | 11600 Century Oaks Terr. (Burnet Rd.) | 512-836-0500
www.mccormickandschmicks.com

Unless you "get a booth and draw the curtain", it's sea and be seen at this "upscale" chain known for its "succulent seafood" (especially the "impressive" variety of oysters), "ample" wine list and "helpful" staff; revelers reveal "real fun" can be had at the bar, home to "great

happy-hour specials", but landlubbers lament it's a "typical chain" – "seen one, seen 'em all."

Melting Pot *Fondue*

21 | 20 | 21 | $43

Downtown | 305 E. Third St. (bet. San Jacinto Blvd. & Trinity St.) | 512-401-2424
Northwest Austin | 13343 Hwy. 183 N. (Anderson Mill Rd.) | 512-401-2424
www.meltingpot.com

"Change-of-pace" mavens and "do-it-yourself" types are fond of this "novel" fondue franchise for its "interactive" approach, i.e. the chance to "cook your own dinner"; the "long, slow meals" make it appropriate for "first dates" or "large crowds", and although the morsels are "tasty", you'll "end up spending a lot of money" for them.

Meyer's Elgin Smokehouse *BBQ*

21 | 10 | 15 | $12

Elgin | 188 Hwy. 290 E. (Loop 109) | 512-281-3331 | www.meyerselginsausage.com

"First-class Texas BBQ" including "amazing brisket" and "wonderful" housemade sausages are the pride and joy of this "mom-and-pop smokehouse" in the middle of Elgin – a small town just 30 minutes east of Austin; boosters boast it "takes you back to the bygone days" with "order-at-the-counter" service and a "plain" setting with picnic-style seating adding to the overall "authentic" experience.

Mikado Ryotei ⧄ *Japanese*

▽ 24 | 22 | 22 | $35

North Austin | 9033 Research Blvd. (Burnet Rd.) | 512-833-8188 | www.mikadoryotei.com

Though set in an "unassuming" North Austin strip mall, this Japanese "favorite" "soars above fancier Downtown places" with a mix of "traditional and inventive" fare including charcoal-grilled robata dishes and "top-grade" sushi all set down in "stylish" quarters; a "black-clad" staff provides proficient service, but those in-the-know sit at the bar where you're "treated like a king."

Mirabelle ⧄ *American*

25 | 19 | 24 | $35

Northwest Hills | 8127 Mesa Dr. (bet. Spicewood Springs Rd. & Steck Ave.) | 512-346-7900 | www.mirabellerestaurant.com

"Inspired" New American cuisine keeps Northwest Hills crowds coming to this "favorite" "neighborhood" "bistro" where the "creative" plates are "perfectly paired" with "reasonably priced, high-quality" vintages; devotees don't mind the "plain decor" with wood tables and floors because the "stunning food" plus "knowledgeable staff" guarantee it as "a safe bet for a quality meal"; P.S. their twice-monthly wine dinners are a "great value" too

Moonshine *American*

20 | 20 | 19 | $28

Downtown | 303 Red River St. (3rd St.) | 512-236-9599 | www.moonshinegrill.com

The "upscale, creative" American "comfort food" features "cutting-edge twists on some Southern mainstays" at this "quaint", "old rock house" Downtown, a "historic landmark" from the 1850s that's "elegantly comfy" and "romantic, without being stuffy"; highlights in-

clude its "generous" Sunday brunch, a "relaxed, breezy patio", drinks from the old carriage house bar that are "like candy in a glass" and a "caring staff that's anxious to please."

Ms. B's Authentic Creole Restaurant ⊠ *Creole*

| 22 | 17 | 21 | $23 |

Northwest Hills | 8105 Mesa Dr. (Spicewood Springs) | 512-372-9529 | www.msbscreole.com

Surveyors swear they'd "died and gone to heaven (or at least New Orleans)" after a taste of the "fabulous" Creole dishes like seafood gumbo and shrimp étouffée at this "comfortable" Northwest Hills eatery offering "good value" for the money; service may be "leisurely", but owners and staff are exceedingly "friendly"; N.B. the East Austin branch has closed.

NEW Mulberry *American*

| - | - | - | M |

Downtown | 360 Nueces St. (3rd St.) | 512-320-0297 | www.mulberryaustin.com

Hidden in a Downtown cul-de-sac on the street level of the new 360 condo tower, this tony wine bar is already packing 'em in for its inventive menu of New American plates, cheese and meat trays and well-considered selection of vintages; the diminutive space features a central bar and a smattering of tables, with outdoor seating available in warm weather; N.B. weekend brunch is also popular.

Musashino Sushi Dokoro Ⓜ *Japanese*

| 27 | 18 | 19 | $38 |

Northwest Hills | 3407 Greystone Dr. (MoPac Expwy.) | 512-795-8593 | www.musashinosushi.com

Connoisseurs claim "you'd be hard-pressed to find a more authentic Japanese menu" than the one at this Northwest Hills "gem" "hidden" beneath a Chinese restaurant where the "knowledgeable chefs" craft an "amazing selection" of Tokyo-style sushi from "fresh" fish flown in daily from the Tsukiji market; considering it's "one of the best in the city", supporters say it's "easy to go overboard" and end up "spending too much" here.

NEW Nomad *Eclectic*

| - | - | - | I |

Coronado Hills | 1213 Corona Dr. (Cameron Rd.) | 512-628-4288 | www.nomadbar.com

Though relatively new, this Coronado Hills watering hole already has the feel of a longtime neighborhood bar thanks to its friendly barkeeps and wide range of well-priced draft beers, wines and specialty cocktails; the kitchen pumps out Eclectic fare like panini, empanadas and cheese plates – plus a noteworthy Sunday brunch – served either in the roomy interior decorated with mismatched furniture or on the lush landscaped patio.

NoRTH *Italian*

| - | - | - | M |

Northwest Austin | The Domain | 11506 Century Oaks Terr. (bet. Braker Ln. & Burnet Rd.) | 512-339-4400 | www.foxrc.com

This Northwest Austin outpost of a Scottsdale-based chain marries contemporary design with a modern menu of Northern Italian dishes (think wood-fired pizzas and innovative pasta dishes); it

draws a steady stream of hip mall-goers who stop in for a post-shopping boost or a cocktail out on the lively patio.

North by Northwest *American*   18 | 19 | 17 | $24

Great Hills | 10010 N. Capital of Texas Hwy. (Stonelake Blvd.) | 512-467-6969 | www.nxnwbrew.com

"Catering to the young professional set", this Great Hills American bistro/microbrewery is known as the spot "for after-work drinks" and "singles mingling" in a "Pacific Northwestern" "mountain-lodge" setting; folks enjoy "sitting by the fireplace in the winter" or listening to "live music on the patio" (Wednesday–Saturday) while noshing on "upscale pub grub" washed down with "great house brews" at "reasonable prices", even if the "service can be cranky."

Oasis, The *Tex-Mex*   11 | 24 | 14 | $24

Lakeway | 6550 Comanche Trail (Rte. 620) | 512-266-2442 | www.oasis-texas.com

The "stunning views" of Lake Travis are best admired from the "great patio" at this Lakeway Tex-Mex where locals label the food "under-whelming", the drinks "watered down" and the service "marginal"; yet in spite of that and a "crowded", "touristy" "atmosphere that feels like you're at a frat amusement park", most maintain you have to go "at least once" and bask in the "terrific sunsets" on "a warm night."

Oaxacan Tamaleo 🅼 *Mexican*   - | - | - | I

Cedar Creek | 1634 Hwy. 71 (FM 1209) | 512-289-9262 | www.tamaleo.com

Authentic Oaxacan fare is the focus of Leonor and Bill Stoude's homey Cedar Creek Mexican joint turning out a variety of moles and tamales all made from scratch and based on family recipes; although it's no longer BYO only (they now offer beer and wine), tabs are kept as low as ever.

NEW Olivia *French/Italian*   - | - | - | M

South Lamar | 2043 S. Lamar Blvd. (Oltorf St.) | 512-804-2700 | www.olivia-austin.com

Housed in a striking Michael Hsu–designed building on South Lamar, this somewhat pricey newcomer boasts a seasonal French-Italian menu based on ingredients sourced from local farms and dairies; despite its sleek, ultramodern look, the narrow interior with pendant lamps and an open kitchen also includes plenty of cozy nooks for romantic dining.

Opal Divine's *American*   14 | 15 | 16 | $16

Downtown | 700 W. Sixth St. (Rio Grande St.) | 512-477-3308 ◗
North Austin | 12709 MoPac Expwy. N. (Parmer Ln.) | 512-733-5353
South Austin | 3601 S. Congress Ave. (Ben White Blvd.) | 512-707-0237 ◗
www.opaldivines.com

"Popular for its extensive scotch and beer selections", this locally owned American trio serves "standard pub grub"; regulars "quaff quality pints" on "the best patio on lower Sixth Street" at the Downtown original, on the "great deck" at the Penn Field locale or

	FOOD	DECOR	SERVICE	COST

on the boardwalklike setting at The Marina, but all boast a "laid-back ambiance" that's ideal "for groups" – from "happy hour" to late-night.

Opie's Barbecue *BBQ* — ▽ 23 | 6 | 14 | $17

Spicewood | 9504 Hwy. 71 E. (Spur 191) | 830-693-8660 | www.opiesbarbecue.com

"Like the many other famous destination BBQ joints" in Central Texas, chowhounds claim this "friendly, family-owned" Spicewood staple is definitely "worth the drive" for "fantastic" smoked meats, chops, sausages and babyback ribs; patrons pick their grub "off the pit" then head inside the roomy space (which packs loads of good ol' country style) for side dishes and fixin's off the all-you-can-eat bean and condiment bar; N.B. save room for their fab homemade cobbler!

NEW **Paggi House** ☒ *American* — - | - | - | E

Downtown South | 200 Lee Barton Dr. (Riverside Dr.) | 512-473-3700 | www.paggihouse.com

After an extensive renovation, one of the city's oldest buildings has reopened as this Downtown South fine-dining destination serving New American cuisine with international touches; the elegant interior juxtaposes historic and modern elements and opens onto a loungey landscaped deck outfitted with plush seating and wooden bistro-style tables, and boasting views of the skyline and Lady Bird Lake.

Pappadeaux *Seafood* — 23 | 19 | 20 | $29

North Austin | 6319 I-35 N. (Hwy. 290) | 512-452-9363 | www.pappadeaux.com

See review in Houston Directory.

NEW **Parkside** ● *American* — - | - | - | M

Downtown | 301 E. Sixth St. (San Jacinto Blvd.) | 512-474-9898 | www.parkside-austin.com

Shawn Cirkiel, of the late, lamented Jean Luc's, makes his return to the Austin restaurant scene with this Downtown arrival set in the atmospheric storefront that once housed Dan McKlusky's; the seasonal New American menu changes often, and features simple, satisfying items like bar steaks, bone marrow and fresh oysters paired with expertly made cocktails; it's already garnered a following among many local chefs.

Pei Wei Asian Diner *Pan-Asian* — 19 | 15 | 16 | $15

Hyde Park | Hancock Shopping Ctr. | 1000 E. 41st St. (I-35) | 512-382-3860

NEW **Jollyville** | 13429 Hwy. 183 N. (Anderson Mill Rd.) | 512-996-0095

North Austin | Shops at Tech Ridge | 12901 I-35 N. (bet. Howard & Parmer Lns.) | 512-691-3060

NEW **Round Rock** | University Commons Shopping Ctr. | 200 University Blvd. (Westgate Dr.) | 512-863-4087

Southwest Austin | Brodie Oaks Shopping Ctr. | 4200 S. Lamar Blvd. (Capital of Texas Hwy.) | 512-382-2990

www.peiwei.com

See review in Dallas/Ft. Worth Directory.

	FOOD	DECOR	SERVICE	COST

NEW Perry's Steakhouse & Grille 🅢 *Steak* | 25 | 25 | 24 | $45 |

Downtown | 114 W. Seventh St. (Colorado St.) | 512-474-6300 |
www.perryssteakhouse.com
See review in Houston Directory.

P.F. Chang's China Bistro *Chinese* | 22 | 22 | 20 | $27 |

Arboretum | 10114 Jollyville Rd. (Great Hills Trail) | 512-231-0208
Downtown | 201 San Jacinto Blvd. (2nd St.) | 512-457-8300
www.pfchangs.com
See review in Dallas/Ft. Worth Directory.

Player's ● *Burgers* | 19 | 9 | 14 | $10 |

Campus | 300 W. Martin Luther King Jr. Blvd. (Guadalupe St.) |
512-478-9299 | www.austinplayers.com
"Just a hop, skip and a jump from Campus", this "shrine to grease
(the liquid, not the musical)" is a "longtime" "favorite" of "starving
students", who love to "hang out" here, bolting "some of the best
burgers in town" and "not-to-be-missed shakes" while "watching
games" on the big-screen TV or playing "horseshoes in the back";
"there may not be decor" and service is "counter-style", but it's a
cool "dive" – and it's open "late at night."

Polvo's *Mexican* | 21 | 12 | 15 | $16 |

Bouldin Creek | 2004 S. First St. (bet. Johanna & Live Oaks Sts.) |
512-441-5446
A "change of pace from Tex-Mex", this "classic Mexican dive (right
down to the hideous pastel plastered walls)" in Bouldin Creek is
chock-full of "hipsters" in their "thrift-store trendiest" tucking into
"tasty" dishes, "housemade salsas" and "downright lethal margaritas", served on the "cool patio" or within its "funky South Austin"
interior – "all of which is worth" putting up with "the neglect you'll
receive" from the "slow", "occasionally snide" staff.

NEW Primizie Osteria *Italian* | - | - | - | I |

East Austin | 1000 E. 11th St., Ste. 150 (Curve St.) | 512-236-0088 |
www.primizieaustin.com
Tucked into a newly gentrified block of East Austin, this Italian arrival flaunts a lofty, modern interior with high ceilings, concrete
floors and big windows looking out onto the street; its inexpensive
pastas, pizzas and panini are joined by a full lineup of from-The-Boot
vintages, strong coffee and pastries, also available to go.

Quality Seafood Restaurant & | - | - | - | I |
Oyster Bar 🅢 *Seafood*

Hyde Park | 5621 Airport Blvd. (FM 2222) | 512-454-5827 |
www.qualityseafoodmarket.com
Ensconced in a historic North Hyde Park fish market, this inexpensive Cajun-inflected seafooder serves up heaping plates of shrimp,
deep-fried catfish fillets and hearty bowls of gumbo available to eat
in the no-frills interior or packaged to go; there's also a full oyster
bar that's the perfect place to wait out rush hour traffic while relaxing with a pile of bivalves and an icy cold beer.

Ranch 616 *Southwestern*

23	22	20	$35

Downtown | 616 Nueces St. (7th St.) | 512-479-7616 | www.theranch616.com

The "impressive menu" of "unique", "savory" dishes features plenty of "local ingredients" at this "small, locally owned" Downtown Southwestern serving what many call "cowboy cuisine at its best" – and "at a great price"; "cool", "quirky decor", "friendly owners" and staff and a "deft hand in the kitchen" add up to a "wonderful experience", even if the "live country music" (Tuesdays and Thursdays) sometimes "gets too loud for conversation"; N.B. the new patio provides a quieter dining option.

Rather Sweet Bakery & Café ⓩ *Bakery*

▽ 26	17	20	$15

Fredericksburg | 249 E. Main St. (Lincoln St.) | 830-990-0498 | www.rathersweet.com

Her "bread alone is worth driving 100 miles for" declare devotees of chef-owner Rebecca Rather's "small, simply decorated" Fredericksburg cafe where a "light" menu of soups, salads and sandwiches are a "good prelude" to her "fantastic" sweets like decadent chocolate buttercream cake and fruity tarts; early birds applaud the "breakfast items" too, with cinnamon rolls, bacon and cheddar scones and other modestly priced items available till they close at 5 PM.

Reale's Pizza & Cafe ⓩ *Italian*

23	13	19	$18

Jollyville | Plaza 183 | 13450 Hwy. 183 N. (Anderson Mill Rd.) | 512-335-5115 | www.realespizzaandcafe.com

"Genuine New York–style thin-crust pizza" and "down-home Italian fare" can be found at this "family-run business" "somewhat hidden in a strip mall" in Jollyville; its "devoted following of expat Easterners" flocks for its "excellent" veal, chicken and pasta dishes, which are served "at reasonable prices" within a homey atmosphere (right "down to the checkered tablecloths") and can be wonderfully paired with offerings from their "decent wine list."

Real New Orleans Style Restaurant ⓩ *Creole*

-	-	-	I

Round Mountain | 10541 Hwy. 281 N. (R.R. 962) | 830-825-3600 | www.therealneworleansstylerestaurant.com

In the tiny hamlet of Round Mountain (between Marble Falls and Johnson City), this former failing truck stop was taken over by members of a New Orleans congregation whose church and homes were destroyed by Hurricane Katrina; they're bringing Creole cooking and a dash of Big Easy style to the Hill Country, much to the delight of locals and travelers; N.B. it's closed on Sundays, when the staff is 'on fire for the Lord, and smokin' for Jesus.'

Restaurant Jezebel ⓩ *American*

▽ 27	21	23	$52

Downtown | 914 Congress Ave. (9th St.) | 512-499-3999 | www.restaurantjezebel.com

Enthusiasts assert the food is "first rate" at this New American "in the heart of Downtown Austin" whose "interesting" menu draws inspiration from a variety of international cuisines and solicitous serv-

ers help diners navigate the 1,400-label wine list; decor is done up in "dark", deep burgundy and mustard colors with watercolors of nudes adding to the "romantic" atmosphere.

Roaring Fork *Southwestern*

| | 24 | 24 | 23 | $38 |

Downtown | InterContinental Stephen F. Austin Hotel | 701 Congress Ave. (7th St.) | 512-583-0000 | www.eddiev.com

"Hearty" "haute cowboy cuisine" like green chile pork stew and Dr. Pepper-braised short ribs sates the appetites of "congressmen", "lobbyists" and other "businesspeople" at this "convivial" Downtown hangout done up in an "elegant" Old-West style with wrought-iron accents and rustic wood floors; service is suitably "professional", and those who find the tab "a bit high" may want to visit the "inviting" bar where you can make a "whole meal" on reduced-price drinks and apps during the "great happy hour"; N.B. the San Antonio branch is new.

Rocco's Grill *Italian*

| | ▽ 20 | 22 | 20 | $30 |

Lakeway | Lakeway Commons | 900 Ranch Road 620 S. (Lakeway Blvd.) | 512-263-8204 | www.roccosgrill.com

Patrons praise the "beautiful" golf-course views and "nice deck" at this Lakeway eatery offering midpriced Italian specialties as well as mesquite-grilled meats ferried by servers who are generally "up to par"; cons counter that the cuisine is "run-of-the-mill" adding that "the murals on the wall are the most colorful part of the experience" here.

Romeo's *Italian*

| | 17 | 17 | 19 | $22 |

Georgetown | 701 Main St. (W. 7th St.) | 512-868-1300
Zilker | 1500 Barton Springs Rd. (Lamar Blvd.) | 512-476-1090
www.austinromeos.com

"Large portions" of "homestyle Italian" at "reasonable prices" are served by a "friendly staff" at this "cozy spot" on Zilker's Restaurant Row; despite its "kitschy" decor – "grapes growing out of the ceiling" and "fake, plastic flowers" – fans feel the "dimly lit" space manages to be "charming and intimate", with "romantic touches" like live jazz Thursday–Saturday that make it "perfect for a cheap date-night"; P.S. ask to be "seated out on the patio."

R.O.'s Outpost ⊠ Ⓜ ⇄ *BBQ*

| | - | - | - | I |

Spicewood | 22112 Hwy. 71 W. (bet. Crawford Rd. & Hazy Hills Dr.) | 512-264-1169

This tiny, funky BYO shack on Highway 71 in Spicewood (17 miles west of Austin) teems with Texas hospitality and some of the most ardent BBQ fans around; its pecan-smoked brisket, pork ribs, sausage, ham and chicken – not to mention housemade pies – are legendary, as the walls covered in autographed photos of Texas musicians suggest; chicken-fried steak and other Southern dishes round out the menu.

Roy's *Hawaiian*

| | 25 | 24 | 23 | $48 |

Downtown | 340 E. Second St. (Trinity St.) | 512-391-1500 | www.roysrestaurant.com

See review in Dallas/Ft. Worth Directory.

Ruby's BBQ ⏺ *BBQ*

23	13	17	$14

North Campus | 512 W. 29th St. (Guadalupe St.) | 512-477-1651 | www.rubysbbq.com

"Some of the yummiest (and most PC) barbecue in town" can be found at this "quirky" North Campus "joint" whose "beef is billed as hormone-free" with "no antibiotics"; the "tender" cuts are "smoked to perfection" and served with "divine desserts" by a "friendly counter" staff, plus its selection of "tasty veg" dishes means it's the "place for carnivores to take vegetarians and make everyone happy."

Ruth's Chris Steak House *Steak*

25	22	25	$57

Downtown | 107 W. Sixth St. (Congress Ave.) | 512-477-7884 | www.ruthschris.com

See review in San Antonio Directory.

Saba Blue Water *Eclectic*

18	19	16	$28

Warehouse District | 208D W. Fourth St. (bet. Colorado & Lavaca Sts.) | 512-478-7222 | www.sabacafe.com

"It's hard to be blue" at this Warehouse District destination where the modern space with aquatic details sets the tone for an "inventive" menu of Pacific- and Caribbean-influenced plates and creative cocktails; filled with a "lively crowd", it "can get a bit loud, especially later at night" when it morphs into more of a "club"-like environment; P.S. wallet-watchers insist the "happy-hour specials" are a great deal.

Sagra *Italian*

-	-	-	I

Downtown | 1610 San Antonio St. (17th St.) | 512-535-5988 | www.sagrarestaurant.net

Occupying a refurbished cottage Downtown, this Italian eatery turns out affordable regional dishes made from local, seasonal ingredients in a simple, candlelit space with white linen tablecloths; inspired by the food festivals for which it's named, it also plays host to special monthly dinners based around a single ingredient.

Ⓩ Salt Lick *BBQ*

24	18	20	$21

NEW Round Rock | 3350 E. Palm Valley Rd. (Harrell Pkwy.) | 512-386-1044

Driftwood | 18300 FM 1826 (FM 967) | 512-858-4959 ⏚ www.saltlickbbq.com

"The mother of all Texas BBQ places" swear surveyors sweet on this Driftwood "landmark" famed for its "tender", "flavorful" brisket and "rustic" Hill Country setting with "communal" "picnic tables" and live music on weekends; be forewarned, it's BYO (and located in a dry county), so grab a cooler and "pick up a six-pack" of Shiner Bock before you "mosey on over"; N.B. the new Round Rock branch – built from rock quarried at the original – is located in the parking lot of the Dell Diamond and features the same 'cue, plus a full bar.

Sampaio's Restaurant *Brazilian*

20	20	19	$27

Rosedale | Rosedale Shopping Ctr. | 4800 Burnet Rd. (bet. 47th & 49th Sts.) | 512-469-9988 | www.sampaiosrestaurant.com

Locals laud this Rosedale restaurant where moderately priced "nouveau" Brazilian" fare and "tasty" cocktails come together in a "styl-

ish" setting awash in yellows and greens; "top-notch" service adds to the appeal, as does a "quiet", plant-filled patio that proves the perfect escape from the sometimes "noisy" interior.

São Paulo's ☒ *Brazilian* ▽ 21 | 14 | 18 | $20

Campus | 2809 San Jacinto Blvd. (bet. Duval & Speedway Sts.) | 512-473-9988 | www.saopaulos.net

"Brazil meets Tex-Mex" at this "groovy little joint" near Campus that's "popular with university" sorts for its "varied" menu of "authentic" and "tasty" dishes from its namesake city along with some local offerings, all served with "terrific" tropical cocktails like caipirinhas and mojitos by a staff that's "always friendly"; P.S. "great Brazilian music performed on weekends" (Thursday–Saturday nights) is a bonus.

Sarovar Indian Cuisine *Indian* ▽ 21 | 12 | 15 | $18

North Austin | 8440 Burnet Rd. (Penny Ln.) | 512-454-8636 | www.sarovar.net

See review in San Antonio Directory.

Satay *Pan-Asian* 21 | 15 | 17 | $20

Northwest Austin | 3202 W. Anderson Ln. (Shoal Creek Blvd.) | 512-467-6731 | www.satayusa.com

"Fresh, flavorful fare" at a "great price point" characterizes this longtime Northwest Austin favorite that's earned a loyal following with its "good presentations" of "spicy", "interesting" Southeast Asian dishes (mostly Thai, with some Malaysian, Indonesian and Vietnamese mainstays), including "daily specials that are always winners"; though "the owner makes you feel like one of the family", some surveyors still suggest that the "service can vary considerably."

Sazón *Mexican* - | - | - | I

Zilker | 1816 S. Lamar Blvd. (Hether St.) | 512-326-4395 | www.sazonaustin.com

Although not much to look at from the outside (or the inside, for that matter), this family-owned Mexican in Zilker is attracting attention with its authentic regional cuisine, featuring unique dishes – like huitlacoche empanadas made with corn truffle – found nowhere else in town; thanks to its gentle prices, it's already gained a loyal following, especially for weekend breakfast.

Scholz Garten *German* 13 | 16 | 15 | $15

Downtown | 1607 San Jacinto Blvd. (17th St.) | 512-474-1958 | www.scholzgarten.net

Offering up "a bit of Austin as our great-grandparents knew it", this "real 19th-century German biergarten" Downtown, just south of Campus, "creates a decent Oktoberfest atmosphere" within its festive "beer-hall" interior and out on its "picnic table–studded patio"; perhaps most people "don't come here for the food or the service" but it's nevertheless a popular "hangout for students and politicos", and known as "the University of Texas football game-day tailgate" headquarters.

FOOD | DECOR | SERVICE | COST

NEW Segovia Spanish
- | - | - | I

Oak Hill | H.E.B. Shopping Ctr. | 7010 Hwy. 71 W. (Hwy. 290 W.) | 512-579-0726 | www.segoviaaustin.com

This affordable Oak Hill Spaniard belies its suburban strip-mall setting by serving an authentic lineup of tapas alongside paella and other traditional dishes; an adjacent bar offers wine, beer and homemade sangria, while entertainment comes in the form of a flatscreen TV and live flamenco music on weekends.

Serranos Tex-Mex
16 | 14 | 17 | $17

Arboretum | 10000 Research Blvd. (bet. Capital of Texas Hwy. & Great Hills Trail) | 512-250-9555
Cedar Park | 11100 Pecan Park Blvd. (Lakeline Mall Blvd.) | 512-258-3441
Downtown | Symphony Sq. | 1111 Red River St. (11th St.) | 512-322-9080
North Central | Southpark Meadows | 9500 I-35 S. (Turk Ln.) | 512-280-7770
Round Rock | La Frontera Shopping Ctr. | 2701 Parker Rd. (I-35) | 512-218-4888
Southwest Austin | Best Buy Shopping Ctr. | 5030 Hwy. 290 W. (MoPac Expwy.) | 512-891-7592
www.serranos.com

"Popular" for its "two-for-one specials" on Mondays, this "local" chain serves up "huge portions" of "standard Tex-Mex" fare that tends toward the "run-of-the-mill"; although the Downtown location's "great outdoor setting" with "terraced stone steps overlooking the creek" make it a destination to "grab a few margaritas", patrons of the other branches wish they'd "work on that decor, please."

Shady Grove American
19 | 21 | 17 | $17

Zilker | 1624 Barton Springs Rd. (Lamar Blvd.) | 512-474-9991 | www.theshadygrove.com

A "laid-back, relaxed atmosphere" characterizes this "trailer-themed" spot, a "true Austin-style hangout" in Zilker with "something to please everyone" on its "interesting" classic American menu; the "unique decor is just too cool" but the main draw is the "outside seating under the pecan trees", where diners dig "fab margaritas" and "live music under the stars" on Thursdays – but "expect long waits during peak times."

Shanghai Restaurant Chinese
- | - | - | I

North Central | 6718 Middle Fiskville Rd. (Huntland Dr.) | 512-458-8088
This family-owned emporium in North Central Austin features an extensive menu of inexpensive Chinese standards set down in spacious bamboo-accented surroundings; it's a favorite for dim sum on weekends, with a mind-boggling array of offerings brought to your table by friendly cart-pushing servers.

Shoal Creek Saloon Cajun
18 | 15 | 18 | $16

Downtown | 909 N. Lamar Blvd. (9th St.) | 512-474-0805 | www.shoalcreeksaloon.com
Often "overlooked", this "Louisiana-inspired" "hangout" offers "a little New Orleans in Downtown Austin"; it's a spot "to watch sports" or "sit out back" on the patio "overlooking Shoal Creek" while having a

"cheap" "cold beer" and "good Cajun" fare such as "fried seafood" and "po' boys that easily serve two"; P.S. the Wednesday and Friday "all-you-can-eat lunchtime fish fry is popular with the locals."

Shoreline Grill *Continental*

24	24	24	$44

Downtown | San Jacinto Ctr. | 98 San Jacinto Blvd. (Cesar Chavez St.) | 512-477-3300 | www.shorelinegrill.com

An "appealing" menu with "a wide variety" of "exceptional" and "artfully presented" Continental dishes and a "fantastic wine selection" are staples at this Downtown mainstay, which also offers "splendid service that's a perfect balance of professionalism, warmth and courteousness"; further enhancing the experience are the "gorgeous views" from its "lovely room" and "outdoor seating along Lady Bird Lake", making it the ideal place to "watch the bats fly at sunset."

☑ Siena *Italian*

25	27	22	$41

Northwest Hills | 6203 N. Capital of Texas Hwy. (Rte. 2222) | 512-349-7667 | www.sienarestaurant.com

Set in a "lovely" stone building that evokes an "old Italian villa", this Northwest Hills "favorite" charms customers with "scrumptious", "rustic" Tuscan cuisine (think bistecca alla florentina and "lots of wild boar") and an "expansive" regional wine list; service is "attentive, but not hovering", ensuring a "delightful", if "expensive", experience that works for a "quiet lunch" or "romantic dinner."

NEW Silver & Stone ☒ *American*

-	-	-	E

Georgetown | 501 S. Austin Ave. (W. 5th St.) | 512-868-0565 | www.silverstonerestaurant.com

This ambitious newcomer housed in a stately Georgetown building has cemented itself as one of the area's top fine-dining establishments thanks to an adventurous New American menu and an impressive drink list featuring over 200 wine selections, 50 craft beers and an ample selection of scotches and cognacs; the atmosphere is upscale casual, with oak woodwork, high ceilings and stained-glass chandeliers creating a sophisticated atmosphere that gets a lift from live music on weekends.

Silver K Cafe *American*

-	-	-	M

Johnson City | 209 E. Main St. (F Ave.) | 830-868-2911 | www.silverkcafe.com

Housed in a "pretty" historic building with exposed-wood beams and antique light fixtures, this Johnson City cafe proves a "must-visit" in Hill Country for its "inspired" takes on Traditional American fare (signatures include honey-pecan fried chicken and buttermilk pie) and its well-considered selection of Texas wines; service is "good" too, leading regulars to recommend it as a "nice place to stop in" – you'd never expect such a "jewel" "given the small-town location."

Smitty's Market ☞ *BBQ*

▽ 19	10	12	$16

Lockhart | 208 S. Commerce St. (Prairie Lea St.) | 512-398-9344 | www.smittysmarket.com

Another "darn good" BBQ "joint" in Lockhart, this "top-tier" contender occupies the historic building where Kreuz Market once

stood (the two institutions are run by different branches of the same family); fans line up for "wonderful" smoked meats and links served cafeteria-style and then hunker down at one of the long pine tables for an old-fashioned chowdown.

Snow's BBQ ⛌Ⓜ *BBQ*

| - | - | - | I |

Lexington | 516 Main St. (bet. 2nd & 3rd Sts.) | 979-542-8189 | www.snowsbbq.com

Set in Lexington – about an hour northeast of Austin – this quintessential small-town joint struck it big when *Texas Monthly* dubbed it the state's top 'cue contender for its sublimely smoked brisket, ribs and sausage; it's only open on Saturdays, from 8 AM until the meat runs out, so get there early to load up. P.S. those in-the-know call in their order during the week.

South Congress Café *Southwestern*

| 22 | 20 | 21 | $28 |

SoCo | 1600 S. Congress Ave. (Monroe St.) | 512-447-3905 | www.southcongresscafe.com

"Clever" takes on Southwestern cuisine, "great cocktails" and a "knockout brunch" are the hallmarks of this fairly priced SoCo spot set in "bright", "stylish" digs with alligator-skin booths and retro light fixtures; service is "top-notch", but regulars warn of "long waits" to be seated and suggest you "go at off hours because this place is mighty popular."

Southside Market & BBQ *BBQ*

| 24 | 10 | 14 | $15 |

Elgin | 1212 Hwy. 290 E. (Hwy. 95) | 512-281-4650 | www.southsidemarket.com

Supporters salivate over the "excellent sausage" at this family-owned BBQ fixture in Elgin that's been turning out their "spicy" signature links since 1882; a selection of slow-cooked meats, "homemade" sides and hand-dipped ice cream cones round out the inexpensive offerings served up "Texas-style" in a "down-home" setting with communal tables and a full-service butcher shop on-site.

🆕 Southwest Bistro *Southwestern*

| - | - | - | M |

Downtown South | Hyatt Regency Austin | 208 Barton Springs Rd. (Congress Ave.) | 512-477-1234 | www.hyattregencyaustin.com

Into the beautifully transformed space on the second level of the Hyatt Regency Downtown comes this new Southwestern chicly dressed in autumnal tones with windows peeking out onto the Austin skyline; its moderately expensive menu includes smoked pork ribs and hefty steaks backed by well-made cocktails; N.B. there's also a noteworthy breakfast buffet.

Starlite *American*

| 25 | 21 | 22 | $42 |

Warehouse District | 407 Colorado St. (4th St.) | 512-374-9012 | www.starliteaustin.net

This Warehouse District "star" "shines" thanks to a seasonal New American menu showcasing "innovative" dishes plus handcrafted cocktails all served up in an "elegant and modern" interior with vaulted ceilings and an Italian crystal chandelier; "professional" servers and all-around "attention to detail" make it a favorite "date spot."

	FOOD	DECOR	SERVICE	COST

Steeping Room, The *Tearoom* ▽ 21 | 22 | 19 | $16

Northwest Austin | The Domain | 11410 Century Oaks Terr. (bet. Domain Dr. & Frontage Rd.) | 512-977-8337 | www.thesteepingroom.com

Northwest Austinites applaud this "cute little tearoom" ensconced in The Domain serving a long list of drinks alongside "delicious" sandwiches "with the crusts cut off", as well as reasonably priced soups, salads and sweets; even if service sometimes hits a snag, the soothing "Zen atmosphere" makes it "a pleasant place for lunch", a hot drink or a glass of wine at one of the outdoor tables.

ᴺᴱᵂ Steiner Ranch Steakhouse *Steak* - | - | - | E

Steiner Ranch | 5424 Steiner Ranch Blvd. (Hwy. 620 N.) | 512-381-0800 | www.steinersteakhouse.com

This larger-than-life steakhouse in Steiner Ranch inhabits a striking former ranch building constructed from limestone and river rock, and sporting incredible Lake Travis vistas; the kitchen sends out gigantic cuts of meat as well as house specialties like chicken fried elk and miso mahi mahi, all bolstered by an impressive wine and cocktail list and an eager-to-please staff.

Stubb's Ⓜ *BBQ* 20 | 17 | 16 | $18

Downtown | 801 Red River St. (8th St.) | 512-480-8341 | www.stubbsaustin.com

"Beer, barbecue and bands" are the mainstays of this Downtown temple to "live music" and "hearty meals" that are a "fine example of" the genre, featuring "many more options of sides than most joints" of its ilk, all dished out with "fast service" in a "lively, rustic atmosphere"; P.S. "the gospel Sunday brunch is a treat."

Sullivan's Steakhouse *Steak* 24 | 23 | 23 | $53

Warehouse District | 300 Colorado St. (3rd St.) | 512-495-6504 | www.sullivansteakhouse.com

"If you're in the mood for steak" but "don't want a $300 bill", these "dependable" chain links prove some of "the better chophouses" around given their "excellent cuts of beef", "attentive" staffers and retro "big-city" vibe; the "lively" bars are a "swinging" "place to mingle" and are typically "crowded and noisy" after dark.

Sunflower Vietnamese *Vietnamese* ▽ 23 | 8 | 13 | $15

North Austin | 8557 Research Blvd. (Ohlen Dr.) | 512-339-7860

"Someone in the kitchen truly knows what he's doing" at this "find" "in the Little Saigon area" of North Austin featuring "delightful" Vietnamese dishes that are "fresh, hot and well-seasoned"; most don't fret about the "slow service" (or the "strip-mall" location), insisting that "every dish is worth the wait", because "dollar for dollar it's one of the best values in town."

Suzi's China Grill *Chinese* 19 | 17 | 18 | $20

Allandale | 7858 Shoal Creek Blvd. (Anderson Ln.) | 512-302-4600
West Lake Hills | 2745 Bee Caves Rd. (Edgegrove Dr.) | 512-347-7077

(continued)

(continued)

Suzi's China Kitchen ⑤ *Chinese*
South Lamar | 1152 S. Lamar Blvd. (Barton Springs Rd.) | 512-441-8400
www.suzischinagrill.com

"Old standbys that never fail to please", these "upscale Chinese" outposts appeal to those craving "fresh", "fast", "elegant" fare served in a "pleasant" "friendly atmosphere"; the "effervescent" owner has created three distinct eateries: the South Lamar original has a "neighborhood feel", the Allandale location is "a hot spot for those weekday lunches", while the West Lake Hills branch is "spiffier."

Tacodeli *Mexican*
25 | 13 | 20 | $9

Northwest Austin | 12001 Burnet Rd. (MoPac Expwy.) | 512-339-1700
Southwest Austin | 1500 Spyglass Dr. (MoPac Expwy.) | 512-732-0303
www.tacodeli.com

"Crave-worthy tacos", "mouthwatering" daily specials and other inexpensive "authentic" Mexican eats make these area "standouts" Austin's No. 1 Bang for the Buck ("talk about a great meal at a great price"); both the Northwest and Southwest locations offer "order-at-the-counter" service and "cool", "casual" settings, which are "overflowing with regulars" whose only complaint is that they "wish" these "gems" "were open for dinner."

Taco Xpress *Mexican*
21 | 16 | 15 | $10

South Lamar | 2529 S. Lamar Blvd. (Manchaca Rd.) | 512-444-0261 |
www.tacoxpress.com

The epitome of "Austin", this "funky" South Lamar "joint" run by local "icon" Maria Corbalan turns out "yummy" tacos in a "kitschy", "convivial" atmosphere enhanced by "live music" on the "great patio"; though a move some years back imparted a "more modern" look, it remains as "busy" as ever thanks to the "same wonderful food" at "unbeatable" prices.

🆕 Taste Select Wines *American*
- | - | - | E

Downtown | 202 W. Cesar Chavez St. (Colorado St.) | 512-478-2783 |
www.tasteselectwines.com

This new Downtown wine bar flaunts an impressive, ever-evolving selection of vintages ready to be paired with snackable New American bites; it boasts a lofty look with walnut tables, brown leather chairs and bright, white countertops, and there's also a retail portion with a nifty Enomatic dispenser that allows you to purchase tastes before you buy.

Taverna Pizzeria & Risotteria *Italian*
23 | 20 | 20 | $30

Downtown | 258 W. Second St. (Lavaca St.) | 512-477-1001 |
www.tavernabylombardi.com
See review in Dallas/Ft. Worth Directory.

TC Noodle House *Noodle Shop*
- | - | - | I

North Austin | Chinatown Austin | 10901 N. Lamar Blvd. (Kramer Ln.) |
512-873-8235

Noodles of every shape and size are pan-fried, boiled or dunked in soup at this inexpensive Pan-Asian located in the Chinatown Center in

FOOD DECOR SERVICE COST

North Austin; smoked meats, congee, a smattering of Vietnamese-style dishes and a nice selection of teas round out the offerings, which are presented in comfortable, semi-traditional quarters by a congenial staff.

Texas Chili Parlor � *American* | 20 | 18 | 20 | $14 |

Downtown | 1409 Lavaca St. (15th St.) | 512-472-2828

This "dark", "grungy" "Capitol-area" Downtown "hangout" is famed for its "hellfire hot chili", juicy burgers and other "cheap" American grub accompanied by "heavy pours" of "good cold beer"; even if connoisseurs claim the food's "not that great", old-timers insist it's "a must-visit for tradition's sake" thanks to an "authentically Texas" vibe and "gruff service [that's] part of the charm."

Thai Kitchen *Thai* | 20 | 7 | 16 | $14 |

Campus | 3009 Guadalupe St. (30th St.) | 512-474-2575 ❷
South Austin | 801 E. William Cannon Dr. (I-35) | 512-445-4844
West Lake Hills | 3437 Bee Caves Rd. (Blue Ridge Trail) | 512-328-3538 ⊠
www.thaikitchenofaustin.com

"Good, cheap" Thai fare (and some Chinese dishes) – including a "wide selection" of "blissful soups" – is on the menu at these branches of a locally owned chain; still, some say the "service and food quality can be hit-or-miss" and the decor "could use a lot of help", especially at the West Lake Hills and South Austin outposts, which are each "marred by a crummy location."

Thai Noodle House *Thai* | ∇ 17 | 7 | 14 | $11 |

Campus | 2602 Guadalupe St. (26th St.) | 512-494-1011

"Don't expect fancy dining" at this "simple, reliable" Campus noodle house that's frequented by "die-hard fans", despite being "tucked away a bit from The Drag"; its "repeat customers" report that it's "worth the effort to find" for its menu of "basic Thai options" featuring food that's "humble" but full of "flavor", while detractors are "not happy with the service" or similarly "no-frills" decor.

Thai Passion ❷ *Thai* | 20 | 16 | 19 | $19 |

Downtown | 620 Congress Ave. (7th St.) | 512-472-1244 |
www.thaipassion.com

"Beautifully plated" and "tasty" cuisine is "attentively served" by a "gracious" staff in a "serene setting" (especially the glass-topped "courtyard dining room") at this Downtown Thai eatery with "historic ambiance"; its "good value" makes it a "favorite lunch spot", and its "late-night hours" (open nightly till 3 AM) are another plus.

Thistle Café *American* | 18 | 18 | 16 | $24 |

Downtown | 300 W. Sixth St. (Lavaca St.) | 512-275-9777
West Lake Hills | Davenport Vill. | 3801 Capital of Texas Hwy. N. (Westlake Dr.) | 512-347-1000
www.thistlecafe.com

A varied menu of "healthy" American options prove "more than acceptable" to local lunchers at these order-at-the-counter twins Downtown (sleeker with more space) and in West Lake Hills (offering full dinner service); yet while some regulars report they've had

"good" experiences, the majority maintains it "could be a lot better", attesting that "unconcerned" service and "soulless" decor are among the downsides.

Threadgill's *Southern*

19 | 19 | 18 | $18

Crestview | 6416 N. Lamar Blvd. (bet. Hwy. 183 & Rte. 2222) | 512-451-5440
Downtown South | 301 W. Riverside Dr. (Barton Springs Rd.) | 512-472-9304
www.threadgills.com

"You'll think you're at grandma's" when you visit these "homestyle Southern" spots that are "legendary for live music" and "old-fashioned comfort food that makes mouths happy"; "history was made at the original" Crestview site (Janis Joplin got her start here in the 1960s), while the newer Downtown South branch is "filled to the rafters with rock memorabilia", and features a "fine Sunday gospel brunch."

III Forks 🅱 *Steak*

25 | 24 | 24 | $60

Downtown | 111 Lavaca St. (1st St.) | 512-474-1776 | www.3forks.com
Bring "a full wallet and an empty stomach" to these Austin and Dallas-area "temples of beef" searing "excellent steaks" "cooked to perfection" and accompanied by "fabulous fixin's" like duchess potatoes and "the best creamed corn ever"; a "gracious" staff and "over-the-top" marble-and-wood decor "give it an elegant" feel, so even if critics cry it's "gaudy" and "overhyped", it still ranks as a "favorite" for "special occasions."

Tokai Japanese Hibachi *Japanese*

- | - | - | M

Cedar Park | Railyard Shopping Ctr. | 601 E. Whitestone Blvd. (Hwy. 183 N.) | 512-528-8282 | www.tokaihibachi.com
Blink and you just might miss this petite Japanese newcomer nestled in a shopping center in Cedar Park; the modestly priced menu features teppanyaki in a myriad of meat and veggie combinations, well-stocked bento boxes and a full lineup of sushi featuring adventurous rolls with an American spin.

Torchy's Tacos *Mexican*

- | - | - | I

Bouldin Creek | 1311 S. First St. (W. Elizabeth St.) | 512-366-0537
NEW Bouldin Creek | 2809 S. First St. (El Paso St.) | 512-444-0300
NEW Campus | 2801 Guadalupe St. (28th St.) | 512-494-8226
www.torchystacos.com

Originating out of a trailer in Bouldin Creek, this Mexican trio traffics in quirky, gut-busting tacos (think fried avocado and Jamaican jerk chicken) topped with a variety of salsas that range from mild to volcanic; loaded breakfast tortillas are also available at all three locations, two of which are housed indoors in cafelike settings; N.B. plans are afoot to open more outposts in 2009.

Trattoria Lisina *Italian*

- | - | - | M

Driftwood | Mandola Estate Winery | 13308 FM 150 W. (FM 1826) | 512-894-3111 | www.trattorialisina.com
Resembling a Tuscan stone villa, this lovely Driftwood Italian from chef Damian Mandola proffers a variety of moderately priced rustic

specialties like osso buco and roast suckling pig; the romantic interior features well-worn concrete floors, wooden chairs and copper accents while the enclosed patio perched on the edge of the family's adjacent vineyard offers a superb seat for taking in a Hill Country sunset.

☑ TRIO *American* 27 | 24 | 26 | $52

Downtown | Four Seasons Hotel | 98 San Jacinto Blvd. (1st St.) | 512-685-8300 | www.fourseasons.com

It's "not just 'hotel food'" insist enthusiasts of the "delicious" fare at this dining room in Downtown's Four Seasons where the New American menu focuses on premium steaks, seafood and wine (60 available by the glass) and the "elegant" interior is dressed in warm red tones and outfitted with mahogany tables; considering it still offers a luxurious Sunday brunch and a "fab view" of Lady Bird Lake, it's no wonder some suggest it "reflects the best of the 'new' Austin."

Trudy's ● *Tex-Mex* 20 | 16 | 18 | $17

North Austin | 8820 Burnet Rd. (Hwy. 183) | 512-454-1474
North Campus | 409 W. 30th St. (Guadalupe St.) | 512-477-2935
South Austin | 901 Little Texas Ln. (I-35) | 512-326-9899
www.trudys.com

"Still going strong after more than 25 years", this "popular" Tex-Mex mini-chain "hits the spot" with "fresh" south-of-the-border eats served in a "crowded", "family-friendly" atmosphere; some diners demur on the "fraternity party" bar scene and service that can be "variable", but most misgivings are pushed aside once you toss back one of their famously "potent" Mexican martinis (only two per customer because "they'll really knock you on your you-know-what").

Truluck's *Seafood* 23 | 22 | 23 | $44

Arboretum | 10225 Research Blvd. (Great Hills Trail) | 512-794-8300
Warehouse District | 400 Colorado St. (4th St.) | 512-482-9000
www.trulucks.com
See review in Dallas/Ft. Worth Directory.

Turtle Restaurant, The ☒Ⓜ *American* - | - | - | M

Brownwood | 514 Center Ave. (bet. Adams & Chandler Sts.) | 325-646-8200 | www.theturtlerestaurant.com

The quaint Hill Country town of Brownwood is home to this inviting eatery that pays homage to the Slow Food movement with New American dishes crafted from local Texas ingredients, including herbs and veggies from the back garden; the small, candlelit room is decorated with a turtle theme, though the most appealing feature may be the adjacent gelateria turning out 16 seasonal homemade flavors; N.B. it's BYO for now, but soon they'll offer beer and wine in both the restaurant and the adjacent enoteca.

219 West *American* 21 | 19 | 18 | $26

Warehouse District | 219 W. Fourth St. (Lavaca St.) | 512-474-2194 | www.219west.com

"Upscale bar food" plus "a darn good wine list" lure "trendy" tipplers to this "hip" Warehouse District New American featuring one of "the best happy hours in town", with deals on drinks and small

plates from 5–9 PM on weekdays; "service can slow", but plasma TVs and a "cool singles scene" provide ample distraction.

Ⓩ Uchi *Japanese*   28 | 26 | 25 | $48

Zilker | 801 S. Lamar Blvd. (Barton Springs Rd.) | 512-916-4808 | www.uchiaustin.com

"Prepare to be dazzled" at this "chic" Zilker destination that surveyors say is "about as close to perfect as it gets" thanks to "incredible young chef" Tyson Cole's "brilliant" creations that take Japanese cuisine "to a new level" and earn this "jewel" the No. 1 Food score in Austin; a "top-notch" staff "goes out of its way to please" in the "charming, little" house, so even if "endless waits" and "expensive" tabs are par for the course, it all adds up to a "wonderful experience" nonetheless.

NEW Uncorked 🗷 *Eclectic*   – | – | – | I

East Austin | 900 E. Seventh St. (I-35) | 512-524-2809 | www.uncorkedtastingroom.com

After a miraculous transformation, the hilltop East Austin cottage that once housed Angie's is now this chic wine bar and bistro done up in green and grape and divided into numerous cozy rooms, with deck seating offering panoramic views of the skyline; an extensive selection of vino is available by the glass, bottle or in one of their many creative flights, with small plates and cheese boards sharing menu space with more substantial Eclectic plates like pecan-dusted pork chops.

Ventana 🗷Ⓜ *French*   ▽ 23 | 17 | 18 | $30

North Austin | Texas Culinary Academy | 11400 Burnet Rd. (Duval Rd.) | 512-339-3850 | www.tca.edu/restaurant.asp

Staffed by the students and teachers of the Texas Culinary Academy, this North Austin fine-dining room features a "wonderful" "sampling" of classical and contemporary French "delights" accompanied by well-chosen wines all at more-than-reasonable prices; even if a few note that service sometimes hits a snag, consensus is that "when the students hit it right, it's as good or better than anything else in the city"; N.B. open Tuesdays–Fridays.

Ⓩ Vespaio *Italian*   28 | 23 | 24 | $43

SoCo | 1610 S. Congress Ave. (Monroe St.) | 512-441-6100 | www.austinvespaio.com

Equal parts "unpretentious" "neighborhood" hangout and "elegant" "big-city" joint, this "upscale" SoCo "mainstay" – and Austin's Most Popular restaurant – is "almost impossible to get into" thanks to its "fantastic" Italian cuisine ("delicious homemade pastas", "tempting specials") and "great wines" brought from the open kitchen by an "outstanding" staff; because of a no-reservations policy on weekends, there's "always a line", but those in-the-know "steal a seat at the bar" and pass the "waits" with some stellar "people-watching."

NEW Viva Chocolato! *Dessert*   – | – | – | I

Northwest Austin | The Domain | 3401 Esperanza Crossing (Domain Dr.) | 512-339-8482 | www.vivachocolato.com

Chocolate is the star of this Northwest Austin newcomer where panini and salads serve as a prelude to a mind-boggling assortment of

decadent desserts like fondues, bonbons and housemade gelato, plus wines by the glass; sweet-seeking patrons can opt for one of the European-style tables or take out imported and locally made truffles from the display counter up front.

Vivo *Tex-Mex*   19 | 21 | 17 | $21

Cherrywood | 2015 Manor Rd. (Poquito St.) | 512-482-0300 | www.vivo-austin.com

The "cool" crimson interior and paintings of voluptuous nudes set a "sexy" scene at this "crowded" Cherrywood hideaway that's "great for a date" thanks to "fab margaritas", a "beautiful" plant-filled patio and "complimentary roses for each lady"; "fresh" Tex-Mex fare includes "delicious" deep-fried puffy tacos as well as a smattering of "healthy options" all at moderate prices.

Waterloo Ice House *Burgers*   16 | 14 | 16 | $15

Circle C | Escarpment Vill. | 9600 Escarpment Blvd. (Slaughter Ln.) | 512-301-1007

Downtown | 600 N. Lamar Blvd. (6th St.) | 512-472-5400

Jollyville | 14900 Avery Ranch Blvd. (Parmer Ln.) | 512-255-4873

North Austin | 8600 Burnet Rd. (Hwy. 183) | 512-458-6544

NEW **North Central** | Southpark Meadows | 9600 I-35 S. (Slaughter Ln.) | 512-292-7900

Northwest Hills | 6203 N. Capital of Texas Hwy. (Rte. 2222) | 512-418-9700

Rosedale | 1106 W. 38th St. (Medical Pkwy.) | 512-451-5245

www.waterlooicehouse.com

"Juicy", "loaded burgers" and "crispy housemade fries" are the staples at this "fast, friendly", "family-oriented" chain where the little ones get their own menu; "typical", "bland decor" and "inconsistent service" are drawbacks, but the Downtown location has "good live music" on weekends, while "parents can have a beer" from the "extensive selection" as "kids play in the sandbox" at the Northwest Hills branch.

NEW **Whip-In Parlour Café** *Indian*   - | - | - | I

South Austin | 1950 I-35 S. (Riverside Dr.) | 512-442-5337 | www.whipin.com

This offbeat South Austin convenience store now includes a sit-down cafe featuring homemade Indian specialties like naan sandwiches and rice bowls served in a warm space adorned with tapestries and antiques; free WiFi and live music nightly cultivate a congenial scene, soon to be made even more so by the addition of wine and beer.

Wildfire *Southwestern*   ▽ 22 | 17 | 19 | $25

Georgetown | 812 S. Austin Ave. (bet. 8th & 9th Sts.) | 512-869-3473 | www.wildfiretexas.com

"A pleasant surprise in Georgetown", this upscale-casual Southwestern in an "interesting location" across the street from the courthouse offers a "creative menu" showcasing succulent meats (including wild game) cooked in an "oak-fired grill", plus "an excellent selection of fine appetizers" and "Texas wines" at "great prices"; with dark woods and low lighting, the space is "quaint", but it's the "smell of the wood fire burning that brings folks back every time."

	FOOD	DECOR	SERVICE	COST

NEW Wine Cellar
at Barton Creek *American* — | - | - | - | I |

West Lake Hills | Barton Creek Vill. | 2700 Barton Creek Blvd.
(Wimberly Ln.) | 512-330-9119 | www.thewinecellarabc.com

This well-appointed wine bar/shop in West Lake Hills features an expansive list of international pours that pair well with simple American dishes (think sliders, sandwiches and salads), all served in a warm space with leather chairs, dark-wood cocktail tables and a long marble-topped bar; the knowledgeable staff will make anyone feel at home, and they'll also open any bottle from the retail side for a reasonable corkage fee.

Ⓩ Wink ●Ⓩ *American* — 27 | 21 | 26 | $54

Old West Austin | 1014 N. Lamar Blvd. (11th St.) | 512-482-8868 | www.winkrestaurant.com

A "temple for foodies" in Old West Austin, this "super-small" strip-mall eatery "delights" diners with an "amazing" New American menu that shows a "fanatical devotion to fresh, local ingredients" while the equally "wonderful" wine list is loaded with "little-known gems"; on the downside are "small portions", "big prices" and a "cramped" "seating plan that would make a Parisian cafe proud", but "personalized service" means most "can't wait to go back"; P.S. the adjacent wine bar "is worth a visit on its own."

Woodland, The Ⓜ *American* — 18 | 17 | 18 | $24

SoCo | 1716 S. Congress Ave. (Annie St.) | 512-441-6800 | www.woodlandaustin.com

American "home cooking" is updated for "hipsters" at this SoCo spot that mixes gently priced "comfort" classics with "retro" cocktails; the "cute" "sylvan setting" ("yes, that is a tree in there") is trimmed in greens while a "friendly staff" tends to a customer base culled from "neighborhood" "students" and "families."

NEW Yume *Asian Fusion* — - | - | - | M |

North Central | The Triangle | 815 W. 47th St. (Guadalupe St.) | 512-407-9001

A recent addition to The Triangle in North Central Austin, this mid-priced newcomer mixes up sushi with a number of elaborate fusion dishes incorporating Asian and Caribbean flavors (think chicken topped with crab and served with plantain fritters); the earthy interior is sparsely decorated with potted plants and slate tile, but salsa and mambo rhythms in the background create a festive atmosphere.

Zax Pints & Plates *American* — 19 | 17 | 19 | $25

Downtown South | 312 Barton Springs Rd. (Riverside Dr.) | 512-481-0100 | www.zaxaustin.com

You'll find "more than just pints" at this "sleek" "yet comfortable" spot south of Downtown serving "upscale pub grub" and "a decent wine list" at an "excellent value"; it's ideal for "burgers for the kids and something a little better for the parents", or for "a nice lunch with clients", and there's "live jazz" and a "pint-night happy hour" on Wednesdays and a "lovely courtyard."

	FOOD	DECOR	SERVICE	COST

Zoot ⓜ *American*

26 | **22** | **25** | **$48**

Old West Austin | 509 Hearn St. (Lake Austin Blvd.) | 512-477-6535 | www.zootrestaurant.com

"Beautifully prepared" dishes from an "imaginative" market-driven New American menu "attract a great mix" of customers to this Old West Austin "favorite" set in an "elegant", "well-appointed" bungalow exuding a "quiet, relaxing" atmosphere; "unhurried" service from a "first-class" staff means "you can always count on it" for a "romantic" date or any other "special occasion" that calls for a "near-perfect meal"; P.S. insiders say the tasting menus – especially the "amazing" vegetarian one – are "excellent" options.

Z'Tejas *Southwestern*

22 | **20** | **19** | **$26**

Arboretum | 9400 Arboretum Blvd. (Capital of Texas Hwy.) | 512-346-3506
Clarksville | 1110 W. Sixth St. (Lamar Blvd.) | 512-478-5355
Jollyville | 10525 W. Parmer Ln. (Avery Ranch Blvd.) | 512-388-7772
www.ztejas.com

"A loyal following" means "tables are scarce" at these "convivial" "hot spots" offering "delicious" Southwestern fare, "festive" environments (complete with "terrific outside dining") and "friendly staffers"; the Clarksville "original is a hodgepodge of linked 1940s cottages", while the Arboretum offshoot is housed in a "Colorado lodge–style" building that's "big, airy and spacious", and the Jollyville branch boasts a fire pit.

AUSTIN AND THE HILL COUNTRY INDEXES

Cuisines

Includes restaurant names, locations and Food ratings.

AMERICAN (NEW)

Blue Star	**Rosedale**	20
Chez Zee	**NW Hills**	21
NEW Creek Road Café	**Dripping Springs**	-
Crú Wine Bar	**multi.**	20
Z Driskill Grill	**Downtown**	26
Eastside Café	**Cherrywood**	24
NEW Fion Bistro	**Steiner Rch**	-
NEW Grove wine bar	**W Lake**	-
House.Wine.	**Fredericksburg**	-
Z Hudson's	**Lakeway**	28
Z Jasper's	**NW Austin**	24
Z Jeffrey's	**Clarksville**	26
Judges' Hill	**W Campus**	24
Kona Grill	**NW Austin**	20
Mirabelle	**NW Hills**	25
NEW Mulberry	**Downtown**	-
NEW Paggi Hse.	**Downtown S**	-
NEW Parkside	**Downtown**	-
Rest. Jezebel	**Downtown**	27
NEW Silver & Stone	**Georgetown**	-
Starlite	**Warehouse Dist**	25
NEW Taste Wines	**Downtown**	-
Z TRIO	**Downtown**	27
Turtle	**Brownwood**	-
219 West	**Warehouse Dist**	21
Z Wink	**Old W Austin**	27
Woodland	**SoCo**	18
Zoot	**Old W Austin**	26

AMERICAN (TRADITIONAL)

Belmont	**Downtown**	18
Billy's/Burnet	**Rosedale**	20
Cheesecake Factory	**Arboretum**	20
NEW Cuatros	**Campus**	-
Daily Grill	**NW Austin**	24
Dirty Martin's	**W Campus**	21
1886 Café	**Downtown**	22
Houston's	**NW Austin**	23
Hyde Park	**multi.**	21
Magnolia Café	**multi.**	21
Moonshine	**Downtown**	20
North by NW	**Great Hills**	18
Opal Divine's	**multi.**	14
Shady Grove	**Zilker**	19

Silver K	**Johnson City**	-
Texas Chili	**Downtown**	20
Thistle Café	**multi.**	18
NEW Wine Cellar	**W Lake**	-
Zax Pints	**Downtown S**	19

ASIAN

Pei Wei	**Round Rock**	19
NEW Yume	**N Central**	-

ASIAN FUSION

Bistro 88	**W Lake**	25
NEW Yume	**N Central**	-

BAKERIES

1886 Café	**Downtown**	22
Rather Sweet	**Fredericksburg**	26

BARBECUE

Artz Rib Hse.	**S Lamar**	21
Buster's	**Bee Cave**	24
City Market	**Luling**	24
Cooper's	**Llano**	27
County Line	**multi.**	20
Gonzales Mkt.	**Gonzales**	-
Green Mesquite	**Zilker**	18
Iron Works	**Downtown**	22
Kreuz Mkt.	**Lockhart**	26
Lambert's	**Warehouse Dist**	23
Louie Mueller	**Taylor**	25
Meyer's	**Elgin**	21
Opie's BBQ	**Spicewood**	23
R.O.'s Outpost	**Spicewood**	-
Ruby's	**N Campus**	23
Z Salt Lick	**multi.**	24
Smitty's Mkt.	**Lockhart**	19
Snow's BBQ	**Lexington**	-
Southside Mkt.	**Elgin**	24
Stubb's	**Downtown**	20

BRAZILIAN

Estância	**SW Austin**	27
Sampaio's	**Rosedale**	20
São Paulo's	**Campus**	21

BURGERS

Billy's/Burnet	**Rosedale**	20
Dirty Martin's	**W Campus**	21

Menus, photos, voting and more – free at ZAGAT.com

Hut's | **Downtown** 23
Player's | **Campus** 19
Shady Grove | **Zilker** 19
Waterloo Ice Hse. | **multi.** 16

CAJUN

Evangeline Café | **SW Austin** 19
Gene's | **E Austin** 25
Gumbo's | **multi.** 24
Hilltop Café | **Fredericksburg** 23
Pappadeaux | **N Austin** 23
Shoal Creek | **Downtown** 18

CARIBBEAN

Café Josie | **Clarksville** 26

CHINESE

(* dim sum specialist)
Din Ho | **N Austin** 24
First Chinese | **N Austin** 25
Golden Wok* | **N Austin** 22
P.F. Chang's | **multi.** 22
Shanghai Rest.* | **N Central** ‒
Suzi's | **multi.** 19

CONTINENTAL

Green Pastures | **Bouldin Creek** 23
Z Jeffrey's | **Clarksville** 26
Shoreline Grill | **Downtown** 24

CREOLE

Evangeline Café | **SW Austin** 19
Gumbo's | **multi.** 24
Ms. B's | **NW Hills** 22
Real New Orleans | **Round Mtn** ‒

CUBAN

Habana | **multi.** 21

DELIS

Cissi's Mkt. | **SoCo** ‒
Katz's | **Downtown** 19

DESSERT

Aquarelle | **Downtown** 27
Asti Trattoria | **Hyde Pk** 24
Austin Land | **Downtown** 22
Chez Zee | **NW Hills** 21
Z Driskill Grill | **Downtown** 26
1886 Café | **Downtown** 22
Enoteca Vespaio | **SoCo** 25
European Bistro | **Pflugerville** 24
Fino | **W Campus** 23

Moonshine | **Downtown** 20
Starlite | **Warehouse Dist** 25
Steeping Room | **NW Austin** 21
Z TRIO | **Downtown** 27
Z Vespaio | **SoCo** 28
NEW Viva Chocolato! | **NW Austin** ‒

ECLECTIC

August E's | **Fredericksburg** 27
Bess | **Downtown** 17
Eastside Café | **Cherrywood** 24
Hilltop Café | **Fredericksburg** 23
Kerbey Ln. Café | **multi.** 20
NEW Nomad | **Coronado Hills** ‒
Saba Blue | **Warehouse Dist** 18
NEW Uncorked | **E Austin** ‒

EUROPEAN

Bistro 88 | **W Lake** 25
European Bistro | **Pflugerville** 24

FONDUE

Melting Pot | **multi.** 21

FRENCH

Aquarelle | **Downtown** 27
Chez Nous | **Downtown** 25
Flip Happy Crepes | **Zilker** ‒
NEW Olivia | **S Lamar** ‒
Ventana | **N Austin** 23

GERMAN

Scholz Garten | **Downtown** 13

HAWAIIAN

Kona Grill | **NW Austin** 20
Roy's | **Downtown** 25

INDIAN

Clay Pit | **Downtown** 23
Madras Pavilion | **N Austin** 22
Sarovar Indian | **N Austin** 21
NEW Whip-In Parlour | **S Austin** ‒

ITALIAN

(N=Northern)
Andiamo | **N Austin** ‒
Asti Trattoria | **Hyde Pk** 24
Bellagio | **Jester Vill** 21
Brick Oven | **multi.** 19
Carmelo's | **Downtown** 22
Carrabba's | **multi.** 22

Enoteca Vespaio | SoCo	25
Frank & Angie's | Downtown	21
Gypsy Italian | Bouldin Creek	-
Joe DiMaggio's | NW Austin	-
La Traviata | Downtown	24
Mandola's | N Central	22
Mangieri's | Circle C	22
NoRTH | NW Austin	-
NEW Olivia | S Lamar	-
NEW Primizie Osteria | E Austin	-
Reale's | Jollyville	23
Rocco's Grill | Lakeway	20
Romeo's | multi.	17
Sagra | Downtown	-
Z Siena | N | NW Hills	25
Taverna | Downtown	23
Trattoria Lisina | Driftwood	-
Z Vespaio | SoCo	28

JAPANESE
(* sushi specialist)

Hayashi* | multi.	-
Kenichi* | Warehouse Dist	22
Mikado Ryotei* | N Austin	24
Musashino* | NW Hills	27
Tokai* | Cedar Pk	-
Z Uchi* | Zilker	28

JEWISH

Katz's | Downtown	19

KOREAN

Korea Hse. | NW Austin	21

KOSHER/ KOSHER-STYLE

Madras Pavilion | N Austin	22

MEDITERRANEAN

Fino | W Campus	23
Louie's 106 | Downtown	24

MEXICAN

Abuelo's | SW Austin	19
Cantina Laredo | Downtown	21
NEW Corazón | Downtown	-
Curra's Grill | Travis Hts	21
El Chile | Cherrywood	22
El Meson | SE Austin	27
Elsi's | Brentwood	-
El Sol y La Luna | SoCo	19

Z Fonda San Miguel | Highland Pk	26
Guero's | SoCo	20
Las Palomas | W Lake	21
Manuel's | multi.	22
NEW Maria Maria | Warehouse Dist	-
Oaxacan Tamaleo | Cedar Creek	-
Polvo's | Bouldin Creek	21
Sazón | Zilker	-
Tacodeli | multi.	25
Taco Xpress | S Lamar	21
Torchy's Tacos | multi.	-

NOODLE SHOPS

TC Noodle House | N Austin	-
Thai Noodle Hse. | Campus	17

PAN-ASIAN

NEW Imperia | Warehouse Dist	-
Kenichi | Warehouse Dist	22
Pei Wei | multi.	19
Satay | NW Austin	21

PERSIAN

Alborz | NW Austin	21

PIZZA

Brick Oven | multi.	19
Frank & Angie's | Downtown	21
Home Slice | SoCo	23
Mangieri's | Circle C	22
Reale's | Jollyville	23
Taverna | Downtown	23

PUB FOOD

Zax Pints | Downtown S	19

SALVADORAN

Elsi's | Brentwood	-

SEAFOOD

Z Eddie V's | multi.	26
Finn & Porter | Downtown	23
McCormick/Schmick's | multi.	21
Pappadeaux | N Austin	23
NEW Parkside | Downtown	-
Quality Seafood | Hyde Pk	-
III Forks | Downtown	25
Z TRIO | Downtown	27
Truluck's | multi.	23

SMALL PLATES

(See also Spanish tapas specialist)

Cissi's Mkt. | French | SoCo	-
Fino | Med. | W Campus	23
House.Wine. | Amer. | Fredericksburg	-
NEW Imperia | Pan-Asian | Warehouse Dist	-
Louie's 106 | Med. | Downtown	24
NEW Taste Wines | Amer. | Downtown	-
219 West | Amer. | Warehouse Dist	21
NEW Uncorked | Eclectic | E Austin	-

SOUL FOOD

Gene's | E Austin	25
Hoover's | multi.	21

SOUTH AMERICAN

Café Josie | Clarksville	26
Latin Café Austin | Downtown	20

SOUTHERN

Hoover's | multi.	21
Threadgill's | multi.	19

SOUTHWESTERN

Backstage | Spicewood	26
Cool River | NW Austin	19
Ranch 616 | Downtown	23
Roaring Fork | Downtown	24
South Congress | SoCo	22
NEW Southwest Bistro | Downtown S	-
Wildfire | Georgetown	22
Z'Tejas | multi.	22

SPANISH

(* tapas specialist)

Málaga* | Warehouse Dist	20
NEW Segovia* | Oak Hill	-

STEAKHOUSES

August E's | Fredericksburg	27
Austin Land | Downtown	22
Backstage | Spicewood	26
Cedar Grove | Wimberley	-
Cool River | NW Austin	19
Z Eddie V's | multi.	26
Estância | SW Austin	27
Finn & Porter | Downtown	23
Fleming's Prime | Downtown	24
Hoffbrau Steak | Downtown	16
Joe DiMaggio's | NW Austin	-
NEW Perry's Steak | Downtown	25
Ruth's Chris | Downtown	25
NEW Steiner Ranch | Steiner Rch	-
Sullivan's | Warehouse Dist	24
III Forks | Downtown	25
Z TRIO | Downtown	27

TEAROOMS

Steeping Room | NW Austin	21

TEX-MEX

Z Chuy's | multi.	21
El Azteca | E Austin	18
El Mercado | multi.	15
Hula Hut | Old W Austin	18
Iron Cactus | multi.	18
Matt's El Rancho | S Lamar	18
Oasis | Lakeway	11
Serranos | multi.	16
Trudy's | multi.	20
Vivo | Cherrywood	19

THAI

Madam Mam's | multi.	21
Thai Kitchen | multi.	20
Thai Noodle Hse. | Campus	17
Thai Passion | Downtown	20

VEGETARIAN

Madras Pavilion | N Austin	22

VIETNAMESE

NEW Lulu B's | Zilker	-
Sunflower | N Austin	23

Locations

Includes restaurant names, cuisines and Food ratings.

Austin

ALLANDALE

El Mercado | *Tex-Mex* | 15
Suzi's | *Chinese* | 19

ARBORETUM

Carrabba's | *Italian* | 22
Cheesecake Factory | *Amer.* | 20
Z Eddie V's | *Seafood/Steak* | 26
Manuel's | *Mex.* | 22
P.F. Chang's | *Chinese* | 22
Serranos | *Tex-Mex* | 16
Truluck's | *Seafood* | 23
Z'Tejas | *SW* | 22

BEE CAVE

Buster's | *BBQ* | 24
Iron Cactus | *Tex-Mex* | 18

BOULDIN CREEK

El Mercado | *Tex-Mex* | 15
Green Pastures | *Continental* | 23
Gypsy Italian | *Italian* | -
Polvo's | *Mex.* | 21
Torchy's Tacos | *Mex.* | -

BRENTWOOD

Elsi's | *Mex./Salvadoran* | -

BRYKERWOODS

Brick Oven | *Pizza* | 19
Kerbey Ln. Café | *Eclectic* | 20

CAMPUS

NEW Cuatros | *Amer.* | -
Kerbey Ln. Café | *Eclectic* | 20
Madam Mam's | *Thai* | 21
Player's | *Burgers* | 19
São Paulo's | *Brazilian* | 21
Thai Kitchen | *Thai* | 20
Thai Noodle Hse. | *Thai* | 17
Torchy's Tacos | *Mex.* | -

CEDAR CREEK

Oaxacan Tamaleo | *Mex.* | -

CEDAR PARK

Hayashi | *Japanese* | -
Serranos | *Tex-Mex* | 16
Tokai | *Japanese* | -

CHERRYWOOD

Eastside Café | *Amer./Eclectic* | 24
El Chile | *Mex.* | 22
Hoover's | *Southern* | 21
Vivo | *Tex-Mex* | 19

CIRCLE C

Mangieri's | *Pizza* | 22
Waterloo Ice Hse. | *Burgers* | 16

CLARKSVILLE

Café Josie | *Carib.* | 26
Z Jeffrey's | *Amer./Continental* | 26
Z'Tejas | *SW* | 22

CORONADO HILLS

NEW Nomad | *Eclectic* | -

CRESTVIEW

Threadgill's | *Southern* | 19

DOWNTOWN

Aquarelle | *French* | 27
Austin Land | *Steak* | 22
Belmont | *Amer.* | 18
Bess | *Eclectic* | 17
Brick Oven | *Pizza* | 19
Cantina Laredo | *Mex.* | 21
Carmelo's | *Italian* | 22
Chez Nous | *French* | 25
Clay Pit | *Indian* | 23
NEW Corazón | *Mex.* | -
Crú Wine Bar | *Amer.* | 20
Z Driskill Grill | *Amer.* | 26
Z Eddie V's | *Seafood/Steak* | 26
1886 Café | *Amer.* | 22
El Mercado | *Tex-Mex* | 15
Finn & Porter | *Seafood/Steak* | 23
Fleming's Prime | *Steak* | 24
Frank & Angie's | *Pizza* | 21
Gumbo's | *Cajun/Creole* | 24
Habana | *Cuban* | 21
Hoffbrau Steak | *Steak* | 16

Hut's	*Burgers*	23
Iron Cactus	*Tex-Mex*	18
Iron Works	*BBQ*	22
Katz's	*Deli*	19
Latin Café Austin	*S Amer.*	20
La Traviata	*Italian*	24
Louie's 106	*Med.*	24
Manuel's	*Mex.*	22
McCormick/Schmick's	*Seafood*	21
Melting Pot	*Fondue*	21
Moonshine	*Amer.*	20
NEW Mulberry	*Amer.*	-
Opal Divine's	*Amer.*	14
NEW Parkside	*Amer.*	-
NEW Perry's Steak	*Steak*	25
P.F. Chang's	*Chinese*	22
Ranch 616	*SW*	23
Rest. Jezebel	*Amer.*	27
Roaring Fork	*SW*	24
Roy's	*Hawaiian*	25
Ruth's Chris	*Steak*	25
Sagra	*Italian*	-
Scholz Garten	*German*	13
Serranos	*Tex-Mex*	16
Shoal Creek	*Cajun*	18
Shoreline Grill	*Continental*	24
Stubb's	*BBQ*	20
NEW Taste Wines	*Amer.*	-
Taverna	*Italian*	23
Texas Chili	*Amer.*	20
Thai Passion	*Thai*	20
Thistle Café	*Amer.*	18
III Forks	*Steak*	25
Z TRIO	*Amer.*	27
Waterloo Ice Hse.	*Burgers*	16

DOWNTOWN SOUTH

NEW Paggi Hse.	*Amer.*	-
NEW Southwest Bistro	*SW*	-
Threadgill's	*Southern*	19
Zax Pints	*Amer.*	19

EAST AUSTIN

El Azteca	*Tex-Mex*	18
Gene's	*Cajun/Soul Food*	25
NEW Primizie Osteria	*Italian*	-
NEW Uncorked	*Eclectic*	-

ELGIN

Meyer's	*BBQ*	21
Southside Mkt.	*BBQ*	24

GEORGETOWN

Hayashi	*Japanese*	-
Romeo's	*Italian*	17
NEW Silver & Stone	*Amer.*	-
Wildfire	*SW*	22

GONZALES

Gonzales Mkt.	*BBQ*	-

GREAT HILLS

Brick Oven	*Pizza*	19
Iron Cactus	*Tex-Mex*	18
North by NW	*Amer.*	18

HIGHLAND PARK

Z Fonda San Miguel	*Mex.*	26

HYDE PARK

Asti Trattoria	*Italian*	24
Hyde Park	*Amer.*	21
Pei Wei	*Pan-Asian*	19
Quality Seafood	*Seafood*	-

JESTER VILLAGE

Bellagio	*Italian*	21

JOLLYVILLE

Pei Wei	*Pan-Asian*	19
Reale's	*Italian*	23
Waterloo Ice Hse.	*Burgers*	16
Z'Tejas	*Southwestern*	22

LAKEWAY

Z Hudson's	*Amer.*	28
Oasis	*Tex-Mex*	11
Rocco's Grill	*Italian*	20

LEXINGTON

Snow's BBQ	*BBQ*	-

LOCKHART

Kreuz Mkt.	*BBQ*	26
Smitty's Mkt.	*BBQ*	19

LULING

City Market	*BBQ*	24

NORTH AUSTIN

Andiamo	*Ital.*	-
Carrabba's	*Italian*	22
Z Chuy's	*Tex-Mex*	21
Din Ho	*Chinese*	24
First Chinese	*Chinese*	25
Golden Wok	*Chinese*	22

Madras Pavilion	Indian	22
Mikado Ryotei	Japanese	24
Opal Divine's	Amer.	14
Pappadeaux	Seafood	23
Pei Wei	Pan-Asian	19
Sarovar Indian	Indian	21
Sunflower	Viet.	23
TC Noodle House	Noodle Shop	-
Trudy's	Tex-Mex	20
Ventana	French	23
Waterloo Ice Hse.	Burgers	16

NORTH CAMPUS

| Ruby's | BBQ | 23 |
| Trudy's | Tex-Mex | 20 |

NORTH CENTRAL

Mandola's	Italian	22
Serranos	Tex-Mex	16
Shanghai Rest.	Chinese	-
Waterloo Ice Hse.	Burgers	16
NEW Yume	Asian Fusion	-

NORTHWEST AUSTIN

Alborz	Persian	21
Cool River	SW/Steak	19
Crú Wine Bar	Amer.	20
Daily Grill	Amer.	24
Hoover's	Southern	21
Houston's	Amer.	23
Z Jasper's	Amer.	24
Joe DiMaggio's	Italian/Steak	-
Kerbey Ln. Café	Eclectic	20
Kona Grill	Amer.	20
Korea Hse.	Korean	21
McCormick/Schmick's	Seafood	21
Melting Pot	Fondue	21
NoRTH	Italian	-
Satay	Pan-Asian	21
Steeping Room	Tea	21
Tacodeli	Mex.	25
NEW Viva Chocolato!	Dessert	-

NORTHWEST HILLS

Chez Zee	Amer.	21
County Line	BBQ	20
Mirabelle	Amer.	25
Ms. B's	Creole	22
Musashino	Japanese	27
Z Siena	Italian	25
Waterloo Ice Hse.	Burgers	16

OAK HILL

| NEW Segovia | Spanish | - |

OLD WEST AUSTIN

Hula Hut	Tex-Mex	18
Magnolia Café	Amer.	21
Z Wink	Amer.	27
Zoot	Amer.	26

PFLUGERVILLE

| European Bistro | Euro. | 24 |

ROSEDALE

Billy's/Burnet	Amer.	20
Blue Star	Amer.	20
Sampaio's	Brazilian	20
Waterloo Ice Hse.	Burgers	16

ROUND ROCK

Z Chuy's	Tex-Mex	21
Gumbo's	Cajun/Creole	24
Pei Wei	Pan-Asian	19
Z Salt Lick	BBQ	24
Serranos	Tex-Mex	16

SOCO

Cissi's Mkt.	Deli	-
El Sol y La Luna	Mex.	19
Enoteca Vespaio	Italian	25
Guero's	Mex.	20
Home Slice	Pizza	23
Magnolia Café	Amer.	21
South Congress	SW	22
Z Vespaio	Italian	28
Woodland	Amer.	18

SOUTH AUSTIN

Z Chuy's	Tex-Mex	21
Habana	Cuban	21
Opal Divine's	Amer.	14
Thai Kitchen	Thai	20
Trudy's	Tex-Mex	20
NEW Whip-In Parlour	Indian	-

SOUTHEAST AUSTIN

| El Meson | Mex. | 27 |

SOUTH LAMAR

Artz Rib Hse.	BBQ	21
Kerbey Ln. Café	Eclectic	20
NEW Lulu B's	Viet.	-
Matt's El Rancho	Tex-Mex	18

NEW Olivia	*French/Italian*	_
Suzi's	*Chinese*	19
Taco Xpress	*Mex.*	21

SOUTHWEST AUSTIN

Abuelo's	*Mex.*	19
Brick Oven	*Pizza*	19
Estância	*Brazilian/Steak*	27
Evangeline Café	*Cajun/Creole*	19
Hyde Park	*Amer.*	21
Madam Mam's	*Thai*	21
Pei Wei	*Pan-Asian*	19
Serranos	*Tex-Mex*	16
Tacodeli	*Mex.*	25

STEINER RANCH

| NEW Fion Bistro | *Amer.* | _ |
| NEW Steiner Ranch | *Steak* | _ |

TAYLOR

| Louie Mueller | *BBQ* | 25 |

TRAVIS HEIGHTS

| Curra's Grill | *Mex.* | 21 |

WAREHOUSE DISTRICT

NEW Imperia	*Pan-Asian*	_
Kenichi	*Pan-Asian*	22
Lambert's	*BBQ*	23
Málaga	*Spanish*	20
NEW Maria Maria	*Mex.*	_
Saba Blue	*Eclectic*	18
Starlite	*Amer.*	25
Sullivan's	*Steak*	24
Truluck's	*Seafood*	23
219 West	*Amer.*	21

WEST CAMPUS

Dirty Martin's	*Burgers*	21
Fino	*Med.*	23
Judges' Hill	*Amer.*	24

WEST LAKE HILLS

Bistro 88	*Asian/Euro.*	25
County Line	*BBQ*	20
NEW Grove wine bar	*Amer.*	_

Las Palomas	*Mex.*	21
Suzi's	*Chinese*	19
Thai Kitchen	*Thai*	20
Thistle Café	*Amer.*	18
NEW Wine Cellar	*Amer.*	_

WIMBERLEY

| Cedar Grove | *Steak* | _ |

ZILKER

Z Chuy's	*Tex-Mex*	21
Flip Happy Crepes	*French*	_
Green Mesquite	*BBQ*	18
Romeo's	*Italian*	17
Sazón	*Mex.*	_
Shady Grove	*Amer.*	19
Z Uchi	*Japanese*	28

Hill Country

BROWNWOOD

| Turtle | *Amer.* | _ |

DRIFTWOOD

| Z Salt Lick | *BBQ* | 24 |
| Trattoria Lisina | *Italian* | _ |

DRIPPING SPRINGS

| NEW Creek Road Café | *Amer.* | _ |

FREDERICKSBURG

August E's	*Steak*	27
Hilltop Café	*Eclectic*	23
House.Wine.	*Amer.*	_
Rather Sweet	*Bakery*	26

JOHNSON CITY

| Silver K | *Amer.* | _ |

LLANO

| Cooper's | *BBQ* | 27 |

ROUND MOUNTAIN

| Real New Orleans | *Creole* | _ |

SPICEWOOD

Backstage	*Steak*	26
Opie's BBQ	*BBQ*	23
R.O.'s Outpost	*BBQ*	_

Special Features

Listings cover the best in each category and include names, locations and Food ratings. Multi-location restaurants' features may vary by branch.

ADDITIONS

(Properties added since the last edition of the book)

Andiamo	N Austin	-
Cissi's Mkt.	SoCo	-
Corazón	Downtown	-
Creek Road Café	Dripping Springs	-
Cuatros	Campus	-
Fion Bistro	Steiner Rch	-
First Chinese	N Austin	25
Grove wine bar	W Lake	-
Hayashi	multi.	-
House.Wine.	Fredericksburg	-
Imperia	Warehouse Dist	-
Lulu B's	Zilker	-
Maria Maria	Warehouse Dist	-
Mulberry	Downtown	-
Nomad	Coronado Hills	-
Olivia	S Lamar	-
Paggi Hse.	Downtown S	-
Parkside	Downtown	-
Perry's Steak	Downtown	25
Primizie Osteria	E Austin	-
Sazón	Zilker	-
Segovia	Oak Hill	-
Silver & Stone	Georgetown	-
Snow's BBQ	Lexington	-
Southwest Bistro	Downtown S	-
Steiner Ranch	Steiner Rch	-
Taste Wines	Downtown	-
TC Noodle House	N Austin	-
Tokai	Cedar Pk	-
Torchy's Tacos	multi.	-
Uncorked	E Austin	-
Viva Chocolato!	NW Austin	-
Whip-In Parlour	S Austin	-
Wine Cellar	W Lake	-
Yume	N Central	-

BREAKFAST

(See also Hotel Dining)

Curra's Grill	Travis Hts	21
El Mercado	multi.	15
El Meson	SE Austin	27
El Sol y La Luna	SoCo	19
Guero's	SoCo	20
Hoover's	Cherrywood	21
Katz's	Downtown	19
Kerbey Ln. Café	multi.	20
Magnolia Café	multi.	21
Taco Xpress	S Lamar	21
Trudy's	multi.	20
Waterloo Ice Hse.	multi.	16

BRUNCH

Chez Zee	NW Hills	21
Eastside Café	Cherrywood	24
1886 Café	Downtown	22
Enoteca Vespaio	SoCo	25
☒ Fonda San Miguel	Highland Pk	26
Green Pastures	Bouldin Creek	23
Hyde Park	Hyde Pk	21
Judges' Hill	W Campus	24
Katz's	Downtown	19
Manuel's	multi.	22
Moonshine	Downtown	20
Oasis	Lakeway	11
South Congress	SoCo	22
Thistle Café	W Lake	18
Threadgill's	Downtown S	19
Trudy's	N Campus	20
Wildfire	Georgetown	22

BUFFET SERVED

(Check availability)

Alborz	NW Austin	21
Clay Pit	Downtown	23
El Mercado	Downtown	15
Green Pastures	Bouldin Creek	23
Iron Cactus	multi.	18
Lambert's	Warehouse Dist	23
Madras Pavilion	N Austin	22
Sarovar Indian	N Austin	21
Silver K	Johnson City	-
Threadgill's	Downtown S	19
Trudy's	N Austin	20

BUSINESS DINING

Andiamo	N Austin	-
Aquarelle	Downtown	27

Asti Trattoria	**Hyde Pk**	24
August E's	**Fredericksburg**	27
Belmont	**Downtown**	18
Blue Star	**Rosedale**	20
Carmelo's	**Downtown**	22
Cedar Grove	**Wimberley**	-
Cool River	**NW Austin**	19
NEW Corazón	**Downtown**	-
NEW Creek Road Café	**Dripping Springs**	-
Z Driskill Grill	**Downtown**	26
Z Eddie V's	**multi.**	26
1886 Café	**Downtown**	22
Finn & Porter	**Downtown**	23
Fino	**W Campus**	23
Fleming's Prime	**Downtown**	24
Z Fonda San Miguel	**Highland Pk**	26
NEW Grove wine bar	**W Lake**	-
Gumbo's	**Downtown**	24
Gypsy Italian	**Bouldin Creek**	-
Z Hudson's	**Lakeway**	28
NEW Imperia	**Warehouse Dist**	-
Z Jasper's	**NW Austin**	24
Z Jeffrey's	**Clarksville**	26
Joe DiMaggio's	**NW Austin**	-
Judges' Hill	**W Campus**	24
Kenichi	**Warehouse Dist**	22
Louie's 106	**Downtown**	24
Manuel's	**multi.**	22
NEW Maria Maria	**Warehouse Dist**	-
McCormick/Schmick's	**multi.**	21
Mikado Ryotei	**N Austin**	24
Mirabelle	**NW Hills**	25
Musashino	**NW Hills**	27
NoRTH	**NW Austin**	-
NEW Olivia	**S Lamar**	-
NEW Paggi Hse.	**Downtown S**	-
NEW Parkside	**Downtown**	-
NEW Perry's Steak	**Downtown**	25
Rather Sweet	**Fredericksburg**	26
Rest. Jezebel	**Downtown**	27
Roaring Fork	**Downtown**	24
Roy's	**Downtown**	25
Ruth's Chris	**Downtown**	25
Shanghai Rest.	**N Central**	-
Shoreline Grill	**Downtown**	24
Z Siena	**NW Hills**	25
NEW Silver & Stone	**Georgetown**	-
Silver K	**Johnson City**	-
NEW Southwest Bistro	**Downtown S**	-
Starlite	**Warehouse Dist**	25
NEW Steiner Ranch	**Steiner Rch**	-
Sullivan's	**Warehouse Dist**	24
Suzi's	**multi.**	19
Texas Chili	**Downtown**	20
Thistle Café	**Downtown**	18
Z TRIO	**Downtown**	27
Truluck's	**multi.**	23
Z Uchi	**Zilker**	28
NEW Uncorked	**E Austin**	-
Ventana	**N Austin**	23
Wildfire	**Georgetown**	22
Woodland	**SoCo**	18
NEW Yume	**N Central**	-
Zax Pints	**Downtown S**	19
Zoot	**Old W Austin**	26

CELEBRITY CHEFS

Backstage	*Raymond Tatum*	**Spicewood**	26
Z Fonda San Miguel	*Miguel Ravago*	**Highland Pk**	26
Z Hudson's	*Jeff Blank*	**Lakeway**	28
NEW Maria Maria	*Roberto Santibañez*	**Warehouse Dist**	-
Rather Sweet	*Rebecca Rather*	**Fredericksburg**	26
Trattoria Lisina	*Damian Mandola*	**Driftwood**	-
Z Uchi	*Tyson Cole*	**Zilker**	28

CHEF'S TABLE

NEW Silver & Stone	**Georgetown**	-
NEW Southwest Bistro	**Downtown S**	-

CHILD-FRIENDLY

(Alternatives to the usual fast-food places; * children's menu available)

Billy's/Burnet*	**Rosedale**	20
Brick Oven*	**multi.**	19
County Line*	**multi.**	20
Curra's Grill*	**Travis Hts**	21
Din Ho	**N Austin**	24
Eastside Café	**Cherrywood**	24
El Azteca*	**E Austin**	18
El Mercado*	**multi.**	15

El Meson | **SE Austin**	27
El Sol y La Luna* | **SoCo**	19
Evangeline Café* | **SW Austin**	19
Frank & Angie's | **Downtown**	21
Green Mesquite* | **Zilker**	18
Guero's* | **SoCo**	20
Hilltop Café* | **Fredericksburg**	23
Hoover's* | **Cherrywood**	21
Hut's | **Downtown**	23
Hyde Park* | **Hyde Pk**	21
Iron Works | **Downtown**	22
Kerbey Ln. Café* | **multi.**	20
Las Palomas* | **W Lake**	21
Magnolia Café* | **multi.**	21
Matt's El Rancho* | **S Lamar**	18
Oasis* | **Lakeway**	11
Pei Wei* | **multi.**	19
Player's | **Campus**	19
Polvo's* | **Bouldin Creek**	21
Rocco's Grill* | **Lakeway**	20
Romeo's* | **Zilker**	17
Ruby's* | **N Campus**	23
ⓩ Salt Lick* | **Driftwood**	24
Scholz Garten* | **Downtown**	13
Serranos* | **multi.**	16
Shady Grove* | **Zilker**	19
Stubb's* | **Downtown**	20
Suzi's | **multi.**	19
Taco Xpress | **S Lamar**	21
Threadgill's | **Downtown S**	19
Trudy's* | **S Austin**	20
Waterloo Ice Hse. | **multi.**	16
Z'Tejas* | **multi.**	22

CIGARS WELCOME

Cool River | **NW Austin**	19

DELIVERY/TAKEOUT

(D=delivery, T=takeout)

Alborz | T | **NW Austin**	21
Billy's/Burnet | T | **Rosedale**	20
Brick Oven | D, T | **multi.**	19
Chez Zee | T | **NW Hills**	21
ⓩ Chuy's | D | **multi.**	21
County Line | T | **multi.**	20
Curra's Grill | T | **Travis Hts**	21
Din Ho | T | **N Austin**	24
1886 Café | T | **Downtown**	22
El Meson | T | **SE Austin**	27
Frank & Angie's | T | **Downtown**	21

Hoover's | T | **Cherrywood**	21
Hut's | T | **Downtown**	23
Iron Works | T | **Downtown**	22
Katz's | T | **Downtown**	19
Kerbey Ln. Café | T | **multi.**	20
Louie's 106 | T | **Downtown**	24
Madam Mam's | T | **Campus**	21
Madras Pavilion | T | **N Austin**	22
Magnolia Café | T | **multi.**	21
Manuel's | T | **multi.**	22
Matt's El Rancho | T | **S Lamar**	18
North by NW | D, T | **Great Hills**	18
Pei Wei | T | **multi.**	19
P.F. Chang's | T | **Downtown**	22
Player's | T | **Campus**	19
Ruby's | T | **N Campus**	23
ⓩ Salt Lick | D, T | **Driftwood**	24
Satay | D, T | **NW Austin**	21
Shoal Creek | T | **Downtown**	18
Stubb's | T | **Downtown**	20
Sunflower | T | **N Austin**	23
Suzi's | T | **multi.**	19
Taco Xpress | T | **S Lamar**	21
Thai Kitchen | T | **multi.**	20
Thai Noodle Hse. | D, T | **Campus**	17
Thai Passion | T | **Downtown**	20
Thistle Café | T | **multi.**	18
Threadgill's | D, T | **multi.**	19
Waterloo Ice Hse. | T | **multi.**	16

DESSERT

Aquarelle | **Downtown**	27
Asti Trattoria | **Hyde Pk**	24
Austin Land | **Downtown**	22
Chez Zee | **NW Hills**	21
ⓩ Driskill Grill | **Downtown**	26
1886 Café | **Downtown**	22
European Bistro | **Pflugerville**	24
Fino | **W Campus**	23
Moonshine | **Downtown**	20
Starlite | **Warehouse Dist**	25
Steeping Room | **NW Austin**	21
ⓩ TRIO | **Downtown**	27
ⓩ Vespaio | **SoCo**	28

DINING ALONE

(Other than hotels and places with counter service)

Billy's/Burnet | **Rosedale**	20
Chez Nous | **Downtown**	25

🆉 Eddie V's | **Downtown**	26
Enoteca Vespaio | **SoCo**	25
Fino | **W Campus**	23
Fleming's Prime | **Downtown**	24
🆉 Jasper's | **NW Austin**	24
Katz's | **Downtown**	19
La Traviata | **Downtown**	24
Louie's 106 | **Downtown**	24
Málaga | **Warehouse Dist**	20
Opal Divine's | **Downtown**	14
Pei Wei | **multi.**	19
Ranch 616 | **Downtown**	23
Tacodeli | **multi.**	25
🆉 Uchi | **Zilker**	28
🆉 Vespaio | **SoCo**	28
Waterloo Ice Hse. | **Jollyville**	16
Zax Pints | **Downtown S**	19

ENTERTAINMENT

(Call for days and times of performances)

Alborz | belly dancers | **NW Austin**	21
Backstage | varies | **Spicewood**	26
Carmelo's | accordion | **Downtown**	22
Chez Zee | jazz/piano/pop | **NW Hills**	21
Cool River | varies | **NW Austin**	19
County Line | acoustic | **NW Hills**	20
🆉 Driskill Grill | jazz/piano | **Downtown**	26
🆉 Eddie V's | jazz | **Downtown**	26
El Mercado | varies | **Bouldin Creek**	15
El Sol y La Luna | Latin | **SoCo**	19
European Bistro | piano | **Pflugerville**	24
Frank & Angie's | mandolin | **Downtown**	21
Green Mesquite | blues/country/folk | **Zilker**	18
Green Pastures | piano | **Bouldin Creek**	23
Guero's | bands | **SoCo**	20
Habana | varies | **Downtown**	21
Hilltop Café | blues/jazz | **Fredericksburg**	23
Las Palomas | jazz/Latin | **W Lake**	21
Latin Café Austin | Latin | **Downtown**	20

Manuel's | jazz/Latin | **multi.**	22
🆕 Maria Maria | jazz/Latin | **Warehouse Dist**	-
Matt's El Rancho | jazz/Latin | **S Lamar**	18
McCormick/Schmick's | jazz | **Downtown**	21
Mirabelle | jazz | **NW Hills**	25
North by NW | varies | **Great Hills**	18
Oasis | jazz/rock | **Lakeway**	11
Opal Divine's | blues/folk/rock | **multi.**	14
Ranch 616 | country | **Downtown**	23
Romeo's | jazz | **Zilker**	17
🆉 Salt Lick | varies | **Driftwood**	24
Shady Grove | varies | **Zilker**	19
Shoal Creek | varies | **Downtown**	18
Stubb's | varies | **Downtown**	20
Sullivan's | bands/jazz | **Warehouse Dist**	24
Threadgill's | varies | **multi.**	19
Truluck's | jazz/piano | **Arboretum**	23
Vivo | DJ | **Cherrywood**	19
Waterloo Ice Hse. | varies | **multi.**	16
Z'Tejas | varies | **Clarksville**	22

GAME IN SEASON

Asti Trattoria | **Hyde Pk**	24
August E's | **Fredericksburg**	27
Backstage | **Spicewood**	26
Cedar Grove | **Wimberley**	-
Chez Nous | **Downtown**	25
Cool River | **NW Austin**	19
🆉 Driskill Grill | **Downtown**	26
Fino | **W Campus**	23
Green Pastures | **Bouldin Creek**	23
🆉 Hudson's | **Lakeway**	28
🆉 Jeffrey's | **Clarksville**	26
Meyer's | **Elgin**	21
Ranch 616 | **Downtown**	23
Rest. Jezebel | **Downtown**	27
Sampaio's | **Rosedale**	20
🆉 Siena | **NW Hills**	25
🆕 Silver & Stone | **Georgetown**	-
🆕 Taste Wines | **Downtown**	-
Turtle | **Brownwood**	-
Ventana | **N Austin**	23

| Wildfire | **Georgetown** | 22 |
| **Z** Wink | **Old W Austin** | 27 |

HISTORIC PLACES

(Year opened; * building)

1830	Stubb's*	**Downtown**	20
1850	Moonshine*	**Downtown**	20
1859	Thai Passion*	**Downtown**	20
1866	Scholz Garten*	**Downtown**	13
1882	Southside Mkt.	**Elgin**	24
1886	Driskill Grill*	**Downtown**	26
1886	1886 Café*	**Downtown**	22
1894	Green Pastures*	**Bouldin Creek**	23
1900	Guero's*	**SoCo**	20
1900	Hudson's*	**Lakeway**	28
1900	Judges' Hill*	**W Campus**	24
1900	Kreuz Mkt.	**Lockhart**	26
1900	Uncorked*	**E Austin**	-
1904	European Bistro*	**Pflugerville**	24
1918	Bess*	**Downtown**	17
1920	Eastside Café*	**Cherrywood**	24
1920	Green Mesquite*	**Zilker**	18
1920	Zoot*	**Old W Austin**	26
1926	Dirty Martin's*	**W Campus**	21
1930	Hyde Park*	**Hyde Pk**	21
1930	Iron Works*	**Downtown**	22
1933	Threadgill's	**Crestview**	19
1934	Hoffbrau Steak*	**Downtown**	16
1938	Quality Seafood	**Hyde Pk**	-
1939	Hut's*	**Downtown**	23
1949	Louie Mueller	**Taylor**	25
1952	Matt's El Rancho	**S Lamar**	18
1957	City Market	**Luling**	24

HOTEL DINING

Driskill Hotel
| **Z** Driskill Grill | **Downtown** | 26 |
| 1886 Café | **Downtown** | 22 |
Four Seasons Hotel
| **Z** TRIO | **Downtown** | 27 |

Hilton Downtown
| Finn & Porter | **Downtown** | 23 |
Hyatt Regency Austin
| **NEW** Southwest Bistro | **Downtown S** | - |
InterContinental Stephen F. Austin Hotel
| Roaring Fork | **Downtown** | 24 |
Mansion at Judges' Hill
| Judges' Hill | **W Campus** | 24 |

LATE DINING

(Weekday closing hour)

House.Wine.	12 AM	**Fredericksburg**	-
Hyde Park	12 AM	**Hyde Pk**	21
Katz's	24 hrs.	**Downtown**	19
Kerbey Ln. Café	24 hrs.	**multi.**	20
Magnolia Café	24 hrs.	**multi.**	21
Málaga	varies	**Warehouse Dist**	20
Opal Divine's	1 AM	**multi.**	14
NEW Parkside	varies	**Downtown**	-
Player's	3 AM	**Campus**	19
Ruby's	12 AM	**N Campus**	23
Texas Chili	12 AM	**Downtown**	20
Thai Kitchen	12 AM	**Campus**	20
Thai Passion	3 AM	**Downtown**	20
Trudy's	12 AM	**multi.**	20
Z Wink	12 AM	**Old W Austin**	27

MEET FOR A DRINK

Belmont	**Downtown**	18
Bess	**Downtown**	17
Billy's/Burnet	**Rosedale**	20
Z Chuy's	**multi.**	21
Cissi's Mkt.	**SoCo**	-
Cool River	**NW Austin**	19
NEW Corazón	**Downtown**	-
NEW Cuatros	**Campus**	-
Curra's Grill	**Travis Hts**	21
Z Eddie V's	**multi.**	26
El Chile	**Cherrywood**	22
Fino	**W Campus**	23
NEW Fion Bistro	**Steiner Rch**	-
Fleming's Prime	**Downtown**	24
NEW Grove wine bar	**W Lake**	-
Guero's	**SoCo**	20
Habana	**Downtown**	21
House.Wine.	**Fredericksburg**	-
Hula Hut	**Old W Austin**	18

NEW Imperia | **Warehouse Dist** | -
Z Jasper's | **NW Austin** | 24
Joe DiMaggio's | **NW Austin** | -
Latin Café Austin | **Downtown** | 20
Louie's 106 | **Downtown** | 24
Málaga | **Warehouse Dist** | 20
Manuel's | **multi.** | 22
NEW Maria Maria | **Warehouse Dist** | -
Matt's El Rancho | **S Lamar** | 18
McCormick/Schmick's | **NW Austin** | 21
Moonshine | **Downtown** | 20
NEW Mulberry | **Downtown** | -
NEW Nomad | **Coronado Hills** | -
NoRTH | **NW Austin** | -
North by NW | **Great Hills** | 18
Oasis | **Lakeway** | 11
NEW Olivia | **S Lamar** | -
Opal Divine's | **multi.** | 14
NEW Paggi Hse. | **Downtown S** | -
NEW Parkside | **Downtown** | -
NEW Primizie Osteria | **E Austin** | -
Quality Seafood | **Hyde Pk** | -
Ranch 616 | **Downtown** | 23
Roaring Fork | **Downtown** | 24
Saba Blue | **Warehouse Dist** | 18
Sagra | **Downtown** | -
Sampaio's | **Rosedale** | 20
Sazón | **Zilker** | -
Scholz Garten | **Downtown** | 13
NEW Segovia | **Oak Hill** | -
Serranos | **multi.** | 16
Shady Grove | **Zilker** | 19
Shoal Creek | **Downtown** | 18
NEW Silver & Stone | **Georgetown** | -
South Congress | **SoCo** | 22
NEW Southwest Bistro | **Downtown S** | -
Starlite | **Warehouse Dist** | 25
Steeping Room | **NW Austin** | 21
NEW Taste Wines | **Downtown** | -
Texas Chili | **Downtown** | 20
Threadgill's | **Downtown S** | 19
Z TRIO | **Downtown** | 27
Trudy's | **multi.** | 20
Turtle | **Brownwood** | -
NEW Uncorked | **E Austin** | -
Z Vespaio | **SoCo** | 28

NEW Viva Chocolato! | **NW Austin** | -
Waterloo Ice Hse. | **multi.** | 16
NEW Whip-In Parlour | **S Austin** | -
NEW Wine Cellar | **W Lake** | -
Woodland | **SoCo** | 18
NEW Yume | **N Central** | -
Zax Pints | **Downtown S** | 19
Z'Tejas | **multi.** | 22

OUTDOOR DINING

(G=garden; P=patio; S=sidewalk; T=terrace; W=waterside)

Abuelo's | G | **SW Austin** | 19
Backstage | P | **Spicewood** | 26
Billy's/Burnet | P | **Rosedale** | 20
Brick Oven | P | **multi.** | 19
Chez Zee | G | **NW Hills** | 21
Z Chuy's | P | **multi.** | 21
Cool River | P | **NW Austin** | 19
County Line | P | **W Lake** | 20
Crú Wine Bar | P | **Downtown** | 20
Curra's Grill | P | **Travis Hts** | 21
1886 Café | P | **Downtown** | 22
El Azteca | P | **E Austin** | 18
El Chile | P | **Cherrywood** | 22
El Mercado | P | **multi.** | 15
El Sol y La Luna | P | **SoCo** | 19
Evangeline Café | S | **SW Austin** | 19
Fino | T | **W Campus** | 23
Frank & Angie's | P | **Downtown** | 21
Green Mesquite | P | **Zilker** | 18
NEW Grove wine bar | P | **W Lake** | -
Guero's | P | **SoCo** | 20
Habana | P | **Downtown** | 21
Hoffbrau Steak | P | **Downtown** | 16
Z Hudson's | G, P | **Lakeway** | 28
Hula Hut | P, W | **Old W Austin** | 18
Iron Works | P | **Downtown** | 22
Z Jasper's | P | **NW Austin** | 24
Joe DiMaggio's | P | **NW Austin** | -
Kerbey Ln. Café | P | **multi.** | 20
Las Palomas | P | **W Lake** | 21
Latin Café Austin | P | **Downtown** | 20
Manuel's | P | **Arboretum** | 22
Matt's El Rancho | P | **S Lamar** | 18
Moonshine | G, P | **Downtown** | 20
NoRTH | P | **NW Austin** | -

North by NW | P, T | **Great Hills**	18
Oasis | P, T | **Lakeway**	11
Opal Divine's | P, T | **multi.**	14
Pei Wei | P | **SW Austin**	19
P.F. Chang's | P | **Arboretum**	22
Player's | G | **Campus**	19
Polvo's | P | **Bouldin Creek**	21
Rocco's Grill | P, W | **Lakeway**	20
Romeo's | P | **Zilker**	17
Ruby's | P | **N Campus**	23
☑ Salt Lick | P | **Driftwood**	24
São Paulo's | S | **Campus**	21
Satay | G, P | **NW Austin**	21
Scholz Garten | P | **Downtown**	13
Serranos | P | **multi.**	16
Shady Grove | P | **Zilker**	19
Shoal Creek | P | **Downtown**	18
Shoreline Grill | P, W | **Downtown**	24
☑ Siena | P | **NW Hills**	25
Taco Xpress | P | **S Lamar**	21
Thai Noodle Hse. | P | **Campus**	17
Thistle Café | P | **W Lake**	18
Trattoria Lisina | P | **Driftwood**	-
☑ TRIO | T, W | **Downtown**	27
Trudy's | P, T | **multi.**	20
Truluck's | P | **Arboretum**	23
Vivo | P | **Cherrywood**	19
Waterloo Ice Hse. | P | **NW Hills**	16
Zax Pints | P | **Downtown S**	19
Z'Tejas | P | **multi.**	22

POWER SCENES

August E's | **Fredericksburg**	27
Austin Land | **Downtown**	22
Belmont | **Downtown**	18
Bess | **Downtown**	17
Carmelo's | **Downtown**	22
Cedar Grove | **Wimberley**	-
Cool River | **NW Austin**	19
☑ Driskill Grill | **Downtown**	26
☑ Eddie V's | **Downtown**	26
Finn & Porter | **Downtown**	23
Fleming's Prime | **Downtown**	24
NEW Imperia | **Warehouse Dist**	-
☑ Jasper's | **NW Austin**	24
Joe DiMaggio's | **NW Austin**	-
Lambert's | **Warehouse Dist**	23
NEW Maria Maria | **Warehouse Dist**	-
McCormick/Schmick's | **multi.**	21

NoRTH | **NW Austin**	-
NEW Olivia | **S Lamar**	-
NEW Paggi Hse. | **Downtown S**	-
NEW Parkside | **Downtown**	-
NEW Perry's Steak | **Downtown**	25
Rest. Jezebel | **Downtown**	27
Roaring Fork | **Downtown**	24
Ruth's Chris | **Downtown**	25
NEW Southwest Bistro | **Downtown S**	-
NEW Steiner Ranch | **Steiner Rch**	-
Sullivan's | **Warehouse Dist**	24
Texas Chili | **Downtown**	20
☑ TRIO | **Downtown**	27

PRIX FIXE MENUS

(Call for prices and times)

Aquarelle | **Downtown**	27
Chez Nous | **Downtown**	25
☑ Driskill Grill | **Downtown**	26
☑ Jeffrey's | **Clarksville**	26
☑ Salt Lick | **Driftwood**	24
☑ Siena | **NW Hills**	25
Thai Passion | **Downtown**	20
Threadgill's | **Downtown S**	19
☑ Wink | **Old W Austin**	27
Zoot | **Old W Austin**	26

QUIET CONVERSATION

Aquarelle | **Downtown**	27
August E's | **Fredericksburg**	27
Backstage | **Spicewood**	26
Bess | **Downtown**	17
Carmelo's | **Downtown**	22
Cedar Grove | **Wimberley**	-
Chez Nous | **Downtown**	25
NEW Creek Road Café | **Dripping Springs**	-
☑ Driskill Grill | **Downtown**	26
Eastside Café | **Cherrywood**	24
1886 Café | **Downtown**	22
European Bistro | **Pflugerville**	24
NEW Fion Bistro | **Steiner Rch**	-
Gypsy Italian | **Bouldin Creek**	-
☑ Jeffrey's | **Clarksville**	26
Judges' Hill | **W Campus**	24
McCormick/Schmick's | **NW Austin**	21
Mirabelle | **NW Hills**	25

Ms. B's | **NW Hills** `22`
NEW Mulberry | **Downtown** `-`
NEW Paggi Hse. | **Downtown S** `-`
Rather Sweet | **Fredericksburg** `26`
Sagra | **Downtown** `-`
Shoreline Grill | **Downtown** `24`
Z Siena | **NW Hills** `25`
NEW Silver & Stone | **Georgetown** `-`
Silver K | **Johnson City** `-`
NEW Southwest Bistro | **Downtown S** `-`
Starlite | **Warehouse Dist** `25`
Steeping Room | **NW Austin** `21`
NEW Steiner Ranch | **Steiner Rch** `-`
Thistle Café | **Downtown** `18`
Z TRIO | **Downtown** `27`
Turtle | **Brownwood** `-`
Ventana | **N Austin** `23`
NEW Whip-In Parlour | **S Austin** `-`
Woodland | **SoCo** `18`
Zoot | **Old W Austin** `26`

ROMANTIC PLACES

Andiamo | **N Austin** `-`
Aquarelle | **Downtown** `27`
August E's | **Fredericksburg** `27`
Backstage | **Spicewood** `26`
Belmont | **Downtown** `18`
Bess | **Downtown** `17`
Bistro 88 | **W Lake** `25`
Carmelo's | **Downtown** `22`
Cedar Grove | **Wimberley** `-`
Chez Nous | **Downtown** `25`
Clay Pit | **Downtown** `23`
NEW Creek Road Café | **Dripping Springs** `-`
Z Driskill Grill | **Downtown** `26`
Eastside Café | **Cherrywood** `24`
European Bistro | **Pflugerville** `24`
NEW Fion Bistro | **Steiner Rch** `-`
Z Fonda San Miguel | **Highland Pk** `26`
Gypsy Italian | **Bouldin Creek** `-`
House.Wine. | **Fredericksburg** `-`
Z Hudson's | **Lakeway** `28`
Joe DiMaggio's | **NW Austin** `-`
Judges' Hill | **W Campus** `24`
Mirabelle | **NW Hills** `25`
NEW Olivia | **S Lamar** `-`

NEW Paggi Hse. | **Downtown S** `-`
Rest. Jezebel | **Downtown** `27`
Romeo's | **Zilker** `17`
Sagra | **Downtown** `-`
Shoreline Grill | **Downtown** `24`
Z Siena | **NW Hills** `25`
NEW Silver & Stone | **Georgetown** `-`
Silver K | **Johnson City** `-`
Starlite | **Warehouse Dist** `25`
Z TRIO | **Downtown** `27`
Turtle | **Brownwood** `-`
NEW Uncorked | **E Austin** `-`
NEW Viva Chocolato! | **NW Austin** `-`
Wildfire | **Georgetown** `22`
Zoot | **Old W Austin** `26`

SENIOR APPEAL

Andiamo | **N Austin** `-`
Aquarelle | **Downtown** `27`
Austin Land | **Downtown** `22`
Carmelo's | **Downtown** `22`
Cedar Grove | **Wimberley** `-`
City Market | **Luling** `24`
Cooper's | **Llano** `27`
County Line | **multi.** `20`
NEW Creek Road Café | **Dripping Springs** `-`
Z Driskill Grill | **Downtown** `26`
1886 Café | **Downtown** `22`
European Bistro | **Pflugerville** `24`
Gonzales Mkt. | **Gonzales** `-`
Green Pastures | **Bouldin Creek** `23`
Z Hudson's | **Lakeway** `28`
Z Jasper's | **NW Austin** `24`
Joe DiMaggio's | **NW Austin** `-`
Judges' Hill | **W Campus** `24`
Kreuz Mkt. | **Lockhart** `26`
Lambert's | **Warehouse Dist** `23`
Louie Mueller | **Taylor** `25`
Mandola's | **N Central** `22`
Mangieri's | **Circle C** `22`
McCormick/Schmick's | **NW Austin** `21`
Melting Pot | **multi.** `21`
Meyer's | **Elgin** `21`
Ms. B's | **NW Hills** `22`
Opie's BBQ | **Spicewood** `23`
NEW Perry's Steak | **Downtown** `25`

NEW Primizie Osteria | **E Austin**	_
Rather Sweet | **Fredericksburg**	26
Real New Orleans | **Round Mtn**	_
R.O.'s Outpost | **Spicewood**	_
Ruth's Chris | **Downtown**	25
Shoreline Grill | **Downtown**	24
Smitty's Mkt. | **Lockhart**	19
Southside Mkt. | **Elgin**	24
NEW Southwest Bistro | **Downtown S**	_
Steeping Room | **NW Austin**	21
NEW Steiner Ranch | **Steiner Rch**	_
TC Noodle House | **N Austin**	_
Threadgill's | **multi.**	19
Trattoria Lisina | **Driftwood**	_
Z TRIO | **Downtown**	27
Turtle | **Brownwood**	_
Ventana | **N Austin**	23
NEW Viva Chocolato! | **NW Austin**	_
Woodland | **SoCo**	18

SINGLES SCENES

Belmont | **Downtown**	18
Bess | **Downtown**	17
Blue Star | **Rosedale**	20
Z Chuy's | **multi.**	21
Cissi's Mkt. | **SoCo**	_
Cool River | **NW Austin**	19
Z Eddie V's | **multi.**	26
Finn & Porter | **Downtown**	23
Fleming's Prime | **Downtown**	24
Habana | **Downtown**	21
Hula Hut | **Old W Austin**	18
NEW Imperia | **Warehouse Dist**	_
Joe DiMaggio's | **NW Austin**	_
Málaga | **Warehouse Dist**	20
NEW Maria Maria | **Warehouse Dist**	_
NEW Nomad | **Coronado Hills**	_
NoRTH | **NW Austin**	_
North by NW | **Great Hills**	18
NEW Paggi Hse. | **Downtown S**	_
NEW Parkside | **Downtown**	_
Saba Blue | **Warehouse Dist**	18
Serranos | **multi.**	16
South Congress | **SoCo**	22
Sullivan's | **Warehouse Dist**	24

NEW Taste Wines | **Downtown**	_
Torchy's Tacos | **multi.**	_
NEW Uncorked | **E Austin**	_
NEW Yume | **N Central**	_

SLEEPERS

(Good to excellent food, but little known)

August E's | **Fredericksburg**	27
Backstage | **Spicewood**	26
Buster's | **Bee Cave**	24
City Market | **Luling**	24
Daily Grill | **NW Austin**	24
Din Ho | **N Austin**	24
El Meson | **SE Austin**	27
Estância | **SW Austin**	27
European Bistro | **Pflugerville**	24
Finn & Porter | **Downtown**	23
First Chinese | **N Austin**	25
Gene's | **E Austin**	25
Golden Wok | **N Austin**	22
Hilltop Café | **Fredericksburg**	23
Judges' Hill | **W Campus**	24
Louie Mueller | **Taylor**	25
Mangieri's | **Circle C**	22
Mikado Ryotei | **N Austin**	24
Ms. B's | **NW Hills**	22
Opie's BBQ | **Spicewood**	23
Rather Sweet | **Fredericksburg**	26
Reale's | **Jollyville**	23
Rest. Jezebel | **Downtown**	27
Southside Mkt. | **Elgin**	24
Sunflower | **N Austin**	23
Tacodeli | **multi.**	25
Ventana | **N Austin**	23
Wildfire | **Georgetown**	22

TRANSPORTING EXPERIENCES

Aquarelle | **Downtown**	27
Carmelo's | **Downtown**	22
County Line | **multi.**	20
Din Ho | **N Austin**	24
Estância | **SW Austin**	27
European Bistro | **Pflugerville**	24
Z Fonda San Miguel | **Highland Pk**	26
Green Pastures | **Bouldin Creek**	23
Hula Hut | **Old W Austin**	18
Z Siena | **NW Hills**	25

TRENDY

August E's | **Fredericksburg**	27
Belmont | **Downtown**	18
Bess | **Downtown**	17
Finn & Porter | **Downtown**	23
Fino | **W Campus**	23
NEW Imperia | **Warehouse Dist**	–
Z Jasper's | **NW Austin**	24
Joe DiMaggio's | **NW Austin**	–
Lambert's | **Warehouse Dist**	23
NEW Maria Maria | **Warehouse Dist**	–
NEW Mulberry | **Downtown**	–
NoRTH | **NW Austin**	–
NEW Olivia | **S Lamar**	–
NEW Parkside | **Downtown**	–
Rest. Jezebel | **Downtown**	27
Roy's | **Downtown**	25
Starlite | **Warehouse Dist**	25
NEW Taste Wines | **Downtown**	–
Z TRIO | **Downtown**	27
Z Uchi | **Zilker**	28
NEW Uncorked | **E Austin**	–
Z Vespaio | **SoCo**	28
Z Wink | **Old W Austin**	27

VIEWS

Cedar Grove | **Wimberley**	–
County Line | **NW Hills**	20
Z Eddie V's | **multi.**	26
Hilltop Café | **Fredericksburg**	23
Hula Hut | **Old W Austin**	18
Oasis | **Lakeway**	11
NEW Paggi Hse. | **Downtown S**	–
Rocco's Grill | **Lakeway**	20
Z Salt Lick | **Driftwood**	24
Shoreline Grill | **Downtown**	24
NEW Steiner Ranch | **Steiner Rch**	–
Trattoria Lisina | **Driftwood**	–
Z TRIO | **Downtown**	27
Z'Tejas | **multi.**	22

VISITORS ON EXPENSE ACCOUNT

Aquarelle | **Downtown**	27
Carmelo's | **Downtown**	22
Cool River | **NW Austin**	19
Finn & Porter | **Downtown**	23
Fleming's Prime | **Downtown**	24
Z Hudson's | **Lakeway**	28
NEW Imperia | **Warehouse Dist**	–
Z Jeffrey's | **Clarksville**	26
Joe DiMaggio's | **NW Austin**	–
Judges' Hill | **W Campus**	24
Kenichi | **Warehouse Dist**	22
McCormick/Schmick's | **Downtown**	21
NEW Olivia | **S Lamar**	–
NEW Perry's Steak | **Downtown**	25
Rest. Jezebel | **Downtown**	27
Roy's | **Downtown**	25
Ruth's Chris | **Downtown**	25
NEW Steiner Ranch | **Steiner Rch**	–
Z TRIO | **Downtown**	27
Z Uchi | **Zilker**	28
Z Vespaio | **SoCo**	28
Z Wink | **Old W Austin**	27
Zoot | **Old W Austin**	26

WINNING WINE LISTS

Aquarelle | **Downtown**	27
Asti Trattoria | **Hyde Pk**	24
August E's | **Fredericksburg**	27
Bess | **Downtown**	17
Blue Star | **Rosedale**	20
Carmelo's | **Downtown**	22
Cedar Grove | **Wimberley**	–
Cissi's Mkt. | **SoCo**	–
NEW Creek Road Café | **Dripping Springs**	–
Z Driskill Grill | **Downtown**	26
Enoteca Vespaio | **SoCo**	25
Estância | **SW Austin**	27
Finn & Porter | **Downtown**	23
Fino | **W Campus**	23
NEW Fion Bistro | **Steiner Rch**	–
Fleming's Prime | **Downtown**	24
Z Hudson's | **Lakeway**	28
Z Jasper's | **NW Austin**	24
Z Jeffrey's | **Clarksville**	26
Joe DiMaggio's | **NW Austin**	–
La Traviata | **Downtown**	24
Louie's 106 | **Downtown**	24
Mirabelle | **NW Hills**	25
NEW Mulberry | **Downtown**	–
NEW Olivia | **S Lamar**	–
NEW Paggi Hse. | **Downtown S**	–

NEW Parkside | **Downtown**	-
NEW Perry's Steak | **Downtown**	25
Roaring Fork | **Downtown**	24
Roy's | **Downtown**	25
Ruth's Chris | **Downtown**	25
Z Siena | **NW Hills**	25
NEW Taste Wines | **Downtown**	-
Z TRIO | **Downtown**	27
Z Uchi | **Zilker**	28
NEW Uncorked | **E Austin**	-
Z Vespaio | **SoCo**	28
Wildfire | **Georgetown**	22
NEW Wine Cellar | **W Lake**	-
Z Wink | **Old W Austin**	27
Zoot | **Old W Austin**	26

WORTH A TRIP

Driftwood	
Z Salt Lick	24
Fredericksburg	
Hilltop Café	23
Georgetown	
NEW Silver & Stone	-
Wildfire	22
Lexington	
Snow's BBQ	-
Pfluggerville	
European Bistro	24
Spicewood	
Backstage	26
Opie's BBQ	23

DALLAS/FT. WORTH

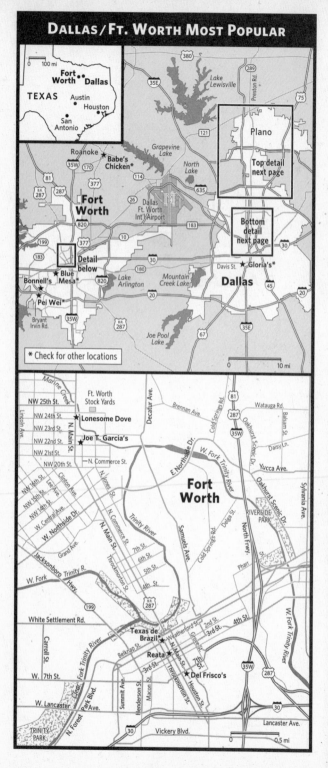

DALLAS/FT. WORTH MOST POPULAR

TEXAS

Fort Worth • • Dallas

Austin •
Houston •

San Antonio •

Roanoke ★ Babe's Chicken*

Grapevine Lake

North Lake

Plano

Top detail next page

Fort Worth

Dallas Ft. Worth Int'l Airport

Bottom detail next page

Davis St. ★ Gloria's*

Bonnell's ★ ★ Blue Mesa*

Dallas

★ Pei Wei*

Bryant Irvin Rd.

Lake Arlington

Mountain Creek Lake

Joe Pool Lake

* Check for other locations

0   10 mi

Marine Creek

Ft. Worth Stock Yards

NW 25th St.
NW 24th St.   ★ Lonesome Dove
NW 23rd St.
NW 22nd St.   ★ Joe T. Garcia's
NW 21st St.
NW 20th St.   — N. Commerce St.

Fort Worth

RIVERSIDE PARK

White Settlement Rd.

Texas de Brazil ★

Reata ★

★ Del Frisco's

W. 7th St.

W. Lancaster Ave.

TRINITY PARK

Vickery Blvd.

0   0.5 mi

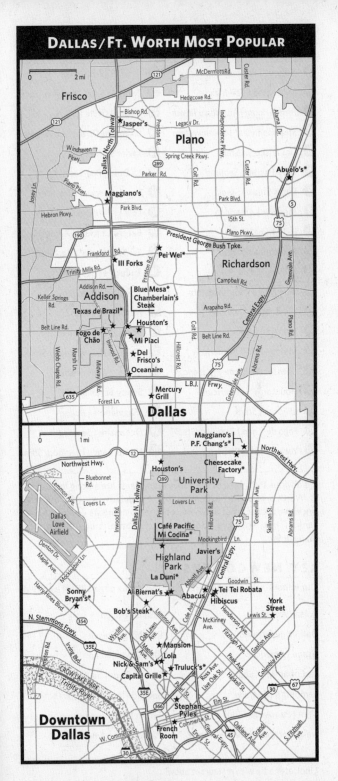

Frisco

(121)

McDermottt Rd.

Custer Rd.

Hedgcoxe Rd.

Bishop Rd.

★ Jasper's

Legacy Dr.

Preston Rd.

Plano

Independence Pkwy.

Alma Dr.

Windhaven Pkwy.

Spring Creek Pkwy.

(289)

Plano Pkwy.

Josey Ln.

Parker Rd.

Colit Rd.

Custer Rd.

★ Abuelo's*

(5)

Hebron Pkwy.

★ Maggiano's

Park Blvd.

Park Blvd.

75

15th St.

Plano Pkwy.

Greenville Ave.

190

President George Bush Tpke.

Frankford Rd.

★ Pei Wei*

Richardson

★★ III Forks

Preston Rd.

Trinity Mills Rd.

Central Expy.

Plano Rd.

Campbell Rd.

Addison Rd.

Blue Mesa*

Keller Springs Rd.

Addison

Chamberlain's Steak

Arapaho Rd.

★ Texas de Brazil*

Houston's

Colit Rd.

Belt Line Rd.

Belt Line Rd.

Webb Chapel Rd.

Fogo de Chão

★ Mi Piaci

Hillcrest Rd.

75

Marsh Ln.

Midway Rd.

Inwood Rd.

★ Del Frisco's

Abrams Rd.

Oceanaire

L.B.J. Frwy.

Greenville Ave.

635

Forest Ln.

Mercury Grill

Dallas

Maggiano's

P.F. Chang's*

12

Northwest Hwy.

Northwest Hwy.

Houston's

Cheesecake Factory*

(289)

University Park

Bluebonnet Rd.

Preston Rd.

Lovers Ln.

Dallas N. Tollway

Lovers Ln.

Hillcrest Rd.

75

Greenville Ave.

Skillman St.

Abrams Rd.

Dallas Love Airfield

Café Pacific

Denton Dr.

Mi Cocina*

Mockingbird Ln.

Maple Ave.

Highland Park

Javier's

Central Expy.

Mockingbird Ln.

Harry Hines Blvd.

La Duni*

Abbott Ave.

Goodwin St.

Sonny Bryan's*

★ Al Biernat's

★ Abacus

Tei Tei Robata

N. Stemmons Frwy.

Bob's Steak*

Hibiscus

York Street

354

Lewis St.

35E

Wycliff Ave.

Oak Lawn Ave.

Cole Ave.

McKinney Ave.

Henderson Ave.

Gaston Ave.

N. Hampton Rd.

Irving Blvd.

Maple Ave.

Mansion

Lola

Fitzhugh Ave.

Peak Ave.

Columbia Ave.

CROW LAKE PARK Trinity River

Nick & Sam's

★ Truluck's*

Ross Ave.

Live Oak St.

Haskell St.

67

Capital Grille

30

35E

366

Elm St.

Central Expy.

Oakland Ave.

Grand Ave.

S. Fitzhugh Ave.

Downtown Dallas

Stephan Pyles

French Room

Commerce St.

45

W. Commerce St.

30

Most Popular

1	Abacus | *Eclectic*	**21**	Gloria's | *Salvadoran/Tex-Mex*
2	Mi Cocina | *Tex-Mex*	**22**	Texas de Brazil | *Brazilian/Steak*
3	French Room | *American/French*	**23**	Capital Grille | *Steak*
4	Stephan Pyles* | *Southwestern*	**24**	Lonesome Dove | *Southwestern*
5	Del Frisco's | *Steak*	**25**	Javier's | *Mexican*
6	Cafe Pacific | *Seafood*	**26**	La Duni | *Pan-Latin*
7	Bob's Steak | *Steak*	**27**	Joe T. Garcia's | *Tex-Mex*
8	Jasper's | *American*	**28**	Lola | *American*
9	P.F. Chang's | *Chinese*	**29**	Babe's Chicken | *American*
10	Al Biernat's | *Steak*	**30**	Tei Tei Robata* | *Japanese*
11	Pei Wei* | *Pan-Asian*	**31**	Truluck's | *Seafood*
12	Blue Mesa | *Southwestern*	**32**	Abuelo's | *Mexican*
13	Hibiscus* | *American*	**33**	Mi Piaci* | *Italian*
14	Mansion | *American*	**34**	Bonnell's | *Southwestern*
15	Mercury Grill | *American*	**35**	Chamberlain's Steak | *Steak*
16	Cheesecake Factory | *American*	**36**	Reata* | *Southwestern*
17	Houston's* | *American*	**37**	Sonny Bryan's | *BBQ*
18	III Forks | *Steak*	**38**	Maggiano's | *Italian*
19	Fogo de Chão | *Brazilian/Steak*	**39**	Oceanaire | *Seafood*
20	York Street | *American*	**40**	Nick & Sam's | *Seafood/Steak*

It's obvious that many of the above restaurants are among the Dallas/Ft. Worth area's most expensive, but if popularity were calibrated to price, we suspect that a number of other restaurants would join their ranks. Thus, we have added two lists comprising 40 Best Buys on page 90.

KEY NEWCOMERS

Our editors' take on the year's top arrivals. See page 175 for a full list.

Bolsa | *American*	Nonna | *Italian*
Dali Wine Bar | *Amer.*	Rise N° 1 | *French*
Grace | *American*	Rist. Cibus | *Italian*
La Cubanita | *Cuban*	Screen Door | *Southern*
Lambert's | *Seafood*	Second Floor | *Amer./French*
Mint | *Pan-Asian/Thai*	Tei An | *Japanese*
Neighborhood Services | *Amer.*	Woodlands | *American*

* Indicates a tie with restaurant above

Top Food Ratings

Excludes places with low votes, unless indicated by a ▽.

28] French Room | *Amer./French*
Tei Tei Robata | *Japanese*
Local | *American*
Teppo Yakitori | *Japanese*
Abacus | *Eclectic*

27] York Street | *American*
Saint-Emilion | *French*
Yutaka | *Japanese*
Bonnell's | *Southwestern*
Lanny's | *Eclectic/Mexican*
Aurora | *American*
Bijoux | *French*
Stephan Pyles | *Southwestern*
Del Frisco's | *Steak*
Mercury Grill | *American*
Amici | *Italian*
Nana* | *American*
Lola | *American*
Pappas Bros. | *Steak*

26] Mercury Chop | *Steak*
Lonesome Dove | *Southwestern*

Suze | *Mediterranean*
Café Pacific | *Seafood*
Ristorante La Piazza | *Italian*
Mansion | *American*
Al Biernat's | *Steak*
Fearing's | *Southwestern*
Bistro Louise | *American/Med.*
St. Martin's | *American/French*
Fogo de Chão | *Brazilian/Steak*

25] Hibiscus | *American*
Chamberlain's Steak | *Steak*
First Chinese BBQ | *Chinese*
Hattie's | *American*
Piranha | *Japanese*
Nick & Sam's | *Seafood/Steak*
Capital Grille | *Steak*
Babe's Chicken | *American*
Ruth's Chris | *Steak*
Parigi | *American/Med.*
Salum* | *American*
Shinsei | *Pan-Asian*

BY CUISINE

AMERICAN (NEW)

28] Local
27] York Street
Aurora
Mercury Grill
Nana

AMERICAN (TRAD.)

25] Babe's Chicken
23] Houston's
Sevy's
Paris Coffee Shop
22] Porch

BARBECUE

24] Angelo's BBQ
22] Railhead Smokehouse
Peggy Sue BBQ
Sonny Bryan's
21] Cousin's BBQ

CHINESE

25] First Chinese BBQ
22] P.F. Chang's
20] Howard Wang's
Szechuan Chinese*
19] Empress of China

ECLECTIC

28] Abacus
27] Lanny's
24] Sapristi!
23] 2900
22] Café Modern

FRENCH

28] French Room
27] Saint-Emilion
Bijoux
26] St. Martin's
25] Cacharel

INDIAN

23] India Palace
Clay Pit
22] Madras Pavilion
18] Roti Grill
Masala

ITALIAN

27] Amici
26] Ristorante La Piazza
24] Mi Piaci
Nicola's
Daniele

JAPANESE

28 Tei Tei Robata
   Teppo Yakitori
27 Yutaka
25 Piranha
   Steel

MEDITERRANEAN

26 Canary Cafe∇
   Suze
   Bistro Louise
25 Parigi
21 Palomino

MEXICAN

27 Lanny's
24 Esperanza's
   La Familia
   Veracruz
22 Javier's

SEAFOOD

26 Café Pacific
24 Oceanaire
23 Chamberlain's Fish
   Truluck's
   S&D Oyster Co.

SOUTHWESTERN

27 Bonnell's
   Stephan Pyles
26 Lonesome Dove
   Fearing's
24 Reata

STEAKHOUSES

27 Del Frisco's
   Pappas Bros.
26 Mercury Chop
   Al Biernat's
   Fogo de Chão

TEX-MEX

24 Mia's
21 Matt's Rancho Martinez
   Gloria's
   Mi Cocina
   Chuy's

THAI

24 Samui Thai
23 Royal Thai
   Chow Thai
   Asian Mint
21 Mango Thai

BY SPECIAL FEATURE

BREAKFAST

23 Main St. Bistro
23 Paris Coffee Shop
22 Bread Winners Cafe
21 Mama's Daughters'
19 Café Brazil

BRUNCH

27 Mercury Grill
26 Bistro Louise
   St. Martin's
25 Hattie's
   Parigi

BUSINESS DINING

28 Abacus
27 Saint-Emilion
   Stephan Pyles
   Del Frisco's
   Pappas Bros.

CHILD-FRIENDLY

25 Babe's
21 Mi Cocina
19 H.P. Pharmacy
17 Zoë's Kitchen
14 Purple Cow

HOTEL DINING

28 French Room
     (Hotel Adolphus)
27 Nana (Hilton Anatole)
26 Mansion
   Fearing's (Ritz-Carlton)
25 Craft (W Hotel)

MEET FOR A DRINK

27 Stephan Pyles
   Mercury Grill
26 Mansion
24 Reata
21 Fuse

OFFBEAT

25 Babe's
23 Spiral Diner
22 Cosmic Café
21 Fuse
19 Trader Vic's

PEOPLE-WATCHING

28 French Room
   Abacus
26 Fearing's
   Lonesome Dove
25 Craft

Menus, photos, voting and more – free at ZAGAT.com

QUICK BITES

23	Kincaid's
19	H.P. Pharmacy
	Pei Wei
18	Café Express
17	Zoë's Kitchen

QUIET CONVERSATION

28	French Room
27	Saint-Emilion
	Bonnell's
	Nana
25	Grape

TRENDY

27	Lanny's
26	Fearing's
24	ALÓ
22	Kenichi
21	Trece

WINNING WINE LISTS

28	French Room
	Abacus
27	Pappas Bros.
	Del Frisco's
	Lola

WORTH A TRIP

25	Hattie's
	Oak Cliff
24	Jasper's
	Plano
	Culpepper
	Rockwall
	Goodhues▽
	McKinney

BY LOCATION

DALLAS

DOWNTOWN

28	French Room
25	Morton's Steak
24	Zodiac
22	Sonny Bryan's
21	Fuse

GREENVILLE AVENUE

28	Teppo Yakitori
26	St. Martin's
25	Grape
24	Kirby's
23	Royal Thai

KNOX-HENDERSON

28	Tei Tei Robata
	Abacus
25	Hibiscus
24	ALÓ
	La Duni

LOVE FIELD AREA

27	Pappas Bros.
23	Avila's
22	Sonny Bryan's
21	Mama's Daughters'
	Celebration

NORTH DALLAS

27	Del Frisco's
25	Ruth's Chris

	Ill Forks
24	Lawry's
	Lavendou Bistro

NORTHPARK

22	P.F. Chang's
21	McCormick & Schmick's
20	Blue Mesa
	Luna de Noche
	Maggiano's

OAK LAWN

27	Aurora
26	Al Biernat's
25	Parigi
	Steel
24	Silver Fox

UPTOWN

27	Yutaka
	Lola
26	Mansion
	Fearing's
25	Nick & Sam's

WEST LOVERS LANE

27	Bijoux
25	Shinsei
22	Bread Winners Cafe
	Sonny Bryan's
21	Café Istanbul

WEST VILLAGE

23 Campania
21 Mi Cocina

20 Fish
Taco Diner*
Crú Wine Bar

FT. WORTH

CULTURAL DISTRICT

27 Saint-Emilion
Lanny's
24 Michaels
Buffet at the Kimbell
22 Café Modern

SOUTHWEST

27 Bonnell's
26 Bistro Louise
21 Keg Steak
Cousin's BBQ
20 Szechuan Chinese

OTHER AREAS

ADDISON

26 Fogo de Chão
25 Chamberlain's Steak
24 Texas de Brazil
Mi Piaci
23 Houston's

LAS COLINAS

24 Café on the Green
23 Blue Fish
Via Reál
22 I Fratelli
21 Café Cipriani

FRISCO

24 Silver Fox
21 Cantina Laredo
Gloria's
Jinbeh
20 Terilli's

PLANO

25 First Chinese BBQ
Bob's Steak
Roy's
24 Jasper's
Samui Thai

GRAPEVINE

25 Bob's Steak
24 Silver Fox
Boi Na Braza
23 Main St. Bistro
Ferrari's

RICHARDSON

25 First Chinese BBQ
24 Silver Fox
23 Pappadeaux
Main St. Bistro
22 Madras Pavilion

Top Decor Ratings

29	French Room	24	Bistro Louise
28	Stephan Pyles		Café Ashton
27	Nana		Saint-Emilion
	Fearing's		Café Pacific
	Mansion		III Forks
26	Café Modern		St. Martin's
	ALÓ		Del Frisco's
	Abacus		Mi Piaci
	Mercy		Nobu
	Trader Vic's		Pappas Bros.
25	Reata		Local
	Café on the Green		N9ne Steak
	Lanny's		Old Warsaw
	Jasper's		Roy's
	Tillman's		Buffet at the Kimbell
	Craft		Aurora
	Bijoux	23	Arthur's
	Nicola's		Steel
	Capital Grille		Al Biernat's
	Ristorante La Piazza		Bonnell's

OUTDOORS

Brio		Joe T. Garcia's
Coal Vines		Mansion
Dakota's		Patrizio
Ferre		Reata
Fuse		Rough Creek Lodge

ROMANCE

Aurora		Lola
Bijoux		Lonesome Dove
French Room		Mansion
Grape		Nana
Hôtel St. Germain		Saint-Emilion

ROOMS

Abacus		Mercury Grill
Central 214		Nana
City Café		Pappas Bros.
Maggiano's		Reata
Mansion		Stephan Pyles

VIEWS

Cacharel		Nana
Café Modern		Primo's B&G (Garland)
Café Nasher		Reata
Mansion		Rist. Cibus
Mi Piaci		Rough Creek Lodge

Top Service Ratings

29	French Room		Bijoux
27	Nana		Pappas Bros.
	Saint-Emilion		Al Biernat's
	Aurora		St. Martin's
	Abacus		Ruth's Chris
26	Stephan Pyles		Fearing's
	Bonnell's		Nick & Sam's
	Café Pacific		Boi Na Braza
	Mansion	24	Chamberlain's Steak
	Café on the Green		Palm
	Old Warsaw		Mercury Grill
	La Familia		Bugatti
	Lanny's		Suze*
	York Street		Texas de Brazil
	Fogo de Chão		Hattie's
25	Del Frisco's		Amici
	Local		Edelweiss*
	Capital Grille		Cacharel
	Lola		Lawry's*
	Teppo Yakitori		III Forks

Best Buys

In order of Bang for the Buck rating.

1. H.P. Pharmacy
2. Paris Coffee Shop
3. Kincaid's
4. Buffet at the Kimbell
5. Esperanza's
6. Love Shack
7. Cousin's BBQ
8. La Familia
9. Carshon's Deli
10. Babe's Chicken
11. Bubba's
12. Mama's Daughters'
13. Angelo's BBQ
14. Cosmic Café
15. Railhead Smokehouse
16. Billy Miner's
17. Benito's
18. Main St. Bistro
19. Greenz
20. Masala

OTHER GOOD VALUES

Amici
Bread Winners
Café Brazil
Celebration
Charleston's
Chic from Barcelona
First Chinese BBQ
Gloria's
Green Papaya
Kathleen's Sky Diner
Kuby's
Maggiano's
Mango Thai
Mia's
Neuhaus Café
Peggy Sue BBQ
Pei Wei
Roti Grill
Taco Diner
Zeke's

Menus, photos, voting and more – free at ZAGAT.com

Dallas/Ft. Worth

Z Abacus ⊠ *Eclectic*   28 | 26 | 27 | $66

Knox-Henderson | 4511 McKinney Ave. (Armstrong Ave.) | Dallas | 214-559-3111 | www.kentrathbun.com

"Hands down one of the best restaurants in town" hail fans of this "inventive" Knox-Henderson Eclectic (indeed it's Dallas/Ft. Worth's Most Popular) helmed by Kent Rathbun, whose "truly memorable" "Californian, French and Asian"–style dishes – including signature lobster shooters that "deserve the hype" – "never fail to delight or impress"; service is "meticulous" as well, so the only downside is that it's so "expensive", you may "need an abacus to total the bill"; N.B. the Decor score does not reflect a recent redo.

Abuelo's *Mexican*   19 | 21 | 19 | $21

Plano | 3420 N. Central Expwy. (Parker Rd.) | 972-423-9290
Plano | 3701 Dallas Pkwy. (Parker Rd.) | 972-781-1613
Lewisville | 2520 S. Stemmons Frwy. (Rte. 121) | 972-315-6057
Arlington | 1041 I-20 W. (Matlock Rd.) | 817-468-2622
Hurst | 824 Airport Frwy. (Precinct Line Rd.) | 817-514-9355
www.abuelos.com

See review in Austin and the Hill Country Directory.

Addison Cafe *American*   23 | 20 | 24 | $39

Addison | 5290 Belt Line Rd. (Montfort Dr.) | 972-991-8824 | www.addisoncafe.com

After "many years in business", this "quaint little bistro" in Addison is "still a wonderful experience", with a "solid, steady" "French-themed" New American menu and servers so "attentive" that, after you dine there "only a couple times", they'll "know your name and favorite drink"; "best for business lunches and dates", it has a "cozy", "classy" interior that takes some "back to the elegance of the '50s and '60s" – and even those who can't "get over" the location concede it's "nice for a shopping-strip" venue.

Adelmo's ⊠ *Italian*   23 | 18 | 22 | $42

Knox-Henderson | 4537 Cole Ave. (Knox St.) | Dallas | 214-559-0325 | www.adelmos.com

Adelmo Banchetti's eatery in Knox-Henderson is "just what a good Italian neighborhood restaurant ought to be": "unpretentious", with "no gimmicks – just a nice place to enjoy good food" and wines that "will satisfy connoisseurs without emptying the bank account"; backed by a "staff-to-diner ratio" that's "insane" (in a good way), Adelmo "tends bar and greets you" within the "cozy" interior of a "charming" building with "lace curtains" that feels "like grandma's."

Aija ⊠ *American*   ▽ 19 | 15 | 19 | $20

Arts District | Trammell Crow Ctr. | 2001 Ross Ave. (bet. Harwood & Olive Sts.) | Dallas | 214-979-3111 | www.artsdistrictbanquets.com

Downtowners in-the-know scamper to this "great bargain", lunch-only eatery in a "beautiful setting" at the Trammell Crow Center in the Arts District, where the all-buffet offerings include a "nice vari-

ety" of "innovative" Asian-influenced American dishes; locals eat their "quick bite" at tables that are decked in white linen, backdropped by a stunning mural; N.B. closed Saturdays and Sundays.

Z Al Biernat's *Steak* | 26 | 23 | 25 | $57 |

Oak Lawn | 4217 Oak Lawn Ave. (Herschel Ave.) | Dallas | 214-219-2201 | www.albiernats.com

A "magnet for the rich and famous", this "always-crowded" Oak Lawn steakhouse is a "loud but welcoming" "classic" that proffers "very solid" "power lunches and dinners"; advocates admire the "social" ambiance that's encouraged by owner Al Biernat as he works the room and greets guests by name, and if the "prices set your heart aflame", given the "outstanding" service and "snazzelicious" vibe, they're "worth the hole they burn in your pocket."

Z ALÓ *Mexican/Peruvian* | 24 | 26 | 19 | $34 |

Knox-Henderson | 4447 N. Central Expwy. (Garrett Ave.) | Dallas | 214-520-9711 | www.alodallas.com

The La Duni duo brings "fabulously unique" "Peruvian-Mexican fusion" to Knox-Henderson with this "delightful" cantina and its "clever, unusual" "small plates"; the cool modern surroundings (complete with flat-screen cooking demos and stone accents) win raves, though a few frugal-minded feasters argue that it's "supposed to be street food, but the cost is out of proportion", especially given the sometimes "haphazard" service.

Ama Lur *Southwestern* | ∇ 23 | 23 | 23 | $51 |

Grapevine | Gaylord Texan Resort | 1501 Gaylord Trail (Rte. 26) | 817-778-2215 | www.gaylordhotels.com

Though the fare at this "expensive" Southwestern restaurant in Grapevine's Gaylord Texan Resort is "still good", disappointed sorts bemoan that it's slipped since "many of the faves were taken off the menu", making it "not nearly as good as when it first opened"; still, it's a popular gathering spot, set under an atrium, and the margarita bar and salsa band distract from a somewhat "inconsistent" staff.

NEW American Girl
Boutique & Bistro *American* | - | - | - | I |

Galleria | 13464 Dallas Pkwy. (Alpha Rd.) | Dallas | 888-777-0010 | www.americangirl.com

Set within the wildly popular toy emporium, this pretty-in-pink Galleria cafe attracts gaggles of girls (and their favorite dolls) for kid-friendly Traditional American menu items like cheese fondue, heart-shaped ravioli and indulgent desserts, all offered à la carte or in a fixed-price format; private rooms are available for birthdays and tea parties and come pre-decorated with favors; N.B. reservations essential on weekends and school holidays.

Amici ⧉Ⓜ *Italian* | 27 | 17 | 24 | $42 |

Carrollton | 1022 S. Broadway Rd. (Belt Line Rd.) | 972-245-3191 | www.amicisignature.com

A "delightful find" rave fans of this Carrollton "hideaway" overseen by a "charming chef-owner" who sends out "first-class" French-inflected

	FOOD	DECOR	SERVICE	COST

Italian cuisine with "excellent game specials"; the dining room is "dark" and modern (and, it's worth noting, located up a "steep flight of stairs"), and because it's BYO, prices are a relative "bargain."

Andiamo ☒ *Italian* | 21 | 17 | 20 | $31 |

Addison | 4151 Belt Line Rd. (Midway Rd.) | 972-233-1515 | www.andiamogrill.com

"For many years", enthusiasts have enjoyed "pleasant" "repeat visits" to this "cozy" "neighborhood restaurant" in Addison, where "moderately priced" and "well-prepared classic Italian" fare is served by an "attentive staff" amid "charming" (if "typical") decor; though it's "free from the usual North Dallas hype", "do call ahead" since "without a reservation, you may not get a table."

Angela's Bistro 51 ☒ *American* | ▽ 22 | 19 | 21 | $46 |

Uptown | 2701 Guillot St. (Boll St.) | Dallas | 214-979-0051 | www.angelasbistro51.com

Expect "well-executed", "upscale home cooking" at this Uptown New American that's a "great neighborhooder", serving fast-paced pre-theater dinners as well as leisurely lunches; surveyors "love the art" on the walls (made by local talent) and the polish that radiates from the restored hardwood floors inside this "hidden treasure."

Angelo's Barbecue ☒✏ *BBQ* | 24 | 14 | 15 | $13 |

Near West | 2533 White Settlement Rd. (bet. N. Henderson St. & University Dr.) | Ft. Worth | 817-332-0357 | www.angelosbbq.com

This "classic" Near West Ft. Worth spot is "a longtime institution" and an "almighty shrine to smoked meat", dishing up "Texas beef at its very finest" along with "schooners of cold draft beer"; with its "authentic Texana surroundings", including a weathered wood interior and an infamous "big bear in the foyer" that "kids love", it "may look like a hole-in-the-wall, but isn't that usually where one finds the best BBQ?"

Arcodoro & Pomodoro Ⓜ *Italian* | 21 | 21 | 19 | $43 |

Uptown | 2708 Routh St. (bet. McKinney Ave. & Howell St.) | Dallas | 214-871-1924 | www.arcodoro.com

The "authentic Sardinian" cuisine is a departure "from standard Italian fare" at this Uptown "see-and-be-seen" spot that gets special nods for its "awesome pastas" and "delicious thin-crust pizza" made in a "wood-burning oven"; it also boasts "beautiful villa decor" and a "romantic outdoor patio", but surveyors are split on the "well-dressed staff" – some finding it "snooty", others "as enchanting as the food"; N.B. they plan to move to Crescent Court in 2009.

Arthur's Prime Steaks & Seafood ☒ *Seafood/Steak* | 23 | 23 | 21 | $53 |

Addison | 15175 Quorum Dr. (Belt Line Rd.) | 972-385-0800 | www.arthursdallas.com

Take "a step into the past" at this "elegant" steak-and-seafood house in Addison, whose "dark and quiet" interior is a "good place for a special dinner or just treating yourself" to a "nice all-around meal" accompanied by a "well-made" cocktail; its "huge bar" is "a

gathering place for mature adults", with an "active lounge" featuring "great bands" (Monday–Saturday) and a dance floor that affords prime "people-watching."

Asian Mint *Pan-Asian/Thai*

| 23 | 14 | 18 | $23 |

Medical City | 11617 N. Central Expwy. (Forest Ln.) | Dallas | 214-363-6655 | www.asianmint.com

Mint, The ⑤ *Pan-Asian/Thai*

NEW **Highland Park Village** | Shops of Highland Park | 4246 Oak Lawn Ave. (Herschel Ave.) | Dallas | 214-219-6468 | www.themintdallas.com

An "oasis" tucked into an "unattractive shopping center", this local "treasure" near Medical City charms chowhounds with "wonderful", "affordable" Thai and Pan-Asian dishes plus "inventive cocktails" and desserts you'll want to "leave room for"; though a few find the "trendy" quarters don't offer "much ambiance for dinner", "smooth service" ensures a pleasant time nonetheless; N.B. the Highland Park outpost is new.

☑ Aurora ⑤ *American*

| 27 | 24 | 27 | $89 |

Oak Lawn | 4216 Oak Lawn Ave. (Wycliff Ave.) | Dallas | 214-528-9400 | www.auroradallas.com

Diners don't hesitate to "max out [their] credit cards" at this "over-the-top" Oak Lawn New American that "stands out among the many temples of haute cuisine" thanks to "master" chef Avner Samuel, who serves up "beautifully presented" plates matched with wine from an "outstanding" 600-label list; bejeweled cognoscenti fill the art deco–inspired space and coo over its "luxury, sophistication and polish", though some find the "strip-center" drive-up an incongruous welcome.

Avanti *Italian/Mediterranean*

| 20 | 19 | 19 | $35 |

Downtown Dallas | Fountain Pl. | 1445 Ross Ave. (Field St.) | Dallas | 214-965-0055 ⑤
Uptown | 2720 McKinney Ave. (Worthington St.) | Dallas | 214-871-4955
Addison | Addison Circle | 5001 Addison Circle (bet. Airport Pkwy. & McEntire Pl.) | 972-386-7800 ⑤
www.avantirestaurants.com

A "charming" trio, these "reliable" eateries offer "very good Italian-Med food" in a variety of "intimate", "sophisticated" atmospheres; big-city émigrés find the Uptown branch "a great place to go for late evenings" on weekends, with a "fabulous after-hours breakfast" for "in-the-know" eaters, and there's "good live music" at the Addison and McKinney Avenue locations.

Avila's ⑤ *Mexican*

| 23 | 15 | 21 | $18 |

Love Field | 4714 Maple Ave. (Kings Rd.) | Dallas | 214-520-2700
"Don't go for the ambiance – go for" the "fresh", "authentic" fare at this "awesome hole-in-the-wall Mexican" near Love Field, where "you feel like family" thanks to the welcoming Avila clan; they now serve hard liquor, with handcrafted margaritas (along with beer and wine) proving the perfect complement to the "wonderful" food.

	FOOD	DECOR	SERVICE	COST

Awaji *Japanese* — 24 | 15 | 21 | $33

Plano | Berkley Sq. | 4701 W. Park Blvd. (Ohio Dr.) | 972-519-1688 |
www.awajiplano.com

"Spectacular" sushi crafted from "quality fish" is the draw at this
Japanese in western Plano also featuring "fairly creative" specialty
dishes; moderate tabs and a "warm" welcome from the "polite" staff
overcome its strip-center setting and "long-in-the-tooth" decor.

Babe's Chicken Dinner House *American* — 25 | 17 | 22 | $16

Carrollton | 1006 W. Main St. (S. Broadway St.) | 972-245-7773
NEW Frisco | 6475 Page St. (Church St.) | 214-387-9500
Garland | 1456 Belt Line Rd. (Garland Ave.) | 972-496-1041
Sanger | 204 N. Fourth St. (Cherry St.) | 940-458-0000 Ⓜ
Roanoke | 104 N. Oak St. (Main St.) | 817-491-2900
Burleson | 120 S. Main St. (Ellison St.) | 817-447-3400
Granbury | 114 W. Pearl St. (Houston St.) | 817-573-9777
www.babeschicken.com

The "fried chicken puts your mother's to shame" at this "kitschy"
homegrown Texas chain where the "old-fashioned" American cooking comes with "all-you-can-eat" "fixings" (like "great" homemade
biscuits) passed "family-style"; regulars report the Roanoke original
reigns, but all outposts offer the same modest tabs plus plenty of
"kids", "noise" and occasional "waits"; N.B. they're BYO.

Bavarian Grill Ⓢ Ⓜ *German* — 20 | 18 | 20 | $23

Plano | Ruisseau Vill. | 221 W. Parker Rd. (Central Expwy.) | 972-881-0705 |
www.bavariangrill.com

"Come hungry, as the portions are huge" at this Plano parlor – one
of the few area German spots – whose popular biergarten boasts
"all the basics: brats, schnitzels" and a "great selection of draft
beers"; perhaps the "decor is a bit worn", but "you can have a fine,
if somewhat hokey, meal" – as long as "you don't mind the accordion, ever-present chicken dance" and "fun polka bands" that "add
to the atmosphere" of "good cheer."

Bella Italia Ⓢ *Italian* — ▽ 24 | 17 | 24 | $34

West | 5139 Camp Bowie Blvd. (Merrick St.) | Ft. Worth | 817-738-1700 |
www.restaurant.com/bellaitalia

"If you like game, this is your place" say fans of this "neighborhood
gem", a quaint, homey hideaway in West Ft. Worth that's one of the
rare Italian places to specialize in that wild provender; regulars insist
that the "specials are always the best" bet (some would "have them
every night"), and other attractions are an "excellent wine list" and
a personable staff that makes you feel "like you're eating at home."

NEW Bene Bene Ristorante Ⓢ *Italian* — - | - | - | M

North Dallas | Frankford Crossing | 4727 Frankford Rd.
(Dallas N. Tollway) | Dallas | 972-267-2363 |
www.benebeneristorante.com

Chef-owner Rino Brigliadori (once of Modo Mio and Positano) re-
turns to North Dallas with this midpriced arrival serving Italian
dishes – including a noteworthy chicken ravioli with brown butter

sage sauce – all prepared with a light touch; a cheerful staff works the mustard-hued room under the watchful eye of the chef, often spotted roaming among the tables in his sauce-stained apron.

Benihana *Japanese/Steak*   20 | 18 | 21 | $32

Medical City | 7775 Banner Dr. (Merit Dr.) | Dallas | 972-387-4404 | www.benihana.com

Las Colinas | 5400 Whitehall St. (Walnut Hill Ln.) | Irving | 972-550-0060 | www.benihana.com

NEW **Plano** | Shops at Legacy | 5840 Legacy Circle (Bishop Rd.) | 469-467-2242

They "have a good sense of humor" at this "kitschy" national Japanese steakhouse chain "where the personable staff cooks your food in front of you on giant grills"; "fun with a group", they're "great places to entertain 13-year-old boys who love to see food thrown" ("the flying shrimp" that "go from the grill to the chef's toque" or are "flipped into a pocket" are particular favorites), but the fare's also "tasty" – "good lunch specials too."

Benito's *Mexican*   18 | 12 | 19 | $13

Hospital District | 1450 W. Magnolia Ave. (Fairmount Ave.) | Ft. Worth | 817-332-8633

It's "nothing fancy", but this "authentic" Mexican in Ft. Worth's Hospital District pleases local lunchers with "solid" fare at reasonable prices (you'll have to pay for your chips and salsa, though); the "old-school" atmosphere "hasn't changed in years", but is enlivened on weekends when it draws a "late-night" crowd till 2 AM.

☑ Bijoux ☒ *French*   27 | 25 | 25 | $77

West Lovers Lane | Inwood Vill. | 5450 W. Lovers Ln. (Inwood Rd.) | Dallas | 214-350-6100 | www.bijouxrestaurant.com

Expect "impeccable everything" at Scott Gottlich's "consistently superb" West Lovers Lane "star that has not lost its luster", luring foodies and "special-occasion" celebrators with "ultrarefined" French food and "fabulous, attentive service"; the "tables are spaced nicely" in the artful, "sedate" space, so your conversation is your own, just know that prix fixe menus (which can be paired with "affordable wines") are the only dining option.

Billy Miner's *Burgers*   19 | 15 | 15 | $13

Sundance Square | 150 W. Third St. (bet. Houston & Main Sts.) | Ft. Worth | 817-877-3301 | www.cyberrodeo.com

Locals laud the "delicious burgers" and solid American grub at this "friendly" saloon in Downtown Ft. Worth's Sundance Square; "cheap" prices pull in local "families", while "drink specials" and plenty of "ice-cold beer" draw a rowdier bar crowd later on.

Bistro Louise *American/Mediterranean*   26 | 24 | 22 | $43

Southwest | Stonegate Commons | 2900 S. Hulen St. (Oak Park Ln.) | Ft. Worth | 817-922-9244 | www.bistrolouise.com

"Marvelous" New American–Med cuisine served in "pretty" surroundings by "attentive" servers make chef-owner Louise Lamensdorf's "expensive" Southwest Ft. Worth boîte a "wonderful

find" that's "worth returning" to; it's especially favored by "ladies who lunch", while denizens declare that brunch is "exquisite" too.

Blackfinn *Pub Food*

| 13 | 17 | 13 | $21 |

Addison | 4440 Beltline Rd. (Midway Rd.) | 469-374-7667 | www.blackfinndallas.com

The "lively bar scene" is the best thing going for this "friendly" Addison chain link catering to a "younger crowd" with "happy-hour" specials, TV screens blaring and "eye candy" galore; considering the Irish-American pub grub is only "ok", most patrons propose you "go for a drink, but pass on the food."

Blue Fish *Japanese*

| 23 | 18 | 19 | $33 |

Greenville Avenue | 3519 Greenville Ave. (McCommas Blvd.) | Dallas | 214-824-3474

North Dallas | 18149 N. Dallas Pkwy. (Frankford Rd.) | Dallas | 972-250-3474

Las Colinas | Las Colinas Vill. | 925 W. John Carpenter Frwy. (MacArthur Blvd.) | Irving | 972-385-3474

www.thebluefishsushi.com

This Japanese micro-chain is a "surprising find", a "hip, happening kind of place" with "creative" fin fare, "fusion-type rolls", and "tempura and bento boxes" that are "right on"; thanks to its "bustling" "clublike atmosphere with thumping music and intimate lighting" and "Asian-eclectic decor", it's "not your typical, quiet sushi place"; N.B. a Watters Creek branch will open soon.

☑ Blue Mesa *Southwestern*

| 20 | 19 | 19 | $24 |

NorthPark | Lincoln Park | 7700 W. Northwest Hwy. (Central Expwy.) | Dallas | 214-378-8686

Addison | Village on the Pkwy. | 5100 Belt Line Rd. (Dallas N. Tollway) | 972-934-0165

Plano | Granite Park | 8200 N. Dallas Pkwy. (Hwy. 121) | 214-387-4407

University Area | University Park Vill. | 1600 S. University Dr. (bet. Old University Dr. & River Run) | Ft. Worth | 817-332-6372

Southlake | Southlake Town Sq. | 1586 E. Southlake Blvd. (Carroll Ave.) | 817-416-0055

www.bluemesagrill.com

"A taste of Santa Fe" comes to Texas via this "popular" mini-chain drawing plenty of "crowds" for "affordable", "palate-pleasing" Southwestern dishes, "addictive sweet potato chips", "killer" blue margaritas and a "fantastic Sunday brunch buffet"; the vibe is "comfortable" and staff "accommodating to large groups", so the only downside is that it "can be hard to get in."

☑ Bob's Steak & Chop House ☒ *Steak*

| 25 | 20 | 23 | $59 |

Lemmon Avenue | 4300 Lemmon Ave. (Wycliff Ave.) | Dallas | 214-528-9446

Plano | Shops at Legacy | 5760 Legacy Dr. (Bishop Rd.) | 972-608-2627

Grapevine | 1255 South Main St. (Hwy. 114) | 817-481-5555

www.bobs-steakandchop.com

"Manly high-end dining" is alive and well at these "clubby" chophouse "institutions" where "yuppies" on "expense accounts" "tackle" "perfectly seared" steaks garnished with an "enormous"

signature glazed carrot; all locations feature "noisy" environs, while the Lemmon Avenue branch offers "frequent Dallas Cowboy sightings" as an added appeasement; N.B. a branch in Ft. Worth's Omni Hotel is coming in 2009.

Boi Na Braza *Brazilian/Steak*

| 24 | 22 | 25 | $55 |

Grapevine | 4025 William D. Tate Ave. (Hall Johnson Rd.) | 817-329-5514 | www.boinabraza.com

Those "hungry for meat" march over to this all-you-can-eat Grapevine churrascaria where gaucho-clad waiters "carve" "delicious" morsels from a "mind-boggling" array of skewered cuts while an extensive salad bar satisfies grazers; it's "top-shelf" all the way from the handsome wood-accented decor to cigar-friendly bar and "expensive" prices.

NEW Bolsa *American*

| - | - | - | M |

Oak Cliff | 614 W. Davis St. (N. Llewellyn Ave.) | Dallas | 214-367-9367 | www.bolsadallas.com

On the outskirts of the Bishop Street Arts District in Oak Cliff, this new arrival integrates restaurant, market and wine bar into one contemporary space where organic and local ingredients are assembled in New American dishes like savory flatbread pizzas and pork BBQ with cheese grits – a refined antidote to Texas beef with red sauce and fries; a laid-back staff and stylishly spare design (it was formerly an auto repair shop) give it an effortless cool feel.

☑ Bonnell's ☒Ⓜ *Southwestern*

| 27 | 23 | 26 | $44 |

Southwest | 4259 Bryant Irvin Rd. (Southwest Blvd.) | Ft. Worth | 817-738-5489 | www.bonnellstexas.com

"A safari of fine foods" is rounded up by "wonderfully inventive" chef-owner Jon Bonnell, who is "true to Texas cuisine" at this moderately priced Southwestern "favorite" where "innovative" wild game preparations wow "adventurous" and timid types alike; "don't be fooled by the outside appearance" "next to the freeway" on the Southwest side of town, "inside is cozier", trimmed in stylish "cowboy and Western motifs", and serviced by a "top-quality" staff.

Bread Winners
Cafe & Bakery *American/Bakery*

| 22 | 18 | 17 | $21 |

West Lovers Lane | Inwood Vill. | 5560 W. Lovers Ln. (Inwood Rd.) | Dallas | 214-351-3339
Uptown | 3301 McKinney Ave. (Hall St.) | Dallas | 214-754-4940
Plano | Lakeside Mkt. | 4021 Preston Rd. (bet. Parker Rd. & Spring Creek Pkwy.) | 972-312-9300
www.breadwinnerscafe.com

"Fabulous lunches and brunches" are the main event at this trio of cafes that "also presents a delicious dinner"; each sports a "huge menu" of "amazing bakery items" plus "consistently good" New American salads, sandwiches and soups; still, some say their "lively atmosphere" can translate into a vibe that's "rushed" and "loud", and on weekends when it's a mob scene, "the wait could kill your appetite."

	FOOD	DECOR	SERVICE	COST

Brio Tuscan Grille *Italian* | 21 | 23 | 20 | $31 |

NEW **Allen** | Watters Creek at Montgomery Farm | 810 Central Expwy. (W. Bethany Dr.) | 214-383-5556
Southlake | Southlake Town Sq. | 1431 Plaza Pl. (Grand Ave.) | 817-310-3136
www.brioitalian.com

A "wide selection" of "simple" Tuscan fare makes these "lively", "child-friendly" chain links in the Dallas area and Houston "dependable" picks for a "reasonably priced" meal; spacious, "high-style" decor gets a boost from "fabulous" outdoor seating at both locations, though regulars report service that swings between "sometimes great and sometimes not."

NEW **Brix** *Pizza* | - | - | - | I |

Southwest | 2747 S. Hulen St. (Stonegate Blvd.) | Ft. Worth | 817-924-2749 | www.brixpizzeria.com

Sicilian emissary Daniele Puleo (Daniele Osteria) expands his territory to the Southwest side of Ft. Worth with this casual pizzeria and wine bar; a glowing oven is the heart of the burgundy-hued room where pies, panini and pastas come to the table piping hot and synch up with well-priced vinos; light-on-the-wallet prices and a pleasant patio make it a natural for work lunches and weekend gatherings.

Bruno's ⧅ *Italian* | 22 | 17 | 21 | $31 |

Irving | 9462 N. MacArthur Blvd. (bet. Cimarron & Santa Fe Trails) | 972-556-2465 | www.brunosristorante.com

The "warm welcome" from owner Bruno Ceka adds to the "homey" feel of this "local" Italian in the Valley Ranch section of Irving; with "wonderful" food, moderate prices and a view of the canals, "it's particularly nice for a romantic evening" with live music on weekends as an added virtue.

Bubba's *Southern* | 23 | 10 | 15 | $12 |

Park Cities | Snider Plaza | 6617 Hillcrest Ave. (bet. Daniel & Rosedale Aves.) | Dallas | 214-373-6527 | www.babeschicken.com

"Skip the Colonel" and head straight to this Snider Plaza "comfortfood" joint (and sib of Babe's) for "damn good fried chicken", "huge yeast rolls" and other rib-sticking dishes at appropriately downhome prices; though many opt for takeout or drive-thru, inside has a "retro" feel thanks to order-at-the-counter service and its setting in a converted 1920s service station.

Buffet at the Kimbell Ⓜ *American* | 24 | 24 | 16 | $15 |

Cultural District | Kimbell Art Museum | 3333 Camp Bowie Blvd. (Arch Adams St.) | Ft. Worth | 817-332-8451 | www.kimbellart.org

"As classy and refined as" the Kimbell Art Museum that houses it, this Traditional American in Ft. Worth's Cultural District features an "excellent buffet" comprising a "lovely selection of salads, sandwiches, soups, quiches and desserts"; though some see the menu as "limited", all agree it's "carefully prepared", and "to top it off, you're surrounded by some of the finest artworks in the world"; N.B. dinner on Fridays only.

Bugatti Ristorante *Italian*

21 | 17 | 24 | $30

Love Field | 3802 W. Northwest Hwy. (Lemmon Ave.) | Dallas | 214-350-2470 | www.bugattis.net

"They always remember your name" at this Love Field "neighborhood restaurant" where the faithful flock for "inspiring" Italian food at moderate prices; the "quiet" Mediterranean-styled quarters with adjoining patio work for business meetings and "romantic" interludes alike.

Byblos Lebanese 🗷 *Lebanese*

21 | 15 | 17 | $23

North Side | 1406 N. Main St. (Central Ave.) | Ft. Worth | 817-625-9667 | www.byblostx.com

Befitting a member of the Hedary family of Med eateries, the "delectable" "traditional" Lebanese fare "does not disappoint" at this "informal and cheap" North Sider with a "wonderful buffet" at lunch (Monday–Saturday) – plus "available hookahs" and "belly dancing on certain nights" add to a "fun experience" that's "certainly different from most in Ft. Worth"; N.B. open till 2 AM on weekends.

Cacharel 🗷 *French*

25 | 23 | 24 | $54

Arlington | Brookhollow Tower Two | 2221 E. Lamar Blvd. (Ballpark Way) | 817-640-9981

"Everything a French restaurant should be" avow admirers of this longtime Arlington eatery nestled on the ninth floor of an office building where "excellent", "classic" cuisine is delivered by an equally "top-notch" staff; it's "perfect for that special night out" with "elegant" provincial decor heightened by "fantastic" panoramic views.

Cadillac Bar *Mexican*

18 | 18 | 18 | $25

West End | 1800 North Mkt. (Corbin St.) | Dallas | 214-999-0662 | www.cadillacbar.com

See review in Houston Directory.

Café Ashton *American*

24 | 24 | 21 | $46

Downtown Ft. Worth | Ashton Hotel | 610 Main St. (6th St.) | Ft. Worth | 817-332-0100 | www.theashtonhotel.com

A "charming" respite in Downtown Ft. Worth's historic Ashton Hotel, this "intimate" New American delights diners with a "romantic" ambiance enhanced by live piano (Thursday–Saturday) and a fireplace; service can be "slightly slow", but "consistently good" fare redeems, making it a "lovely" choice for dinner or an "elegant" afternoon tea; N.B. the Decor score does not reflect a recent revamp.

Cafe Aspen 🗷 *American*

21 | 17 | 21 | $32

West | 6103 Camp Bowie Blvd. (Bryant Irvin Rd.) | Ft. Worth | 817-738-0838 | www.cafeaspen.com

How nice for West Ft. Worth to have this "popular spot" with "consistently" "excellent" New American fare, a "knowledgeable staff" and a "wonderful community feeling", where people know one another and the owner knows everyone" – be it the "blue-haired ladies at lunch" or those seeking "a great place for a business or pleasure" meal; some say the "setting leaves a bit to be desired", but more find the "nice, soothing decor" "charming."

	FOOD	DECOR	SERVICE	COST

Café Brazil *Coffeehouse* | 19 | 14 | 17 | $17

Deep Ellum | 2815 Elm St. (Malcolm X Blvd.) | Dallas | 214-747-2730
Greenville Avenue | 2900 Greenville Ave. (Goodwin Ave.) | Dallas | 214-841-0900 ◗
Park Cities | 6420 N. Central Expwy. (Fondren Dr.) | Dallas | 214-691-7791 ◗
Oak Lawn | 3847 Cedar Springs Rd. (Oak Lawn Ave.) | Dallas | 214-461-8762 ◗
NEW Oak Cliff | 611 N. Bishop Ave. (W. Davis St.) | Dallas | 214-946-7927
Addison | Quorum II Plaza | 4930 Belt Line Rd. (Addison Rd.) | 972-386-7966
Richardson | 2071 N. Central Expwy. (Campbell Rd.) | 972-783-9011 ◗
McKinney | 3190 S. Central Expwy. (Eldorado Pkwy.) | 972-984-1259
Carrollton | 2510 N. Josey Ln. (Trinity Mills Rd.) | 972-242-8228
Plano | 200 Coit Rd. (President George Bush Tpke.) | 469-229-9140
www.cafebrazil.com

An "eclectic" mix of "hipsters", "students" and "typical Dallas yuppies" comes together at these "funky" coffeehouses to "hang out" and fill up on "exceptional" java and "hearty breakfasts" or "sober up" after a night out (some branches are open 24/7); the "tattooed" staff is "friendly, if not always professional", but a little "quirkiness" is no matter when prices are this "affordable."

Café Cipriani ⓩ *Italian* | 21 | 17 | 22 | $41

Las Colinas | 220 E. Las Colinas Blvd. (O'Connor Blvd.) | Irving | 972-869-0713 | www.cafecipriani.com

You'll be "treated as a regular, even if it's your first time" at this "dependable" Italian in Las Colinas, where the modus operandi is to lavish the customer with "warm, personal attention"; the "homestyle food" is both "affordable" and "very good", making it a popular "business-lunch" spot, but the big curiosity is the "elevator you take down to" the "basement dining room."

Café Express *Eclectic* | 18 | 14 | 14 | $15

Mockingbird Station | Mockingbird Station | 5307 E. Mockingbird Ln. (I-75) | Dallas | 214-841-9444
West Lovers Lane | Pavilion Ctr. | 5600 W. Lovers Ln. (Inwood Rd.) | Dallas | 214-352-2211
Uptown | 3230 McKinney Ave. (Bowen St.) | Dallas | 214-999-9444
Plano | Shops at Legacy | 5800 Legacy Dr. (Bishop Rd.) | 972-378-9444
Southlake | Southlake Town Sq. | 1472 Main St. (Fountain Pl.) | 817-251-0063
www.cafe-express.com
See review in Houston Directory.

Café Istanbul Ⓜ *Turkish* | 21 | 15 | 18 | $24

West Lovers Lane | Inwood Vill. | 5450 W. Lovers Ln. (Inwood Rd.) | Dallas | 214-902-0919 | www.cafe-istanbul.net
NEW Plano | 7300 Lone Star Dr. (bet. Postal Way & Terre Colony Ct.)ⓩ

"Seductive flavors" "tickle the tongue" at this "authentic" Turkish "favorite" on West Lovers Lane where "inexpensive" prices (including "affordable wines") and a "warm" welcome from the staff in-

creases the appeal; those craving quiet may want to "watch out for weekends" when belly dancers enhance the already "lively" atmosphere; N.B. the Plano branch is new.

Café Italia *Italian*   21 | 19 | 20 | $31

Love Field | 4615 W. Lovers Ln. (bet. Inwood & Midway Rds.) | Dallas | 214-357-4200

The idiosyncrasy at this "Italian bistro" near Love Field is the "Texan twist" to its "inventive menu", but regulars advise "don't laugh at the odd combos until you try some"; some say its offbeat site (a former motorcycle rental place) lacks appeal, and the "tables are a little close", but "chandeliers and a glowing interior" help smooth edges.

Café Lago *Eclectic*   - | - | - | I

Lake Highlands | 9219 Garland Rd. (Lunar Ln.) | Dallas | 214-320-0726 | www.cafe-lago.com

Regulars of this "quaint", "unexpectedly good" Lake Highlands cantina "really like" it as a "fun little spot" for breakfast or a lunch of "great sandwiches and salads" or a "casual dinner", saying they've "yet to find something they don't like" on its Eclectic menu.

Café Madrid ☒ *Spanish*   21 | 16 | 19 | $28

Knox-Henderson | 4501 Travis St. (Armstrong Ave.) | Dallas | 214-528-1731

Oak Cliff | 408 N. Bishop Ave. (8th St.) | Dallas | 214-942-8272 www.cafemadrid-dallas.com

"Hang for a couple hours and dine on wonderful tapas", a "traditional" "taste of Spain", paired with "pitchers of sangria" or "inexpensive" Iberian wines served "in ordinary glasses (very European)" at these Knox-Henderson and Oak Cliff snackeries; the "warm, inviting vibe" and "efficient service" make it a favorite "gathering place" that's "fun for a party or date"; N.B. the Travis Street location also features a hopping patio-and-bar scene.

☑ Café Modern ☒ *Eclectic*   22 | 26 | 20 | $25

Cultural District | Modern Art Museum | 3200 Darnell St. (University Dr.) | Ft. Worth | 817-840-2157 | www.themodern.org

Gallery-goers make a beeline for this "chic" canteen with "cool" "water views" housed in the "magnificent" Tadao Ando–designed Modern Art Museum in Ft. Worth's Cultural District; the seasonal Eclectic menu offers "creative" midpriced lunch and brunch options as well as a selection of coffees and sandwiches available for those on the go; N.B. dinner is served the first Friday of every month.

Café Nasher by   18 | 22 | 16 | $24
Wolfgang Puck ☒ *American*

Arts District | Nasher Sculpture Ctr. | 2001 Flora St. (Olive St.) | Dallas | 214-242-5118 | www.nashersculpturecenter.org

The "spacious and airy" digs overlooking the grounds of the "stunning" Nasher Sculpture Center in the Arts District win raves from those who say it's a "nice place" for New American "comfort food" like signature salads and "soup and sandwich fare" after "checking out some great work"; others opine it "doesn't deserve Wolfgang

Puck's name" with "not-that-great" fare, cafeteria-style service and tabs they find "expensive"; N.B. admission to the museum is required to dine here.

Café on the Green *American*   24 | 25 | 26 | $59

Las Colinas | Four Seasons Resort & Club | 4150 N. MacArthur Blvd. (Northgate Dr.) | Irving | 972-717-2420 | www.fourseasons.com
"As if you needed another reason to stay at the Four Seasons" in Las Colinas, you'll find it in the "great overall experience" at this "elegant hotel restaurant": between its "wonderful service", "serene atmosphere", "beautiful vistas" and "enticing" American menu of "excellent, innovative" dishes, it's no wonder it's a pick for a "business power dinner", "romantic evening" or "excellent Sunday brunch."

☑ Café Pacific *Seafood*   26 | 24 | 26 | $51

Park Cities | 24 Highland Park Vill. (bet. Mockingbird Ln. & Preston Rd.) | Dallas | 214-526-1170 | www.cafepacificdallas.com
"Rub elbows" with "old money" matrons and a "who's who" of "society" types at this "tony" Highland Park Village eatery ensconced in "clubby" quarters with polished marble floors and a "classic 1920s feel"; "top-tier" seafood plates are set down by a staff that "caters to your every need", though a few critics charge it's "stuffy" and add "you better be a regular if you want even average service."

NEW Café R+D *American*   - | - | - | M

Preston Center | Preston Center Plaza | 8300 Preston Center Plaza (Wentwood Dr.) | Dallas | 214-890-7900 | www.hillstone.com
This prototype eatery from the folks behind the always overflowing Houston's creates a traffic snarl of its own with a similar formula of crowd-pleasing, moderately priced New American fare and creative cocktails attracting a tony local crowd; expect mountainous Asian chicken salads, sandwiches and sushi served up in the bright, art-filled interior or out on the umbrella-dotted patio, which has already become a popular trysting spot in the Preston Center area.

Campania *Pizza*   23 | 12 | 14 | $18

West Village | Mondrian | 3800 Blackburn St. (McKinney Ave.) | Dallas | 214-780-0605
Southlake | 291 Grand Ave. (Civic Pl.) | 817-310-3116
www.campaniapizza.com
Pieheads praise the "amazing" Neapolitan pizza made from "imported Italian ingredients" at this well-priced West Village BYO with "funky mosaic tables", a streetside patio and a "laid-back" vibe; even with "mediocre" service, converts claim it's "definitely worth a visit"; N.B. the Southlake branch is newer and features live music on Friday and Saturday nights.

Campisi's *Pizza*   19 | 14 | 17 | $19

Downtown Dallas | Stone Street Gdns. | 1520 Elm St. (bet. Akard & Erway Sts.) | Dallas | 214-752-0141 ⓢ
Greenville Avenue | Kroger's Food Court | 5665 E. Mockingbird Ln. (Greenville Ave.) | Dallas | 214-821-4741

(continued)

(continued)

Campisi's

West Lovers Lane | 5405 W. Lovers Ln. (Inwood Rd.) | Dallas |
214-350-2595 🅼

North Dallas | 7632 W. Campbell Rd. (Coit Rd.) | Dallas | 972-931-2267

Plano | 3115 W. Parker Rd. (Independence Pkwy.) | 972-612-1177

Plano | 8100 N. Dallas Pkwy. (Granite Pkwy.) | 214-387-0233

Campisi's Egyptian *Pizza*

Greenville Avenue | 5610 E. Mockingbird Ln. (Greenville Ave.) |
Dallas | 214-827-0355
www.campisis.us

"A mainstay since the 1940s", this "landmark" near Greenville
Avenue has appeal that goes beyond its "unique", "thin, rectangular
pizza"; yes, it's "dated inside", but its "funky" interior, "like walking
onto the set of a Scorsese movie", is "filled with character" – and
characters, such as its "old-school waitresses", who are "part of the
charm"; there are several newer outposts, but enthusiasts attest
"the original has the best atmosphere."

Canary Cafe 🅼 Ⓜ *Mediterranean* ▽ 26 | 18 | 24 | $36

Addison | Village on the Pkwy. | 5100 Belt Line Rd. (Dallas N. Tollway) |
972-503-7080 | www.canarycafeaddison.com

Enthusiasts applaud the evening-only performances at this moderately priced Addison Mediterranean where chef-owner Mansour
Gorji "is always there" turning out "delicious" dishes that play off of
"unusual combinations of ingredients"; though it's set in a strip mall,
the "candlelit" room creates a "cozy" atmosphere that's "perfect"
for a "relaxed" meal or "special occasion."

Cantina Laredo *Mexican* 21 | 20 | 20 | $23

Lakewood | 2031 Abrams Rd. (Gaston Ave.) | Dallas | 214-821-5785

Preston Royal | 6025 Royal Ln. (Preston Rd.) | Dallas | 214-265-1610

West Lovers Lane | 165 Inwood Vill. (Lovers Ln.) | Dallas | 214-350-5227

Addison | 4546 Belt Line Rd. (Beltway Dr.) | 972-458-0962

North Dallas | 17808 Dallas Pkwy. (Briargrove Ln.) | Dallas | 469-828-4818

Frisco | 1125 Legacy Dr. (Hwy. 121) | 214-618-9860

Sundance Square | 530 Throckmorton St. (bet. 4th & 5th Sts.) |
Ft. Worth | 817-810-0773

Lewisville | 2225 S. Stemmons Frwy. (bet. Corporate Dr. & Hebron Pkwy.) |
972-315-8100

Grapevine | 4020 William D. Tate Ave. (Hall Johnson Rd.) | 817-358-0505
www.cantinalaredo.com

"Creative" Mexican fare including "guacamole made tableside" elevates these "reliable" outposts "a step above" the typical chain experience; the decor is "upscale" too, though some sticklers suggest
they're "overpriced" and add that "service can be lacking" as well.

Capital Grille, The *Steak* 25 | 25 | 25 | $58

Uptown | Crescent Shops & Galleries | 500 Crescent Ct.
(bet. Cedar Springs Rd. & Maple Ave.) | Dallas | 214-303-0500 |
www.thecapitalgrille.com

"Everything a steakhouse ought to be", this decidedly "upscale"
chain lures "buttoned-down" "power" players with "flavorful",

FOOD | DECOR | SERVICE | COST

"artfully presented" chops; the "low-lit, dark-wood" digs and "attentive" service are "ideal for a special occasion or a business dinner", and even though the bill can be "way expensive", "you get what you pay for" here.

Carrabba's Italian Grill *Italian*
22 | 19 | 22 | $28

North Dallas | 17548 Dallas Pkwy. (Trinity Mills Rd.) | Dallas | 972-732-7752
Plano | 3400 N. Central Expwy. (Parker Rd.) | 972-516-9900
Hurst | 1101 Melbourne Rd. (bet. Bedford Euless & Pipeline Rds.) | 817-595-3345
Grapevine | 1701 Crossroads Dr. (Hwy. 114) | 817-410-8461
www.carrabbas.com
See review in Houston Directory.

Carshon's Delicatessen ⊠⇔ *Deli*
23 | 12 | 18 | $13

University Area | 3133 Cleburne Rd. (bet. 8th & McCart Aves.) | Ft. Worth | 817-923-1907 | www.carshons.com
Corned beef connoisseurs head to this "classic" (circa 1929) deli in Ft. Worth's University Area for "great sandwiches" and other "top-quality" noshes like bagels and soups with a "New York feel"; "proficient service" keeps the line moving at the counter while the seating area is decked out with "vintage chrome and Formica decor" and historic photos of the city.

Cattlemen's Steakhouse *Steak*
23 | 18 | 21 | $36

Stockyards | 2458 N. Main St. (Exchange Ave.) | Ft. Worth | 817-624-3945 | www.cattlemenssteakhouse.com
"If nostalgia counts for anything" this Ft. Worth "classic" from 1947 set in the historic Stockyards District is "still worth a visit" claim "cowboys" clamoring for "outrageous" charbroiled steaks and sides rustled to the table by "sweet waitresses with big hair"; even if a few find there are "better beef options" elsewhere, it's still worthwhile if only for a beer and to soak in the "old-style" decor with "pictures of cattle" plastered on the walls.

Celebration *American*
21 | 15 | 20 | $21

Love Field | 4503 W. Lovers Ln. (bet. Inwood Rd. & Lemmon Ave.) | Dallas | 214-358-0612 | www.celebrationrestaurant.com
"The granddaddy of all Dallas home-cooking restaurants", this "old standby" has been serving generous portions of "solid, consistent" "comfort food" "in a homey setting" for over 30 years; set "in a series of houses" near Love Field (like "grandma's house, without the grandma"), it's a "great" spot for "large groups", a "post-finals hangout for SMU students" and a "quaint place to slow down with family" "after church on Sundays."

Central 214 *American*
24 | 23 | 21 | $50

Park Cities | Hotel Palomar | 5680 N. Central Expwy. (Mockingbird Ln.) | Dallas | 214-443-9339 | www.central214.com
A "cool Beverly Hills vibe" emanates from this "sleek, modern" venue in Park Cities' "trendy" Hotel Palomar where "hipsters" and blue bloods are "blown away by" the "excellent" New American cuisine; "the staff aims to please", though you'll pay for it with prices

	FOOD	DECOR	SERVICE	COST

that several diners dub "expensive"; N.B. the Food score does not reflect the departure of chef Tom Fleming.

Chamberlain's Fish Market Grill *Seafood*

| 23 | 21 | 23 | $44 |

Addison | 4525 Belt Line Rd. (bet. Dallas N. Tollway & Midway Rd.) | 972-503-3474 | www.chefchamberlain.com

Sister to Chamberlain's Steak & Chop House down the street, this "outstanding (and busy) seafood" spot in Addison features "nicely cooked and presented" fin fare "so fresh, you'd think you were in Cape Cod instead of Texas"; some say it lacks "the flair you'd expect, given the prices", but most maintain it's simply "superior", plus the "pleasant (if not fancy)" setting and "super, laid-back service" elevate it "beyond the standard fish house."

Chamberlain's Steak & Chop House *Steak*

| 25 | 22 | 24 | $54 |

Addison | 5330 Belt Line Rd. (Montfort Dr.) | 972-934-2467 | www.chamberlainsrestaurant.com

"A standout among the many cow palaces of Dallas" proclaim patrons of this big-ticket Addison chophouse (and sister to Chamberlain's Fish Market Grill) searing "fine" dry-aged steaks so "succulent", it "should be a crime" not to order one; it's a "class act" all around, from the "top-notch" service to the "quiet, clubby atmosphere" that makes for "a most enjoyable evening on every occasion."

Charleston's *American*

| 18 | 18 | 19 | $23 |

Southwest | 3020 S. Hulen St. (Bellaire Dr.) | Ft. Worth | 817-735-8900 | www.charlestons.com

Whether "for lunch" or "a quick dinner with family", you'll find "consistently good food and service" at this "casual American" on Ft. Worth's Southwest Side, a branch of an Oklahoma-based chain; its menu of steaks, seafood and other basics is "varied for all tastes" – in fact, its "mac 'n' cheese is big with the adults as well as the preschool set."

Charlie Palmer at the Joule *American*

| - | - | - | VE |

Downtown Dallas | Joule Hotel | 1530 Main St. (bet. Akard & Ervay Sts.) | Dallas | 214-261-4600 | www.charliepalmer.com

Acclaimed chef Charlie Palmer adds star power to this vibrant Downtown venue in the Joule Hotel; though the Adam Tihany-designed decor is themed on wind energy (with an earthy color scheme and turbine ceiling features to convey the message), it's the New American food that makes the bolder statement, along with an exceptional wine list that comes to the table in an electronic tablet; prices are high, but appropriate, given the top-tier experience; N.B. the adjacent wine shop and bar features selections from the restaurant.

Cheesecake Factory *American*

| 20 | 20 | 18 | $26 |

NorthPark | Lincoln Park | 7700 W. Northwest Hwy. (Central Expwy.) | Dallas | 214-373-4844

NEW **Allen** | Watters Creek at Montgomery Farm | 820 Central Expwy. (Bethany Dr.) | 972-908-3900

Frisco | Stonebriar Ctr. | 2601 Preston Rd. (Rte. 121) | 972-731-7799

FOOD | DECOR | SERVICE | COST

(continued)

Cheesecake Factory

Arlington | Parks at Arlington Mall | 3811 S. Cooper St. (W. Arbrook Blvd.) | 817-465-2211

Southlake | Southlake Town Sq. | 1440 Plaza Pl. (Grand Ave.) | 817-310-0050

www.thecheesecakefactory.com

See review in Houston Directory.

Chic from Barcelona ⌧ *Spanish*   18 | 18 | 18 | $22

Preston Forest | 11909 Preston Rd. (Forest Ln.) | Dallas | 972-239-2442 | www.chicbarcelona.com

The "fantastic" rotisserie chicken alone is "worth the trip" to this "cheap" Preston Forest "find" featuring a "limited" menu of "unusual" Catalan choices served by a "friendly" (if sometimes "slow") staff; the "strip-center" space is "big on charm" with the "cool decor" cast in upbeat yellow tones and adorned with customer decorated plates while there's a "nice patio" outside too.

Chow Thai *Thai*   23 | 19 | 19 | $25

Addison | 5290 Belt Line Rd. (Montfort Dr.) | 972-960-2999

Plano | 3309 Dallas Pkwy. (Parker Rd.) | 972-608-1883

www.chowthai.com

"Go once and you'll be hooked" by these "upscale" spots owned by West Coast transplants Vinnie and Sam Virasin, a husband-and-wife duo that delivers with "wonderful" food that's a "fresh, Californian-style Thai (i.e. don't expect authentic)"; "despite the strip-mall location" at both the Addison and Plano branches, each is a "quiet place, perfect for lunch or dinner", with "lightning-fast service" and "fun decor."

Chubby's *Diner*   ∇ 18 | 11 | 19 | $12

Lake Highlands | 11331 E. Northwest Hwy. (Jupiter Rd.) | Dallas | 214-348-6065

NEW Duncanville | 7474 S. Cockrell Hill Rd. (Skyline Dr.) | 972-298-1270

Lancaster | 3307 W. Pleasant Run Rd. (I-35) | 972-228-4101

Plano | 910 W. Parker Rd. (bet. Alma & Premier Drs.) | 972-881-1348

"No frills here", just "hearty", "home-cooked" all-day breakfasts plus "standard" American lunches and dinners doled out by "friendly" waitresses at these "old-fashioned diners" in Duncanville, Lake Highlands, Lancaster and Plano; all deliver "quick" in-and-out service "even on busy weekends" with prices so "affordable" there's enough left for the "don't-miss cakes and pies."

Chuy's *Tex-Mex*   21 | 19 | 19 | $18

Knox-Henderson | 4544 McKinney Ave. (bet. Armstrong Ave. & Knox St.) | Dallas | 214-559-2489

NEW Plano | 3408 Central Expwy. (E. Parker Rd.) | 469-241-9393

www.chuys.com

See review in Austin and the Hill Country Directory.

	FOOD	DECOR	SERVICE	COST

Cindi's New York Style Deli *Deli*
17 | 9 | 16 | $15

NEW **Downtown Dallas** | 306 S. Houston St. (Jackson St.) | Dallas | 214-744-4745 🛇
Medical City | 11111 N. Central Expwy. (Northhaven Rd.) | Dallas | 214-739-0918
Richardson | 7522 Campbell Rd. (Lauder Ln.) | 972-248-0608
Carrollton | 2001 Midway Rd. (Belt Line Rd.) | 972-458-7740
www.cindisnydeli.com

Its menu may be "more Midwest than Midtown", but this "NY-style deli" chainlet still satisfies with "credible bagels", "matzo ball soup" and other "solid", "homestyle" fare all at "reasonable" prices; waitresses may be "sassy", but they let you "stay and chat" even when there's a "long wait" during "Sunday brunch."

City Café *American*
– | – | – | M

West Lovers Lane | 5757 W. Lovers Ln. (Dallas N. Tollway) | Dallas | 214-351-2233 | www.thecitycafedallas.com

Tucked into a multistory shopping center in the shadow of the Tollway, this West Lovers Lane landmark proves its staying power with an approachable, if pricey, menu of New American dishes; the simple-yet-elegant white-tablecloth decor suits the well-heeled locals who find the adjacent casual take-out shop (with tables for daytime service) a fabulous alternative when they are too hurried to linger.

Classic Cafe at Roanoke 🛇 *American*
∇ 28 | 21 | 27 | $40

Roanoke | 504 N. Oak St. (Denton St.) | 817-430-8185 | www.theclassiccafe.com

"A small-town jewel", this "intimate" New American is where "haute cuisine meets Texas – and with great success"; though some say its upscale profile seems "kind of out of place in Roanoke", and its old converted house is somewhat "underwhelming from the outside", the "inviting atmosphere" within complements the "wonderful staff and exquisite food", making it a keeper, especially for "special occasions."

Clay Pit: Contemporary Indian Cuisine *Indian*
23 | 20 | 19 | $25

Addison | 4460 Belt Line Rd. (Midway Rd.) | 972-233-0111 | www.claypit.com

See review in Austin and the Hill Country Directory.

Coal Vines *Italian*
24 | 19 | 18 | $25

Uptown | 2404 Cedar Springs Rd. (Maple Ave.) | Dallas | 214-855-4999 ☾
Southlake | 1251 E. Southlake Blvd. (Carroll Ave.) | 817-310-0850
www.coalvines.com

"New York transplants" tout the "delectable thin-crust" pies, "fresh salads" and "affordable wines" at this "trendy" Uptown Italian catering to a "yuppie" crowd with "late" hours on weekends and a "lively" bar scene; those who complain they feel "stuffed" into the rustic, brick-walled quarters seek out the Southlake branch that offers an alternative to the Cedar Springs Road location's "uncomfortable" seating and "annoying waits."

Cool River Cafe *Southwestern/Steak*
19 | 21 | 20 | $38

Las Colinas | 1045 Hidden Ridge (MacArthur Blvd.) | Irving |
972-871-8881 | www.coolrivercafe.com
See review in Austin and the Hill Country Directory.

Cosmic Café *Eclectic*
22 | 19 | 17 | $15

Oak Lawn | 2912 Oak Lawn Ave. (Cedar Springs Rd.) | Dallas |
214-521-6157 | www.cosmiccafedallas.com
"One of the few all vegetarian/vegan places in Dallas", this "fun"
spot "in an old home" in Oak Lawn features an Eclectic menu of
physically and "metaphysically pleasing food" enlivened by "Indian
spices throughout" and served within a "quaint, quirky setting"; a
"Nepali hippie Zen-yoga feel" that "defines laid-back" adds to the
"mystical, surreal experience", prompting patrons to proclaim that
"just being there calms your soul" – and also provides some corre-
spondingly "great people-watching."

Cousin's Bar-B-Q ☒ *BBQ*
21 | 15 | 17 | $13

Southwest | 5125 Bryant Irvin Rd. (bet. Overton Ridge Blvd. &
Trailview Dr.) | Ft. Worth | 817-346-3999
South Side | 6262 McCart Ave. (Westcreek Dr.) | Ft. Worth | 817-346-2511
Keller | 535 Keller Pkwy. (Cindy St.) | 817-379-0306
www.cousinsbbq.com
"Tender" brisket and ribs plus plentiful sides and sweet tea await at
this "family-owned" chain of "hometown" BBQ joints scattered
around Tarrant County; a "friendly staff", "fast" "cafeteria line" service and a "relaxed atmosphere" with "middle-of-the-road prices"
make it "a great place to take the kids" or pick up some solid takeout; N.B. the Keller branch is drive-thru only.

Craft Dallas *American*
25 | 25 | 23 | $67

Victory Park | W Hotel | 2440 Victory Park Ln. (Olive St.) | Dallas |
214-397-4111 | www.craftrestaurant.com
"Deceptively simple" New American dishes showcasing "sublime"
ingredients win the favor of "foodies" at this Victory Park outpost
from NYC chef-owner Tom Colicchio that's set in a "glossy, sumptuous" ground-floor space with a beige and black color scheme in the
W Hotel; though a "trendy" crowd thrives on the "buzz" and "swank
atmosphere", detractors declare "some of the adventure doesn't
quite work out" with "snooty service" and "outrageous prices" leaving "much to be desired."

Cristina's *Mexican*
18 | 17 | 17 | $15

Addison | 4933 Beltline Rd. (Runyon Rd.) | 972-386-0082
McKinney | 2811 Craig Dr. (Eldorado Pkwy.) | 214-544-2800
NEW **Frisco** | 5105 Eldorado Pkwy. (Dallas Tollway N.) | 469-362-8177
Frisco | 8210 Hwy. 121 (Parkwood Blvd.) | 214-618-8230
Garland | 4107 Lavon Dr. (Firewheel Pkwy.) | 972-476-7555
Plano | 3432 Hebron Pkwy. (Park Blvd.) | 972-380-8844
Flower Mound | 6424 Cross Timbers Rd. (Shiloh Rd.) | 817-430-3669
Lewisville | 360 E. Round Grove Rd. (Rockbrook Dr.) | 972-315-3126
Trophy Club | 2003 Hwy. 114 (Trophy Club Dr.) | 817-430-4545

(continued)

(continued)

Cristina's

Grapevine | 2707 E. Southlake Blvd. (Nolan Dr.) | 817-488-2095
www.cristinasmex.com

"Just one will do it" toast tequila lovers sipping the "biggest margaritas you ever saw" at this "reliable" chain with an "extensive menu"
of "well-made" dishes from Central Mexico brought out by "attentive servers"; all locations thrive on inexpensive prices and a casual
atmosphere brightened with sun-themed Latin art.

Crú Wine Bar *American*   20 | 23 | 21 | $34

West Village | West Vill. | 3699 McKinney Ave. (Lemmon Ave.) |
Dallas | 214-526-9463

NEW **Allen** | Watters Creek at Montgomery Farm | 842 Market St.
(Bethany Rd.) | 972-908-2532

Plano | Shops at Legacy | 7201 Bishop Rd. (Legacy Dr.) | 972-312-9463 ●
www.cruawinebar.com

Oenophiles "enjoy a glass of vino", indulge in "creative" New American
snacks "after shopping or a movie", or perch on a seat and "people-
watch" at these "atmospheric" outposts of a Dallas-based wine bar
chain; they're "sophisticated", candlelit spots with a "swanky library"
feel, though some detractors demur on tabs they find "pricey" and
say there's "room for improvement" when it comes to service too.

Cuba Libre *Caribbean*   20 | 19 | 18 | $26

Knox-Henderson | 2822 N. Henderson Ave. (Willis Ave.) | Dallas |
214-827-2820 | www.cubalibredallas.com

"Be ready for a wait" at this "lively" Caribbean in Knox-Henderson, as
its "large portions" of "fun, flirty food" (at "easy-on-the-pocket
prices"), "tasty Cuban-inspired cocktails" and "vibrant atmosphere"
preserve its position as a "perennial hot spot" that attracts an "eclectic
crowd", with "lots of hotties" and "beautiful people" among its
"young professionals, families and sophisticated seniors"; another
"bonus – the kitchen is open late" Fridays and Saturdays.

Culpepper Steakhouse *Steak*   24 | 21 | 23 | $47

Rockwall | 309 I-30 E. (Horizon Rd.) | 972-771-1001 |
www.culpeppersteakhouse.com

This venerable Rockwall beef emporium fires up "excellent" steaks
and teams them with "fantastic wines" in "Texas-themed" surroundings decked out in animal hides and outfitted with a huge fireplace; add in solid service, moderate prices and live music on
weekends and it's no wonder converts count on it as a "place to
bring visitors" for a "traditional" Lone Star state experience.

Dakota's Steakhouse Ⓢ *Steak*   22 | 21 | 20 | $50

Arts District | 600 N. Akard St. (Ross Ave.) | Dallas | 214-740-4001 |
www.dakotasrestaurant.com

While acknowledged as "another great steakhouse" – with "big,
juicy" cuts of meat, "excellent" seafood and an "attentive staff" –
what sets apart this "upscale" "gem" is its "unique" underground
setting, with a "dark, elegant" atmosphere and "romantic patio"

complete with "waterfall and hanging plants"; it's a "place to take tourists" or "special dates", and its Arts District location Downtown makes it "very good for business lunches" as well.

NEW Dali Wine Bar & Cellar *American* | - | - | - | M |

Arts District | One Arts Plaza | 1722 Routh St. (Flora St.) | Dallas | 469-385-9360 | www.daliwinebar.com

Dallas dining scene mainstay Paul Pinnell (ex Nana) is behind this ambitious wine bar, restaurant and retail shop based in the burgeoning Arts District and set in a minimalist space with a custom-made cork-embedded bar; big-flavored New American plates like panroasted duck are paired with an intriguing list of small production and hard-to-find vintages all selected with the help of extremely capable stewards; N.B. live music nightly.

Dallas Fish Market Ⓢ *American/Seafood*   ▽ | 24 | 22 | 24 | $48 |

Downtown Dallas | 1501 Main St. (Akard St.) | Dallas | 214-744-3474 | www.dallasfishmarket.com

Seafood comes to "meat country" via this swank Downtown entry ensconced in an "airy, modern" space with a sushi bar and wine room filled with a "well-edited" selection of boutique vinos (26 are available by the glass); patrons proclaim the sea-centric New American cuisine "creative" and "fresh", and if it's "too soon to know" how it'll all shape up, it certainly "has potential."

Daniele Osteria Ⓜ *Italian* | 24 | 17 | 23 | $39 |

Oak Lawn | 3300 Oak Lawn Ave. (Hall St.) | Dallas | 214-443-9420 | www.danieleosteria.com

Local gastronomes are grateful this midpriced Oak Lawn hideaway "remains under the radar" (it's quite literally "hidden away" below street level) so they can enjoy "simple", "flavorful" Sicilian meals with "no delays" in a "romantic" candlelit setting; "personable" chefowner Daniele Puleo packs the place with a "posh mixed crowd" that practices its "Texas-accented Italian" with the "friendly" staff.

ⓏDel Frisco's Double Eagle Steak House *Steak* | 27 | 24 | 25 | $69 |

North Dallas | 5251 Spring Valley Rd. (Dallas N. Tollway) | Dallas | 972-490-9000

Downtown Ft. Worth | 812 Main St. (8th St.) | Ft. Worth | 817-877-3999 www.delfriscos.com

Born in Dallas, this "high-end" franchise attracts a "see-and-beseen" crowd with its "Texas-size" steaks and sides backed up by a "fantastic wine list"; sure, it's "way expensive", but in return you get sleek settings, "flawless service" from "attractive" staffers and a "no-chain feeling."

Deli News *Deli* | 22 | 13 | 17 | $17 |

North Dallas | 17062 Preston Rd. (Campbell Rd.) | Dallas | 972-733-3354 | www.dallasdelinews.com

This "really good" "New York–style deli" in North Dallas offers "outstanding meats and desserts" plus "bagels flown in from New York", specifically H&H of *Sex and the City* fame; it features a

"crowded, dinerlike atmosphere", providing a "valid option for" Manhattan expats – well, "almost", quip those who say the "servers are too polite."

Dixie House *Southern*

18 | 14 | 18 | $15

Lakewood | 6400 Gaston Ave. (Abrams Pkwy.) | Dallas | 214-826-2412 | www.theblackeyedpea.com

Lakewood's "comfort-food headquarters", this "authentic" Southerner still feels like a "neighborhood venue" in spite of its kinship with the Black-Eyed Pea restaurant chain (it's the original outpost); supporters say it's a "reliable family place" with fried and grilled specialties to fit every diet and a "friendly atmosphere" with sweet service, and gentle pricing.

Dragonfly *American*

19 | 23 | 18 | $47

Uptown | Hotel ZaZa | 2332 Leonard St. (McKinney Ave.) | Dallas | 214-468-8399 | www.hotelzaza.com

"You can't beat the people-watching" at this "Uptown hot spot" in the "sexy" Hotel ZaZa, a "happening" New American eatery with an "awesome interior"and "a fantastic wine list"; still, some can't get past the "stereotypical Dallas pretty people" peopling the place, quipping that it's "better known for what celebrity is falling into the pool" "than for its food."

Dream Café *American*

18 | 13 | 15 | $19

Uptown | Quadrangle | 2800 Routh St. (Howell St.) | Dallas | 214-954-0486
Addison | Village on the Pkwy. | 5100 Belt Line Rd. (Dallas N. Tollway) | 972-503-7326
www.thedreamcafe.com

Bringing an "Austin attitude to Dallas", this pair of "healthy alternatives" purveys "cheap, casual" New American eats, including "lots of choices for vegetarians"; its forte is its "hectic" Sunday brunch, when families descend on the "kid-friendly", "dog-friendly" Addison branch with its patio and jungle gym, and "large crowds" throng the the Quadrangle location, "as hip a setting as possible in Uptown."

East Wind *Pan-Asian*

21 | 18 | 21 | $28

Uptown | Quadrangle | 2800 Routh St. (Howell St.) | Dallas | 214-745-5554 | www.eastwinddallas.com

"There's always a warm reception from the gracious owner" at this Uptown Pan-Asian featuring a "treasure trove" of well-priced Eastern specialties that go "far beyond the typical Thai" with sushi and Vietnamese dishes rounding out the offerings; lunches are "busy", but the vibe is "soothing" thanks to a warm interior with fresh flowers on the tables and paintings on the walls.

Edelweiss 🗵 Ⓜ *German*

20 | 20 | 24 | $25

West | 3801 Southwest Blvd. (Desert Ridge Dr.) | Ft. Worth | 817-738-5934 | www.edelweissrestaurant.com

Don the lederhosen and head to the West side of Ft. Worth for this "old-world" eatery that satisfies schnitzel lovers with "hearty" German "grub" and pitchers of imported brews; an "oompah band" every night adds to the authenticity of the "mountain lodge" setting.

	FOOD	DECOR	SERVICE	COST

8.0 Restaurant & Bar *American*

14 | **17** | **15** | **$27**

Sundance Square | Sundance Sq. | 111 E. Third St. (bet. Commerce & Houston Sts.) | Ft. Worth | 817-336-0880 | www.eightobar.com

"Grab a quick bite" at this "casual" "hangout" that "draws a hip crowd" of "lively post-work" "professionals" and "singles" who "enjoy the live music", "great drinks" and American "bar staples"; some deem the eats "average" and say the staffers are "hired only on the basis of their good looks", but the "popular patio" provides some of the "best people-watching in Sundance Square."

El Rancho Grande 🖾 *Mexican*

20 | **15** | **21** | **$18**

North Side | 1400 N. Main St. (Central Ave.) | Ft. Worth | 817-624-9206

"Ignore the decor and focus on the food" at this no-frills Mexican on the North Side of Ft. Worth where the "great" housemade chips are the perfect prelude to "traditional" dishes like fajitas and chalupas; service is swift, but those in-the-know insist you "come early" since "there's always a lineup" on "weekends" and at "lunch."

Empress of China *Chinese*

19 | **14** | **19** | **$18**

Las Colinas | Grande Shopping Ctr. | 2648 N. Belt Line Rd. (Grande Bulevar) | Irving | 972-252-7677

Flower Mound | 1913 Justin Rd. (Valley Ridge Ln.) | 972-691-1628

Grapevine | 2030 Glade Rd. (bet. Hwy. 360 & W. Airfield Dr.) | 817-442-0088

www.eocrestaurant.com

It may not rival "NYC or San Francisco", but this trio of "dependable" Chinese eateries does a "pretty darn good" job serving Flower Mound, Grapevine and Las Colinas with "tasty" dishes made from "fresh" "top-quality ingredients"; as a welcome "change from mega-buffets" nearby, the "waiters remember your favorites" here – a personal touch that overcomes the "spartan atmosphere" and strip-mall locations without leaving you with a higher tab.

Esperanza's Mexican Bakery & Café *Mexican*

24 | **14** | **19** | **$14**

Hospital District | 1601 Park Place Ave. (8th Ave.) | Ft. Worth | 817-923-1961

North Side | 2122 N. Main St. (21st St.) | Ft. Worth | 817-626-5770 🖾

www.joets.com

Part of "the famous Joe T. Garcia–LanCarte family", this pair of "Ft. Worth staples" has long been serving up "no-frills", "authentic Mexican dishes" at an "affordable price"; its Hospital District location "is not the prettiest" (the Main Street branch is nicer), but both get the thumbs-up for their "great breakfasts" and "excellent bakery items."

🖾 Fearing's *Southwestern*

26 | **27** | **25** | **$77**

Uptown | Ritz-Carlton Hotel | 2121 McKinney Ave. (Olive St.) | Dallas | 214-922-4848 | www.fearingsrestaurant.com

Chef-owner Dean Fearing (ex Mansion on Turtle Creek) takes Southwestern cuisine "to a new level" claim those who "can't get enough" of his "fantastic" food at this fine-dining room in Uptown's Ritz-Carlton Hotel, where the "mesmerizing interior" is separated

into seven "chic" areas abuzz with a glittery crowd and some of "Dallas' finest plastic surgery on display"; some find the prices "excessive" and note a few "kinks" with the otherwise "courteous" service, but insiders insist it's "destined to become a destination."

Ferrari's Italian Villa *Italian*

| 23 | 18 | 23 | $37 |

Addison | 14831 Midway Rd. (bet. Belt Line & Spring Valley Rds.) | 972-980-9898
Grapevine | 1200 William D. Tate Ave. (Ira E. Woods Ave.) | 817-251-2525 Ⓢ
www.ferrerestaurant.com

The Secchis "make you feel like you're family" at their Sardinia-themed Italian in Addison, where "extraordinarily talented chef" Stefano turns out "fresh, delicious pasta" and "outstanding bread", baked in an "open-hearth" "wood-burning oven strategically positioned" in the center of the dining room; "tableside creations" and an impressive antipasto table contribute to the "charming atmosphere"; N.B. the Grapevine location is newer and has a martini and wine bar.

Ferre Ristorante e Bar Ⓢ *Italian*

| 21 | 21 | 19 | $38 |

Sundance Square | Sundance Sq. | 215 E. Fourth St. (bet. Calhoun & Commerce Sts.) | Ft. Worth | 817-332-0033 | www.ferrerestaurant.com

You'll find "surprisingly good food at this hip spot in Sundance Square, a "see-and-be-seen" scene with "creative" Northern Italian fare; regulars also "love" the "Manhattan-like" vibe and "attentive staff", but its "popularity" means it "can be louder than a rock concert", so "sit outside" on the patio where people-watching is its own entertainment.

Fireside Pies *Pizza*

| 23 | 17 | 18 | $24 |

Knox-Henderson | 2820 N. Henderson Ave. (Milam St.) | Dallas | 214-370-3916 ◖
West Lovers Lane | 7709 Inwood Rd. (W. Lovers Ln.) | Dallas | 214-357-3800
Plano | Shops at Legacy | 5717 Legacy Dr. (Dallas N. Tollway) | 972-398-2700
Grapevine | 1285 S. Main St. (Hwy. 114) | 817-416-1285
www.firesidepies.com

"Fantastic, gourmet pizzas" coupled with "creative salads" "make it worth" the sometimes "two-hour wait" at these "hip spots (at least "they don't rush you once you've been seated"); some sigh it's "too bad" the "cramped inside spaces" are "so small", though, suggesting you "sit on the patio if you can – it's even heated during the winter."

First Chinese BBQ ⊅ *Chinese*

| 25 | 9 | 12 | $15 |

Richardson | 111 S. Greenville Ave. (Belt Line Rd.) | 972-680-8216
NEW **Carrollton** | 1927 E. Belt Line Rd. (Metrocrest Dr.) | 972-478-7228
NEW **Garland** | 3405 W. Walnut St. (Jupiter Rd.) | 972-494-3430
Plano | 3304 Coit Rd. (Parker Rd.) | 972-758-2988
Arlington | 2214 S. Collins St. (Pioneer Pkwy.) | 817-469-8876
www.firstchinesebbq.com

"You'll be eating leftover pork for days" after a visit to these "authentic" Cantonese standbys attracting a steady stream of chowhounds and the occasional celeb chef for roast meats and "awesome" noodles

at "bargain prices"; never mind that there's no alcohol, "service could be better" and decor doesn't amount to much more than the "ducks hanging in the window", insiders insist "you will not be disappointed" with your meal; N.B. cash only, except at the Austin branch.

Fish, The *Japanese* | 20 | 17 | 15 | $37 |

West Village | 3636 McKinney Ave. (Cityplace West Blvd.) | Dallas | 214-522-0071 | www.thefishdallas.com
See review in Houston Directory.

Fogo de Chão *Brazilian/Steak* | 26 | 22 | 26 | $55 |

Addison | 4300 Belt Line Rd. (Midway Rd.) | 972-503-7300 | www.fogodechao.com
See review in Houston Directory.

Franki's Li'l Europe Ⓜ *E European* ▽ | 21 | 15 | 19 | $33 |

Lake Highlands | Casa Linda Plaza | 362 Casa Linda Plaza (Garland Rd.) | Dallas | 214-320-0426 | www.frankislileurope.com
This "neighborhood cafe" in Lake Highlands boasts a "delicious" "varied menu" where dishes "from all over the continent" are presented alongside Eastern European mainstays; with an "inexpensive wine list", "personable service" and a "cozy" ambiance, it's no wonder the "area's best-kept secret isn't so secret anymore."

☑ French Room Ⓢ Ⓜ *American/French* | 28 | 29 | 29 | $87 |

Downtown Dallas | Hotel Adolphus | 1321 Commerce St. (Field St.) | Dallas | 214-742-8200 | www.hoteladolphus.com
"Smitten" surveyors salute an "off-the-charts experience" at this Downtown "icon", voted No. 1 for Food, Decor and Service in Dallas/ Ft. Worth, where "stupendous" French–New American cuisine is served with "unparalleled attention to detail" inside the "opulent" crystal-chandeliered dining room of the Hotel Adolphus; sure, it's "expensive", but "close to perfect" for an "old-fashioned splurge" – especially if you opt for the tasting menu with "excellent" wine pairings.

Fuji Steakhouse & Sushi Bar *Japanese* ▽ | 20 | 15 | 19 | $26 |

Preston Forest | 12817 Preston Rd. (Lyndon B. Johnson Frwy.) | Dallas | 972-661-5662 | www.fujidallas.com
The hibachi takes center stage at this North Dallas "favorite" where knife-wielding chefs "put on a show for the kids" and expertly cook up an array of seafood and beef dishes; a "surprisingly good neighborhood sushi bar" in the back pleases finicky fish fiends while all are appeased by modest tabs, if not the simply decorated surroundings.

Fuse Ⓢ *Pan-Asian/Southwestern* | 21 | 22 | 20 | $42 |

Downtown Dallas | Dallas Power and Light Bldg. | 1512 Commerce St. (Akard St.) | Dallas | 214-742-3873 | www.fusedallas.com
This "hip", high-wattage Downtown hub reengineered from a space once home to Dallas Power and Light boasts a "cool layout" of multi-level eating spaces capped by a "rooftop, pool-side bar" proffering "fanciful drinks"; the wild mix of Pan-Asian and Southwestern cuisine "sounds strange, but works well", though service strikes some as "spotty" while tabs can feel "overpriced" too.

	FOOD	DECOR	SERVICE	COST

Gloria's *Salvadoran/Tex-Mex* | 21 | 18 | 19 | $21 |

Greenville Avenue | 3715 Greenville Ave. (bet. Martel & Matalee Aves.) | Dallas | 214-874-0088

Lemmon Avenue | 4140 Lemmon Ave. (Douglas Ave.) | Dallas | 214-521-7576

Oak Cliff | 600 W. Davis St. (bet. Bishop Ave. & Tyler St.) | Dallas | 214-948-3672

Addison | Village on the Pkwy. | 5100 Belt Line Rd. (Dallas N. Tollway) | 972-387-8442

Frisco | 8600 Gaylord Pkwy. (Preston Rd.) | 972-668-1555

Garland | Firewheel Town Ctr. | 360 Coneflower Dr. (Town Center Blvd.) | 972-526-5290

Rockwall | 2079 Summer Lee Dr. (Rockwall Pkwy.) | 972-772-4088

Near West | Montgomery Plaza | 2600 W. Seventh St. (Carroll St.) | Ft. Worth | 817-332-8800

NEW Arlington | Arlington Highlands | 3901 Arlington Highlands Blvd. (Matlock Rd.) | 817-701-2981

Colleyville | 5611 Colleyville Blvd. (Church St.) | 817-656-1784
www.gloriasrestaurants.com

Fanatics "can't get enough" of the complimentary warm black bean dip at this "popular" chain of cantinas with a menu that marries "authentic Salvadoran" cuisine with "solid Tex-Mex" cooking; the "friendly", "tropical atmosphere" and "excellent happy-hour prices" make it a "festive place to kick off the night", though some opt to "stick around for the salsa dancing" ("it's quite a show") or the live entertainment that varies by location.

Go Fish Ocean Club *American/Seafood* | 21 | - | 19 | $37 |

Galleria | 5301 Alpha Rd. (Noel St.) | Dallas | 972-980-1919 | www.gofishoceanclub.com

Afishionados applaud the "imaginative" presentations at this "upscale" seafooder that clings to a few favored New American selections after relocating from landlocked Addison to the Galleria; lime and charcoal colors punch up the vibe in the multilevel space where a well-heeled crowd demands servers keep a lively pace; additions of a sushi bar, glass-encased wine tower and dual fireplace patio are all reflected in the tab.

Goodhues Wood Fired Grill ⑤ *American*   ▽ | 24 | 21 | 20 | $39 |

McKinney | 204 W. Virginia St. (Church St.) | 972-562-7570 | www.goodhuesgrill.com

Ensconced in a historic neighborhood "just off the square in McKinney", this upmarket eatery conjures up a "nice atmosphere" thanks to its setting in a 1920s building with lots of brick and exposed wood beams; the midpriced New American menu showcases "great" signatures like steaks and seafood grilled over pecan and mesquite wood, but regulars report the "specials rock" too.

NEW Grace ⑤ *American* | - | - | - | E |

Downtown Ft. Worth | 777 Main St. (7th St.) | Ft. Worth | 817-877-3388 | www.gracefortworth.com

Former Del Frisco's GM Adam Jones strikes out on his own with this high-style New American in a Downtown Ft. Worth skyscraper fea-

turing a beef- and seafood-heavy menu from chef Blaine Staniford (ex Fuse in Dallas); the sleek, neutral dining room sports a soaring glass wine cave, while a lively bar abetted by well-crafted cocktails makes an apt setting to impress a date or clinch a deal.

Grand Lux Cafe *Eclectic*

19 | 22 | 18 | $29

Galleria | Galleria | 13420 N. Dallas Pkwy. (Alpha Rd.) | Dallas | 972-385-3114 | www.grandluxcafe.com

With an Eclectic menu so "amazingly long" it "takes 15 minutes to read", this Galleria "spin-off of the ever-popular Cheesecake Factory" is "good for kids, picky eaters and those with huge appetites"; foes say that the portions are "obscenely large", the "cavernous space" is "loud" and the "overenthusiastic service" gets "a little annoying" – but none of that stops it from getting "crazy on the weekends."

Grape, The *American*

25 | 20 | 23 | $35

Greenville Avenue | 2808 Greenville Ave. (Vickery Blvd.) | Dallas | 214-828-1981 | www.thegraperestaurant.com

"One of the darkest and oldest wine bars in Dallas", this "intimate" Greenville Avenue "neighborhood bistro" is a "foodie favorite", boasting "terrific" New American fare that's "consistently good, even with different chefs over the years"; "comparatively low mark-ups" on its vino and an "educated, attentive staff" are other selling points, and the "romantic atmosphere" with its "cozy, close quarters" makes it a "perfect place to get engaged."

Green Papaya *Vietnamese*

21 | 12 | 18 | $21

Oak Lawn | 3211 Oak Lawn Ave. (Cedar Springs Rd.) | Dallas | 214-521-4811 | www.greenpapayarestaurants.com

"Excellent Vietnamese at a reasonable price" is the draw at this Oak Lawn storefront specializing in "good, healthy Asian" fare; other than a "beautiful fish tank set in the wall like a picture frame", the feel of this "tiny, crowded place" is "no-frills", but the smitten shrug "so what?"

Greenz 🅴 *American*

20 | 13 | 16 | $14

Uptown | 2808 McKinney Ave. (Allen St.) | Dallas | 214-720-7788
Addison | 15615 Quorum Dr. (Addison Circle) | 972-385-7721
www.greenzsalads.com

As the name suggests, "the major attraction is salads" – and "inventive" ones too – at this duo of "quick, healthy" New Americans; they may be "small and crowded", but they're still "lunch favorites", whether "on the run or at your desk", a status abetted by the fact that "any salad can be rolled into a wrap" for maximum portability; P.S. the Uptown location has "a definite parking problem."

Grill on the Alley, The *American*

21 | 23 | 22 | $50

Galleria | Galleria | 13270 N. Dallas Pkwy. (Alpha Rd.) | Dallas | 214-459-1601 | www.thegrill.com

Dealmakers declare the tony Galleria outpost of this Beverly Hills original a "convenient" option for "power-lunching" on an "expense account" in appropriately handsome dark-wood surroundings; the "professional" staff dispatches traditional cocktails and an "expansive" selection of "perfectly executed" American dishes on cue, so

even though some beef "it's a bit pricey", most maintain, "if you can afford it", "it's a sure bet."

NEW Grimaldi's *Pizza*

-	-	-	I

West Village | 3636 McKinney Ave. (Cityplace West Blvd.) | Dallas | 214-559-4611
Allen | Watters Creek at Montgomery Farm | 836 Market St. (W. Bethany Dr.) | 214-383-9703
www.grimaldispizzeria.com

An offshoot of the venerable New York City pizzeria, this new Dallas-area duo serves up similarly thin-crust pies straight from an old-fashioned coal-fired brick oven; a zany staff delivers the goods – along with beer and wine – at lightning speed to tables filled with diners of all ages gathered to cheer on their favorite sports teams; N.B. the expansion roll will continue with branches in Houston and San Antonio in 2009.

Hattie's *American*

25	23	24	$32

Oak Cliff | 418 N. Bishop Ave. (8th St.) | Dallas | 214-942-7400 | www.hatties.net

"A place with character in a sea of urban sprawl", this "contemporary Southern" belle housed in a "quaint" 1920s Oak Cliff storefront charms customers with "inventive" New American "home cooking" like "shrimp and grits to die for" and "addictive pecan-crusted catfish"; the "reasonably priced" dishes all come with a side of "fabulous service", keeping this "popular" spot "packed every night" (in other words: "make a reservation").

Hector's on Henderson ⑤ *American*

22	18	21	$47

Knox-Henderson | 2929 N. Henderson Ave. (Miller Ave.) | Dallas | 214-821-0432 | www.hectorsonhenderson.com

Diners "thankful for the exploding Knox-Henderson food scene" consider this "snappy, fun place" "another top-notch example" of the trend; the New American cuisine "with a Texas accent" is "memorable", and owner Hector Garcia is "the ultimate host", and "quite the singer" too – he sometimes "spontaneously belts out a song" with musicians who play nightly in its "noisy, lively" space.

Hedary's Mediterranean Ⓜ *Mediterranean*

▽ 22	17	15	$24

West | 6323 Shopping Ctr. | 3308 Fairfield Ave. (Camp Bowie Blvd.) | Ft. Worth | 817-731-6961 | www.hedarys.com

Those with a hankering for "authentic" Lebanese specialties head to this West Ft. Worth stalwart where the Middle Eastern "food is always good" (and cheap) and has been for decades; it recently benefited from a "much-needed face-lift" reenergizing the interior, yet followers fume that "uneven" service could use a similar boost.

ⓩ Hibiscus ⑤ *American*

25	23	24	$54

Knox-Henderson | 2927 N. Henderson Ave. (Miller Ave.) | Dallas | 214-827-2927 | www.hibiscusdallas.com

"No meal is complete" without a helping of the "amazing mac 'n' cheese" at this "happening" Knox-Henderson New American where the "dark", "swanky" decor "is a mere backdrop for some of the best

food in the city"; the service team "works very hard to make you feel special", so even if the prices are "expensive", it still "lives up to every penny"; P.S. if there's no room for dessert, satisfy your sweet tooth with "great eye candy" in all flavors.

Highland Park Cafeteria *American*

− | − | − | I

Lake Highlands | Casa Linda Plaza | 1200 N. Buckner Blvd. (Garland Rd.) | Dallas | 214-324-5000 | www.highlandparkcafeteria.com

Though shuttered for over a decade, this Dallas institution reopened in 2007 in Lake Highlands' Casa Linda Plaza; traditionalists take comfort in the well-stocked cafeteria line of homestyle American entrees, salads (with Jell-O, natch) and an endless array of veggies, breads and desserts; the Kelly green–and–white dining room attracts a wide range of customers from old folks to young families and professionals enjoying a square meal at a reasonable price; N.B. takeaway is also available via a separate entrance.

Highland Park Pharmacy *American*

19 | 16 | 19 | $10

Knox-Henderson | 3229 Knox St. (Travis St.) | Dallas | 214-521-2126

You "never know who you might sit next to" at this "classic soda fountain", "a staple of life" in Knox-Henderson since 1912 that's ranked Best Bang for the Buck among Dallas/Ft. Worth restaurants; it's a "throwback to the days before automation and sensitive staffs", "so don't expect gourmet, but do expect to be called 'hon'" as you "enjoy the meanest milkshake and grilled cheese sandwich in town."

Hot Damn, Tamales! ⓢ *Tex-Mex*

▽ 26 | 9 | 19 | $13

Hospital District | 713 W. Magnolia Ave. (Hemphill St.) | Ft. Worth | 817-926-9909 | www.hotdamntamales.com

"Hot damn, these are good tamales!" exclaim fans of these "mighty tasty" hand-pressed treats that "great people" turn out of a Hospital District storefront in an "unbelievable selection of flavors" from poblano chicken to chocolate cherry; with just a few booths and cafeteria-style service, it's "not primarily a dine-in place" but locals are more than content to grab one (or a "dozen") to take on the go; P.S. the "lard-free" recipes mean even "vegetarians" can indulge.

Hôtel St. Germain ⓢ Ⓜ *Continental/French*

▽ 25 | 26 | 26 | $132

Uptown | Hôtel St. Germain | 2516 Maple Ave. (bet. Cedar Springs Rd. & McKinney Ave.) | Dallas | 214-871-2516 | www.hotelstgermain.com

Set within a "beautiful hotel" "in an old Victorian house" Uptown, this "romantic getaway" is a "perfect" "place to celebrate" any "special occasion" thanks to a "well-thought-out" prix fixe French-Continental menu of "fantastic food" served by a host of "waiters in white gloves"; reserve "weeks in advance" and your reward will be an "elegant", "formal dining experience" (jacket and tie required).

House of Blues ◑ *Southern*

19 | 23 | 19 | $30

Victory Park | White Swan Bldg. | 2200 N. Lamar St. (Houston St.) | Dallas | 214-978-2583 | www.hob.com

This "down-home, feel-good" chain link in Victory Park purveys a "standard" selection of "Southern comfort-food" items in faux

honky-tonk settings goosed up by "live band performances"; "loud, bustling" and always jammed with "tourists", it may be "nothing to write home about", though disciples sing "hallelujah for the Sunday gospel brunch."

Houston's *American* | 23 | 20 | 22 | $30 |

Preston Center | 8300 Preston Rd. (Wentwood Dr.) | Dallas | 214-691-8991
Addison | 5318 Belt Line Rd. (Dallas N. Tollway) | 972-960-1752
www.hillstone.com
See review in Houston Directory.

Howard Wang's China Grill *Chinese* | 20 | 15 | 18 | $21 |

Preston Hollow | Villages of Preston Hollow | 4343 W. Northwest Hwy. (Midway Rd.) | Dallas | 214-366-1606 | www.hwchinagrill.com
"Little brother to the Empress of China", this Preston Hollow eatery serves "very good Chinese food" – "not the traditional American" version, but a "sleek, modern" interpretation "with a cosmopolitan twist" "as well as some of the old favorites" – "in a contemporary setting"; some suggest the "service veers between rushed and lackadaisical at times", but those who "make it a regular stop" report it's "improving with each visit."

H3 Ranch *Steak* | 20 | 21 | 18 | $29 |

Stockyards | 109 E. Exchange Ave. (Main St.) | Ft. Worth | 817-624-1246 | www.h3ranch.com
This Stockyards steakhouse is a "pretty darn good pardner" for roping up "awesome steaks" with all the "trimmings" as well as "rockin' breakfasts" on weekends; the "Texas-themed environment" complete with saddle-topped stools and "stuffed buffalo heads on one side and buffalo butts on the other" make it a "must-go" "tourist attraction" for "out-of-towners" who also appreciate the moderate prices.

I Fratelli Ristorante & Wine Bar *Italian* | 22 | 19 | 19 | $21 |

Las Colinas | 7701 N. MacArthur Blvd. (Lyndon B. Johnson Frwy.) | Irving | 972-501-9700 | www.ifratelli.net
Piezani praise the "killer pizzas" with "excellent thin crusts" and "just the right amount of toppings" at this "suburban oasis" in Las Colinas also offering "traditional" Italian "comfort food" paired with wines from a "well-thought-out" list; it packs a crowd with "nice ambiance" and "bargain" lunch specials while the delivery outlets from Grapevine to Lewisville are on everyone's speed dial.

India Palace *Indian* | 23 | 17 | 22 | $27 |

Preston Forest | 12817 Preston Rd. (Lyndon B. Johnson Frwy.) | Dallas | 972-392-0190 | www.indiapalacedallas.com
"One of the most reliable Indian places" in the area, this "traditional establishment" in Preston Forest "has been around a long time" thanks to "authentic" "flavorful and fragrant" fare ferried by "servers who are very nice about explaining the choices"; "white tablecloths and quiet, subdued lighting" exhibit a flair for atmosphere not seen at some of its competitors.

Iron Cactus *Tex-Mex* | 18 | 19 | 18 | $25 |

Downtown Dallas | 1520 Main St. (bet. Akard & Ervay Sts.) | Dallas | 214-749-4766 | www.ironcactus.com

See review in Austin and the Hill Country Directory.

Isabella's *Italian* ▽ 21 | 24 | 23 | $32 |

Frisco | Stonebriar Ctr. | 1279 Legacy Dr. (Rte. 121) | 214-618-3384 | www.isabellasfrisco.com

You'll feel as if you've "stepped out of Frisco and into Italy" at this upscale eatery in Stonebriar Commons ensconced in a tasteful setting enlivened by "wonderful contemporary art" and an active fountain outside; admirers applaud the "excellent" menu items that hail from Lombardy, Piedmont, Tuscany and the Veneto Region, while "accommodating" "individualized" service adds a "warm" touch to the evening.

J & J Oyster Bar *Cajun/Creole* ▽ 21 | 10 | 18 | $16 |

Cultural District | 612 N. University Dr. (bet. 5th & 6th Sts.) | Ft. Worth | 817-335-2756 | www.jjbluesbar.com

For more than 30 years, this "hole-in-the-wall" "dive" in Ft. Worth's Cultural District has been dishing up "great" Cajun-Creole seafood "at a reasonable price", along with "cold beer or iced tea"; with "rolls of paper towels on every table to make cleanup easy", it's strictly a "no-frills" vibe, but "if you like things fried this is the place for you."

Japanese Palace *Japanese* ▽ 26 | 18 | 23 | $33 |

West | 8445 Camp Bowie W. (Brandon Ln.) | Ft. Worth | 817-244-0144 | www.japanesepalace.net

Noble flavors reign at this midpriced West Ft. Worth Japanese where chefs behind hibachi tables cook up "stellar" sukiyaki and the sushi bar sends out a wide variety of fresh fin fare; some say the decor's a bit dated, but even if the "bar feels like a relic from the *Love Boat*", the "attentive" staff makes it a "fun" place for "kids and adults" alike.

Z Jasper's *American* | 24 | 25 | 24 | $42 |

Plano | Shops at Legacy | 7161 Bishop Rd. (Legacy Dr.) | 469-229-9111 | www.kentrathbun.com

See review in Austin and the Hill Country Directory.

Javier's *Mexican* | 22 | 21 | 21 | $39 |

Knox-Henderson | 4912 Cole Ave. (Harvard Ave.) | Dallas | 214-521-4211 | www.javiers.net

An "old Dallas hangout" for over 30 years, this "established" temple of "haute Mexican" cuisine on the edge of Knox-Henderson presents "top-notch margaritas" and "wonderfully authentic" fare to a "clubby", "loud-voiced" crowd; some wags warn it's "pricey" and "overrated", but the "zigzag maze" of "dark" "well-decorated dining rooms" and cigar bar filled with "old-timers and their trophies" mean it's "hard to beat" "for drinks, apps and people-watching"; P.S. "have a reservation or plan to wait."

	FOOD	DECOR	SERVICE	COST

Jinbeh *Japanese*

21 | 18 | 20 | $29

Frisco | Shafer Plaza | 2693 Preston Rd. (Warren Pkwy.) | 214-619-1200
Las Colinas | 301 E. Las Colinas Blvd. (O'Connor Blvd.) | Irving | 972-869-4011
Lewisville | 2440A S. Stemmons Frwy. (Vista Ridge Blvd.) | 214-488-2224
www.jinbeh.com

A "very good local" mini-chain, this "solid performer" is "popular" for its "excellent sushi", all the more noteworthy since its audience consists mostly of "families with kids" who come for the "great hibachi"; perhaps the "decor is a little lacking", but the "theatrics" of the "tableside cooking", such as the "fire-blowing onions", are "worth the price of admission" alone – so expect "some long waits."

Joe T. Garcia's ⊕ *Tex-Mex*

19 | 22 | 20 | $21

North Side | 2201 N. Commerce St. (22nd St.) | Ft. Worth | 817-626-4356 | www.joets.com

An "awesome patio" overlooking a "beautiful garden" and "tranquil" fountain make this rambling North Side Ft. Worth hacienda a "perennial favorite", especially for "out-of-town guests" (translation: beware of "long lines"); yet in spite of the "delightful atmosphere" and "friendly service", a number of naysayers label the Tex-Mex fare only "ok", though they admit that after a couple of the "potent margaritas", even the pickiest patron "may not care"; N.B. cash only.

Jorg's Café Vienna ⊠ M *Austrian*

▽ 25 | 17 | 22 | $22

Plano | 1037 E. 15th St. (K Ave.) | 972-509-5966 | www.cafevienna.us

"A slice of Vienna" comes to Plano via this "real nice neighborhood spot" where a basket of homemade pretzels sets the mood for a full array of well-priced "down-home" Austrian specialties paired with a "great" selection of brews on tap; brick walls and checkered tablecloths conjure up old-world charm while the beer garden proves a festive respite especially during Oktoberfest; N.B. open Wednesday–Saturday.

J. R.'s Steakhouse ⊠ *Steak*

23 | 21 | 23 | $59

Colleyville | 5400 Hwy. 121 (Hall Johnson St.) | 817-355-1414 | www.jrssteaks.com

Carnivores claim "everything is done well" at this "pricey" Colleyville chophouse where "prime" steaks and "excellent" American dishes are kicked into high gear by an extensive martini selection; a "pleasant" staff warms up the sophisticated setting as does a working fireplace and "good jazz at the right volume" Thursdays–Saturdays.

Kathleen's Sky Diner *Eclectic*

20 | 16 | 17 | $24

Park Cities | 4424 Lovers Ln. (Armstrong Pkwy.) | Dallas | 214-691-2355 | www.kathleensartcafe.com

You'll find "some very original food" on the "varied" Eclectic menu at this "convenient", inexpensive Park Cities restaurant, including "delicious desserts" and an "awesome Sunday brunch"; still, some surveyors say the "quality depends on what you order", adding that "service is unfortunately slow."

	FOOD	DECOR	SERVICE	COST

Keg Steakhouse & Bar *Steak*   21 | 20 | 22 | $38

Las Colinas | 859 W. John Carpenter Frwy. (MacArthur Blvd.) |
Irving | 972-556-9188
Plano | Shops at Willow Bend | 6101 W. Park Blvd. (Dallas Pkwy.) |
972-403-0430
Southwest | 5760 SW Loop 820 (Bryant Irvin Rd.) | Ft. Worth |
817-731-3534
NEW **Arlington** | 4001 Arlington Highlands Blvd. (Airport Frwy.) |
817-465-3700
www.kegsteakhouse.com

Bravely venturing into well-trodden territory with "steaks substantially
cheaper than" some of their competitors', these chain outposts can
claim quality that's "surprisingly good" – "without the à la carte sky-
high prices and snootiness"; their classy lodge decor and good bars
make for a "fun environment" that's also fine "for a business lunch."

Kenichi *Pan-Asian*   22 | 22 | 19 | $43

Victory Park | 2400 Victory Park Ln. (Museum Way) | Dallas |
214-871-8883 | www.kenichirestaurants.com
See review in Austin and the Hill Country Directory.

Kincaid's Hamburgers *Burgers*   23 | 13 | 16 | $11

Southwest | 4825 Overton Ridge Blvd. (Hulen St.) | Ft. Worth |
817-370-6400
West | 4901 Camp Bowie Blvd. (Eldridge St.) | Ft. Worth |
817-732-2881 ⓢ
Arlington | 3900 Arlington Highlands Blvd. (Matlock Rd.) | 817-466-4211
Southlake | 100 N. Kimball Ave. (Southlake Blvd.) | 817-416-2573
www.kincaidshamburgers.com

Occupying a "former small grocery store" since 1946, this "landmark" brings foodies to West Ft. Worth (and to Arlington, Southlake
and Southwest Ft. Worth) for "gooey, juicy, melt-in-your-mouth
burgers" made from "fresh" beef, "not frozen premade patties"; sitting communally "at long picnic tables, next to people getting just as
messy as you, somehow adds to the flavor."

Kirby's Steakhouse *Steak*   24 | 22 | 23 | $50

Greenville Avenue | 3525 Greenville Ave. (McCommas Blvd.) |
Dallas | 214-821-2122
Southlake | 3305 E. Hwy. 114 (Southlake Blvd.) | 817-410-2221
www.kirbyssteakhouse.com

Enjoy "excellent steaks", "fresh seafood", "strong cocktails and
great service" from an "accommodating staff" within the "laid-back
atmosphere" of these outposts of a "great medium-priced steakhouse" micro-chain; their decor is done "in the style of the old supper clubs", with "tasteful wood paneling", and don't forget the
"great bar" ("with piano music" at the Southlake branch) – plus
they're "open Sunday when many others aren't."

Kona Grill *American*   20 | 21 | 18 | $27

NorthPark | NorthPark Ctr. | 8687 N. Central Expwy. (Park Ln.) |
Dallas | 214-369-7600 | www.konagrill.com
See review in Houston Directory.

	FOOD	DECOR	SERVICE	COST

Kozy Kitchen ⊠ *Eclectic*

▽ 25 | 12 | 24 | $24

Knox-Henderson | 4433 McKinney Ave. (bet. Armstrong Ave. & Oliver St.) | Dallas | 214-219-5044 | www.thekozy.net

Those seeking "good, healthy food" find it at this Knox-Henderson "jewel" serving up "fresh and delicious" Eclectic dishes that make use of grass-fed meat, wild seafood and organic produce (they also offer a full line of gluten-free baked goods); colorful quarters and a "friendly" vibe make it a "favorite", especially for lunch; N.B. they now serve beer and wine.

Kuby's Sausage House *German*

22 | 11 | 17 | $18

Park Cities | Snider Plaza | 6601 Snider Plaza (Daniel Ave.) | Dallas | 214-363-2231 | www.kubys.com

"If you're a fan of German food, you'll find all the standards and then some" at this "small, modest" "neighborhood place" in the Snider Plaza area of Park Cities "with a great butcher and gourmet shop attached"; specializing in "awesome sausages", it's a Teutonic "food lover's heaven", and regulars report that "the hearty breakfast" is the highlight; N.B. dinner served only on Fridays and Saturdays.

La Calle Doce *Mexican*

21 | 16 | 19 | $19

Oak Cliff | 415 W. 12th St. (Bishop Ave.) | Dallas | 214-941-4304 | www.lacalledoce-dallas.com

Serving "Veracruz-style seafood at its best", this "modest" family-owned Mexican "hole-in-the-wall" in Oak Cliff has been in business for more than 25 years; it boasts a "casual and crowded" vibe that can sometimes tax the servers, resulting in "slow service", "but they're friendly", nonetheless.

NEW La Cubanita *Cuban*

- | - | - | I

Knox-Henderson | 4444 McKinney Ave. (Armstrong Ave.) | Dallas | 214-520-0100 | www.lacubanitadallas.com

A hip crowd populates the wraparound porch and casual quarters of this inexpensive Knox-Henderson Cuban from the Lombardi restaurant clan that's decked out in pre-Castro era memorabilia with *I Love Lucy* episodes dominating the flat-screen TV; an array of flavored mojitos complements the menu, which includes their signature arroz con pollo, late-night bites (till 1 AM on weekends) and a sizzlin' Sunday brunch; N.B. a second location will open at the Shops at Legacy.

La Duni Latin Cafe Ⓜ *Pan-Latin*

24 | 21 | 19 | $30

Knox-Henderson | 4620 McKinney Ave. (Knox St.) | Dallas | 214-520-7300

La Duni Latin Kitchen *Pan-Latin*
Oak Lawn | 4264 Oak Lawn Ave. (Herschel Ave.) | Dallas | 214-520-6888

La Duni Latin Kitchen & Coffee Studio *Pan-Latin*
NEW **NorthPark** | NorthPark Mall | 8687 N. Central Expwy. (bet. Northwest Hwy. & Park Ln.) | Dallas | 214-987-2260 www.laduni.com

Supporters swoon over chef-owners Espartaco and Dunia Borga's "cosmopolitan" Pan-Latin cuisine, "fabulous coffee drinks" and

	FOOD	DECOR	SERVICE	COST

"magnificent desserts" ("don't leave without a piece of the quatro leches cake") at this "lively" Oak Lawn and Knox-Henderson cafe duo; in spite of "spotty" service and a "noisy" setting, regulars report it's a solid "bet for budget challenged foodies"; N.B. the NorthPark Center outpost is new.

La Familia 🅱 *Mexican* | 24 | 22 | 26 | $18 |

Near West | 841 Foch St. (1 block west of Carroll St.) | Ft. Worth | 817-870-2002

"You're always greeted with a handshake" from owner Al Cavazos at this Near West Ft. Worth Mexican offering "excellent" dishes like enchiladas that are "spiced just right"; dark, "cozy" decor decked out with family photos and cowhides on display brightens up when flaming margaritas are brought over by the "friendly" staff.

NEW Lambert's *Steak* | - | - | - | E |

Near West | 2731 White Settlement Rd. (Foch St.) | Ft. Worth | 817-882-1161 | www.lambertsfortworth.com

An offshoot of Lou Lambert's namesake BBQ joint in Austin, this Ft. Worth outpost focuses more on steaks and seafood served in a rustically chic space appointed with cedar wood touches and saddle chandeliers; the rest of the menu pushes beyond traditional chophouse fare with brown sugar-crusted rib-eyes and south-of-the-border entrees like quail relleno rounding out the pricey offerings.

L'Ancestral 🅱 *French* | 23 | 20 | 24 | $43 |

Knox-Henderson | Travis Walk | 4514 Travis St. (Knox St.) | Dallas | 214-528-1081

"Nostalgic" Francophiles favor this "romantic" Knox-Henderson "staple" serving up "consistently wonderful" Gallic classics like escargots and steak au poivre in a "low-key" setting decorated in a "cozy" country style; even if a few find it's "showing its age", it's a "charming" spot enhanced by "professional" if "slightly gruff waiters who are actually softies."

Landmark, The *American* | - | - | - | E |

Oak Lawn | Warwick Melrose Hotel | 3015 Oak Lawn Ave. (Cedar Springs Rd.) | Dallas | 214-224-3152 | www.warwickmelrosedallas.com

The venerable Warwick Melrose Hotel's remake of its dining venue retains its white-tablecloth stature with polished service, an acclaimed wine list and a sophisticated menu; New American dishes (like Texas partridge with leek confit risotto) share menu space with Asian-inflected items, all set down in a stylish setting quiet enough for business conversations or romantic exchanges; N.B. regulars suggest a stop at the Library Bar to start or round out the evening.

🅩 Lanny's Alta Cocina | 27 | 25 | 26 | $56 |
Mexicana 🅱 🅜 *Eclectic/Mexican*

Cultural District | 3405 W. Seventh St. (Boland St.) | Ft. Worth | 817-850-9996 | www.lannyskitchen.com

"Simply awesome" declare those dazzled by chef Lanny Lancarte's "haute" Eclectic-Mexican eatery in Ft. Worth's Cultural District of-

fering "clever takes" on south-of-the-border classics (like elk mole and pomegranate margaritas) plus "inventive" international dishes all served by a "friendly and efficient" staff; yes, it's "expensive", but an "inviting" atmosphere with a "beautiful patio" makes it all "worth it."

La Playa Maya *Mexican*

| 23 | 17 | 20 | $20 |

West | 6209 Sunset Dr. (bet. Fairfield & Westridge Aves.) | Ft. Worth | 817-738-3329
South Side | 3200 Hemphill St. (Devitt St.) | Ft. Worth | 817-924-0698
Stockyards | 1540 N. Main St. (14th St.) | Ft. Worth | 817-624-8411
Weatherford | 1445 Ft. Worth Hwy. (Hazel Hwy.) | 817-613-8686
www.laplayamaya.com

"Go for" the "authentic ceviche" and other "Mexican seafood specialties" at these "popular" "bright" spots on the Texas horizon, outposts of a "local semi-chain" that also feature a few "great Tex-Mex" dishes; all offer a "fun atmosphere", and they're "quick at lunch" too.

Lavendou 🗷 *French*

| 24 | 23 | 22 | $42 |

North Dallas | 19009 Preston Rd. (bet. Frankford Rd. & President George Bush Tpke.) | Dallas | 972-248-1911 | www.lavendou.com

For "a touch of France", visit this far North Dallas bistro, a "lovely, serene place" offering "the feel and taste of Provence", with a "nice country interior" and "plants on the patio that screen the traffic noise and view of the parking lot well enough that you can forget you are in a strip shopping center"; some say the staff "occasionally exhibits a little bit of attitude", but the service is generally "caring."

Lawry's The Prime Rib *Steak*

| 24 | 21 | 24 | $53 |

North Dallas | 14655 Dallas Pkwy. (Spring Valley Rd.) | Dallas | 972-503-6688 | www.lawrysonline.com

Like the name says, it's all about the "first-class prime rib" at this "old-fashioned", "high-quality" steakhouse chain where the signature dish is "carved tableside" by an "attentive" crew; what with the "1970s-all-over-again vibe", it's a magnet for the "senior set", though folks of all ages agree its "quaint style" makes for a "unique dining experience."

Legacy Naan *Japanese/Korean*

| 22 | 20 | 18 | $35 |

Plano | Shops at Legacy | 7161 Bishop Rd. (Legacy Dr.) | 972-943-9288 | www.legacynaan.com

"A departure from the usual", this "upscale" "combo Korean-Japanese place" situated within Plano's tony Shops at Legacy features an "interesting" menu with a "totally original" "twist on Asian fusion" fare, including unique "sushi creations"; a "helpful" staff and a "nice-looking space" with "cool modern decor" and "a large bar" also add appeal, even if the "food is a little over the edge" for less adventurous eaters.

Lili's Bistro 🗷 *American*

| - | - | - | M |

Hospital District | 1310 W. Magnolia Ave. (bet. Lake St. & 6th Ave.) | Ft. Worth | 817-877-0700 | www.lilisbistro.com

There's often a full house at this funky Ft. Worth Hospital District bistro whose distressed brick walls bear nostalgic Mrs. Baird's

Bread ads; by day it features a menu of reasonably priced sandwiches and simple entrees, which, come night, are replaced with more complex New American fare like their signature rabbit ravioli and nut-crusted flounder.

Little Katana *Asian Fusion*　　　23 | 15 | 18 | $33

Knox-Henderson | 4527 Travis St. (Knox St.) | Dallas | 214-443-9600

Little Katana Sushi Bar *Japanese*

Galleria | Galleria | 13350 N. Dallas Pkwy. (Lyndon B. Johnson Frwy.) | Dallas | 972-991-1122

www.littlekatana.com

"Shhh – don't tell anybody" say secretive supporters of this "small" Asian fusion bôite in Knox-Henderson offering a "diverse menu" drawing from Japanese, Korean, Thai and American cuisines plus a "great" 40-plus bottle sake list; in spite of the "very good food", the less starry-eyed claim that "cramped" conditions and "slow service" prompt them to seek out "lower priced options" elsewhere; N.B. the Galleria original offers sushi only.

Z Local ⊠M *American*　　　28 | 24 | 25 | $51

Deep Ellum | 2936 Elm St. (1 block west of Hall St.) | Dallas | 214-752-7500 | www.localdallas.com

A "hidden gem" in Deep Ellum, chef Tracy Miller's "funky, modern" venue set in the historic Boyd Hotel building charms connoisseurs with "great wines" and a "zingy, fresh-flavored" New American menu that utilizes "local, seasonal ingredients", with fans calling it "one of the few places in Dallas where it's possible to eat both healthy and well"; solid service is a plus, though some find the tabs "pretty pricey" for the area; N.B. there's private parking adjacent to the restaurant.

Lola ⊠M *American*　　　27 | 23 | 25 | $67

Uptown | 2917 Fairmount St. (Cedar Springs Rd.) | Dallas | 214-855-0700 | www.lola4dinner.com

"Romantics", "out-of-towners" and business execs all adore this "quaint old house" Uptown where "outstanding" New American cuisine is presented in "exquisite" prix fixe menus and matched with wines from an "incredible", "reasonably priced" list; add in high-level service, and it's the "perfect spot for a special evening"; P.S. the separate chef's tasting room with a 10-course menu is "one of the city's great fine-dining experiences."

Lonesome Dove　　　26 | 23 | 23 | $51
Western Bistro ⊠ *Southwestern*

Stockyards | 2406 N. Main St. (24th St.) | Ft. Worth | 817-740-8810 | www.lovestyleinc.com

Celebrity chef-owner Tim Love's "haute cowboy cuisine" earns legions of fans at this fine-dining "treasure" in Ft. Worth's Stockyards that "hits the mark" with "huge portions" of "impressive", "experimental" Southwestern specialties like braised wild boar ribs and buffalo rib-eye; given the "sophisticated" saloon setting and staff

that lays on the "Texas charm", it's "a must" for visitors, especially those on an "expense account."

Love & War in Texas *Southwestern* `16` `17` `16` `$24`

Plano | 601 E. Plano Pkwy. (Rte. 75) | 972-422-6201
Grapevine | Grapevine Mills | 2505 E. Grapevine Mills Circle (Hwy. 121) | 972-724-5557
www.loveandwarintexas.com

Boot-scooting types gather at these "funky roadhouses" in east Plano and Grapevine for "gargantuan portions" of regional-style "cowboy food" like chicken-fried steak and fajitas and kick up their heels on weekends to "live music"; the "down-home atmosphere" at both locations is "loud" and "energetic" making it a good fit for large groups.

Love Shack ⊄ *American* `22` `14` `13` `$12`

Stockyards | 110 E. Exchange Ave. (Main St.) | Ft. Worth | 817-740-8812 | www.shakeyourloveshack.com

"Burgers and music" come together at Lonesome Dove chef-owner Tim Love's "quirky" venture in Ft. Worth's Stockyards offering "memorable" patties crafted from ground brisket and tenderloin plus hot dogs, hand-cut onion rings, ice-cold beer and a rotating selection of milkshakes; the "open-air" setting plays host to live bands at lunch and on weekends, though folks can also opt to "grab [their] grub to go."

Lucile's Stateside Bistro *American* `18` `16` `17` `$23`

West | 4700 Camp Bowie Blvd. (Hulen St.) | Ft. Worth | 817-738-4761
West Ft. Worthers appreciate the "convenience" of this "venerable" favorite featuring "excellent" American cuisine and "friendly" service – "the way things used to be"; it's a "casual" kind of "place for simple, straightforward, slightly Southern-inspired dishes", and it wins special raves for its "great lobster dishes", "wood-oven pizzas" and "nice brunch" on Saturdays and Sundays.

Lucky's Café *American* `20` `14` `19` `$16`

Oak Lawn | 3531 Oak Lawn Ave. (Lemmon Ave.) | Dallas | 214-522-3500 | www.croinc.com

When you're "craving" "a hearty breakfast" after a night on the town or "classic diner-type" fare and "mom's not cooking", drop into this Oak Lawn Traditional American where the "comfort food" is "simple but great" and "service can be slow if they are busy"; its "gay-friendly" milieu showcases the "scene, truly a mix of all walks of life" who chat it up in line together on the weekends.

Luna de Noche *Tex-Mex* `20` `18` `19` `$23`

Medical City | 7927 Forest Ln. (Central Expwy.) | Dallas | 972-233-1880
NorthPark | NorthPark Ctr. | 8687 N. Central Expwy. (Park Ln.) | Dallas | 214-389-9520
Victory Park | 2300 Victory Park Ln. (Lamar St.) | Dallas | 214-420-3050
Garland | 7602 N. Jupiter Rd. (Lookout Dr.) | 972-414-3616
Plano | 1401 Preston Rd. (Plano Pkwy.) | 972-818-2727
www.lunadenoche.net

"Creative" Tex-Mex cuisine draws in Dallas denizens at this "fancy" (read: "pricey") chain of cantinas seeded across town where diners

devour "heavenly guacamole" prepared tableside and "delicious salsa"; though service can be "uneven", the "inviting" contemporary digs with "twinkling lights" draw crowds for "romantic" dates and happy-hour margaritas.

Madras Pavilion *Indian*

| 22 | 11 | 14 | $17 |

Richardson | Dalrich Shopping Ctr. | 101 S. Colt Rd. (Belt Line Rd.) | 972-671-3672 | www.madraspavilion.us
See review in Houston Directory.

Maggiano's Little Italy *Italian*

| 20 | 20 | 20 | $30 |

NorthPark | NorthPark Ctr. | 8687 N. Central Expwy. (Northwest Hwy.) | Dallas | 214-360-0707
Plano | Shops at Willow Bend | 6001 W. Park Blvd. (Dallas Pkwy.) | 972-781-0776
www.maggianos.com

You almost "expect to see Sinatra walk in behind you" at this "1940s-esque", checkered-tablecloth chain where "monster portions" of "red-sauce" Italiana are dished out in "enjoyably hectic" surroundings; some dub it a "mixed bag", citing a "mass-production", "quantity-trumps-quality" approach, but fans tout this "crowd-pleaser" as a "big night out" for "not a lot of money."

Maguire's *American*

| 23 | 21 | 22 | $36 |

North Dallas | 17552 Dallas Pkwy. (Trinity Mills Rd.) | Dallas | 972-818-0068 | www.maguiresdallas.com

"Always reliable", this North Dallas clubhouse is "a habit" with area residents, the kind of "place the locals call home" thanks to "always-great" Traditional American fare and "dependable service" offered in a "casual yet trendy setting" – plus a "big bar that's a gathering place for mature adults"; clearly, "they're doing something right"; N.B. the Decor score does not reflect a recent remodel.

Main Street Bistro & Bakery *French*

| 23 | 17 | 17 | $15 |

Richardson | Shire | 3600 Shire Blvd. (Jupiter Rd.) | 972-578-0294
Plano | Shops at Legacy | 7200 Bishop Rd. (Legacy Dr.) | 972-309-0404
Grapevine | 316 S. Main St. (bet. Dallas Rd. & Northwest Hwy.) | 817-424-4333
www.themainbakery.com

Set "in historic Downtown Grapevine", this "intimate sidewalk cafe" is "good for salad and sandwiches", with a "casual French bakery" component that "smells of fresh baked bread and has beautiful pastries"; its younger sibling is also a "popular place", and "a little slice of Europe in Plano", but "be prepared to wait in line" and endure "disappointing service" at both branches; N.B. the Richardson branch is newer.

Mama's Daughters' Diner *Diner*

| 21 | 11 | 20 | $13 |

Market Center | 2014 Irving Blvd. (bet. Turtle Creek Blvd. & Wycliff Ave.) | Dallas | 214-742-8646 | www.mamasdaughtersdiner.com
Love Field | 2610 Royal Ln. (Harry Hines Blvd.) | Dallas | 972-241-8646 | www.mamasdiner.com 🖼

(continued)

(continued)

Mama's Daughters' Diner

Irving | 2412 W. Shady Grove Rd. (Story Rd.) | 972-790-2778 |
www.mamasdaughtersdiner.com
Lewisville | 1288 W. Main St. (Old Orchard Ln.) | 972-353-5955 |
www.mamasdaughtersdiner.com ⑤

"Down-home cookin'" "just like mama makes" keeps this chain of
"old-fashioned" diners "packed" with patrons praising the "rib-
sticking" breakfasts and "homemade pies" not to mention the "good
value for the money"; decor is "simple", so most of the local color
comes from "veteran waitresses" who take no sass ("they're ornery
and proud of it") and provide "efficient", "to the point" service.

Mamma Emilia's Ⓜ *Italian*
18 | 20 | 20 | $28

McKinney | 119 W. Virginia St. (Wood St.) | 972-562-1102 |
www.mammaemiliasonline.com

"Nice Italian fare" "fits the bill" for "neighborhood" denizens at this
"attractive eatery" on the Square in McKinney, presenting solid,
moderately priced cuisine from staff and owners who "take pride in
what they do"; the old-world decor prompts a mixed response with
the dining room deemed "charming" and "comfortable" for some,
and a bit too "dark" and "moody" for others.

Mango Thai *Thai*
21 | 15 | 19 | $23

Park Cities | 4448 E. Lovers Ln. (Dallas N. Tollway) | Dallas | 214-265-9996
Plano | Berkley Sq. | 4701 W. Park Blvd. (Ohio Dr.) | 972-599-0289
www.mangothaicuisine.com

Surveyors salute these "solidly performing" Thai "staples" in Park
Cities and Plano (sibs of Chow Thai) offering "consistently good" –
if "Americanized" – South Asian specialties; decor is "casual" and
"modern" though insiders insist it's a "go-to place for takeout" too.

Ⓩ Mansion, The *American*
26 | 27 | 26 | $77

Uptown | Rosewood Mansion on Turtle Creek | 2821 Turtle Creek Blvd.
(Gillespie St.) | Dallas | 214-559-2100 | www.mansiononturtlecreek.com

"Still the grande dame of Dallas" proclaim proponents of this
Uptown "institution" sending out "superb" New American dishes
that make use of locally sourced ingredients; in recent years, a major renovation divided the "elegant" interior into three rooms done
up in dark woods with contemporary art on the walls, added a bar
menu and relaxed the dress code (except in the more formal 20-seat
Chef's Room); "extremely accommodating service" and "upscale"
pricing, however, remain constants; N.B. the Food score does not reflect the Jan. 2009 departure of chef John Tesar.

Margaux's Ⓢ *Cajun/Creole*
▽ 25 | 22 | 24 | $38

Market Center | 150 Turtle Creek Blvd. (Irving Blvd.) | Dallas |
214-740-1985 | www.margauxsdallas.com

A "charming" detour ensconced in Dallas' Design District, this
"quirky local place" draws a loyal lunchtime following for contemporary Cajun-Creole cuisine (think crawfish and shrimp enchiladas)
that "never disappoints"; white-walled decor is enhanced by enor-

FOOD | DECOR | SERVICE | COST

mous floral prints, fresh flowers on each table as well as "friendly" service; N.B. open for dinner Saturdays only.

Mariposa American
▽ 23 | 23 | 22 | $27

Plano | Shops at Willow Bend | 2201 Dallas Pkwy. (Park Blvd.) | 972-629-1718 | www.neimanmarcus.com

A "jewel in the crown of Neiman Marcus", this upscale daytime-only New American noshery inside the store at Plano's Shops at Willow Bend offers an "excellent repast", with "food and service that rank with the quality of the merchandise" nearby; it's a "lovely place to lunch with the ladies" and a "great end to a fun day of shopping", and high points include "real Texas women with big hair and big jewels, and the best popovers in the world."

Masala Chinese/Indian
18 | 12 | 15 | $13

Irving | 7447 N. MacArthur Blvd. (Mimosa Dr.) | 972-409-0000

Masala Wok Chinese/Indian
Richardson | 1310 W. Campbell Rd. (Coit Rd.) | 972-644-9000
Plano | 8404 Preston Rd. (Rte. 121) | 469-362-5586
www.masalawok.com

"Mix and match" at these links in a regional chain, a "quick", "casual" stop for a "cheap" and "satisfying" fix of Indian and Chinese (with more weight on the former); the "concept" yields some "unusual combinations" and "oddball seasonings", but the "servers are helpful with first-timers."

Matt's Rancho Martinez Tex-Mex
21 | 16 | 19 | $20

Lakewood | 6332 La Vista Dr. (Gaston Ave.) | Dallas | 214-823-5517 | www.thetexmexchef.com

"When you want some carb loading, there's nothing like a meal" at this "good Lakewood spot" that "has grown into an East Dallas staple" for "fab" Tex-Mex fare; perhaps the "space isn't very inviting" (some say it feels "almost like eating in a warehouse") and the service is just "good", "not great" – but ya "gotta love" "grabbing a table on the patio and enjoying" a few of their "strong margaritas" "while kicking back with friends."

McCormick & Schmick's Seafood
21 | 21 | 20 | $41

NorthPark | NorthPark Ctr. | 307 Northpark Ctr. (Northwest Hwy.) | Dallas | 214-891-0100 | www.mccormickandschmicks.com
See review in Austin and the Hill Country Directory.

Melting Pot Fondue
21 | 20 | 21 | $43

Addison | Quorum II Plaza | 4900 Belt Line Rd. (Landmark Blvd.) | 972-960-7028 | www.meltingpot.com
See review in Austin and the Hill Country Directory.

Mercury Chophouse Steak
26 | 23 | 23 | $43

Sundance Square | 301 Main St. (2nd St.) | Ft. Worth | 817-336-4129 | www.mcrowd.com

There's "never a bad meal" at this "solid" Downtown steakhouse in Sundance Square (owned by the M Crowd restaurant group) that's "excellent for a business lunch" and "one of the best in Ft. Worth for

conversation"; the "great" fare features a "perfect filet", and the "intimate" room is both "comfortable and luxurious", with "velvety drapes" and "club chairs" to bring you "back to the '40s."

☒ Mercury Grill American   27 | 23 | 24 | $50

Preston Forest | 11909 Preston Rd. (Forest Ln.) | Dallas | 972-960-7774 | www.mcrowd.com

"Talented" chef Chris Ward "gets it right" at this "fashionable" Preston Forest "place to be seen" with his "sublime" New American menu from which loyalists recite their litany of "favorites" ("heavenly mushroom risotto", braised short ribs); despite the fact that it's "tucked into a strip center", this is "one happening spot", with a staff so personable "we wished our waiter could have joined us for the meal" – just "watch out for the tab."; N.B there's a spacious lounge and rooms for private groups.

☒ Mercy, A Wine Bar French   19 | 26 | 22 | $36

Addison | Village on the Pkwy. | 5100 Belt Line Rd. (Dallas N. Tollway) | 972-702-9463 | www.mercywinebar.com

You'll need to "elbow your way through the young and beautiful" at this Addison "oasis" where the "dark", "loungey" room and "extensive" wine selection (over 100 available by the glass) is conducive to sipping and lingering "all night long"; "knowledgeable" servers pair your vinos with "tasty" shareable French plates, but wallet-watchers should be aware of a "pricey" tab that can creep up on you.

Mia's Tex-Mex   24 | 13 | 19 | $17

Lemmon Avenue | 4322 Lemmon Ave. (Wycliff Ave.) | Dallas | 214-526-1020 | www.miastexmex.com

Groupies "guarantee a good night out" at this "quintessential" Tex-Mexer on Lemmon Avenue where the "nuclear-strength margaritas" and "justifiably famous brisket tacos" come at prices that won't bust your budget; "service is fast" while the "cramped", "casual" quarters have been known to include a "Dallas Cowboy" or two.

Michaels Rest. &   24 | 18 | 19 | $37
Ancho Chile Bar ☒ Southwestern

Cultural District | 3413 W. Seventh St. (bet. Montgomery & University Sts.) | Ft. Worth | 817-877-3413 | www.michaelscuisine.com

"Those who like it hot" say chef-owner Michael Thompson's namesake restaurant "tucked away in a shopping center" in Ft. Worth's Cultural District sizzles with "inventive" "Southwestern ranch" dishes, an "excellent wine" list and solid service; the sleek low-lit dining room features local art on the walls while the adjacent Ancho Chile Bar is a "late-night hangout" where "over-30" singles and cigar smokers are well received.

☒ Mi Cocina Tex-Mex   21 | 19 | 20 | $23

Galleria | Galleria | 13350 N. Dallas Pkwy. (Lyndon B. Johnson Frwy.) | Dallas | 972-239-6426
Lake Highlands | 7201 Skillman St. (Kingsley Rd.) | Dallas | 214-503-6426
Park Cities | Highland Park Vill. | 77 Highland Park Vill. (bet. Mockingbird Ln. & Preston Rd.) | Dallas | 214-521-6426

(continued)

Mi Cocina

Preston Forest | Preston Forest Vill. | 11661 Preston Rd. (Forest Ln.) | Dallas | 214-265-7704
West Village | West Vill. | 3699 McKinney Ave. (Lemmon Ave.) | Dallas | 469-533-5663
Las Colinas | 7750 N. MacArthur Blvd. (Lyndon B. Johnson Frwy.) | Irving | 469-621-0452
Plano | Lakeside Mkt. | 4001 Preston Rd. (Lorimar Dr.) | 469-467-8655
Plano | Shops at Legacy | 5760 Legacy Dr. (Bishop Rd.) | 972-473-8745
Sundance Square | Sundance Sq. | 509 Main St. (bet. 4th & 5th Sts.) | Ft. Worth | 817-877-3600
Southlake | Southlake Town Sq. | 1276 S. Main St. (Carroll Ave.) | 817-410-6426
www.mcrowd.com
Additional locations throughout the Dallas/Ft. Worth area
Admirers assert this "upscale" chain with locations in Highland Park, North Dallas and all the nearby suburbs is the "standard setter" for Tex-Mex cuisine with "light", "fresh-tasting" "contemporary" fare and "killer 'ritas" attracting a "noisy" crowd of "pretty folk" and their offspring; "modern" atmosphere (no "south-of-the-border clichés" here) plus "solid value", even considering the "expensive drinks", mean you can "go to any of them and leave satisfied."

Mignon *French*

22 | 22 | 20 | $48

Plano | Lakeside Mkt. | 4005 Preston Rd. (Lorimar Dr.) | 972-943-3372 | www.mignonplano.com
Locals label this Plano bistro a "fine place for impressing your client as well as your date" with "excellent" "real" French fare and steaks delivered to your table by a staff that "tries hard"; curved booths and mod wood decor evoke "early 1960s" Paris, though "high" prices are a more modern touch.

Mi Piaci Ristorante *Italian*

24 | 24 | 22 | $44

Addison | 14854 Montfort Dr. (Belt Line Rd.) | 972-934-8424 | www.mipiaci-dallas.com
For "a business dinner or a special date", diners declare this long-standing "favorite" "in the heart of Addison" proves "never less than wonderful" with "refined" Northern Italian cuisine, a "terrific" from-The-Boot wine list and "attentive" service from a "caring" staff; the "luxurious" setting includes a "gorgeous" patio overlooking a pond and trees, which is a "nice" respite from the sometimes "noisy" interior.

Mirabelle ⊠Ⓜ *American*

∇ 28 | 23 | 28 | $64

North Dallas | 17610 Midway Rd. (Trinity Mills Rd.) | Dallas | 972-733-0202
Chef Joseph Maher "attends to you personally" at this "extraordinary" North Dallas "neighborhood" spot serving "perfectly executed" New American dishes from a "small, but always innovative menu"; add in a "quiet", "intimate" space accented with an aquarium and colorful art, and it "feels like dining in a private home", in spite of its "strip-mall" location.

	FOOD	DECOR	SERVICE	COST

Momo's Pasta *Italian*

19 | 14 | 18 | $26

Knox-Henderson | 3312 Knox St. (Travis St.) | Dallas | 214-521-3009
Addison | 5290 Belt Line Rd. (Montfort Dr.) | 972-386-7373
www.momospasta.com

"Long established", this duo in Addison and Knox-Henderson offers "consistent", "good Italian comfort food" that is "not overpriced" (another "plus": "you can bring your own wine" for a $10 corkage fee) and is ferried by a "fast, friendly" staff; with decor that's just "ok", their interiors are "nothing fancy", but many say they're still "worth" a visit.

Monica's Aca y Alla Ⓜ *Mexican*

23 | 19 | 21 | $24

Deep Ellum | 2914 Main St. (bet. Hall St. & Malcolm X Blvd.) | Dallas | 214-748-7140 | www.monicas.com

"Monica Greene is a Dallas original", and her cosmopolitan Mexican restaurant in Deep Ellum is an "institution" with a "creative" menu featuring lots of "fantastic specials" to sweeten the deal (plus "fabulous margaritas"); there's "great people-watching" every night, but the "cozy, comfortable and fun" atmosphere is "especially enjoyable with the live music" on weekends.

Morton's The Steakhouse *Steak*

25 | 21 | 23 | $62

Downtown Dallas | 501 Elm St. (Houston St.) | Dallas | 214-741-2277 | www.mortons.com
See review in Houston Directory.

My Martini Wine & Bistro *Eclectic*

∇ 23 | 22 | 20 | $33

Arlington | 859 NE Green Oaks Blvd. (Collins St.) | 817-461-4424 | www.mymartinibistro.com

"As the name suggests", "delish" martinis – along with "excellent" small plates of multiethnic fusion fare and a selection of updated chophouse entrees – are on offer at this Arlington Eclectic; though most are "impressed with the quality of food and the service", some think of the "classy" hipster "mostly for the wine" and as "a place to be seen", since it's "one of the coolest in the mid-cities."

Nakamoto Japanese Cuisine *Japanese*

∇ 24 | 18 | 25 | $38

Plano | 3309 N. Central Expwy. (Parker Rd.) | 972-881-0328
Sushi mavens maintain this east Plano Japanese is the "preferred" "local" "choice" for "creative" fin fare and cooked dishes at moderate prices; though dissenters decry the "drab" "1980s decor", "friendly" service and moderate prices have kept the customers coming back "for over 20 years."

Ⓩ Nana *American*

27 | 27 | 27 | $73

Market Center | Hilton Anatole Hotel | 2201 Stemmons Frwy. (Market Center Blvd.) | Dallas | 214-761-7470 | www.nanarestaurant.com
It's tough to compete with "absolutely stunning" "panoramic" views of Downtown Dallas, yet chef Anthony Bombaci captivates diners with equally "amazing" New American dishes prepared in "imaginative" ways (think ahi tuna tartare with wasabi ice cream) at this elegant aerie atop the Hilton Anatole Hotel in Market Center; prices

| | FOOD | DECOR | SERVICE | COST |

are "expensive", but the "superb" staff "executes at a high level", making it a top ticket for "special occasions."

NEW Neighborhood Services *American* — | — | — | M

West Lovers Lane | 5027 W. Lovers Ln. (Inwood Rd.) | Dallas | 214-350-5027 | www.neighborhoodservicesdallas.com

An unassuming name and discreet entrance on the edge of the Lovers Lane shopping district belie the whirr within at this New American comfort fooder from chef Nick Badovinus (Hibiscus, Fireside Pies); an enthusiastic staff in old-school collegiate sweaters and cheerful midcentury decor add to the overall convivial vibe.

Neuhaus Café *American/Dessert* 17 | 10 | 15 | $17

Preston Royal | 626 Preston Royal Shopping Ctr. (Royal Ln.) | Dallas | 214-739-4600 | www.neuhauscafe.com

Chocoholics claim they "just can't resist" the assorted Belgian bon bons and "wonderful desserts" at this coffee shop/"neighborhood sandwich and salad place" in the Preston Royal shopping area; it's "solid in all the basics", so even if the brightly lit quarters could stand to be "toned down a bit", it still works for an inexpensive meal or a quick snack.

Newport's Seafood *Seafood* 21 | 20 | 20 | $42

West End | 703 McKinney Ave. (I-35) | Dallas | 214-954-0220 | www.newports.us

"Even people who are on the fence about seafood" rave about the "reasonably priced", "fresh" fare at this "hard-to-find" but "delightful place" in the touristy West End that's "great for power lunches or intimate dinners"; lauders also "love the brick interior" of its "converted-brewery" setting "with an old well" "in the center of the dining room" that "makes for unique decor."

Nick & Sam's *Seafood/Steak* 25 | 23 | 25 | $61

Uptown | 3008 Maple Ave. (bet. Carlisle & Wolf Sts.) | Dallas | 214-871-7444 | www.nick-sams.com

Surveyors salute this Uptown meat "mecca" – the "standard bearer" for Dallas beeferies – where "sublime seafood and steaks" come together with "waistline-busting" sides and a 500-label wine list in "dark", "clubby" quarters with a baby grand piano and "great bar" adding to the palpable "buzz"; the "knowledgeable staff" elevates it to among "the best in town" – "just be prepared for a bill as big as the bone-in rib-eye."

Nicola's *Italian* 24 | 25 | 22 | $40

Plano | Shops at Legacy | 5800 Legacy Dr. (Bishop Rd.) | 972-608-4455 | www.nicolaslegacy.com

Plano patrons "find *amore*" at this "sophisticated" spot where the "customer is always taken care of" and the "handmade pastas" win raves, as do more "innovative" offerings on the "pricey" Northern Italian menu; the "beautiful" two-story space is dressed in burgundy tones and accented with wrought-iron chandeliers, but the "energetic vibe" means that sometimes "it can be so noisy you can't hear yourself think."

	FOOD	DECOR	SERVICE	COST

N9ne Steakhouse Ⓩ *Steak* | 22 | 24 | 22 | $66 |

Victory Park | 3090 Olive St. (Houston St.) | Dallas | 214-720-9901 |
www.n9negroup.com

A "sceney" take on the classic steakhouse, this Victory Park "hot spot" (with outposts in Chicago and Sin City) piles on the "Vegas glitz" with "swanky" contemporary decor with suede booths, a "very noisy" clublike ambiance and a young "see-and-be-seen" crowd; yet while high rollers hail the "high-quality beef" and "inventive sides", the less starry-eyed claim it's "all hype" and "overpriced" to boot.

Nobu Dallas *Japanese* | 24 | 24 | 20 | $67 |

Uptown | Rosewood Crescent Hotel | 400 Crescent Ct.
(bet. Cedar Springs Rd. & Maple Ave.) | Dallas | 214-252-7000 |
www.noburestaurants.com

Dallas foodies feel "lucky to have this" "world-class" restaurant in Uptown's Crescent Court complex, an outpost of Nobu Matsuhisa's "famous" Peruvian-influenced Japanese chain and a "true dining experience" thanks to "fabulous food" (including "awesome" "melt-in-your-mouth sushi") and "way-cool decor"; be warned, though, that the "noise" from the "trendy" clientele can make it "hard to converse", while the "outrageous" "expense-account pricing" has some insisting that "better value can be found elsewhere."

NEW Nonna *Italian* | - | - | - | M |

Lemmon Avenue | 4115 Lomo Alto Dr. (bet. Bowser & Lemmon Aves.) |
Dallas | 214-521-1800 | www.nonnadallas.com

Park Cities foodies already seem smitten with this Lemmon Avenue Italian where an adventurous young chef offers an ever-changing menu of antipasti, handmade pastas and plates of halibut and porchetta, straight from the wood-burning oven; it's set in a low-key neighborhood storefront where brick walls, close tables and an open kitchen culminate in a satisfied dining din.

Nonna Tata Ⓜ⊅ *Italian* | - | - | - | M |

Hospital District | 1400 W. Magnolia Ave. (6th Ave.) | Ft. Worth |
817-332-0250

It's nearly impossible to snag one of the dozen tables at this no-reservations, cash-only, BYO trattoria in Ft. Worth's Hospital District; armed with no prior experience but a passion for cooking, chef-owner Donatella Trotti draws a loyal following thanks to her homey Italian cooking created from recipes handed down from her *nonna*.

Nuevo Leon Ⓩ *Mexican* | 22 | 13 | 20 | $20 |

Farmers Branch | 12895 Josey Ln. (Valley View Ln.) | 972-488-1984 |
www.nuevoleonrestaurant.net

"Buried in a Farmers Branch shopping center", this "locals" cantina "doesn't look like much", but customers claim the inexpensive, "authentic" Mexican dishes have had them "coming back for years"; though "nostalgics" "miss the original location" (lost in a fire some years ago), the "small" Josey Lane outpost decorated with Frida Kahlo paintings gets a boost from friendly service.

	FOOD	DECOR	SERVICE	COST

Oceanaire Seafood Room *Seafood* 24 | 23 | 23 | $51

Galleria | Westin Galleria Hotel | 13340 N. Dallas Pkwy.
(Lyndon B. Johnson Frwy.) | Dallas | 972-759-2277 |
www.theoceanaire.com
See review in Houston Directory.

Old Hickory Steakhouse *Steak* ▽ 21 | 21 | 22 | $73

Grapevine | Gaylord Texan Resort | 1501 Gaylord Trail (Rte. 26) |
817-778-1000 | www.gaylordhotels.com
Conventioneers corralled at the Gaylord Texan, a megaresort in
Grapevine, chow down at this top-of-the-line steakhouse where
chef Joanne Bondy (ex Ciudad) turns out "excellent" filets and a selection of seafood in a wood-paneled salon overlooking a tiny vineyard; though it's "not that popular with locals", it holds it own "in its
category" with courteous service pleasing the patrons.

Old Warsaw, The *Continental/French* 24 | 24 | 26 | $67

Uptown | 2610 Maple Ave. (bet. Cedar Springs Rd. & McKinney Ave.) |
Dallas | 214-528-0032 | www.theoldwarsaw.com
This 60-year-old Uptown bastion of "fine dining" continues to hold
court in a "romantic" "old-world" setting with a tuxedo-clad staff
and nightly piano and violin music adding to the overall "impeccable" level of service; even if it's not exactly "on the cutting-edge", it
still "serves up some of the best food in Dallas" with "exquisite"
Continental-French cuisine complemented by "wonderful wines";
N.B. jackets preferred.

Olenjack's Grille *American* ▽ 26 | 18 | 26 | $31

Arlington | Lincoln Sq. | 770 E. Road to Six Flags (Collins St.) |
817-226-2600 | www.olenjacksgrille.com
"A winner!" proclaim patrons of this Arlington entry where chef-
owner Brian Olenjack (of Reata) "takes pride in his food and it
shows" in the "creative" American cuisine that emphasizes local ingredients; add in "kid-friendly" service and fans find it's an "excellent value", even if some note the "shopping-center" setting doesn't
do it justice.

Olivella's *Pizza* 22 | 12 | 16 | $20

Park Cities | 3406 McFarlin Blvd. (Hillcrest Rd.) | Dallas | 214-528-7070 |
www.olivellas.com
"Finally, real pizza in Dallas" sigh those savoring the "superb" "thin-
crust" Neapolitan-style pies crafted from "fresh" ingredients and
fired in a wood-burning brick oven at this "welcome addition" to
Park Cities; "cute SMU" waitresses work the "crowded", "quirky"
slice of a restaurant, but with only seven tables of seating inside
(plus extras on the sidewalk), takeout is sometimes the best option.

Opa! Grille *Greek* ▽ 19 | 13 | 21 | $21

Preston Forest | 12829 Preston Rd. (Lyndon B. Johnson Frwy.) |
Dallas | 972-661-0134 | www.opagrille.com
The "tasty Greek dishes are prepared with care" and "reasonably
priced" at this "delightful mom and pop" near Preston Forest that ca-

ters to those who "just want a good meal"; some suggest "the decor is bizarre", but most say the "casual" space has a "coffee-shop appeal", and it earns more points still among the thrifty for its BYO policy.

Original Market Diner *Diner*

∇ 20 | 16 | 22 | $13

Market Center | 4434 Harry Hines Blvd. (Market Center Blvd.) | Dallas | 214-521-0992

"If you're on a budget and don't care about calories", this Market Center fixture is "the place to go" for "true Texas" staples – "from grits to chicken-fried steak" – dished out daily for breakfast and lunch; the "authentic" experience is further enhanced by "sassy" "beehived" waitresses providing sweet service.

Ovation *Southern*

- | - | - | M

West | 6115 Camp Bowie Blvd. (Bryant Irvin Rd.) | Ft. Worth | 817-732-8900 | www.ovationrestaurant.com

Ft. Worth diners are putting their hands together for this snazzy Camp Bowie venue where a diverse crowd of music lovers convenes for upscale soul food (like fried chicken and waffles or shrimp and jalapeño cheese grits) served to the tune of live jazz, rock and blues nightly; its colorful interior is lined with photos of performers ensuring there's plenty to please the eyes as well as the ears; N.B. on Sundays they host a gospel brunch.

Palm, The *Seafood/Steak*

24 | 19 | 24 | $56

West End | 701 Ross Ave. (Market St.) | Dallas | 214-698-0470 | www.thepalm.com

See review in San Antonio Directory.

Palomino *American/Mediterranean*

21 | 21 | 21 | $39

Uptown | 500 Crescent Ct. (bet. Cedar Springs Rd. & Maple Ave.) | Dallas | 214-999-1222 | www.palomino.com

"You'll never get a bad meal" at this national chain link, a New American–Med powerhouse at Uptown's Crescent Court complex, where all the "anything-but-commonplace" menu items "sound delicious – and are"; perhaps it's "not the scene" it once was, "but it's still a beautiful room" with "dependable service" and a "contemporary" feel that's ideal "for a power lunch" (and for happy hour too).

Pan Acean *Pan-Asian*

20 | 18 | 18 | $19

Coppell | 777 S. MacArthur Blvd. (Belt Line Rd.) | 972-745-7788 | www.panaceancoppell.com

"A smorgasbord" of "affordable" Asian options is what you'll find at this Coppell canteen catering to "neighborhood" denizens with a plethora of "fresh" options from Korea, Japan, Thailand and Vietnam; a "friendly" staff "makes [you] feel at home" in the casual "strip-mall" space while "delivery service" at night is a convenient bonus.

Pappadeaux *Seafood*

23 | 19 | 20 | $29

Oak Lawn | 3520 Oak Lawn Ave. (Lemmon Ave.) | Dallas | 214-521-4700
Duncanville | 800 Hwy. 67 E. (Cockrell Hill Rd.) | 972-572-0580
North Dallas | 10428 Lombardy Ln. (Northwest Hwy.) | Dallas | 214-358-1912

(continued)

Pappadeaux

North Dallas | 18349 N. Dallas Pkwy. (Frankford Rd.) | Dallas | 972-447-9616
Richardson | 725 S. Central Expwy. (Floyds Rd.) | 972-235-1181
Forest Park | 2708 West Frwy. (Park View Dr.) | Ft. Worth | 817-877-8843
Arlington | 1304 Copeland Rd. (Six Flags Dr.) | 817-543-0545
Bedford | 2121 Airport Frwy. (Central Dr.) | 817-571-4696
www.pappadeaux.com
See review in Houston Directory.

Pappas Bros. Steakhouse ☒ Steak | 27 | 24 | 25 | $62 |

Love Field | 10477 Lombardy Ln. (Northwest Hwy.) | Dallas | 214-366-2000 | www.pappasbros.com
See review in Houston Directory.

Parigi American/Mediterranean | 25 | 22 | 23 | $39 |

Oak Lawn | 3311 Oak Lawn Ave. (Hall St.) | Dallas | 214-521-0295 | www.parigirestaurant.com

"On the cutting-edge for over 25 years" this "urban" Oak Lawn boîte has a name that conjures up "gay Paree", but the "wonderful" menu actually tilts toward "unique" New American–Med dishes; it "packs a crowd" of "longtime residents" (some trying to "impress a date") thanks to servers who "make you feel like family" and a "charming" interior decorated with paintings by local artists.

Paris Coffee Shop ☒ American | 23 | 12 | 22 | $11 |

Hospital District | 704 W. Magnolia Ave. (Hemphill St.) | Ft. Worth | 817-335-2041 | www.pariscoffeeshop.net

"Basic diner food and decor, but good value" – that's how to become a "Ft. Worth institution", and this "legendary" "Traditional" American in the Hospital District has been doing just that since the 1920s, serving up "excellent old-fashioned, down-home cooking for breakfast and lunch" (sorry – no dinner service); when you're gorging on those "favorite chicken 'n' dumplings", though, "be sure to leave room for the sinful home-baked pies."

Park Cities Prime ☒ Steak | ▽ 16 | 21 | 22 | $56 |

Preston Center | 8411 Preston Rd. (Villanova Dr.) | Dallas | 214-691-7763 | www.parkcitiesprime.com

Maybe it's not quite "prime", but some surveyors say they still like this "pleasant" steakhouse in Preston Center (from the same owners of PoPoLos Cafe) set in a "beautifully" decorated space done up in a "clubby", "masculine" style; so even if regulars report the food is only "average", "live piano" (Monday–Saturday) and "attentive" barkeeps have turned it into a "local hangout" all the same.

Pasand Indian Cuisine Indian | ▽ 21 | 11 | 15 | $18 |

Richardson | 1377 W. Campbell Rd. (Coit Rd.) | 972-644-4447
Irving | 2600 N. Belt Line Rd. (Hwy. 183) | 972-594-0693
www.pasand.net

With branches in Irving and Richardson, this pair has "earned a reputation" for "excellent", "expertly spiced" North and South Indian

offerings; the "popular" "places are packed every lunch"-time since the "extensive buffet" is "a fabulous value", boasting a "good selection of both meat and vegetable dishes" and "flavorsome naan."

Pastazio's *Pizza*   22 | 12 | 17 | $16

Uptown | 3028 N. Hall St. (bet. Cole & McKinney Aves.) | Dallas | 214-969-5959
Addison | Addison Circle | 5026 Addison Circle (Spectrum Dr.) | 972-386-9200
www.pastazios.com

It's all about the pizza at these separately owned Addison and Uptown counter-service eateries where boosters boast the "huge", "thin-crust" slices taste like they came "right off the streets of Manhattan"; prices are "inexpensive" and delivery is a plus, so some say the biggest drawback is that they're "not open late" "after the bars close."

Patrizio *Italian*   21 | 20 | 19 | $28

Park Cities | Highland Park Vill. | 25 Highland Park Vill.
(bet. Livingston Ave. & Mockingbird Ln.) | Dallas | 214-522-7878
NEW Cedar Hill | Uptown Village Shopping Ctr. | 305 W. FM 1382 (Uptown Blvd.) | 972-291-2600
Plano | 1900 Preston Park Blvd. (Park Blvd.) | 972-964-2200
Highland Village | Shops at Highland Vill. | 4131 Deer Creek (2499 & FM 407) | 972-966-0809
www.patrizios.net

"Amazing pasta at surprisingly reasonable prices", and in portions that "could almost serve two people", draws crowds to this Italian trio, the original a "favorite spot in Highland Park Village" and younger siblings in Cedar Hill, Park Cities and Plano that present solid "value"; each is "popular at both lunch and dinner", so "be prepared for a wait" (and "sometimes slow service"), and if you find them too "noisy" inside, "sit out on" their "fabulous patios."

Peggy Sue BBQ *BBQ*   22 | 13 | 19 | $18

Park Cities | Snider Plaza | 6600 Snider Plaza (Daniel Ave.) | Dallas | 214-987-9188 | www.peggysuebbq.com

BBQ fans find the "down-home" grub "very tasty" at this "local" "fixture" in Snider Plaza specializing in oak-smoked meats enhanced with "spicy sauce" and offering a salad bar and a full lineup of veggies and sides; the "small", "homey" "'50s-flashback"-style space with cowhide tablecloths is "always crowded" with "families, students and couples" who appreciate the friendly "sit-down service" and "cheap" prices.

☑ Pei Wei Asian Diner *Pan-Asian*   19 | 15 | 16 | $15

Knox-Henderson | 3001 Knox St. (N. Central Expwy.) | Dallas | 214-219-0000
Preston Center | Preston Center Pavilion | 8305 Westchester Dr. (Luther Ln.) | Dallas | 214-765-9911
Addison | 4801 Belt Line Rd. (Addison Rd.) | 972-764-0844
North Dallas | 18204 Preston Rd. (Frankford Rd.) | Dallas | 972-985-0090
Allen | 1008 W. McDermott Dr. (I-75) | 469-675-2266
Irving | 7600 N. MacArthur Blvd. (bet. I-635 & President George Bush Tpke.) | 972-373-8000

(continued)

Pei Wei Asian Diner

Cultural District | Montgomery Plaza | 2600 W. Seventh St. (Carroll St.) | Ft. Worth | 817-806-9950

Southwest | 5900 Overton Ridge Rd. (Bryant Irvin Rd.) | Ft. Worth | 817-294-0808

Arlington | Village by the Parks | 4133 E. Cooper St. (Pleasant Ridge Rd.) | 817-466-4545

Southlake | 1582 E. Southlake Blvd. (Central Ave.) | 817-722-0070
www.peiwei.com
Additional locations throughout the Dallas/Ft. Worth area

There's "always a crowd" at this Pan-Asian chain (a "downscale" "little cousin" of P.F. Chang's), where the chow is "tasty", the menu "limited" and the service primarily "cafeteria-style"; a few sigh "boring", but "kids like it", the food "seems healthy" and, not incidentally, the "prices are really good."

Penne Pomodoro *Italian* | 19 | 15 | 17 | $23 |

Park Cities | Snider Plaza | 6815 Snider Plaza (Lovers Ln.) | Dallas | 214-373-9911

Preston Forest | Preston Forest Vill. | 11661 Preston Rd. (Forest Ln.) | Dallas | 214-368-3100
www.pennepomodoro.com

A "variety" of "reliable" Italian dishes attracts couples and "kids" to Alberto Lombardi's "down-to-earth" duo in the Park Cities and Preston Forest where "quality" wood-fired pizzas and pastas are turned out in "comfortable" shopping-center settings; "prompt service" and "low prices" make them a "solid option for a casual night out."

Pepe & Mito's Mexican Café *Mexican* | ∇ 22 | 16 | 25 | $15 |

Deep Ellum | 2911 Elm St. (bet. Malcolm X Blvd. & Walton St.) | Dallas | 214-741-1901

Supporters say this "locals'" cantina in Deep Ellum cooks up "tasty" Mexican and Tex-Mex specialties that keep them "coming back" for more; it's a "favorite" thanks to gentle prices, a colorful setting outfitted with a patio and a warm welcome from the family owners ("the nicest people you'll meet").

Perry's ⊠ *Steak* | 24 | 22 | 23 | $57 |

Uptown | 2911 Routh St. (Cedar Springs Rd.) | Dallas | 214-871-9991
www.perrys-dallas.com

Chef Travis Henderson is the "wizard in the kitchen" of this Uptown steakhouse, a "favorite" of many thirtysomethings, and his "expertise shines in both the seafood and beef departments"; the "clubby, dark and romantic" atmosphere makes it "better for intimate dinners than most" competitors, plus the "excellent bar" is a "great place to take a date or meet colleagues" – "without the noise and pretense" of the "singles scene that flocks to similar restaurants."

⊠ P.F. Chang's China Bistro *Chinese* | 22 | 22 | 20 | $27 |

NorthPark | NorthPark Ctr. | 225 Northpark Ctr. (Northwest Hwy.) | Dallas | 214-265-8669

(continued)

(continued)

P.F. Chang's China Bistro

North Dallas | 18323 N. Dallas Pkwy. (Frankford Rd.) | Dallas | 972-818-3336

Allen | Watters Creek at Montgomery Farm | 915 W. Bethany Dr. (Rte. 75) | 972-390-1040

Sundance Square | Bank One Bldg. | 400 Throckmorton St. (3rd St.) | Ft. Worth | 817-840-2450

Arlington | Arlington Highlands | 215 I-20 E. (Matlock Rd.) | 817-375-8690

Grapevine | 650 Hwy. 114 (bet. Main St. & William D. Tate Ave.) | 817-421-6658

www.pfchangs.com

Expect "major hustle-bustle" at this "noisy" Chinese chain where the "sanitized", "mass-produced" menus "aren't really authentic" yet do "appeal to most palates" (when in doubt, the "lettuce wraps rule"); no one minds the "spotty" service and "ersatz" Sino decor since they "have the formula down" – starting with "nothing-fancy" prices and an overall "fun" vibe.

Piccolo Mondo *Italian* ▽ 21 | 19 | 22 | $32

Arlington | Parkway Central Ctr. | 829 E. Lamar Blvd. (Collins St.) | 817-265-9174 | www.piccolomondo.com

Regulars report they're "never disappointed" at this "longtime" Arlington Italian turning out "well-prepared" dishes at moderate prices; in spite of its "nondescript strip-mall location", it remains a "neighborhood" standby thanks to "witty waiters", fair prices and live piano (Tuesday–Saturday).

Piranha Killer Sushi *Japanese* 25 | 21 | 20 | $36

Sundance Square | 335 W. Third St. (Throckmorton St.) | Ft. Worth | 817-348-0200

NEW **Arlington** | 309 Curtis Mathes Way (bet. Highlander Blvd. & Matlock Rd.) | 817-465-6455

Arlington | 851 NE Green Oaks Blvd. (Collins St.) | 817-261-1636

www.piranhakillersushi.com

"Killer sushi" is bested only by the "imaginative" maki in "wild" combinations (like shrimp tempura with avocado and pico de gallo) at these "lively" Japanese eateries that converts claim serve "the best" fish around; the "trendy" Sundance Square outpost boasts a "hip" scene for "twenty to thirtysomethings" that's as "vibrant" as the food, while the Arlington branch is more of an understated "find"; both boast the same "great" (if sometimes "slow") service and somewhat "pricey" tabs; N.B. the Curtis Mathes Way branch is new.

Poor Richard's Café *American* ▽ 20 | 9 | 21 | $11

Plano | 2442 K Ave. (Park Blvd.) | 972-423-1524 | www.poorrichardscafe.com

"Down-home" American cooking hits the spot for fans of this east Plano "classic" serving "tasty" breakfasts and lunches in a "noisy" setting decorated with "cute quotes" from Poor Richard's Almanac; it's a "friendly, hometown place" enhanced by "old-fashioned" touches like cheap tabs and "fast" service from "waitresses who call you 'hon.'"

	FOOD	DECOR	SERVICE	COST

PoPoLos Cafe *Italian*
20 | 18 | 21 | $38

Preston Royal | Preston Royal Shopping Ctr. | 5959 Royal Ln. (Preston Rd.) | Dallas | 214-692-5497 | www.popolos.com

A "convenient" stop for Preston Royal locals for more than a decade, this "neighborhood" Italian is "good for dates, business dinners or a family night out"; with its Med touches, the food is "reliably good" (if "not memorable"), plus the room is "seldom overcrowded" and there's "jazz to accompany the meal" Tuesday–Saturday nights.

Porch, The *American*
22 | 20 | 22 | $31

Knox-Henderson | 2912 N. Henderson Ave. (bet. Miller & Willis Aves.) | Dallas | 214-828-2916 | www.theporchrestaurant.com

A "young, hip" flock roosts at this Knox-Henderson "hot spot" from restaurateur Tristan Simon (Hibiscus and Cuba Libre) turning out "edgy" American "comfort food" – like brisket sliders and short-rib stroganoff – at prices so "affordable" habitués have adopted it as their new "casual" hangout; it can be "loud" and there are frequent "waits", so some suggest you pass the time with an "innovative" cocktail and some "great people-watching."

Positano 🖂 *Italian*
▽ 22 | 22 | 23 | $40

North Dallas | 18111 Preston Rd. (Frankford Rd.) | Dallas | 972-407-9180 | www.positanodallas.com

The warm "welcome" from chef-owner Antonio Avona kicks off an "enjoyable experience" at this "excellent" midpriced North Dallas eatery featuring a wide-ranging Italian menu; the "fabulous staff" adds to the appeal as does the warm interior with tile floors and vaulted ceilings that manages to be both "elegant" and "comfortable" at the same time.

Primo's Bar & Grille ● *Tex-Mex*
18 | 13 | 16 | $19

Uptown | 3309 McKinney Ave. (Hall St.) | Dallas | 214-220-0510
NEW **Garland** | 4861 Bass Pro Dr. (Chaha St.) | 972-226-8100

While its "dependable Tex-Mex" fare is certainly "good", this Uptown "hangout" "is all about getting to know your table-neighbor" – hence its rep as a "happenin' spot" for "twentysomethings who conduct mating rituals" "while sipping potent Meltdown margaritas" on the "popular patio"; still, those who find the grub "standard", the service "iffy" and the decor "lacking" see "no apparent reason" for its perpetually "packed" state; N.B. the Garland branch is new.

Purple Cow Diner *Diner*
14 | 15 | 15 | $14

Preston Royal | Preston Royal Vill. | 110 Royal Ln. (Preston St.) | Dallas | 214-373-0037
Plano | Lakeside Mkt. | 5809 Preston Rd. (bet. Parker Rd. & Spring Creek Pkwy.) | 972-473-6100
West | 4601 West Frwy. (Rte. 30) | Ft. Worth | 817-737-7177

It's "kiddie city" at this "family"-oriented mini-chain styled after a "1950s soda shop" with a jukebox spinning vintage tunes and a somewhat "generic" selection of American grub (burgers, chicken fingers) plus "decadent" "signature" milkshakes with "liquored up" versions for the adults; prices are "inexpensive", and though

service may be "slow", at least they handle the young 'uns with "humor and patience."

Pyramid Restaurant & Bar *American*

| - | - | - | E |

Arts District | Fairmont Dallas | 1717 N. Akard St. (Ross Ave.) | Dallas | 214-720-5249 | www.fairmont.com/dallas

A triangular napkin and diagonally placed flatware give a nod to its longtime moniker, but all else is renewed in this Arts District luxury hotel venue whose recent renovation imparted a sleek look with beige walls, polished wood floors, treelike sculptures and open wine storage; the locavore-leaning chef assembles New American dishes using regional ingredients like West Texas antelope and Wagyu strip loin enhanced by herbs and vegetables from the terrace garden; poised service and expense-account pricing complete the picture.

☑ Railhead Smokehouse Ⓢ *BBQ*

| 22 | 14 | 14 | $14 |

Cultural District | 2900 Montgomery St. (I-30) | Ft. Worth | 817-738-9808 | www.railheadonline.com

"Bikers", "attorneys" and other assorted "Tuppies (Texas urban professionals)" converge on this "lively" BBQ "institution" in Ft. Worth's Cultural District for "fallin'-off-the-bone-good" ribs and "tender" brisket washed down with "very cold beer"; "long" cafeteria-style "lines are typical, but flow quickly", even on Thursdays, when the bar fills up and this meat market quite literally turns into a "meet market"; N.B. drive-thru is also available.

Reata *Southwestern*

| 24 | 25 | 23 | $43 |

Sundance Square | 310 Houston St. (3rd St.) | Ft. Worth | 817-336-1009 | www.reata.net

"No cowboy ever ate so good" say those savoring the "fancied up ranch cuisine" at this "unique" eatery in Downtown Ft. Worth's Sundance Square where the "superb" Southwestern cuisine (especially "the to-die-for" tenderloin tamales) represents "upscale" "camp cooking at its best"; loads of "out-of-towners" fill the "over-the-top" cowhide-appointed interior rendering it rather "loud", so those in-the-know scamper to the rooftop bar for a quieter atmosphere in addition to "remarkable views" of the city skyline.

Red's Patio Grill *American*

| 20 | 18 | 19 | $22 |

Plano | Lakeside Mkt. | 4005 Preston Rd. (Lorimar Dr.) | 469-229-0098 | www.redspatiogrill.com

The "excellent margaritas" take center stage at this western Plano canteen boasting a collection of over 100 tequilas and a "lovely" "lakeside" patio that's the perfect spot for sipping; Traditional American entrees include rotisserie chicken and "great burgers" all at prices low enough to make it an easy pick for friends and "families" on the run.

Remington's Seafood Grill *Seafood*

| 21 | 15 | 20 | $30 |

Addison | 4580 Belt Line Rd. (Addison Rd.) | 972-386-0122 | www.remingtonseafoodgrill.com

For almost 30 years, the Remington family has been serving "consistently" "excellent" "fresh-fish" fare at this Addison "standby" fa-

vored by an "older" clientele; the decor may be "a bit tired", but "for the hungry seafood lover looking for value", such things pale next to "classic" cuisine, "friendly" service and "reasonable prices."

Rick's Chop House *Southern/Steak*

▽ 21 | 25 | 21 | $49

McKinney | Grand Hotel | 107 N. Kentucky St. (Louisianna St.) | 214-726-9251 | www.rickschophouse.com

Champions cheer this "great addition" to Downtown McKinney, the Grand Hotel's upscale steakhouse with a Southern-leaning menu featuring fried green tomatoes and smoked chicken plus a full lineup of steaks; set in the space that was once an opera house (circa 1885), it features a pressed tin ceiling and gas lanterns illuminating the "beautiful" room while it hangs onto a "small-town feel" thanks to a "knowledgeable staff" offering "accommodating" service.

NEW Rise N° 1 *French*

- | - | - | M

West Lovers Lane | Inwood Vill. | 5360 W. Lovers Ln. (Inwood Rd.) | Dallas | 214-366-9900 | www.risesouffle.com

It's all about the egg, from the shape of the room to what's rising in the ovens at this stylish French cafe on West Lovers Lane sporting a whimsical sprouting of birch trees in the center of the restaurant; the wallet-friendly menu focuses on both savory and sweet soufflés (it also offers sandwiches and salads) backed by a well-considered list of wines, which can be ordered by the glass, bottle or taste.

NEW Ristorante Cibus Caffé *Italian*

- | - | - | M

NorthPark | NorthPark Ctr. | 8687 N. Central Expwy. (Park Ln.) | Dallas | 214-692-0001 | www.cibusdallas.com

Part quick-bite cafe and part full-service ristorante, this Northern Italian trendsetter from Alberto Lombardi offers mall shoppers salads, panini and gelato as well as more involved preparations like risotto and sirloin with Gorgonzola butter; insulated from the frenetic shopping center that surrounds it, the sophisticated interior is accented with flaming orange Murano glass chandeliers and opens onto the serene sculpture garden of NorthPark Center; N.B. a second location will open at the Shops at Legacy.

Ristorante La Piazza *Italian*

26 | 25 | 22 | $49

University Area | University Park Vill. | 1600 S. University Dr. (bet. Old University Dr. & River Run) | Ft. Worth | 817-334-0000 | www.lapiazzafw.com

"A feast for the senses" awaits at this "elegant" University Area enclave where Ft. Worth's "upper crust" gathers for "incredible" "classic Italian" cuisine in a "transporting" setting with "opera playing quietly in the background"; though regulars report "marvelous" treatment, those not on the A-list find service "pretentious" and say the "stuffy" attitude "spoils" an otherwise pleasant experience; N.B. jacket suggested.

Roti Grill *Indian*

18 | 10 | 15 | $15

Knox-Henderson | 4438 McKinney Ave. (bet. Armstrong Ave. & Oliver St.) | Dallas | 214-521-3655

(continued)

(continued)

Roti Grill

Plano | 6509 W. Park Blvd. (Midway Blvd.) | 972-403-7600
www.freshindianfood.com

An "oasis" in the "virtual desert" of Dallas-area Indian options, this "casual" order-at-the-counter duo curries favor with fans thanks to "quality" "low-cost" masalas and tandooris served up "fast"; it works "in a pinch", though "nondescript" environs mean many opt for "takeout"; P.S. the Plano branch is BYO and has a "great lunch buffet."

Rough Creek Lodge *American* ▽ 27 | 28 | 28 | $60

Glen Rose | Rough Creek Lodge & Resort | County Rd. 2013 (U.S. 67) |
254-918-2550 | www.roughcreek.com

The "dramatic contemporary Western setting" of the Rough Creek Lodge & Resort affords "breathtaking views" of the landscape, but it's really the "superb" food that's "worth the trip" to this New American in Glen Rose; of course, there's also "excellent service" from an "attentive", "tireless staff", as well as the "rustic elegance" of its "wonderful atmosphere", which reminds some "of a secluded hunting lodge" where "nobility coming in from the hunt celebrate in grand style."

Royal Thai *Thai* 23 | 19 | 21 | $23

Greenville Avenue | 5500 Greenville Ave. (Lovers Ln.) | Dallas |
214-691-3555 | www.royalthaitexas.com

This Greenville Avenue Thai temple is "different from a lot of others" – "more of an elegant sit-down-and-linger-over-dinner kind of place"; we're talking "top-notch food at an incredibly inexpensive price" and "well presented" by a "wonderful restrained" staff, so "prepare to wait during prime hours on a Friday or Saturday."

Roy's *Hawaiian* 25 | 24 | 23 | $48

Plano | 2840 Dallas Pkwy. (bet. Park Blvd. & Parker Rd.) | 817-722-1533 |
www.roysrestaurant.com

The "next best thing to being oceanside in Maui", this "haute Hawaiian" chain via celeb chef Roy Yamaguchi is "fine dining" personified thanks to a "top-shelf" fusion menu that's as "eye-pleasing as it is palate-pleasing"; "great" service and "upscale-casual" atmospheres add to its luster, though given the "upmarket pricing", it does "taste better when someone else is paying."

Ruffino's Ristorante Italiano 🗷 *Italian* 22 | 18 | 23 | $30

Forest Park | 2455 Forest Park Blvd. (Park Hill Dr.) | Ft. Worth |
817-923-0522 | www.ruffinosfinedining.com

"After many years", this "old-world" "romantic Italian bistro" in Ft. Worth's Forest Park section "still doesn't disappoint" thanks to an "authentic menu" including "housemade pastas with fresh ingredients"; "its fine-dining atmosphere belies the casual, friendly service" of staffers who are so diligent "they practically greet you at your car."

Ruggeri's *Italian* 20 | 19 | 21 | $47

Preston Royal | 5950 Royal Ln. (Preston Rd.) | Dallas | 214-750-0111 |
www.ruggerisrestaurant.net

(continued)

Ruggeri's Colleyville *Italian*

Colleyville | 32 Village Ln. (Main St.) | 817-503-7373

This "neighborhood" Italian in Preston Royal from "friendly" owner Tom Ruggeri pleases loyal patrons who praise the "well-executed" fare, which they deem "worth it" even if it "won't knock your socks off"; still, some longtimers lament they miss the "older" incarnation and label the menu "mediocre" and the tabs "pricey" too; N.B. scores may not reflect the independently operated Colleyville branch.

Ruth's Chris Steak House *Steak* | 25 | 22 | 25 | $57 |

North Dallas | 17840 Dallas Pkwy. (bet. Frankford & Trinity Mills Rds.) | Dallas | 972-250-2244
NEW **Downtown Ft. Worth** | 813 Main St. (7th St.) | Ft. Worth | 817-348-0080
www.ruthschris.com
See review in San Antonio Directory.

Saffron House *Indian* | ▽ 20 | 21 | 18 | $25 |

Addison | Village on the Pkwy. | 5100 Belt Line Rd. (Dallas N. Tollway) | 972-239-1800 | www.thesaffronhouse.com

This Addison entry "raises the bar" for "Dallas-area" Indian food with "perfectly seasoned" curries in addition to an array of more "refined" dishes; diners deem the vividly colored decor "exotic without venturing toward tacky" and service seems "genuinely helpful", so the only downside, say sticklers, is "inconsistency."

⬛ Saint-Emilion ⬛Ⓜ *French* | 27 | 24 | 27 | $54 |

Cultural District | 3617 W. Seventh St. (Montgomery St.) | Ft. Worth | 817-737-2781

A "country French delight" in Ft. Worth's Cultural District, this "jewel" warmed by brick walls and a wood-beamed ceiling is "perfect for dates", presenting "amazing" "blackboard specials" matched by a "fabulous" wine list and "hospitality on the same delicious level as the food"; fans say the prix fixe option offers a real "value in dining" and, as tables are limited, recommend making "reservations."

Salum ⬛ *American* | 25 | 22 | 22 | $54 |

Uptown | 4152 Cole Ave. (Fitzhugh Ave.) | Dallas | 214-252-9604 | www.salumrestaurant.com

Admirers adore this "friendly, little" Uptown bistro helmed by chef-owner Abraham Salum whose "sophisticated" takes on "seasonal" New American cooking come at "reasonable" prices making it a "wonderful neighborhood spot"; don't be "deterred" by the strip-mall location because supporters say the "nondescript" exterior doesn't do justice to the "lovely", "understated room", or the "terrific" food.

Sambuca *Eclectic* | 21 | 23 | 19 | $38 |

Uptown | 2120 McKinney Ave. (Pearl St.) | Dallas | 214-744-0820
Addison | 15207 Addison Rd. (Belt Line Rd.) | 972-385-8455
www.sambucarestaurant.com

"Unwind" with "classy jazz" at this Dallas-based "supper club" chain, where "super" "live entertainment" enhances a "something-

for-everyone" lineup of "fusion-style" Eclectic cuisine; "lounge" habitués laud the "sophisticated" (if "loud") atmosphere, though some who claim it's "a little expensive for what you get" foodwise swing by solely "for the music" and "lively" "bar scene."

Sammy's Bar-B-Q ☒ BBQ — | - | - | I

Uptown | 2126 Leonard St. (Woodall Rodgers Frwy.) | Dallas | 214-880-9064 | www.sammysbbq.com

When it comes to slow-smoked meats slathered in piquant sauce, this lunch-only eatery is a top choice among local 'cue critics; now that the Preston Center locale has closed, the only choice for fans is the Uptown campsite (in the shadows of the Federal Reserve Bank), which caters to power brokers who fling their Hermès neckwear over their shoulder to avoid telltale grease stains.

Samui Thai Thai 24 | 23 | 23 | $25

Allen | Twin Creek Shopping Ctr. | 906 W. McDermott Dr. (I-75) | 972-747-7452

Plano | 5700 Legacy Dr. (Dallas N. Tollway) | 972-398-2807

www.samuithai.com

"Good enough to convert the picky", this pair of "friendly seafood-themed Thai places" in Allen and Plano features an "incredible menu with more choices than" many in the genre, all with "nary a trace of grease and oil"; it's "amazing what they did with strip-mall spaces", and the "great lunch specials" add to their "reasonable" rep.

S & D Oyster Company ☒ Seafood 23 | 16 | 22 | $25

Uptown | 2701 McKinney Ave. (Boll St.) | Dallas | 214-880-0111 | www.sdoyster.com

"For a bit of nostalgia, try this holdout" Uptown that's been serving "New Orleans–style" "seafood and oysters on the half shell" for 30-plus years; though it's a "no-frills place", the "loud" room's "unpretentious, old-timey" vibe is definitely part of the "fun", and the "superb staff" will really make "you feel at home."

Sangria Tapas y Bar Spanish 17 | 19 | 17 | $31

Knox-Henderson | 4524 Cole Ave. (Knox St.) | Dallas | 214-520-4863 | www.sangriatapasybar.com

"Trendy" foodies cram into this "noisy" Knox-Henderson site for a "little taste of Spain" thanks to "innovative" tapas and a festive, "crowded" interior decked out in imported Iberian tiles; yet while some customers cheer the "happening" scene, critics knock "inconsistent" fare that "costs too much" and say they "should have better sangria given their name."

Sapristi! Ⓜ Eclectic 24 | 20 | 21 | $31

Forest Park | 2418 Forest Park Blvd. (Park Hill Dr.) | Ft. Worth | 817-924-7231 | www.sapristibistro.com

"Cheery" and "relaxed", this "cute neighborhood bistro" is a "venerable" part of Ft. Worth's Forest Park district, with "fabulous, European-inspired" Eclectic cuisine that tastes "homemade"; "service can be a little slow for some city folks", but the "friendly and knowledgeable" staff will help you navigate the "ever-changing" list

	FOOD	DECOR	SERVICE	COST

of "fantastic, inexpensive" wines "selected for quality and value, and available for chump change."

Sardines Ristorante Italiano *Italian*

18	15	19	$27

Cultural District | 509 University Dr. (5th St.) | Ft. Worth | 817-332-9937

"Surprisingly good" Italian food is jazzed up by live music nightly at this "old mainstay" in Ft. Worth's Cultural District; "very dark" ("some say cozy") digs feature lots of "memorabilia" on the walls, though grousers who gripe they "can't see the menu" find the patio – now outfitted with a koi pond – a more agreeable and less "noisy" solution.

NEW Screen Door *Southern*

-	-	-	E

Arts District | One Arts Plaza | 1722 Routh St. (Flora St.) | Dallas | 214-720-9111 | www.screendoordallas.com

Southern cooking is elevated to white-tablecloth status at this gracious newcomer in One Arts Plaza inhabiting meticulous celery-and-wheat-hued digs decorated with both modern and homey touches; the gussied up dishes include chicken and dumplings and deconstructed lobster pot pie, which can be paired with wines or iced tea sided with shots of flavorful sweetening syrups; P.S. don't miss the decadent house dessert: a chocolate moon pie with an RC Cola chaser.

NEW Second Floor *American/French*

-	-	-	E

Galleria | Westin Galleria Hotel | 13340 N. Dallas Pkwy. (Lyndon B. Johnson Frwy.) | Dallas | 972-450-2978 | www.thesecondfloorrestaurant.com

This posh entry inside the recently renovated Westin Galleria serves up breakfast, lunch, dinner and bar bites in a glass-enclosed space dressed in soothing green tones; overseen by consulting chef Scott Gottlich (Bijoux), the French–New American menu roams from omelets to gourmet pizzas to shortribs – all artistically plated; N.B. it also offers over 80 varieties of scotch, available in glasses or flights.

Seventeen Seventeen Ⓜ *Eclectic*

22	21	20	$35

Arts District | Dallas Museum of Art | 1717 N. Harwood St. (Ross Ave.) | Dallas | 214-922-1858 | www.wynnwood.com

As "you'd expect", this "great place" in the Dallas Museum of Art is known for the "artfully" presented and "well-prepared Eclectic choices" on its "seasonal menu"; "relaxed service" is also a plus, but in the end, it's the "stylish decor" that makes it "very, very special" – perhaps even the "most elegant lunch spot in town"?

Sevy's Grill *American*

23	22	23	$40

Preston Center | 8201 Preston Rd. (Sherry Ln.) | Dallas | 214-265-7389 | www.sevys.com

Chef Jim 'Sevy' Severson is an "independent who excels at his work", namely creating "stellar food" at this "upscale-casual" Preston Center "neighborhood hangout" that fans feel is "the definition of what an American bistro should be"; regulars are also "fond of" the "even-keeled service" from the "professional" staff, including "bartenders who remember your name" and "really know how to pour a drink" – one reason for the "active bar scene."

Shinsei 🗷 *Pan-Asian*

25 | 23 | 22 | $49

West Lovers Lane | 7713 Inwood Rd. (W. Lovers Ln.) | Dallas | 214-352-0005 | www.shinseirestaurant.com

"Sexy atmosphere, sexy people, sexy food" sum up surveyors who "dress to the nines" for this "beautifully decorated" West Lovers Lane boîte backed by Lynae Fearing and Tracy Rathbun (wives of Dean and Kent); sure, it's a "swanky" scene, but surveyors swear the food is "phenomenal" too with "artfully presented" Pan-Asian dishes showcasing "brilliant flavors" plus "amazing service" and "designer libations" adding up to a "don't-miss" experience.

Silver Fox Steakhouse 🗷 *Steak*

24 | 22 | 23 | $54

Oak Lawn | Centrum Bldg. | 3102 Oak Lawn Ave. (Cedar Springs Rd.) | Dallas | 214-559-2442

Richardson | 3650 Shire Blvd. (Jupiter Rd.) | 972-423-8121

Frisco | 1303 Legacy Dr. (Hwy. 121) | 214-618-5220

University Area | 1651 S. University Dr. (I-30) | Ft. Worth | 817-332-9060

Grapevine | 1235 William D. Tate Ave. (Hwy. 114) | 817-329-6995 www.silverfoxsteakhouse.com

"If you want a fancy steak dinner without being expected to dress up", these "crowded" younger siblings of III Forks do the trick; with an "impeccable menu, superior service" and a "dark, romantic atmosphere", they offer a "more modern Texas steakhouse" experience, and their "value" also sets them apart – "side dishes are included with the price of the meal."

Sonny Bryan's Smokehouse *BBQ*

22 | 12 | 16 | $16

Downtown Dallas | Republic Ctr. | 325 N. St. Paul St. (Pacific Ave.) | Dallas | 214-979-0102 🗷

West End | 302 N. Market St. (Pacific Ave.) | Dallas | 214-744-1610

Galleria | 13375 Noel Rd. (bet. James Temple Dr. & Peterson Ln.) | Dallas | 214-295-1497 🗷

Love Field | 2202 Inwood Rd. (Harry Hines Blvd.) | Dallas | 214-357-7120 🗷

Preston Forest | Preston Forest Vill. | 11661 Preston Rd. (Forest Ln.) | Dallas | 214-234-0888

West Lovers Lane | 5519 W. Lovers Ln. (Inwood Rd.) | Dallas | 214-351-2024

Richardson | Pavilion Park Ctr. | 1251 W. Campbell Rd. (Coit Rd.) | 972-664-9494

Las Colinas | Las Colinas Plaza | 4030 N. MacArthur Blvd. (Northgate Dr.) | Irving | 972-650-9564

Alliance | Alliance Ctr. | 2421 Westport Pkwy. (I-35) | Ft. Worth | 817-224-9191 www.sonnybryans.com

"It'd be hard to find better BBQ" – "served without decor or great service, just like it should be" – than at this Love Field–area "institution" that's spawned a slew of satellites; "a true melting pot of Dallas", it's peopled by everyone "from day laborers to billionaires", all tucking into "reliable beef sandwiches, monster onion rings" and "ice-cold beers" plunked down on "grease-stained picnic tables" by servers "with an attitude" in "a shack right out of central casting."

	FOOD	DECOR	SERVICE	COST

Sonoma Grill & Wine Bar 🗷 *American* ▽ 22 | 19 | 19 | $37

Flower Mound | Parker Sq. | 380 Parker Sq. (Main St.) | 972-899-8989 | www.sonomagrill-winebar.com

"Lucky" Flower Mound is home to this "little gem" in the Parker Square shopping center where the "fabulous" New American fare is bested only by the "strong selection" of Northern California vinos; regulars who bask on the covered patio insist you'll "feel you've been whisked off to wine country" with coddling service adding to the appeal.

Spiral Diner & Bakery Ⓜ *Diner/Vegetarian* ▽ 23 | 22 | 21 | $14

NEW | **Oak Cliff** | 1101 N. Beckley Ave. (Zang Blvd.) | Dallas | 214-948-4747

Hospital District | 1314 W. Magnolia Ave. (6th Ave.) | Ft. Worth | 817-332-8834

www.spiraldiner.com

"Vegetarians", "your friends from California" and even "carnivores" all appreciate the "imaginative", "delicious" vegan fare and "socially conscious" vibe at this "funky" outpost in an "up-and-coming" area around Ft. Worth's Hospital District; 1950s-style diner digs get a modern kick from the tattooed staff, while prices remain delightfully retro; N.B. the Oak Cliff branch is new.

State & Allen Lounge *American* ▽ 19 | 16 | 19 | $22

Uptown | 2400 Allen St. (State St.) | Dallas | 214-239-1990 | www.stateandallen.com

Chef-owners Jonathan Calabrese and Joseph Hickey migrated from their shuttered Savory in Lakewood to launch this New American bistro in Uptown, featuring "delicious" "cutting-edge creations" and a broad wine list boasting "all kinds and all prices"; adding to the allure are a "friendly staff" and a "charming atmosphere", all of which makes many willing to overlook the fact that it's somewhat "expensive."

Steel *Japanese/Vietnamese* 25 | 23 | 21 | $50

Oak Lawn | Centrum Bldg. | 3102 Oak Lawn Ave. (Cedar Springs Rd.) | Dallas | 214-219-9908 | www.steeldallas.com

Yes, this "trendy" Oak Lawn "place to be seen" is filled with "sports figures" and "young", "beautiful people", but supporters insist its "sexy", "urban-chic decor", "fantastic wine list" and "amazing" Japanese-Vietnamese cuisine (including "creatively presented sushi") "back up the flash"; a few find it "pretentious" and "noisy", but more maintain it's "a favorite place to take out-of-towners, who are surprised to find something other than steak in Dallas."

🆉 Stephan Pyles 🗷 *Southwestern* 27 | 28 | 26 | $65

Arts District | 1807 Ross Ave. (St. Paul St.) | Dallas | 214-580-7000 | www.stephanpyles.com

"Father of Southwestern cuisine" Stephan Pyles "has his groove back" say fans of this "elegant but relaxed" Dallas Arts District "hot spot" where he reprises some of his "classic" menu items while also "branching out into newer territory", mixing ingredients "you never expect to mesh"; though some say it can get "way too noisy", most

concur that the "great lighting and architecture" create a "beyond phenomenal" package that's "classy down to the waiter's attire", making it "worth every cent and more."

Steve Fields Steak & Lobster Lounge *Seafood/Steak*

| 23 | 22 | 23 | $52 |

Plano | 5013 W. Park Blvd. (Preston Rd.) | 972-596-7100 | www.stevefieldsrestaurant.com

Carnivores claim this western Plano beefery lives up to "everything a steak place should be" with "first-rate" filets and seafood sent out in a "smart" space hosted by namesake Steve Fields who "personally drops by your table" ensuring an "all-around" "great experience"; despite a few quibbles about "noise level", the white-tablecloth setting fits the bill for an adult night out with "premium" prices to match.

St. Martin's Wine Bistro *American/French*

| 26 | 24 | 25 | $39 |

Greenville Avenue | 3020 Greenville Ave. (Monticello Ave.) | Dallas | 214-826-0940 | www.stmartinswinebistro.com

Regulars report this "elegant" hideaway "tucked in an unassuming row of shops on Lower Greenville" "has it all" from a "delightful" French-accented American menu to a "romantic" "softly lit" mahogany-trimmed room where live "piano is a plus"; a "welcoming" team ensures a "pleasant" atmosphere, making it a "reliable" well-priced pick for "anniversary dinners" or for a "nice", leisurely brunch.

Sullivan's Steakhouse *Steak*

| 24 | 23 | 23 | $53 |

North Dallas | 17795 Dallas Pkwy. (Briargrove Ln.) | Dallas | 972-267-9393 | www.sullivanssteakhouse.com

See review in Austin and the Hill Country Directory.

NEW Sushi Axiom *Japanese*

| - | - | - | M |

Knox-Henderson | 2323 N. Henderson Ave. (Capitol Ave.) | Dallas | 214-828-2288
Southwest | Chapel Hill Ctr. | 4625 Donnelly Ave. (Hulen St.) | Ft. Worth | 817-735-9100
www.sushiaxiom.net

Riding the region's sushi swell, this avant-garde duo in Dallas and Southwest Ft. Worth seeks to satisfy the hipster contingent with an array of Japanese preparations from raw fare to beef tenderloin with pepper sauce; both serve up the well-priced eats with signature cocktails in moderately stylish surroundings; N.B. the Henderson Avenue branch also offers happy-hour specials.

Sushi Zushi *Japanese*

| 21 | 20 | 17 | $29 |

Oak Lawn | Turtle Creek Shopping Ctr. | 3858 Oak Lawn Ave. (Blackburn St.) | Dallas | 214-522-7253 | www.sushizushi.com

See review in San Antonio Directory.

Suze 🗷 Ⓜ *Mediterranean*

| 26 | 19 | 24 | $41 |

Preston Hollow | Villages of Preston Hollow | 4345 W. Northwest Hwy. (Midway Rd.) | Dallas | 214-350-6135 | www.suzerestaurant.net

"Expertly prepared" dishes from a "frequently changing" Med menu keep crowds coming to this "upscale" "little neighborhood jewel"

"hidden" in a Preston Hollow strip center; it "never fails to deliver" thanks to "quiet", "cozy digs", a "courteous" staff and "personal attention" from chef-owner Gilbert Garza.

Sweet Basil *Italian*   ▽ 23 | 19 | 24 | $24

North Dallas | 17610 Midway Rd. (Trinity Mills Rd.) | Dallas | 972-733-1500 | www.sweetbasilitalian.com

A "rare find" in North Dallas, this family-friendly Italian standby differentiates itself from the nearby chains with "attentive" servers who always "remember you" and solid takes on old-school "classics" like shrimp scampi and eggplant parmigiana; a few find it "bland", but the "affordable" prices usually win them over.

Szechuan Chinese *Chinese*   20 | 14 | 19 | $18

Southwest | 4750 Bryant Irvin Rd. (I-20) | Ft. Worth | 817-346-6111
West | 5712 Locke Ave. (bet. Camp Bowie Blvd. & Horne St.) | Ft. Worth | 817-738-7300 | www.entreesontrays.com

Aficionados aver "you can't go wrong" at this Chinese staple in West Ft. Worth or its Southwest spin-off, each of which has a "long track record" for "reliable food", "consistent service" and a "quiet" setting that's "good for the soul"; modernists might fault the fare as "not cutting-edge", but traditionalists testify that it's "excellent Sichuan"; P.S. don't miss the "value-priced lunches."

Taco Diner *Mexican*   20 | 17 | 18 | $20

Preston Center | 4011 Villanova St. (Preston Center Pl.) | Dallas | 214-696-4944
West Village | West Vill. | 3699 McKinney Ave. (Lemmon Ave.) | Dallas | 214-521-3669
Las Colinas | 5904 N. MacArthur Blvd. (Hwy. 114) | Irving | 972-401-2691
Plano | Shops at Legacy | 7201 Bishop Rd. (Legacy Dr.) | 469-241-9945
Southlake | Southlake Town Sq. | 432 Grand Ave. W. (Southlake Blvd.) | 682-651-6426
www.mcrowd.com

Brought to you by the M Crowd, who also own Mi Cocina and Mercury Grill, these members of an "authentic Mexico City taqueria" family bring "a citified and healthful flair" to the "pretty food" they purvey to "pretty people" within a "modern atmosphere" that's "more upscale than your typical Mexican place"; perhaps the "service could be better at times", but not to worry – "the people-watching is superb."

Taverna Pizzeria & Risotteria *Italian*   23 | 20 | 20 | $30

Knox-Henderson | 3210 Armstrong Ave. (Travis St.) | Dallas | 214-520-9933
Sundance Square | Sundance Sq. | 450 Throckmorton St. (4th St.) | Ft. Worth | 817-885-7502
www.tavernabylombardi.com

"The Lombardi family really got it right" with these "hip, upscale" "favorites" focused on "fantastic Italian food" including "to-die-for risotto" and "tasty, thin-crust pizza"; the "bustling urban-style setting" and "cute, attentive waiters" make it "wonderful for meeting friends and lovers" – "the only problems are the wait" and "noise."

	FOOD	DECOR	SERVICE	COST

NEW Tei An 🚫 *Japanese* — — — M

Arts District | One Arts Plaza | 1722 Routh St. (Flora St.) | Dallas | 214-220-2828

Chef-owner Teiichi Sakurai, who introduced Dallas to top-drawer sushi and robata at Teppo and Tei Tei, brings another Japanese first to town, this Arts District soba house crafting slurpilicious strands of buckwheat pasta served hot or cold with an array of dipping sauces and broths; a limited lineup of sushi and tempura plus sho-chu, sake and cocktails complete the offerings, which are presented in a tranquil dining room with a window peeking onto the noodle-makers in action.

Z Tei Tei Robata Bar M *Japanese* — 28 | 23 | 23 | $48

Knox-Henderson | 2906 N. Henderson Ave. (Willis Ave.) | Dallas | 214-828-2400 | www.teiteirobata.com

"Some of the best sushi in Dallas" shout aficionados at this "noisy" Knox-Henderson Japanese catering to a "hip" crowd with "fantas-tic" fish and a "wonderful" selection of grilled dishes served by a "warm" staff; it's "often very crowded", but fans find it's "worth the wait" and the somewhat "pricey" tabs.

Z Teppo Yakitori & Sushi Bar M *Japanese* — 28 | 22 | 25 | $45

Greenville Avenue | 2014 Greenville Ave. (Prospect Ave.) | Dallas | 214-826-8989 | www.teppo.com

It's "like a top yakitori restaurant in Tokyo" rave devotees of this "real-deal" Greenville Avenue Japanese that dishes out "killer sushi" and "great grilled" meats by chefs who clearly show "care in the preparation" of "fresh, fresh, fresh" food; adding to the "wonderful experience", its minimally decorated space (with semi-private tatami rooms for parties) feels "swanky yet comfortable", prices are "reasonable" and the staff is "welcoming" – just "be prepared for a long wait."

Terilli's *Italian* — 20 | 18 | 19 | $31

Greenville Avenue | 2815 Greenville Ave. (Vickery Blvd.) | Dallas | 214-827-3993

Frisco | 4226 Preston Rd. (bet. Lebanon Rd. & Warren Pkwy.) | 214-387-4600

www.terillis.com

"Heavenly" signature "Italian nachos" stand out among the "down-to-earth Italian fare" at Jeannie Terilli's twin "standbys" in Frisco and the Greenville Avenue area; served by staffers "you can depend on", the eats are complemented by the "coldest martinis in town" and "reasonably priced" wines, while "live jazz music" ("a great bonus", if sometimes "a little loud") and breezy patios augment the "inti-mate" feel of the dark, candlelit interiors.

Texas de Brazil *Brazilian/Steak* — 24 | 23 | 24 | $52

Uptown | 2727 Cedar Springs Rd. (bet. Carlisle & Woodrow Sts.) | Dallas | 214-720-1414

Addison | 15101 Addison Rd. (Belt Line Rd.) | 972-385-1000

	FOOD	DECOR	SERVICE	COST

(continued)

Texas de Brazil

Downtown Ft. Worth | 101 N. Houston St. (Weatherford St.) | Ft. Worth | 817-882-9500
www.texasdebrazil.com

Bring a "Texas-sized appetite" to these all-you-can-eat Brazilian steakhouses - a veritable "meat orgy" where an "unending" parade of "delicious" cuts are proffered by "gaucho"-clad servers and "even a vegetarian" "won't leave hungry" thanks to the "huge" salad bar stocked with "fabulous" goodies; though the less-impressed label them "gimmicky" and "overpriced", backers boast that "considering the amount you get for your money" "at least you won't leave hungry."

III Forks *Steak* 25 | 24 | 24 | $60

North Dallas | 17776 Dallas Pkwy. (bet. Frankford & Trinity Mills Rds.) | Dallas | 972-267-1776 | www.3forks.com

See review in Austin and the Hill Country Directory.

Tillman's Roadhouse [S] [M] *American* 23 | 25 | 22 | $33

Oak Cliff | 324 W. Seventh St. (Madison Ave.) | Dallas | 214-942-0988 |
www.tillmansroadhouse.com

"Diners south of the Trinity" are singing praises for "roadhouse mama" Sara Tillman's "sassy" Oak Cliff creation - a revamp of her original Tillman's Corner - that's "getting better all the time" thanks to chef Dan Landsberg's "adventurous" American comfort food and equally "daring", "over-the-top" Western-style decor fancied up with crystal chandeliers; though lauded as a "breath of fresh air" in the emerging Bishop Arts District, wallet-watchers lament it's "more expensive" than they were expecting given the "funky" setting.

Tipperary Inn *Pub Food* ∇ 18 | 22 | 19 | $17

Lakewood | 5815 Live Oak St. (Skillman St.) | Dallas | 214-821-6500 |
www.tippinn.com

More a "great bar" than an eatery, this classic-looking, dark-wood Emerald Isle pub in Lakewood gets its patrons' Irish up with the help of an "international beer selection", live Celtic music, dartboards and a "lively atmosphere"; still, tasters attest that downing "a pint of Guinness" and a "heaping helping of fish 'n' chips" will make you "feel like you're no longer in Dallas."

Tom Tom Asian Grill & Sushi Bar *Pan-Asian* 20 | 18 | 16 | $26

West Village | West Vill. | 3699 McKinney Ave. (Lemmon Ave.) |
Dallas | 214-522-9866 | www.tomtomasiangrill.com

Devotees beat the drum for this "trendy" boîte in McKinney Avenue's "über-hip West Village" shopping center, calling its Pan-Asian provender "tasty, easy on the wallet" and fine for a "quick bite"; the modern, "minimalist-Zen" interiors are "pleasant" but alfresco fans particularly recommend "dining on the patio" and "watching the cool crowd walk by"; disappointed dissenters dis "declining" service and "wish their food were as hot as their spot."

Toulouse Café & Bar *French*

19 | 20 | 18 | $35

Knox-Henderson | 3314 Knox St. (Travis St.) | Dallas | 214-520-8999 | www.toulousecafeandbar.com

"Very Parisian" proclaim patrons of this "bustling" bistro nestled in Knox-Henderson that buzzes with "beautiful people" munching "well-prepared" French specialties (like mussels cooked four different ways) in a "noisy" space outfitted with cushy red booths and a lively streetside patio; despite some quibbles about "inconsistent" service, most diners deem it "quite enjoyable" for a leisurely brunch, an "afternoon drink" or an "easy night out."

⚡ Trader Vic's *Polynesian*

19 | 26 | 20 | $46

Park Cities | Hotel Palomar | 5330 E. Mockingbird Ln. (Homer St.) | Dallas | 214-823-0600 | www.tradervicsdallas.com

"Shuttered for 20 years", this "kitschy" Polynesian paradise reopened in its original location adjacent to Park Cities' Hotel Palomar and was immediately embraced by nostalgic Dallasites delighting in the "overflowing rum drinks" and "glorious faux-island decor"; a few pooh-pooh the "mediocre" food (although "the pupu platter is a must"), but supporters swear they "love" this "tiki time warp" that takes you "back to the '60s", that is, at least "until you get the check."

Tramontana 🅂 Ⓜ *American*

23 | 19 | 22 | $47

Preston Center | Preston Center Pavilion | 8220 Westchester Dr. (bet. Luther & Sherry Lns.) | Dallas | 214-368-4188 | www.mybistro.net

A "wonderful, intimate dining experience" awaits at this "charming" "chef-owned neighborhood" bistro "tucked away" in Preston Center with a "creative menu" of New American fare featuring "refined country-style French" and Italian influences, along with a list of "well-priced wines"; its dark, casual environment is "without pretense", plus the "attentive service" makes eating here "like dining in the home of good friends."

Trece *Mexican/Southwestern*

21 | 21 | 20 | $41

Knox-Henderson | 4513 Travis St. (bet. Armstrong Ave. & Knox St.) | Dallas | 214-780-1900 | www.trecerestaurant.com

It's "quite the scene" at this "chic" Knox-Henderson hangout catering to a "chichi crowd" with "innovative" Southwestern and Mexican dishes (the lobster nachos are a "favorite") and "enticing cocktails" crafted from over 100 tequilas; some diners demur on "uneven service" and "expensive" tabs, but "trendy" types tout it as a "fun" experience as long as you're prepared for the "ear-splitting" acoustics.

Truluck's *Seafood*

23 | 22 | 23 | $44

Uptown | 2401 McKinney Ave. (Maple Ave.) | Dallas | 214-220-2401
Addison | 5001 Belt Line Rd. (Quorum Dr.) | 972-503-3079
Southlake | Southlake Town Sq. | 1420 Plaza Pl. (Grand Ave.) | 817-912-0500
www.trulucks.com

Those in need of a "stone crab fix" seek out this "popular" chain of upscale seafood specialists where the "incredible" crustaceans are "the highlight" of a "satisfying" lineup of "fresh fish", "quality

steaks" and a "marvelous" collection of wines; "handsome" decor and "attentive" service add to the appeal, though a chorus of critics claim it's "not impressed" with what it dubs "mediocre" eats and an overall "formulaic" experience.

2900 🖥 Ⓜ *American/Eclectic* | 23 | 18 | 20 | $44 |

Uptown | 2900 Thomas Ave. (Allen St.) | Dallas | 214-303-0400 | www.2900restaurant.com

Behind this unadorned Uptown facade lies one of the "best moderately priced" restaurants around exclaim enthusiasts who "absolutely love the manchego stuffed beef tenderloin" and other "unique, high-end" New American–Eclectic eats; with a "quaint" interior, "friendly" service and "good-value" tabs, it's "great before the symphony", with a "date" or on a casual night out.

Uncle Buck's Brewery & Steakhouse *Steak* | 19 | 21 | 20 | $36 |

Grapevine | 2501 Bass Pro Dr. (Hwy. 121) | 214-513-2337 | www.unclebucks.com

Hunters are in heaven at this larger-than-life lodge-themed steakhouse adjacent to the Bass Pro sporting goods shop in Grapevine featuring "cowboy"-sized steaks and house brews on tap all at moderate prices; the "festive" atmosphere makes it especially "good for groups."

Veracruz Café *Mexican* | 24 | 21 | 21 | $25 |

Oak Cliff | 408 N. Bishop Ave. (8th St.) | Dallas | 214-948-4746

"Excellent, original Mexican cuisine" "with a twist" is on the menu at this Oak Cliff spot in the Bishop Arts District, where "everything tastes homemade", including "coastal dishes that are a refreshing change" of pace; a limited number of seats makes it "perennially packed" – and leads some to sigh that it's just "too small" – but at least you get "nice, personal service from the owners."

Via Reál *Mexican* | 23 | 20 | 21 | $34 |

Las Colinas | 4020 N. MacArthur Blvd. (Byron Nelson Way) | Irving | 972-650-9001 | www.viareal.com

It's "not just the standard Mexican cuisine" among the "novel offerings" at this "classy" cantina that's "still a favorite" after more than 20 years, as the "nice variety" on its menu also includes "wonderful Southwestern cuisine"; its "nice, tableclothed" Las Colinas setting is "relaxing and attractive", with a distinct Santa Fe vibe, and the "so-attentive" staffers ensure a "perfect work lunch or special meal."

Victory Tavern City Grille 🖥 *American* | 15 | 18 | 17 | $29 |

Victory Park | 2501 N. Houston St. (Olive St.) | Dallas | 214-432-1900 | www.victorytavern.com

"Much nicer" looking than the name suggests, this sleek, minimalist eatery in Victory Park proffers "solid", "upscale" takes on American "bar food" and pairs them with an "excellent" selection of wines by the glass; yet "save for the gorgeous decor" several sum up the experience as "disappointing" though they admit it works for "a quick bite" "before or after one of the events at the American Airlines center."

NEW Villa-O *Italian*

| | | | M |

Knox-Henderson | Travis Walk | 4514 Travis St. (Knox St.) | Dallas | 214-780-1880 | www.villaorestaurant.com

Restaurateur Robert Colombo is behind this nautically themed Knox-Henderson Italian right across from buzzing sib Trece, where tony passengers come aboard for wood-fired pizzas and handmade pastas made from organic ingredients plus half-bottles of wines and the signature frozen peach Bellinis; though prices aren't cheap, the three-course Sunday night family special – boasting free meals for kids – is sure to be a hit with wallet-watchers.

Watel's Allen Street Cottage Ⓜ *French*

| 24 | 20 | 21 | $47 |

Uptown | 2207 Allen St. (bet. Hallsville & Thomas Sts.) | Dallas | 214-720-0323 | www.watels.com

Tucked into a charming cottage, this "traditional" country French "is a nice change of pace" in trendy Uptown, and the "perfect romantic date" spot; "chef-owner René Peeters knows his stuff for sure", turning out a "great variety" of "consistently delicious dishes", including "to-die-for sweetbreads" (it's "the place for offal"); some cluck that he "should learn how to do more vegetables", but factor in "nice service" and it all adds up to "real value."

Who's Who Burgers *Burgers*

| 18 | 9 | 13 | $14 |

Park Cities | Highland Park Vill. | 69 Highland Park Vill. (bet. Mockingbird Ln. & Preston Rd.) | Dallas | 214-522-1980 | www.whoswhoburgers.com

"Kobe beef" patties clinch it for the "well-heeled clientele" at this Highland Park Village "gourmet" burger "joint" with a plethora of "tasty" between-the-bun offerings plus sea-salt sprinkled fries and thick shakes all at "expensive" prices befitting its ritzy address; order-at-the-counter service is "fast", but with only a smattering of stools inside, many maintain it's "better for takeout."

NEW Woodlands *American*

| | | | M |

Preston Forest | 6073 Forest Ln. (Preston Rd.) | Dallas | 972-239-2024
Allen | Watters Creek at Montgomery Farm | 932 Garden Park Dr. (W. Bethany Dr.) | 214-495-7000
www.woodlands-grill.com

These new chain outposts in Allen and Preston Forest offer up a wide-spanning American menu featuring items like Kobe brisket sliders and roast chicken paired with well-priced wines and intriguing cocktails; both inhabit striking Frank Lloyd Wright–inspired digs with lots of stacked stone, hardwood floors and heated patios, making them both casual enough for a gathering of friends, but also suitable for business dinners.

Y.O. Ranch Steakhouse *Steak*

| ▽ 19 | 21 | 19 | $41 |

West End | 702 Ross Ave. (Market St.) | Dallas | 214-744-3287 | www.yoranchsteakhouse.com

Branded with the name of a "famous" Kerrville ranch, this "upscale" West End steakhouse is "the place to go for game", prime cuts of beef and other "creative cowboy" dishes served in a "nostalgic, chuck

wagon" setting decorated with artifacts from its namesake inspiration; prices are comparable to other cow palaces making it a concierge's choice for conventiongoers and other "tourists."

⚖ York Street ⚧Ⓜ American | 27 | 20 | 26 | $58 |

Lakewood | 6047 Lewis St. (Skillman St.) | Dallas | 214-826-0968 |
www.yorkstreetdallas.com

Chef-owner Sharon Hage's "artistry" makes for "beautifully conceived and executed" New American dishes incorporating "locally fresh" ingredients at this "teeny-tiny", hard-to-find "old house" on the outskirts of Lakewood; while some find the space "sparse" and "cramped", most agree the servers are "wonderful" (even if they sometimes "concentrate on regulars") and the food offers "substantial rewards" at "fair prices" for those willing to "reserve well in advance."

⚖ Yutaka Sushi Bistro ⚧ Japanese | 27 | 19 | 22 | $45 |

Uptown | 2633 McKinney Ave. (Boll St.) | Dallas | 214-969-5533 |
www.yutakasushibistro.com

"Locals" lament "the secret is out" at this Uptown Japanese that's "packed" with fin-addicts feasting on "outstanding sushi" and "phenomenal grilled dishes", all best appreciated via an "omakase meal" that's "to die for"; the space is "small", but "down-to-earth prices" and a "friendly" staff compensate for occasional "waits."

Zander's House Vietnamese | ∇ 23 | 18 | 23 | $24 |

Plano | 2300 N. Central Expwy. (Park Blvd.) | 972-943-9199 |
www.zandershouse.com

Relocated from the Big Apple, this relative newcomer to the Plano dining scene captures a neighborhood crowd with an "interesting variety" of "well-done" Vietnamese dishes (like "beautifully cooked fish") tagged with prices that won't bust your budget; though it's set off of I-75, it cultivates a "nice atmosphere" thanks to its whitewashed setting and "friendly service" from the family owners.

Zeke's Fish & Chips Seafood | ∇ 24 | 13 | 14 | $13 |

West | 5920 Curzon Ave. (Camp Bowie Blvd.) | Ft. Worth | 817-731-3321 |
www.zekesfishandchips.com

Fry fetishists seek out this "hole-in-the-wall" seafooder in West Ft. Worth where the "crisp", "nongreasy" fish 'n' chips earn raves from even the pickiest Brit; prices are cheap, and order-at-the-counter and drive-thru service efficient, so even if it may not be the most "healthy" experience (though they do offer some "good" clam chowder and shrimp gumbo), converts claim you'll always leave here "happy and full"; N.B. there's also an outdoor beer garden.

Ziziki's Restaurant & Bar Greek | 24 | 19 | 21 | $32 |

Knox-Henderson | Travis Walk | 4514 Travis St. (Knox St.) | Dallas |
214-521-2233
Preston Forest | Preston Forest Vill. | 11661 Preston Rd. (Forest Ln.) |
Dallas | 469-232-9922
www.zizikis.com

It's a consensus: "excellent Greek cuisine" blesses both the original Knox-Henderson location and the Preston Forest spin-off of this

"always-reliable" pair whose "upbeat" environments are "great for a big group"; the "warm", "friendly staffers" provide "attentive" service, but be warned that the spaces are so "small" that "you might get to know the folks at the next table before the night's over."

Zodiac, The 🗷 *American* | 24 | 22 | 23 | $30

Downtown Dallas | Neiman Marcus | 1618 Main St. (bet. Akard & Ervay Sts.) | Dallas | 214-573-5800 | www.neimanmarcus.com

"A Dallas institution inside a Dallas institution", this "elegant" dining room in Downtown's Neiman Marcus department store attracts a crowd of blue bloods and "blue hairs" with a "truly great" New American menu that works for lunch, a "late afternoon meal" or a post-shopping pick-me-up; the "famous" "popovers with strawberry butter" and "consommé" alone are "reason enough to go", but "gracious service" and "people-watching" supply added enticement.

Zoë's Kitchen *American* | ▽ 17 | 12 | 15 | $17

Park Cities | Snider Plaza | 6800 Snider Plaza (Milton Ave.) | Dallas | 214-987-1020

West Lovers Lane | 5710 Lovers Ln. (Eastern Ave.) | Dallas | 214-357-0100 | www.zoeskitchen.com

This bevy of "cute", "very basic" kitchens are linked to a Southeastern chain specializing in "quality" casual New American cuisine – like soups, sandwiches, salads and take-out chicken dinners – dispensed fast and with a healthy twist; "loud enough for kids" and priced for the family budget, they "hit the spot" for perpetually pressed moms.

DALLAS/FT. WORTH INDEXES

Cuisines

Includes restaurant names, locations and Food ratings.

AMERICAN (NEW)

Addison Cafe | **Addison**	23
Aija | **Arts Dist**	19
Angela's | **Uptown**	22
☑ Aurora | **Oak Lawn**	27
Bistro Louise | **SW**	26
🆕 Bolsa | **Oak Cliff**	-
Bread Winners | **multi.**	22
Café Ashton | **Downtown FW**	24
Cafe Aspen | **West**	21
Café Nasher | **Arts Dist**	18
🆕 Café R+D | **Preston Ctr**	-
Central 214 | **Park Cities**	24
Charlie Palmer | **Downtown D**	-
City Café | **W Lovers Ln**	-
Classic Cafe at Roanoke | **Roanoke**	28
Craft Dallas | **Victory Pk**	25
Crú Wine Bar | **multi.**	20
🆕 Dali | **Arts Dist**	-
Dallas Fish | **Downtown D**	24
Dragonfly | **Uptown**	19
Dream Café | **multi.**	18
☑ French Rm. | **Downtown D**	28
Go Fish | **Galleria**	21
Goodhues | **McKinney**	24
🆕 Grace | **Downtown FW**	-
Grape | **Greenville Ave**	25
Greenz | **multi.**	20
Hattie's | **Oak Cliff**	25
Hector's | **Knox-Henderson**	22
☑ Hibiscus | **Knox-Henderson**	25
☑ Jasper's | **Plano**	24
Kona Grill | **NorthPark**	20
Landmark | **Oak Lawn**	-
Lili's Bistro | **Hospital Dist**	-
☑ Local | **Deep Ellum**	28
Lola | **Uptown**	27
☑ Mansion | **Uptown**	26
Mariposa | **Plano**	23
☑ Mercury Grill | **Preston Forest**	27
Mirabelle | **N Dallas**	28
☑ Nana | **Market Ctr**	27

🆕 Neighborhood Services | **W Lovers Ln**	-
Palomino | **Uptown**	21
Parigi | **Oak Lawn**	25
Pyramid | **Arts Dist**	-
Rough Creek | **Glen Rose**	27
Salum | **Uptown**	25
🆕 Second Floor | **Galleria**	-
Sonoma Grill | **Flower Mound**	22
State & Allen | **Uptown**	19
Tramontana | **Preston Ctr**	23
2900 | **Uptown**	23
Victory Tav. | **Victory Pk**	15
☑ York St. | **Lakewood**	27
Zodiac | **Downtown D**	24
Zoë's | **multi.**	17

AMERICAN (TRADITIONAL)

🆕 American Girl | **Galleria**	-
Babe's | **multi.**	25
Billy Miner's | **Sundance Sq**	19
Buffet/Kimbell | **Cultural Dist**	24
Café on Green | **Las Colinas**	24
Celebration | **Love Field**	21
Charleston's | **SW**	18
Cheesecake Factory | **multi.**	20
Chubby's | **multi.**	18
Cindi's NY | **multi.**	17
Deli News | **N Dallas**	22
8.0 | **Sundance Sq**	14
Grill/Alley | **Galleria**	21
H.P. Cafeteria | **Lake Highlands**	-
H.P. Pharmacy | **Knox-Henderson**	19
Houston's | **multi.**	23
Love Shack | **Stockyards**	22
Lucile's Stateside Bistro | **West**	18
Lucky's | **Oak Lawn**	20
Maguire's | **N Dallas**	23
Mama's Daughters' | **multi.**	21
Neuhaus Café | **Preston Royal**	17
Olenjack's Grille | **Arlington**	26
Paris Coffee | **Hospital Dist**	23

Poor Richard's | **Plano**	20
Porch, The | **Knox-Henderson**	22
Purple Cow | **multi.**	14
Red's | **Plano**	20
Sevy's | **Preston Ctr**	23
St. Martin's | **Greenville Ave**	26
Tillman's | **Oak Cliff**	23
NEW Woodlands | **multi.**	-

ASIAN FUSION

Little Katana | **Knox-Henderson**	23

AUSTRIAN

Jorg's | **Plano**	25

BAKERIES

Bread Winners | **multi.**	22
Esperanza's | **multi.**	24
Main St. Bistro | **multi.**	23

BARBECUE

Angelo's | **Near W**	24
Cousin's | **multi.**	21
Peggy Sue BBQ | **Park Cities**	22
Z Railhead Smokehse. | **Cultural Dist**	22
Sammy's BBQ | **Uptown**	-
Sonny Bryan's | **multi.**	22

BRAZILIAN

Boi Na Braza | **Grapevine**	24
Fogo de Chão | **Addison**	26
Texas de Brazil | **multi.**	24

BURGERS

Billy Miner's | **Sundance Sq**	19
Kincaid's | **multi.**	23
Love Shack | **Stockyards**	22
Red's | **Plano**	20
Who's Who | **Park Cities**	18

CAJUN

J&J Oyster | **Cultural Dist**	21
Margaux's | **Market Ctr**	25
Pappadeaux | **multi.**	23

CARIBBEAN

Cuba Libre | **Knox-Henderson**	20

CHINESE

Empress of China | **multi.**	19
First Chinese | **multi.**	25

Howard Wang's | **Preston Hollow**	20
Masala Wok | **multi.**	18
Z P.F. Chang's | **multi.**	22
Szechuan Chinese | **multi.**	20

COFFEE SHOPS/DINERS

Café Brazil | **multi.**	19
Chubby's | **multi.**	18
H.P. Cafeteria | **Lake Highlands**	-
Mama's Daughters' | **multi.**	21
Original Mkt. | **Market Ctr**	20
Poor Richard's | **Plano**	20
Purple Cow | **multi.**	14
Spiral Diner | **multi.**	23

CONTINENTAL

Hôtel St. Germain | **Uptown**	25
Old Warsaw | **Uptown**	24

CREOLE

J&J Oyster | **Cultural Dist**	21
Margaux's | **Market Ctr**	25

CUBAN

NEW La Cubanita | **Knox-Henderson**	-

DELIS

Carshon's | **University Area**	23
Cindi's NY | **multi.**	17
Deli News | **N Dallas**	22

DESSERT

La Duni | **multi.**	24
Neuhaus Café | **Preston Royal**	17

EASTERN EUROPEAN

Franki's | **Lake Highlands**	21

ECLECTIC

Z Abacus | **Knox-Henderson**	28
Café Express | **multi.**	18
Café Lago | **Lake Highlands**	-
Z Café Modern | **Cultural Dist**	22
Cosmic Café | **Oak Lawn**	22
Grand Lux | **Galleria**	19
Kathleen's | **Park Cities**	20
Kozy Kitchen | **Knox-Henderson**	25
Z Lanny's | **Cultural Dist**	27
My Martini | **Arlington**	23
Sambuca | **multi.**	21

Sapristi!	**Forest Pk**	24
Seventeen Seventeen	**Arts Dist**	22
2900	**Uptown**	23

FONDUE

Melting Pot	**Addison**	21

FRENCH

Z Bijoux	**W Lovers Ln**	27
Cacharel	**Arlington**	25
Z French Rm.	**Downtown D**	28
Hôtel St. Germain	**Uptown**	25
L'Ancestral	**Knox-Henderson**	23
Lavendou	**N Dallas**	24
Main St. Bistro	**multi.**	23
Z Mercy	**Addison**	19
Mignon	**Plano**	22
Old Warsaw	**Uptown**	24
NEW Rise N° 1	**W Lovers Ln**	-
Z Saint-Emilion	**Cultural Dist**	27
NEW Second Floor	**Galleria**	-
St. Martin's	**Greenville Ave**	26
Toulouse	**Knox-Henderson**	19
Watel's	**Uptown**	24

GERMAN

Bavarian Grill	**Plano**	20
Edelweiss	**West**	20
Kuby's	**Park Cities**	22

GREEK

Opa! Grille	**Preston Forest**	19
Ziziki's	**multi.**	24

HAWAIIAN

Kona Grill	**NorthPark**	20
Roy's	**Plano**	25

HEALTH FOOD

(See also Vegetarian)

Kozy Kitchen	**Knox-Henderson**	25
Zoë's	**multi.**	17

ICE CREAM PARLORS

H.P. Pharmacy	**Knox-Henderson**	19
Purple Cow	**multi.**	14

INDIAN

Clay Pit	**Addison**	23
India Palace	**Preston Forest**	23
Madras Pavilion	**Richardson**	22
Masala Wok	**multi.**	18
Pasand Indian	**multi.**	21
Roti Grill	**multi.**	18
Saffron Hse.	**Addison**	20

IRISH

Tipperary Inn	**Lakewood**	18

ITALIAN

(N=Northern; S=Southern)

Adelmo's	**Knox-Henderson**	23
Amici	**Carrollton**	27
Andiamo	**Addison**	21
Arcodoro/Pomodoro	**Uptown**	21
Avanti	**multi.**	20
Bella Italia	**West**	24
NEW Bene Bene	**N Dallas**	-
Brio	**multi.**	21
Bruno's	**Irving**	22
Bugatti	**Love Field**	21
Café Cipriani	N	**Las Colinas**	21
Café Italia	S	**Love Field**	21
Campisi's	**multi.**	19
Carrabba's	**multi.**	22
Coal Vines	**multi.**	24
Daniele	S	**Oak Lawn**	24
Ferrari's	**multi.**	23
Ferre	N	**Sundance Sq**	21
Isabella's	**Frisco**	21
Maggiano's	**multi.**	20
Mamma Emilia's	**McKinney**	18
Mi Piaci	N	**Addison**	24
Momo's Pasta	**multi.**	19
Nicola's	N	**Plano**	24
NEW Nonna	**Lemmon Ave**	-
Nonna Tata	**Hospital Dist**	-
Pastazio's	**multi.**	22
Patrizio	**multi.**	21
Penne Pomodoro	**multi.**	19
Piccolo Mondo	**Arlington**	21
PoPoLos	**Preston Royal**	20
Positano	N	**N Dallas**	22
NEW Rist. Cibus	N	**NorthPark**	-
Rist. La Piazza	**University Area**	26
Ruffino's	**Forest Pk**	22
Ruggeri's	N	**multi.**	20
Sardines	**Cultural Dist**	18
Sweet Basil	**N Dallas**	23

Taverna	**multi.**	23
Terilli's	**multi.**	20
NEW Villa-O	**Knox-Henderson**	-

JAPANESE

(* sushi specialist)

Awaji*	**Plano**	24
Benihana	**multi.**	20
Blue Fish*	**multi.**	23
East Wind*	**Uptown**	21
Fish*	**W Vill**	20
Fuji Steak*	**Preston Forest**	20
Japanese Palace*	**West**	26
Jinbeh*	**multi.**	21
Kenichi*	**Victory Pk**	22
Legacy Naan*	**Plano**	22
Little Katana*	**multi.**	23
My Martini*	**Arlington**	23
Nakamoto	**Plano**	24
Nobu*	**Uptown**	24
Piranha*	**multi.**	25
Shinsei*	**W Lovers Ln**	25
Steel	**Oak Lawn**	25
NEW Sushi Axiom*	**multi.**	-
Sushi Zushi*	**Oak Lawn**	21
NEW Tei An*	**Arts Dist**	-
☑ Tei Tei Robata*	**Knox-Henderson**	28
☑ Teppo*	**Greenville Ave**	28
☑ Yutaka	**Uptown**	27

KOREAN

Legacy Naan	**Plano**	22

KOSHER/ KOSHER-STYLE

Madras Pavilion	**Richardson**	22

LEBANESE

Byblos	**N Side**	21
Hedary's	**West**	22

MEDITERRANEAN

Avanti	**multi.**	20
Bistro Louise	**SW**	26
Canary Cafe	**Addison**	26
Hedary's	**West**	22
Palomino	**Uptown**	21
Parigi	**Oak Lawn**	25
Suze	**Preston Hollow**	26

MEXICAN

Abuelo's	**multi.**	19
☑ ALÓ	**Knox-Henderson**	24
Avila's	**Love Field**	23
Benito's	**Hospital Dist**	18
Cadillac Bar	**W End**	18
Cantina Laredo	**multi.**	21
Cristina's	**multi.**	18
El Rancho Grande	**N Side**	20
Esperanza's	**multi.**	24
Javier's	**Knox-Henderson**	22
La Calle Doce	**Oak Cliff**	21
La Familia	**Near W**	24
☑ Lanny's	**Cultural Dist**	27
La Playa Maya	**multi.**	23
☑ Mi Cocina	**Galleria**	21
Monica's Aca	**Deep Ellum**	23
Nuevo Leon	**Farmers Branch**	22
Pepe & Mito's	**Deep Ellum**	22
Taco Diner	**multi.**	20
Trece	**Knox-Henderson**	21
Veracruz	**Oak Cliff**	24
Via Reál	**Las Colinas**	23

PAN-ASIAN

Asian Mint/Mint	**multi.**	23
East Wind	**Uptown**	21
Fuse	**Downtown D**	21
Kenichi	**Victory Pk**	22
Pan Acean	**Coppell**	20
☑ Pei Wei	**multi.**	19
Shinsei	**W Lovers Ln**	25
Tom Tom Asian	**W Vill**	20

PAN-LATIN

La Duni	**multi.**	24

PERUVIAN

☑ ALÓ	**Knox-Henderson**	24

PIZZA

Arcodoro/Pomodoro	**Uptown**	21
NEW Brix	**SW**	-
Campania	**multi.**	23
Campisi's	**multi.**	19
Coal Vines	**multi.**	24
Fireside Pies	**multi.**	23
NEW Grimaldi's	**multi.**	-

I Fratelli | **Las Colinas**	22
Olivella's | **Park Cities**	22
Pastazio's | **multi.**	22
Taverna | **multi.**	23

POLYNESIAN

Z Trader Vic's | **Park Cities**	19

PUB FOOD

Blackfinn | **Addison**	13
Porch, The | **Knox-Henderson**	22
Tipperary Inn | **Lakewood**	18

SALVADORAN

Gloria's | **multi.**	21

SEAFOOD

Arthur's | **Addison**	23
Z Café Pacific | **Park Cities**	26
Chamberlain's Fish | **Addison**	23
Dallas Fish | **Downtown D**	24
Go Fish | **Galleria**	21
J&J Oyster | **Cultural Dist**	21
McCormick/Schmick's | **NorthPark**	21
Newport's | **W End**	21
Nick & Sam's | **Uptown**	25
Oceanaire | **Galleria**	24
Palm | **W End**	24
Pappadeaux | **multi.**	23
Remington's | **Addison**	21
S&D Oyster | **Uptown**	23
Steve Fields | **Plano**	23
III Forks | **N Dallas**	25
Truluck's | **multi.**	23
Zeke's | **West**	24

SMALL PLATES

(See also Spanish tapas specialist)

Café Madrid | Spanish | **multi.**	21
NEW Dali | Eclectic | **Arts Dist**	–
Z Mercy | French | **Addison**	19
My Martini | Eclectic | **Arlington**	23
Sangria Tapas | Spanish | **Knox-Henderson**	17

SOUTHERN

Bubba's | **Park Cities**	23
Dixie House | **Lakewood**	18
House of Blues | **Victory Pk**	19

Ovation | **West**	–
Rick's | **McKinney**	21
NEW Screen Door | **Arts Dist**	–

SOUTHWESTERN

Ama Lur | **Grapevine**	23
Z Blue Mesa | **multi.**	20
Z Bonnell's | **SW**	27
Cool River | **Las Colinas**	19
Z Fearing's | **Uptown**	26
Fuse | **Downtown D**	21
Lonesome Dove | **Stockyards**	26
Love & War | **multi.**	16
Michaels | **Cultural Dist**	24
Reata | **Sundance Sq**	24
Z Stephan Pyles | **Arts Dist**	27
Trece | **Knox-Henderson**	21
Via Reál | **Las Colinas**	23

SPANISH

(* tapas specialist)

Café Madrid* | **multi.**	21
Chic from Barcelona | **Preston Forest**	18
Sangria Tapas* | **Knox-Henderson**	17

STEAKHOUSES

Z Al Biernat's | **Oak Lawn**	26
Arthur's | **Addison**	23
Benihana | **multi.**	20
Z Bob's Steak | **multi.**	25
Boi Na Braza | **Grapevine**	24
Capital Grille | **Uptown**	25
Cattlemen's | **Stockyards**	23
Chamberlain's Steak | **Addison**	25
Cool River | **Las Colinas**	19
Culpepper | **Rockwall**	24
Dakota's | **Arts Dist**	22
Z Del Frisco's | **multi.**	27
Fogo de Chão | **Addison**	26
H3 Ranch | **Stockyards**	20
J.R.'s Steak | **Colleyville**	23
Keg | **multi.**	21
Kirby's | **multi.**	24
NEW Lambert's | **Near W**	–
Lawry's | **N Dallas**	24
Mercury Chop | **Sundance Sq**	26

Morton's Steak | **Downtown D** 25

Nick & Sam's | **Uptown** 25

N9ne | **Victory Pk** 22

Old Hickory | **Grapevine** 21

Palm | **W End** 24

Pappas Bros. | **Love Field** 27

Park Cities Prime | **Preston Ctr** 16

Perry's | **Uptown** 24

Rick's | **McKinney** 21

Ruth's Chris | **multi.** 25

Silver Fox | **multi.** 24

Steve Fields | **Plano** 23

Sullivan's | **N Dallas** 24

Texas de Brazil | **multi.** 24

III Forks | **N Dallas** 25

Uncle Buck's | **Grapevine** 19

Y.O. Ranch | **W End** 19

TEX-MEX

Chuy's | **Knox-Henderson** 21

Gloria's | **Arlington** 21

Hot Damn, Tamales! | 26
  Hospital Dist

Iron Cactus | **Downtown D** 18

Joe T. Garcia's | **N Side** 19

Luna de Noche | **multi.** 20

Matt's Rancho | **Lakewood** 21

Mia's | **Lemmon Ave** 24

Z Mi Cocina | **multi.** 21

Primo's | **multi.** 18

THAI

Asian Mint/Mint | **multi.** 23

Chow Thai | **multi.** 23

Mango | **multi.** 21

Royal Thai | **Greenville Ave** 23

Samui Thai | **multi.** 24

TURKISH

Café Istanbul | **W Lovers Ln** 21

VEGETARIAN

(* vegan)

Cosmic Café* | **Oak Lawn** 22

Madras Pavilion | **Richardson** 22

Spiral Diner* | **multi.** 23

VIETNAMESE

Green Papaya | **Oak Lawn** 21

Steel | **Oak Lawn** 25

Zander's Hse. | **Plano** 23

Locations

Includes restaurant names, cuisines and Food ratings.

Dallas

ARTS DISTRICT

Aija | *Amer.* — 19
Café Nasher | *Amer.* — 18
Dakota's | *Steak* — 22
NEW Dali | *Amer.* — -
Pyramid | *Amer.* — -
NEW Screen Door | *Southern* — -
Seventeen Seventeen | *Eclectic* — 22
Z Stephan Pyles | *SW* — 27
NEW Tei An | *Japanese* — -

DEEP ELLUM/ DOWNTOWN/ MARKET CENTER/ WEST END

Avanti | *Italian/Med.* — 20
Cadillac Bar | *Mex.* — 18
Café Brazil | *Coffee* — 19
Campisi's | *Pizza* — 19
Charlie Palmer | *Amer.* — -
Cindi's NY | *Deli* — 17
Dallas Fish | *Amer./Seafood* — 24
Z French Rm. | *Amer./French* — 28
Fuse | *Pan-Asian/SW* — 21
Iron Cactus | *Tex-Mex* — 18
Z Local | *Amer.* — 28
Mama's Daughters' | *Diner* — 21
Margaux's | *Cajun/Creole* — 25
Monica's Aca | *Mex.* — 23
Morton's Steak | *Steak* — 25
Z Nana | *Amer.* — 27
Newport's | *Seafood* — 21
Original Mkt. | *Diner* — 20
Palm | *Seafood/Steak* — 24
Pepe & Mito's | *Mex.* — 22
Sonny Bryan's | *BBQ* — 22
Y.O. Ranch | *Steak* — 19
Zodiac | *Amer.* — 24

GALLERIA

NEW American Girl | *Amer.* — -
Go Fish | *Amer./Seafood* — 21
Grand Lux | *Eclectic* — 19
Grill/Alley | *Amer.* — 21
Little Katana | *Japanese* — 23
Z Mi Cocina | *Tex-Mex* — 21
Oceanaire | *Seafood* — 24
NEW Second Floor | *Amer./French* — -
Sonny Bryan's | *BBQ* — 22

GREENVILLE AVE./ LAKE HIGHLANDS/ LAKEWOOD

Blue Fish | *Japanese* — 23
Café Brazil | *Coffee* — 19
Café Lago | *Eclectic* — -
Campisi's | *Pizza* — 19
Cantina Laredo | *Mex.* — 21
Chubby's | *Diner* — 18
Dixie House | *Southern* — 18
Franki's | *E Euro.* — 21
Gloria's | *Salvadoran/Tex-Mex* — 21
Grape | *Amer.* — 25
H.P. Cafeteria | *Amer.* — -
Kirby's | *Steak* — 24
Matt's Rancho | *Tex-Mex* — 21
Z Mi Cocina | *Tex-Mex* — 21
Royal Thai | *Thai* — 23
St. Martin's | *Amer./French* — 26
Z Teppo | *Japanese* — 28
Terilli's | *Italian* — 20
Tipperary Inn | *Pub* — 18
Z York St. | *Amer.* — 27

HIGHLAND PARK VILL./MOCKINGBIRD STA./PARK CITIES

Bubba's | *Southern* — 23
Café Brazil | *Coffee* — 19
Café Express | *Eclectic* — 18
Z Café Pacific | *Seafood* — 26
Central 214 | *Amer.* — 24
Kathleen's | *Eclectic* — 20
Kuby's | *German* — 22
Mango | *Thai* — 21

☒ Mi Cocina	*Tex-Mex*	21
Asian Mint/Mint	*Pan-Asian/Thai*	23
Olivella's	*Pizza*	22
Patrizio	*Italian*	21
Peggy Sue BBQ	*BBQ*	22
Penne Pomodoro	*Italian*	19
☒ Trader Vic's	*Polynesian*	19
Who's Who	*Burgers*	18
Zoë's	*Amer.*	17

KNOX-HENDERSON

☒ Abacus	*Eclectic*	28
Adelmo's	*Italian*	23
☒ ALÓ	*Mex./Peruvian*	24
Café Madrid	*Spanish*	21
Chuy's	*Tex-Mex*	21
Cuba Libre	*Carib.*	20
Fireside Pies	*Pizza*	23
Hector's	*Amer.*	22
☒ Hibiscus	*Amer.*	25
H.P. Pharmacy	*Amer.*	19
Javier's	*Mex.*	22
Kozy Kitchen	*Eclectic*	25
NEW La Cubanita	*Cuban*	-
La Duni	*Pan-Latin*	24
L'Ancestral	*French*	23
Little Katana	*Asian Fusion*	23
Momo's Pasta	*Italian*	19
☒ Pei Wei	*Pan-Asian*	19
Porch, The	*Amer.*	22
Roti Grill	*Indian*	18
Sangria Tapas	*Spanish*	17
NEW Sushi Axiom	*Japanese*	-
Taverna	*Italian*	23
☒ Tei Tei Robata	*Japanese*	28
Toulouse	*French*	19
Trece	*Mex./SW*	21
NEW Villa-O	*Italian*	-
Ziziki's	*Greek*	24

LEMMON AVE./ OAK LAWN

☒ Al Biernat's	*Steak*	26
☒ Aurora	*Amer.*	27
☒ Bob's Steak	*Steak*	25
Café Brazil	*Coffee*	19

Cosmic Café	*Eclectic*	22
Daniele	*Italian*	24
Gloria's	*Salvadoran/Tex-Mex*	21
Green Papaya	*Viet.*	21
La Duni	*Pan-Latin*	24
Landmark	*Amer.*	-
Lucky's	*Amer.*	20
Mia's	*Tex-Mex*	24
NEW Nonna	*Italian*	-
Pappadeaux	*Seafood*	23
Parigi	*Amer./Med.*	25
Silver Fox	*Steak*	24
Steel	*Japanese/Viet.*	25
Sushi Zushi	*Japanese*	21

LOVE FIELD AREA/ NORTHPARK/ PRESTON/ WEST LOVERS LN.

Asian Mint/Mint	*Pan-Asian/Thai*	23
Avila's	*Mex.*	23
Benihana	*Japanese/Steak*	20
☒ Bijoux	*French*	27
☒ Blue Mesa	*SW*	20
Bread Winners	*Amer./Bakery*	22
Bugatti	*Italian*	21
Café Express	*Eclectic*	18
Café Istanbul	*Turkish*	21
Café Italia	*Italian*	21
NEW Café R+D	*Amer.*	-
Campisi's	*Pizza*	19
Cantina Laredo	*Mex.*	21
Celebration	*Amer.*	21
Cheesecake Factory	*Amer.*	20
Chic from Barcelona	*Spanish*	18
Cindi's NY	*Deli*	17
City Café	*Amer.*	-
Fireside Pies	*Pizza*	23
Fuji Steak	*Japanese*	20
Houston's	*Amer.*	23
India Palace	*Indian*	23
Kona Grill	*Amer.*	20
La Duni	*Pan-Latin*	24
Luna de Noche	*Tex-Mex*	20
Maggiano's	*Italian*	20
Mama's Daughters'	*Diner*	21

McCormick/Schmick's	Seafood	21
🄴 Mercury Grill	Amer.	27
🄴 Mi Cocina	Tex-Mex	21
NEW Neighborhood Services	Amer.	–
Neuhaus Café	Amer./Dessert	17
Opa! Grille	Greek	19
Pappas Bros.	Steak	27
Park Cities Prime	Steak	16
🄴 Pei Wei	Pan-Asian	19
Penne Pomodoro	Italian	19
🄴 P.F. Chang's	Chinese	22
PoPoLos	Italian	20
Purple Cow	Diner	14
NEW Rise Nº 1	French	–
NEW Rist. Cibus	Italian	–
Ruggeri's	Italian	20
Sevy's	Amer.	23
Shinsei	Pan-Asian	25
Sonny Bryan's	BBQ	22
Taco Diner	Mex.	20
Tramontana	Amer.	23
NEW Woodlands	Amer.	–
Ziziki's	Greek	24
Zoë's	Amer.	17

MCKINNEY AVE./ QUADRANGLE/ UPTOWN/WEST VILLAGE (NORTH OF DOWNTOWN)

Angela's	Amer.	22
Arcodoro/Pomodoro	Italian	21
Avanti	Italian/Med.	20
Bread Winners	Amer./Bakery	22
Café Express	Eclectic	18
Campania	Pizza	23
Capital Grille	Steak	25
Coal Vines	Italian	24
Crú Wine Bar	Amer.	20
Dragonfly	Amer.	19
Dream Café	Amer.	18
East Wind	Pan-Asian	21
🄴 Fearing's	SW	26
Fish	Japanese	20
Greenz	Amer.	20
NEW Grimaldi's	Pizza	–

Hôtel St. Germain	Continental/French	25
Lola	Amer.	27
🄴 Mansion	Amer.	26
🄴 Mi Cocina	Tex-Mex	21
Nick & Sam's	Seafood/Steak	25
Nobu	Japanese	24
Old Warsaw	Continental/French	24
Palomino	Amer./Med.	21
Pastazio's	Pizza	22
Perry's	Steak	24
Primo's	Tex-Mex	18
Salum	Amer.	25
Sambuca	Eclectic	21
Sammy's BBQ	BBQ	–
S&D Oyster	Seafood	23
State & Allen	Amer.	19
Taco Diner	Mex.	20
Texas de Brazil	Brazilian/Steak	24
Tom Tom Asian	Pan-Asian	20
Truluck's	Seafood	23
2900	Amer./Eclectic	23
Watel's	French	24
🄴 Yutaka	Japanese	27

PRESTON HOLLOW

Howard Wang's	Chinese	20
Suze	Med.	26

VICTORY PARK

Craft Dallas	Amer.	25
House of Blues	Southern	19
Kenichi	Pan-Asian	22
Luna de Noche	Tex-Mex	20
N9ne	Steak	22
Victory Tav.	Amer.	15

South Dallas

CEDAR HILL

Patrizio	Italian	21

DUNCANVILLE

Chubby's	Diner	18
Pappadeaux	Seafood	23

LANCASTER

Chubby's	Diner	18

OAK CLIFF

NEW Bolsa | *Amer.*	-
Café Brazil | *Coffee*	19
Café Madrid | *Spanish*	21
Gloria's | *Salvadoran/Tex-Mex*	21
Hattie's | *Amer.*	25
La Calle Doce | *Mex.*	21
Spiral Diner | *Diner/Vegetarian*	23
Tillman's | *Amer.*	23
Veracruz | *Mex.*	24

Outlying Dallas

ADDISON/ NORTH DALLAS/ RICHARDSON

Addison Cafe | *Amer.*	23
Andiamo | *Italian*	21
Arthur's | *Seafood/Steak*	23
Avanti | *Italian/Med.*	20
NEW Bene Bene | *Ital.*	-
Blackfinn | *Pub*	13
Blue Fish | *Japanese*	23
Z Blue Mesa | *SW*	20
Café Brazil | *Coffee*	19
Campisi's | *Pizza*	19
Canary Cafe | *Med.*	26
Cantina Laredo | *Mex.*	21
Carrabba's | *Italian*	22
Chamberlain's Fish | *Seafood*	23
Chamberlain's Steak | *Steak*	25
Chow Thai | *Thai*	23
Cindi's NY | *Deli*	17
Clay Pit | *Indian*	23
Cristina's | *Mex.*	18
Z Del Frisco's | *Steak*	27
Deli News | *Deli*	22
Dream Café | *Amer.*	18
Ferrari's | *Italian*	23
First Chinese | *Chinese*	25
Fogo de Chão | *Brazilian/Steak*	26
Gloria's | *Salvadoran/Tex-Mex*	21
Greenz | *Amer.*	20
Houston's | *Amer.*	23
Lavendou | *French*	24
Lawry's | *Steak*	24
Madras Pavilion | *Indian*	22

Maguire's | *Amer.*	23
Main St. Bistro | *French*	23
Masala Wok | *Chinese/Indian*	18
Melting Pot | *Fondue*	21
Z Mercy | *French*	19
Mi Piaci | *Italian*	24
Mirabelle | *Amer.*	28
Momo's Pasta | *Italian*	19
Pappadeaux | *Seafood*	23
Pasand Indian | *Indian*	21
Pastazio's | *Pizza*	22
Z Pei Wei | *Pan-Asian*	19
Z P.F. Chang's | *Chinese*	22
Positano | *Italian*	22
Remington's | *Seafood*	21
Ruth's Chris | *Steak*	25
Saffron Hse. | *Indian*	20
Sambuca | *Eclectic*	21
Silver Fox | *Steak*	24
Sonny Bryan's | *BBQ*	22
Sullivan's | *Steak*	24
Sweet Basil | *Italian*	23
Texas de Brazil | *Brazilian/Steak*	24
III Forks | *Steak*	25
Truluck's | *Seafood*	23

ALLEN/MCKINNEY

Brio | *Italian*	21
Café Brazil | *Coffee*	19
Cheesecake Factory | *Amer.*	20
Cristina's | *Mex.*	18
Crú Wine Bar | *Amer.*	20
Goodhues | *Amer.*	24
NEW Grimaldi's | *Pizza*	-
Mamma Emilia's | *Italian*	18
Z Pei Wei | *Pan-Asian*	19
Z P.F. Chang's | *Chinese*	22
Rick's | *Southern/Steak*	21
Samui Thai | *Thai*	24
NEW Woodlands | *Amer.*	-

CARROLLTON/ FARMERS BRANCH

Amici | *Italian*	27
Babe's | *Amer.*	25
Café Brazil | *Coffee*	19
Cindi's NY | *Deli*	17

First Chinese | *Chinese* 25
Nuevo Leon | *Mex.* 22

FRISCO

Babe's | *Amer.* 25
Cantina Laredo | *Mex.* 21
Cheesecake Factory | *Amer.* 20
Cristina's | *Mex.* 18
Gloria's | *Salvadoran/Tex-Mex* 21
Isabella's | *Italian* 21
Jinbeh | *Japanese* 21
Silver Fox | *Steak* 24
Terilli's | *Italian* 20

GARLAND/ MESQUITE

Babe's | *Amer.* 25
Cristina's | *Mex.* 18
First Chinese | *Chinese* 25
Gloria's | *Salvadoran/Tex-Mex* 21
Luna de Noche | *Tex-Mex* 20
Primo's | *Tex-Mex* 18

IRVING/ LAS COLINAS

Benihana | *Japanese/Steak* 20
Blue Fish | *Japanese* 23
Bruno's | *Italian* 22
Café Cipriani | *Italian* 21
Café on Green | *Amer.* 24
Cool River | *SW/Steak* 19
Empress of China | *Chinese* 19
I Fratelli | *Italian* 22
Jinbeh | *Japanese* 21
Keg | *Steak* 21
Mama's Daughters' | *Diner* 21
Masala Wok | *Chinese/Indian* 18
Z Mi Cocina | *Tex-Mex* 21
Pasand Indian | *Indian* 21
Z Pei Wei | *Pan-Asian* 19
Sonny Bryan's | *BBQ* 22
Taco Diner | *Mex.* 20
Via Reál | *Mex.* 23

PLANO

Abuelo's | *Mex.* 19
Awaji | *Japanese* 24
Bavarian Grill | *German* 20
Benihana | *Japanese/Steak* 20

Z Blue Mesa | *SW* 20
Z Bob's Steak | *Steak* 25
Bread Winners | *Amer./Bakery* 22
Café Brazil | *Coffee* 19
Café Express | *Eclectic* 18
Café Istanbul | *Turkish* 21
Campisi's | *Pizza* 19
Carrabba's | *Italian* 22
Chow Thai | *Thai* 23
Chubby's | *Diner* 18
Chuy's | *Tex-Mex* 21
Cristina's | *Mex.* 18
Crú Wine Bar | *Amer.* 20
Fireside Pies | *Pizza* 23
First Chinese | *Chinese* 25
Z Jasper's | *Amer.* 24
Jorg's | *Austrian* 25
Keg | *Steak* 21
Legacy Naan | *Japanese/Korean* 22
Love & War | *SW* 16
Luna de Noche | *Tex-Mex* 20
Maggiano's | *Italian* 20
Main St. Bistro | *French* 23
Mango | *Thai* 21
Mariposa | *Amer.* 23
Masala Wok | *Chinese/Indian* 18
Z Mi Cocina | *Tex-Mex* 21
Mignon | *French* 22
Nakamoto | *Japanese* 24
Nicola's | *Italian* 24
Patrizio | *Italian* 21
Poor Richard's | *Amer.* 20
Purple Cow | *Diner* 14
Red's | *Amer.* 20
Roti Grill | *Indian* 18
Roy's | *Hawaiian* 25
Samui Thai | *Thai* 24
Steve Fields | *Seafood/Steak* 23
Taco Diner | *Mex.* 20
Zander's Hse. | *Viet.* 23

ROCKWALL

Culpepper | *Steak* 24
Gloria's | *Salvadoran/Tex-Mex* 21

SANGER

Babe's | *Amer.* 25

Menus, photos, voting and more – free at ZAGAT.com

Ft. Worth

CULTURAL DISTRICT/ NEAR WEST/ SOUTHWEST/WEST

Angelo's	BBQ	24
Bella Italia	Italian	24
Bistro Louise	Amer./Med.	26
⚡ Bonnell's	SW	27
NEW Brix	Pizza	-
Buffet/Kimbell	Amer.	24
Cafe Aspen	Amer.	21
⚡ Café Modern	Eclectic	22
Charleston's	Amer.	18
Cousin's	BBQ	21
Edelweiss	German	20
Gloria's	Salvadoran/Tex-Mex	21
Hedary's	Med.	22
J&J Oyster	Cajun/Creole	21
Japanese Palace	Japanese	26
Keg	Steak	21
Kincaid's	Burgers	23
La Familia	Mex.	24
NEW Lambert's	Steak	-
⚡ Lanny's	Eclectic/Mex.	27
La Playa Maya	Mex.	23
Lucile's Stateside Bistro	Amer.	18
Michaels	SW	24
Ovation	Southern	-
⚡ Pei Wei	Pan-Asian	19
Purple Cow	Diner	14
⚡ Railhead Smokehse.	BBQ	22
⚡ Saint-Emilion	French	27
Sardines	Italian	18
NEW Sushi Axiom	Japanese	-
Szechuan Chinese	Chinese	20
Zeke's	Seafood	24

DOWNTOWN/ SUNDANCE SQUARE

Billy Miner's	Burgers	19
Café Ashton	Amer.	24
Cantina Laredo	Mex.	21
⚡ Del Frisco's	Steak	27
8.0	Amer.	14
Ferre	Italian	21
NEW Grace	Amer.	-

Mercury Chop	Steak	26
⚡ Mi Cocina	Tex-Mex	21
⚡ P.F. Chang's	Chinese	22
Piranha	Japanese	25
Reata	SW	24
Ruth's Chris	Steak	25
Taverna	Italian	23
Texas de Brazil	Brazilian/Steak	24

FOREST PARK/ HOSPITAL DISTRICT/ SOUTH SIDE/ UNIVERSITY AREA

Benito's	Mex.	18
⚡ Blue Mesa	SW	20
Carshon's	Deli	23
Cousin's	BBQ	21
Esperanza's	Mex.	24
Hot Damn, Tamales!	Tex-Mex	26
La Playa Maya	Mex.	23
Lili's Bistro	Amer.	-
Nonna Tata	Italian	-
Pappadeaux	Seafood	23
Paris Coffee	Amer.	23
Rist. La Piazza	Italian	26
Ruffino's	Italian	22
Sapristi!	Eclectic	24
Silver Fox	Steak	24
Spiral Diner	Diner/Veg.	23

NORTH SIDE/ STOCKYARDS

Byblos	Lebanese	21
Cattlemen's	Steak	23
El Rancho Grande	Mex.	20
Esperanza's	Mex.	24
H3 Ranch	Steak	20
Joe T. Garcia's	Tex-Mex	19
La Playa Maya	Mex.	23
Lonesome Dove	SW	26
Love Shack	Amer.	22

Denton County

FLOWER MOUND

Cristina's	Mex.	18
Empress of China	Chinese	19
Sonoma Grill	Amer.	22

HIGHLAND VILLAGE

Patrizio | *Italian* — 21

LEWISVILLE

Abuelo's | *Mex.* — 19
Cantina Laredo | *Mex.* — 21
Cristina's | *Mex.* — 18
Jinbeh | *Japanese* — 21
Mama's Daughters' | *Diner* — 21

ROANOKE

Babe's | *Amer.* — 25
Classic Cafe at Roanoke | *Amer.* — 28

TROPHY CLUB

Cristina's | *Mex.* — 18

Mid-Cities

ARLINGTON

Abuelo's | *Mex.* — 19
Cacharel | *French* — 25
Cheesecake Factory | *Amer.* — 20
First Chinese | *Chinese* — 25
Gloria's | *Salvadoran/Tex-Mex* — 21
Keg | *Steak* — 21
Kincaid's | *Burgers* — 23
My Martini | *Eclectic* — 23
Olenjack's Grille | *Amer.* — 26
Pappadeaux | *Seafood* — 23
Z Pei Wei | *Pan-Asian* — 19
Z P.F. Chang's | *Chinese* — 22
Piccolo Mondo | *Italian* — 21
Piranha | *Japanese* — 25

BEDFORD

Pappadeaux | *Seafood* — 23

HURST

Abuelo's | *Mex.* — 19
Carrabba's | *Italian* — 22

Northeast Tarrant County

ALLIANCE

Sonny Bryan's | *BBQ* — 22

COLLEYVILLE

Gloria's | *Salvadoran/Tex-Mex* — 21
J.R.'s Steak | *Steak* — 23
Ruggeri's | *Italian* — 20

COPPELL

Pan Acean | *Pan-Asian* — 20

GRAPEVINE

Ama Lur | *SW* — 23
Z Bob's Steak | *Steak* — 25
Boi Na Braza | *Brazilian/Steak* — 24
Cantina Laredo | *Mex.* — 21
Carrabba's | *Italian* — 22
Cristina's | *Mex.* — 18
Empress of China | *Chinese* — 19
Ferrari's | *Italian* — 23
Fireside Pies | *Pizza* — 23
Love & War | *SW* — 16
Main St. Bistro | *French* — 23
Old Hickory | *Steak* — 21
Z P.F. Chang's | *Chinese* — 22
Silver Fox | *Steak* — 24
Uncle Buck's | *Steak* — 19

KELLER

Cousin's | *BBQ* — 21

SOUTHLAKE

Z Blue Mesa | *SW* — 20
Brio | *Italian* — 21
Café Express | *Eclectic* — 18
Campania | *Pizza* — 23
Cheesecake Factory | *Amer.* — 20
Coal Vines | *Italian* — 24
Kincaid's | *Burgers* — 23
Kirby's | *Steak* — 24
Z Mi Cocina | *Tex-Mex* — 21
Z Pei Wei | *Pan-Asian* — 19
Taco Diner | *Mex.* — 20
Truluck's | *Seafood* — 23

Rural

BURLESON

Babe's | *Amer.* — 25

GLEN ROSE

Rough Creek | *Amer.* — 27

GRANBURY

Babe's | *Amer.* — 25

WEATHERFORD

La Playa Maya | *Mex.* — 23

Special Features

Listings cover the best in each category and include names, locations and Food ratings. Multi-location restaurants' features may vary by branch.

ADDITIONS

(Properties added since the last edition of the book)

American Girl	**Galleria**	-
Bene Bene	**N Dallas**	-
Bolsa	**Oak Cliff**	-
Brix	**SW**	-
Café R+D	**Preston Ctr**	-
Dali	**Arts Dist**	-
Grace	**Downtown FW**	-
Grimaldi's	**multi.**	-
La Cubanita	**Knox-Henderson**	-
Lambert's	**Near W**	-
Lili's Bistro	**Hospital Dist**	-
Neighborhood Services	**W Lovers Ln**	-
Nonna	**Lemmon Ave**	-
Ovation	**West**	-
Pyramid	**Arts Dist**	-
Rise Nº 1	**W Lovers Ln**	-
Rist. Cibus	**NorthPark**	-
Screen Door	**Arts Dist**	-
Second Floor	**Galleria**	-
Sushi Axiom	**multi.**	-
Tei An	**Arts Dist**	-
Villa-O	**Knox-Henderson**	-
Woodlands	**multi.**	-

BREAKFAST

(See also Hotel Dining)

Bread Winners	**multi.**	22
Café Brazil	**multi.**	19
Café Lago	**Lake Highlands**	-
Deli News	**N Dallas**	22
Dream Café	**multi.**	18
H.P. Pharmacy	**Knox-Henderson**	19
H3 Ranch	**Stockyards**	20
Kathleen's	**Park Cities**	20
Kuby's	**Park Cities**	22
La Duni	**Oak Lawn**	24
Lucky's	**Oak Lawn**	20
Main St. Bistro	**multi.**	23

Mama's Daughters'	**multi.**	21
Opa! Grille	**Preston Forest**	19
Original Mkt.	**Market Ctr**	20
Paris Coffee	**Hospital Dist**	23
Poor Richard's	**Plano**	20

BRUNCH

Bistro Louise	**SW**	26
☑ Blue Mesa	**multi.**	20
Bread Winners	**multi.**	22
Café on Green	**Las Colinas**	24
Carshon's	**University Area**	23
Cheesecake Factory	**NorthPark**	20
City Café	**W Lovers Ln**	-
Cool River	**Las Colinas**	19
☑ Fearing's	**Uptown**	26
Grand Lux	**Galleria**	19
Hattie's	**Oak Cliff**	25
Hedary's	**West**	22
House of Blues	**Victory Pk**	19
Kuby's	**Park Cities**	22
La Calle Doce	**Oak Cliff**	21
La Duni	**multi.**	24
Landmark	**Oak Lawn**	-
Lawry's	**N Dallas**	24
Lucile's Stateside Bistro	**West**	18
Maguire's	**N Dallas**	23
Mamma Emilia's	**McKinney**	18
☑ Mercury Grill	**Preston Forest**	27
Monica's Aca	**Deep Ellum**	23
Palomino	**Uptown**	21
Parigi	**Oak Lawn**	25
PoPoLos	**Preston Royal**	20
Reata	**Sundance Sq**	24
Rough Creek	**Glen Rose**	27
Saffron Hse.	**Addison**	20
Sapristi!	**Forest Pk**	24
St. Martin's	**Greenville Ave**	26
Terilli's	**multi.**	20
Texas de Brazil	**Addison**	24
Veracruz	**Oak Cliff**	24
Via Reál	**Las Colinas**	23

Watel's | **Uptown**	24
Ziziki's | **multi.**	24

BUFFET SERVED
(Check availability)

Aija | **Arts Dist**	19
Z Blue Mesa | **multi.**	20
Buffet/Kimbell | **Cultural Dist**	24
Café on Green | **Las Colinas**	24
Clay Pit | **Addison**	23
Hedary's | **West**	22
H.P. Cafeteria | **Lake Highlands**	-
India Palace | **Preston Forest**	23
Iron Cactus | **Downtown D**	18
Madras Pavilion | **Richardson**	22
Mamma Emilia's | **McKinney**	18
Pasand Indian | **multi.**	21
Roti Grill | **Plano**	18
Saffron Hse. | **Addison**	20
Texas de Brazil | **multi.**	24
NEW Woodlands | **Allen**	-

BUSINESS DINING

Z Abacus | **Knox-Henderson**	28
Z Al Biernat's | **Oak Lawn**	26
NEW Bene Bene | **N Dallas**	-
Z Bob's Steak | **multi.**	25
Brio | **Southlake**	21
Cacharel | **Arlington**	25
Café Ashton | **Downtown FW**	24
Café on Green | **Las Colinas**	24
Z Café Pacific | **Park Cities**	26
NEW Café R+D | **Preston Ctr**	-
Capital Grille | **Uptown**	25
Chamberlain's Steak | **Addison**	25
Charlie Palmer | **Downtown D**	-
City Café | **W Lovers Ln**	-
Cool River | **Las Colinas**	19
Dakota's | **Arts Dist**	22
NEW Dali | **Arts Dist**	-
Z Del Frisco's | **multi.**	27
Z Fearing's | **Uptown**	26
Grill/Alley | **Galleria**	21
Z Jasper's | **Plano**	24
Kenichi | **Victory Pk**	22
NEW Lambert's | **Near W**	-
Lavendou | **N Dallas**	24

Lola | **Uptown**	27
Z Mansion | **Uptown**	26
Mercury Chop | **Sundance Sq**	26
Z Mercury Grill | **Preston Forest**	27
Mi Piaci | **Addison**	24
Z Nana | **Market Ctr**	27
Nick & Sam's | **Uptown**	25
N9ne | **Victory Pk**	22
Nobu | **Uptown**	24
Oceanaire | **Galleria**	24
Olenjack's Grille | **Arlington**	26
Palm | **W End**	24
Palomino | **Uptown**	21
Pappas Bros. | **Love Field**	27
Perry's | **Uptown**	24
PoPoLos | **Preston Royal**	20
Pyramid | **Arts Dist**	-
Reata | **Sundance Sq**	24
Rist. La Piazza | **University Area**	26
Z Saint-Emilion | **Cultural Dist**	27
NEW Screen Door | **Arts Dist**	-
NEW Second Floor | **Galleria**	-
Sevy's | **Preston Ctr**	23
Silver Fox | **multi.**	24
Sonny Bryan's | **Love Field**	22
Steel | **Oak Lawn**	25
Z Stephan Pyles | **Arts Dist**	27
Steve Fields | **Plano**	23
III Forks | **N Dallas**	25
Truluck's | **multi.**	23
NEW Woodlands | **Preston Forest**	-

CELEBRITY CHEFS

Z Abacus | *Kent Rathbun* | **Knox-Henderson**	28
Z Aurora | *Avner Samuel* | **Oak Lawn**	27
Z Bijoux | *Scott Gottlich* | **W Lovers Ln**	27
Bistro Louise | *Louise Lamensdorf* | **SW**	26
Z Bonnell's | *Jon Bonnell* | **SW**	27
Charlie Palmer | *Charlie Palmer* | **Downtown D**	-
Craft Dallas | *Tom Colicchio* | **Victory Pk**	25

Z Fearing's | *Dean Fearing* | **Uptown** — 26

Z Lanny's | *Lanny Lancarte* | **Cultural Dist** — 27

Lonesome Dove | *Tim Love* | **Stockyards** — 26

Z Mansion | *John Tesar* | **Uptown** — 26

Mercury Chop | *Chris Ward* | **Sundance Sq** — 26

Z Mercury Grill | *Chris Ward* | **Preston Forest** — 27

Z Nana | *Anthony Bombaci* | **Market Ctr** — 27

NEW Neighborhood Services | *Nick Badavinus* | **W Lovers Ln** — ‑

Nobu | *Nobu Matsuhisa* | **Uptown** — 24

Olenjack's Grille | *Brian Olenjack* | **Arlington** — 26

Z Stephan Pyles | *Stephan Pyles* | **Arts Dist** — 27

NEW Tei An | *Teiichi Sakurai* | **Arts Dist** — ‑

Z York St. | *Sharon Hage* | **Lakewood** — 27

CHEF'S TABLE

Z Abacus | **Knox-Henderson** — 28

Daniele | **Oak Lawn** — 24

Z Fearing's | **Uptown** — 26

NEW Lambert's | **Near W** — ‑

Tramontana | **Preston Ctr** — 23

CHILD-FRIENDLY

(Alternatives to the usual fast-food places; * children's menu available)

Avila's* | **Love Field** — 23

Babe's* | **multi.** — 25

Benihana* | **multi.** — 20

Benito's* | **Hospital Dist** — 18

Z Blue Mesa* | **multi.** — 20

Bread Winners* | **multi.** — 22

Café Brazil* | **multi.** — 19

Café Express* | **multi.** — 18

Campisi's* | **Greenville Ave** — 19

Celebration* | **Love Field** — 21

Charleston's* | **SW** — 18

Cheesecake Factory | **multi.** — 20

Classic Cafe at Roanoke* | **Roanoke** — 28

Cousin's* | **multi.** — 21

Deli News* | **N Dallas** — 22

Dream Café* | **multi.** — 18

Edelweiss* | **West** — 20

El Rancho Grande* | **N Side** — 20

Ferrari's* | **Addison** — 23

Fireside Pies* | **multi.** — 23

Fuji Steak* | **Preston Forest** — 20

Gloria's* | **multi.** — 21

Hedary's | **West** — 22

H.P. Cafeteria | **Lake Highlands** — ‑

H.P. Pharmacy | **Knox-Henderson** — 19

Houston's* | **multi.** — 23

Howard Wang's* | **Preston Hollow** — 20

H3 Ranch* | **Stockyards** — 20

I Fratelli* | **Las Colinas** — 22

India Palace* | **Preston Forest** — 23

Japanese Palace* | **West** — 26

Joe T. Garcia's* | **N Side** — 19

Keg* | **multi.** — 21

Kincaid's | **multi.** — 23

La Familia* | **Near W** — 24

Lucile's Stateside Bistro* | **West** — 18

Maggiano's* | **multi.** — 20

Maguire's | **N Dallas** — 23

Main St. Bistro* | **multi.** — 23

Mama's Daughters'* | **multi.** — 21

Mamma Emilia's* | **McKinney** — 18

Z Mi Cocina* | **multi.** — 21

Nuevo Leon* | **Farmers Branch** — 22

Pasand Indian | **multi.** — 21

Z Pei Wei* | **multi.** — 19

Z P.F. Chang's | **multi.** — 22

Purple Cow* | **multi.** — 14

Z Railhead Smokehse. | **Cultural Dist** — 22

Roti Grill* | **multi.** — 18

Samui Thai* | **multi.** — 24

Sevy's* | **Preston Ctr** — 23

Sonny Bryan's* | **multi.** — 22

Sonoma Grill* | **Flower Mound** — 22

Sweet Basil* | **N Dallas** — 23

Uncle Buck's* | **Grapevine** — 19

Via Reál* | **Las Colinas** — 23

Y.O. Ranch* | **W End**	19
Zeke's | **West**	24
Zoë's* | **multi.**	17

CIGARS WELCOME

Boi Na Braza | **Grapevine**	24
Chamberlain's Steak | **Addison**	25
Cool River | **Las Colinas**	19
Javier's | **Knox-Henderson**	22
Michaels | **Cultural Dist**	24
Pappas Bros. | **Love Field**	27
☒ Railhead Smokehse. | **Cultural Dist**	22

DELIVERY/TAKEOUT

(D=delivery, T=takeout)

Abuelo's | D, T | **multi.**	19
Amici | T | **Carrollton**	27
Andiamo | T | **Addison**	21
Angelo's | T | **Near W**	24
Asian Mint/Mint | D, T | **Medical City**	23
Avila's | T | **Love Field**	23
Babe's | T | **Roanoke**	25
☒ Blue Mesa | D, T | **multi.**	20
Bread Winners | T | **multi.**	22
Byblos | T | **N Side**	21
Café Ashton | T | **Downtown FW**	24
Café Express | T | **multi.**	18
Café Lago | T | **Lake Highlands**	-
Campania | D, T | **multi.**	23
Campisi's | D, T | **multi.**	19
Carshon's | D, T | **University Area**	23
Celebration | T | **Love Field**	21
Chamberlain's Fish | T | **Addison**	23
Charleston's | T | **SW**	18
Cheesecake Factory | T | **multi.**	20
Chow Thai | T | **multi.**	23
Chuy's | D | **Knox-Henderson**	21
City Café | D, T | **W Lovers Ln**	-
Classic Cafe at Roanoke | T | **Roanoke**	28
Clay Pit | D, T | **Addison**	23
Coal Vines | D, T | **multi.**	24
Cosmic Café | T | **Oak Lawn**	22
Cousin's | T | **multi.**	21

Deli News | D, T | **N Dallas**	22
Dixie House | T | **Lakewood**	18
Dream Café | T | **multi.**	18
East Wind | T | **Uptown**	21
8.0 | D, T | **Sundance Sq**	14
El Rancho Grande | T | **N Side**	20
Empress of China | D, T | **Las Colinas**	19
Esperanza's | T | **N Side**	24
Fireside Pies | T | **Knox-Henderson**	23
First Chinese | D | **multi.**	25
Gloria's | T | **multi.**	21
Grand Lux | T | **Galleria**	19
Green Papaya | T | **Oak Lawn**	21
Greenz | T | **multi.**	20
H.P. Cafeteria | T | **Lake Highlands**	-
Howard Wang's | D, T | **Preston Hollow**	20
H3 Ranch | T | **Stockyards**	20
I Fratelli | T | **Las Colinas**	22
India Palace | T | **Preston Forest**	23
☒ Jasper's | T | **Plano**	24
Jinbeh | T | **multi.**	21
Kincaid's | T | **multi.**	23
Kuby's | T | **Park Cities**	22
La Calle Doce | T | **Oak Cliff**	21
Lucky's | D, T | **Oak Lawn**	20
Maggiano's | T | **multi.**	20
Maguire's | D, T | **N Dallas**	23
Main St. Bistro | D, T | **multi.**	23
Mama's Daughters' | T | **multi.**	21
Mamma Emilia's | T | **McKinney**	18
Mariposa | D, T | **Plano**	23
Matt's Rancho | T | **Lakewood**	21
☒ Mi Cocina | T | **multi.**	21
Monica's Aca | T | **Deep Ellum**	23
Nuevo Leon | T | **Farmers Branch**	22
Olivella's | D | **Park Cities**	22
Opa! Grille | D, T | **Preston Forest**	19
Original Mkt. | D, T | **Market Ctr**	20
Palomino | T | **Uptown**	21
Pan Acean | D, T | **Coppell**	20
Paris Coffee | T | **Hospital Dist**	23
Pasand Indian | T | **multi.**	21
Pastazio's | T | **multi.**	22

☑ Pei Wei | T | **multi.**	19
☑ P.F. Chang's | T | **multi.**	22
Purple Cow | D, T | **multi.**	14
☑ Railhead Smokehse. | T | **Cultural Dist**	22
Roti Grill | D, T | **Knox-Henderson**	18
Royal Thai | D, T | **Greenville Ave**	23
Samui Thai | T | **multi.**	24
S&D Oyster | T | **Uptown**	23
Sapristi! | T | **Forest Pk**	24
Sardines | D, T | **Cultural Dist**	18
Sonny Bryan's | D, T | **multi.**	22
Sonoma Grill | T | **Flower Mound**	22
Spiral Diner | T | **Hospital Dist**	23
State & Allen | T | **Uptown**	19
Sushi Zushi | D, T | **Oak Lawn**	21
Suze | T | **Preston Hollow**	26
Szechuan Chinese | D, T | **multi.**	20
Taco Diner | T | **multi.**	20
Taverna | T | **Knox-Henderson**	23
Via Reál | T | **Las Colinas**	23
Y.O. Ranch | T | **W End**	19
Zeke's | D, T | **West**	24
Ziziki's | T | **multi.**	24
Zoë's | D | **multi.**	17

DESSERT

Bistro Louise | **SW**	26
☑ Bonnell's | **SW**	27
Bread Winners | **multi.**	22
Capital Grille | **Uptown**	25
Cheesecake Factory | **multi.**	20
Dream Café | **multi.**	18
Grand Lux | **Galleria**	19
☑ Hibiscus | **Knox-Henderson**	25
La Duni | **multi.**	24
Main St. Bistro | **multi.**	23
☑ Mansion | **Uptown**	26
☑ Nana | **Market Ctr**	27
Pappas Bros. | **Love Field**	27
☑ Saint-Emilion | **Cultural Dist**	27

DINING ALONE

(Other than hotels and places with counter service)

☑ ALÓ | **Knox-Henderson**	24
Asian Mint/Mint | **Medical City**	23

Bread Winners | **multi.**	22
Buffet/Kimbell | **Cultural Dist**	24
Cafe Aspen | **West**	21
Café Brazil | **multi.**	19
Campisi's | **multi.**	19
Chic from Barcelona | **Preston Forest**	18
City Café | **W Lovers Ln**	-
Classic Cafe at Roanoke | **Roanoke**	28
Coal Vines | **multi.**	24
Cosmic Café | **Oak Lawn**	22
Deli News | **N Dallas**	22
Dream Café | **multi.**	18
Ferre | **Sundance Sq**	21
Fireside Pies | **multi.**	23
First Chinese | **Richardson**	25
Gloria's | **multi.**	21
Greenz | **multi.**	20
H.P. Pharmacy | **Knox-Henderson**	19
H3 Ranch | **Stockyards**	20
I Fratelli | **Las Colinas**	22
Kincaid's | **multi.**	23
La Duni | **multi.**	24
La Familia | **Near W**	24
L'Ancestral | **Knox-Henderson**	23
Lavendou | **N Dallas**	24
Little Katana | **multi.**	23
Luna de Noche | **multi.**	20
Mango | **Park Cities**	21
Masala Wok | **multi.**	18
Mia's | **Lemmon Ave**	24
Neuhaus Café | **Preston Royal**	17
Nonna Tata | **Hospital Dist**	-
Olenjack's Grille | **Arlington**	26
Olivella's | **Park Cities**	22
☑ Pei Wei | **multi.**	19
Penne Pomodoro | **multi.**	19
☑ Railhead Smokehse. | **Cultural Dist**	22
Reata | **Sundance Sq**	24
NEW Rist. Cibus | **NorthPark**	-
Sonny Bryan's | **multi.**	22
☑ Stephan Pyles | **Arts Dist**	27
Tramontana | **Preston Ctr**	23
NEW Woodlands | **multi.**	-

Yutaka | **Uptown**	27
Zander's Hse. | **Plano**	23
Zoë's | **W Lovers Ln**	17

ENTERTAINMENT

(Call for days and times of performances)

Ama Lur | salsa | **Grapevine**	23
Arthur's | bands | **Addison**	23
Avanti | jazz/Latin | **multi.**	20
Bavarian Grill | varies | **Plano**	20
Bella Italia | guitar | **West**	24
Bread Winners | jazz | **Uptown**	22
Bruno's | piano | **Irving**	22
Buffet/Kimbell | jazz | **Cultural Dist**	24
Byblos | belly dancers | **N Side**	21
Café Ashton | piano | **Downtown FW**	24
Cafe Aspen | jazz/piano | **West**	21
Café Istanbul | belly dancers | **W Lovers Ln**	21
Café Madrid | flamenco | **Knox-Henderson**	21
Café on Green | saxophonist | **Las Colinas**	24
Celebration | jazz | **Love Field**	21
Clay Pit | varies | **Addison**	23
Cool River | varies | **Las Colinas**	19
Cosmic Café | varies | **Oak Lawn**	22
Culpepper | varies | **Rockwall**	24
NEW Dali | live music | **Arts Dist**	-
Del Frisco's | piano | **N Dallas**	27
Edelweiss | German | **West**	20
8.0 | varies | **Sundance Sq**	14
French Rm. | jazz | **Downtown D**	28
Gloria's | varies | **multi.**	21
Hector's | varies | **Knox-Henderson**	22
House of Blues | live music | **Victory Pk**	19
Joe T. Garcia's | mariachi | **N Side**	19
J.R.'s Steak | blues/jazz | **Colleyville**	23
Kirby's | live music | **Southlake**	24
Kuby's | accordion | **Park Cities**	22

La Calle Doce | varies | **Oak Cliff**	21
Maggiano's | piano/vocals | **NorthPark**	20
Maguire's | jazz | **N Dallas**	23
Main St. Bistro | varies | **Plano**	23
Mansion | jazz | **Uptown**	26
Monica's Aca | jazz/Latin | **Deep Ellum**	23
My Martini | jazz | **Arlington**	23
Nana | jazz | **Market Ctr**	27
Nick & Sam's | piano | **Uptown**	25
Old Warsaw | piano/violin | **Uptown**	24
Ovation | varies | **West**	-
Pappas Bros. | piano | **Love Field**	27
PoPoLos | jazz | **Preston Royal**	20
Reata | gospel | **Sundance Sq**	24
Ruffino's | piano | **Forest Pk**	22
Sambuca | varies | **multi.**	21
Sardines | jazz | **Cultural Dist**	18
St. Martin's | piano | **Greenville Ave**	26
Sullivan's | bands/jazz | **N Dallas**	24
Terilli's | jazz | **multi.**	20
III Forks | varies | **N Dallas**	25
Tipperary Inn | Irish | **Lakewood**	18
Watel's | jazz | **Uptown**	24
Zeke's | bands | **West**	24

GAME IN SEASON

Abacus | **Knox-Henderson**	28
Addison Cafe | **Addison**	23
Adelmo's | **Knox-Henderson**	23
Amici | **Carrollton**	27
Arcodoro/Pomodoro | **Uptown**	21
Arthur's | **Addison**	23
Aurora | **Oak Lawn**	27
Bella Italia | **West**	24
Bijoux | **W Lovers Ln**	27
Bistro Louise | **SW**	26
NEW Bolsa | **Oak Cliff**	-
Bonnell's | **SW**	27
Bruno's | **Irving**	22
Cacharel | **Arlington**	25
Café Madrid | **multi.**	21
Chamberlain's Steak | **Addison**	25

Classic Cafe at Roanoke | **Roanoke** `28`

Culpepper | **Rockwall** `24`

Franki's | **Lake Highlands** `21`

Gloria's | **multi.** `21`

Grape | **Greenville Ave** `25`

Hattie's | **Oak Cliff** `25`

Hôtel St. Germain | **Uptown** `25`

Kuby's | **Park Cities** `22`

Z Lanny's | **Cultural Dist** `27`

Lonesome Dove | **Stockyards** `26`

Mi Piaci | **Addison** `24`

Mirabelle | **N Dallas** `28`

Pyramid | **Arts Dist** `-`

Rough Creek | **Glen Rose** `27`

Z Saint-Emilion | **Cultural Dist** `27`

Sapristi! | **Forest Pk** `24`

NEW Screen Door | **Arts Dist** `-`

NEW Second Floor | **Galleria** `-`

State & Allen | **Uptown** `19`

Uncle Buck's | **Grapevine** `19`

Watel's | **Uptown** `24`

Y.O. Ranch | **W End** `19`

Z York St. | **Lakewood** `27`

HISTORIC PLACES

(Year opened; * building)

1885 | Rick's* | **McKinney** `21`

1891 | S&D Oyster* | **Uptown** `23`

1906 | Hôtel St. Germain* | **Uptown** `25`

1908 | Local* | **Deep Ellum** `28`

1912 | French Rm.* | **Downtown D** `28`

1912 | H.P. Pharmacy | **Knox-Henderson** `19`

1920 | Goodhues* | **McKinney** `24`

1920 | Hattie's* | **Oak Cliff** `25`

1926 | Lucile's Stateside Bistro* | **West** `18`

1926 | Paris Coffee | **Hospital Dist** `23`

1929 | Carshon's | **University Area** `23`

1930 | Fuse* | **Downtown D** `21`

1932 | Spiral Diner* | **Hospital Dist** `23`

1935 | Esperanza's | **Hospital Dist** `24`

1935 | Joe T. Garcia's | **N Side** `19`

1946 | Campisi's | **multi.** `19`

1946 | Kincaid's | **West** `23`

1947 | Cattlemen's | **Stockyards** `23`

1948 | Arthur's | **Addison** `23`

1948 | Old Warsaw | **Uptown** `24`

1954 | Kirby's | **Greenville Ave** `24`

1957 | Zodiac | **Downtown D** `24`

1958 | Angelo's | **Near W** `24`

1958 | Mama's Daughters' | **Market Ctr** `21`

1958 | Sonny Bryan's | **multi.** `22`

HOTEL DINING

Adolphus Hotel

  Z French Rm. | **Downtown D** `28`

Ashton Hotel

  Café Ashton | **Downtown FW** `24`

Fairmont Dallas

  Pyramid | **Arts Dist** `-`

Four Seasons Resort & Club

  Café on Green | **Las Colinas** `24`

Gaylord Texan Resort

  Ama Lur | **Grapevine** `23`

  Old Hickory | **Grapevine** `21`

Grand Hotel

  Rick's | **McKinney** `21`

Hilton Anatole Hotel

  Z Nana | **Market Ctr** `27`

Hotel Palomar

  Central 214 | **Park Cities** `24`

  Z Trader Vic's | **Park Cities** `19`

Joule Hotel

  Charlie Palmer | **Downtown D** `-`

Ritz-Carlton Hotel

  Z Fearing's | **Uptown** `26`

Rosewood Crescent Hotel

  Nobu | **Uptown** `24`

Rosewood Mansion on Turtle Creek

  Z Mansion | **Uptown** `26`

Rough Creek Lodge

  Rough Creek | **Glen Rose** `27`

St. Germain Hôtel

  Hôtel St. Germain | **Uptown** `25`

Warwick Melrose Hotel	
Landmark | **Oak Lawn**	–
Westin Galleria Hotel	
Oceanaire | **Galleria**	24
NEW Second Floor | **Galleria**	–
W Hotel	
Craft Dallas | **Victory Pk**	25
ZaZa Hotel	
Dragonfly | **Uptown**	19

JACKET REQUIRED

(* Tie also required)

Z French Rm. | **Downtown D**	28
Hôtel St. Germain* | **Uptown**	25

LATE DINING

(Weekday closing hour)

Café Brazil | 12 AM | **multi.**	19
Coal Vines | varies | **Uptown**	24
Crú Wine Bar | 12 AM | **Plano**	20
Fireside Pies | 12 AM | **Knox-Henderson**	23
House of Blues | 12 AM | **Victory Pk**	19
Primo's | varies | **multi.**	18

MEET FOR A DRINK

Z ALÓ | **Knox-Henderson**	24
Ama Lur | **Grapevine**	23
Blackfinn | **Addison**	13
Brio | **Southlake**	21
Z Café Pacific | **Park Cities**	26
NEW Café R+D | **Preston Ctr**	–
Capital Grille | **Uptown**	25
Central 214 | **Park Cities**	24
Charlie Palmer | **Downtown D**	–
Chuy's | **Knox-Henderson**	21
Cool River | **Las Colinas**	19
Cristina's | **multi.**	18
Crú Wine Bar | **multi.**	20
Cuba Libre | **Knox-Henderson**	20
NEW Dali | **Arts Dist**	–
Dallas Fish | **Downtown D**	24
Z Del Frisco's | **multi.**	27
El Rancho Grande | **N Side**	20
Z Fearing's | **Uptown**	26
Ferre | **Sundance Sq**	21
Fireside Pies | **W Lovers Ln**	23
Fuse | **Downtown D**	21

Grape | **Greenville Ave**	25
Grill/Alley | **Galleria**	21
House of Blues | **Victory Pk**	19
H3 Ranch | **Stockyards**	20
Iron Cactus | **Downtown D**	18
Z Jasper's | **Plano**	24
Joe T. Garcia's | **N Side**	19
Keg | **SW**	21
Kenichi | **Victory Pk**	22
Landmark | **Oak Lawn**	–
Love Shack | **Stockyards**	22
Luna de Noche | **Victory Pk**	20
Maguire's | **N Dallas**	23
Z Mansion | **Uptown**	26
Mercury Chop | **Sundance Sq**	26
Z Mercury Grill | **Preston Forest**	27
Z Mercy | **Addison**	19
Z Mi Cocina | **multi.**	21
Monica's Aca | **Deep Ellum**	23
Z Nana | **Market Ctr**	27
Nick & Sam's | **Uptown**	25
N9ne | **Victory Pk**	22
Olenjack's Grille | **Arlington**	26
Palm | **W End**	24
Palomino | **Uptown**	21
Porch, The | **Knox-Henderson**	22
Primo's | **Uptown**	18
Reata | **Sundance Sq**	24
Sambuca | **multi.**	21
Sangria Tapas | **Knox-Henderson**	17
Sapristi! | **Forest Pk**	24
Sevy's | **Preston Ctr**	23
Steel | **Oak Lawn**	25
Z Stephan Pyles | **Arts Dist**	27
Sullivan's | **N Dallas**	24
Tipperary Inn | **Lakewood**	18
Z Trader Vic's | **Park Cities**	19
Trece | **Knox-Henderson**	21
Victory Tav. | **Victory Pk**	15
NEW Villa-O | **Knox-Henderson**	–

OUTDOOR DINING

(G=garden; P=patio; S=sidewalk; T=terrace; W=waterside)

Abuelo's | P | **multi.**	19
Angela's | P | **Uptown**	22

Arcodoro/Pomodoro | P | **Uptown** — 21

Bavarian Grill | G | **Plano** — 20

NEW Bolsa | P | **Oak Cliff** — -

Bread Winners | G, P | **multi.** — 22

Brio | P, T | **multi.** — 21

NEW Brix | P | **SW** — -

Bruno's | P, W | **Irving** — 22

Buffet/Kimbell | G | **Cultural Dist** — 24

Cafe Aspen | P | **West** — 21

Café Express | G, P, S | **multi.** — 18

Café Lago | P | **Lake Highlands** — -

Z Café Modern | P | **Cultural Dist** — 22

Celebration | P | **Love Field** — 21

Chuy's | P | **Knox-Henderson** — 21

Clay Pit | P | **Addison** — 23

Coal Vines | P | **multi.** — 24

Cosmic Café | P | **Oak Lawn** — 22

Cousin's | P, S | **multi.** — 21

Crú Wine Bar | P | **multi.** — 20

Cuba Libre | P | **Knox-Henderson** — 20

Culpepper | G, T | **Rockwall** — 24

Dakota's | P | **Arts Dist** — 22

NEW Dali | P | **Arts Dist** — -

Dragonfly | P, W | **Uptown** — 19

Dream Café | P | **multi.** — 18

8.0 | P | **Sundance Sq** — 14

Z Fearing's | P | **Uptown** — 26

Ferre | P | **Sundance Sq** — 21

Fireside Pies | P | **Knox-Henderson** — 23

Fuse | P | **Downtown D** — 21

Gloria's | P | **multi.** — 21

Go Fish | P | **Galleria** — 21

NEW Grimaldi's | P | **multi.** — -

Z Jasper's | P | **Plano** — 24

Joe T. Garcia's | P | **N Side** — 19

La Calle Doce | P | **Oak Cliff** — 21

Lavendou | P | **N Dallas** — 24

Z Mansion | T | **Uptown** — 26

Mignon | W | **Plano** — 22

Mi Piaci | P, W | **Addison** — 24

Nonna Tata | S | **Hospital Dist** — -

Parigi | P | **Oak Lawn** — 25

Patrizio | G, P | **multi.** — 21

Primo's | P | **Uptown** — 18

Reata | P | **Sundance Sq** — 24

Red's | P, W | **Plano** — 20

NEW Rist. Cibus | P | **NorthPark** — -

Rough Creek | T, W | **Glen Rose** — 27

Sambuca | P | **Uptown** — 21

Sapristi! | P | **Forest Pk** — 24

Sardines | P | **Cultural Dist** — 18

State & Allen | S | **Uptown** — 19

NEW Sushi Axiom | P | **multi.** — -

Taco Diner | P | **multi.** — 20

Taverna | P | **Knox-Henderson** — 23

Terilli's | P | **multi.** — 20

Tipperary Inn | P | **Lakewood** — 18

Tom Tom Asian | P | **W Vill** — 20

Watel's | P | **Uptown** — 24

NEW Woodlands | P | **multi.** — -

POWER SCENES

Z Abacus | **Knox-Henderson** — 28

Z Al Biernat's | **Oak Lawn** — 26

Z Bijoux | **W Lovers Ln** — 27

Z Bob's Steak | **multi.** — 25

Z Café Pacific | **Park Cities** — 26

NEW Café R+D | **Preston Ctr** — -

Capital Grille | **Uptown** — 25

Charlie Palmer | **Downtown D** — -

Craft Dallas | **Victory Pk** — 25

Z Del Frisco's | **multi.** — 27

Z Fearing's | **Uptown** — 26

Z French Rm. | **Downtown D** — 28

NEW Grace | **Downtown FW** — -

Z Jasper's | **Plano** — 24

Kenichi | **Victory Pk** — 22

NEW Lambert's | **Near W** — -

Z Lanny's | **Cultural Dist** — 27

Lola | **Uptown** — 27

Lonesome Dove | **Stockyards** — 26

Z Mansion | **Uptown** — 26

Z Mercury Grill | **Preston Forest** — 27

Mi Piaci | **Addison** — 24

Morton's Steak | **Downtown D** — 25

Z Nana | **Market Ctr** — 27

Nick & Sam's | **Uptown** — 25

N9ne | **Victory Pk** — 22

Nobu | **Uptown** — 24

Oceanaire | **Galleria**	24
Palm | **W End**	24
Pappas Bros. | **Love Field**	27
Rist. La Piazza | **University Area**	26
Z Saint-Emilion | **Cultural Dist**	27
Sammy's BBQ | **Uptown**	–
Shinsei | **W Lovers Ln**	25
Silver Fox | **multi.**	24
Steel | **Oak Lawn**	25
Z Stephan Pyles | **Arts Dist**	27

PRIX FIXE MENUS

(Call for prices and times)

Z Abacus | **Knox-Henderson**	28
Z Bijoux | **W Lovers Ln**	27
Cacharel | **Arlington**	25
Fogo de Chão | **Addison**	26
Z French Rm. | **Downtown D**	28
Hôtel St. Germain | **Uptown**	25
Lola | **Uptown**	27
Z Mansion | **Uptown**	26
Z Nana | **Market Ctr**	27
Nobu | **Uptown**	24
Old Warsaw | **Uptown**	24
Palm | **W End**	24
Z Saint-Emilion | **Cultural Dist**	27
Tramontana | **Preston Ctr**	23

QUIET CONVERSATION

Adelmo's | **Knox-Henderson**	23
Z Bijoux | **W Lovers Ln**	27
Bistro Louise | **SW**	26
Z Bonnell's | **SW**	27
Bugatti | **Love Field**	21
Cacharel | **Arlington**	25
Café Cipriani | **Las Colinas**	21
Café on Green | **Las Colinas**	24
City Café | **W Lovers Ln**	–
Classic Cafe at Roanoke | **Roanoke**	28
Daniele | **Oak Lawn**	24
Z French Rm. | **Downtown D**	28
Grape | **Greenville Ave**	25
Hôtel St. Germain | **Uptown**	25
L'Ancestral | **Knox-Henderson**	23
Landmark | **Oak Lawn**	–

Lavendou | **N Dallas**	24
Lonesome Dove | **Stockyards**	26
Z Mansion | **Uptown**	26
Mi Piaci | **Addison**	24
Z Nana | **Market Ctr**	27
NEW Nonna | **Lemmon Ave**	–
Old Warsaw | **Uptown**	24
NEW Rise Nº 1 | **W Lovers Ln**	–
Rist. La Piazza | **University Area**	26
Rough Creek | **Glen Rose**	27
Ruffino's | **Forest Pk**	22
Ruggeri's | **Preston Royal**	20
Z Saint-Emilion | **Cultural Dist**	27
Sapristi! | **Forest Pk**	24
NEW Second Floor | **Galleria**	–
Seventeen Seventeen | **Arts Dist**	22
Tramontana | **Preston Ctr**	23
Zodiac | **Downtown D**	24

ROMANTIC PLACES

Addison Cafe | **Addison**	23
Z Aurora | **Oak Lawn**	27
Z Bijoux | **W Lovers Ln**	27
Cacharel | **Arlington**	25
Café Ashton | **Downtown FW**	24
Classic Cafe at Roanoke | **Roanoke**	28
NEW Dali | **Arts Dist**	–
Z French Rm. | **Downtown D**	28
Grape | **Greenville Ave**	25
Hôtel St. Germain | **Uptown**	25
Isabella's | **Frisco**	21
L'Ancestral | **Knox-Henderson**	23
Z Local | **Deep Ellum**	28
Lola | **Uptown**	27
Lonesome Dove | **Stockyards**	26
Z Mansion | **Uptown**	26
Mi Piaci | **Addison**	24
Z Nana | **Market Ctr**	27
Old Warsaw | **Uptown**	24
Perry's | **Uptown**	24
NEW Rise Nº 1 | **W Lovers Ln**	–
NEW Rist. Cibus | **NorthPark**	–
Rough Creek | **Glen Rose**	27
Ruffino's | **Forest Pk**	22
Ruggeri's | **Preston Royal**	20

Z Saint-Emilion | **Cultural Dist**	27
Sapristi! | **Forest Pk**	24
NEW Second Floor | **Galleria**	-
Watel's | **Uptown**	24
Z York St. | **Lakewood**	27

SENIOR APPEAL

Adelmo's | **Knox-Henderson**	23
Babe's | **multi.**	25
Bistro Louise | **SW**	26
Bubba's | **Park Cities**	23
Cacharel | **Arlington**	25
Café Ashton | **Downtown FW**	24
Z Café Modern | **Cultural Dist**	22
Z Café Pacific | **Park Cities**	26
Celebration | **Love Field**	21
Chubby's | **multi.**	18
City Café | **W Lovers Ln**	-
Deli News | **N Dallas**	22
H.P. Cafeteria | **Lake Highlands**	-
H.P. Pharmacy | **Knox-Henderson**	19
Kuby's | **Park Cities**	22
L'Ancestral | **Knox-Henderson**	23
Lawry's | **N Dallas**	24
Mama's Daughters' | **multi.**	21
Old Warsaw | **Uptown**	24
Patrizio | **multi.**	21
Poor Richard's | **Plano**	20
Ruggeri's | **Preston Royal**	20
Zodiac | **Downtown D**	24

SINGLES SCENES

Z ALÓ | **Knox-Henderson**	24
Blackfinn | **Addison**	13
Z Blue Mesa | **Southlake**	20
NEW Café R+D | **Preston Ctr**	-
Chuy's | **Knox-Henderson**	21
Cool River | **Las Colinas**	19
Cristina's | **multi.**	18
Crú Wine Bar | **multi.**	20
Cuba Libre | **Knox-Henderson**	20
Dallas Fish | **Downtown D**	24
Z Del Frisco's | **multi.**	27
Dragonfly | **Uptown**	19
Fireside Pies | **multi.**	23
Fuse | **Downtown D**	21

Gloria's | **multi.**	21
NEW Grimaldi's | **multi.**	-
House of Blues | **Victory Pk**	19
Iron Cactus | **Downtown D**	18
Kenichi | **Victory Pk**	22
Z Mercy | **Addison**	19
Z Mi Cocina | **multi.**	21
NEW Neighborhood Services | **W Lovers Ln**	-
Porch, The | **Knox-Henderson**	22
Primo's | **Uptown**	18
Red's | **Plano**	20
Sambuca | **multi.**	21
Sangria Tapas | **Knox-Henderson**	17
Sevy's | **Preston Ctr**	23
Steel | **Oak Lawn**	25
Sullivan's | **N Dallas**	24
Z Teppo | **Greenville Ave**	28
Texas de Brazil | **Downtown FW**	24
Tom Tom Asian | **W Vill**	20
Z Trader Vic's | **Park Cities**	19
Trece | **Knox-Henderson**	21
Victory Tav. | **Victory Pk**	15
NEW Villa-O | **Knox-Henderson**	-

SLEEPERS

(Good to excellent food, but little known)

Addison Cafe | **Addison**	23
Adelmo's | **Knox-Henderson**	23
Amici | **Carrollton**	27
Arthur's | **Addison**	23
Awaji | **Plano**	24
Bella Italia | **West**	24
Campania | **multi.**	23
Canary Cafe | **Addison**	26
Classic Cafe at Roanoke | **Roanoke**	28
Dallas Fish | **Downtown D**	24
Daniele | **Oak Lawn**	24
First Chinese | **multi.**	25
Goodhues | **McKinney**	24
Hot Damn, Tamales! | **Hospital Dist**	26
India Palace | **Preston Forest**	23
Jorg's | **Plano**	25

J.R.'s Steak | **Colleyville**	23
Kozy Kitchen | **Knox-Henderson**	25
L'Ancestral | **Knox-Henderson**	23
Little Katana | **multi.**	23
Main St. Bistro | **multi.**	23
Margaux's | **Market Ctr**	25
Mirabelle | **N Dallas**	28
My Martini | **Arlington**	23
Olenjack's Grille | **Arlington**	26
Parigi | **Oak Lawn**	25
Rist. La Piazza | **University Area**	26
Rough Creek | **Glen Rose**	27
Royal Thai | **Greenville Ave**	23
Salum | **Uptown**	25
Spiral Diner | **multi.**	23
Sweet Basil | **N Dallas**	23
Tramontana | **Preston Ctr**	23
2900 | **Uptown**	23
Watel's | **Uptown**	24
Zander's Hse. | **Plano**	23

TRANSPORTING EXPERIENCES

☑ Abacus | **Knox-Henderson**	28
☑ Aurora | **Oak Lawn**	27
☑ Café Modern | **Cultural Dist**	22
Charlie Palmer | **Downtown D**	–
☑ French Rm. | **Downtown D**	28
Lola | **Uptown**	27
☑ Nana | **Market Ctr**	27
Nobu | **Uptown**	24
Reata | **Sundance Sq**	24
NEW Rise N° 1 | **W Lovers Ln**	–
Rough Creek | **Glen Rose**	27
☑ Saint-Emilion | **Cultural Dist**	27
Seventeen Seventeen | **Arts Dist**	22
☑ Stephan Pyles | **Arts Dist**	27
NEW Tei An | **Arts Dist**	–
☑ Trader Vic's | **Park Cities**	19

TRENDY

☑ Abacus | **Knox-Henderson**	28
☑ ALÓ | **Knox-Henderson**	24
NEW Bolsa | **Oak Cliff**	–
NEW Café R+D | **Preston Ctr**	–
Central 214 | **Park Cities**	24

Charlie Palmer | **Downtown D**	–
Craft Dallas | **Victory Pk**	25
NEW Dali | **Arts Dist**	–
Dallas Fish | **Downtown D**	24
☑ Del Frisco's | **multi.**	27
☑ Fearing's | **Uptown**	26
Fireside Pies | **multi.**	23
Fuse | **Downtown D**	21
NEW Grace | **Downtown FW**	–
Hattie's | **Oak Cliff**	25
☑ Hibiscus | **Knox-Henderson**	25
House of Blues | **Victory Pk**	19
Kenichi | **Victory Pk**	22
NEW La Cubanita | **Knox-Henderson**	–
NEW Lambert's | **Near W**	–
☑ Lanny's | **Cultural Dist**	27
Little Katana | **multi.**	23
Love Shack | **Stockyards**	22
☑ Mercy | **Addison**	19
NEW Neighborhood Services | **W Lovers Ln**	–
N9ne | **Victory Pk**	22
Nobu | **Uptown**	24
NEW Nonna | **Lemmon Ave**	–
Nonna Tata | **Hospital Dist**	–
Porch, The | **Knox-Henderson**	22
NEW Rist. Cibus | **NorthPark**	–
Sangria Tapas | **Knox-Henderson**	17
NEW Screen Door | **Arts Dist**	–
Shinsei | **W Lovers Ln**	25
☑ Stephan Pyles | **Arts Dist**	27
NEW Tei An | **Arts Dist**	–
Tillman's | **Oak Cliff**	23
☑ Trader Vic's | **Park Cities**	19
Trece | **Knox-Henderson**	21
NEW Villa-O | **Knox-Henderson**	–
☑ Yutaka | **Uptown**	27

VIEWS

Aija | **Arts Dist**	19
Cacharel | **Arlington**	25
☑ Café Modern | **Cultural Dist**	22
Café Nasher | **Arts Dist**	18
Iron Cactus | **Downtown D**	18

Menus, photos, voting and more – free at ZAGAT.com

Z Mansion | **Uptown**	26
Mignon | **Plano**	22
Mi Piaci | **Addison**	24
Z Nana | **Market Ctr**	27
Primo's | **Garland**	18
Reata | **Sundance Sq**	24
NEW Rist. Cibus | **NorthPark**	-
Rough Creek | **Glen Rose**	27

VISITORS ON EXPENSE ACCOUNT

Z Abacus | **Knox-Henderson**	28
Z Al Biernat's | **Oak Lawn**	26
Z Aurora | **Oak Lawn**	27
Z Bijoux | **W Lovers Ln**	27
Z Bob's Steak | **multi.**	25
Z Café Pacific | **Park Cities**	26
Capital Grille | **Uptown**	25
Charlie Palmer | **Downtown D**	-
Craft Dallas | **Victory Pk**	25
Z Del Frisco's | **multi.**	27
Z Fearing's | **Uptown**	26
Z French Rm. | **Downtown D**	28
NEW Grace | **Downtown FW**	-
Grill/Alley | **Galleria**	21
Hôtel St. Germain | **Uptown**	25
Kenichi | **Victory Pk**	22
Lola | **Uptown**	27
Z Mansion | **Uptown**	26
Z Mercury Grill | **Preston Forest**	27
Mi Piaci | **Addison**	24
Z Nana | **Market Ctr**	27
Nick & Sam's | **Uptown**	25
N9ne | **Victory Pk**	22
Nobu | **Uptown**	24
Oceanaire | **Galleria**	24
Old Hickory | **Grapevine**	21
Pappas Bros. | **Love Field**	27
Perry's | **Uptown**	24
Pyramid | **Arts Dist**	-
Z Saint-Emilion | **Cultural Dist**	27
NEW Screen Door | **Arts Dist**	-
Silver Fox | **multi.**	24
Steel | **Oak Lawn**	25
Z Stephan Pyles | **Arts Dist**	27
Texas de Brazil | **multi.**	24

III Forks | **N Dallas**	25
Z York St. | **Lakewood**	27

WINNING WINE LISTS

Z Abacus | **Knox-Henderson**	28
Adelmo's | **Knox-Henderson**	23
Z Al Biernat's | **Oak Lawn**	26
Arcodoro/Pomodoro | **Uptown**	21
Z Aurora | **Oak Lawn**	27
Café on Green | **Las Colinas**	24
Z Café Pacific | **Park Cities**	26
Capital Grille | **Uptown**	25
Chamberlain's Steak | **Addison**	25
Charlie Palmer | **Downtown D**	-
Craft Dallas | **Victory Pk**	25
Crú Wine Bar | **multi.**	20
Dakota's | **Arts Dist**	22
NEW Dali | **Arts Dist**	-
Z Del Frisco's | **multi.**	27
Z Fearing's | **Uptown**	26
Ferre | **Sundance Sq**	21
Z French Rm. | **Downtown D**	28
NEW Grace | **Downtown FW**	-
Grape | **Greenville Ave**	25
Houston's | **Addison**	23
Kenichi | **Victory Pk**	22
Landmark | **Oak Lawn**	-
Lawry's | **N Dallas**	24
Lola | **Uptown**	27
Maguire's | **N Dallas**	23
Z Mansion | **Uptown**	26
Z Mercury Grill | **Preston Forest**	27
Z Mercy | **Addison**	19
Mi Piaci | **Addison**	24
Morton's Steak | **Downtown D**	25
My Martini | **Arlington**	23
Z Nana | **Market Ctr**	27
Newport's | **W End**	21
Nick & Sam's | **Uptown**	25
N9ne | **Victory Pk**	22
Oceanaire | **Galleria**	24
Old Hickory | **Grapevine**	21
Old Warsaw | **Uptown**	24
Palm | **W End**	24
Pappas Bros. | **Love Field**	27

Perry's | **Uptown** 24

PoPoLos | **Preston Royal** 20

Pyramid | **Arts Dist** -

Rough Creek | **Glen Rose** 27

Ruth's Chris | **N Dallas** 25

Z Saint-Emilion | **Cultural Dist** 27

Sapristi! | **Forest Pk** 24

Sonoma Grill | **Flower Mound** 22

State & Allen | **Uptown** 19

Steel | **Oak Lawn** 25

Z Stephan Pyles | **Arts Dist** 27

St. Martin's | **Greenville Ave** 26

Sullivan's | **N Dallas** 24

III Forks | **N Dallas** 25

Truluck's | **Uptown** 23

NEW Villa-O | -
Knox-Henderson

Z York St. | **Lakewood** 27

Ziziki's | **multi.** 24

WORTH A TRIP

Glen Rose
  Rough Creek 27

McKinney
  Goodhues 24

Oak Cliff
  NEW Bolsa -
  Hattie's 25

Plano
  Z Jasper's 24

Roanoke
  Classic Cafe at Roanoke 28

Rockwall
  Culpepper 24

HOUSTON

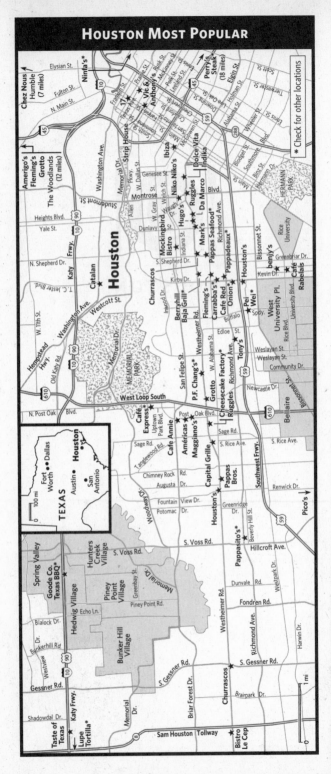

HOUSTON MOST POPULAR

Chez Nous Humble (7 miles)

Elysian St.

Ninfa's*

Fulton St.

N. Main St.

Nolda St.

Black St.

McKinney St.

Enid St.

Elgin St.

Scott St.

Prairie St.

Polk St.

Leeland St.

Holman St.

Ennis St.

Travis St.

Vic & Anthony's

Perry's Steak (18 miles)

Amerigo's Fleming's Grotto

The Woodlands (12 miles)

Washington Ave.

Memorial Dr.

Strip House

W. Dallas St.

Genesee St.

Smith St.

Crawford St.

Wheeler Ave.

Ibiza

Dolce Vita

Indika

Alabama St.

Southmore Blvd.

Binz St.

Blodget St.

Montrose

Niko Niko's

Ruggles

Da Marco

Blvd.

Main St.

HERMANN PARK

Heights Blvd.

Yale St.

Studemont St.

Allen

Dunlavy

W. Gray

Welch St.

Waugh Dr.

Hugo's

Mark's

Richmond Ave.

Hermann Dr.

Rice University

Mockingbird Bistro

Indiana St.

Pappas Seafood*

Pappadeaux

Houston's

benjy's

Bissonnet St.

Greenbriar Dr.

Café Rabelais

N. Shepherd Dr.

Catalan

T.C. Jester Blvd.

S. Shepherd Dr.

Kirby Dr.

Inwood Dr.

Churrascos

Berryhill Baja Grill*

Fleming's

Cafe Red Onion

Pei Wei

Kevin Dr.

University Blvd.

West University Pl.

Houston

Carrabba's

Buffalo

Spdy.

Rice Blvd.

Katy Frwy.

W. 11th St.

Westcott St.

Memorial Dr.

Edloe St.

Tony's

Weslayan St.

Weslayan St.

Community Dr.

Hempstead Hwy.

Old Katy Rd.

San Felipe St.

Grotto

W. Alabama St.

P.F. Chang's*

Cheesecake Factory*

Ruggles

Richmond Ave.

Newcastle Dr.

Bissonnet St.

MEMORIAL PARK

West Loop South

Post Oak Blvd.

Café Express

Uptown Park Blvd.

Américas

Maggiano's

Sage Rd.

Bellaire Blvd.

N. Post Oak Blvd.

Sage Rd.

Tanglewood Dr.

Cafe Annie

Capital Grille

S. Rice Ave.

S. Rice Ave.

Chimney Rock Rd.

Augusta

Pappas Bros.

Houston's

Renwick Dr.

Fountain View Dr.

Potomac Dr.

Greenridge Dr.

Pico's

Beverly Hill St.

Woodway Dr.

Spring Valley

Hunters Creek Village

S. Voss Rd.

S. Voss Rd.

Hillcroft Ave.

Pappasito's*

Goode Co. Texas BBQ*

Piney Point Village

Memorial Dr.

Greenbay St.

Piney Point Rd.

Dunvale Rd.

Westpark Dr.

Hedwig Village

Blalock Dr.

Echo Ln.

Fondren Rd.

Richmond Ave.

Bunkerhill Rd.

Westview

Bunker Hill Village

Harwin Dr.

Gessner Rd.

S. Gessner Rd.

S. Gessner Rd.

Shadowdal Dr.

Katy Frwy.

Memorial Dr.

Briar Forest Dr.

Churrascos

Brairpark Dr.

Taste of Texas

Lupe Tortilla*

Sam Houston Tollway

Bistro Le Cep

TEXAS

Fort Worth

Dallas

Houston

Austin

San Antonio

100 mi

Menus, photos, voting and more – free at ZAGAT.com

Most Popular

1. Mark's | *American*
2. Carrabba's | *Italian*
3. Cafe Annie | *Southwestern*
4. Perry's Steak | *Steak*
5. Da Marco | *Italian*
6. Pappasito's | *Tex-Mex*
7. Pappadeaux | *Seafood*
8. Américas | *S American*
9. Pappas Bros. | *Steak*
10. P.F. Chang's | *Chinese*
11. Lupe Tortilla | *Mexican*
12. Churrascos | *S American*
13. Hugo's | *Mexican*
14. Goode Co. Texas BBQ | *BBQ*
15. Tony's | *Italian*
16. Fleming's | *Steak*
17. Ibiza* | *Mediterranean*
18. Cafe Red Onion | *Pan-Latin*
19. Cheesecake Factory | *American*
20. Grotto | *Italian*
21. Vic & Anthony's | *Steak*
22. Capital Grille | *Steak*
23. Taste of Texas* | *Steak*
24. Café Rabelais | *French*
25. Ruggles* | *American*
26. Pappas Seafood | *Seafood*
27. Niko Niko's | *Greek*
28. Mockingbird Bistro | *American*
29. Berryhill Baja Grill | *Mexican*
30. Indika | *Indian*
31. Ninfa's/Orig. Ninfa's | *Tex-Mex*
32. 17 | *American*
33. Chez Nous | *French*
34. Dolce Vita | *Italian*
35. Catalan | *American/Spanish*
36. Pico's | *Mexican*
37. Café Express | *Eclectic*
38. Pei Wei* | *Pan-Asian*
39. Strip House* | *Steak*
40. Amerigo's | *Italian*
41. Bistro Le Cep* | *French*
42. benjy's | *American*
43. Houston's* | *American*
44. Maggiano's | *Italian*

It's obvious that many of the above restaurants are among the Houston area's most expensive, but if popularity were calibrated to price, we suspect that a number of other restaurants would join their ranks. Thus, we have added two lists comprising 80 Best Buys on page 198.

KEY NEWCOMERS

Our editors' take on the year's top arrivals. See page 282 for a full list.

BB's Kitchen | *Cajun*

Bedford | *American*

Cullen's | *American*

Feast | *British*

Frank's | *Steak*

Gigi's | *Pan-Asian*

Hue | *Vietnamese*

Little Bigs | *Burgers*

Rist. Cavour | *Italian*

Russo's | *Italian*

Textile | *American*

Voice | *American*

* Indicates a tie with restaurant above

Top Food Ratings

Excludes places with low votes, unless indicated by a ∇.

28	Mark's	*American*
	Da Marco	*Italian*
27	Tony's	*Italian*
	Kanomwan	*Thai*
	China View	*Chinese*
	Pappas Bros.	*Steak*
26	Cafe Annie	*Southwestern*
	Vic & Anthony's	*Steak*
	Nielsen's Deli	*Deli*
	Japaneiro's	*Japanese/S Amer.*
	Chez Nous	*French*
	Hugo's	*Mexican*
	Lynn's Steak	*Steak*
	Fogo de Chão	*Brazilian/Steak*
	Jimmy Wilson's	*Seafood*
	Red Onion*	*Seafood*
	Café Rabelais	*French*
	Le Mistral	*French*
	Uptown Sushi	*Japanese*
25	Brenner's	*Steak*

Churrascos | *S American*
Bistro Le Cep | *French*
Indika | *Indian*
Kubo's | *Japanese*
Capital Grille | *Steak*
Reef | *Seafood*
Fung's Kitchen | *Chinese/Sea.*
Ruth's Chris | *Steak*
t'afia | *American*
Mockingbird Bistro | *American*
Remington | *American*
Ibiza | *Mediterranean*
Kiran's | *Indian*
17 | *American*
Glass Wall | *American*
Goode Co. Texas BBQ | *BBQ*
Shade | *American*
Artista | *American*
Perry's Steak | *Steak*
Piatto | *Italian*

BY CUISINE

AMERICAN (NEW)
28	Mark's
25	t'afia
	Mockingbird Bistro
	Remington
	17

AMERICAN (TRAD.)
23	Houston's
	Cleburne Cafeteria
	Lankford Grocery
	Breakfast Klub
22	Dessert Gallery

BARBECUE
25	Goode Co. Texas BBQ
24	Swinging Door
	Pizzitola's BBQ∇
23	Luling City Mkt.
	Thelma's BBQ∇

BURGERS
23	Pappas Burgers
	Lankford Grocery
22	Becks Prime
	Goode Co. Hamburgers
21	Bellaire Burger

CHINESE
27	China View
25	Fung's Kitchen
23	Yum Yum Cha
	Daniel Wong's
	Kim Son

CREOLE/CAJUN
24	Tony Mandola's
	Treebeards
23	Pappadeaux
22	Floyd's
21	Ragin' Cajun

ECLECTIC
21	Barnaby's Café
	Hobbit Cafe
	Sambuca
	Raven Grill
	Max's

FRENCH
26	Chez Nous
	Café Rabelais
	Le Mistral
25	Bistro Le Cep
24	Chez Georges

INDIAN

25 Indika
   Kiran's
24 Ashiana
23 Khyber North Indian
22 Madras Pavilion

ITALIAN

28 Da Marco
27 Tony's
25 Piatto
24 Dolce Vita
   Nino's

JAPANESE

26 Japaneiro's
   Uptown Sushi
25 Kubo's
23 Sushi King
   Azuma/Azumi

MEDITERRANEAN

25 Ibiza
23 Phoenicia Deli
   Café Benedicte▽
21 Fadi's
18 Dimassi's

MEXICAN

26 Hugo's
24 Pico's
22 Irma's
21 Tila's
20 Las Alamedas

SEAFOOD

26 Jimmy Wilson's
   Red Onion Seafood
25 Reef
   Fung's Kitchen
24 Oceanaire

SOUTH AMERICAN

26 Japaneiro's
   Red Onion Seafood
25 Churrascos
24 Américas
   Café Red Onion

SOUTHERN/ SOUTHWESTERN

26 Cafe Annie
24 Treebeards
23 Cleburne Cafeteria
   Burning Pear
   Ouisie's Table

STEAKHOUSES

27 Pappas Bros.
26 Vic & Anthony's
   Lynn's Steak
   Fogo de Chão
25 Brenner's

TEX-MEX

23 Pappasito's
22 Ninfa's/Original Ninfa's
   El Tiempo
21 Sylvia's
   Chuy's

THAI

27 Kanomwan
24 Thai Gourmet
23 Mai Thai
21 Nit Noi
18 Thai Pepper

VIETNAMESE

23 Mai's
22 Kim Son
   Miss Saigon
20 Mo Mong
   Vietopia

BY SPECIAL FEATURE

BREAKFAST

25 Remington
   17
24 Pico's
   Kenny & Ziggy's
23 Lankford Grocery

BRUNCH

26 Hugo's
25 Bistro Le Cep
   Shade
24 Ashiana
   Michelangelo's

BUSINESS DINING

28 Mark's
27 Tony's
   Pappas Bros.
26 Cafe Annie
   Vic & Anthony's

CHILD-FRIENDLY

25 Goode Co. Texas BBQ
24 Swinging Door
   Taste of Texas
   Pico's
   Cafe Red Onion

HOTEL DINING

25 Remington (St. Regis)
   17 (Alden Houston)
23 Quattro (Four Seasons)
22 Noé (Omni Hotel)
21 Rio Ranch (Westchase Hilton)

MEET FOR A DRINK

26 Uptown Sushi
25 t'afia
   Remington
   Ibiza
   17

OFFBEAT

25 Goode Co. Texas BBQ
24 Swinging Door
23 Yum Yum Cha
   Niko Niko's
   Star Pizza

PEOPLE-WATCHING

28 Mark's
27 Tony's
26 Vic & Antony's
   Uptown Sushi
25 t'afia

POWER SCENES

28 Mark's
27 Tony's
   Pappas Bros.
26 Cafe Annie
   Vic & Anthony's

QUICK BITES

24 Frenchie's
23 Kahn's Deli
   Lankford Grocery
   Ruggles
22 Becks Prime

TRENDY

28 Mark's
26 Uptown Sushi
25 Reef
   t'afia
   Mockingbird Bistro

WINNING WINE LISTS

28 Mark's
   Da Marco
27 Tony's
   Pappas Bros.
26 Cafe Annie

WORTH A TRIP

26 Chez Nous
      Humble
24 Swinging Door
      Richmond
   Frenchie's
      Clear Lake
22 Amerigo's
      The Woodlands
   Gaido's
      Galveston

BY LOCATION

DOWNTOWN

26 Vic & Anthony's
25 17
   Artista
   Morton's Steak
24 Strip House

GALLERIA

27 Pappas Bros.
26 Cafe Annie
   Nielsen's Deli
25 Capital Grille
   Ruth's Chris

HEIGHTS

25 Glass Wall
   Shade
24 Catalan
23 Star Pizza
   Rainbow Lodge

LOWER SHEPHERD

25 Churrascos
23 Star Pizza
22 divino
   Mission Burritos
21 Hobbit Cafe

MEMORIAL

25 Brenner's
   Goode Co. Texas BBQ
   Perry's Steak
24 Taste of Texas
23 Pappadeaux

MIDTOWN

25 Reef
   t'afia
   Ibiza
23 Charivari
   Mai's

MONTROSE

- 28 | Mark's
- Da Marco
- 26 | Hugo's
- 25 | Indika
- 24 | Dolce Vita

RICE VILLAGE

- 26 | Café Rabelais
- 25 | Kubo's
- 23 | Yum Yum Cha
- Prego
- Kahn's Deli

RIVER OAKS

- 25 | Brenner's
- Mockingbird Bistro
- 24 | Fleming's
- 23 | Tony Mandola's
- Thierry André

SUGAR LAND

- 26 | Japaneiro's
- 25 | Perry's Steak
- 24 | Amici
- 23 | Pappasito's
- 22 | Carrabba's

SW HOUSTON

- 25 | Churrascos
- Fung's Kitchen
- 23 | Rudi Lechner's

- 21 | Rio Ranch
- Ragin' Cajun

THE WOODLANDS

- 25 | Perry's Steak
- 24 | Jasper's
- Kirby's Steak
- Fleming's
- 23 | Pappadeaux

UPPER KIRBY DISTRICT

- 24 | Cafe Red Onion
- 23 | Houston's
- Pappadeaux
- Mai Thai
- Sushi King

WEST HOUSTON

- 27 | China View
- 26 | Lynn's Steak
- Le Mistral
- 25 | Bistro Le Cep
- 24 | Ashiana

WEST U

- 25 | Goode Co. Texas BBQ
- 24 | Antica Osteria
- 23 | Cleburne Cafeteria
- Goode Co. Texas Seafood
- 22 | Goode Co. Hamburgers

Top Decor Ratings

27] La Colombe d'Or
Tony's

26] 17
Rainbow Lodge
Mark's
Café Le Jadeite

25] Artista
Américas
Jasper's
Strip House
Perry's Steak
Las Alamedas
Remington*
Vic & Anthony's
Capital Grille
Trevisio

24] Vargo's
Brenner's
Uptown Sushi*
Zula*
Cafe Annie

Amici
Masraff's
Pappas Bros.
Sorrento
Fleming's

23] Hugo's
Oceanaire
Sambuca
Lynn's Steak
Quattro
Crú Wine Bar
Brio
Sullivan's*
Grappino di Nino
Pesce

22] Kiran's
Shade
Noé
Arturo's
Indika*
Churrascos

OUTDOORS

Baba Yega
Backstreet Café
Brasil
Daily Review
Dolce Vita

El Pueblito
Empire Café
Grappino di Nino
Grove
Hugo's

ROMANCE

Artista
Cafe Annie
Café Le Jadeite
Chez Nous
Da Marco

La Colombe d'Or
Mark's
Rainbow Lodge
Rist. Cavour
Tony's

ROOMS

Arcodoro
Cafe Annie
Mark's
Masraff's
Ouisie's Table

Pappas Bros.
Quattro
Rainbow Lodge
Smith & Wollensky
Vic & Anthony's

VIEWS

Artista
Brenner's
Del Frisco's
Grove
Las Alamedas

Monarch
Rainbow Lodge
Reef
Trevisio
Vargo's

Menus, photos, voting and more – free at ZAGAT.com

Top Service Ratings

27 Tony's
Mark's

26 Cafe Annie
Chez Nous
Da Marco
Fogo de Chão

25 Capital Grille
Pappas Bros.
Remington
Ruth's Chris

24 Vic & Anthony's
Charivari
Lynn's Steak
Palm
Masraff's
Rudi Lechner's
La Colombe d'Or
Brenner's
Perry's Steak
Jasper's

23 Churrascos
Kirby's Steak
Sullivan's
Bistro Le Cep
Jimmy Wilson's*
Michelangelo's*
Rioja Tapas*
Fleming's
Morton's Steak
Mockingbird Bistro
17
Amerigo's
Taste of Texas
Quattro
Strip House
Oceanaire
Reef
Noé
Truluck's
Piatto

Best Buys

In order of Bang for the Buck rating.

1. Bellaire Burger
2. Mission Burritos
3. Nielsen's Deli
4. 100% Taquito
5. Kahn's Deli
6. Treebeards
7. Lankford Grocery
8. Becks Prime
9. Cleburne Cafeteria
10. Chinese Café
11. Swinging Door
12. Jax Grill
13. Goode Co. Texas BBQ
14. Dessert Gallery
15. Fadi's
16. Daniel Wong's
17. China View
18. Mama's Café
19. 59 Diner
20. Leibman's
21. Sylvia's Enchilada
22. Niko Niko's
23. Avalon Drug Co.
24. Breakfast Klub
25. Buffalo Grille
26. Barnaby's
27. Masala
28. Black Walnut Café
29. Istanbul Grill
30. Empire Café
31. Pappas Burgers
32. Star Pizza
33. Berryhill Baja
34. Pei Wei
35. Van Loc
36. Chuy's
37. McGonigel's
38. Christian's Tailgate
39. Barry's Pizza
40. Phoenicia Deli

OTHER GOOD VALUES

Baba Yega
Blue Nile
Brasil
Café Express
Dimassi's
Don Carlos
Droubi's
Empanadas by Marini
Goode Co. Hamburgers
Hobbit Cafe
Jarro Café
Jasmine
Jenni's Noodle Hse.
Kasra
Kenneally's
Kenny & Ziggy's
Kim Son
La Mexicana
Little Bigs
Luling City Mkt.

Lyndon's Pit BBQ
Mai Thai
Market Sq. B&G
Mexico's Deli
One's A Meal
Otilia's
Pizzitola's
Pronto Cucinino
Rudi Lechner's
Russo's NY Pizza
Sawadee
Sichuan Cuisine
Spanish Flowers
Tan Tan
Teotihuacan
Thelma's
This is It
Tiny Boxwoods
Vieng Thai
Vietopia

Houston

	FOOD	DECOR	SERVICE	COST

Aka Japanese Cuisine *Japanese*   ▽ 23 | 21 | 17 | $27
West Houston | 1460 Eldridge Pkwy. (bet. Forkland & Westerloch Drs.) | 281-558-8900
Aka Sushi House *Japanese*
Upper Kirby District | 2390 W. Alabama St. (bet. Kirby & Shepherd Drs.) | 713-807-7875
www.akasushi.net
This plush West Houston eatery is the sushi spot of choice for nearby Energy Corridor executives seeking "innovative" Japanese dishes at lunch; after dark, happy-hour specials and flat-screen TVs at the bar draw post-work revelers for fruity sake cocktails, snacks and more substantial meals; N.B. the Upper Kirby District sibling is newer.

Alexander the Great *Greek*   24 | 17 | 21 | $27
Galleria | 3055 Sage Rd. (Hidalgo St.) | 713-622-2778 | www.alexanderthegreat.cc
Supporters say it's worth seeking out this "hard-to-find" Hellenic where the "tasty", "well-priced" food is served in "large portions" and sets the "gold standard" for Galleria-area Greek; traditional decor may be "underwhelming" but it gets a boost from live music and belly dancing Friday–Saturday.

Amazón Grill *S American*   18 | 15 | 14 | $16
West U | Woodlake Sq. | 5114 Kirby Dr. (Bissonnet St.) | 713-522-5888 | www.cordua.com
Another "home run" for the Cordúa family (Churrascos), this counter-service West U eatery is "fun for a casual meal" thanks to "inexpensive" and "unusual" South American dishes in "carefree" environs; many deem it "one of Houston's best bargains", though a few holdouts aren't bananas about the "screaming kids and funny food."

Z Américas *S American*   24 | 25 | 22 | $42
Galleria | The Pavilion | 1800 Post Oak Blvd. (bet. San Felipe St. & Westheimer Rd.) | 713-961-1492 ⓢ
NEW **The Woodlands** | 21 Waterway Ave. (Timberloch Pl.) | 281-367-1492
www.cordua.com
"Whimsical" doesn't even begin to describe the "over-the-top" decor at this Cordúa family Galleria-area "mainstay" where the "dark, cavernous" interior conjures up a "psychedelic" fantasyland that diners liken to a "full-scale production at Disney World"; "imaginative" South American cuisine is "well done" too and service "surpasses your expectations", so the "only complaint" is that the "noise level is extremely high"; N.B. the newer Woodlands branch is more subdued.

Amerigo's Grille *Italian*   22 | 22 | 23 | $51
The Woodlands | Grogan's Park | 25250 Grogan's Park Dr. (Sawdust Rd.) | 281-362-0808 | www.amerigos.com
A comparative "oldie in The Woodlands" (since 1994) amid a host of "high-end" "chain" newcomers, this rustic-looking "hometown

	FOOD	DECOR	SERVICE	COST

fave" is still respected for its "attractive, tasty" Italian eats and "excellent wine selections", all enhanced by "first-class service"; locals label it "lovely for special lunches or dinners" and a "nice break from the suburban sprawl"; N.B. there's also occasional live music.

Amici *Italian*
24 | 24 | 23 | $38

Sugar Land | Sugar Land Town Sq. | 16089 City Walk (Plaza Dr.) | 281-242-2800 | www.amicitownsquare.com

"Excellent" Italian entrees with a Neapolitan "twist" plus "outstanding antipasto" and plenty of "traditional favorites" make the Vallone family's moderately priced Sugar Land venture "a big hit" with local "families"; though critics call it "too loud", the outdoor patio is a quieter respite where "great people-watching" is a plus.

NEW Andrea Ristorante
‒ | ‒ | ‒ | M

Italiano ⌧ *Italian*

West Houston | 12513 Westheimer Rd. (S. Dairy Ashford St.) | 281-496-9443 | www.andrearistorante.com

Chef-owner Andrea Pintus (ex Patrenella's) strikes out on his own with this rustic Italian newcomer in West Houston; its comforting vibe extends from the cozy Tuscan-inspired environs to the moderately priced menu, which features fresh seafood pastas and thick lamb chops backed by an array of regional wines.

Antica Osteria ⌧ *Italian*
24 | 19 | 21 | $40

West U | 2311 Bissonnet St. (Greenbriar Dr.) | 713-521-1155 | www.anticarestaurant.com

Set in a "cozy" space that was once a rare-books shop, this rustic West U trattoria has become a best-seller among the "local power crowd" for its "authentic Italian cuisine" and "nice owners"; fans find it a "romantic fave", but critics claim it's nothing novel ("you can do better for your money in the area"); P.S. "eat early" before the "awesome specials" "get erased from the chalkboard."

Arcodoro *Italian*
20 | 20 | 19 | $44

Galleria | Centre at Post Oak | 5000 Westheimer Rd. (Post Oak Blvd.) | 713-621-6888 | www.arcodoro.com

"Actual Italians would approve" of the "friendly service" and "reliable" dishes (including "exotic Sardinian specialties") at this "upmarket" – read: "expensive" – ristorante near the Galleria; during the day it's a "convenient" haven for "business-lunchers" and "shopping tourists", while the "hopping" bar is popular "after work" and as a "late-night watering hole for Gen-Xers"; N.B. there's a Dallas sibling named Arcodoro & Pomodoro.

Armadillo Palace ◑ *Pub Food*
▽ 21 | 23 | 18 | $17

West U | 5015 Kirby Dr. (Bartlett St.) | 713-526-9700 | www.thearmadillopalace.com

A giant stainless-steel armadillo out front welcomes folks to this "energetic" West U eatery, an "Old West–type saloon" with "casual" Traditional American fare and "better-than-average live country music"; pleased pardners like to "hang out after work" on the patio, but if the "mayhem" gets "maddening" or the food seems

"off" it's easy to mosey across the street to corporate sibling Goode Co. Texas BBQ.

Armandos *Tex-Mex*

| 14 | 18 | 15 | $40 |

River Oaks | 2630 Westheimer Rd. (Kirby Dr.) | 713-520-1738 | www.armandosrestaurant.com

After a long hiatus, "local celebrity" Armando Palacios has re-created his eponymous Tex-Mex hangout, now in River Oaks digs decked out with gilded mirrors, Hispanic art and "loud music" on the speakers; it's "popular with the social set", even if critics maintain it's "more about the 'scene' than the food", pointing to "uninspired" fare, "expensive" tabs and "mediocre service."

☑ Artista ⑤ *American*

| 25 | 25 | 22 | $43 |

Downtown | Hobby Center for the Performing Arts | 800 Bagby St. (Walker St.) | 713-278-4782 | www.cordua.com

Another Cordúa family "favorite", this "theater district" "standout" features a "creative" New American menu that allows patrons to "mix-and-match sides and sauces", adding a "fun element of experimentation" to any meal; it may be "pricey", and "service can be hit-or-miss", but the "elegant" setting on the second floor of the Hobby Center offers a "glorious view" of the Downtown skyline, making it "perfect before a show" or "an excellent place to impress out-of-towners"; N.B. outdoor terrace seating is also available.

Arturo's Uptown Italiano ⑤ *Italian*

| 19 | 22 | 21 | $42 |

Uptown | Uptown Park | 1180 Uptown Park Blvd. (San Felipe St.) | 713-621-1180 | www.arturosuptown.com

Arturo Boada's (ex Beso) "inviting" Uptowner thrives on a "lively" atmosphere thanks to an "elegant" interior done up in warm Tuscan tones and an active bar scene "for the well-heeled, over-40 set"; prices are "reasonable" considering the posh address and "parking lot dotted with Ferraris and Rolls-Royces", but a number of skeptics say they're left disappointed" by Italian cuisine that doesn't "live up to its surroundings" or its noted chef.

Ashiana *Indian*

| 24 | 18 | 20 | $29 |

West Houston | 12610 Briar Forest Dr. (Dairy Ashford Rd.) | 281-679-5555 | www.ashiana.cc

Even "dedicated Inner-Loopers" readily trek out to West Houston for the "superb variety" of "excellent" Indian eats at this "fine" establishment, where there's an "incredible lunch buffet" and staffers can "recommend the right wine" from an "impressive" list; sticklers suggest "don't show up in jeans" because atmosphere is on the "upscale" side.

Au Petit Paris ⑤ *French*

| - | - | - | E |

Lower Shepherd | 2048 Colquitt St. (Shepherd Dr.) | 713-524-7070 | www.aupetitparisrestaurant.com

Tucked into a converted bungalow on a gentrified strip of Lower Shepherd, this midpriced French yearling echoes Paris with a classic menu featuring foie gras made in-house and duck confit; the appropriately *petit* interior is divided into three cream-colored dining rooms and includes a charming bar area that seats five.

	FOOD	DECOR	SERVICE	COST

Aura 🗓Ⓜ American
| | - | - | - | M |

Missouri City | 3340 FM 1092 Rd. (Hwy. 6) | 281-403-2872 |
www.aura-restaurant.com

Frédéric Perrier (ex Ruggles Grille 5115) has resurfaced in a Missouri
City strip mall with this French-influenced New American eatery
that exhibits modern sensibilities both in its sleek setting and innovative menu featuring enticing dishes like bison sliders with seared
foie gras; it's already drawing a loyal local following thanks to its
moderate prices and eager-to-please staff.

Avalon Drug Co. & Diner American
| | 16 | 12 | 15 | $12 |

River Oaks | 2417 Westheimer Rd. (Revere St.) | 713-527-8900
Stafford | The Fountains, Stafford | 12810 Southwest Frwy.
(Fountain Lake Circle) | 281-240-0213
www.avalondiner.com

"Generations" have "savored" the "great old drugstore food"
(e.g. "hearty" American breakfasts) at this River Oaks institution,
which also has a licensed namesake in Stafford; you'll "rub shoulders" with "people you read about in *Texas Monthly*" but you may
also get "service with a grimace."

Azuma Japanese
| | 23 | 20 | 18 | $32 |

Downtown | 909 Texas St. (909 Texas Ave.) | 713-223-0909
Rice Village | 5600 Kirby Dr. (Nottingham St.) | 713-432-9649
Azumi 🗓 Japanese
Medical Center | Baylor College of Medicine | 1709 Dryden Rd.
(Main St.) | 713-790-9997

Sushi-seekers say this "upmarket" threesome "really works" thanks
to "fabulously fresh fish", a list of "exotic rolls" that "reads like 31
Flavors" and the "unusual" opportunity to "cook your own meat on
hot rocks"; "contemporary" Asian-inflected decor and "mean martinis" attract "trendies" and "couples on dates" who'll overlook the
"pricey" tabs and sometimes "slow" service; N.B. the scaled-down
Azumi, in the Medical Center, is more take-out oriented.

Baba Yega American
| | 20 | 19 | 18 | $20 |

Montrose | 2607 Grant St. (Missouri St.) | 713-522-0042 |
www.babayega.com

"Flamboyant staffers" and "Montrose characters" make for "good
people-watching" at this "funky" "house-turned-restaurant" that's become a "local institution" in Houston; denizens dig into "deliciously
fresh", vegetarian-friendly Traditional American fare and find "comfort" in the "cozy" setting that "looks like your great-aunt's living
room"; bonus: a patio overlooking lush, "tranquil" gardens.

Backstreet Café American
| | 22 | 20 | 21 | $37 |

River Oaks | 1103 S. Shepherd Dr. (Clay St.) | 713-521-2239 |
www.backstreetcafe.net

Loyalists "love everything about" this River Oaks "neighborhood bistro", from the "well-prepared" New American cuisine with a Southern
"kick" to the "lovely", "shaded" patio where you can enjoy a "romantic dinner" attended by a "knowledgeable" staff; though it's gener-

ally quiet ("you can actually have a conversation here"), "brunch is prime time", with live jazz music bringing in a "more festive crowd."

Barnaby's Café *American/Eclectic* | 21 | 16 | 20 | $16 |

NEW Briargrove | 5750 Woodway Dr. (Bering Dr.) | 713-266-0046
Midtown | 414 W. Gray St. (bet. Stanford & Taft Sts.) | 713-522-8898
Montrose | 604 Fairview St. (Hopkins St.) | 713-522-0106
River Oaks | 1701 S. Shepherd Dr. (Haddon St.) | 713-520-5131
Baby Barnaby's *American/Eclectic*
Montrose | 602 Fairview St. (Hopkins St.) | 713-522-4229
www.barnabyscafe.com

"Salads bigger than most gardens" and "excellent meatloaf" are among the "hearty" Eclectic–Traditional American eats served at this "colorful", canine-themed local chain ("too nice to be called a dive, but just as comfortable"); best friends say "super prices" make it a "no-brainer" for "fun" family meals, even if, like dogs, the service is "friendly" yet "spotty"; N.B. Baby Barnaby's in Montrose serves only breakfast; its big brother next door handles lunch and dinner.

Barry's Pizza *Pizza* | 20 | 12 | 17 | $15 |

Briargrove | 6003 Richmond Ave. (Fountain View Dr.) | 713-266-8692
Stafford | The Fountains, Stafford | 11303 Fountain Lake Dr.
(Fountain Lake Circle) | 281-494-0666
www.barryspizza.com

This duet of extremely casual, "user-friendly" parlors in Briargrove and Stafford is best known for its "good" pizza, including a thick-crusted Sicilian pie that some say is the "best deep-dish" in the area; with cheap prices and TVs on-site, these are also "terrific places to watch sports."

NEW **BB's Kitchen** ❷ *Cajun* | - | - | - | I |

Montrose | 2710 Montrose Blvd. (Westheimer Rd.) | 713-524-4499 |
www.bbscajuncafe.com

To a hopping stretch of Montrose Boulevard comes this tiny new Cajun kitchen turning out affordable grub like po' boys and shrimp étouffée, plus daiquiris to go; on weekends they serve into the wee hours (till 4 AM), and breakfast is offered all day – every day – which especially comes in handy after those late nights.

Beaver's Ⓜ *BBQ* | - | - | - | I |

Heights | 2310 Decatur St. (Washington Ave.) | 713-864-2328 |
www.beavershouston.com

Monica Pope (t'afia) takes on Texas BBQ at her casual joint near the Heights offering a wide-ranging menu featuring smoked brisket and shredded pork shoulder alongside more unusual selections like quail stuffed with jalapeño cream cheese and bison meatloaf; with unusual cocktails and 75 varieties of beer, the modern roadhouse setting plays host to a busy bar scene as well.

Becks Prime *Burgers* | 22 | 13 | 17 | $13 |

Briargrove | 2615 Augusta Dr. (Westheimer Rd.) | 713-266-9901
Downtown | 919 Milam St. (Walker St.) | 713-659-6122 🛃

(continued)

(continued)

Becks Prime

Memorial | Memorial Park Golf Course Clubhouse | 1001 E. Memorial Loop (Westcott St.) | 713-863-8188

NEW **Memorial** | Memorial City Mall | 514 Memorial City Way (Gessner Dr.) | 713-463-4486

Upper Kirby District | 2902 Kirby Dr. (Kipling St.) | 713-524-7085

West Houston | 11000 Westheimer Rd. (Wilcrest Dr.) | 713-952-2325

West Houston | 1202 Dairy Ashford St. (Katy Frwy.) | 281-493-3806

Sugar Land | 1822 Hwy. 6 S. (Southwest Frwy.) | 281-242-6300

The Woodlands | Grogan's Mill Village Ctr. | 2120 Buckthorne Pl. (Grogans Mill Rd.) | 281-367-3600

www.becksprime.com

Patty people "can't drive by" any of this chain's locations "without salivating" for "flavorful" burgers, "real" fries and "heavenly" milkshakes; interiors are "zero"-frills, but outdoor seating draws kudos, especially Augusta's "giant oak tree" and Memorial Park's "lovely golf-course views"; wallet-watchers warn it's "pricey for fast food."

NEW **Bedford** *American* | - | - | - | E |

Heights | 1001 Studewood St. (Merrill St.) | 713-880-1001 | www.bedfordrestaurant.com

Taking its name from the birthplace of chef-owner Robert Gadsby (ex Noé), this swanky arrival is revving up to be another hot spot for the formerly forlorn Heights area; its global array of seasonal New American dishes can be served in the brick-accented dining area, at the emerald-studded bar or at Table One – the chef's restaurant-within-a-restaurant – featuring seven- and nine-course tasting menus.

Bellaire Broiler Burger ⭐ *Burgers* | 21 | 6 | 16 | $9 |

Bellaire | 5216 Bellaire Blvd. (Bissonnet St.) | 713-668-8171 | www.houstonbizdir.com/bbb

This "Bellaire institution" has been "pumping out" "flavorful and juicy" flame-broiled burgers for the past half-century; sure, it's "a dive" with "decor that time warps to the '50s" and service that's sometimes "unpleasant", but it remains a "favorite" among "locals" who rank it as the No. 1 Best Buy in the Houston area.

Benihana *Japanese/Steak* | 20 | 18 | 21 | $32 |

Downtown | 1318 Louisiana St. (bet. Cray & Polk Sts.) | 713-659-8231

Southwest Houston | 9707 Westheimer Rd. (Gessner Rd.) | 713-789-4962

Sugar Land | 2579 Town Center Blvd. (Hwy. 6) | 281-565-8888

The Woodlands | Pinecroft Town Ctr. | 1720 Lake Woodlands Dr. (Six Pines Dr.) | 281-292-0061

www.benihana.com

See review in Dallas/Ft. Worth Directory.

benjy's *American* | 23 | 19 | 21 | $32 |

Rice Village | 2424 Dunstan St. (Kelvin Dr.) | 713-522-7602 | www.benjys.com

A "stark"-looking space in Rice Village, this New American retains its "devoted following" with a "classy" menu of "creative", "tasty"

multinational munchies (including a "terrific" weekend brunch) and a "cool lounge" upstairs; still, some say the eats are "overshadowed" by the "see-and-be-seen" scene ("the better you look, the better time you'll have") and the servers, though "knowledgeable" and "cheerful", can be "detached."

Berryhill Baja Grill *Mexican* | 19 | 15 | 15 | $15 |

West U | 5110 Buffalo Spdwy. (Westpark Dr.) | 713-667-8226
Champions | Champions Forest | 5482 FM 1960 W. (Champions Vill.) | 281-444-8844
Galleria | 1717 Post Oak Blvd. (San Felipe St.) | 713-871-8226
Heights | 702 E. 11th St. (Beverly St.) | 713-225-2252
NEW Memorial | Memorial City Mall | 731 Memorial City Way (bet. Katy Frwy. & Future Gaylord Dr.) | 713-932-8226
Montrose | Hawthorne Sq. | 3407 Montrose Blvd. (Hawthorne St.) | 713-523-8226
River Oaks | 2639 Revere St. (Westheimer Rd.) | 713-526-8080
NEW Katy | 22756 Westheimer Pkwy. (S. Peek Rd.) | 281-392-8400
Sugar Land | 13703 Southwest Frwy. (Sugar Creek Blvd.) | 281-313-8226
The Woodlands | Market St. | 9595 Six Pines Dr. (Lake Woodlands Dr.) | 281-298-8226
www.berryhillbajagrill.com
Additional locations throughout the Houston area
"Phenomenal fish tacos" are the main draw at this "popular" local chain offering "tasty" Mexican eats, "casual" digs and "quick" order-at-the-counter service; insiders insist that "some locations" – like "the original on Revere" – are better than others, but all "still get packed", especially at "happy hour."

Bibas Greek Pizza *Greek/Pizza* | ∇ 18 | 7 | 19 | $17 |

Heights | 5526 Memorial Dr. (bet. Shepherd Dr. & Westcott St.) | 713-861-2266
"Unique" pizzas plus "some of the best gyros in town" head up the menu at this inexpensive Greek in the lower Heights; nondescript digs are elevated by a friendly staff that makes it a "great place to stop after a softball game" at nearby Memorial Park.

Bistro Calais M *French* | ∇ 23 | 22 | 21 | $32 |

River Oaks | 2811 Bammel Ln. (Westheimer Rd.) | 713-529-1314 | www.bistrocalais.com
Supporters say this "quiet, little" bistro in River Oaks "keeps getting better" with country-style French and Continental fare and a "great" Sunday buffet brunch plus a well-priced selection of wines to match; servers "who care" tend to customers in the light-filled converted cottage setting while live cabaret on Wednesdays and some Fridays adds additional appeal.

NEW Bistro Don Camillo S *French/Italian* | - | - | - | M |

Briargrove | 6510 Del Monte Dr. (S. Voss Rd.) | 713-782-3011 | www.bistrodoncamillo.com
From the family behind Bistro Provence comes this Briargrove entry matching southern French flavors with the cuisine of neighboring Italy; expect duck confit, oxtail ravioli and pizzas all coexisting on a

FOOD | DECOR | SERVICE | COST

midpriced menu served in an unpretentious strip-mall space warmed
up by a brick oven and colorful tablecloths.

Bistro Lancaster *American* | 20 | 20 | 20 | $42 |

Downtown | Lancaster Hotel | 701 Texas Ave. (Louisiana St.) |
713-228-9500 | www.thelancaster.com

It's an "easy walk to all live performance" venues from this Downtown
Lancaster Hotel longtimer, but that's not the only thing that has admirers applauding – they also laud its "unpretentious, fresh and
well-prepared" New American cuisine, "comfortable" "old-world
charm" and "cool" jazz piano music on weekends; trendier types
term it "stuffy", though, and add that "service should be faster";
N.B. the Food score does not reflect a 2008 chef change.

Bistro Le Cep *French* | 25 | 21 | 23 | $34 |

West Houston | 11112 Westheimer Rd. (Wilcrest Dr.) | 713-783-3985 |
www.bistrolecep.com

"Amiable" chef-owner Joe Mannke "makes everyone feel welcome" at
his "charming" West Houston bistro where "delicious", "beautifully
presented" French dishes and "wonderful" wines (over 50 by the glass)
come at "moderate prices"; "quaint" "country" quarters may get "a
might crowded", but it's all so "delightful" that no one seems to mind.

Bistro Provence 🗷 *French* | 23 | 20 | 23 | $32 |

West Houston | 13616 Memorial Dr. (bet. Kirkwood Rd. & Wilcrest Dr.) |
713-827-8008 | www.bistroprovence.us

"Comfort food" for Francophiles wins raves at this "family-run" "gem"
set in a West Houston strip mall where "first-rate bread from a wood-
burning oven" proves a promising start to a meal of "scrumptious"
bistro classics; the "cozy" digs get a "rustic" feel from exposed wood
beams, and while a few fret over "crowded" conditions and a no-
reservations policy, gentle prices keep everything "*très bien.*"

Black Labrador Pub *Pub Food* | 17 | 21 | 18 | $20 |

Montrose | 4100 Montrose Blvd. (W. Main St.) | 713-529-1199 |
www.blacklabradorpub.com

Expats and Tex-pats alike patronize this "proper pub" in Montrose
for the sake of its "authentic", "warming" British "comfort food"
(shepherd's pie, fish 'n' chips, trifle) and "great selection" of draft
beers and scotches; it's a "charming" (if slightly "stereotypical")
"bit of Merrie Olde England" replete with a "friendly staff", a "cozy
fireplace" and an attractive patio with a giant chess set – now "all
they need is cricket on the telly."

Black Walnut Café *Eclectic/Italian* | 20 | 20 | 16 | $16 |

Rice Village | 5510 Morningside Dr. (University Blvd.) | 713-526-5551
Sugar Land | First Colony Mall | 16535 Southwest Frwy. (Hwy. 6) |
281-565-7800
The Woodlands | 2520 Research Forest Dr. (Grogans Mill Rd.) |
281-362-1678
www.blackwalnutcafe.com

These self-styled 'fast-casual' Eclectic-Italians in Rice Village, Sugar
Land and The Woodlands proffer a "fun" menu of "consistent" fare

	FOOD	DECOR	SERVICE	COST

(including "excellent" breakfasts) for "every kind of appetite"; their wood-paneled "conversation areas" are a "pleasant" compensation for the "informal" counter service.

Blue Nile *Ethiopian* | - | - | - | I |

Southwest Houston | 9400 Richmond Ave. (Westerland Dr.) | 713-782-6882 | www.bluenilerestaurant.com

"What an experience for the taste buds!" exclaim admirers of this Southwest Houston "destination" featuring "exotic" Ethiopian dishes presented with spongy injera bread; bright-colored decor may not be much to speak of, but with a cordial staff there to "guide you" through the menu, it's a "favorable" experience overall.

Bombay Brasserie *Indian* | 18 | 14 | 17 | $23 |

NEW Galleria | 3005 W. Loop Frwy. S. (Oakshire Dr.) | 713-622-2005

Rice Village | Rice Village Arcade | 2414 University Blvd. (Morningside Dr.) | 713-355-2000

www.thebombaybrasserie.com

Locals laud the "authentic" "mix of old standards and a wildcard dish or two" at these modestly priced Galleria and Rice Village Indians featuring a lunch buffet that some say is "the best in the area"; decor isn't fancy at either spot, but they have a "pleasant", "neighborhood" feel nonetheless.

Brasil ● *Coffeehouse* | 20 | 19 | 16 | $17 |

Montrose | 2604 Dunlavy St. (Westheimer Rd.) | 713-528-1993

This "funky" Montrose hangout caters to an "arty crowd" – "cool tattoos and piercings" abound – with "great" sandwiches and salads, vegetarian-friendly offerings, well-chosen bottled beers and wines and what many surveyors deem "the best house coffee around"; it's all dished up in art-filled, bare-brick quarters boasting live music and movies some nights; P.S. just "people-watch and pretend you're studying."

Brasserie Max & Julie ⧮ *French* | - | - | - | M |

Montrose | 4315 Montrose Blvd. (Richmond Ave.) | 713-524-0070 | www.caferabelais.com

Set in the Montrose spot that acclaimed Aires previously occupied, this moderately priced eatery from the owners of Café Rabelais dishes up comforting Gallic cooking like cassoulet and boeuf bourguignon; the wine list is all-French, as is the homey decor with its lace curtains and polished brass fixtures.

Breakfast Klub, The ⧮ *Soul Food* | 23 | 12 | 19 | $15 |

Midtown | 3711 Travis St. (Alabama St.) | 713-528-8561 | www.thebreakfastklub.com

Don't you "forget about" this "funky" Midtown "hot spot", which "outguns IHOP and Denny's" with "housemade soul food" (i.e. "real-deal" "chicken wings and waffles, catfish and grits") that's so "excellent" the "nonexistent decor" hardly matters – witness the "enormous lines on weekends"; so what if these folks "kan't spell, they sure kan kook!"

	FOOD	DECOR	SERVICE	COST

Brenner's *Steak*

25 | **24** | **24** | **$55**

Memorial | 10911 Katy Frwy. (bet. Brittmoore Rd. & Wilcrest Dr.) | 713-465-2901 | www.brennerssteakhouse.com
River Oaks | 1 Birdsall St. (Memorial Dr.) | 713-868-4444 | www.brennersonthebayou.com

Longtime fans laud this "traditional", "high-end" Memorial steakhouse that's "held true" since 1936 (despite its acquisition by the Landry's empire) with "wonderfully aged" beef and "impeccable" service; prices may be high, but "inviting" decor with a working fireplace and a "pretty garden" make it a "memorable" pick for "special occasions"; N.B. scores may not reflect the newer River Oaks branch.

Brio Tuscan Grille *Italian*

21 | **23** | **20** | **$31**

The Woodlands | Woodlands Mall | 1201 Lake Woodlands Dr. (I-45) | 281-465-8993 | www.brioitalian.com
See review in Dallas/Ft. Worth Directory.

Buffalo Grille, The *American*

20 | **13** | **15** | **$14**

West U | 3116 Bissonnet St. (Buffalo Spdwy.) | 713-661-3663
Briargrove | 1301 S. Voss Rd. (bet. San Felipe St. & Woodway Dr.) | 713-784-3663
www.thebuffalogrille.com

"Unbelievable breakfasts" (especially the "plate-sized flapjacks") dished up all day long bring "white-collar yuppies", "dreadlocked college students" and "kids, parents and grandparents" to this "hectic but friendly" Tex-Mex-flavored American duo in Briargrove and West U; given these spots' "affordable" tabs and "neighborhoody" vibe, it's no surprise there are "lines out the door" on weekends; P.S. "good buffalo burgers too", natch.

Burning Pear, The *Southwestern/Steak*

▽ **23** | **18** | **21** | **$34**

Sugar Land | Marriott Hotel | 16090 City Walk (Alvin-Sugar Land Rd.) | 281-275-5925 | www.theburningpear.com

This "really creative" Southwestern steakhouse in Sugar Land gets burned by hotelophobes who claim "this place is great, shame it's in the Marriott", but thanks to "excellent" personnel proffering "Texas grub at its best" – including a "lovely Sunday brunch buffet" – most munchers don't mind the somewhat impersonal earth-toned environs.

Cabo Mix-Mex Grill ● *Tex-Mex*

14 | **14** | **12** | **$17**

Downtown | 419 Travis St. (Prairie St.) | 713-225-2060 | www.cabomixmex.com

"Average" Tex-Mex meals and "hit-or-miss" service "much slower than the pickup scene" don't dissuade loyalists from mixing it up at this "cool hangout spot" Downtown, especially if they can sit on the "great balcony" while downing "fresh-squeezed margaritas" ("imbibe with caution!") and "nice cold beers"; baseball fans find it a convenient stop "before an Astros game."

Cadillac Bar *Mexican*

18 | **18** | **18** | **$25**

Heights | 1802 Shepherd Dr. (I-10) | 713-862-2020

(continued)

Cadillac Bar

Kemah | 100 Bradford St. (3rd St.) | 281-334-9049 **M**
www.cadillacbar.com

Strong margaritas fuel the "incredible bar scene" at these "boister-ous" cantinas in Dallas and Houston serving up solid, if not exactly "authentic" Mexican eats; the "lively" atmosphere plus spacious seating and reasonable prices make it "perfect for large groups."

Z Cafe Annie **S** *Southwestern*   26 | 24 | 26 | $60

Galleria | 1728 Post Oak Blvd. (San Felipe St.) | 713-840-1111 |
www.cafe-annie.com

Robert Del Grande "still has it" declare devotees of his "fabulous" Galleria-area destination where "businessmen" and "Chanel-clad la-dies" sup on "exquisite" Southwestern cuisine ferried by "impeccable" servers in an "elegant" dining room; though the less starry-eyed de-clare it "overpriced" and "overrated", most maintain that even with "occasional lapses", this is still among "the best in the city."

Café Benedicte *Mediterranean*   23 | 20 | 21 | $30

West Houston | 15455 Memorial Dr. (bet. Eldridge Pkwy. & Hwy. 6) |
281-558-6607 | www.cafebenedicte.com

This West Houston "neighborhood favorite" proffers well-prepared dishes from just about "any country bordering the [Mediterranean]" – including Spain, France, Italy, Morocco and Greece – in a "very pleas-ing atmosphere" that includes a "quaint view" of a small pond; it shares owners with Lynn's Steakhouse, so diners can expect "nice wine flights", plus service that's "personable", if sometimes "uneven."

Café Caspian **M** *Persian*   22 | 18 | 20 | $23

West Houston | Gray Falls | 12126 Westheimer Rd. (Gray Falls Dr.) |
281-493-4000 | www.cafecaspian.com

"Reliably" well-prepared meals begin with freshly made taftoon, a "wonderful bread" that's paired with bountiful herbs and a fetalike cheese at this West Houston Persian; "friendly service" and modest tabs boost the appeal of the casual, cafe-style setting in a strip mall off busy Westheimer.

Café Chino *Chinese*   22 | 17 | 20 | $22

Rice Village | 6140 Village Pkwy. (bet. Amherst St. & Times Blvd.) |
713-524-4433 | www.cafechinohouston.com

Comparatively "attractive decor" helps make this Chinese in Rice Village a "favorite" for folks craving "fresh", "consistent" and "rela-tively inexpensive" eats served by "quick, friendly" staffers with "never a wait."

Café Express *Eclectic*   18 | 14 | 14 | $15

Briargrove | 6570 Woodway Dr. (Voss Rd.) | 713-935-9222
Champions | Champions Vill. | 5311 FM 1960 W. (Champions Vill.) |
832-484-9222
Downtown | 650 Main St. (bet. Capitol St. & Texas Ave.) |
713-237-9222 **S**

(continued)

(continued)

Café Express

Uptown | Uptown Park | 1101 Uptown Park Blvd. (Post Oak Blvd.) |
713-963-9222 🕐

Meyerland | Meyerland Plaza | 210 Meyerland Plaza (I-610) |
713-349-9222

Montrose | Museum of Fine Arts | 5601 S. Main St. (Binz St.) |
713-639-7370 Ⓜ

River Oaks | 1422 W. Gray St. (Waugh Dr.) | 713-522-3100

Upper Kirby District | 3200 Kirby Dr. (Main St.) | 713-522-3994

Webster | 19443 Gulf Frwy. (Bay Area Blvd.) | 281-554-6999

Sugar Land | First Colony Mall | 15930 City Walk Blvd. (bet. Rte. 6 &
Sweetwater Blvd.) | 281-980-9222

www.cafe-express.com

Additional locations throughout the Houston area

Surveyors salute the "fresh, healthy meals" at these chain links that
kick "fast food" "up a notch" with a "wholesome" array of Eclectic
sandwiches and salads plus a "large condiment bar" to customize
your order and "happy-hour specials" on wine too; prices are
"cheap", though "noisy" digs and order-at-the-counter service have
some relegating it to "takeout" only.

Café Japon 🕐 *Japanese*   22 | 18 | 18 | $23

Upper Kirby District | 3915 Kirby Dr. (bet. Richmond Ave. &
Southwest Frwy.) | 713-529-1668

This long-running Upper Kirby Japanese remains "a favorite" for its
"good-value" sushi ("the jazz roll deserves homage"); however, aesthetes assert the "somewhat run-down" furnishings "need remodel-
ing" and the servers, though "nice", can be slow ("are there staffers
in the building?"); N.B. open till 2 AM on weekends.

Ⓩ Café Le Jadeite *Pacific Rim*   22 | 26 | 22 | $36

River Oaks | River Oaks Ctr. | 1952 W. Gray St. (Driscoll St.) |
713-528-4288 | www.cafelejadeite.biz

"Sublime" Pacific Rim cuisine awaits at this "top-notch" Asian eatery in River Oaks; loyalists liken the "over-the-top" decor decked out
with lacquer, jade and "ancient treasures" to "eating in a museum",
creating an "elegant" atmosphere aided by live piano (Tuesday-
Saturday) and a "wonderful staff."

Cafe Lili Ⓢ *Lebanese*   24 | 12 | 21 | $19

Galleria | 5757 Westheimer Rd. (bet. Chimney Rock Rd. &
Fountain View Dr.) | 713-952-6969 | www.cafelili.com

"The hosts make everyone feel at home" at this "mom-and-pop"
Galleria Lebanese "favorite" turning out "fantastic" food like "top-
quality grilled meats" and "addictive" appetizers; there may not be
"much in the way of decor" (and service is order-at-the-counter),
but fans swear that for an "inexpensive" meal, "it can't be beat."

Cafe Piquet *Cuban*   ▽ 21 | 17 | 19 | $16

Bellaire | 5757 Bissonnet St. (Chimney Rock Rd.) | 713-664-1031

This Bellaire mainstay pleases local patrons with "outstanding
Cuban food" like long-cooked roast pork, ropa vieja and whole fried

red snapper; even if prices have been "raised" in recent years, tabs are still quite reasonable while service remains "pleasant" and efficient.

☑ Café Rabelais ⊠ *French*   26 | 20 | 22 | $36

Rice Village | 2442 Times Blvd. (bet. Kelvin St. & Morningside Dr.) | 713-520-8841 | www.caferabelais.com

"Authentic" bistro cooking like "amazing mussels" and frites "to die for" "transports" diners to Paris at this "charming" Rice Village French that also pleases with "phenomenal wines" and a "knowledgeable" staff; "the crowd is friendly" and prices a "great value", but "tables are tight" and they don't take reservations, so "get there early or expect to wait."

☑ Cafe Red Onion ⊠ *Pan-Latin*   24 | 17 | 19 | $23

Northwest Houston | 12440 Northwest Frwy. (43rd St.) | 713-957-0957
Upper Kirby District | 3910 Kirby Dr. (bet. Richmond Ave. & Southwest Frwy.) | 713-807-1122
West Houston | 1111 Eldridge Pkwy. (Enclave Pkwy.) | 281-293-7500
www.caferedonion.com

It's "always a fiesta" at this trio of "festive", "casual" "favorites" featuring "imaginative" "Latin fusion" cuisine plus South/Central American standards set out in "beautiful presentations" (also notable are the "wonderful chips and pineapple salsa to munch on"); in spite of a few grumbles about "noisy" environs and "sometimes slow" service, they remain "unique" spots "worth a visit."

Cantina Laredo   *Mexican*   21 | 20 | 20 | $23

West Houston | 11129 Westheimer Rd. (Wilcrest Dr.) | 713-952-3287 | www.cantinalaredo.com
See review in Dallas/Ft. Worth Directory.

Capital Grille, The   *Steak*   25 | 25 | 25 | $58

Galleria | 5365 Westheimer Rd. (Yorktown St.) | 713-623-4600 | www.thecapitalgrille.com
See review in Dallas/Ft. Worth Directory.

Carmelo's   *Italian*   22 | 22 | 22 | $35

West Houston | 14795 Memorial Dr. (bet. Dairy Ashford Rd. & Eldridge Pkwy.) | 281-531-0696 | www.carmelosrestaurant.com
See review in Austin and the Hill Country Directory.

☑ Carrabba's Italian Grill   *Italian*   22 | 19 | 22 | $28

Briargrove | 1399 S. Voss Rd. (bet. San Felipe St. & Woodway Dr.) | 713-468-0868
Champions | Champions Vill. | 5440 FM 1960 W. (Champion Forest Dr.) | 281-397-8255
Northwest Houston | 7540 Hwy. 6 N. (Longenbaugh Dr.) | 281-859-9700
Upper Kirby District | 3115 Kirby Dr. (Branard St.) | 713-522-3131
West Houston | 11339 Katy Frwy. (bet. N. Kirkwood Rd. & N. Wildcrest Dr.) | 713-464-6595
Webster | 502 W. Bay Area Blvd. (I-45) | 281-338-0574
Kingwood | 750 Kingwood Dr. (Chestnut Ridge Dr.) | 281-358-5580

(continued)

(continued)

Carrabba's Italian Grill

Sugar Land | 2335 Hwy. 6 S. (Southwest Frwy.) | 281-980-4433
The Woodlands | 25665 North Frwy. (Rayford Rd.) | 281-367-9423
www.carrabbas.com

For over 20 years these "dependable" "fixtures" have been "beloved by families with small children" for "solid", "midrange" Italian "without pretension" presented in "large portions"; insiders insist the Outback-controlled branches "can't compare" to the original "family-owned" outposts (Upper Kirby District and Briargrove in Houston), though all locations remain "noisy" and "crowded."

Catalan Food and Wine Ⓜ *American/Spanish* | 24 | 21 | 21 | $43 |

Heights | 5555 Washington Ave. (TC Jester Blvd.) | 713-426-4260 |
www.catalanfoodandwine.com

"What a wonderful addition to the neighborhood" exclaim enthusiasts of this "hip" Heights Spaniard (and sib to Ibiza) where "outstanding" tapas and "cutting-edge" New American entrees are complemented by a "thoughtful" selection of wines "with some of the best prices in the city"; though the brick-arched, candlelit dining room may get "crowded" and "loud", "friendly and informed servers" ensure a "fabulous experience all around."

Cava Bistro Ⓢ *American* | 21 | 21 | 22 | $34 |

Downtown | 301 Main St. (Congress St.) | 713-223-4068 |
www.bellarestaurants.com

The few who've found this often-"overlooked" Downtowner aren't cavalier about it; they praise its "innovative" New American fare served by a "friendly", "quirky" crew and dig the "cool, cavelike" wine-cellar setting with its "delightful" patio; located near a light-rail stop, this "great date" spot is also convenient for pre-theater dining.

Charivari Ⓢ *Continental* | 23 | 18 | 24 | $39 |

Midtown | 2521 Bagby St. (McGowen St.) | 713-521-7231 |
www.charivarirest.com

"Step into old-world Europe" at this "quaint", "high-class" Midtowner that "truly honors" Continental cuisine with "superbly prepared" plates of Wiener schnitzel and "standout" Transylvanian specialties; "service is impeccable", although a few find the "subdued" atmosphere too "serious" and urge the owners to "loosen it up a little."

Ⓩ Cheesecake Factory *American* | 20 | 20 | 18 | $26 |

Galleria | 5015 Westheimer Rd. (Post Oak Blvd.) | 713-840-0600
Sugar Land | First Colony Mall | 16535 Southwest Frwy. (Hwy. 6) |
281-313-9500
The Woodlands | Woodlands Mall | 1201 Lake Woodlands Dr. (I-45) |
281-419-3400
www.thecheesecakefactory.com

The menu's "mammoth" – and "so are the crowds" – at this "family-pleasing" chain where the "endless" American options arrive in equally "colossal" portions (ironically, "they give you so much there's no room" for their "heavenly" namesake desserts); despite

"ordinary" settings, "spotty" staffing and "lots of commotion", these "well-oiled machines" are so "busy, busy, busy" that they're best accessed "off-hours" to avoid a "long wait."

☑ Chez Nous ⊠ French   26 | 21 | 26 | $51

Humble | 217 S. Ave. G (Main St.) | 281-446-6717 | www.cheznousfrenchrestaurant.com

"A hidden treasure" that's "worth the drive to Humble" proclaim patrons of this "special-occasion" destination set in a converted home and serving "exceptional" "classic French cooking" featuring "fresh herbs and vegetables from their own garden"; the "charming" ambiance gets a boost from "top-notch" servers who lavish "personal attention" on diners, so even if a few lament it's "slipped just a bit", most maintain it's "still an all-time favorite"; N.B. jacket suggested.

☑ China View   Chinese   27 | 16 | 22 | $18

West Houston | 11113½ Katy Frwy. (bet. Kirkwood Rd. & Wilcrest Dr.) | 713-464-2728 | www.chinaview.us

Helmed by "creative" and "caring" chef-owner Robin Luo, this West Houston "culinary pearl" "stands out", compensating for its somewhat "dismal setting" with "exquisite" Chinese dishes that utilize local produce and seafood; add in "very friendly service" and "bargain prices", and it's no wonder fans swear they "go there at least once a week."

Chinese Café   Chinese   22 | 6 | 13 | $11

Alief | 9352 Bellaire Blvd. (Manchester) | 713-771-4330
Galleria | 5092 Richmond Ave. (Post Oak Blvd.) | 713-621-2888
Chowhounds choose these "no-frills" Chinese twins for "quick" Cantonese meals that are always "good 'n' cheap"; even if service is "sullen" and decor "nothing fancy", they're a "safe bet" for "lunch", "takeout" or a "weekday dinner."

Christian's Tailgate Bar & Grill   Burgers   19 | 12 | 15 | $14

Memorial | 7340 Washington Ave. (Katy Frwy.) | 713-864-9744 ⊠
Midtown | 2000 Bagby St. (Gray St.) | 713-527-0261 | www.christianstailgate.com ●

Some of the "best hamburgers in Texas" plus frosty mugs of beer keep the "tailgating crowd" coming to these Memorial-area and Midtown "dives"; service may be "variable", but "sports on TV" and a congenial atmosphere make them fine places for "hanging out."

☑ Churrascos   S American   25 | 22 | 23 | $38

Lower Shepherd | 2055 Westheimer Rd. (Shepherd Dr.) | 713-527-8300
Southwest Houston | 9705 Westheimer Rd. (Gessner Rd.) | 713-952-1988
www.cordua.com

"The namesake steak" "melts in your mouth" at Michael Cordúa's Southwest Houston mainstays where "large portions" of "flavorful" South American cuisine are matched with "fabulous" wines and "phenomenal" desserts ("save room for the tres leches cake!"); "helpful" servers work the "oversized" contemporary dining

rooms, so even if tabs are a bit "pricey", boosters boast it's "always a winner" nonetheless.

Chuy's *Tex-Mex*   21 | 19 | 19 | $18

NEW **Northwest Houston** | 19827 Northwest Frwy. (Westward St.) | 281-970-0341

River Oaks | 2706 Westheimer Rd. (Kirby Dr.) | 713-524-1700

NEW **Humble** | 20502 Hwy. 59 N. (Cantertrot Dr.) | 281-540-7778

Spring | 18035 I-45 (FM 1960) | 936-321-4440

www.chuys.com

See review in Austin and the Hill Country Directory.

Ciro's *Italian*   20 | 20 | 20 | $24

Memorial | 9755 Katy Frwy. (Bunker Hill Rd.) | 713-467-9336 | www.ciros.com

Supporters "stick with the pasta dishes" at this "popular" Memorial Italian offering "reliable" eats at modest prices; though service is "smooth" and it's often "crowded", some sticklers suggest it's "unremarkable" and add that it "lost its charisma" when it moved across the freeway to "bigger digs" some years back.

Cleburne Cafeteria ⊅ *American*   23 | 13 | 18 | $14

West U | 3606 Bissonnet St. (Mercer St.) | 713-667-2386 | www.cleburnecafeteria.com

Size does matter at this West U "cafeteria on steroids", where the "fresh", "exceptional" Southern-style American "comfort food" comes in "gigantic" portions ("cakes the size of small dogs"); family-owned and -run, the "quaint" place is an "institution", so be prepared for "long lines after church on Sundays"; N.B. closed Saturdays.

Collina's *Italian*   18 | 12 | 17 | $17

Greenway Plaza Area | 3835 Richmond Ave. (Weslayan St.) | 713-621-8844 | www.collinas.com

Heights | 502 W. 19th St. (Nicholson Dr.) | 713-869-0492 | www.collinas.com

Memorial | 8800 Katy Frwy. (bet. Campbell & Voss Rds.) | 713-365-9497 | www.collinas.com

Meyerland | 4990 Beechnut St. (Rice Ave.) | 713-349-9040 | www.collinasitaliancafe.com

Rice Village | 2400 Times Blvd. (Morningside Dr.) | 713-526-4499 | www.collinasitaliancafe.com

"Fabulous" for "multigenerational groups", this "reliable" local chain turns out "down-home" Italian fare ("out-of-this-world" "gourmet pizza") in "casual" surroundings; the "best part" is that the BYOB policy, with a modest corkage fee, makes for "great value" – almost worth the "annoyance" of "haphazard" service and high decibel levels; N.B. the Meyerland and Rice Village branches are separately owned.

Cova *American*   19 | 19 | 19 | $31

West U | 5600 Kirby Dr. (Nottingham St.) | 713-838-0700 ☽

Heights | 5555 Washington Ave. (TC Jester Blvd.) | 713-868-3366 www.covawines.com

This lower Heights and West U pair of "cool", "casual" vino bars/restaurants/wine shops offers a "solid" American menu of

"small" bites that work for a "light meal", "before-party pick-me-up" or "after-hours" snack; though service is "helpful", critics carp that the "extensive" list of pours "by the glass" comes at too "extravagant" a price.

Crapitto's Cucina Italiana ☒ *Italian*

| 21 | 18 | 22 | $34 |

Galleria | 2400 Mid Lane St. (Westheimer Rd.) | 713-961-1161 | www.crapittos.com

"Get past the unfortunate name" – this "fine" venue in the Galleria area proffers "delicious" Italian cuisine and "well-priced" wines in a "lovely, romantic" restored 1915 house; service is generally "attentive", but generation-gappers wonder whether "anyone under 60" can find this "hidden" eatery; P.S. "request a table under the live oaks outside" on the patio.

Crú Wine Bar *American*

| 20 | 23 | 21 | $34 |

The Woodlands | Market St. | 9595 Six Pines Dr. (Lake Woodlands Dr.) | 281-465-9463 | www.cruawinebar.com
See review in Dallas/Ft. Worth Directory.

NEW Cullen's Upscale American Grille *American*

| - | - | - | E |

Clear Lake | 11500 Space Center Blvd. (Genoa Red Bluff Rd.) | 281-481-3463 | www.cullenshouston.com

The Clear Lake dining scene heats up with this flashy newcomer with Texas-sized ambitions whose dramatically designed interior features a cavernous dining room decked out with digital artwork plus several private eating areas, including a glassed-in one that appears suspended in air; its expensive Traditional American menu includes prime rib and chicken pot pie while the sizable vino collection can be accessed by a computerized tablet; additional draws include a lounge, billiards tables, live weekend music and a boozy brunch.

Cyclone Anaya's *Mexican*

| 20 | 18 | 18 | $23 |

Briargrove | 5761 Woodway Dr. (Augusta Dr.) | 713-339-4552
Heights | 1710 Durham Dr. (Inker St.) | 713-862-3209
Midtown | 309 Gray St. (Bagby St.) | 713-520-6969
www.cycloneanaya.com

"You'll have to wrestle your way in" to these "yuppified" Mexican joints (revivals of a 1960s Houston-area classic) set in "upscale" digs with exposed brick, white tablecloths and a "festive atmosphere"; "tasty" fare and "awesome margaritas" are strong points, though a few fret about "noisy" environs and tabs they find "a bit expensive."

Daily Grind *Coffeehouse*

| 14 | 13 | 17 | $14 |

Heights | 4115 Washington Ave. (Bonner St.) | 713-861-4558 | www.dailygrindunwind.com

Caffeine-crazed locals laud this "funky", "neighborhood" coffee shop in the lower Heights for its "great" java and satisfying breakfasts and lunches; the decor may be on the "shabby" side, but it's still a "comfy" place with "good people-watching" and free WiFi drawing plenty of "businesspeople" and "students on laptops."

	FOOD	DECOR	SERVICE	COST

Daily Review Café *American* 20 | 17 | 17 | $30

River Oaks | 3412 W. Lamar St. (Dunlavy St.) | 713-520-9217 |
www.dailyreviewcafe.com

This "quiet and unpretentious" River Oaks eatery pleases patrons
with "modestly priced" Traditional American fare (and a "great Sunday
brunch") that fans favor in warm weather "when you can sit outdoors" on the "beautiful" patio; some quibble about "tight" quarters inside while others are left wishing that "service were better."

☑ Da Marco ☒Ⓜ *Italian* 28 | 22 | 26 | $57

Montrose | 1520 Westheimer Rd. (bet. Ridgewood & Windsor Sts.) |
713-807-8857 | www.damarcohouston.com

Aficionados "indulge" in "exemplary" Italian cuisine prepared
from "the freshest ingredients" (including "superb pastas" "worth
saving your carbs for") and sip wines from a "world-class" list at
chef/co-owner Marco Wiles' pricey Montrose destination; its setting
in a converted home cultivates a "cozy", "romantic" vibe, so even if
"tables are too close together" and the "attentive" service sometimes feels "rushed", it still "stands out" as "one of Houston's finest."

Damian's Cucina Italiana ☒ *Italian* 21 | 20 | 22 | $44

Midtown | 3011 Smith St. (Rosalie St.) | 713-522-0439 |
www.damians.com

"Everybody is somebody" at this Midtown "fixture" where "polished, efficient" staffers proffer "old-school", "high-end" Italian cuisine and "fine" regional wines in a setting "just on the comfortable
side of stuffy"; now that the "old standby" is in its third decade, however, some surveyors sigh it's "tired" and in need of an "update."

D'Amico's Italian Market Café *Italian* 21 | 15 | 18 | $22

Rice Village | 5510 Morningside Dr. (bet. Rice & University Blvds.) |
713-526-3400 | www.damico-cafe.com

Half grocery, half Italian cafe, this Rice Villager is a "favorite haunt" for
locals who love its "straightforward" cooking (like "awesome" pizza);
"pleasant" staffers foster a "family-friendly" vibe, so many settle in
"on the patio with a glass of wine, some fresh tortellini" and the kids.

Daniel Wong's Kitchen *Chinese* 23 | 13 | 19 | $15

Bellaire | 4566 Bissonnet St. (Ave. B) | 713-663-6665 |
www.danielwongskitchen.com

For over a decade, this easy-on-the-wallet Bellaire eatery has been
dishing up "inventive" Chinese fare that's often "healthy" thanks to
its "fresh ingredients"; if fans wonder why it "isn't jam-packed during
dinner", it may be because, says one surveyor, "the decor and lighting are horrendous", causing some to opt for the "great" carryout.

Danton's Gulf Coast Seafood Kitchen ☒ *Seafood* - | - | - | M

Montrose | 4611 Montrose Blvd. (Hwy. 59) | 713-807-8883 |
dantonsseafood.com

This Gulf Coast-centric seafooder in Montrose plies patrons with oysters, overstuffed po' boys, seafood gumbo and plates of grilled and

fried fish, as well as Louisiana classics like shrimp étouffée; its down-to-earth vibe is enhanced by the family photos and antique maps adorning the walls and welcoming staffers who are eager-to-please.

Del Frisco's Double Eagle

| 27 | 24 | 25 | $69 |

Steak House *Steak*

Galleria | Galleria | 5061 Westheimer Rd. (McCue Rd.) | 713-355-2600 | www.delfriscos.com

See review in Dallas/Ft. Worth Directory.

Denis' Seafood House *Seafood*

| 21 | 19 | 21 | $30 |

Memorial | 9777 Katy Frwy. (Memorial City Way) | 713-464-6900

"Not flashy but excellent" seafood dishes – spiced up with "hellaciously good" sauces and "priced right" – have habitués hooked on this Cajun-accented Memorial restaurant, where "helpful" staffers "provide expert advice" on the menu; adding to the appeal are "sleek" decor and live zydeco music on the patio on Thursday nights.

Dessert Gallery

| 22 | 13 | 16 | $14 |

Bakery & Café *American/Dessert*

Galleria | 1616 Post Oak Blvd. (Westbriar Ln.) | 713-622-0007
Upper Kirby District | 3200 Kirby Dr. (Main St.) | 713-522-9999
Sugar Land | First Colony Mall | 2260 Lone Star Dr. (Town Center Blvd.) | 713-797-8000
www.dessertgallery.com

Unsurprisingly, owing to their "overwhelming selection of delectable desserts" ("the carrot cake makes you want to eat your vegetables"), this trio of "chocoholics' dream" spots continues to be a "crowd-pleaser"; surveyors also appreciate the Traditional American meals and report that "upbeat" staffers and board games at every table help make it "fun for all ages."

Dharma Café ⓜ *Eclectic*

| ▽ 21 | 16 | 22 | $29 |

Neartown | 1718 Houston Ave. (bet. Crockett & Summer Sts.) | 713-222-6996 | www.dharmacafehouston.com

"Fresh", "simple" and "healthy" Eclectic fare (think wraps at lunch and more substantial dishes like salmon at dinner) is prepared with a "personal" touch at this arty neighborhood eatery at the edge of Neartown; "service is informal and funky" and tabs are modest, meaning locals are more than content to keep it their own little "secret."

Dimassi's

| 18 | 10 | 12 | $14 |

Mediterranean Buffet *Mediterranean*

Medical Center | 8236 Kirby Dr. (La Concha Ln.) | 713-526-5111
Galleria | 5064 Richmond Ave. (Post Oak Blvd.) | 713-439-7481
West Houston | 11335 Katy Frwy. (bet. N. Kirkwood Rd. & N. Wildcrest Dr.) | 713-465-8222
West Houston | 6802 Hwy. 6 S. (Bellaire Blvd.) | 281-530-0033
NEW Webster | 1039 W. Bay Area Blvd. (Gulf Frwy.) | 281-332-9295
The Woodlands | 1640 Lake Woodlands Dr. (Pinecroft Dr.) | 281-363-0200
www.dimassisbuffet.com

"Succulent lamb", "chunky cucumber salad" and "fresh pita" are the stars at these "wondrous" all-you-can-eat Mediterranean buffets

	FOOD	DECOR	SERVICE	COST

featuring a tremendous "variety" of "honest", "reliable" Middle Eastern choices; "there's not much decor" and service is strictly "cafeteria-style", but the easy-on-the-wallet tabs offer "good bang for the buck."

divino 🗵 *Italian* | 22 | 16 | 20 | $31 |

Lower Shepherd | 1830 W. Alabama St. (bet. Hazard & Woodhead Sts.) | 713-807-1123 | www.divinohouston.com

"Excellent-value" vinos are vaunted at this "charming", "quiet" Lower Shepherd spot, a "neighborhood favorite" for its "well-thought-out", "reliable" and "reasonably priced" Northern Italian dishes; the menu may be "limited", but portions are "sized for a human, not a horse" and service is "personal" so the roomful of "regulars" feel like they're dining "at a friend's house."

Dolce Vita Pizzeria Enoteca Ⓜ *Italian* | 24 | 16 | 19 | $28 |

Montrose | 500 Westheimer Rd. (Whitney St.) | 713-520-8222 | www.dolcevitahouston.com

Right in the middle of Montrose, this "lively", "casual cousin of Da Marco" features "amazing Italian-style" "thin-crust" pizzas topped with an "offbeat but delicious variety of toppings", resulting in some of the "best pies in town"; its "pasta specials and appetizers" are "wonderful" too, as is the "great wine list" with choices from throughout The Boot, though "pricey" tabs and service that's "not consistent" temper the experience.

Don Carlos *Tex-Mex* | - | - | - | I |

Sharpstown | 6500 Southwest Frwy. (Harwin Dr.) | 713-776-2891
Hobby | 8385 Broadway St. (Bellfort Ave.) | 713-641-2084
Neartown | 416 N. 76th St. (Sherman St.) | 713-923-1906

Free-flowing margaritas and "well-prepared" *comida* are bolstered by mariachi (on Fridays) and happy-hour specials at this earthy Tex-Mex trio; "reasonable" prices and "quick" service keep customers coming "over and over again" to all locations, though a few favor the Neartown branch for its more festive feel.

Droubi's *Mediterranean* | ▽ 21 | 8 | 14 | $12 |

Briargrove | 2721 Hillcroft St. (Westheimer Rd.) | 713-334-1829
Southwest Houston | 7333 Hillcroft St. (Evergreen St.) | 713-988-5897

The Droubi brothers' two Med grocery-cum-sandwich shops in Briargrove and Southwest Houston remain handy for a "quick bite" according to surveyors smitten with their "tasty Middle Eastern standards" ("excellent" falafel, "great gyros", "absolute-best" fresh-baked pita) deemed a "blessed departure from the ordinary"; just expect a "complete lack of decor" and "no hugs or kisses" from the staff.

El Meson Restaurant *Pan-Latin* | 19 | 13 | 18 | $23 |

Rice Village | 2425 University Blvd. (Morningside Dr.) | 713-522-9306 | www.elmeson.com

A "family-friendly" "neighborhood standby", this Rice Villager ropes in regulars with a variety of Cuban, Spanish and Tex-Mex options

(almost "too many" say some) plus an "outstanding" collection of wines; the understated room decorated with family photos and oil paintings "isn't fancy", but service is solid and prices affordable too.

El Pueblito Place *Guatemalan/Mexican*   20 | 16 | 17 | $17

Montrose | 1423 Richmond Ave. (Loretto Dr.) | 713-520-6635 | www.elpueblitopatio.com

Its "backyard is reason enough to go" croon cognoscenti who are crazy about the "elaborate" "tropical" patio at this Montrose Mexican-Guatemalan; happily, its "imaginative" seafood dishes (at "modest prices") and "fine margaritas" also shine – though just like other "popular" places it can be "noisy at night", especially on weekends when there's live flamenco and salsa; N.B. check out the cabana that seats 15.

El Tiempo 1308 Cantina *Tex-Mex*   22 | 17 | 18 | $26

Montrose | 1308 Montrose Blvd. (W. Clay St.) | 713-807-8996
El Tiempo Cantina *Tex-Mex*
Greenway Plaza Area | 3130 Richmond Ave. (Eastside St.) | 713-807-1600
Memorial | 5602 Washington Ave. (Asbury St.) | 713-681-3645
www.eltiempocantina.com

The Laurenzo family (offspring of Mama Ninfa's founder) is behind these three "high-end" Tex-Mex cantinas in the Greenway Plaza area, Montrose and Memorial, where "fabulous grilled meats" and "fresh" salsas and sides embody a "refreshing fusion of flavors and textures" and service is "frantic yet friendly"; the bar scene is "excellent" for "meeting friends" or scoping out the "A-list" crowd, but be warned that the "potent" margaritas "pack a powerful punch."

Empanadas by Marini *Argentinean*   ▽ 23 | 14 | 21 | $10

Southwest Houston | Carillon Sq. | 10001 Westheimer Rd. (Briarpark Dr.) | 713-266-2729 🛇
Katy | 3522 S. Mason Rd. (Westheimer Pkwy.) | 281-391-4273 Ⓜ
www.theoriginalmarinisempanadahouse.com

An "amazing variety" of sweet and savory "handmade Argentine-style empanadas" make for a "good lunch" or a toothsome dessert at these inexpensive order-at-the-counter Katy and Southwest Houston "mom-and-pop" shops; specialty sandwiches and salads round out the menu, while shaded patio tables provide the perfect perch at either location.

Empire Café *American*   20 | 19 | 16 | $16

Montrose | 1732 Westheimer Rd. (bet. Dunlavy & Woodhead Sts.) | 713-528-5282 | www.empirecafe.net

Yes, the New American entrees are "delicious" and the weekend breakfast specials are a "must", but at this rustic counter-service Montrose "roadside cafe" – once a gas station – it's really "all about the cake": "enormous", "delectable" desserts you can wash down with "great coffee"; "friendly" staffers and a "hip atmosphere" also help attract a "trendy crowd"; P.S. the streetside patio is "perfect for lounging in the sun" and people-watching.

	FOOD	DECOR	SERVICE	COST

Empire Turkish Grill *Turkish*   ▽ 24 | 16 | 23 | $23

West Houston | 12448 Memorial Dr. (bet. Benigus & Gessner Rds.) |
713-827-7475 | www.empiretrgrill.com

Sultans who swing by this "find" at a West Houston strip mall savor
its "flavorful", "authentic" Turkish fare, the regional artifacts on the
walls and the "service with a smile"; often filled with expats at din-
nertime, it feels "very much like Istanbul."

Fadi's Mediterranean *Mediterranean*   21 | 14 | 15 | $14

Briargrove | 8383 Westheimer Rd. (Dunvale Rd.) | 713-532-0666
Meyerland | 4738 Beechnut St. (W. Loop Frwy.) | 713-666-4644
www.fadiscuisine.com

"Crowds" craving "divine" Med munchies ("excellent" brick-oven
pita, "exceptional lamb", lots of veggie-friendly items) gather at
these two "fast" cafeteria-style spots in Briargrove and Meyerland;
true, there's "not much atmosphere" but tabs are low, naturally
leading to the presence of "many young children" – a fact that disappoints some who are seeking "a peaceful, quiet meal."

Farrago *Eclectic*   19 | 17 | 17 | $27

Midtown | 318 Gray St. (Bagby St.) | 713-523-6404 |
www.farragohouston.com

Look for "great surprises" on the "inventive" Eclectic menu at this
"super-cool", "modern" Midtown "hot spot", where a "young",
"pretty" clientele gathers in the "lovely" courtyard for "perfectly
mixed" cocktails, "huge burgers" "before a ballgame" or Sunday
brunch ("quite a party"); prices are "reasonable" too, though service can be "awkward."

NEW Feast *British*   - | - | - | M

Montrose | 219 Westheimer Rd. (Bagby St.) | 713-529-7788 |
www.feasthouston.com

'Nose to tail' eating comes to Houston via this midpriced Montrose
addition featuring a rustic, but modern, British menu with a focus on
forgotten cuts, courtesy of co-chef James Silk, who trained under
English offal-master Fergus Henderson; with its cheeky old cookbook photos, the tavernlike interior is an appropriately comfortable
space for the hearty fare; N.B. closed Tuesdays.

Fernando's Latin Cuisine Ⓢ Ⓜ *Pan-Latin*   - | - | - | M

Sugar Land | 14135 Southwest Frwy. (One Sugar Place Blvd.) |
281-494-9087 | www.fernandosrestaurants.com

Raising the level of dining in Sugar Land is this upscale Pan-Latin
eatery set in a handsome wood-trimmed space evoking an old-
fashioned supper club, especially on weekends, when a guitarist
takes to the stage; the cuisine ranges from ceviche to pastas to
char-grilled steaks, which pair nicely with the wide selection of
South American wines.

59 Diner ◑ *Diner*   16 | 16 | 16 | $14

Lower Shepherd | 3801 Farnham St. (Sandman St.) | 713-523-2333
Northwest Houston | 17695 Tomball Pkwy. (Gessner Rd.) | 832-237-7559

(continued)

59 Diner

West Houston | 10407 Katy Frwy. (Sam Houston Tollway) | 713-984-2500
Stafford | 12550 Southwest Frwy. (Kirkwood Rd.) | 281-242-5900
www.59diner.com

"Sometimes you need a diner", and at those times hungry Houstonians opt for these four "nostalgia places" in town; the Traditional American fare ("shakes that make you forget your hardening arteries", "chocolate-chip pancakes better than sex") is kid-friendly and affordable, though skeptics shrug it's just "comfort food at its worst."

Fish, The *Japanese*

20 | 17 | 15 | $37

Midtown | 309 Gray St. (Bagby St.) | 713-526-5294 |
www.thefishhouston.com

"There's "eye candy aplenty" at this "trendy", moderately priced Midtown Houston Japanese where a "young crowd" munches on "creative rolls" in a "lively" (some say "deafening") interior done up in sleek reds and blacks; skeptics say the "scene" trumps the sushi and add that service can be "inconsistent" too; N.B. the Dallas branch is newer.

ⓩ Fleming's Prime Steakhouse & Wine Bar *Steak*

24 | 24 | 23 | $54

River Oaks | River Oaks Ctr. | 2405 W. Alabama St. (Kirby Dr.) |
713-520-5959
The Woodlands | Woodlands Mall | 1201 Lake Woodlands Dr. (I-45) |
281-362-0103
www.flemingssteakhouse.com

"Not as stuffy" as the competition, this "inviting" chophouse chain purveys "classic" steaks and sides in "relaxed", "clubby" digs conducive to both "business and romance"; "low-profile" service and an "excellent wine-by-the-glass program" add to its allure, but since "everything's à la carte", be prepared for "high-end" tabs.

Floyd's Cajun Seafood House *Cajun/Seafood*

▽ 22 | 14 | 18 | $19

Webster | 20760 Gulf Frwy. (Nasa Rd. 1) | 281-332-7474 |
www.floydscajun.com

"The Big Easy" comes to Houston via this Cajun seafooder set in boat-shaped digs on the Gulf Freeway in Webster and sending out "generous portions" of fried shrimp, crab and frogs' legs that "beer drinkers" wash down with mugs of icy Abita; the "kitchen can be a little slow", but "exceptional values" keep the "crowds" happy.

ⓩ Fogo de Chão *Brazilian/Steak*

26 | 22 | 26 | $55

Briargrove | 8250 Westheimer Rd. (Dunvale Rd.) | 713-978-6500 |
www.fogodechao.com

"Paradise for Atkins diet–lovers", this churrascaria chain imported from Brazil rolls out all-you-can-eat meats on skewers for folks seeking to "embrace their inner caveperson"; the "meal-in-itself" salad bar is equally "tasty" and the drinks sure "pack a punch", but be careful and "pace yourself" to avoid the inevitable "protein swoon."

	FOOD	DECOR	SERVICE	COST

NEW Frank's Chop House ⑤ *Steak* — | — | — | E

Greenway Plaza Area | 3736 Westheimer Rd. (bet. Timmons Ln. & Weslayan St.) | 713-572-8600 | www.frankschophouse.com

Into a Greenway Plaza storefront that has seen its share of steak-houses over the years comes this brand-new eatery serving up lo-cally sourced cuts, including flavorful filets and maple-brined pork chops, alongside seasonal New American entrees; its comfortable setup eschews the traditional chophouse decor for a softer look, with an inviting bar and outdoor seating in warm weather.

Frenchie's ⑤ *Italian* 24 | 13 | 18 | $22

Clear Lake | 1041 Nasa Pkwy. (El Camino Real) | 281-486-7144 | www.villacaprionclearlake.com

"Despite the name", Italian's the game at this "casual", family-owned and family-friendly Clear Lake "standard" where "NASA eats lunch" and astronaut pics adorn the walls; regulars "treasure" the "tasty" *cucina* that comes in "huge", "steaming-hot" portions, and though the "popular" place can be a "zoo", service is usually "fast."

NEW Fuegovivo Churrascaria *Brazilian* — | — | — | E

West Houston | 11681 Westheimer Rd. (Cresent Park Dr.) | 281-597-8108 | www.fuegovivo.com

Part of a Florida-based mini-chain, this all-you-can-eat Brazilian BBQ on the West side is well situated, not just in beef-loving Houston, but it's also just a stone's throw from the American head-quarters of Brazil's national oil company; as per the classic churras-caria formula, an expansive salad bar prefaces the constant advance of grilled skewered meats (beef, pork, lamb, chicken, sausages) that are the prime attraction here.

Fung's Kitchen *Chinese/Seafood* 25 | 19 | 18 | $23

Southwest Houston | 7320 Southwest Frwy. (Fondren Rd.) | 713-779-2288 | www.fungskitchen.com

Just east of New Chinatown, this sprawling, "authentic" Southwest Houston favorite offers what may be "the best dim sum between San Francisco and New York" along with a "huge" menu of "Hong Kong–style" "fresh fish" and other "delights"; the space features chandeliers and "mini-landscapes" on the walls, and is "always crowded with Chinese patrons" and other "adventurous eaters" who don't seem to mind the often "inconsistent service."

Gaido's *Seafood* 22 | 17 | 20 | $32

Galveston | 3800 Seawall Blvd. (37th St.) | 409-762-9625 | www.gaidosofgalveston.com

"Get seated by the window" for a "great view" of the Gulf advise ad-mirers of this Galveston "grande dame", "serving quality seafood" since "before fish had fins" (since 1911, actually); it's still "depend-able" for "incredibly fresh" seafood, "generous bread baskets" and "pecan pie to die for", along with service that's "kind" if sometimes "spotty", so though a few cutting-edge critics carp about an "out-dated" interior and "overpriced" fare at this "ossified institution", most urge "don't change a thing."

	FOOD	DECOR	SERVICE	COST

🆕 Gigi's Asian Bistro & Dumpling Bar *Pan-Asian*

| - | - | - | M |

Galleria | Galleria | 5085 Westheimer Rd. (McCue Rd.) | 713-629-8889 |
www.gigisasianbistro.com

Gigi Huang, whose family ran the popular Uptown Hunan restaurant for several decades, is behind this stylish Galleria newcomer whose refined Pan-Asian menu showcases shumai and potstickers alongside kicked-up Vietnamese and Thai standards; its modern-edged setting boats several separate dining areas, including a long, narrow lounge studded with semi-private booths and a dramatic central room decorated with pink cherry blossoms.

Ginza *Japanese*

| - | - | - | M |

Briargrove | 5868 San Felipe St. (bet. Chimney Rock Rd. & Fountain View Dr.) | 713-785-0332

"Japanese expats" choose this "small" spot in Briargrove for "quality" homestyle dishes like tempura, soba and udon, plus sushi so "fresh" "it nearly jumps off the plate"; traditional decor with paper screens is on the plain side, but it gets a lift from moderate prices and "pleasant" service from the staff.

Glass Wall 🅂🅼 *American*

| 25 | 22 | 22 | $42 |

Heights | 933 Studewood St. (bet. E. 10th & Omar Sts.) | 713-868-7930 |
www.glasswalltherestaurant.com

An "inspired" menu of "seasonal" New American dishes is served in a "striking" interior decorated with river rock and aqua tile at chef-owner Lance Fegen's "high-end" surf-inspired eatery that Heights denizens are hailing as a "great entry" in the local dining scene; "knowledgeable" servers are a definite plus, but on the downside is a room so "noisy" that some suggest "earplugs should be placed next to the silverware."

Goode Co. Hamburgers & Taqueria *Burgers*

| 22 | 12 | 15 | $16 |

West U | 4902 Kirby Dr. (Westpark Dr.) | 713-520-9153 |
www.goodecompany.com

As a member of the eponymous empire, this "friendly" West U "staple" benefits from built-in Goode will ("anything that's Goode has got to be great") but holds its own with "pure-Texas" mesquite-grilled burgers, meat and fish, "delicious" Tex-Mex breakfasts (weekends only) and "nice, cold margaritas"; with its "reasonable" prices and easy counter service, this "laid-back joint" provides "great value" for "family outings."

🆉 Goode Co. Texas BBQ *BBQ*

| 25 | 17 | 17 | $16 |

West U | 5109 Kirby Dr. (bet. Bissonnet St. & Westpark Dr.) | 713-522-2530
Memorial | 8911 Katy Frwy. (Campbell Rd.) | 713-464-1901
🆕 **Northwest Houston** | 20102 US-290 W (FM 1960) |
832-678-3562
www.goodecompany.com

Quite possibly "the gold standard in Houston BBQ", this West U "institution" dishes up "tender" mesquite-smoked meats, "fresh-baked

FOOD DECOR SERVICE COST

jalapeño cornbread" and "pecan pie" that just might "make you cry" to "day workers and land barons" who "rub shoulders" at the "communal" picnic tables outside; the "spunky" counter staff keeps the lines moving "fast" at both the "larger" Memorial offshoot and the more "down-home" original; N.B. the Northwest branch is new.

Goode Co. Texas Seafood Seafood

23	17	20	$27

West U | 2621 Westpark Dr. (Kirby Dr.) | 713-523-7154
Memorial | 10211 Katy Frwy. (Gessner Dr.) | 713-464-7933
www.goodecompany.com

Goode friends gloat this piscatory pair "proves that Texas food can be excellent even if it's not barbecue or Mexican"; the "fresh", "perfectly seasoned" fish comes in many forms ("don't leave without trying" the signature campechana) along with other Gulf Coast specialties ("good-as-it-gets" gumbo) ferried by "quick" servers; also transporting is the decor – West U's "neat old" converted train car and an "antique racing boat" at the "more upscale" Memorial location.

Grand Lux Cafe Eclectic

19	22	18	$29

Galleria | Centre at Post Oak | 5000 Westheimer Rd. (Post Oak Blvd.) | 713-626-1700 | www.grandluxcafe.com
See review in Dallas/Ft. Worth Directory.

Grappino di Nino ⊠ Italian

20	23	19	$34

Montrose | 2817 W. Dallas St. (La Rue St.) | 713-528-7002 | www.ninos-vincents.com

"On a nice evening" you can enjoy a glass of wine and soak up the ambiance on the "great patio" at this most casual of the three adjacent Vincent Mandola–owned Montrose eateries (Nino's and Vincent's) where live jazz Thursday–Saturday adds to the appeal; Italian cuisine comes in "tasty" "small plates" as well as "heartier" entrees all at prices that enthusiasts assure are "reasonable" too.

Gravitas American

21	18	18	$36

Neartown | 807 Taft St. (bet. Allen Pkwy. & W. Dallas St.) | 713-522-0995 | www.gravitasrestaurant.com

Co-owner-slash–"food genius" Scott Tycer lends his air of gravitas to this "hot" Neartown bistro, a "hip", "stark" space spotlighting "inventive" New American fare and "interesting" wines; prices are "reasonable" and "prospects look bright" but for now many diagnose "growing pains", as evidenced by "uneven" service and "terrible acoustics."

Grotto Italian

22	21	21	$34

Galleria | 4715 Westheimer Rd. (Westcreek Ln.) | 713-622-3663
The Woodlands | 9595 Six Pines Dr. (Lake Woodlands Dr.) | 281-419-4252
www.grottohouston.com

Though loyalists lament this Galleria/Woodlands duo has "lost its edge" since owner Tony Vallone sold it to Landry's, fans still find it "worth a visit" for "solid", "midpriced" Neapolitan-inspired dishes, "great" antipasto and "thin and crusty" pizzas ferried by a "somewhat attentive" staff; both locations thrive in "noisy", "crowded" environs with a "see-and-be-seen" vibe, especially at the bar.

	FOOD	DECOR	SERVICE	COST

Grove, The *American*

| - | - | - | E |

Downtown | Discovery Green | 1611 Lamar St. (Crawford St.) | 713-337-7321 | www.thegrovehouston.com

Chefs Robert Del Grande (Cafe Annie) and Ryan Pera (ex 17) teamed up on the ambitious American menu at this highly anticipated arrival in Downtown Houston's new Discovery Green Park inhabiting a showstopping two-story, glass-enclosed space; its moderately expensive rotisserie dishes are joined by shareable items like duck meatloaf and free-range deviled eggs.

Hard Rock Cafe ❶ *American*

| 14 | 21 | 14 | $26 |

Downtown | 502 Texas Ave. (bet. Bagby & Smith Sts.) | 713-227-1392 | www.hardrock.com

An "iconic part of the tourist landscape", this rock 'n' roll–themed American chain was "cool in the '80s", but many feel it's "past its sell date", citing "mundane" grub, "haphazard" service and "way too loud" acoustics; despite a "surprisingly decent burger" and all that "fun music memorabilia", it may be better to "buy the T-shirt" instead.

Hobbit Cafe *Eclectic*

| 21 | 13 | 15 | $16 |

Lower Shepherd | 2243 Richmond Ave. (Greenbriar Dr.) | 713-526-5460

"Long before Peter Jackson" brought Middle Earth to the big screen, hobbits ruled at this *Lord of the Rings*–themed cafe, an "offbeat" "geeks' paradise" in an old house in Lower Shepherd; among the "cozy nooks" that are adorned with "amusing" Tolkien memorabilia, a "granola" staff feeds the "hippielike" habitués an Eclectic array of "mile-high sandwiches" and other "healthy" veggie-friendly vittles.

Hollywood Vietnamese & Chinese ❷ *Chinese/Vietnamese*

| - | - | - | I |

Montrose | 2409 Montrose Blvd. (Fairview St.) | 713-523-8808

Montrose denizens are delighted by the "huge" selection of "fresh and delicious" Chinese and Vietnamese items on offer at this sprawling spot that's "fun with a large crowd"; gentle prices and late hours (they're open till 2 AM on weekends) boost the appeal, as does the bamboo-bedecked patio that's especially festive.

Houston's *American*

| 23 | 20 | 22 | $30 |

Galleria | 5888 Westheimer Rd. (Fountain View Dr.) | 713-975-1947
Upper Kirby District | 4848 Kirby Dr. (Westpark Dr.) | 713-529-2386
www.hillstone.com

A "chain that doesn't feel like one", this "reliable" national franchise "clicks" thanks to a "pretty darn good" menu of "all-American comfort" items (including a notoriously "addicting spinach dip") and a "modern metropolitan" ambiance that brings in "mingling singles" after work; despite debate on the cost – "inexpensive" vs. "overpriced" – most report "solid quality" here.

NEW Hue *Vietnamese*

| - | - | - | M |

Upper Kirby District | 3600 Kirby Dr. (Richmond Ave.) | 713-526-8858

Though it takes its name from the historic Vietnamese city, the look of this Upper Kirby newcomer is anything but traditional, with a con-

temporary clean-lined dining room done up in light woods and accented with greenery; prices may be slightly higher than others of its ilk, but the menu is more ambitious as well with dishes like crispy quail with watercress and grilled pork short ribs joined up with a smart wine list.

☑ Hugo's *Mexican*

| 26 | 23 | 22 | $35 |

Montrose | 1600 Westheimer Rd. (Mandell St.) | 713-524-7744 | www.hugosrestaurant.net

This stylish Montrose "class act" provides "gourmet, designer Mexican" that's both "innovative and traditional", making it "a great alternative" for chile-hounds "who want Latin cuisine but are tired of the old Tex-Mex"; "excellent handmade margaritas", a "great wine list", "cool setting" (though the noise-averse warn it has the "acoustics of an airplane hangar") and capable staff add to the allure; P.S. Sunday brunch is its "best-kept secret here."

Hunan ⊠ *Chinese*

| ▽ 21 | 15 | 18 | $34 |

Downtown | 812 Capitol St. (Milam St.) | 713-227-8999

Tucked among the towering skyscrapers, this Downtown Sino convenient to the convention center earns kudos from fans for its "upscale" Chinese cuisine; it draws a "good lunch crowd" so those who aren't "prepared to wait" may want to opt for takeout.

Hungry's Café & Bistro *Eclectic*

| 19 | 15 | 17 | $17 |

Rice Village | 2356 Rice Blvd. (bet. Greenbriar & Morningside Drs.) | 713-523-8652

West Houston | 14714 Memorial Dr. (Dairy Ashford Rd.) | 281-493-1520 www.hungryscafe.com

Admirers with an appetite appreciate this Eclectic pair in Rice Village and West Houston, dubbing them "kid-friendly" "neighborhood staples" for their "healthy", "well-prepared" and "inexpensive" eats and "straightforward" decor; servers are "inexperienced but eager to please", and both locations offer home delivery for a small fee.

☑ Ibiza Ⓜ *Mediterranean*

| 25 | 21 | 22 | $40 |

Midtown | 2450 Louisiana St. (McGowen St.) | 713-524-0004 | www.ibizafoodandwinebar.com

"A favorite of the 'in' crowd", this "happening" Midtown Med helmed by chef Charles Clark is famed for "imaginative", "consistently delicious" "tapas-style" dishes, though it's the "incomparable" wine list that wins the most raves with a 500-label collection filled with "great values"; servers are "responsive", but regulars report "it can get a little noisy", especially on weekends, so lunch is a more "relaxing" option; N.B. adjacent is the plush Ibiza Lounge, offering a similarly extensive wine list plus a full bar.

India's Restaurant *Indian*

| 21 | 17 | 18 | $25 |

Galleria | 5704 Richmond Ave. (Chimney Rock Rd.) | 713-266-0131 | www.indiasrestauranthouston.com

Masala mavens hail the "constantly improving menu" at this Galleria Indian offering "seriously spiced dishes" alongside "lean" healthy-heart options in serene surroundings with wall hangings and fresh

| | FOOD | DECOR | SERVICE | COST |

flowers; a few find fault with service that needs "improving", but on the whole locals laud it as a "friendly" spot that's a "great value."

Indika ⓜ Indian
| 25 | 22 | 22 | $37 |

Montrose | 516 Westheimer Rd. (Whitney St.) | 713-984-1725 | www.indikausa.com

Gastronomes gush over the "delicious", "delicately spiced" Indian dishes prepared with "intelligent", "modern twists" at "charming" chef-owner Anita Jaisinghani's "upmarket" Montrose "jewel"; "gracious" servers work the "cool" and contemporary room where saffron-yellow walls and colorful curtains add a soft touch.

Irma's Ⓢ Mexican
| 22 | 17 | 21 | $21 |

Downtown | 22 N. Chenevert St. (Ruiz St.) | 713-222-0767

At this Downtown "institution" "close to Minute Maid Park", "politicos, courthouse types" and other regulars happily step up to the plate for Irma Galvan's "uncomplicated" Mexican fare and a glass of her "legendary lemonade"; quirks of the "funky-shabby" spot include "quaint oral menus" and the "upbeat" staff's use of an "honor system" to total up the tab; N.B. closed evenings and weekends.

Irma's Southwest Grill Ⓢ Tex-Mex
| 21 | 16 | 18 | $23 |

Downtown | 1314 Texas Ave. (Austin St.) | 713-247-9651 | www.irmassouthwest.com

"Easier to get to" and a little "pricier", this Downtown offspring of Irma's "lacks its mother's character", but the "authentic Tex-Mex" fare (including "delicious" seafood and the "signature lemonade") is just as "enjoyable"; with "efficient" service and decor that's "a bit nicer" than the original, it's equally "great before a ball game" – especially now that it has doubled in size.

Isla Coquí ⓜ Puerto Rican
| - | - | - | M |

Heights | 1801 Durham Dr. (I-10) | 713-861-1000 | www.islacoquipr.com

"Home-cooked Puerto Rican food" (think sweet plantain-beef pie) draws an eclectic crowd to this moderately priced Heights area newbie; though the spacious room appointed with white ceiling fans is "sparsely decorated", it grooves on a festive vibe, thanks to tropical drinks and live jazz and salsa on Friday nights.

Istanbul Grill ⓜ Turkish
| 22 | 14 | 21 | $17 |

Rice Village | 5613 Morningside Dr. (University Blvd.) | 713-526-2800 | www.istanbulgrill.com

This "unpretentious" Rice Village Turk provides "excellent value" with "fresh, delicious" and "authentic" Middle Eastern eats served by an "attentive staff"; the decor is "nothing much to look at", but the vibe is "casual and fun" – just know that parking can be a "nightmare."

🆉 Japaneiro's Sushi Bistro & Latin Grill Japanese/S American
| 26 | 20 | 22 | $24 |

Sugar Land | Sugar Land Town Sq. | 2168 Texas Dr. (Hwy. 59) | 281-242-1121 | www.japaneiro.com

"It works!" exclaim initiates impressed by the "fusion of Japanese and Latin" at this colorful original on the Town Square in Sugar Land,

FOOD · DECOR · SERVICE · COST

where the "interesting" "balance of tastes" yields "excellent" eating and "lots of things to choose from"; generous portions provide "value" for the quality, and the "service is great as well."

Jarro Café *Mexican*

| - | - | - | I |

Spring Branch | 1521 Gessner Dr. (Hazelhurst Dr.) | 713-827-0373 | www.jarrocafe.com

The taco truck in front of this Spring Branch counter-service Mexican is all you need to know about its roots, which are even more evident in its "awesome tacos" and the array of "six or so salsas" (some fiery) that give the goods an authentic kick; jarringly, the frill-free interior sports decor that's more Beatlemania than taqueria.

Jasmine Asian Cuisine *Vietnamese*

| - | - | - | I |

Alief | 9938 Bellaire Blvd. (Sam Houston Pkwy.) | 713-272-8188 | www.jasmineasiancuisine.com

Tucked into a shopping center in Alief's New Chinatown, this surprisingly spacious and stylish Vietnamese (think Indochine-era ceiling fans and lots of bamboo) offers one of the broadest menus around, including seldom-found specialties like seven courses of beef or fish; its lunch specials rank among the best deals in town.

Jasper's *American*

| 24 | 25 | 24 | $42 |

The Woodlands | Market St. | 9595 Six Pines Dr. (Lake Woodlands Dr.) | 281-298-6600 | www.kentrathbun.com

See review in Austin and the Hill Country Directory.

Jax Grill *Southern*

| 19 | 12 | 16 | $13 |

Bellaire | 6510 S. Rice Ave. (Bissonnet St.) | 713-668-3606
Heights | 1613 Shepherd Dr. (Eigel St.) | 713-861-5529
www.jax-grill.com

This casual pair of "local grills with personality" boasts a "huge menu" of "good" "basic" Southern fare doled out "serve-yourself"-style, which helps keep prices "cheap"; "zydeco dancing on Friday and Saturday nights" is a draw at the lower Heights location, while the Bellaire outpost is "ultra-kid-friendly", which means it's "always packed on weekends and evenings" with the "soccer mom" crowd.

Jenni's Noodle House *Vietnamese*

| ▽ 21 | 10 | 16 | $15 |

Lower Shepherd | 3111 S. Sheperd Dr. (Alabama St.) | 713-523-7600 | www.noodlesrule.com

It's now installed in spiffier new digs in Lower Shepherd, but "yummy" "noodles in wonderfully flavorful soups" are still the main attraction at this "bargain" Vietnamese; fans find it jennuinely "cool" and "accommodating", though a few less-than-thrilled purists plead for "better instead of hipper."

⧩ Jimmy Wilson's Seafood & Chop House *Seafood*

| 26 | 20 | 23 | $30 |

Briargrove | 5161 San Felipe St. (bet. Post Oak Blvd. & Sage Rd.) | 713-960-0333 | www.jimmywilsons.com

A rep for "excellent Cajun seafood" like the trademark gumbo precedes this Briargrove eatery, home to "the freshest" fish and a menu

"chock-full of seasonal delicacies" from the Gulf and beyond; with "friendly and efficient" service, it's "like a short trip to Louisiana" even if (or maybe because) the site's rustic room "is a little tired."

Joyce's Ocean Grill 🗷 *Seafood* | 19 | 15 | 20 | $30 |

Briargrove | 6415 San Felipe St. (Winrock Blvd.) | 713-975-9902 | www.joycesoceangrill.com

This "friendly neighborhood" Briargrove seafooder serves "fresh", "consistent" "Gulf Coast–style" cuisine and more, making it "a locals' favorite" even if the unconvinced carp "overrated"; it's "tucked away in a shopping center, so look hard" or you may just miss it; N.B. the Greenway Plaza branch has closed.

Julia's Bistro 🗷 *Nuevo Latino* | 19 | 14 | 19 | $33 |

Midtown | 3722 Main St. (Alabama St.) | 713-807-0090 | www.juliasbistro.com

A "modern" "urban" bistro with the MetroRail line outside its front window, this midsized Midtowner plies "innovative" Nuevo Latino cooking in a "stark, loftlike" space; most applaud the "inventive and fresh dishes" and "unusual picks" on the wine list, though holdouts hint at a "noisy background" and "erratic" service.

Kahn's Deli *Deli* | 23 | 10 | 18 | $13 |

Rice Village | The Village | 2429 Rice Blvd. (Morningside Dr.) | 713-529-2891 | www.kahnsdeli.com

This 25-year-old Rice Village deli is a counter-service "continuation of the Kahn family tradition" featuring "generous" top-notch "NY sandwiches" for a fair price; keep in mind that somewhat "surly" help comes with the "authentic" territory; N.B. the Decor score does not reflect a major remodel in 2008.

Kam's Fine Chinese Cuisine *Chinese* | 20 | 13 | 20 | $18 |

Montrose | 4500 Montrose Blvd. (I-59) | 713-529-5057

A "loyal local" following makes this Montrose Chinese a "neighborhood" "staple" for "quality" chow that won't break the bank; happy kampers add the "service is always friendly", and if the dark-paneled decor's "not fancy", the goods are also "spot-on to go."

Kaneyama *Japanese* | ∇ 27 | 17 | 21 | $36 |

West Houston | 9527 Westheimer Rd. (Rockyridge Dr.) | 713-784-5168

After a decade and a half, this West Houston Japanese "keeps its standards" with an "imaginative" menu of "great sushi" leading an "excellent" lineup that's paired with "impeccable" service; insiders sense it's "underappreciated" (maybe due to the nondescript stripcenter setting), but it's a "better bargain" than many.

🗷 Kanomwan 🗷 *Thai* | 27 | 7 | 11 | $18 |

Neartown | 736½ Telephone Rd. (Dumble St.) | 713-923-4230

Fans of this Neartown BYO (aka the 'Telephone Thai') fervently proclaim the "intensely flavored" Siamese eats "the best" in town "hands down"; the "lackluster room" is "nothing to look at" and service is often "grumpy", but at least a trip here "won't break the bank."

Karl's at the Riverbend Ⓜ *American/Continental*

▽ 27 | 21 | 26 | $43

Richmond | 5011 FM 723 (FM 359) | 281-238-9300 | www.karlsrb.com

Those in-the-know declare it's "definitely worth the drive" to this rustic Richmond roost, a "wonderful" "find" for "traditional" American-Continental fare ("game dishes are the main attraction") matched with "reasonable wines"; the "friendly staff" is bent on creating a "relaxing" atmo and lays out "an amazing spread" for Sunday brunch.

Kasra Persian Grill *Mideastern*

- | - | - | M

Southwest Houston | 9741 Westheimer Rd. (Gessner Rd.) | 713-975-1810

Complimentary fresh taftoon ("some of the best bread ever") kicks off the Persian excursion at this Southwest Houston strip-center standout, which grills up "large portions" of "delicious" specialties at a moderate cost; the comfy quarters are well attended, and newbies can rest assured the "staff is very helpful explaining the menu."

Katz's Deli ◐ *Deli*

19 | 15 | 16 | $18

Montrose | 616 Westheimer Rd. (Montrose Blvd.) | 713-521-3838

Katz's Express *Deli*

The Woodlands | Portofino Ctr. | 19075 I-45 N. (bet. Research Forest Dr. & Wellman Rd.) | 936-321-1880
www.ilovekatzs.com

See review in Austin and the Hill Country Directory.

Kenneally's Irish Pub ◐ *Pub Food*

▽ 16 | 11 | 16 | $16

Lower Shepherd | 2111 S. Shepherd Dr. (Indiana St.) | 713-630-0486 | www.irishpubkenneallys.com

"Leave it to an Irish pub" to make what many consider "the best thin-crust pizza in town" marvel mates of this Lower Shepherd tavern, which also proffers the usual "proletarian" pub grub to go with plenty of cold beer; add in a patio "for shade and relaxation", a "fun" crowd and bartenders who've "been here forever" and "what else do you need – ambiance?"; N.B. kitchen open till 1 AM nightly.

Kenny & Ziggy's New York Delicatessen *Deli*

24 | 17 | 19 | $20

Galleria | 2327 Post Oak Blvd. (Westheimer Rd.) | 713-871-8883 | www.kennyandziggys.com

"Oy, gevalt" exclaim fressers impressed by the corned beef and pastrami, "fabulous" smoked fish and other "old-fashioned Jewish comfort foods" that make this deli so "authentic" it evokes "Manhattan right in the middle of the Galleria"; also adding a "Big Apple feel" are the "crowded", "boisterous" room, "abrupt but helpful" staffers and the "NYC prices."

NEW Kenzo Sushi Bistro *American/Japanese*

- | - | - | M

Katy | La Centerra Mall | 23501 Cinco Ranch Blvd. (Grand Pkwy.) | 281-371-8200 | www.kenzosushi.com

Katy residents no longer have to travel for quality sushi thanks to this recent arrival occupying an elegant space decorated in rich earth

tones with cream-colored banquettes and bamboo accents; though the raw fish is certainly a draw, the moderately priced menu also includes Asian-accented New American fare like poached salmon with peppercorn cream and Kalbi-style ribs with baby bok choy.

NEW Khun Kay Thai Café *Thai*

- | - | - | I

Montrose | 1209 Montrose Blvd. (bet. W. Clay & Dallas Sts.) | 713-524-9614 | www.khunkaythaicafe.com

Replacing the long-standing Golden Room, this new Thai eatery from the same owners strives to provide similarly authentic fare in a fast-casual format; given the speedy service and gentle prices, it's no surprise that it's entered into the lunch rotation of many Montrose diners.

Khyber North Indian Grill M *Indian*

23 | 16 | 19 | $23

Upper Kirby District | 2510 Richmond Ave. (Kirby Dr.) | 713-942-9424

Don't pass up this Upper Kirby District Indian grill urge regulars who revere its "flavorful" "food with flair" (the lunch buffet "rocks"); most praise the "warm, clubby" scene and "friendly service" as well, so though wallet-watchers find tabs rather "high", fans feel just "chatting with the owner is worth the price of admission."

Killen's Steakhouse Ⓢ *Steak*

- | - | - | E

Pearland | 2804 S. Main St. (Hwy. 518) | 281-485-0844 | www.killenssteakhouse.com

"Wow, what a steak!" clamor carnivores who venture "outside the hustle and bustle" to this "outstanding" cow palace "in Pearland, no less", for "superb" cuts of aged prime beef bolstered by "extremely large sides"; ok, the "minimalist" setting might not strike a chord, but the "creativity goes into the food" and "until you taste it, you won't believe the hype."

Kim Son *Chinese/Vietnamese*

23 | 20 | 19 | $21

Alief | 10603 Bellaire Blvd. (bet. Rogerdale Rd. & Wilcrest Dr.) | 281-598-1777

Downtown | 2001 Jefferson St. (Chartres St.) | 713-222-2461

Stafford | 12750 Southwest Frwy. (Fountain Lake Dr.) | 281-242-3500

This "sprawling" Downtown landmark and its Stafford sibling offer an "extensive", even "overwhelming" menu (more than 400 items) of "good to excellent" Vietnamese and Chinese dishes – both "authentic" and "Americanized" – to suit a mixed clientele in "family-friendly", often crowded settings; on weekends the Southwest Freeway branch also serves "must-try" dim sum; N.B. the Bellaire location is buffet and dim sum only.

Kiran's *Indian*

25 | 22 | 22 | $39

Galleria | 4100 Westheimer Rd. (Midlane St.) | 713-960-8472 | www.kiranshouston.com

Chef-owner Kiran Verma "educates your palate" with "absolutely exceptional" cooking at this "high-end" Galleria-area Indian, where the cuisine introduces an "original" "mix of traditional and new"; with a "top-class" staff and "beautiful, serene surroundings" accented with antiques from the subcontinent, it's "pricey" but "worth every penny."

	FOOD	DECOR	SERVICE	COST

Kirby's Steakhouse *Steak* | 24 | 22 | 23 | $50 |

The Woodlands | 1111 Timberloch Pl. (I-45) | 281-362-1121 |
www.kirbyssteakhouse.com
See review in Dallas/Ft. Worth Directory.

Kona Grill *American* | 20 | 21 | 18 | $27 |

Galleria | 5061 Westheimer Rd. (Post Oak Blvd.) | 713-877-9191
Sugar Land | First Colony Mall | 16535 Southwest Frwy. (Hwy. 6) |
281-242-7000
www.konagrill.com
"Yuppies" enjoy the "see-and-be-seen" scene at these New
Americans, connecting over drinks and a "wide menu" with Hawaiian
leanings shored up by "contemporary sushi"; converts claim "everything's a little surprising" here – "not bad for a chain."

Kubo's *Japanese* | 25 | 20 | 21 | $31 |

Rice Village | Rice Village Arcade | 2414 University Blvd. (Morningside Dr.) |
713-528-7878 | www.kubos-sushi.com
Sushiphiles lavish kudos on this "true Japanese" hot spot upstairs in a retail center in Rice Village, where chefs trained in the
homeland slice "super-fresh" fish of the "highest quality", including numerous more "exotic items"; the unadorned setting
keeps the focus on the food, which "continues to deliver" at "top-
notch" levels – "*arigato*."

☑ La Colombe d'Or *Continental/French* | 21 | 27 | 24 | $56 |

Montrose | La Colombe d'Or | 3410 Montrose Blvd. (bet. Harold &
Hawthorne Sts.) | 713-524-7999 | www.lacolombedor.com
Diners delight in the "romantic" surroundings at this Montrose
mainstay housed in a "beautiful" "historically preserved" 1923
mansion-turned-hotel (it's rated No. 1 for Decor in Houston); yet
while the "wonderful" flower-filled interior wins raves, detractors
declare the "classic" French-Continental menu "needs invigora-
tion" and say sometimes "spotty" service doesn't live up to the
"extremely expensive" tabs.

La Griglia *Italian* | 21 | 22 | 20 | $40 |

River Oaks | River Oaks Ctr. | 2002 W. Gray St. (bet. McDuffie St. &
Shepherd Dr.) | 713-526-4700 | www.lagrigliarestaurant.com
Paesani praise this "boisterous", mural-filled River Oaks Italian for
the "finest seafood" and "excellent" free pizza bread, ably served to
an "elite" clientele; the "fabulous" bar is a "hot scene" as well, but
din-sensitive diners should "bring earplugs"; P.S. since its sale to the
Landry's empire, some find the place "about the same", yet many
fret quality and service have "dropped like a lead balloon."

La Mexicana *Mexican* | 19 | 12 | 17 | $17 |

Montrose | 1018 Fairview St. (Montrose Blvd.) | 713-521-0963 |
www.lamexicanarestaurant.com
"For a hangover, take two tacos" and in an hour "you'll be ready to repeat the sins of the previous evening" report respondents who also rely
on the "great Mexican breakfasts" and other "old-school" *comida* at
this "casual" Montrose "standby", a "neighborhood" "favorite."

	FOOD	DECOR	SERVICE	COST

Lankford Grocery & Market 🖪🗭 *Burgers* | 23 | 10 | 15 | $12 |

Midtown | 88 Dennis St. (Boston St.) | 713-522-9555

This old, family-run, Midtown daytime "locals' dive" has surveyors swearing by its burgers and other "cheap and greasy" comfort food; they couldn't care less that staffers sometimes act like "grumpy parents" or that the space has "zero" decor.

Las Alamedas *Mexican* | 20 | 25 | 22 | $33 |

Memorial | 8615 Katy Frwy. (Bingle Rd.) | 713-461-1503 | www.lasalamedas.com

"Intriguing interiors" with huge "windows overlooking the lush bayou" make this Memorial hacienda feel like a "beautiful oasis right beside a major freeway"; proponents praise the "classy" "gourmet" Mexican dishes – especially at the "quite nice" Sunday brunch and at happy hour with its "wonderful" free buffet – and "accommodating" staff, but critics lament that the "mediocre" fare and service are "no match for the view."

La Strada 🅼 *Italian* | 19 | 19 | 18 | $34 |

Montrose | 322 Westheimer Rd. (Taft St.) | 713-523-1014 | www.lastradahouston.com

Fans of this Montrose Italian dig its "excellent food", "pleasant" staff and "hip" atmosphere – especially the "debaucherous", "decadent" Sunday brunch (a "gigantic party"); but critics blast the "noisy, crowded" "zoo" with its "uninspiring food" and "inattentive service": "overpriced, overdone, over."

La Trattoria *Italian* ∇ | 20 | 16 | 16 | $34 |

Briargrove | 6504 Westheimer Rd. (bet. Briargrove Dr. & Voss. Rd.) | 713-782-1324 | www.latrattoria-houston.com

A Briargrove fixture for over 25 years, this Northern Italian features "homemade" pastas and fresh seafood "prepared simply" in a "quiet setting" equipped with a wine cellar and a patio; "service can be spotty", but "the owner is such a character" that partisans pardon "the occasional lapses."

Laurier Café & Wine 🖪 *American* | 25 | 19 | 21 | $37 |

Greenway Plaza Area | 3139 Richmond Ave. (Eastside St.) | 713-807-1632 | www.lauriercafe.com

This "quaint, cute, cozy" cafe near Greenway Plaza pleases with "fantastic" midpriced New American cookery and bistro classics like "outstanding steak frites", accompanied by an "inspired wine list"; the "intimate setting" includes a small patio, making this a prime place for "a quiet meal with someone special."

La Vista *American/Italian* | 23 | 14 | 20 | $27 |

Briargrove | 1936 Fountain View Dr. (San Felipe St.) | 713-787-9899

Memorial | 12665 Memorial Dr. (Broken Bough Dr.) | 713-973-7374 | www.fatbutter.com

"Casual restaurants with un-casual food", this "neighborhood" New American pair is lauded for "wonderful" cooking incorporating "cre-

ative Italian" touches and a "super" BYO policy with a "more-than-fair" "$7 corkage fee" ("they have a wine list" too); some take a dim view of the "bare-bones" spaces, but their "lively spirit" makes them "local" "favorites."

Leibman's *Deli*   21 | 16 | 16 | $15
West Houston | 14529 Memorial Dr. (Dairy Ashford Rd.) | 281-493-3663 | www.leibmans.com

Deli, "wine shop" and "gourmet foods" emporium are bundled into one at this West Houston vet, an ever-"popular" stop for its "fab selection" of overstuffed sandwiches and "made-from-scratch soups, salads and desserts"; since customers queue to "order at the counter" and seating is functional, many opt to "carry out."

☑ Le Mistral *French*   26 | 18 | 22 | $43
West Houston | 1400 Eldridge Pkwy. (Briar Forest Dr.) | 832-379-8322 | www.lemistralhouston.com

"The Denis brothers bring St. Tropez to West Houston" at this "wonderful bistro", home to "fabulous" Provençal-inflected French fare proffered by "friendly" folks with an "unassuming" style; "neighborhood" Francophiles who make it a "favorite" acknowledge it's "a bit pricey, but worth it every time"; N.B. a post-Survey relocation puts the Decor score into question.

Lemongrass Café *Asian Fusion*   21 | 19 | 21 | $24
Bellaire | 5109 Bellaire Blvd. (Rice Ave.) | 713-664-6698 | www.lemongrass-cafe.com

"Near-gourmet" Asian fusion cuisine that's "innovative" but "stays in the comfort zone" delights those diners who have "discovered" this "true find" in Bellaire; there's also a "well-selected" wine collection and an "eager if not expert" staff to help foster a "pleasant" atmosphere, though hearty eaters harrumph the "small portions" are too "pricey."

Lemon Tree Ⓜ *Peruvian*   - | - | - | I
West Houston | 12591 Whittington Dr. (Dairy Ashford Rd.) | 281-556-0690 | www.lemontreeonline.com

A "unique" niche for "excellent ceviche" and other "authentic" plates, this West Houston strip-center Peruvian's diminutive dining room is typically filled with expats; most root for the "interesting", "reasonably priced" eating even if "below-par" decor and "sometimes clueless" service strike sour notes; P.S. it's BYO only ("no corkage fee!").

Le Viet *Vietnamese*   ▽ 21 | 15 | 17 | $19
Royal Oaks | 11328 Westheimer Rd. (Hayes Rd.) | 281-293-8883 | www.le-viet.com

This "unassuming" restaurant on Westheimer near Royal Oaks fills the neighborhood need for Vietnamese with a "great variety" of "flavorful" choices centered on seafood (the "lobster dishes are always good"); its allies appreciate the "friendly" atmosphere and modest pricing, though the modern-esque setting could use some polishing.

Lexington Grille, The ⊠ *Continental* ▽ 21 | 20 | 21 | $36

Lower Shepherd | 2005 Lexington St. (Shepherd Dr.) | 713-524-9877 | www.lexingtongrille.com

Get away from the nearby hustle and bustle at this "quaint" "little" Lower Shepherd "find", whose short but "varied menu" features Continental cooking so "delicious" it "should be illegal"; given the flattering lighting and "quiet", "romantic" vibes, romeos rank it among the "best locations for dinner with your date."

NEW Little Bigs *Burgers* – | – | – | I

Montrose | 2703 Montrose Blvd. (Westheimer Ave.) | 713-521-2447 | www.littlebigshouston.com

Capitalizing on the raves received for their sliders at Reef, owners Bill Floyd and Bryan Caswell have focused their attention on America's favorite food with this new burger shack featuring beefy bite-sized patties alongside a fine selection of beers, wines and cocktails (like "The Dude", a frozen White Russian); set near the heart of Montrose, this casual spot is another in the small, but growing ranks of late-night options long needed by Houstonians.

López ⊠ *Mexican* – | – | – | I

Alief | 11606 S. Wilcrest Dr. (bet. Bellfort Ave. & Hwy. 59) | 281-495-2436 | www.vivalopez.com

Lóyal lócals say "mmm . . . is all you need to know" about this family-run Alief favorite, for three decades a "dependable" source of "solid Mexican" at a fair price; when paired with a casual, kid-friendly atmosphere and capable service, it's no surprise the sprawling setup is often packed.

Luling City Market *BBQ* 23 | 11 | 13 | $15

Galleria | 4726 Richmond Ave. (I-610) | 713-871-1903 | www.lulingcitymarket.com

Folks are fired up about this Galleria-area "hole-in-the-wall" barbecue joint because of its brisket ("tender as a mother's love"), ribs that "don't need sauce" and "delicious" sides, served counter-style on butcher paper; chatting with "interesting locals" at the "smoky" bar also befits the "traditional" treats, but skeptics wonder what's with the "Wonder Bread" – "good Texas 'cue deserves better!"

⊠ Lupe Tortilla *Mexican* 21 | 17 | 17 | $19

West U | 2414 Southwest Frwy. (Kirby Dr.) | 713-522-4420
North Houston | 15315 North Frwy. (Richey Rd.) | 281-873-6220
Northwest Houston | 22465 Tomball Pkwy. (Spring-Cypress Rd.) | 832-843-0004
West Houston | 318 Stafford St. (I-10) | 281-496-7580
Webster | 891 W. Bay Area Blvd. (I-45) | 281-338-2711
Sugar Land | 15801 Southwest Frwy. (Hwy. 6) | 281-265-7500
The Woodlands | 19437 I-45 S. (bet. Oak Ridge School Rd. & Research Forest Dr.) | 281-298-5274
www.lupetortillas.com

"Divine" beef fajitas and "homemade tortillas" lead the lineup at this area chain of big, "crowded and loud" Tex-Mexers, where the "relatively cheap" prices and "fun for families" ensure little ones are

"everywhere"; on the flip side, there's "usually a wait" ("drop the kids in the sandbox and enjoy a 'rita") and purists posit the "yuppie" clientele and pidgin-menu shtick are "embarrassing."

Lyndon's Pit Bar-B-Q *BBQ*

| - | - | - | I |

Northwest Houston | 13165 Northwest Frwy. (Hollister Rd.) | 713-690-2112

Maybe it's "not a traditional Texas brisket house", but 'cue connoisseurs consider this BBQ joint's "pulled-pork approach" a "tasty" "change of pace" that's "worth a trip" to a "nondescript strip mall" in Northwest Houston; more typical touches include "fantastic" sides, reasonable prices and rustically tacky decor.

☑ Lynn's Steakhouse ⓢ *Steak*

| 26 | 23 | 24 | $53 |

West Houston | 955 Dairy Ashford St. (bet. I-10 & Memorial Dr.) | 281-870-0807 | www.lynnssteakhouse.com

Catering to "the expense-account crowd", this "high-end" West Houston meatery rewards the "well-heeled" with "delectable" prime beef and "first-rate" seafood complemented by "superior service" and an "extensive wine list" boasting over 900 labels; the office-park exterior belies a "warm", "intimate setting" suitable for "that romantic dinner."

Madras Pavilion *Indian*

| 22 | 11 | 14 | $17 |

Upper Kirby District | 3910 Kirby Dr. (bet. Richmond Ave. & Southwest Frwy.) | 713-521-2617
Sugar Land | 16260 Kensington Dr. (bet. Hwy. 6 & I-59) | 281-491-3672
www.madraspavilion.us

This no-frills multicity chainlet pleases "hungry" spice cadets seeking "great-tasting" Indian eats "with a bite" ("interesting" midday buffets and "huge" dosas "are a must"); service, though, is "hit-or-miss" ("terrible" vs. "bearable"); N.B. the North Austin and Richardson branches are vegetarian, kosher and BYO.

Maggiano's Little Italy *Italian*

| 20 | 20 | 20 | $30 |

Galleria | 2019 Post Oak Blvd. (bet. San Felipe St. & Westheimer Rd.) | 713-961-2700 | www.maggianos.com

See review in Dallas/Ft. Worth Directory.

Magnolia Bar & Grill *Cajun/Seafood*

| ▽ 20 | 17 | 17 | $26 |

Briargrove | 6000 Richmond Ave. (Fountain View Dr.) | 713-781-6207 | www.magnolia-grill.com

A "reliable" stop for over 25 years and a "crawfish lover's paradise" in season, this Briargrove Cajun specializes in South Louisiana faves like Gulf seafood, étouffée and bread pudding; but though the fairly priced fare's still "consistent", the old-school setting is "getting worn around the edges."

Mai's Restaurant ◑ *Vietnamese*

| 23 | 11 | 17 | $17 |

Midtown | 3403 Milam St. (Francis St.) | 713-520-7684 | www.maisrestauranttx.com

"Terrific value" makes decor "irrelevant" at this Midtown Vietnamese "landmark" offering a "novel-size" menu of "wonderful", "spicy"

| | FOOD | DECOR | SERVICE | COST |

specialties for "cheap"; "touch-and-go" service ranges from "quick" to "notoriously bad", but the kitchen stays open until 4 AM on weekends, making this "people-watching" spot "salvation" for "insomniacs", "college students" and "clubbers leaving the bars Downtown."

Mai Thai ☒ Thai | 23 | 16 | 23 | $19 |
Upper Kirby District | 3819 Kirby Dr. (bet. Hwy. 59 & Richmond Ave.) | 713-522-6707 | www.maithaihouston.com
Despite its pink-hued exterior and location in the bustling Upper Kirby District, this "tried-and-true" Thai is still "a hidden gem" serving "exemplary" Siamese classics in "quiet", "simple surroundings"; the "quality" chow and "impeccably" "polite" staff have admirers pronouncing it "a great neighborhood place."

Mama's Café ● American | 19 | 14 | 18 | $14 |
Briargrove | 6019 Westheimer Rd. (bet. Fountain View & Greenridge Drs.) | 713-266-8514 | www.mamascafe.net
See review in San Antonio Directory.

Mambo Seafood Seafood | 20 | 10 | 16 | $16 |
NEW **Greenpoint** | 12333 E. Frwy. (Federal Rd.) | 713-637-0553
Sharpstown | 6697 Hillcroft St. (Dashwood Dr.) | 713-541-3666
Spring Branch | 10002 Long Point Rd. (Witte Rd.) | 713-465-5009
North Houston | 10810 N. Frwy. (Kingswood Ln.) | 281-820-3300
North Houston | 6101 Airline Dr. (Dunham Dr.) | 713-691-9700
Northwest Houston | 13485 Hwy. 290 (Tidwell Rd.) | 713-462-0777
www.mamborestaurants.com
Brightly bedecked and "casual", this local chain is known for "great, cheap seafood" prepared Mexican-style and washed down with *micheladas* (spicy south-of-the-border beer drinks); in keeping with the "value" orientation, their interiors "leave something to be desired."

Mardi Gras Grill Cajun/Seafood | ∇ 18 | 12 | 18 | $20 |
Heights | 1200 Durham Dr. (Nett St.) | 713-864-5600 | www.mardigrasgrill.net
"Good ol'" Cajun fin fare is the forte at this Lower Heights hideout, a "master" at crab bisque, fried seafood, seasonal boiled crawfish and other "down-home" delights; the "low-key, comfortable" digs may not evoke Bourbon Street, but they still complement the rustic eats.

Market Square Bar & Grill ☒ American | - | - | - | I |
Downtown | 311 Travis St. (Preston St.) | 713-224-6133
A square deal for "fine" American fare including the "best burger" around, this "locals' hangout" occupies an old brick building where the "shabby-chic ambiance" "makes everything taste better"; plus the patio out back lets desk jockeys "escape Downtown for an hour."

☒ Mark's American Cuisine American | 28 | 26 | 27 | $59 |
Montrose | 1658 Westheimer Rd. (bet. Dunlavy & Ralph Sts.) | 713-523-3800 | www.marks1658.com
"The old church still produces heavenly dishes" declare the faithful at this "upper-echelon" Montrose New American (voted Most

Popular and No. 1 for Food in Houston) in a "beautifully converted" fane, where "master chef" Mark Cox fuses the finest in "fresh ingredients" into "exquisite" seasonal fare that's "expensive but so worth it"; "attentive" "but not stuffy" service and a "vibrant", upscale setting "truly bring the meal to the next level", marking this one as "tops" for "special occasions."

Mary'z Mediterranean Cuisine *Mediterranean*

▽ 21 | 11 | 13 | $22

Galleria | 5825 Richmond Ave. (bet. Chimney Rock Rd. & Fountain View Dr.) | 832-251-1955 | www.maryzcuisine.com

This Galleria-area Mediterranean is an "authentic enough" source of "decent Lebanese" featuring kebabs, shawarmas and other viands of the Levant; it draws "large groups that congregate to socialize and smoke hookahs" on the expansive patio, and if "service is a bit slow", it's always "friendly."

Masala Wok *Chinese/Indian*

18 | 12 | 15 | $13

Southwest Houston | Carillion Sq. | 10001 Westheimer Rd. (Briarpark Dr.) | 713-784-8811 | www.masalawok.com
See review in Dallas/Ft. Worth Directory.

Masraff's *Continental*

23 | 24 | 24 | $50

Uptown | 1025 S. Post Oak Ln. (bet. San Felipe St. & Woodway Dr.) | 713-355-1975 | www.masraffs.com

Set in a "classy" stand-alone building, this "sophisticated" Uptowner earns wide recognition for its "superb" "Euro-American cuisine" and "especially attentive service" led by a "genial host"; a "beautiful setting" hung with Murano chandeliers creates a "fashionable atmosphere" that's a natural "for a special event" or just "to stop for a drink" and enjoy the "live piano."

Massa's Restaurant 🅂 *Seafood*

19 | 14 | 18 | $31

Downtown | 1160 Smith St. (Dallas St.) | 713-650-0837

Massa's Seafood Grill 🅂 *Seafood*

Downtown | 1331 Lamar St. (bet. Austin & Caroline Sts.) | 713-655-9100
www.massas.com

These family-owned Downtown seafood restaurants are fraternal, not identical, twins; the "dimly lit, relaxed" Smith Street locale offers turf as well as surf, while the amply windowed Seafood Grill cooks with a "Creole-Cajun flair", but both please their "power-lunching" patrons.

Max's Wine Dive *Eclectic*

21 | 15 | 17 | $32

Heights | 4720 Washington Ave. (Shepherd Dr.) | 713-880-8737 | www.maxswinedive.com

"Comfort food to the nth degree" chased with 180 "super wines by the glass" keeps this "casual", diner-ish Heights-area "hot spot" filled to the max as a "loud", "fun crowd" flocks in for "funky" Eclectic eats like fried chicken and 'haute dogs'; maybe the "service doesn't measure up to the food", but you'll still have to "come early" "if you expect to sit down."

	FOOD	DECOR	SERVICE	COST

McCormick & Schmick's *Seafood*

| 21 | 21 | 20 | $41 |

NEW Downtown | Houston Pavilions | 1201 Fannin St. (Dallas Ave.) | 713-658-8100
Uptown | Uptown Park | 1151 Uptown Park Blvd. (Post Oak Blvd.) | 713-840-7900
www.mccormickandschmicks.com
See review in Austin and the Hill Country Directory.

McGonigel's Mucky Duck *Pub Food*

| 16 | 21 | 18 | $17 |

Upper Kirby District | 2425 Norfolk St. (bet. Park & Revere Sts.) | 713-528-5999 | www.mcgonigels.com

"Surprisingly good pub food" shares the bill with "amazing music" at this Upper Kirby Anglo-Irish tavern, an intimate showcase where top regional acts (Alejandro Escovedo, Jack Ingram, etc.) perform most nights of the week; it's easy to duck in "for uncrowded lunches", and the "great beer selection" is poured in proper Imperial pints.

Melting Pot *Fondue*

| 21 | 20 | 21 | $43 |

Galleria | Briar Grove Plaza | 6100 Westheimer Rd. (bet. Chimney Rock & S. Voss Rds.) | 713-532-5011 | www.meltingpot.com
See review in Austin and the Hill Country Directory.

Mexico's Deli *Deli/Mexican*

| - | - | - | I |

West Houston | 2374 Dairy Ashford St. (Westheimer Rd.) | 281-679-7790

"This is authentic Mexican" cheer compadres of this West Houston deli known for bounteous tortas (grilled sandwiches) that deliver hearty combos of meats and cheese at a fantastic value; the agua frescas ("fresh fruit drinks") are a "right-on" complement to the chow.

Mia Bella Trattoria *Italian*

| 22 | 18 | 21 | $28 |

Downtown | 320 Main St. (Preston St.) | 713-237-0505
Greenway Plaza Area | 2006 Lexington St. (bet. Hwy. 59 & Shepherd Dr.) | 713-523-2428
www.miabellatrattoria.com

At these two "easygoing" eateries Downtown and in the Greenway Plaza Area, Italian aficionados find the chow *bella* – "not just tomato sauce and garlic", it's "high-end fare at low-end prices"; *amici* are satisfied with the "friendly, prompt" service and "authentic" atmosphere and say the Main Street branch is "good for a quick bite" before the theater or an evening of "bar-hopping"; N.B. new branches will be opening at Houston Pavilions and Vintage Park in 2009.

Michelangelo's *Italian*

| 24 | 22 | 23 | $36 |

Montrose | 307 Westheimer Rd. (Mason St.) | 713-524-7836 | www.michelangelosrestaurant.com

Nearly 40 years "hasn't changed much in the atmosphere or quality" at this "romantic" Montrose Italian, where loyalists trek for the "excellent food" and "wonderful ambiance" centered around a dining room that uniquely features a "tree growing through the roof"; it's the picture of a "charming" "date place" and a "family favorite" for brunch.

Mi Luna *Spanish*

19 | 17 | 16 | $27

Rice Village | 2441 University Blvd. (Kelvin Dr.) | 713-520-5025
Sugar Land | First Colony Mall | 2298 Texas Dr. (N. Town Ctr. Blvd.) |
281-277-8272
The Woodlands | 6777 Woodlands Pkwy. (Kuykendahl Rd.) |
281-419-0330
www.mi-luna.com

The topic is tapas at this Spanish trio in Rice Village, Sugar Land and
The Woodlands where amigos come en masse to "sample a number"
of "tasty", "creative" morsels and "potent" sangria; luna-tics particularly love the evenings with live music and dancing, which may be
why these "informal" venues are "always festive" (aka "loud" and
"chaotic") and often "crowded" with "glittery" "twentysomethings."

Mint Café *Mediterranean*

▽ 19 | 13 | 16 | $18

Galleria | 2800 Sage Rd. (Alabama St.) | 713-622-3434 |
www.mintcafehouston.com

Recently minted in the shadow of the Galleria, this "small", minimalist Mediterranean dishes up "plentiful" plates of Lebanese specialties ("the kebabs are great") at a moderate cost; but those not in
tune with the counter-service setup demur "nothing special."

Mission Burritos *Mexican*

22 | 12 | 17 | $11

Heights | 1609 Durham Dr. (Eigel St.) | 713-426-6634 |
www.missionburritos.com
Lower Shepherd | 2245 W. Alabama St. (Greenbriar Dr.) | 713-529-0535 |
www.missionburritos.com
NEW Rice Village | Village Arcade II | 5510 Morningside Dr.
(bet. Times & University Blvds.) | 713-520-7240 |
www.missionburritos.com
NEW West Houston | 6168 Hwy. 6 N (W. Little York Rd.) | 281-856-0344
NEW Humble | 7025 Humble-Huffman Rd. (W. Lake Houston Pkwy.) |
281-852-5603
NEW Katy | 23501 Cinco Ranch Blvd. (Grand Pkwy.) | 281-371-7150 |
www.missionburritos.com

These "fast", "friendly" "counter-service" Mexicans "blow the doors
off the bigger chains" with their "huge" "Californian-style burritos",
"made to order" with "fresh" fixings at a "bargain" price; if the interiors are missin' something, there's a "great patio" at each address.

Miss Saigon Café ⊠ *Vietnamese*

22 | 16 | 21 | $24

Rice Village | 5503 Kelvin St. (Times Blvd.) | 713-942-0108

"Small" but "comfortable", this "charming" Rice Village Vietnamese
wins kudos for its "simple" "home-cooked" dishes served by a
"friendly" crew; though it runs a bit "more expensive" than some competitors, regulars regard this "fave" as "a sweet little date spot."

Mockingbird Bistro Wine Bar *American*

25 | 20 | 23 | $44

River Oaks | 1985 Welch St. (McDuffie St.) | 713-533-0200 |
www.mockingbirdbistro.com

"Chef-owner John Sheely is a genius" twitter awestruck admirers
who "consider moving closer" to this "excellent" New American
"tucked away" in River Oaks, which "consistently delivers" with its

"delightful" "seasonal menu" and "fabulous" 500-label wine list; it glides on the wings of "professional" service, and the "low-lit" space with medieval accents lends a "funky" feel.

Mo Mong   *Vietnamese* | 20 | 16 | 16 | $22 |

Montrose | 1201 Westheimer Rd. (Waugh Dr.) | 713-524-5664 | www.mo-mong.com

This "swinging" "spring roll–martini nexus" in Montrose draws an "urban" clientele hungry for its "delicious", not-quite-authentic Vietnamese cuisine; "accommodating" servers are "sometimes sassy" and food is somewhat "expensive", but the "funky" scene makes some folks feel they're "in San Francisco, not Houston."

Monarch   *American* | ▽ 21 | 25 | 24 | $55 |

Medical Center | Hotel ZaZa | 5701 Main St. (Ewing St.) | 713-527-1800 | www.hotelzaza.com/houston

The "trendy" Hotel ZaZa near the Medical Center is home to this "gorgeous", "romantic" New American where "higher-end" types can "see and be seen" enjoying a "fun and functional" menu and "lovely views of the Mecom fountain" outside; but though loyal subjects find it "fabulous", others protest the "premium cost" for an operation that's "still working to get it right."

Morton's The Steakhouse   *Steak* | 25 | 21 | 23 | $62 |

Downtown | 1001 McKinney St. (Fannin St.) | 713-659-3700
Galleria | Centre at Post Oak | 5000 Westheimer Rd. (Post Oak Blvd.) | 713-629-1946
www.mortons.com

"Consistency abounds" at this "can't-go-wrong" steakhouse chain pairing "well-prepared" chops that "hang off the plate" with "seriously powerful martinis"; "arm-and-a-leg" pricing comes with the territory, along with a "Saran-wrapped presentation" of raw meats (accompanied by an instructional "recitation" by the waiter) – a "shtick" that many find "tired."

NEW Mo's... A Place for Steaks   *Steak* | - | - | - | E |

Galleria | 1801 Post Oak Blvd. (bet. San Felipe St. & Westheimer Rd.) | 713-877-0720 | www.mosaplaceforsteaks.com

Taking over the Galleria storefront that was long home to Tony's, this Milwaukee-based chain proffers expensive beef and cocktails for business travelers and well-heeled locals alike; the decor reflects an elegant take on the classic steakhouse look, while the menu features standbys like Texas cowboy rib-eye as well as more unusual items like grass-fed Australian beef and Wagyu filets.

Moveable Feast, A ✉ *American* | ▽ 22 | 9 | 18 | $13 |

Memorial | 9341 Katy Frwy. (Echo Ln.) | 713-365-0368 | www.amoveablefeast.com

"Are they sure this is health food?" ask amazed admirers of this "comfortable", long-established Memorial natural foods store and cafe who assert its "variety" of "good-tasting" Traditional American eats proves such fare "doesn't have to be boring"; feasters are also moved to comment on the crew's "great hospitality."

	FOOD	DECOR	SERVICE	COST

Nelore Churrascaria ⓜ *Brazilian/Steak* ▽ 20 | 19 | 25 | $42

Montrose | 4412 Montrose Blvd. (Richmond Ave.) | 713-395-1050 |
www.nelorechurrascaria.com

"Only meat lovers need come (and come hungry)" to this Montrose
all-you-can-eat Brazilian steakhouse, where a "caring staff" is afoot
to "ensure your favorite cuts" are "only seconds away"; set in a
comfy old casa with "minimal" frills, its midpriced blowout is "a
whole lot cheaper" than the more upscale competition's.

New York Coffee Shop *Diner* - | - | - | I

Meyerland | 9720 Hillcroft St. (Braeswood Blvd.) | 713-723-8650
In "time-honored" coffee-shop "tradition", this Formica-lined
Meyerland mainstay dishes up "great breakfasts", deli specials and
"real NY-style bagels" that are "some of the best" in town; low
prices lead to "lines on the weekends" and a regular morning crowd
at the adjoining bakery; N.B. closes at 3 PM daily.

☒ Nielsen's Delicatessen *Deli* 26 | 4 | 18 | $11

Galleria | 4500 Richmond Ave. (Mid Lane St.) | 713-963-8005
After more than half a century, Nielsen ratings are still high for the
"wonderful" deviled eggs, "great sandwiches" and "creamy potato
salad" – all with that "famous" housemade mayonnaise – served at
this "traditional" counter-service deli in the Galleria area; less of a
hit is the no-frills, no-tips, no-space setting that suggests all the energy is channeled into the food: "consider carryout" or delivery.

Niko Niko's *Greek* 23 | 13 | 16 | $15

Montrose | 2520 Montrose Blvd. (Missouri St.) | 713-528-1308 |
www.nikonikos.com

"Yum yum" echo enthusiasts at this "wildly popular" Montrose "staple", an "H-town classic" where the "giant portions" of "amazing"
eats are "as good as Greek gets" and the "utilitarian" "self-serve"
setup is "always a full house"; it's "indispensable" to those "on a
budget", and thanks to renovations in recent years, the "long lines"
now "move fast."

Ninfa's *Tex-Mex* 22 | 15 | 20 | $22

Hobby | 8553 Gulf Frwy. (I-45) | 713-943-3183
Bellaire | 5423 Bellaire Blvd. (Chimney Rock Rd.) | 713-432-0003
Downtown | 600 Travis St. (Texas St.) | 713-228-6200 ☒
Galleria | 5923 Westheimer Rd. (Fountain View Dr.) | 713-781-2740
Uptown | 1650 Post Oak Blvd. (San Felipe St.) | 713-623-6060
Memorial | 9401 Katy Frwy. (Echo Ln.) | 713-932-8760
Northwest Houston | 9507 Jones Rd. (West Rd.) | 281-517-0600
Upper Kirby District | 3601 Kirby Dr. (Richmond Ave.) | 713-520-0203
Missouri City | 5730 Hwy. 6 (bet. Riverstone & S. University Blvds.) |
281-497-5100
Additional locations throughout the Houston area

Original Ninfa's on Navigation *Tex-Mex*

Neartown | 2704 Navigation Blvd. (bet. Delano & Nagle Sts.) |
713-228-1175 | www.mamaninfas.com

This "bustling" Neartown grande dame of "traditional Tex-Mex" inspired a chain of spin-offs, but consensus says "the other locations

fall short" of the "awesome" "authentic" likes of its legendary faji-tas, "made-by-hand" tortillas and "unmatched" Ninfaritas; the backdrop may be "ramshackle", but the "colorful atmosphere" is still "worth a trip to the neighborhood" and "a must for visitors"; N.B. the original on Navigation is an independent operation.

Nino's 🅂 *Italian*

| 24 | 22 | 22 | $34 |

Montrose | 2817 W. Dallas St. (La Rue St.) | 713-522-5120 | www.ninos-vincents.com

"It hasn't lost any of its touch over the years" say steadfast support-ers of this '70s-era Montrose Italian, where the Mandola family serves up "terrific food" in a "pretty" "old house" that shares a court-yard with its sib, Vincent's; notwithstanding the rustic, "homestyle feel", this is the toniest of the three eateries on the site.

Nippon 🅼 *Japanese*

| - | - | - | M |

Montrose | 4464 Montrose Blvd. (bet. Hwy. 59 & Richmond Ave.) | 713-523-3939

For a "more authentic" sushi experience, this "real Japanese" joint in Montrose claims a 23-year history of slicing "incredibly fresh" fish to real-deal specifications (though "some excellent 'American' rolls" make the cut too); prices are fair for the quality, but some suggest the unassuming digs "need to be updated."

Nit Noi *Thai*

| 21 | 17 | 18 | $19 |

Champions | Red Oak Shopping Ctr. | 850 FM 1960 W. (Red Oak Dr.) | 281-444-7650 🅂
Memorial | Woodway Sq. | 6395 Woodway Dr. (Voss Rd.) | 713-789-1711
West Houston | Royal Oaks Vill. | 11807 Westheimer Rd. (Kirkwood Dr.) | 281-597-8200
The Woodlands | 6700 Woodlands Pkwy. (Kuykendahl Rd.) | 281-367-3355
www.nitnoithai.com

Nit Noi Cafe *Thai*

Bellaire | 4703 Richmond Ave. (Morningside) | 713-524-8114
Downtown | 2020 Louisiana St. (I-45) | 713-652-5855
West Houston | 1005 Dairy Ashford St. (south of I-10) | 281-496-9200 🅂
www.nitnoithai.com

This "popular" homegrown Thai mini-chain satisfies devotees of Siamese cooking with its "consistently" "delicious" "standards" (in-cluding "perfect" spring rolls) that can be "toned down" "for the ten-der of tongue" if need be; "great lunch specials" deliver added value, while service tends toward the "friendly, if not overly quick."

Noé *American*

| 22 | 22 | 23 | $71 |

Uptown | Omni Hotel Houston | 4 Riverway Dr. (Hwy. 610) | 713-871-8177 | www.noerestaurant.com

Ensconced in Uptown's Omni Hotel, this New American is deemed "fantastic" by enthusiasts of its "superb", "over-the-top" New American cuisine with a Japanese twist; most maintain that, given its "romantic" vibe and "impeccable" service, "you get more than you pay for", even though a less-impressed minority finds it a little "pretentious."

	FOOD	DECOR	SERVICE	COST

Oceanaire Seafood Room *Seafood* — 24 | 23 | 23 | $51

Galleria | Galleria | 5061 Westheimer Rd. (Post Oak Blvd.) |
832-487-8862 | www.theoceanaire.com

"So good that it's hard to believe it's a chain", this "exceptional" seafood franchise with outposts in Dallas and the Galleria shopping center in Houston features "all the exuberance of a steakhouse in a fish house", starting with its "bountiful menu" and "fine wine list"; "happening" bar scenes, "1930s" "ocean liner"–like settings and "big prices" reflect the overall "classy" mood.

Ocean Palace *Chinese* — ▽ 23 | 14 | 19 | $18

Bellaire | Hong Kong City Mall | 11215 Bellaire Blvd. (Boone Rd.) |
281-988-8898 | www.oceanpalacerest.com

"Visitors are always impressed" with this vast Sino seafood emporium located in a busy shopping mall in Bellaire; its "wonderful displays" of fin fare (especially "dinner banquets") have appeal, but the magnet for most is the "extensive" array of dim sum – on weekends, the 1,800-plus seats are "packed with Chinese families" and others "craving" the savory bites brought around via "quick carts."

Old Heidelberg *German* — ▽ 21 | 16 | 19 | $28

Briargrove | 1810 Fountain View Dr. (San Felipe St.) | 713-781-3581 |
www.theoldheidelberg.com

Teutonic tastes in this burg turn to this longtime Galleria-area German for "wonderful" wursts, Wiener schnitzel and other filling fare served with a "friendly" demeanor that makes it a "family favorite"; then again, the *echt*-retro "interior needs an update" and trendsters taunt "old is the key word" here.

Olivette *American* — - | - | - | E

Uptown | The Houstonian | 111 N. Post Oak Ln. (bet. Memorial & Woodway Drs.) | 713-685-6713 | www.houstonian.com

Tucked inside the Houstonian hotel, this secluded Uptown mainstay has long been a destination for guests and discriminating locals alike for high-end New American dishes like sea scallops with foie gras; an open kitchen provides a lively counterpoint to the otherwise subdued, softly lit setting, while cocktails at the adjacent bar provide a perfect complement, either before or after a meal.

100% Taquito *Mexican* — 18 | 14 | 15 | $11

West U | 3245 Southwest Frwy. (Buffalo Spdwy.) | 713-665-2900 |
www.100taquito.com

"A real find" assert amigos of this "authentic" sit-down taqueria across the Southwest Freeway where a variety of "mix-and-match" homey Mexican specialties make for a "fast", "fresh" meal; decor is strictly "no-frills", but prices are so "cheap" that no one seems to mind.

One's A Meal ◑ *Greek* — 18 | - | 17 | $14
(fka Bibas One's A Meal)

Montrose | 812 Westheimer Ave. (Montrose Blvd.) | 713-523-0425
An "unpretentious' spot for "solid" Greek "standbys", this "homey" Montrose "joint" draws a "line out the door" at lunch, when

"Houstonians" crowd in for a cheap and "filling" meal served by longtime waiters ("John is a gem"); it's open 24/7, meaning it works for "post-drinking munchies" "after a night out" as well; N.B. a recent move has outdated the above Decor score.

Osaka Japanese Restaurant *Japanese*   ▽ 24 | 19 | 22 | $26

West U | 4001 Bellaire Blvd. (Stella Link Rd.) | 713-838-9812
Montrose | 515 Westheimer Rd. (Stanford St.) | 713-533-9098

It's "always a pleasure" to sit down to the "top sushi" at this Montrose Japanese according to adherents who appreciate the "huge" portions and "lunch specials"; the "deliciously bossy" owner charms customers, who also cheer to hear it's "open late", till 12:30 AM on weekends; N.B. the smaller West U branch closes earlier.

Otilia's Ⓜ *Mexican*   ▽ 22 | 11 | 16 | $21

Spring Branch | 7710 Long Point Rd. (Wirt Rd.) | 713-681-7203 | www.otiliasrestaurant.com

Cravers of "authentic" "interior Mexican" have a "reason to drive out to Spring Branch" to sample the "real" thing at this casual cantina; sí, the service and decor are merely functional, but the payoff to the palate remains "very, very good" "for the price."

Ouisie's Table *Southern*   23 | 22 | 21 | $39

River Oaks | 3939 San Felipe St. (bet. Drexel Dr. & Willowick Rd.) | 713-528-2264 | www.ouisiestable.com

Loyalists love this "sophisticated" River Oaks "favorite" for its "creative menu" of "refined Southern comfort food" and "superb wine list" proffered by a "well-mannered" staff; dissenters deem the experience "uneven" and "expensive", with more than a few citing a "haughty" "attitude" from personnel that inspires "gnashing of teeth."

Palazzo's *Italian*   20 | 16 | 19 | $23

Briargrove | Briar Ridge Ctr. | 2620 Briar Ridge Dr. (Westheimer Rd.) | 713-784-8110 Ⓢ
NEW **River Oaks** | 2300 Westheimer Rd. (bet. Kirby & S. Shepherd Drs.) | 713-522-6777
West Houston | 10455 Briar Forest Dr. (Beltway 8) | 713-785-8800
www.palazzoscafe.com

Families flock to these casual Italians for "well-prepared, beautifully presented" pastas and pizzas at "great prices", even if a few feel the wine list "could be improved"; for those disturbed by "minimal decor" and uneven service ("great" vs. "abominable") there's a "convenient" solution: "they deliver!"

Palm, The *Steak*   24 | 19 | 24 | $56

Galleria | Briar Grove Plaza | 6100 Westheimer Rd. (bet. Chimney Rock & S. Voss Rds.) | 713-977-2544 | www.thepalm.com

See review in San Antonio Directory.

NEW Pan y Agua Ⓢ *Seafood/Steak*   - | - | - | M

River Oaks | 3215 Westheimer Rd. (bet. Buffalo Spdwy. & Kirby Dr.) | 713-523-4500 | www.panyagua.us

There's much more than just bread and water on the menu at this River Oaks newcomer specializing in Latin-inflected dishes utilizing

Gulf Coast seafood and meats; expect midpriced plates of mesquite grilled steaks, ceviche, filet à la pasilla and popular desserts like tres leches cake and crème brûlée set down in a dimly lit white-table-cloth space that manages to be both upscale and casual at the same time; N.B. don't miss the extensive margarita list.

Z Pappadeaux *Seafood* 23 | 19 | 20 | $29
(aka Café Pappadeaux)

Medical Center | 2525 S. Loop W. (S. Main St.) | 713-665-3155
Champions | 7110 FM 1960 W. (Cutten Rd.) | 281-580-5245
FM 1960 | 2226 FM 1960 Rd. W. (Kuykendahl Rd.) | 281-893-0206
Galleria | 6015 Westheimer Rd. (Greenridge Dr.) | 713-782-6310
Memorial | 10499 Katy Frwy. (Sam Houston Pkwy.) | 713-722-0221
Northwest Houston | 13080 Hwy. 290 (Hollister St.) | 713-460-1203
Upper Kirby District | 2410 Richmond Ave. (Kirby Dr.) | 713-527-9137
Seabrook | 309 Waterfront Dr. (Houston Ave.) | 281-291-9932
Stafford | 12711 Southwest Frwy. (Corporate Dr.) | 281-240-5533
The Woodlands | 18165 I-45 N. (Shenandoah Park Dr.) | 936-321-4200
www.pappadeaux.com
Additional locations throughout the Houston area

"Bring your appetite" to the Pappas clan's locally spawned seafood chain, an "uptempo" outfit known for "consistent", "nicely spiced" Louisiana-style cooking, "gaudy Cajun decor" and "huge portions" (there's "always enough to take home"); the less impressed acknowledge the "dependable, if unexciting, food" but grouse the "packed", sprawling dining rooms are "just too loud."

Z Pappas Bros. Steakhouse ⑧ *Steak* 27 | 24 | 25 | $62
Galleria | 5839 Westheimer Rd. (Bering Dr.) | 713-780-7352 |
www.pappasbros.com

"The Pappas family does it right" at these "standout" meateries in Dallas and Houston that keep "packing them in" to their "sumptuous" quarters for a "phenomenal" combo of "awesome" beef, "killer wines" and "outstanding service" that's "worth every dollar" of the "high" prices; the "warm" ambiance is "great for business dinners or a night out with the guys", so expect a strong showing of "men in suits."

Pappas Burgers *Burgers* 23 | 14 | 18 | $16
Galleria | 5815 Westheimer Rd. (bet. Chimney Rock Rd. &
Fountain View Dr.) | 713-975-6082 | www.pappasburger.com
The name says it all at this Galleria spot, where the "juicy", "Texas-sized" burgers and "fresh-cut" fries rank with "the best", likely since the beef comes "from their steakhouse next door"; though the order-at-the-counter setup "isn't fancy", it's "perfect" for "beer and sports."

Pappas Grill Steakhouse *Steak* ∇ 28 | 25 | 27 | $50
Stafford | 12000 Hwy. 59 S. (Wilcrest Dr.) | 281-277-9292 |
www.pappasgrillhouston.com
"Despite its second-fiddle status in the Pappas steakhouse world", this "upscale" outpost in suburban Stafford "matches its glossier cousins in quality" with "fantastic" cuts of beef and a "more-than-adequate" wine lineup to ensure "you get what you pay for"; advocates add the "service is less snooty and there's rarely a wait."

	FOOD	DECOR	SERVICE	COST

☒ Pappasito's *Tex-Mex* — 23 | 18 | 20 | $24

Medical Center | 2515 S. Loop W. (bet. Buffalo Spdwy. & Kirby Dr.) | 713-668-5756
Briargrove | 6445 Richmond Ave. (Hillcroft Ave.) | 713-784-5253
FM 1960 | 7050 W. FM 1960 (Cutten Rd.) | 281-893-5030
Memorial | 10409 Katy Frwy. (Sam Houston Tollway) | 713-468-1913
North Houston | 15280 I-45 N. (Lockhaven Dr.) | 281-821-4505
Northwest Houston | 13070 Hwy. 290 (Langfield Rd.) | 713-462-0245
Upper Kirby District | 2536 Richmond Ave. (Kirby Dr.) | 713-520-5066
Webster | 20099 I-45 (Nasa Rd. 1) | 281-338-2885
Humble | 10005 FM 1960 Bypass W. (Hwy. 59) | 281-540-8664
Sugar Land | 13750 Southwest Frwy. (Dairy Ashford Rd.) | 281-565-9797
www.pappasitos.com
Additional locations throughout the Houston area

"It's always busy" at any of the "cavernous" locations of this "mainstream" chain, but amigos are "prepared to wait" for the "generous portions" of "consistently" "solid Tex-Mex", especially the "benchmark" beef fajitas; they're "lively" (if "loud") faves "for out-of-town guests", though those who charge "quantity over quality" is the rule contend "there are better options" "for half the price."

Pappas Seafood *Seafood* — 23 | 18 | 20 | $30

Sharpstown | 6894 Southwest Frwy. (Bellerive Dr.) | 713-784-4729
Almeda | 6945 I-45 S. (Woodridge Dr.) | 713-641-0318
Lower Shepherd | 3001 S. Shepherd Dr. (W. Alabama St.) | 713-522-4595
North Houston | 11301 I-45 N. (Aldine Bender Rd.) | 281-999-9928
Webster | 19991 I-45 S. (Bay Area Blvd.) | 281-332-7546
Humble | 20410 Hwy. 59 N. (Townsen Blvd.) | 281-446-7707
Galena Park | 12010 I-10 E. (Federal Rd.) | 713-453-3265
www.pappasseafood.com

This "family-owned chain" of "casual" but "high-quality" seafooders is reckoned a "good fallback" for "large portions" of fin fare from a "wide" "menu of Gulf Coast favorites" that includes some of the "best fried" fish around; "as with all Pappas restaurants", they're "dependable", "noisy" and "a tad pricey."

Pasha ☒ *Mediterranean* — ∇ 25 | 18 | 22 | $20

Rice Village | 2325 University Blvd. (bet. Greenbriar & Morningside Drs.) | 713-592-0020 | www.epasha.com

An "untapped neighborhood treasure" to those in-the-know, this "quaint little" Turk "hidden" away near Rice Village specializes in "excellent", "fresh" Mediterranean bites; posh it's not, but the "relaxing", ruby-hued setting is warmed by a "wonderfully friendly" staff and an affordable lineup of Turkish wines.

Patrenella's ☒☒ *Italian* — 17 | 14 | 19 | $29

Heights | 813 Jackson Hill St. (Washington Ave.) | 713-863-8223 | www.patrenellas.net

Sited in a "cozy" house in the lower Heights, this "old-fashioned Italian" "local" is a "family-type" "standby" that dishes up "decent" red- and white-sauce dishes at a fair price; its faithful patrons can "feel the love", though more insensitive sorts scoff "mediocre."

	FOOD	DECOR	SERVICE	COST

Paulie's *Italian*

| | 19 | 12 | 16 | $17 |

West U | 2617 W. Holcombe Blvd. (Kirby Dr.) | 713-660-7057
Montrose | 1834 Westheimer Rd. (bet. Driscoll & Morse Sts.) |
713-807-7271 ⑤
www.pauliesrestaurant.com

Shortbread cookies decorated for the season are the "best thing in
the place", but supporters of this self-service pair in Montrose and
West U also polish off "gourmet" salads, panini and Italian entrees;
"reasonable" prices and a "simple" "diner/cafeteria" setting help
make this a "great place for kids."

Pei Wei Asian Diner *Pan-Asian*

| | 19 | 15 | 16 | $15 |

West U | Plaza in the Park | 5110 Buffalo Spdwy. (Westpark Dr.) |
713-661-0900
Champions | Champions Vill. | 5203 FM 1960 W. (Champion Forest Dr.) |
281-885-5430
Memorial | 1413 S. Voss Rd. | 713-785-1620 ⑤ Ⓜ
Montrose | 1005 Waugh Dr. (bet. Clay & Dallas Sts.) | 713-353-7366
Northwest Houston | 12020 FM 1960 W. (bet. Eldridge Pkwy. &
Fallbrook Dr.) | 281-571-4990
West Houston | 14008 Memorial Dr. | 281-506-3500 ⑤ Ⓜ
Webster | 19411 Gulf Frwy. (Bay Area Blvd.) | 281-554-9876
Kingwood | Kingwood Commons | 702 Kingwood Dr. (Chestnut Ridge Dr.) |
281-318-2877
Katy | Highland Town Ctr. | 1590 S. Mason Rd. (Highland Knolls Dr.) |
281-392-1410
Sugar Land | Town Center Lakeside | 16101 Kensington Dr. (Hwy. 6) |
281-240-1931
www.peiwei.com
Additional locations throughout the Houston area
See review in Dallas/Ft. Worth Directory.

Perbacco Cucina Caprese ⑤ Ⓜ *Italian*

| | ▽ 23 | 13 | 21 | $26 |

Downtown | 700 Milam St. (Capitol St.) | 713-224-2422

Touted as "the best Italian restaurant no one knows", this "small"
hideaway in Downtown's Pennzoil Building is "not to be missed" for
"garlic-laden" classics by way of the Bay of Naples at "surprisingly
reasonable prices"; "quick", "personal service" renders it a "lunch
favorite", and as for the "very understated room", some shrug "good
food, no atmosphere."

ⓩ Perry's Steakhouse & Grille *Steak*

| | 25 | 25 | 24 | $45 |

Champions | 9730 Cypresswood Dr. (Cutten Rd.) | 281-970-5999
Memorial | 9827 Katy Frwy. (bet. I-10 HOV Ln. & Memorial City Way) |
832-358-9000
Clear Lake | 487 Bay Area Blvd. (Rte. 3) | 281-286-8800
Sugar Land | Sugar Land Town Sq. | 2115 Town Square Pl.
(Southwest Frwy.) | 281-565-2727
The Woodlands | 6700 Woodlands Pkwy. (Kuykendahl Rd.) |
281-362-0569
www.perryssteakhouse.com

"Superb for the suburbs", this locally based "chophouse chain" is a
"classy but not stuffy" haven for those far from the city center that's

"distinctive" for its "awesome meats" (including the "massive" "specialty" pork chop); the "sleek, stylish" space and "super service" make for a "top-notch" "night out", "especially on someone else's tab."

Pesce ⛿ *Seafood* | 21 | 23 | 21 | $52 |

Upper Kirby District | Upper Kirby Shopping Ctr. | 3029 Kirby Dr. (Alabama St.) | 713-522-4858 | www.pescehouston.com
Acclaimed chef Mark Holley mans the helm at this Upper Kirby District seafooder from the Landry's fleet, an upmarket harbor for "fantastic" fish served by a "very knowledgeable staff"; a "posh" back-drop featuring a "great marble bar" contributes to "the wow factor", though pesky critics call it "noisy", "pretentious" and "overpriced."

⛿ P.F. Chang's China Bistro *Chinese* | 22 | 22 | 20 | $27 |

Galleria | Highland Vill. | 4094 Westheimer Rd. (bet. I-610 & Willowick Rd.) | 713-627-7220
Northwest Houston | Willowbrook | 18250 Tomball Pkwy. (Willow Chase Blvd.) | 281-571-4050
West Houston | 11685 Westheimer Rd. (Cresent Park Dr.) | 281-920-3553
Sugar Land | 2120 Lone Star Dr. (Hwy. 6) | 281-313-8650
The Woodlands | Woodlands Mall | 1201 Lake Woodlands Dr. (I-45) | 281-203-6350
www.pfchangs.com
See review in Dallas/Ft. Worth Directory.

Phoenicia Deli ⛿ *Mediterranean* | 23 | 10 | 14 | $14 |

Royal Oaks | 12116 Westheimer Rd. (Gray Falls Dr.) | 281-558-0416 | www.phoenicia-deli.com
The "best chicken shawarma" and other "fresh and authentic" de-lights make this counter-service "hole-in-the-wall" near Royal Oaks the Med deli of choice for many, including choosy "vegetarians"; its casualness and low cost keep it crowded at lunch, but as there's "no decor" there's every reason to "take away."

Piatto *Italian* | 25 | 20 | 23 | $30 |

Galleria | 4925 W. Alabama St. (Post Oak Blvd.) | 713-871-9722 ⛿
Royal Oaks | 11693 Westheimer Rd. (Cresent Park Dr.) | 281-759-7500
www.piattoristorante.com
Each of these "family-run" fraternal twins offers a "cheery environ-ment" (the original even musters "neighborhood appeal in the mid-dle of the Galleria") to match their "quality" Italian dishes, best prefaced by the "amazing asparagus and lump crabmeat appetizer"; champions of the "simple" style and "reasonable prices" consider them "real sleepers."

Pico's Mex-Mex *Mexican* | 24 | 15 | 21 | $20 |

Bellaire | 5941 Bellaire Blvd. (Renwick Dr.) | 713-662-8383 | www.picos.net
"Escape from Tex-Mex" at this "out-of-the-way" Bellaire "icon", "for many years" an "exemplary" source of "real-deal" "interior Mexican" cooking (including "fresh seafood") and "awesome margaritas" in a casual roadside setting; few are piqued at the

FOOD | DECOR | SERVICE | COST

"quite plain" decor since the "value" is "well worth the trip" ("not luxurious, not expensive").

Pizzitola's Bar-B-Que ☒ BBQ ▽ 24 | 9 | 21 | $17

Heights | 1703 Shepherd Dr. (I-10) | 713-227-2283 | www.pizzitolas.com

The food's the thing at this no-frills lower Heights bastion of BBQ where one of the oldest working pits around smokes what some call the "best 'cue in town", including inexpensive "old-style ribs cooked the way they should be"; the "friendly staff" that "treats everyone like a regular and the regulars like family" makes up for the space, which even fans concur is "nothing pretty."

Polo's ☒ American 20 | 22 | 21 | $49

Greenway Plaza Area | 3800 Southwest Frwy. (Cummins St.) | 713-626-8100 | www.polosignature.com

Take a "date whom you're trying to impress" to this "inviting" Greenway Plaza New American from chef-owner Polo Becerra, where the "innovative menu", "efficient" service and "elegant supper-club" ambiance exude "a bit of the Houston social-society vibe"; meanwhile, an unmoved few maintain there's "nothing wrong, but nothing special" either, "for the price."

Post Oak Grill American 21 | 19 | 21 | $38

Downtown | 1111 Louisiana St. (Lamar St.) | 713-650-1700 ☒
Galleria | 1415 S. Post Oak Ln. (Cedar Creek Dr.) | 713-993-9966 ☒
NEW Midtown | 3017 Milam St. (Anita St.) | 713-523-1010
NEW Sugar Land | 4524 Hwy. 6 S. (Austin Parkway Blvd.) | 281-491-2901 ☒
www.postoakgrill.com

"Savory" traditional fare, "dependable service" and "genteel surroundings" qualify this upscale American quartet as "favorite spots for a power lunch" ("business or social"); proponents postulate they're "pricey but deliver good value", though trendsetters see a "warhorse" outfit that's "past its prime" and "needs some updating fast."

Prego Italian 23 | 19 | 21 | $36

Rice Village | 2520 Amherst St. (Kirby Dr.) | 713-529-2420 | www.prego-houston.com

There's a "wonderful, big-city feel" to this "bustling" trattoria in Rice Village, which keeps a "loyal" following for its "consistently strong" Italian "classics", its "fabulous" cellar and its "accommodating" service; the 100-seat spot gets "crowded" and "noisy" at peak hours, so insiders suggest large parties "ask for the wine room" for a quieter ambiance.

Pronto Cucinino Italian 19 | 16 | 18 | $17

Medical Center | 3191 W. Holcombe Blvd. (Buffalo Spdwy.) | 713-592-8646
Montrose | 1401 Montrose Blvd. (Clay St.) | 713-528-8646
www.pronto-2-go.com

"What a great concept!" cheer fans of Vincent Mandola's "fast-food Italian" duo, a "casual", "convenient" supplier of "reliable" "comfort food" (including "many of the dishes from Nino's and

Vincent's") at "bargain" prices; the "efficiently designed" setups are "great for families" and well-suited to "take out or eat in" – so "what's not to like?"

Quattro *Italian* | 23 | 23 | 23 | $46 |

Downtown | Four Seasons Hotel | 1300 Lamar St. (Austin St.) | 713-276-4700 | www.fourseasons.com

You'll "forget you're in a hotel" at the Four Seasons' "sophisticated" Downtown showcase for "Italian flair", which merges a "terrific" menu and "excellent" service in a "fabulous" "modern" setting that's equally inviting for a "business meal or an intimate celebration"; but holdouts "miss the old-school" approach and deem it "overpriced."

Ragin' Cajun *Cajun* | 21 | 13 | 16 | $17 |

Downtown | McKinney Tunnel | 930 Main St. (McKinney St. & Travis St.) | 713-571-2422 ⓢ
Galleria | 4302 Richmond Ave. (West Ln.) | 713-623-6321
Southwest Houston | Woodlake Sq. | 9600 Westheimer Rd. (Gessner Rd.) | 832-251-7171
Sugar Land | 16100 Kensington Dr. (Hwy. 6) | 281-277-0704
www.ragin-cajun.com

Loyalists like this counter-service Cajun mini-chain, which may well be the "closest thing to N'Awlins in Houston" thanks to "classic" po' boys and "super-spicy" crawfish (in season); the "fun", "loud" venues have "homey" decor to go with their "interactive, messy food" ("ask for seconds, but don't ask for utensils"); N.B. the Downtown Tunnel location opens only for lunch Monday–Friday.

☑ Rainbow Lodge Ⓜ *American* | 23 | 26 | 21 | $43 |

Heights | 2011 Ella Blvd. (TC Jester Blvd.) | 713-861-8666 | www.rainbow-lodge.com

Lodged in a log cabin overlooking a creek near the Heights, this upscale, ultrarustic New American carries on a 30-year tradition with plenty of wild game on the "excellent" menu – as well as "mounted" on the walls; with its "beautiful gardens" and "fabulous bar", it's "worth the steep price", even if those less smitten find the eating "predictable."

Rattan Pan-Asian Bistro ⓢ *Pan-Asian* | - | - | - | M |

West Houston | 1396 Eldridge Pkwy. (Forkland Dr.) | 281-556-9888 | www.rattanbistro.com

This trendy West Houston yearling packs them in with its creative sushi selection and midpriced Pan-Asian dishes; the wine program is a highlight, with an Enomatic preservation system allowing patrons to sample high-end vintages; there's also a patio for leisurely sipping.

Raven Grill *Eclectic* | 21 | 19 | 19 | $26 |

West U | 1916 Bissonnet St. (bet. Hazard & Woodhead Sts.) | 713-521-2027 | www.theravengrill.com

"Reliable", "not overly pricey" and "popular", this kid-friendly West U Eclectic "satisfies most palates" thanks to "comfort food" with "originality"; staffers are "efficient", and the "modern" dining room and "pleasant patio" are "nice for dates or relaxing with friends."

	FOOD	DECOR	SERVICE	COST

Red Lion Pub, The ● *Pub Food*
∇ 19 | 16 | 15 | $21

Lower Shepherd | 2316 S. Shepherd Dr. (Fairview St.) | 713-782-3030 | www.redlionhouston.com

"Get your English on" at this Lower Shepherd British pub where regulars lionize the "surprisingly good" grub "for a bar", from fish 'n' chips to some "unexpected" "Indian selections"; the mood's bolstered by low lighting and dark wood, and not incidentally the tip-top "selection of draught beers" comes in correct Imperial pints.

☒ Red Onion Seafood y Mas ☒ *Seafood*
26 | 22 | 22 | $28

Northwest Houston | 12041 Northwest Frwy. (43rd St.) | 713-957-2232 | www.caferedonion.com

"One of the most original" joints in town, Rafael Galindo's seafood specialist in Northwest Houston boasts an "innovative menu" that draws on Pan-Latin inspiration with "consistently excellent" results; the "beautiful, upscale" decor exudes a stylishly "old-time" feel, with a pianist providing accompaniment on weekends.

Red Onion Taco Cantina ☒ *Mexican*
- | - | - | I

Northwest Houston | 13147 Northwest Fwy. (Hollister Rd.) | 713-690-1403

Providing a modern twist on the traditional taqueria, Rafael Galindo's concept offers refined takes on Mexican street food and serves them up in an inviting crimson-colored space in a NW Houston strip mall; the prices may be higher than your typical cantina, but it's worth it thanks to the high-quality ingredients and incredible array of tequilas.

Reef ☒ *Seafood*
25 | 22 | 23 | $44

Midtown | 2600 Travis St. (McGowen St.) | 713-526-8282 | www.reefhouston.com

Ex-Bank bigwigs Bill Floyd and Bryan Caswell "have done it again" at this "happening" addition to Midtown, a "sleek", "savvy" seafooder featuring "very inventive" preparations of "stellar fish (many unheard of)" that leave diners "extremely satisfied rather than stuffed to the gills"; the "wonderful" "modern decor" and "excellent wine values" shore up the "buzz" that's netting it "a big reputation fast."

Reggae Hut ☒ *Caribbean*
- | - | - | I

Medical Center | 4814 Almeda Rd. (Arbor St.) | 713-520-7171 | www.thereggaehut.com

"Very informal, friendly and authentic", this counter-service cafe just north of the Medical Center dishes up "real Caribbean food" like "excellent jerk and curry" chased with fruity tropical tipples; with a "laid-back" staff that "won't be rushing you out the door", it "feels like Jamaica" and costs only a fraction of a flight.

Remington, The *American*
25 | 25 | 25 | $63

Uptown | St. Regis Hotel | 1919 Briar Oaks Ln. (San Felipe St.) | 713-403-2631 | www.theremingtonrestaurant.com

A "quiet" retreat for "amazing meals", this Galleria-area New American in the St. Regis Hotel is "an exceptional setting" for "a ladies' lunch" or a premium-priced dinner, providing a "stylish" backdrop and "delicious and satisfying" food; it follows through fittingly with

service that's "attentive but unobtrusive"; P.S. the "busier" bar is a "great scene" with "live sounds" and dancing on weekends.

Rickshaw Far East Bistro *Pan-Asian* ▽ | 19 | 19 | 16 | $33

River Oaks | 2810 Westheimer Rd. (Kirby Dr.) | 713-942-7272 | www.rickshawbambu.com

An "urban", "sexy vibe" and weekend DJs who "spin music late into the night" make this River Oaks Pan-Asian a "hipster's paradise"; most report the "nouveau" eats are "terrific", if "a bit costly for what you get."

Rioja Tapas Restaurant Ⓜ *Spanish* 24 | 22 | 23 | $32

West Houston | 11920 Westheimer Rd. (Kirkwood Dr.) | 281-531-5569 | www.riojarestaurant.com

"Wonderful tapas" are the highlight at this "authentic" West Houston Spaniard, which matches its "creative menu" with an "excellent Spanish wine list" and "very enjoyable" surroundings replete with chandeliers, glossy woodwork and a fireplace; salsa and flamenco fans add that "live music on the weekends is a nice touch."

Rio Ranch *Steak* 21 | 21 | 20 | $31

Southwest Houston | Westchase Hilton | 9999 Westheimer Rd. (Briarpark Dr.) | 713-952-5000 | www.rioranch.com

Cowhands confirm prime beef "cooked to perfection" makes for a "hearty meal" at this regionally accented steakhouse attached to Southwest Houston's Westchase Hilton, a rough-hewn hideaway with a "Texas-theme ranch" look built on Hill Country limestone and cedar; it's "a little pricey but well worth it", and some cite the Sunday spread as the "best brunch for the money" in town.

NEW Ristorante Cavour Ⓢ *Italian* - | - | - | E

Uptown | Hotel Granduca | 1080 Uptown Park Blvd. (Post Oak Blvd.) | 713-418-1000 | www.granducahouston.com

Inside the exclusive Hotel Granduca Uptown sits this tony arrival where executive chef David Denis (Le Mistral) oversees the Provençal-inflected Northern Italian menu featuring osso buco, light-as-a-feather gnocchi and briny brodetto (a seafood stew); its snug, antiques-appointed space sets an elegant, old-world tone that extends to the near-impeccable service and upper-end pricing.

Romero's Las Brazas *Mexican* ▽ | 21 | 18 | 19 | $16

Northwest Houston | 15703 Longenbaugh Dr. (Hwy. 6) | 281-463-4661 | www.romeroslasbrazas.com

Favored for "excellent" Mexican at a fair price, this "quiet, quaint" outpost in Northwest Houston is more authentic than most thanks to its homestyle Oaxacan recipes (not to mention 60-plus tequilas); with its folksy knickknacks and tiled floor, the family-friendly space's "laid-back" feel is as genuine as it gets.

Royers Round Top Café Ⓜ⇗ *American* ▽ | 22 | 12 | 17 | $24

Round Top | On the Square | 105 Main St. (bet. FM 1457 & Hwy. 237) | 979-249-3611 | www.royersroundtopcafe.com

"Worth every dollar spent on gas" is what surveyors have to say about this "regional legend" located in Round Top, 95 miles

northwest of Houston; it's a "cozy", "homey", family-run cafe that specializes in "mouthwatering" Traditional American cookery, most notably "don't-miss" "freshly baked" pies, so "pack the car and your appetite" but "leave your diet at the door"; N.B. open Thursday–Sunday only.

Rudi Lechner's ☒ *German* `23` `18` `24` `$22`

Southwest Houston | Woodlake Sq. | 2503 S. Gessner Rd. (Westheimer Rd.) | 713-782-1180 | www.rudilechners.com

Guardians of Teutonic "tradition" just say "*ja*" to this "authentic German" in Southwest Houston, an "old standard" for "fantastic" "home-cooked meals", "beer in liter mugs" and even a "good salad bar"; it's "like a visit to Bavaria" complete with a "polka band" four nights a week, so even with "outdated" decor, "what's not to like?"

Rudyard's ☻ *Pub Food* `-` `-` `-` `I`

Montrose | 2010 Waugh Dr. (Welch St.) | 713-521-0521 | www.rudyards.com

Besides being a "great place for darts and beer", this Montrose pub and "live music" stalwart is "actually pretty good" for all-American "bar food" according to aficionados; just be prepared for downscale digs and rudimentary service that's "inattentive to newcomers."

Ruggles Grille 5115 ☒ *American* `23` `18` `18` `$31`

Galleria | Saks Fifth Ave. | 5115 Westheimer Rd. (McCue Rd.) | 713-963-8067

Ruggles Cafe Bakery *American*

Rice Village | 2365 Rice Blvd. (Morningside Dr.) | 713-520-6662 www.rugglesgrill.com

Fans give the food "high marks for originality and presentation" at these "dependable" New American "favorites"; the Galleria outpost proves an "elegant" respite in the midst of Saks Fifth Avenue, while the newer "order-at-the-counter" Rice Village cafe rivals "its more expensive counterpart" with "creative" burgers, salads and sandwiches and "decadent desserts" well-suited "for a quick lunch"; N.B. the original branch in Montrose has been closed since Hurricane Ike.

NEW Russo's New York `-` `-` `-` `I`
Coal-Fired Pizzeria *Italian*

Northwest Houston | 19817 Northwest Frwy. (Hwy. 6) | 281-477-6002 | www.nypizzeria.com

A rarity in Northwest Houston, this New York–style pizzeria turns out admirably thin-crusted pies and hefty calzones from a coal-stoked oven; its classic parlor-style interior exudes a casual vibe with well-worn wood floors and lots of candlelight plus decorative touches like brick archways and chandeliers throughout; N.B. a Memorial branch will open in 2009.

Ruth's Chris Steak House *Steak* `25` `22` `25` `$57`

Galleria | 6213 Richmond Ave. (bet. Fountain View & Hillcroft Aves.) | 713-789-2333 | www.ruthschris.com

See review in San Antonio Directory.

NEW Sage ●Ⓜ Continental

| - | - | - | M |

Lower Shepherd | 2221 W. Alabama St. (Greenbriar Dr.) | 713-526-6242
Although this Lower Shepherd kitchen first fired up in 2008, the menu is decidedly old-fashioned, spotlighting classic Continental dishes like rack of lamb and chicken with apricot-brandy sauce at moderate prices; its cottagelike setting has a homey feel with low lighting, beamed-wood ceilings and numerous dining areas opening up onto a verdant patio.

Sage 400 Japanese Cuisine _Japanese_

| 22 | 19 | 17 | $34 |

Galleria | 2800 Sage Rd. (Alabama St.) | 713-961-9566 | www.sage400.com
Though "it doesn't have the reputation of some others", this Galleria-area Japanese aims to please with "melt-in-your-mouth fresh" sushi and other "inventive" raw fish served in a "pretty" setting; but while it's stylish enough to be "a bit different", a few fret over "absentee servers" and "a little too much of a singles scene" barside.

Sambuca ● _Eclectic_

| 21 | 23 | 19 | $38 |

Downtown | 909 Texas Ave. (Travis St.) | 713-224-5299 | www.sambucarestaurant.com
See review in Dallas/Ft. Worth Directory.

Sasaki Ⓩ _Japanese_

| - | - | - | M |

Briargrove | 8979 Westheimer Rd. (Fondren Rd.) | 713-266-5768 | www.sasakisushi.com
"Forget all those trendy" contenders urge boosters of this unassuming Briargrove Japanese, where the sushi is "phenomenally fresh" and the "atmosphere and service are as authentic as they come"; "despite its strip-center location", it's overseen by a "master" chef who honed his skills in the homeland.

Sawadee _Thai_

| ▽ 24 | 16 | 23 | $19 |

West U | 6719 Weslayan St. (Bellaire Blvd.) | 713-666-7872
A "best-kept secret", this "quiet" West U Thai is a "reliable" resource that wins raves for its "excellent" cooking ("phenomenal vegetarian fare" included); if the pedestrian decor presents less to brag about, it's readily offset by the "charming" staff and "good value."

Segari's Ⓩ _Seafood/Steak_

| - | - | - | M |

Heights | 1503 Shepherd Dr. (Maxie St.) | 713-880-2470 | www.segarisrestaurant.com
Likened to "a real speakeasy", this tiny "no-sign place" ensconced in a "pleasantly cozy" house lures insiders to the Lower Heights to partake of a "limited" menu featuring some of the "best seafood" "anywhere"; idiosyncratic founder Sam Segari's "spirit is still here", and his legacy carries on as "a great Houston secret."

Ⓩ 17 _American_

| 25 | 26 | 23 | $54 |

Downtown | Alden Houston Hotel | 1117 Prairie St. (San Jacinto St.) | 832-200-8888 | www.aldenhotels.com
This "posh" Downtown "escape" set in the boutique Alden Hotel beguiles guests with "deliciously decadent" New American "big-city

fare" and a "superb wine list", both befitting a "special night out"; the "intimate", "luxuriously understated room" illuminated with "gorgeous chandeliers" is enhanced by "attentive" service, setting the scene for a truly "transporting" meal.

Shade *American*

| 25 | 22 | 22 | $34 |

Heights | 250 W. 19th St. (Rutland St.) | 713-863-7500 | www.shadeheights.com

"Adult" diners have it "made in the shade" at this "jewel in the Heights", a "top-rate" destination for "creative" New American fare with "delightful" "seasonal variations" plus "one of the most interesting wine lists in town"; the "minimalist" setup is as "pleasing" as the "attentive" service, and the "awesome" weekend brunch rounds out an "unpretentious" but "cool" scene.

Shanghai River *Chinese*

| ∇ 22 | 18 | 21 | $24 |

River Oaks | 2407 Westheimer Rd. (Revere St.) | 713-528-5528 | www.shanghairiverrestaurant.com

Purists pooh-pooh the chow as "Americanized", but devotees still stream into this "friendly", "relaxing" River Oaks Chinese for its "delicious" "well-priced" wares ("lunch specials are a great deal"); in a "quiet", "elegant" dining room hung with Asian art, the family of proprietors makes everyone "feel at home."

Shawarma King *Lebanese*

| - | - | - | I |

Briargrove | 3121 Hillcroft Rd. (Richmond Ave.) | 713-784-8882 | www.shawarmakingonline.com

For a "quick" Mideastern "munch" that's "far above fast food", this bare-bones Briargrove joint serves "very solid chicken shawarma" and other "authentic and tasty" grub right over the counter; its lieges esteem the "great prices", but since "you don't visit for ambiance" they often opt "for takeout."

Shiva Indian Restaurant *Indian*

| 20 | 15 | 17 | $20 |

Rice Village | 2514 Times Blvd. (Kirby Dr.) | 713-523-4753
Sugar Land | 16556 Southwest Frwy. (Colony Square Blvd.) | 281-494-2981
www.shivarestaurant.com

A "staple" for "all the staples", this Rice Village Indian and its Sugar Land spin-off provide "tasty" and "authentic" eats served by "attentive" staffers; some regulars rate the lunch-buffet "deal" "just ok", but dinner "doesn't disappoint" with its "good portion sizes" and dimmed lights to tone down the perfunctory decor.

Sichuan Cuisine *Chinese*

| - | - | - | I |

Alief | 9114 Bellaire Blvd. (bet. Gessner & Ranchester Rds.) | 713-771-6868

It's "not for the faint of heart (or stomach)", but this small, spare strip-center Chinese eatery in Alief's New Chinatown stands apart for its "incredibly authentic Sichuan" dishes, including many spiced with the "hot, hot" peppers from that region; connoisseurs claim they are "impressed", and its BYO policy makes it cheap to check out.

NEW Sage ◐ M _Continental_

| - | - | - | M |

	FOOD	DECOR	SERVICE	COST

Simposio ☒ *Italian*

24 **17** **21** **$36**

Briargrove | 8401 Westheimer Rd. (Dunvale Rd.) | 713-532-0550 |
www.simposioristorante.com

This Briargrove Italian lures neighborhood patrons for a midpriced
meal served in an attractive, airy setting; its young Tuscan chef
whips up an array of Northern-area specialties, like their signature
osso buco, along with with toothsome pastas and risottos.

Sinh Sinh ☾ *Chinese*

– **–** **–** **I**

Alief | 9788 Bellaire Blvd. (Corporate Dr.) | 713-541-0888

"Sinfully delicious" Sino fare marks this "hot-pot" hot spot in Alief's
New Chinatown, which appeals to "seafood lovers" with an array
displayed in "tanks around the restaurant"; the decor and staff are
less impressive ("expect bad service and you won't be disappointed"), but seekers of the "authentic" "crave it again and again."

Smith & Wollensky ☾ *Seafood/Steak*

20 **19** **19** **$57**

Galleria | Highland Vill. | 4007 Westheimer Rd. (Drexler Ave.) |
713-621-7555 | www.smithandwollensky.com

"Love the classic steakhouse atmosphere" enthuse surveyors of this
Galleria outpost of an "upscale" NYC-bred chain, where "tender
steaks" and "excellent seafood" are served in "enormous portions" by
"helpful" servers; still, cost-watchers worry that it's "way too expensive", saying it's "best to be on an expense account" when you visit.

Soma *American/Japanese*

– **–** **–** **E**

Heights | 4820 Washington Ave. (bet. Durham & Shepherd Drs.) |
713-861-2726

This chic, spacious canteen in the Heights regularly packs a crowd
into its showy black-and-red interior; considering it's a joint venture
with the owners of Azuma, expect high-end sushi and sashimi along
with a lineup of intriguing French-inspired American dishes like foie
gras with tuna terrine.

NEW Sophia Ⓜ *American*

– **–** **–** **I**

Montrose | 1601 W. Main St. (Mandell St.) | 713-942-7970 |
www.sophiahouston.com

Opening just before Hurricane Ike in Montrose digs near the Menil
museum, this new kitchen turns out imaginative New American
dishes like mussels in apple brandy sauce in a modest space decorated with small framed photographs; it's pulling in a neighborhood
crowd, drawn in part by appealingly low tabs; N.B. it's BYO for now.

Sorrento *Italian*

21 **24** **21** **$45**

Montrose | 415 Westheimer Rd. (Whitney St.) | 713-527-0609 |
www.sorrentohouston.com

"Located on restaurant alley" in Montrose, this "gracious" Italian
stands apart from its neighbors with "delicious" "classical" cuisine,
"personal service" and "lovely" atmospherics augmented with "live
piano music"; a minority moans the kitchen is "not consistent", but
fans of the "charming feel" keep it "busy"; P.S. the Sunday brunch is
a "great value" for the quality.

SoVino 🗷 *Eclectic*

| - | - | - | M |

Montrose | 507 Westheimer Rd. (Whitney St.) | 713-524-1000 |
www.sovinowines.com

Montrose's Restaurant Row continues to heat up with this sultry
wine bar and bistro where a sexy crowd sinks into the plush booths
and nibbles vino-friendly cheeses and charcuterie (there's also a
brief selection of entrees); though the menu is global, the wine list
focuses on the Southern Hemisphere, with well-priced picks from
South America, New Zealand and South Africa.

Spanish Flowers ● *Tex-Mex*

| 19 | 12 | 17 | $15 |

Heights | 4701 N. Main St. (Airline Blvd.) | 713-869-1706 |
www.spanish-flowers.com

When it's "midnight and you need a Mexican fix, this is the place"
claim compadres of this Heights-area vet, which grounds its "great
reputation" on "homemade tortillas", "all-day breakfasts" and "ex-
tended hours" (it's 24/7 except for Tuesdays); those not so simpat-
ico reckon it's "unremarkable", if always wallet-friendly.

Spanish Village 🗷 Ⓜ *Tex-Mex*

| ▽ 19 | 15 | 20 | $21 |

Medical Center | 4720 Almeda Rd. (Wentworth St.) | 713-523-2861 |
www.spanishvillagerestaurant.com

A "favorite of natives and old-timers", this "charmingly funky", half-
century-old Medical Center mainstay serves up "consistent", "good
ol'" Tex-Mex, "outstanding" margaritas and "must-have" fried chicken
("yes, fried chicken – don't ask"); still-reasonable prices and staffers "who've spent their lives there" help keep it a local "institution."

Spencer's For Steaks & Chops *Steak*

| ▽ 21 | 17 | 22 | $64 |

Downtown | Hilton Americas Hotel | 1600 Lamar St. (Crawford St.) |
713-577-8325 | www.hilton.com

Meat eaters disagree about this modern steakhouse at Downtown's
Hilton Americas; proponents find its "hearty" chops "terrific", but
dissenters deem them just "average", so it's either "exceptionally
good for a hotel restaurant" or merely "typical."

Star Pizza *Pizza*

| 23 | 12 | 18 | $16 |

Heights | 77 Harvard St. (Washington Ave.) | 713-869-1241
Lower Shepherd | 2111 Norfolk St. (Shepherd Dr.) | 713-523-0800
www.starpizza.net

Experts attest "the best pizza in town" qualifies this stellar pair as an
area "classic", with 30-plus years of producing "fantastic" pies (thin
crust or "Chicago-style deep dish") adorned with "extremely tasty"
toppings in many "original" variations; of the two, "the Shepherd location is much more hip", "but don't expect any elegance" at either.

Strip House *Steak*

| 24 | 25 | 23 | $54 |

Downtown | Shops at Houston Ctr. | 1200 McKinney St. (San Jacinto St.) |
713-659-6000 | www.theglaziergroup.com

"Arguably the best steakhouse" Downtown, this "pricey" NYC "im-
port" appeals to "biz" types with its "top-notch" beef, "fab" sides,
"reasonable noise level" and "sexy" "two-martini atmosphere"; it's

	FOOD	DECOR	SERVICE	COST

also noteworthy for its "risqué" "red-and-black decor" scheme, "tastefully" tarted up with "photos of vintage burlesque beauties."

Sudie's Catfish & Seafood House *Seafood*

| 20 | 15 | 20 | $17 |

Pasadena | 4910 Spencer Hwy. (bet. Beltway 8 & Preston Ave.) | 281-487-0920
League City | 352 Gulf Frwy. N. (off Hwy. 518) | 281-338-5100
www.sudies.com

"If fried catfish is your thing", these "cavernous", country-style and "family-friendly" eateries in Pasadena and League City will float your boat with their "mouthwatering" all-you-can-eat catfish and other seafood specialties (plus the signature fried pickles) at "great" prices; if fried catfish is not your thing, it's all "just ok."

Sullivan's Steakhouse *Steak*

| 24 | 23 | 23 | $53 |

Galleria | 4608 Westheimer Rd. (Westcreek Ln.) | 713-961-0333 | www.sullivanssteakhouse.com
See review in Austin and the Hill Country Directory.

Sushi King *Japanese*

| 23 | 18 | 16 | $34 |

Upper Kirby District | 3401 Kirby Dr. (Richmond Ave.) | 713-528-8998 | www.sushiking.us

Others spots have "hipper names and locations", but this Upper Kirby Japanese boasts "better sushi than most" according to "impressed" admirers of its "wonderfully thick slices" and "clever, creative rolls"; sporting a contempo look and a pianist, it's "nicer on the inside" than the exterior would suggest, though "the service needs some work."

Swinging Door, The Ⓜ *BBQ*

| 24 | 19 | 21 | $18 |

Richmond | 3714 FM 359 (McCrary Rd.) | 281-342-4758 | www.swingingdoor.com

"Worth the trip" claim carnivores who congregate at this "rustic" and affordable barbecue destination in Richmond, 35 miles southwest of Houston; they "crave" the "large portions" of "best-kept-secret" ribs, brisket and "all the fixin's" ("save room" for the "divine" cobblers).

Sylvia's Enchilada Kitchen *Tex-Mex*

| 21 | 18 | 22 | $17 |

West Houston | 12637 Westheimer Rd. (Dairy Ashford Rd.) | 281-679-8300 | www.sylviasenchiladakitchen.com

"Yes, it's out of the way", but this West Houston "neighborhood" joint's "exciting takes" on Tex-Mex showcase an "astounding" selection of "delicious enchiladas" at "reasonable" prices; its "cheerful" crew is led by owner Sylvia Casares Copeland (who "even offers cooking classes" on various days), and only a doubter or two "fails to see what all the fuss is about."

Taco Milagro *Mexican*

| 16 | 16 | 14 | $17 |

Upper Kirby District | 2555 Kirby Dr. (Westheimer Rd.) | 713-522-1999
Webster | 19325 Gulf Frwy. (Bay Area Blvd.) | 281-954-3070
www.taco-milagro.com

Another brainchild of Cafe Annie chef-owner Robert Del Grande, this "popular" counter-service Mex chainlet wins friends with its

"freshly made" and "budget-friendly" (if not exactly miraculous) fare and its 150-label tequila bar under a thatched-palm palapa; what makes it a "prime destination" for "young professionals", though, are the "fabulous happy hour", "excellent" patio and live music at some locations.

t'afia ⊠Ⓜ *American* | 25 | 18 | 22 | $41 |

Midtown | 3701 Travis St. (bet. Alabama & Winbern Sts.) | 713-524-6922 | www.tafia.com

"A savory adventure" awaits courtesy of "genius" chef/co-owner Monica Pope at this "cutting-edge" Midtown New American, where "fresh, seasonal ingredients" are "beautifully prepared" for a "unique" "dining experience" "with a homey touch"; followers applaud the "astute" staff and "relaxed atmosphere", and though the setup "is so minimalist" it can be "a little noisy", at least "you never get bored"; P.S. the Saturday "farmer's market here is a must for serious foodies."

Tampico Seafood *Mexican/Seafood* | - | - | - | I |

North Houston | 10125 I-45 (West Rd.) | 281-445-2525
North Houston | 2115 Airline Dr. (Cavalcade St.) | 713-862-8425
www.tampicoseafood.net

Rightly known for "great Mexican-style seafood", this frill-free North Houston duo specializes in "very fresh grilled" dishes ("pick your own snapper and enjoy") from a lengthy menu of Gulf denizens; finatics declare it's "hard to beat" "at any price" but add "the Tex-Mex dishes don't measure up to the fish."

Tan Tan ◐ *Chinese/Vietnamese* | ▽ 26 | 13 | 18 | $13 |

Alief | 6816 Ranchester Dr. (Bellaire Blvd.) | 713-771-1268 | www.tantanrestaurant.com

With a "tantalizing" menu offering a staggering choice of 400 items, this New Chinatown Sino-Vietnamese is a "consistent" supplier of "excellent food" that leaves loyalists with "no regrets" in spite of "questionable service" and decor; "late-night" hours on the weekends ensure the "lively vibe" lasts "even until 3 in the morning."

Taste of Texas *Steak* | 24 | 21 | 23 | $44 |

Memorial | 10505 Katy Frwy. (bet. Beltway 8 & Gessner Dr.) | 713-932-6901 | www.tasteoftexas.com

"Texan to the core", this "popular" stalwart in "suburban" Memorial ropes in "big eaters" with "more-than-generous" slabs of Angus beef "grilled to perfection" ("love the salad bar too!") and served in a spacious setting steeped in "ranch manor" rusticity; but the "loud", "packed" room "rivals a cattle drive", and antis opine there are "classier places" "at this price level."

Teala's Mexican Restaurant *Mexican* | 18 | 18 | 18 | $23 |

Montrose | 3210 W. Dallas St. (Rosine St.) | 713-520-9292 | www.tealas.com

Providing a "welcome break from traditional Tex-Mex", this Montrose Mexican gives its "consistently" "interesting" fare a Thai twist, as found in "top-notch" salsas and "exotic" margaritas; the

"relaxed but lively" scene includes murals, a "great patio" and a "hopping" Friday happy hour.

Teotihuacan *Tex-Mex*
▽ | 24 | 13 | 20 | $13

Sharpstown | 6579 W. Bellfort St. (Fondren Rd.) | 713-726-9858
Heights | 1511 Airline Dr. (Patton St.) | 713-426-4420
Neartown | 4624 Irvington Blvd. (Cavalcade St.) | 713-695-8757

The "classic" cooking comes in "huge portions" at this "neighborhood Tex-Mex" trio, where an impressive menu of "delicious" items both familiar and less so is bolstered by "homemade corn tortillas" and "friendly" service; "don't be put off by" the modest digs, as the "flavorful" food and "great value" "will make you happy."

Terlingua *Tex-Mex*
18 | 20 | 17 | $19

West U | 3801 Bellaire Blvd. (Southside Pl.) | 713-665-3900
Montrose | 920 Studemont St. (Washington Ave.) |
713-864-3700
www.terlinguatexasbordercafe.com

Fans find a lingering "flair for originality" at this Montrose Tex-Mex *cocina* and its "family-friendly" West U offshoot, where the wide-ranging selections are supplemented by "very potent margaritas" ("beware!"); but holdouts see "nothing spectacular" and tear into service that "can be trying at times."

NEW Textile ⑤Ⓜ *American/French*
- | - | - | VE

Heights | 611 W. 22nd St. (bet. Lawrence St. & N. Shepherd Dr.) |
832-209-7177 | www.textilerestaurant.com

Chef-owner Scott Tycer (Gravitas) marks his return to the kitchen in this ambitious newcomer offering five- and seven-course French-American tasting menus, as well as a limited lineup of seasonal à la carte selections; it's located in a turn-of-the-century textile factory in the Heights, with sheer linen and beige burlap adorning the industrial space that fits just 10 tables.

Thai Bistro *Thai*
- | - | - | M

West U | 3241 Southwest Frwy. (Buffalo Spdwy.) | 713-669-9375

Small and "charming", this West U "gem" serves up "excellent", "reliable" Thai treats; though it's been around for years now, surveyors say it still "seems undiscovered" and note it's rarely crowded.

Thai Gourmet ⑤ *Thai*
24 | 16 | 20 | $20

Galleria | 6324 Richmond Ave. (Hillcroft Ave.) | 713-780-7955 |
www.thaigourmethouston.com

Diners get all fired up over this Galleria-area Siamese because of its "fine selection" of "wonderful", "authentic" dishes "spiced Thai-style" ("crank-up-the-heat") or "American-style"; "friendly" servers help create a pleasant atmosphere despite the eatery's "touristy location."

Thai Pepper *Thai*
18 | 13 | 16 | $22

Lower Shepherd | 2049 W. Alabama St. (Shepherd Dr.) | 713-520-8225 |
www.tealas.com

Patrons of this Lower Shepherd Thai "favorite" (a sib of Teala's) pick it because "nothing changes, and that's a good thing"; the "cheap"

fare is "spicy" and "great for a quick lunch", but those turned off by the "quiet-as-a-library" dining room advise "get it to go."

Thai Restaurant *Thai*
∇ 20 | 12 | 21 | $20

Galleria | 5757 Westheimer Rd. (bet. Chimney Rock Rd. & Fountain View Dr.) | 713-780-0888

A generic name belies the "fresh" preparations (with spice applied "to your liking"), "good-deal" prices and "prompt" service at this Siamese sleeper near the Galleria; meanwhile, straddlers grant it's a "reliable and fast lunch" option but "otherwise nothing special."

Thai Sticks *Thai*
∇ 21 | 22 | 18 | $28

Montrose | 4319 Montrose Blvd. (Richmond Ave.) | 713-529-4500

Non-locals are "wonderfully surprised" to encounter "top-tier" Thai at this "calm" enclave on Montrose, where "relaxing", up-market vibes complement the "delicious" "fusion"-esque cuisine; but some surveyors pronounce it "pricey", especially given occasionally "distracted service."

Thelma's Barbecue ☒ *BBQ*
∇ 21 | 4 | 11 | $12

Neartown | 1020 Live Oak St. (Lamar St.) | 713-228-2262

"You're family here" promise partialists of this "hole-in-the-wall" Neartown BBQ "shack", which plates up "rich, moist and delicious" 'cue in "outright huge" portions at a "very inexpensive" cost; but while "Thelma's a great cook, no doubt", the ultra-"informal" milieu "leaves something to be desired" and "the wait is a killer" at peak times.

Thierry André Tellier Café & Pastry Shop ☒ *French/Swiss*
23 | 16 | 18 | $20

Uptown | Uptown Park | 1101 Uptown Park Blvd. (Post Oak Blvd.) | 713-877-9401
River Oaks | 2515 River Oaks Blvd. (Westheimer Rd.) | 713-524-3863
www.cafeandpastryshop.com

Francophiles favor this "charming" French-Swiss cafe/bakery in River Oaks (and its Uptown sib) for "nice lunches" of "wonderful" soups, salads, sandwiches and quiches, but "the real draws" are the "sophisticated" pastries "that would melt a Parisian's heart"; service can be "slow", especially when it's "crowded on weekends", but that doesn't deter the faithful who claim this "institution" is still one of Houston's "little gems."

This Is it *Soul Food*
21 | 9 | 12 | $14

Midtown | 207 Gray St. (Bagby St.) | 713-659-1608 | www.thisisithouston.com

"If you want to get authentic", "this is it" according to aficionados of the "fatty, greasy, delicious soul food" that makes this joint near Midtown a go-to for "pure" "down-home cookin'"; though it's a "crowded", "cafeteria"-style setup ("don't argue with the line servers"), it's been keeping its customers "full and satisfied" since 1959; N.B. the Decor score does not reflect a recent remodel.

Tila's Restaurante & Bar *Mexican*

| 21 | 17 | 18 | $26 |

River Oaks | 1111 S. Shepherd Dr. (McDuffie St.) | 713-522-7654 | www.tilas.com

"Friendly" and whimsically decorated, this River Oaks cantina serves up "flavorful" Mexican cooking that's "creative" and "reasonably priced"; service ranges from "polite" to "erratic", but parking's basically "terrible" to "impossible" ("you have to valet", but it's complimentary).

NEW Tiny Boxwoods *Eclectic*

| - | - | - | I |

Greenway Plaza Area | 3614 W. Alabama St. (Saint St.) | 713-622-4224 | www.thompsonhanson.com

Occupying a corner of the Thompson + Hanson home and garden shop in the Greenway Plaza area, this chic yet casual Eclectic eatery serves refined cafe fare like grilled cheese with pesto, Cobb salads and coffee drinks; the light-filled space with a marble espresso bar and chalkboard menus fills up with a ladies-who-lunch crowd, and also plays host to a busy weekend brunch scene.

Tokyohana Grill & Sushi Bar *Japanese*

| 19 | 16 | 16 | $26 |

West U | 3239 Southwest Frwy. (Buffalo Spdwy.) | 713-838-9560
North Houston | 15155 North Frwy. (Richey Rd.) | 281-877-8744
www.tokyohana.com

This Japanese pair in West U and North Houston rolls out "diverse" sushi and hibachi dishes and "decent" wines along with the usual teppanyaki chefs' tricks; the "fun" Southwest Freeway location is "extremely popular with children", even hosting magicians on Thursdays and Saturdays, though some do find it "bizarre" ("did Chuck E. Cheese and Benihana mate?"); come evening, the North Freeway location turns into a lounge, complete with DJ on weekends.

Tony Mandola's Gulf Coast Kitchen *Seafood*

| 24 | 18 | 22 | $37 |

River Oaks | River Oaks Ctr. | 1962 W. Gray St. (McDuffie St.) | 713-528-3474 | www.tonymandolas.com

"You can't go wrong" with this "dependable" River Oaks seafooder's "delectable variety" of Gulf Coast–style shellfish, "perfectly seasoned" slaw or gumbo that'll "make you weep"; "Tony runs a tight ship" in this "lively", "friendly" "hangout", so though a few find the fare "overpriced", "no one seems to care."

Z Tony's ☒ *Continental/Italian*

| 27 | 27 | 27 | $64 |

Greenway Plaza Area | 3755 Richmond Ave. (Timmons Ln.) | 713-622-6778 | www.tonyshouston.com

An undisputed "Houston classic" installed in "knockout" Greenway Plaza digs, this "world-class" tribute to "formal dining" "caters to the elite" with "the total package": "exceptional" Continental-Italian fare, the "toniest" service around (rated No. 1 in Houston) and "smart", "art-filled" surroundings; it's "expensive", but "you get what you pay for", and its "moneyed" clientele hardly objects if it's "a little stuffy."

	FOOD	DECOR	SERVICE	COST

Treebeards 🅈 *Cajun/Southern*   24 | 14 | 16 | $13

Downtown | 1100 Louisiana St. (Lamar St.) | 713-752-2601
Downtown | The Cloister | 1117 Texas Ave. (San Jacinto St.) |
713-229-8248
Downtown | Market Sq. | 315 Travis St. (Preston St.) | 713-228-2622
Downtown | Downtown Tunnel | 700 Rusk St. (Milam St.) | 713-224-6677
www.treebeards.com

The four locations of this "Houston classic" – open only for weekday
lunch – dish up "delicious" Cajun-accented Southern "home cooking";
"courteous" service and "comfortable" cafeteria-style digs help make
meals here "worth the money"; N.B. the Market Square and Cloister
venues are notable – the former is in Houston's second oldest building (1870) and the latter in Christ Church Cathedral's social hall.

Trevisio 🅈 *Italian*   21 | 25 | 19 | $39

Medical Center | Texas Medical Ctr. | 6550 Bertner Ave. (Moursund St.) |
713-749-0400 | www.trevisiorestaurant.com

Recuperate with a "quiet, relaxing meal" at this "underutilized" "oasis"
"in the heart of the Medical Center", featuring "classy" Italian fare and
a "lovely" layout with a "lush wall of water" and a "view of the ex-
panse" of facilities below; doctors and staff appreciate the "convenience", though on the downside some diagnose "variable service."

Truluck's *Seafood*   23 | 22 | 23 | $44

Galleria | 5350 Westheimer Rd. (Sage Rd.) | 713-783-7270 |
www.trulucks.com

See review in Dallas/Ft. Worth Directory.

🄏 Uptown Sushi 🅈 *Japanese*   26 | 24 | 18 | $43

Uptown | Uptown Park | 1131-14 Uptown Park Blvd. (Post Oak Blvd.) |
713-871-1200 | www.uptown-sushi.com

"Be sure to dress to impress" for the "upscale" "social scene" at this
"trendy" Uptown Japanese, but "don't let its hipness throw you off"
since it follows through with "top-quality" sushi in an "elegant space";
it's a key place to "see and be seen" and accordingly "pricey", even
if the "party atmosphere" is slightly offset by "hit-or-miss" service.

Van Loc *Vietnamese*   18 | 9 | 17 | $13

Midtown | 3010 Milam St. (Elgin St.) | 713-528-6441

This modest Midtowner satisfies locals via "authentic" Vietnamese
"home cooking" ("excellent" spring rolls, "best pho", "well-prepared
noodle dishes"); to most, the "reliable, cheap eats" "make up" for
"abrupt" service and "bland" surroundings that "lack character."

Vargo's *Continental*   17 | 24 | 19 | $46

Memorial | 2401 Fondren Rd. (Westheimer Rd.) | 713-782-3888 |
www.vargosonline.com

"Lovely gardens" that play "host to peacocks" provide a "serene"
backdrop that surpasses the merely "good food" at this venerable
Memorial-area Continental ("make reservations by the window"); it
still works for "romance" and "wedding receptions", but dissenters
who allege it's "ready for an update" protest paying "big money" "for
too little beyond the glorious grounds."

Via Emilia *Italian* | - | - | - | M |
Northwest Houston | 3731 FM 1960 W. (bet. Falling Creek Dr. & Walters Rd.) | 281-587-9137
The flavor of "real Italian" awaits at this quaint, "family-owned" trattoria in Northwest Houston, where the repertoire covers favorites from osso buco to "tasty homemade pastas"; music fans note there's "great entertainment on weekends" as singers (operatic and otherwise) strut their stuff.

☑ Vic & Anthony's *Steak* | 26 | 25 | 24 | $61 |
Downtown | 1510 Texas Ave. (La Branch St.) | 713-228-1111 | www.vicandanthonys.com
It's "definitely pricey", but this "classic" Downtown steakhouse from "the Landry's empire" "ranks with the best", enticing a "power carnivore" crowd into its "opulent" "dark-oak" digs with "huge" cuts of "fabulous beef, an "amazing wine list" and "top-of-the-line" service; sited "in the shadow of" Minute Maid Park, it's "perfect for the pre- or post–ball game" blowout.

Vieng Thai *Thai* | - | - | - | I |
Spring Branch | 6929 Long Point Rd. (bet. Afton St. & Silber Rd.) | 713-688-9910
Homestyle Thai dishes, some of them unfamiliar to American palates, rule at this modest, family-friendly Spring Branch grocery store-turned-restaurant, where the extensive, authentic menu includes signature papaya salad, basil stir-fry and sticky rice with mango; N.B. its BYO policy and reasonable prices make it a downright bargain.

Vietnam Restaurant, The ☒ *Vietnamese* | ▽ 19 | 8 | 18 | $14 |
Heights | 605 W. 19th St. (Lawrence St.) | 832-618-1668 | www.thevietnamrestaurant.com
Smitten surveyors appreciate this "secret" "neighborhood hangout" in a Heights strip center for its "generous portions" of "fine" Vietnamese fare (they add "just the right amount of spice") and "friendly" staff; the BYO policy "helps" the already "unbelievably low" prices.

Vietopia *Vietnamese* | 20 | 21 | 19 | $22 |
West U | 5176 Buffalo Spdwy. (Westpark Dr.) | 713-664-7303 | www.vietopiarestaurant.com
With "charming" "upscale" surroundings and a "helpful", "nice" staff, this "family-friendly" West U Vietnamese has won the hearts and minds of its contented clientele; the "reliable", "healthy" entrees and "fab lunch specials" are "delicious" too (if perhaps closer to "experiments in fusion" than to "authentic" South Asian vittles), but a vocal few opine this "overpriced" place is "not utopia."

Vincent's ☒ *Italian* | 22 | 20 | 21 | $34 |
Montrose | 2701 W. Dallas St. (Eberhard St.) | 713-528-4313 | www.ninos-vincents.com
Next door to its sibling, Nino's – with which it shares a courtyard – this "casual", "dependable" Montrose Italian still wins friends after more than two decades with its "super" signature dishes (e.g. "juicy,

flavorful" rotisserie chicken, "divine veal Vincent") and "friendly", "competent" service; the unfulfilled bemoan "amazingly small" ("for Texas") portions.

NEW **Voice** *American*   – | – | – | E

Downtown | Hotel Icon | 220 Main St. (bet. Congress & Franklin Sts.) | 832-667-4470 | www.hotelicon.com

Inside the revamped dining room in the Hotel Icon sits this tony destination where chef Michael Kramer (ex Mansion at Turtle Creek) offers up a varied, modern American menu that puts the focus on locally sourced ingredients; its striking setting features high ceilings, red banquettes and expansive windows that make it feel part of Downtown while still remaining pleasantly outside the fray.

NEW **Waza Sushi &**   – | – | – | M
Robata Grill *Japanese*

Champions | 6927 FM 1960 W. (bet. Cutten & Haynes Rds.) | 281-580-8858

A hip addition to Champions, this sushi/robata hybrid specializes in gargantuan sushi rolls and grilled meats pumped out of an open kitchen; thanks to its boisterous bar scene and the appearance of weekend DJs, it's no surprise that it's already become a magnet for trendy twentysomethings.

Yao Restaurant & Bar *Chinese*   19 | 20 | 20 | $23

Southwest Houston | 9755 Westheimer Rd. (Gessner Rd.) | 832-251-2588 | www.yaorestaurant.com

"A real surprise" in Southwest Houston, this "upscale" "Chinese restaurant owned by an NBA star" (that's Rockets center Yao Ming) scores with "better-than-average" "traditional" cuisine and "polite, efficient service"; opponents counter it's "a little over-priced" for "ordinary" eating, but even they acknowledge that the lounge can be a "great sports bar"; N.B. a second location is set to open in the Houston Pavilions.

Yatra Brasserie *Indian*   ▽ 24 | 17 | 18 | $27

Downtown | 706 Main St. (bet. Capitol & Rusk Sts.) | 713-224-6700 | www.yatrausa.com

This newish Downtown taste of India is "worth its weight in curry" to champions of the "consistent" kitchen, which turns out dishes "flavorful" enough to "make you dance" around the stylish space; the original resides in London's ritzy Mayfair district, and its stateside sib aims to be a fashionable place to "make a night of it."

Yia Yia Mary's *Greek*   18 | 14 | 16 | $22

Galleria | 4747 San Felipe St. (I-610) | 713-840-8665 | www.yiayiamarys.com

Count on "typical Pappas quality" from this "quick", "casual" Galleria Mediterranean eatery's "tasty" "take on Greek", featuring a "traditional" lineup with "lots of things to choose from" all for a "reasonable price"; meanwhile, naysayers natter about "loud, loud" acoustics and chow that's "a little too Americanized" for purist palates.

	FOOD	DECOR	SERVICE	COST

Yildizlar ⑤ *Mideastern* ▽ 21 | 9 | 14 | $13

Upper Kirby District | Richmond Kirby Shopping Ctr. | 3419 Kirby Dr. (Richmond Ave.) | 713-524-7735

Globe-trotters like to graze at this Upper Kirby Middle Eastern "hole-in-the-wall" where both vegetarians and carnivores can enjoy the "authentically wonderful" fare; "try a little of everything" urge fans who frequent this cafeteria-style "quick lunch stop."

Yum Yum Cha Café *Chinese* 23 | 8 | 17 | $16

Rice Village | 2435 Times Blvd. (Kelvin Dr.) | 713-527-8455

Launched by a "charming", "personable" father-daughter team, this Chinese "little treasure" in Rice Village serves up "piping-hot", made-to-order dim sum "any day of the week at any time" ("no carts"); "be patient" counsel connoisseurs, who consider the "fresh", "upscale" fare "worth the 15-minute wait" and somewhat "slow" service; N.B. it's BYO.

Zoë's Kitchen *American* ▽ 17 | 12 | 15 | $17

Upper Kirby District | 3701 S. Shepherd Dr. (Richmond Ave.) | 713-522-7447 | www.zoeskitchen.com

See review in Dallas/Ft. Worth Directory.

Zula ⑤ *American* 23 | 24 | 21 | $53

Downtown | St. Germain Bldg. | 705 Main St. (Capitol St.) | 713-227-7052 | www.zulahouston.com

This "glitzy", "extravagant", high-ceilinged Downtowner "attracts those with bling, and those who want those with bling"; fans applaud "creative", "satisfying" New American eats and appreciate staffers' "pampering", while foes shrug that this "overpriced" place "tries too hard to be hip" and now feels "dated."

HOUSTON
INDEXES

Cuisines

Includes restaurant names, locations and Food ratings.

AMERICAN (NEW)

Ƶ Artista | **Downtown**	25
Aura | **Missouri City**	-
Backstreet Café | **River Oaks**	22
NEW Bedford | **Heights**	-
benjy's | **Rice Vill**	23
Bistro Lancaster | **Downtown**	20
Catalan | **Heights**	24
Cava Bistro | **Downtown**	21
Cova | **multi.**	19
Crú Wine Bar | **Woodlands**	20
Empire Café | **Montrose**	20
NEW Frank's | **Greenway Plaza**	-
Glass Wall | **Heights**	25
Gravitas | **Neartown**	21
Jasper's | **Woodlands**	24
NEW Kenzo | **Katy**	-
Kona Grill | **multi.**	20
Laurier Café | **Greenway Plaza**	25
La Vista | **multi.**	23
Ƶ Mark's | **Montrose**	28
Max's | **Heights**	21
Mockingbird Bistro | **River Oaks**	25
Monarch | **Medical Ctr**	21
Noé | **Uptown**	22
Olivette | **Uptown**	-
Polo's | **Greenway Plaza**	20
Ƶ Rainbow Lodge | **Heights**	23
Remington | **Uptown**	25
Ruggles | **multi.**	23
Ƶ 17 | **Downtown**	25
Shade | **Heights**	25
Soma | **Heights**	-
NEW Sophia | **Montrose**	-
t'afia | **Midtown**	25
NEW Textile | **Heights**	-
NEW Voice | **Downtown**	-
Zoë's | **Upper Kirby**	17
Zula | **Downtown**	23

AMERICAN (TRADITIONAL)

Armadillo Palace | **West U**	21
Avalon Diner | **multi.**	16
Baba Yega | **Montrose**	20
Barnaby's | **multi.**	21
Becks Prime | **Memorial**	22
Breakfast Klub | **Midtown**	23
Buffalo Grille | **multi.**	20
Ƶ Cheesecake Factory | **multi.**	20
Christian's | **multi.**	19

Cleburne | **West U**	23
NEW Cullen's | **Clear Lake**	-
Daily Grind | **Heights**	14
Daily Review | **River Oaks**	20
Dessert Gallery | **multi.**	22
59 Diner | **multi.**	16
Grove | **Downtown**	-
Hard Rock | **Downtown**	14
Houston's | **multi.**	23
Karl's | **Richmond**	27
Lankford Grocery | **Midtown**	23
NEW Little Bigs | **Montrose**	-
Mama's Café | **Briargrove**	19
Market Sq. | **Downtown**	-
Moveable Feast | **Memorial**	22
Post Oak Grill | **multi.**	21
Royers Round Top | **Round Top**	22
Rudyard's | **Montrose**	-

ARGENTINEAN

Empanadas by Marini | **multi.**	23

ASIAN FUSION

Lemongrass | **Bellaire**	21

BAKERIES

NY Coffee Shop | **Meyerland**	-
Thierry André | **multi.**	23

BARBECUE

Beaver's | **Heights**	-
Ƶ Goode Co. TX BBQ | **multi.**	25
Luling City Mkt. | **Galleria**	23
Lyndon's | **NW Houston**	-
Pizzitola's | **Heights**	24
Swinging Door | **Richmond**	24
Thelma's BBQ | **Neartown**	21

BRAZILIAN

Ƶ Fogo de Chão | **Briargrove**	26
NEW Fuegovivo | **W Houston**	-
Nelore | **Montrose**	20

BRITISH

Black Labrador | **Montrose**	17
NEW Feast | **Montrose**	-
McGonigel's | **Upper Kirby**	16
Red Lion | **Lower Shepherd**	19

BURGERS

Becks Prime | **multi.**	22
Bellaire Burger | **Bellaire**	21
Christian's | **multi.**	19

Goode Co. Burgers	**West U**	22
Lankford Grocery	**Midtown**	23
NEW Little Bigs	**Montrose**	–
Pappas Burgers	**Galleria**	23

CAJUN

NEW BB's Kitchen	**Montrose**	–
Danton's	**Montrose**	–
Floyd's	**Webster**	22
Magnolia B&G	**Briargrove**	20
Mardi Gras	**Heights**	18
Z Pappadeaux	**multi.**	23
Ragin' Cajun	**multi.**	21
Tony Mandola's	**River Oaks**	24
Treebeards	**Downtown**	24

CARIBBEAN

Reggae Hut	**Medical Ctr**	–

CENTRAL AMERICAN

Z Américas	**multi.**	24

CHINESE

(* dim sum specialist)

Café Chino	**Rice Vill**	22
Z China View	**W Houston**	27
Chinese Café	**multi.**	22
Daniel Wong's	**Bellaire**	23
Fung's*	**SW Houston**	25
Hollywood	**Montrose**	–
Hunan	**Downtown**	21
Kam's	**Montrose**	20
Kim Son*	**multi.**	23
Masala Wok	**SW Houston**	18
Ocean Palace*	**Bellaire**	23
Z P.F. Chang's	**multi.**	22
Shanghai River	**River Oaks**	22
Sichuan Cuisine	**Alief**	–
Sinh Sinh	**Alief**	–
Tan Tan	**Alief**	26
Yao	**SW Houston**	19
Yum Yum Cha*	**Rice Vill**	23

COFFEEHOUSES

Brasil	**Montrose**	20
Daily Grind	**Heights**	14

COFFEE SHOPS/ DINERS

Avalon Diner	**multi.**	16
Buffalo Grille	**multi.**	20
59 Diner	**multi.**	16
NY Coffee Shop	**Meyerland**	–

CONTINENTAL

Charivari	**Midtown**	23
Karl's	**Richmond**	27

Z La Colombe d'Or	**Montrose**	21
Lexington Grille	**Lower Shepherd**	21
Masraff's	**Uptown**	23
NEW Sage	**Lower Shepherd**	–
Z Tony's	**Greenway Plaza**	27
Vargo's	**Memorial**	17

CUBAN

Cafe Piquet	**Bellaire**	21

DELIS

Kahn's Deli	**Rice Vill**	23
Katz's	**multi.**	19
Kenny & Ziggy's	**Galleria**	24
Leibman's	**W Houston**	21
Mexico's Deli	**W Houston**	–
Z Nielsen's	**Galleria**	26

DESSERT

benjy's	**Rice Vill**	23
Z Churrascos	**multi.**	25
Dessert Gallery	**multi.**	22
Empire Café	**Montrose**	20
Quattro	**Downtown**	23
Ruggles	**Rice Vill**	23
Thierry André	**multi.**	23

ECLECTIC

Barnaby's	**multi.**	21
Black Walnut	**multi.**	20
Café Express	**multi.**	18
Dharma Café	**Neartown**	21
Farrago	**Midtown**	19
Grand Lux	**Galleria**	19
Hobbit Cafe	**Lower Shepherd**	21
Hungry's	**multi.**	19
Max's	**Heights**	21
Raven Grill	**West U**	21
Sambuca	**Downtown**	21
SoVino	**Montrose**	–
NEW Tiny Boxwoods	**Greenway Plaza**	–

ETHIOPIAN

Blue Nile	**SW Houston**	–

FONDUE

Melting Pot	**Galleria**	21

FRENCH

Au Petit Paris	**Lower Shepherd**	–
Bistro Calais	**River Oaks**	23
Brass. Max & Julie	**Montrose**	–
Z Chez Nous	**Humble**	26
Z La Colombe d'Or	**Montrose**	21
Z Le Mistral	**W Houston**	26

FRENCH (BISTRO)

NEW Bistro Don Camillo | Briargrove	-
Bistro Le Cep | **W Houston**	25
Bistro Provence | **W Houston**	23
Z Café Rabelais | **Rice Vill**	26
Thierry André | **multi.**	23

GERMAN

Old Heidelberg | **Briargrove**	21
Rudi Lechner's | **SW Houston**	23

GREEK

Alexander | **Galleria**	24
Bibas Greek | **Heights**	18
Niko Niko's | **Montrose**	23
One's A Meal | **Montrose**	18
Yia Yia Mary's | **Galleria**	18

GUATEMALAN

El Pueblito | **Montrose**	20

HAWAIIAN

Kona Grill | **multi.**	20

INDIAN

Ashiana | **W Houston**	24
Bombay Brass. | **multi.**	18
India's | **Galleria**	21
Indika | **Montrose**	25
Khyber | **Upper Kirby**	23
Kiran's | **Galleria**	25
Madras Pavilion | **multi.**	22
Masala Wok | **SW Houston**	18
Shiva Indian | **multi.**	20
Yatra | **Downtown**	24

ITALIAN

(N=Northern; S=Southern)

Amerigo's | **Woodlands**	22
Amici | S | **Sugar Land**	24
NEW Andrea | **W Houston**	-
Antica Osteria | **West U**	24
Arcodoro | S | **Galleria**	20
Arturo's | **Uptown**	19
NEW Bistro Don Camillo | Briargrove	-
Black Walnut | **multi.**	20
Brio | **Woodlands**	21
Carmelo's | S | **W Houston**	22
Z Carrabba's | **multi.**	22
Ciro's | **Memorial**	20
Collina's | **multi.**	18
Crapitto's | **Galleria**	21
Z Da Marco | **Montrose**	28

Damian's | **Midtown**	21
D'Amico's | **Rice Vill**	21
divino | N | **Lower Shepherd**	22
Dolce Vita | **Montrose**	24
Frenchie's | **Clear Lake**	24
Grappino di Nino | **Montrose**	20
Grotto | S | **multi.**	22
La Griglia | **River Oaks**	21
La Strada | **Montrose**	19
La Trattoria | N | **Briargrove**	20
La Vista | **multi.**	23
Maggiano's | **Galleria**	20
Mia Bella | **multi.**	22
Michelangelo's | **Montrose**	24
Nino's | **Montrose**	24
Palazzo's | **multi.**	20
Patrenella's | **Heights**	17
Paulie's | **multi.**	19
Perbacco | S | **Downtown**	23
Piatto | **multi.**	25
Prego | **Rice Vill**	23
Pronto Cucinino | **multi.**	19
Quattro | **Downtown**	23
NEW Rist. Cavour | N | **Uptown**	-
NEW Russo's | **NW Houston**	-
Simposio | N | **Briargrove**	24
Sorrento | **Montrose**	21
Z Tony's | **Greenway Plaza**	27
Trevisio | **Medical Ctr**	21
Via Emilia | **NW Houston**	-
Vincent's | **Montrose**	22

JAPANESE

(* sushi specialist)

Aka* | **multi.**	23
Azuma/Azumi* | **multi.**	23
Benihana | **multi.**	20
Café Japon* | **Upper Kirby**	22
Fish* | **Midtown**	20
Ginza* | **Briargrove**	-
Z Japaneiro's* | **Sugar Land**	26
Kaneyama* | **W Houston**	27
NEW Kenzo* | **Katy**	-
Kubo's* | **Rice Vill**	25
Nippon* | **Montrose**	-
Osaka* | **multi.**	24
Rickshaw Far East* | **River Oaks**	19
Sage 400* | **Galleria**	22
Sasaki* | **Briargrove**	-
Soma* | **Heights**	-
Sushi King* | **Upper Kirby**	23
Tokyohana* | **multi.**	19
Z Uptown Sushi* | **Uptown**	26
NEW Waza* | **Champions**	-

Menus, photos, voting and more - free at ZAGAT.com

JEWISH

Kahn's Deli	**Rice Vill**	23
Katz's	**multi.**	19
Kenny & Ziggy's	**Galleria**	24
NY Coffee Shop	**Meyerland**	–

LEBANESE

Cafe Lili	**Galleria**	24
Shawarma King	**Briargrove**	–

MEDITERRANEAN

Café Benedicte	**W Houston**	23
Dimassi's	**multi.**	18
Droubi	**multi.**	21
Fadi's	**multi.**	21
☑ Ibiza	**Midtown**	25
Mary'z	**Galleria**	21
Mint Café	**Galleria**	19
Phoenicia Deli	**Royal Oaks**	23

MEXICAN

Berryhill Baja	**multi.**	19
Cadillac Bar	**multi.**	18
Cantina Laredo	**W Houston**	21
Cyclone Anaya's	**multi.**	20
El Pueblito	**Montrose**	20
☑ Hugo's	**Montrose**	26
Irma's	**Downtown**	22
Jarro Café	**Spring Branch**	–
La Mexicana	**Montrose**	19
Las Alamedas	**Memorial**	20
López	**Alief**	–
Mexico's Deli	**W Houston**	–
Mission Burritos	**multi.**	22
100% Taquito	**West U**	18
Otilia's	**Spring Branch**	22
Pico's	**Bellaire**	24
Red Onion Taco	**NW Houston**	–
Romero's	**NW Houston**	21
Taco Milagro	**multi.**	16
Tampico	**N Houston**	–
Teala's	**Montrose**	18
Teotihuacan	**multi.**	24
Tila's	**River Oaks**	21

MIDDLE EASTERN

Dimassi's	**multi.**	18
Droubi	**multi.**	21
Mary'z	**Galleria**	21
Mint Café	**Galleria**	19
Yildizlar	**Upper Kirby**	21

NUEVO LATINO

Julia's	**Midtown**	19

PACIFIC RIM

☑ Café Le Jadeite	**River Oaks**	22

PAN-ASIAN

NEW Gigi's	**Galleria**	–
Pei Wei	**multi.**	19
Rattan	**W Houston**	–
Rickshaw Far East	**River Oaks**	19

PAN-LATIN

☑ Cafe Red Onion	**multi.**	24
El Meson	**Rice Vill**	19
Fernando's Latin	**Sugar Land**	–
☑ Red Onion	**NW Houston**	26

PERSIAN

Café Caspian	**W Houston**	22
Kasra	**SW Houston**	–

PERUVIAN

Lemon Tree	**W Houston**	–

PIZZA

Barry's	**multi.**	20
Bibas Greek	**Heights**	18
Dolce Vita	**Montrose**	24
Kenneally's	**Lower Shepherd**	16
NEW Russo's	**NW Houston**	–
Star Pizza	**multi.**	23

PUB FOOD

Armadillo Palace	**West U**	21
Black Labrador	**Montrose**	17
Kenneally's	**Lower Shepherd**	16
McGonigel's	**Upper Kirby**	16
Red Lion	**Lower Shepherd**	19
Rudyard's	**Montrose**	–

PUERTO RICAN

Isla Coquí	**Heights**	–

SEAFOOD

Danton's	**Montrose**	–
Denis' Seafood	**Memorial**	21
Floyd's	**Webster**	22
Fung's	**SW Houston**	25
Gaido's	**Galveston**	22
Goode Co. TX Seafood	**multi.**	23
☑ Jimmy Wilson's	**Briargrove**	26
Joyce's	**Briargrove**	19
☑ Lynn's	**W Houston**	26
Magnolia B&G	**Briargrove**	20
Mambo	**multi.**	20
Mardi Gras	**Heights**	18
Massa's	**Downtown**	19

McCormick/Schmick's | multi.	21
Oceanaire | Galleria	24
Ocean Palace | Bellaire	23
NEW Pan y Agua | River Oaks	-
Z Pappadeaux | multi.	23
Pappas Seafood | multi.	23
Pesce | Upper Kirby	21
Z Red Onion | NW Houston	26
Reef | Midtown	25
Segari's | Heights	-
Smith & Wollensky | Galleria	20
Sudie's | multi.	20
Tampico | N Houston	-
Tony Mandola's | River Oaks	24
Truluck's | Galleria	23

SMALL PLATES

(See also Spanish tapas specialist)

Catalan | Amer. | Heights	24
Cova | Amer. | multi.	19
divino | Italian | Lower Shepherd	22
Z Ibiza | Med. | Midtown	25
Mi Luna | Spanish | multi.	19
SoVino | Eclectic | Montrose	-

SOUL FOOD

Breakfast Klub | Midtown	23
This Is it | Midtown	21

SOUTH AMERICAN

Amazón Grill | West U	18
Z Américas | multi.	24
Z Churrascos | multi.	25
Z Japaneiro's | Sugar Land	26

SOUTHERN

Cleburne | West U	23
Jax Grill | multi.	19
Ouisie's | River Oaks	23
Treebeards | Downtown	24

SOUTHWESTERN

Burning Pear | Sugar Land	23
Z Cafe Annie | Galleria	26

SPANISH

(* tapas specialist)

Catalan | Heights	24
Mi Luna* | multi.	19
Rioja* | W Houston	24

STEAKHOUSES

Benihana | multi.	20
Brenner's | multi.	25
Burning Pear | Sugar Land	23

Capital Grille | Galleria	25
Z Churrascos | multi.	25
Del Frisco's | Galleria	27
Z Fleming's Prime | multi.	24
Z Fogo de Chão | Briargrove	26
NEW Frank's | Greenway Plaza	-
Killen's | Pearland	-
Kirby's | Woodlands	24
Z Lynn's | W Houston	26
Morton's Steak | multi.	25
NEW Mo's... | Galleria	-
Nelore | Montrose	20
Palm | Galleria	24
NEW Pan y Agua | River Oaks	-
Z Pappas Bros. | Galleria	27
Pappas Grill | Stafford	28
Z Perry's Steak | multi.	25
Rio Ranch | SW Houston	21
Ruth's Chris | Galleria	25
Segari's | Heights	-
Smith & Wollensky | Galleria	20
Spencer's | Downtown	21
Strip Hse. | Downtown	24
Sullivan's | Galleria	24
Taste of TX | Memorial	24
Z Vic & Antony's | Downtown	26

SWISS

Thierry André | multi.	23

TEX-MEX

Armandos | River Oaks	14
Buffalo Grille | multi.	20
Cabo | Downtown	14
Chuy's | multi.	21
Don Carlos | multi.	-
El Tiempo | multi.	22
Goode Co. Burgers | West U	22
Irma's SW | Downtown	21
Z Lupe Tortilla | multi.	21
Ninfa's/Original Ninfa's | multi.	22
Z Pappasito's Cantina | multi.	23
Spanish Flowers | Heights	19
Spanish Vill. | Medical Ctr	19
Sylvia's | W Houston	21
Teotihuacan | Heights	24
Terlingua | multi.	18

THAI

Z Kanomwan | Neartown	27
NEW Khun Kay | Montrose	-
Mai Thai | Upper Kirby	23
Nit Noi | multi.	21
Sawadee | West U	24
Thai Bistro | West U	-

Thai Gourmet | **Galleria** 24
Thai Pepper | **Lower Shepherd** 18
Thai Rest. | **Galleria** 20
Thai Sticks | **Montrose** 21
Vieng Thai | **Spring Branch** -

TURKISH

Empire Turkish | **W Houston** 24
Istanbul Grill | **Rice Vill** 22
Pasha | **Rice Vill** 25

VEGETARIAN

Brasil | **Montrose** 20
Hobbit Cafe | **Lower Shepherd** 21
Madras Pavilion | **Upper Kirby** 22

VIETNAMESE

Hollywood | **Montrose** -
NEW Hue | **Upper Kirby** -
Jasmine | **Alief** -
Jenni's Noodle | **Lower Shepherd** 21
Kim Son | **multi.** 23
Le Viet | **Royal Oaks** 21
Mai's | **Midtown** 23
Miss Saigon | **Rice Vill** 22
Mo Mong | **Montrose** 20
Tan Tan | **Alief** 26
Van Loc | **Midtown** 18
Vietnam | **Heights** 19
Vietopia | **West U** 20

Locations

Includes restaurant names, cuisines and Food ratings.

Houston

ALDINE/GREENSPOINT

Mambo	*Seafood*	20

ALIEF/SHARPSTOWN

Chinese Café	*Chinese*	22
Don Carlos	*Tex-Mex*	-
Jasmine	*Viet.*	-
Kim Son	*Chinese/Viet.*	23
López	*Mex.*	-
Mambo	*Seafood*	20
Pappas Seafood	*Seafood*	23
Sichuan Cuisine	*Chinese*	-
Sinh Sinh	*Chinese*	-
Tan Tan	*Chinese/Viet.*	26
Teotihuacan	*Tex-Mex*	24

ALMEDA/HOBBY/PASADENA

Don Carlos	*Tex-Mex*	-
Ninfa's/Original Ninfa's	*Tex-Mex*	22
Pappas Seafood	*Seafood*	23
Sudie's	*Seafood*	20

BELLAIRE/MEDICAL CENTER/WEST U

Amazón Grill	*S Amer.*	18
Antica Osteria	*Italian*	24
Armadillo Palace	*Pub*	21
Azuma/Azumi	*Japanese*	23
Bellaire Burger	*Burgers*	21
Berryhill Baja	*Mex.*	19
Buffalo Grille	*Amer.*	20
Cafe Piquet	*Cuban*	21
Cleburne	*Amer.*	23
Cova	*Amer.*	19
Daniel Wong's	*Chinese*	23
Dimassi's	*Med.*	18
Goode Co. Burgers	*Burgers*	22
Ⓩ Goode Co. TX BBQ	*BBQ*	25
Goode Co. TX Seafood	*Seafood*	23
Jax Grill	*Southern*	19
Lemongrass	*Asian Fusion*	21
Ⓩ Lupe Tortilla	*Tex-Mex*	21
Monarch	*Amer.*	21
Ninfa's/Original Ninfa's	*Tex-Mex*	22
Nit Noi	*Thai*	21

Ocean Palace	*Chinese*	23
100% Taquito	*Mex.*	18
Osaka	*Japanese*	24
Ⓩ Pappadeaux	*Seafood*	23
Ⓩ Pappasito's Cantina	*Tex-Mex*	23
Paulie's	*Italian*	19
Pei Wei	*Pan-Asian*	19
Pico's	*Mex.*	24
Pronto Cucinino	*Italian*	19
Raven Grill	*Eclectic*	21
Reggae Hut	*Carib.*	-
Sawadee	*Thai*	24
Spanish Vill.	*Tex-Mex*	19
Terlingua	*Tex-Mex*	18
Thai Bistro	*Thai*	-
Tokyohana	*Japanese*	19
Trevisio	*Italian*	21
Vietopia	*Viet.*	20

BRIARGROVE

Barnaby's	*Amer./Eclectic*	21
Barry's	*Pizza*	20
Becks Prime	*Burgers*	22
NEW Bistro Don Camillo	*French/Ital.*	-
Buffalo Grille	*Amer.*	20
Café Express	*Eclectic*	18
Ⓩ Carrabba's	*Italian*	22
Cyclone Anaya's	*Mex.*	20
Droubi	*Med.*	21
Fadi's	*Med.*	21
Ⓩ Fogo de Chão	*Brazilian/Steak*	26
Ginza	*Japanese*	-
Ⓩ Jimmy Wilson's	*Seafood*	26
Joyce's	*Seafood*	19
La Trattoria	*Italian*	20
La Vista	*Amer./Italian*	23
Magnolia B&G	*Cajun/Seafood*	20
Mama's Café	*Amer.*	19
Old Heidelberg	*German*	21
Palazzo's	*Italian*	20
Ⓩ Pappasito's Cantina	*Tex-Mex*	23
Sasaki	*Japanese*	-
Shawarma King	*Lebanese*	-
Simposio	*Italian*	24

CHAMPIONS

Berryhill Baja	*Mex.*	19
Café Express	*Eclectic*	18
Ⓩ Carrabba's	*Italian*	22
Nit Noi	*Thai*	21

Ɛ Pappadeaux | *Seafood*	23
Pei Wei | *Pan-Asian*	19
Ɛ Perry's Steak | *Steak*	25
NEW Waza | *Japanese*	-

DOWNTOWN

Ɛ Artista | *Amer.*	25
Azuma/Azumi | *Japanese*	23
Becks Prime | *Burgers*	22
Benihana | *Japanese/Steak*	20
Bistro Lancaster | *Amer.*	20
Cabo | *Tex-Mex*	14
Café Express | *Eclectic*	18
Cava Bistro | *Amer.*	21
Grove | *Amer.*	-
Hard Rock | *Amer.*	14
Hunan | *Chinese*	21
Irma's | *Mex.*	22
Irma's SW | *Tex-Mex*	21
Kim Son | *Chinese/Viet.*	23
Market Sq. | *Amer.*	-
Massa's | *Seafood*	19
McCormick/Schmick's | *Seafood*	21
Mia Bella | *Italian*	22
Morton's Steak | *Steak*	25
Ninfa's/Original Ninfa's | *Tex-Mex*	22
Nit Noi | *Thai*	21
Perbacco | *Italian*	23
Post Oak Grill | *Amer.*	21
Quattro | *Italian*	23
Ragin' Cajun | *Cajun*	21
Sambuca | *Eclectic*	21
Ɛ 17 | *Amer.*	25
Spencer's | *Steak*	21
Strip Hse. | *Steak*	24
Treebeards | *Cajun/Southern*	24
Ɛ Vic & Antony's | *Steak*	26
NEW Voice | *Amer.*	-
Yatra | *Indian*	24
Zula | *Amer.*	23

FM 1960/KLEIN

Ɛ Pappadeaux | *Seafood*	23
Ɛ Pappasito's Cantina | *Tex-Mex*	23

GALLERIA/UPTOWN

Alexander | *Greek*	24
Ɛ Américas | *S Amer.*	24
Arcodoro | *Italian*	20
Arturo's | *Italian*	19
Berryhill Baja | *Mex.*	19
Bombay Brass. | *Indian*	18
Ɛ Cafe Annie | *SW*	26

Café Express | *Eclectic*	18
Cafe Lili | *Lebanese*	24
Capital Grille | *Steak*	25
Ɛ Cheesecake Factory | *Amer.*	20
Chinese Café | *Chinese*	22
Crapitto's | *Italian*	21
Del Frisco's | *Steak*	27
Dessert Gallery | *Amer./Dessert*	22
Dimassi's | *Med.*	18
NEW Gigi's | *Pan-Asian*	-
Grand Lux | *Eclectic*	19
Grotto | *Italian*	22
Houston's | *Amer.*	23
India's | *Indian*	21
Kenny & Ziggy's | *Deli*	24
Kiran's | *Indian*	25
Kona Grill | *Amer.*	20
Luling City Mkt. | *BBQ*	23
Maggiano's | *Italian*	20
Mary'z | *Med.*	21
Masraff's | *Continental*	23
McCormick/Schmick's | *Seafood*	21
Melting Pot | *Fondue*	21
Mint Café | *Med.*	19
Morton's Steak | *Steak*	25
NEW Mo's... | *Steak*	-
Ɛ Nielsen's | *Deli*	26
Ninfa's/Original Ninfa's | *Tex-Mex*	22
Noé | *Amer.*	22
Oceanaire | *Seafood*	24
Olivette | *Amer.*	-
Palm | *Steak*	24
Ɛ Pappadeaux | *Seafood*	23
Ɛ Pappas Bros. | *Steak*	27
Pappas Burgers | *Burgers*	23
Ɛ P.F. Chang's | *Chinese*	22
Piatto | *Italian*	25
Post Oak Grill | *Amer.*	21
Ragin' Cajun | *Cajun*	21
Remington | *Amer.*	25
NEW Rist. Cavour | *Italian*	-
Ruggles | *Amer.*	23
Ruth's Chris | *Steak*	25
Sage 400 | *Japanese*	22
Smith & Wollensky | *Seafood/Steak*	20
Sullivan's | *Steak*	24
Thai Gourmet | *Thai*	24
Thai Rest. | *Thai*	20
Thierry André | *French/Swiss*	23
Truluck's | *Seafood*	23
Ɛ Uptown Sushi | *Japanese*	26
Yia Yia Mary's | *Greek*	18

GREENWAY PLAZA AREA

Collina's	*Italian*	18
El Tiempo	*Tex-Mex*	22
NEW Frank's	*Steak*	-
Laurier Café	*Amer.*	25
Polo's	*Amer.*	20
NEW Tiny Boxwoods	*Eclectic*	-
Z Tony's	*Continental/Italian*	27

HEIGHTS

Beaver's	*BBQ*	-
NEW Bedford	*Amer.*	-
Berryhill Baja	*Mex.*	19
Bibas Greek	*Greek/Pizza*	18
Cadillac Bar	*Mex.*	18
Catalan	*Amer./Spanish*	24
Collina's	*Italian*	18
Cova	*Amer.*	19
Cyclone Anaya's	*Mex.*	20
Daily Grind	*Coffee*	14
Glass Wall	*Amer.*	25
Isla Coquí	*Puerto Rican*	-
Jax Grill	*Southern*	19
Mardi Gras	*Cajun/Seafood*	18
Max's	*Eclectic*	21
Mission Burritos	*Mex.*	22
Patrenella's	*Italian*	17
Pizzitola's	*BBQ*	24
Z Rainbow Lodge	*Amer.*	23
Segari's	*Seafood/Steak*	-
Shade	*Amer.*	25
Soma	*Amer./Japanese*	-
Spanish Flowers	*Tex-Mex*	19
Star Pizza	*Pizza*	23
Teotihuacan	*Tex-Mex*	24
NEW Textile	*Amer./French*	-
Vietnam	*Viet.*	19

LOWER SHEPHERD

Au Petit Paris	*French*	-
Z Churrascos	*S Amer.*	25
divino	*Italian*	22
59 Diner	*Diner*	16
Hobbit Cafe	*Eclectic*	21
Jenni's Noodle	*Viet.*	21
Kenneally's	*Pub*	16
Lexington Grille	*Continental*	21
Mia Bella	*Italian*	22
Mission Burritos	*Mex.*	22
Pappas Seafood	*Seafood*	23
Red Lion	*Pub*	19
NEW Sage	*Cont.*	-
Star Pizza	*Pizza*	23
Thai Pepper	*Thai*	18

MEMORIAL/ SPRING BRANCH

Becks Prime	*Burgers*	22
Berryhill Baja	*Mex.*	19
Brenner's	*Steak*	25
Christian's	*Burgers*	19
Ciro's	*Italian*	20
Collina's	*Italian*	18
Denis' Seafood	*Seafood*	21
El Tiempo	*Tex-Mex*	22
Z Goode Co. TX BBQ	*BBQ*	25
Goode Co. TX Seafood	*Seafood*	23
Jarro Café	*Mex.*	-
Las Alamedas	*Mex.*	20
La Vista	*Amer./Italian*	23
Mambo	*Seafood*	20
Moveable Feast	*Amer.*	22
Ninfa's/Original Ninfa's	*Tex-Mex*	22
Nit Noi	*Thai*	21
Otilia's	*Mex.*	22
Z Pappadeaux	*Seafood*	23
Z Pappasito's Cantina	*Tex-Mex*	23
Pei Wei Asian Diner	*Pan-Asian*	19
Z Perry's Steak	*Steak*	25
Taste of TX	*Steak*	24
Vargo's	*Continental*	17
Vieng Thai	*Thai*	-

MEYERLAND/ WESTBURY

Café Express	*Eclectic*	18
Collina's	*Italian*	18
Fadi's	*Med.*	21
NY Coffee Shop	*Diner*	-

MIDTOWN

Barnaby's	*Amer./Eclectic*	21
Breakfast Klub	*Soul Food*	23
Charivari	*Continental*	23
Christian's	*Burgers*	19
Cyclone Anaya's	*Mex.*	20
Damian's	*Italian*	21
Farrago	*Eclectic*	19
Fish	*Japanese*	20
Z Ibiza	*Med.*	25
Julia's	*Nuevo Latino*	19
Lankford Grocery	*Burgers*	23
Mai's	*Viet.*	23
Post Oak Grill	*Amer.*	21
Reef	*Seafood*	25
t'afia	*Amer.*	25
This Is it	*Soul Food*	21
Van Loc	*Viet.*	18

MONTROSE

Baba Yega	Amer.	20
Barnaby's	Amer./Eclectic	21
NEW BB's Kitchen	Cajun	-
Berryhill Baja	Mex.	19
Black Labrador	Pub	17
Brasil	Coffee	20
Brass. Max & Julie	French	-
Café Express	Eclectic	18
☑ Da Marco	Italian	28
Danton's	Seafood	-
Dolce Vita	Italian	24
El Pueblito	Guatemalan/Mex.	20
El Tiempo	Tex-Mex	22
Empire Café	Amer.	20
NEW Feast	British	-
Grappino di Nino	Italian	20
Hollywood	Chinese/Viet.	-
☑ Hugo's	Mex.	26
Indika	Indian	25
Kam's	Chinese	20
Katz's	Deli	19
NEW Khun Kay	Thai	-
☑ La Colombe d'Or	Continental/French	21
La Mexicana	Mex.	19
La Strada	Italian	19
NEW Little Bigs	Burgers	-
☑ Mark's	Amer.	28
Michelangelo's	Italian	24
Mo Mong	Viet.	20
Nelore	Brazilian/Steak	20
Niko Niko's	Greek	23
Nino's	Italian	24
Nippon	Japanese	-
One's A Meal	Greek	18
Osaka	Japanese	24
Paulie's	Italian	19
Pei Wei	Pan-Asian	19
Pronto Cucinino	Italian	19
Rudyard's	Pub	-
NEW Sophia	Amer.	-
Sorrento	Italian	21
SoVino	Eclectic	-
Teala's	Mex.	18
Terlingua	Tex-Mex	18
Thai Sticks	Thai	21
Vincent's	Italian	22

NEARTOWN

Dharma Café	Eclectic	21
Don Carlos	Tex-Mex	-
Gravitas	Amer.	21
☑ Kanomwan	Thai	27
Ninfa's/Original Ninfa's	Tex-Mex	22

Teotihuacan	Tex-Mex	24
Thelma's BBQ	BBQ	21

NORTH HOUSTON

☑ Lupe Tortilla	Tex-Mex	21
Mambo	Seafood	20
☑ Pappasito's Cantina	Tex-Mex	23
Pappas Seafood	Seafood	23
Tampico	Mex./Seafood	-
Tokyohana	Japanese	19

NORTHWEST HOUSTON

☑ Cafe Red Onion	Pan-Latin	24
☑ Carrabba's	Italian	22
Chuy's	Tex-Mex	21
59 Diner	Diner	16
☑ Goode Co. Texas BBQ	BBQ	25
☑ Lupe Tortilla	Tex-Mex	21
Lyndon's	BBQ	-
Mambo	Seafood	20
Ninfa's/Original Ninfa's	Tex-Mex	22
☑ Pappadeaux	Seafood	23
☑ Pappasito's Cantina	Tex-Mex	23
Pei Wei	Pan-Asian	19
☑ P.F. Chang's	Chinese	22
☑ Red Onion	Seafood	26
Red Onion Taco	Mex.	-
Romero's	Mex.	21
NEW Russo's	Italian	-
Via Emilia	Italian	-

RICE VILLAGE

Azuma/Azumi	Japanese	23
benjy's	Amer.	23
Black Walnut	Eclectic/Italian	20
Bombay Brass.	Indian	18
Café Chino	Chinese	22
☑ Café Rabelais	French	26
Collina's	Italian	18
D'Amico's	Italian	21
El Meson	Pan-Latin	19
Hungry's	Eclectic	19
Istanbul Grill	Turkish	22
Kahn's Deli	Deli	23
Kubo's	Japanese	25
Mi Luna	Spanish	19
Mission Burritos	Mex.	22
Miss Saigon	Viet.	22
Pasha	Med.	25
Prego	Italian	23
Ruggles	Amer.	23
Shiva Indian	Indian	20
Yum Yum Cha	Chinese	23

HOUSTON

LOCATIONS

RIVER OAKS

Armandos | *Tex-Mex*	14
Avalon Diner | *Amer.*	16
Backstreet Café | *Amer.*	22
Barnaby's | *Amer./Eclectic*	21
Berryhill Baja | *Mex.*	19
Bistro Calais | *French*	23
Brenner's | *Steak*	25
Café Express | *Eclectic*	18
☑ Café Le Jadeite | *Pac. Rim*	22
Chuy's | *Tex-Mex*	21
Daily Review | *Amer.*	20
☑ Fleming's Prime | *Steak*	24
La Griglia | *Italian*	21
Mockingbird Bistro | *Amer.*	25
Ouisie's | *Southern*	23
Palazzo's | *Italian*	20
NEW Pan y Agua | *Seafood/Steak*	-
Rickshaw Far East | *Pan-Asian*	19
Shanghai River | *Chinese*	22
Thierry André | *French/Swiss*	23
Tila's | *Mex.*	21
Tony Mandola's | *Seafood*	24

ROYAL OAKS

Le Viet | *Viet.*	21
Phoenicia Deli | *Med.*	23
Piatto | *Italian*	25

SOUTHWEST HOUSTON

Benihana | *Japanese/Steak*	20
Blue Nile | *Ethiopian*	-
☑ Churrascos | *S Amer.*	25
Droubi's | *Med.*	21
Empanadas by Marini | *Argent.*	23
Fung's | *Chinese/Seafood*	25
Kasra | *Mideast.*	-
Masala Wok | *Chinese/Indian*	18
Ragin' Cajun | *Cajun*	21
Rio Ranch | *Steak*	21
Rudi Lechner's | *German*	23
Yao | *Chinese*	19

UPPER KIRBY DISTRICT

Aka | *Japanese*	23
Becks Prime | *Burgers*	22
Café Express | *Eclectic*	18
Café Japon | *Japanese*	22
☑ Cafe Red Onion | *Pan-Latin*	24
☑ Carrabba's | *Italian*	22
Dessert Gallery | *Amer./Dessert*	22
Houston's | *Amer.*	23
NEW Hue | *Viet.*	-
Khyber | *Indian*	23

Madras Pavilion | *Indian*	22
Mai Thai | *Thai*	23
McGonigel's | *Pub*	16
Ninfa's/Original Ninfa's | *Tex-Mex*	22
☑ Pappadeaux | *Seafood*	23
☑ Pappasito's Cantina | *Tex-Mex*	23
Pesce | *Seafood*	21
Sushi King | *Japanese*	23
Taco Milagro | *Mex.*	16
Yildizlar | *Mideast.*	21
Zoë's | *Amer.*	17

WEST HOUSTON

Aka | *Japanese*	23
NEW Andrea | *Ital.*	-
Ashiana | *Indian*	24
Becks Prime | *Burgers*	22
Bistro Le Cep | *French*	25
Bistro Provence | *French*	23
Café Benedicte | *Med.*	23
Café Caspian | *Persian*	22
☑ Cafe Red Onion | *Pan-Latin*	24
Cantina Laredo | *Mex.*	21
Carmelo's | *Italian*	22
☑ Carrabba's | *Italian*	22
☑ China View | *Chinese*	27
Dimassi's | *Med.*	18
Empire Turkish | *Turkish*	24
59 Diner | *Diner*	16
NEW Fuegovivo | *Brazilian*	-
Hungry's | *Eclectic*	19
Kaneyama | *Japanese*	27
Leibman's | *Deli*	21
☑ Le Mistral | *French*	26
Lemon Tree | *Peruvian*	-
☑ Lupe Tortilla | *Tex-Mex*	21
☑ Lynn's | *Steak*	26
Mexico's Deli | *Deli/Mex.*	-
Mission Burritos | *Mex.*	22
Nit Noi | *Thai*	21
Palazzo's | *Italian*	20
Pei Wei Asian Diner | *Pan-Asian*	19
☑ P.F. Chang's | *Chinese*	22
Rattan | *Pan-Asian*	-
Rioja | *Spanish*	24
Sylvia's | *Tex-Mex*	21

Bay Area

CLEAR LAKE/ LEAGUE CITY/ WEBSTER

Café Express | *Eclectic*	18
☑ Carrabba's | *Italian*	22
NEW Cullen's | *Amer.*	-

Dimassi's | *Med.* 18
Floyd's | *Cajun/Seafood* 22
Frenchie's | *Italian* 24
Z Lupe Tortilla | *Tex-Mex* 21
Z Pappasito's Cantina | *Tex-Mex* 23
Pappas Seafood | *Seafood* 23
Pei Wei | *Pan-Asian* 19
Z Perry's Steak | *Steak* 25
Sudie's | *Seafood* 20
Taco Milagro | *Mex.* 16

KEMAH

Cadillac Bar | *Mex.* 18

SEABROOK

Z Pappadeaux | *Seafood* 23

Outlying Areas

**ATASCOCITA/
HUMBLE/KINGWOOD**

Z Carrabba's | *Italian* 22
Z Chez Nous | *French* 26
Chuy's | *Tex-Mex* 21
Mission Burritos | *Mex.* 22
Z Pappasito's Cantina | *Tex-Mex* 23
Pappas Seafood | *Seafood* 23
Pei Wei | *Pan-Asian* 19

GALENA PARK

Pappas Seafood | *Seafood* 23

GALVESTON

Gaido's | *Seafood* 22

KATY/BROOKSHIRE

Berryhill Baja | *Mex.* 19
Empanadas by Marini | *Argent.* 23
NEW Kenzo | *Amer./Japanese* -
Mission Burritos | *Mex.* 22
Pei Wei | *Pan-Asian* 19

**MISSOURI CITY/
RICHMOND/
STAFFORD/
SUGAR LAND**

Amici | *Italian* 24
Aura | *Amer.* -
Avalon Diner | *Amer.* 16
Barry's | *Pizza* 20
Becks Prime | *Burgers* 22
Benihana | *Japanese/Steak* 20
Berryhill Baja | *Mex.* 19
Black Walnut | *Eclectic/Italian* 20
Burning Pear | *Steak/SW* 23
Café Express | *Eclectic* 18
Z Carrabba's | *Italian* 22

Z Cheesecake Factory | *Amer.* 20
Dessert Gallery | *Amer./Dessert* 22
Fernando's Latin | *Pan-Latin* -
59 Diner | *Diner* 16
Z Japaneiro's | *Japanese/S Amer.* 26
Karl's | *American/Continental* 27
Kim Son | *Chinese/Viet.* 23
Kona Grill | *Amer.* 20
Z Lupe Tortilla | *Tex-Mex* 21
Madras Pavilion | *Indian* 22
Mi Luna | *Spanish* 19
Ninfa's/Original Ninfa's | *Tex-Mex* 22
Z Pappadeaux | *Seafood* 23
Pappas Grill | *Steak* 28
Z Pappasito's Cantina | *Tex-Mex* 23
Pei Wei | *Pan-Asian* 19
Z Perry's Steak | *Steak* 25
Z P.F. Chang's | *Chinese* 22
Post Oak Grill | *Amer.* 21
Ragin' Cajun | *Cajun* 21
Shiva Indian | *Indian* 20
Swinging Door | *BBQ* 24

PEARLAND

Killen's | *Steak* -

ROUND TOP

Royers Round Top | *Amer.* 22

**SPRING/
THE WOODLANDS**

Z Américas | *S Amer.* 24
Amerigo's | *Italian* 22
Becks Prime | *Burgers* 22
Benihana | *Japanese/Steak* 20
Berryhill Baja | *Mex.* 19
Black Walnut | *Eclectic/Italian* 20
Brio | *Italian* 21
Z Carrabba's | *Italian* 22
Z Cheesecake Factory | *Amer.* 20
Chuy's | *Tex-Mex* 21
Crú Wine Bar | *Amer.* 20
Dimassi's | *Med.* 18
Z Fleming's Prime | *Steak* 24
Grotto | *Italian* 22
Jasper's | *Amer.* 24
Katz's | *Deli* 19
Kirby's | *Steak* 24
Z Lupe Tortilla | *Tex-Mex* 21
Mi Luna | *Spanish* 19
Nit Noi | *Thai* 21
Z Pappadeaux | *Seafood* 23
Z Perry's Steak | *Steak* 25
Z P.F. Chang's | *Chinese* 22

Special Features

Listings cover the best in each category and include names, locations and Food ratings. Multi-location restaurants' features may vary by branch.

ADDITIONS

(Properties added since the last edition of the book)

Andrea | W Houston	–
BB's Kitchen | Montrose	–
Bedford | Heights	–
Bistro Don Camillo | Briargrove	–
Feast | Montrose	–
Frank's | Greenway Plaza	–
Fuegovivo | W Houston	–
Gigi's | Galleria	–
Hue | Upper Kirby	–
Kenzo | Katy	–
Khun Kay | Montrose	–
Little Bigs | Montrose	–
Mo's... | Galleria	–
Olivette | Uptown	–
Pan y Agua | River Oaks	–
Rist. Cavour | Uptown	–
Russo's | NW Houston	–
Sage | Lower Shepherd	–
Sophia | Montrose	–
Textile | Heights	–
Tiny Boxwoods | Greenway Plaza	–
Voice | Downtown	–
Waza | Champions	–

BREAKFAST

(See also Hotel Dining)

Avalon Diner | multi.	16
Barnaby's | multi.	21
Becks Prime | Memorial	22
Berryhill Baja | multi.	19
Black Walnut | multi.	20
Brasil | Montrose	20
Breakfast Klub | Midtown	23
Buffalo Grille | multi.	20
☑ Cheesecake Factory | Galleria	20
El Pueblito | Montrose	20
El Tiempo | multi.	22
Empire Café | Montrose	20
59 Diner | multi.	16
Goode Co. Burgers | West U	22
Irma's | Downtown	22
Irma's SW | Downtown	21
Katz's | multi.	19
Kenny & Ziggy's | Galleria	24
La Mexicana | Montrose	19
Lankford Grocery | Midtown	23

Mama's Café | Briargrove	19
Pico's | Bellaire	24
Thierry André | multi.	23
Tila's | River Oaks	21
NEW Tiny Boxwoods | Greenway Plaza	–

BRUNCH

Arcodoro | Galleria	20
Ashiana | W Houston	24
Baba Yega | Montrose	20
Backstreet Café | River Oaks	22
benjy's | Rice Vill	23
Bistro Calais | River Oaks	23
Bistro Le Cep | W Houston	25
Black Labrador | Montrose	17
Burning Pear | Sugar Land	23
Cadillac Bar | Heights	18
☑ Cheesecake Factory | Galleria	20
Daily Review | River Oaks	20
Dharma Café | Neartown	21
Farrago | Midtown	19
Grand Lux | Galleria	19
Gravitas | Neartown	21
Hobbit Cafe | Lower Shepherd	21
☑ Hugo's | Montrose	26
Hungry's | multi.	19
Las Alamedas | Memorial	20
La Strada | Montrose	19
Magnolia B&G | Briargrove	20
Masraff's | Uptown	23
Max's | Heights	21
Michelangelo's | Montrose	24
Mi Luna | multi.	19
Ouisie's | River Oaks	23
Prego | Rice Vill	23
Quattro | Downtown	23
☑ Rainbow Lodge | Heights	23
Shade | Heights	25
NEW Sophia | Montrose	–
Sorrento | Montrose	21
Vargo's | Memorial	17

BUFFET SERVED

(Check availability)

Ashiana | W Houston	24
Baba Yega | Montrose	20
Bistro Calais | River Oaks	23
Bombay Brass. | multi.	18

Burning Pear | **Sugar Land**	23
Cadillac Bar | **Heights**	18
☑ China View | **W Houston**	27
Dharma Café | **Neartown**	21
Dimassi's | **multi.**	18
Droubi | **Briargrove**	21
☑ Hugo's | **Montrose**	26
India's | **Galleria**	21
Karl's | **Richmond**	27
Khyber | **Upper Kirby**	23
Kim Son | **Alief**	23
Las Alamedas | **Memorial**	20
Madras Pavilion | **multi.**	22
Magnolia B&G | **Briargrove**	20
Mi Luna | **multi.**	19
Nelore | **Montrose**	20
Quattro | **Downtown**	23
Shiva Indian | **multi.**	20

BUSINESS DINING

☑ Américas | **Galleria**	24
NEW Bedford | **Heights**	-
Brenner's | **River Oaks**	25
☑ Cafe Annie | **Galleria**	26
Café Benedicte | **W Houston**	23
Capital Grille | **Galleria**	25
Carmelo's | **W Houston**	22
☑ Churrascos | **multi.**	25
☑ Da Marco | **Montrose**	28
Damian's | **Midtown**	21
☑ Fleming's Prime | **River Oaks**	24
NEW Frank's | **Greenway Plaza**	-
Grove | **Downtown**	-
☑ Ibiza | **Midtown**	25
Jasper's | **Woodlands**	24
Julia's | **Midtown**	19
☑ La Colombe d'Or | **Montrose**	21
☑ Mark's | **Montrose**	28
Massa's | **Downtown**	19
McCormick/Schmick's | **Downtown**	21
Monarch | **Medical Ctr**	21
Morton's Steak | **Galleria**	25
NEW Mo's... | **Galleria**	-
Nelore | **Montrose**	20
Nino's | **Montrose**	24
Oceanaire | **Galleria**	24
Olivette | **Uptown**	-
Palm | **Galleria**	24
☑ Pappas Bros. | **Galleria**	27
Pappas Grill | **Stafford**	28
☑ Perry's Steak | **multi.**	25
Polo's | **Greenway Plaza**	20
Post Oak Grill | **multi.**	21
Quattro | **Downtown**	23

Reef | **Midtown**	25
Remington | **Uptown**	25
NEW Rist. Cavour | **Uptown**	-
Ruggles | **Galleria**	23
Ruth's Chris | **Galleria**	25
☑ 17 | **Downtown**	25
Smith & Wollensky | **Galleria**	20
Strip Hse. | **Downtown**	24
Sullivan's | **Galleria**	24
Tony Mandola's | **River Oaks**	24
☑ Tony's | **Greenway Plaza**	27
Trevisio | **Medical Ctr**	21
Truluck's | **Galleria**	23
☑ Vic & Antony's | **Downtown**	26
Yatra | **Downtown**	24

CELEBRITY CHEFS

Beaver's | *Monica Pope* | **Heights**	-
NEW Bedford | *Robert Gadsby* | **Heights**	-
☑ Cafe Annie | *Robert Del Grande* | **Galleria**	26
Catalan | *Chris Sheperd* | **Heights**	24
☑ Da Marco | *Marco Wiles* | **Montrose**	28
Glass Wall | *Lance Fegen* | **Heights**	25
Gravitas | *Scott Tycer/ Jason Gould* | **Neartown**	21
Grove | *Ryan Pera* | **Downtown**	-
☑ Hugo's | *Hugo Ortega* | **Montrose**	26
☑ Ibiza | *Charles Clark* | **Midtown**	25
Indika | *Anita Jaisinghani* | **Montrose**	25
Killen's | *Ron Killen* | **Pearland**	-
☑ Le Mistral | *David Denis* | **W Houston**	26
NEW Little Bigs | *Bryan Caswell* | **Montrose**	-
☑ Mark's | *Mark Cox* | **Montrose**	28
Mockingbird Bistro | *John Sheely* | **River Oaks**	25
Pesce | *Mark Holley* | **Upper Kirby**	21
Reef | *Bryan Caswell* | **Midtown**	25
NEW Rist. Cavour | *David Denis* | **Uptown**	-
Soma | *Robert Gadsby* | **Heights**	25
t'afia | *Monica Pope* | **Midtown**	25
NEW Textile | *Scott Tycer* | **Heights**	-

CHEF'S TABLE

Au Petit Paris | **Lower Shepherd**	-
NEW Bedford | **Heights**	-

Bistro Calais | **River Oaks**	23
Damian's | **Midtown**	21
Glass Wall | **Heights**	25
Masraff's | **Uptown**	23
Polo's | **Greenway Plaza**	20
Quattro | **Downtown**	23
Remington | **Uptown**	25
🆕 Textile | **Heights**	-

CHILD-FRIENDLY

(Alternatives to the usual fast-food places; * children's menu available)

Amazón Grill* | **West U**	18
Avalon Diner* | **Stafford**	16
Baba Yega | **Montrose**	20
Barnaby's* | **multi.**	21
Becks Prime* | **multi.**	22
Benihana* | **multi.**	20
Berryhill Baja | **River Oaks**	19
Black Walnut* | **multi.**	20
Breakfast Klub | **Midtown**	23
Café Express* | **multi.**	18
Café Japon | **Upper Kirby**	22
Z Cafe Red Onion* | **multi.**	24
Z Carrabba's* | **multi.**	22
Z Cheesecake Factory | **Galleria**	20
Ciro's* | **Memorial**	20
Cleburne* | **West U**	23
Collina's | **multi.**	18
D'Amico's | **Rice Vill**	21
Dessert Gallery* | **multi.**	22
Droubi | **multi.**	21
El Meson | **Rice Vill**	19
El Pueblito* | **Montrose**	20
59 Diner* | **multi.**	16
Gaido's* | **Galveston**	22
Goode Co. Burgers* | **West U**	22
Z Goode Co. TX BBQ | **West U**	25
Grotto* | **multi.**	22
Hard Rock* | **Downtown**	14
Hobbit Cafe* | **Lower Shepherd**	21
Hungry's* | **multi.**	19
Kim Son | **multi.**	23
La Mexicana* | **Montrose**	19
Z Lupe Tortilla* | **multi.**	21
Mama's Café* | **Briargrove**	19
Mambo | **multi.**	20
Moveable Feast* | **Memorial**	22
Niko Niko's* | **Montrose**	23
Ninfa's/Original Ninfa's* | **multi.**	22
Nit Noi | **multi.**	21
100% Taquito | **West U**	18
Otilia's* | **Spring Branch**	22
Palazzo's* | **Briargrove**	20

Z Pappasito's Cantina* | **Upper Kirby**	23
Paulie's* | **multi.**	19
Pei Wei* | **multi.**	19
Z P.F. Chang's | **multi.**	22
Pico's* | **Bellaire**	24
Ragin' Cajun* | **multi.**	21
Raven Grill* | **West U**	21
Rio Ranch* | **SW Houston**	21
Royers Round Top* | **Round Top**	22
Rudi Lechner's* | **SW Houston**	23
Shanghai River | **River Oaks**	22
Shiva Indian | **multi.**	20
Star Pizza | **multi.**	23
Sudie's* | **multi.**	20
Swinging Door | **Richmond**	24
Sylvia's* | **W Houston**	21
Taco Milagro* | **Upper Kirby**	16
Tampico* | **N Houston**	-
Taste of TX* | **Memorial**	24
Teotihuacan* | **multi.**	24
Terlingua* | **multi.**	18
Thierry André | **multi.**	23
Tokyohana* | **West U**	19
Zoë's | **Upper Kirby**	17

CIGARS WELCOME

Kirby's | **Woodlands**	24

DELIVERY/TAKEOUT

(D=delivery, T=takeout)

Z Américas | D, T | **Galleria**	24
Z Artista | D, T | **Downtown**	25
Avalon Diner | T | **Stafford**	16
Barnaby's | T | **multi.**	21
Becks Prime | T | **multi.**	22
Berryhill Baja | D, T | **multi.**	19
Black Walnut | T | **multi.**	20
Bombay Brass. | D, T | **Rice Vill**	18
Breakfast Klub | T | **Midtown**	23
Buffalo Grille | D, T | **multi.**	20
Cadillac Bar | T | **Heights**	18
Café Caspian | T | **W Houston**	22
Café Chino | T | **Rice Vill**	22
Café Express | T | **multi.**	18
Z Carrabba's | T | **multi.**	22
Cava Bistro | T | **Downtown**	21
Z Cheesecake Factory | T | **Galleria**	20
Z Churrascos | D, T | **multi.**	25
Chuy's | D | **River Oaks**	21
Cleburne | T | **West U**	23
Collina's | D, T | **multi.**	18
D'Amico's | T | **Rice Vill**	21
Dessert Gallery | D, T | **multi.**	22
Dimassi's | T | **multi.**	18

Droubi | T | **multi.** `21`
El Tiempo | D, T | **multi.** `22`
Empire Turkish | T |
  W Houston `24`
Goode Co. Burgers | T | **West U** `22`
🅉 Goode Co. TX BBQ | T |
  multi. `25`
Goode Co. TX Seafood | T |
  multi. `23`
Grappino di Nino | T | **Montrose** `20`
Gravitas | T | **Neartown** `21`
Grotto | T | **multi.** `22`
Hobbit Cafe | T |
  Lower Shepherd `21`
Hungry's | T | **multi.** `19`
India's | T | **Galleria** `21`
Irma's SW | T | **Downtown** `21`
Istanbul Grill | T | **Rice Vill** `22`
Jenni's Noodle | T |
  Lower Shepherd `21`
Kahn's Deli | T | **Rice Vill** `23`
Kenneally's | T | **Lower Shepherd** `16`
Kenny & Ziggy's | T | **Galleria** `24`
Khyber | T | **Upper Kirby** `23`
Kim Son | T | **multi.** `23`
Kiran's | D, T | **Galleria** `25`
Lankford Grocery | T |
  Midtown `23`
La Strada | D, T | **Montrose** `19`
Luling City Mkt. | T | **Galleria** `23`
Lyndon's | T | **NW Houston** `-`
Michelangelo's | T | **Montrose** `24`
Miss Saigon | T | **Rice Vill** `22`
Moveable Feast | T | **Memorial** `22`
🅉 Nielsen's | T | **Galleria** `26`
Niko Niko's | T | **Montrose** `23`
Ninfa's/Original Ninfa's | D, T |
  multi. `22`
Nit Noi | D, T | **multi.** `21`
Ocean Palace | T | **Bellaire** `23`
100% Taquito | T | **West U** `18`
Palazzo's | T | **Briargrove** `20`
Paulie's | T | **multi.** `19`
Pei Wei | T | **multi.** `19`
Pizzitola's | T | **Heights** `24`
Polo's | D, T | **Greenway Plaza** `20`
Post Oak Grill | D, T | **multi.** `21`
Ragin' Cajun | T | **multi.** `21`
Royers Round Top | T | **Round Top** `22`
Sawadee | T | **West U** `24`
Shanghai River | D, T | **River Oaks** `22`
Shiva Indian | T | **multi.** `20`
Star Pizza | D, T | **multi.** `23`
Sudie's | T | **multi.** `20`
Swinging Door | T | **Richmond** `24`
Sylvia's | D, T | **W Houston** `21`

Taco Milagro | T | **Upper Kirby** `16`
Thierry André | T | **multi.** `23`
This Is it | T | **Midtown** `21`
Treebeards | T | **Downtown** `24`
Van Loc | T | **Midtown** `18`
Vietopia | D, T | **West U** `20`
Yildizlar | T | **Upper Kirby** `21`
Yum Yum Cha | T | **Rice Vill** `23`
Zoë's | D | **Upper Kirby** `17`

DESSERT

🅉 Américas | **Galleria** `24`
benjy's | **Rice Vill** `23`
🅉 Cafe Annie | **Galleria** `26`
🅉 Cheesecake Factory | **Galleria** `20`
🅉 Churrascos | **multi.** `25`
🅉 Da Marco | **Montrose** `28`
Dessert Gallery | **multi.** `22`
Empire Café | **Montrose** `20`
Quattro | **Downtown** `23`
Royers Round Top | **Round Top** `22`
Ruggles | **Rice Vill** `23`
NEW Textile | **Heights** `-`
Thierry André | **multi.** `23`
🅉 Tony's | **Greenway Plaza** `27`

DINING ALONE

(Other than hotels and places with
counter service)
Avalon Diner | **multi.** `16`
Barnaby's | **multi.** `21`
Bellaire Burger | **Bellaire** `21`
Bibas Greek | **Heights** `18`
Black Walnut | **Sugar Land** `20`
🅉 Café Rabelais | **Rice Vill** `26`
Chinese Café | **multi.** `22`
Christian's | **multi.** `19`
🅉 Churrascos | **multi.** `25`
Daily Grind | **Heights** `14`
Dimassi's | **Medical Ctr** `18`
El Meson | **Rice Vill** `19`
Empanadas by Marini | **multi.** `23`
59 Diner | **multi.** `16`
Goode Co. TX Seafood | **multi.** `23`
Hobbit Cafe | **Lower Shepherd** `21`
🅉 Hugo's | **Montrose** `26`
Hunan | **Downtown** `21`
Hungry's | **multi.** `19`
India's | **Galleria** `21`
Indika | **Montrose** `25`
Katz's | **multi.** `19`
Kenny & Ziggy's | **Galleria** `24`
Leibman's | **W Houston** `21`
Mambo | **multi.** `20`
Market Sq. | **Downtown** `-`

Masala Wok | **SW Houston**	18
Mexico's Deli | **W Houston**	-
Mia Bella | **multi.**	22
Mint Café | **Galleria**	19
Mission Burritos | **multi.**	22
One's A Meal | **Montrose**	18
Otilia's | **Spring Branch**	22
Pei Wei | **multi.**	19
Perbacco | **Downtown**	23
Pronto Cucinino | **Medical Ctr**	19
Reef | **Midtown**	25
Sage 400 | **Galleria**	22
Sasaki | **Briargrove**	-
Shanghai River | **River Oaks**	22
Shawarma King | **Briargrove**	-
Simposio | **Briargrove**	24
Sinh Sinh | **Alief**	-
Taco Milagro | **Webster**	16
Tony Mandola's | **River Oaks**	24
Vietopia | **West U**	20
Yum Yum Cha | **Rice Vill**	23

ENTERTAINMENT

(Call for days and times of performances)

Alexander | belly dancers | **Galleria**	24
Amerigo's | piano | **Woodlands**	22
Armadillo Palace | varies | **West U**	21
☑ Artista | piano | **Downtown**	25
Backstreet Café | jazz | **River Oaks**	22
Berryhill Baja | varies | **multi.**	19
Bistro Calais | jazz | **River Oaks**	23
Bistro Le Cep | accordion | **W Houston**	25
Brasil | varies | **Montrose**	20
Breakfast Klub | varies | **Midtown**	23
Cadillac Bar | varies | **Kemah**	18
☑ Café Le Jadeite | piano | **River Oaks**	22
Carmelo's | accordion | **W Houston**	22
Daily Review | guitar/jazz | **River Oaks**	20
Denis' Seafood | Cajun/zydeco | **Memorial**	21
El Meson | guitar | **Rice Vill**	19
El Pueblito | flamenco/salsa | **Montrose**	20
Grappino di Nino | jazz | **Montrose**	20
Gravitas | DJ | **Neartown**	21
☑ Hugo's | Mexican | **Montrose**	26
Jax Grill | zydeco | **Heights**	19

Las Alamedas | guitar | **Memorial**	20
Masraff's | jazz/piano | **Uptown**	23
Michelangelo's | piano | **Montrose**	24
Mi Luna | jazz/Latin/soul | **multi.**	19
Ouisie's | jazz | **River Oaks**	23
☑ Pappas Bros. | piano | **Galleria**	27
Pico's | guitar/harp | **Bellaire**	24
☑ Red Onion | piano | **NW Houston**	26
Rickshaw Far East | varies | **River Oaks**	19
Rioja | flamenco/salsa | **W Houston**	24
Rudi Lechner's | polka | **SW Houston**	23
Sambuca | varies | **Downtown**	21
Sullivan's | bands/jazz | **Galleria**	24
Taco Milagro | varies | **Upper Kirby**	16
Tokyohana | DJ | **N Houston**	19
☑ Tony's | piano | **Greenway Plaza**	27
Trevisio | jazz | **Medical Ctr**	21
Via Emilia | vocals | **NW Houston**	-
☑ Vic & Antony's | piano | **Downtown**	26

GAME IN SEASON

Amerigo's | **Woodlands**	22
Antica Osteria | **West U**	24
Arcodoro | **Galleria**	20
Armadillo Palace | **West U**	21
Beaver's | **Heights**	-
Bistro Calais | **River Oaks**	23
NEW Bistro Don Camillo | **Briargrove**	-
Bistro Le Cep | **W Houston**	25
Bistro Provence | **W Houston**	23
Brass. Max & Julie | **Montrose**	-
Brenner's | **Memorial**	25
☑ Cafe Annie | **Galleria**	26
☑ Café Rabelais | **Rice Vill**	26
Charivari | **Midtown**	23
☑ Chez Nous | **Humble**	26
Floyd's | **Webster**	22
Glass Wall | **Heights**	25
Gravitas | **Neartown**	21
☑ Ibiza | **Midtown**	25
Indika | **Montrose**	25
Karl's | **Richmond**	27
☑ La Colombe d'Or | **Montrose**	21
Masraff's | **Uptown**	23
Olivette | **Uptown**	-

☑ Rainbow Lodge	Heights	23
Rioja	W Houston	24
NEW Rist. Cavour	Uptown	–
Royers Round Top	Round Top	22
t'afia	Midtown	25
NEW Textile	Heights	–
☑ Vic & Antony's	Downtown	26

HISTORIC PLACES

(Year opened; * building)

1870	Treebeards*	Downtown	24
1889	Cava Bistro*	Downtown	21
1894	Market Sq.*	Downtown	–
1900	t'afia*	Midtown	25
1911	Gaido's	Galveston	22
1915	Crapitto's*	Galleria	21
1924	17*	Downtown	25
1926	Bistro Lancaster*	Downtown	20
1930	Shade*	Heights	25
1936	Brenner's	Memorial	25
1936	Pizzitola's	Heights	24
1937	Christian's	multi.	19
1939	Lankford Grocery	Midtown	23
1941	Cleburne	West U	23
1944	Massa's	Downtown	19
1952	Nielsen's	Galleria	26
1953	Spanish Vill.	Medical Ctr	19
1957	Bellaire Burger	Bellaire	21

HOTEL DINING

Alden Houston Hotel	
☑ 17	Downtown	25
Four Seasons Hotel	
Quattro	Downtown	23
Hilton Americas Hotel	
Spencer's	Downtown	21
Hotel Granduca	
NEW Rist. Cavour	Uptown	–
Hotel Icon	
NEW Voice	Downtown	–
Hotel ZaZa	
Monarch	Medical Ctr	21
La Colombe d'Or	
☑ La Colombe d'Or	Montrose	21
Lancaster Hotel	
Bistro Lancaster	Downtown	20
Marriott Hotel	
Burning Pear	Sugar Land	23
Omni Hotel Houston	
Noé	Uptown	22
St. Regis Hotel	
Remington	Uptown	25
Westchase Hilton	
Rio Ranch	SW Houston	21

LATE DINING

(Weekday closing hour)

Armadillo Palace	12 AM	West U	21
NEW BB's Kitchen	varies	Montrose	–
Brasil	12 AM	Montrose	20
Cabo	12 AM	Downtown	14
Café Japon	12 AM	Upper Kirby	22
Christian's	12 AM	Midtown	19
Cova	varies	West U	19
59 Diner	24 hrs.	multi.	16
Hard Rock	12 AM	Downtown	14
Hollywood	varies	Montrose	–
Katz's	24 hrs.	Montrose	19
Kenneally's	1 AM	Lower Shepherd	16
Mai's	4 AM	Midtown	23
Mama's Café	2 AM	Briargrove	19
One's A Meal	24 hrs.	Montrose	18
Red Lion	2 AM	Lower Shepherd	19
Rudyard's	12 AM	Montrose	–
Sambuca	varies	Downtown	21
Sinh Sinh	2 AM	Alief	–
Smith & Wollensky	2 AM	Galleria	20
Spanish Flowers	24 hrs.	Heights	19
Tan Tan	varies	Alief	26

MEET FOR A DRINK

☑ Américas	Galleria	24
Amici	Sugar Land	24
Arcodoro	Galleria	20
Armadillo Palace	West U	21
Armandos	River Oaks	14
Arturo's	Uptown	19
benjy's	Rice Vill	23
Black Labrador	Montrose	17
Brasil	Montrose	20
Cabo	Downtown	14
Cadillac Bar	multi.	18
Christian's	multi.	19
Cyclone Anaya's	multi.	20
Del Frisco's	Galleria	27
Dolce Vita	Montrose	24
El Tiempo	Montrose	22
Farrago	Midtown	19
☑ Fleming's Prime	River Oaks	24
Grappino di Nino	Montrose	20
Gravitas	Neartown	21
☑ Ibiza	Midtown	25
Kenneally's	Lower Shepherd	16
La Griglia	River Oaks	21

SPECIAL FEATURES

Las Alamedas | **Memorial**	20
La Strada | **Montrose**	19
Market Sq. | **Downtown**	-
Max's | **Heights**	21
McCormick/Schmick's | **Uptown**	21
McGonigel's | **Upper Kirby**	16
Mi Luna | **Sugar Land**	19
Monarch | **Medical Ctr**	21
NEW Mo's... | **Galleria**	-
Olivette | **Uptown**	-
Palm | **Galleria**	24
☑ Pappadeaux | **multi.**	23
Pappas Grill | **Stafford**	28
☑ Pappasito's Cantina | **multi.**	23
Pico's | **Bellaire**	24
Red Lion | **Lower Shepherd**	19
Reef | **Midtown**	25
Remington | **Uptown**	25
Rickshaw Far East | **River Oaks**	19
Rudyard's | **Montrose**	-
Sambuca | **Downtown**	21
☑ 17 | **Downtown**	25
Smith & Wollensky | **Galleria**	20
Sorrento | **Montrose**	21
Sullivan's | **Galleria**	24
Taco Milagro | **Upper Kirby**	16
t'afia | **Midtown**	25
Teala's | **Montrose**	18
☑ Uptown Sushi | **Uptown**	26
Yatra | **Downtown**	24

OUTDOOR DINING

(G=garden; P=patio; S=sidewalk;
T=terrace; W=waterside)

Amazón Grill | P | **West U**	18
Arcodoro | P | **Galleria**	20
Armadillo Palace | P | **West U**	21
☑ Artista | T | **Downtown**	25
Ashiana | P | **W Houston**	24
Baba Yega | P | **Montrose**	20
Barnaby's | P | **multi.**	21
Backstreet Café | G, P | **River Oaks**	22
Becks Prime | P | **multi.**	22
Berryhill Baja | P | **multi.**	19
Black Labrador | P | **Montrose**	17
Black Walnut | P | **multi.**	20
Brasil | P | **Montrose**	20
Brio | P | **Woodlands**	21
Cabo | P | **Downtown**	14
Café Express | P | **multi.**	18
Cava Bistro | P | **Downtown**	21
Chuy's | P | **River Oaks**	21
Crapitto's | P | **Galleria**	21

Crú Wine Bar | P | **Woodlands**	20
Daily Review | G, P | **River Oaks**	20
D'Amico's | P | **Rice Vill**	21
Denis' Seafood | G | **Memorial**	21
Dolce Vita | P | **Montrose**	24
El Pueblito | P | **Montrose**	20
El Tiempo | P | **multi.**	22
Empire Café | P | **Montrose**	20
Farrago | G | **Midtown**	19
Goode Co. Burgers | P | **West U**	22
☑ Goode Co. TX BBQ | P | **West U**	25
Grappino di Nino | P | **Montrose**	20
Grotto | P | **Woodlands**	22
Grove | P | **Downtown**	-
Hard Rock | P | **Downtown**	14
Hobbit Cafe | P | **Lower Shepherd**	21
☑ Hugo's | P | **Montrose**	26
☑ Ibiza | P | **Midtown**	25
Indika | P | **Montrose**	25
Istanbul Grill | P | **Rice Vill**	22
Jasper's | P | **Woodlands**	24
Kenneally's | P | **Lower Shepherd**	16
La Griglia | P | **River Oaks**	21
La Mexicana | P | **Montrose**	19
Lankford Grocery | T | **Midtown**	23
La Strada | P | **Montrose**	19
Market Sq. | P | **Downtown**	-
Masraff's | P | **Uptown**	23
Mia Bella | P, S | **multi.**	22
Michelangelo's | P | **Montrose**	24
Niko Niko's | P | **Montrose**	23
Ninfa's/Original Ninfa's | P | **Neartown**	22
Nino's | P | **Montrose**	24
Otilia's | P | **Spring Branch**	22
Ouisie's | G, P | **River Oaks**	23
☑ P.F. Chang's | P, W | **multi.**	22
Pico's | P | **Bellaire**	24
☑ Rainbow Lodge | G, P, T, W | **Heights**	23
Raven Grill | P | **West U**	21
Red Lion | P | **Lower Shepherd**	19
Sambuca | P | **Downtown**	21
Star Pizza | P | **multi.**	23
Sylvia's | P | **W Houston**	21
Taco Milagro | P | **Upper Kirby**	16
t'afia | P | **Midtown**	25
Teala's | P | **Montrose**	18
Thai Sticks | P | **Montrose**	21
Tila's | P | **River Oaks**	21
Tony Mandola's | P | **River Oaks**	24
Treebeards | P, T | **Downtown**	24
Trevisio | P | **Medical Ctr**	21
Vincent's | P | **Montrose**	22

POWER SCENES

NEW Bedford | **Heights**	-
Brenner's | **multi.**	25
☑ Cafe Annie | **Galleria**	26
Capital Grille | **Galleria**	25
Carmelo's | **W Houston**	22
☑ Da Marco | **Montrose**	28
☑ Ibiza | **Midtown**	25
Irma's | **Downtown**	22
Jasper's | **Woodlands**	24
☑ La Colombe d'Or | **Montrose**	21
La Griglia | **River Oaks**	21
☑ Mark's | **Montrose**	28
Massa's | **Downtown**	19
Monarch | **Medical Ctr**	21
Morton's Steak | **multi.**	25
NEW Mo's... | **Galleria**	-
Palm | **Galleria**	24
☑ Pappas Bros. | **Galleria**	27
Quattro | **Downtown**	23
Remington | **Uptown**	25
NEW Rist. Cavour | **Uptown**	-
Ruth's Chris | **Galleria**	25
☑ 17 | **Downtown**	25
Strip Hse. | **Downtown**	24
Sullivan's | **Galleria**	24
☑ Tony's | **Greenway Plaza**	27
☑ Vic & Antony's | **Downtown**	26
Zula | **Downtown**	23

PRIX FIXE MENUS

(Call for prices and times)

Arcodoro | **Galleria**	20
Ashiana | **W Houston**	24
Bistro Calais | **River Oaks**	23
☑ Fogo de Chão | **Briargrove**	26
Kiran's | **Galleria**	25
☑ Mark's | **Montrose**	28
Masraff's | **Uptown**	23
Nelore | **Montrose**	20
Pesce | **Upper Kirby**	21
☑ Rainbow Lodge | **Heights**	23
t'afia | **Midtown**	25

QUIET CONVERSATION

Amerigo's | **Woodlands**	22
Au Petit Paris | **Lower Shepherd**	-
☑ Café Le Jadeite | **River Oaks**	22
Carmelo's | **W Houston**	22
Charivari | **Midtown**	23
☑ Chez Nous | **Humble**	26
Crapitto's | **Galleria**	21
Damian's | **Midtown**	21

India's | **Galleria**	21
☑ La Colombe d'Or | **Montrose**	21
☑ Le Mistral | **W Houston**	26
Lexington Grille | **Lower Shepherd**	21
☑ Lynn's | **W Houston**	26
Mai Thai | **Upper Kirby**	23
Massa's | **Downtown**	19
Miss Saigon | **Rice Vill**	22
Ouisie's | **River Oaks**	23
Perbacco | **Downtown**	23
Raven Grill | **West U**	21
NEW Rist. Cavour | **Uptown**	-
Ruggles | **Galleria**	23
Ruth's Chris | **Galleria**	25
NEW Sage | **Lower Shepherd**	-
Sawadee | **West U**	24
☑ 17 | **Downtown**	25
Shanghai River | **River Oaks**	22
Thai Bistro | **West U**	-
Thai Sticks | **Montrose**	21
Tila's | **River Oaks**	21
Vargo's | **Memorial**	17
Via Emilia | **NW Houston**	-

ROMANTIC PLACES

Antica Osteria | **West U**	24
☑ Artista | **Downtown**	25
Au Petit Paris | **Lower Shepherd**	-
☑ Cafe Annie | **Galleria**	26
☑ Café Le Jadeite | **River Oaks**	22
Carmelo's | **W Houston**	22
Cava Bistro | **Downtown**	21
☑ Chez Nous | **Humble**	26
Crapitto's | **Galleria**	21
☑ Da Marco | **Montrose**	28
Damian's | **Midtown**	21
☑ La Colombe d'Or | **Montrose**	21
Las Alamedas | **Memorial**	20
☑ Le Mistral | **W Houston**	26
Lexington Grille | **Lower Shepherd**	21
☑ Lynn's | **W Houston**	26
☑ Mark's | **Montrose**	28
Masraff's | **Uptown**	23
Michelangelo's | **Montrose**	24
☑ Rainbow Lodge | **Heights**	23
Remington | **Uptown**	25
NEW Rist. Cavour | **Uptown**	-
Ruggles | **Galleria**	23
NEW Sage | **Lower Shepherd**	-
Thai Sticks | **Montrose**	21
☑ Tony's | **Greenway Plaza**	27
Vargo's | **Memorial**	17
Via Emilia | **NW Houston**	-

SENIOR APPEAL

Bistro Lancaster | **Downtown**	20
Carmelo's | **W Houston**	22
Cleburne | **West U**	23
Crapitto's | **Galleria**	21
59 Diner | **Stafford**	16
Gaido's | **Galveston**	22
Lexington Grille | **Lower Shepherd**	21
Melting Pot | **Galleria**	21
NY Coffee Shop | **Meyerland**	-
Old Heidelberg | **Briargrove**	21
Ouisie's | **River Oaks**	23
Rudi Lechner's | **SW Houston**	23
NEW Sage | **Lower Shepherd**	-
Thierry André | **River Oaks**	23
Vargo's | **Memorial**	17

SINGLES SCENES

Armadillo Palace | **West U**	21
Armandos | **River Oaks**	14
Arturo's | **Uptown**	19
Berryhill Baja | **Montrose**	19
Cabo | **Downtown**	14
Cadillac Bar | **multi.**	18
Cova | **multi.**	19
Cyclone Anaya's | **multi.**	20
Del Frisco's | **Galleria**	27
Dolce Vita | **Montrose**	24
El Tiempo | **Montrose**	22
Empire Café | **Montrose**	20
Farrago | **Midtown**	19
Fish | **Midtown**	20
☑ Fleming's Prime | **multi.**	24
NEW Gigi's | **Galleria**	-
La Griglia | **River Oaks**	21
La Strada | **Montrose**	19
Max's | **Heights**	21
Mi Luna | **multi.**	19
Pesce | **Upper Kirby**	21
Reef | **Midtown**	25
Rickshaw Far East | **River Oaks**	19
Sage 400 | **Galleria**	22
Sambuca | **Downtown**	21
Smith & Wollensky | **Galleria**	20
Sullivan's | **Galleria**	24
Taco Milagro | **Upper Kirby**	16
Teala's | **Montrose**	18
☑ Uptown Sushi | **Uptown**	26
Zula | **Downtown**	23

SLEEPERS

(Good to excellent food, but little known)

Aka | **multi.**	23
Alexander | **Galleria**	24

Ashiana | **W Houston**	24
Bistro Calais | **River Oaks**	23
Bistro Provence | **W Houston**	23
Café Benedicte | **W Houston**	23
Charivari | **Midtown**	23
Daniel Wong's | **Bellaire**	23
Empanadas by Marini | **multi.**	23
Empire Turkish | **W Houston**	24
Frenchie's | **Clear Lake**	24
Fung's | **SW Houston**	25
Kahn's Deli | **Rice Vill**	23
Karl's | **Richmond**	27
Khyber | **Upper Kirby**	23
Laurier Café | **Greenway Plaza**	25
Mai Thai | **Upper Kirby**	23
Ocean Palace | **Bellaire**	23
Pappas Grill | **Stafford**	28
Pasha | **Rice Vill**	25
Perbacco | **Downtown**	23
Remington | **Uptown**	25
Rioja | **W Houston**	24
Sawadee | **West U**	24
Sushi King | **Upper Kirby**	23
Swinging Door | **Richmond**	24
Tan Tan | **Alief**	26
Teotihuacan | **multi.**	24
Thai Gourmet | **Galleria**	24
Thierry André | **multi.**	23
Yatra | **Downtown**	24

TRANSPORTING EXPERIENCES

☑ Américas | **Galleria**	24
☑ Artista | **Downtown**	25
☑ Cafe Annie | **Galleria**	26
Carmelo's | **W Houston**	22
☑ Chez Nous | **Humble**	26
☑ Da Marco | **Montrose**	28
Indika | **Montrose**	25
☑ Mark's | **Montrose**	28
☑ Rainbow Lodge | **Heights**	23
Reef | **Midtown**	25
Shade | **Heights**	25
t'afia | **Midtown**	25
☑ Tony's | **Greenway Plaza**	27

TRENDY

☑ Américas | **multi.**	24
Amici | **Sugar Land**	24
Armandos | **River Oaks**	14
☑ Artista | **Downtown**	25
Arturo's | **Uptown**	19
Beaver's | **Heights**	-
NEW Bedford | **Heights**	-
benjy's | **Rice Vill**	23

Catalan | **Heights**	24
Cyclone Anaya's | **multi.**	20
Del Frisco's | **Galleria**	27
Dolce Vita | **Montrose**	24
El Tiempo | **multi.**	22
Glass Wall | **Heights**	25
Gravitas | **Neartown**	21
Grove | **Downtown**	-
☑ Ibiza | **Midtown**	25
Julia's | **Midtown**	19
La Griglia | **River Oaks**	21
La Strada | **Montrose**	19
☑ Mark's | **Montrose**	28
Max's | **Heights**	21
Mi Luna | **multi.**	19
Mint Café | **Galleria**	19
Mockingbird Bistro | **River Oaks**	25
Monarch | **Medical Ctr**	21
Pesce | **Upper Kirby**	21
☑ P.F. Chang's | **W Houston**	22
Reef | **Midtown**	25
Rickshaw Far East | **River Oaks**	19
Sambuca | **Downtown**	21
Shade | **Heights**	25
Smith & Wollensky | **Galleria**	20
Soma | **Heights**	-
Taco Milagro | **Upper Kirby**	16
t'afia | **Midtown**	25
NEW Textile | **Heights**	-
☑ Uptown Sushi | **Uptown**	26
Zula | **Downtown**	23

VIEWS

☑ Artista | **Downtown**	25
Baba Yega | **Montrose**	20
Brenner's | **River Oaks**	25
Cabo | **Downtown**	14
Cadillac Bar | **Kemah**	18
Del Frisco's | **Galleria**	27
Gaido's | **Galveston**	22
Grove | **Downtown**	-
☑ La Colombe d'Or | **Montrose**	21
Las Alamedas | **Memorial**	20
Monarch | **Medical Ctr**	21
☑ Rainbow Lodge | **Heights**	23
Reef | **Midtown**	25
Trevisio | **Medical Ctr**	21
Vargo's | **Memorial**	17

VISITORS ON EXPENSE ACCOUNT

☑ Américas | **Galleria**	24
NEW Bedford | **Heights**	-
Brenner's | **multi.**	25
☑ Cafe Annie | **Galleria**	26
Capital Grille | **Galleria**	25
Carmelo's | **W Houston**	22
☑ Da Marco | **Montrose**	28
Del Frisco's | **Galleria**	27
Grove | **Downtown**	-
Kirby's | **Woodlands**	24
☑ La Colombe d'Or | **Montrose**	21
☑ Lynn's | **W Houston**	26
☑ Mark's | **Montrose**	28
Mockingbird Bistro | **River Oaks**	25
Monarch | **Medical Ctr**	21
Morton's Steak | **Galleria**	25
Noé | **Uptown**	22
Palm | **Galleria**	24
☑ Pappas Bros. | **Galleria**	27
Pesce | **Upper Kirby**	21
Quattro | **Downtown**	23
Reef | **Midtown**	25
Remington | **Uptown**	25
NEW Rist. Cavour | **Uptown**	-
Ruth's Chris | **Galleria**	25
☑ 17 | **Downtown**	25
Smith & Wollensky | **Galleria**	20
Strip Hse. | **Downtown**	24
NEW Textile | **Heights**	-
☑ Tony's | **Greenway Plaza**	27
☑ Vic & Antony's | **Downtown**	26

WINNING WINE LISTS

☑ Américas | **Galleria**	24
Arcodoro | **Galleria**	20
Ashiana | **W Houston**	24
Backstreet Café | **River Oaks**	22
benjy's | **Rice Vill**	23
Brass. Max & Julie | **Montrose**	-
Brenner's | **River Oaks**	25
☑ Cafe Annie | **Galleria**	26
☑ Café Rabelais | **Rice Vill**	26
Capital Grille | **Galleria**	25
Carmelo's | **W Houston**	22
Catalan | **Heights**	24
☑ Churrascos | **multi.**	25
☑ Da Marco | **Montrose**	28
El Meson | **Rice Vill**	19
Glass Wall | **Heights**	25
☑ Ibiza | **Midtown**	25
Kiran's | **Galleria**	25
Laurier Café | **Greenway Plaza**	25
NEW Little Bigs | **Montrose**	-
☑ Lynn's | **W Houston**	26

☑ Mark's | **Montrose**	28
Mockingbird Bistro | **River Oaks**	25
Morton's Steak | **Galleria**	25
☑ Pappas Bros. | **Galleria**	27
Pesce | **Upper Kirby**	21
Prego | **Rice Vill**	23
Reef | **Midtown**	25
Remington | **Uptown**	25
Simposio | **Briargrove**	24
t'afia | **Midtown**	25
☑ Tony's | **Greenway Plaza**	27
☑ Vic & Antony's | **Downtown**	26

WORTH A TRIP

Clear Lake	
Frenchie's	24
Galveston	
Gaido's	22
Humble	
☑ Chez Nous	26
Richmond	
Karl's	27
Swinging Door	24
Round Top	
Royers Round Top	22
The Woodlands	
Amerigo's	22

SAN ANTONIO

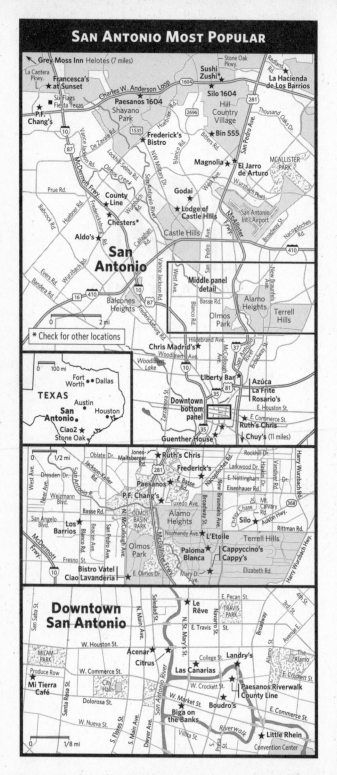

SAN ANTONIO MOST POPULAR

Grey Moss Inn Helotes (7 miles)

La Cantera Pkwy.

★ Francesca's at Sunset

■ Six Flags Fiesta Texas

P.F. Chang's ★

Charles W. Anderson Loop

★ Paesanos 1604

Shavano Park

Stone Oak Pkwy.

Redland Rd.

★ Sushi Zushi*

★ La Hacienda de Los Barrios

★ Silo 1604

Hill Country Village

★ Frederick's Bistro

★ Bin 555

Magnolia ■

■ El Jarro de Arturo

MCALLISTER PARK

Godai ★

County Line ★

Chesters* ★

Aldo's ★

★ Lodge of Castle Hills

San Antonio Int'l Airport

Castle Hills

San Antonio

Middle panel detail

Alamo Heights

Terrell Hills

Balcones Heights

Olmos Park

0   2 mi

* Check for other locations

Chris Madrid's ★

Woodlawn Lake

Liberty Bar ★

★ Azúca
La Frite
Rosario's

0   100 mi

Fort Worth ● ● Dallas

TEXAS

Austin ●

San Antonio ●

Houston ●

Ciao2 ★
Stone Oak

Downtown bottom panel

★ E. Houston St.

Ruth's Chris ★

Guenther House ★

Chuy's (11 miles)

0   1/2 mi

Oblate Dr.

Jones-Maltsberger Rd.

★ Ruth's Chris

★ Frederick's

★ Paesanos

P.F. Chang's ★

Los Barrios ★

OLMOS BASIN PARK

Alamo Heights

★ Silo

Olmos Park

★ L'Etoile

Paloma Blanca ★

★ Cappyccino's Cappy's

Bistro Vatel ★
Ciao Lavanderia ★

Terrell Hills

Downtown San Antonio

★ Le Rêve

TRAVIS PARK

MILAM PARK

Acenar ★
Citrus ★

Landry's ★

Las Canarias ★

The Alamo

Mi Tierra Café ■

City Hall

★ Paesanos Riverwalk
County Line

Boudro's ★

Biga on the Banks ★

Riverwalk

★ Little Rhein
Convention Center

0   1/8 mi

294   Menus, photos, voting and more – free at ZAGAT.com

Most Popular

1. Le Rêve | *French*
2. Biga on the Banks | *American*
3. Boudro's | *Seafood/Steak*
4. Paesanos | *Italian*
5. Paloma Blanca | *Mexican*
6. Lodge of Castle Hills | *Amer.*
7. Liberty Bar | *Eclectic*
8. Silo | *American*
9. Cappy's | *American*
10. L'Etoile | *French/Seafood*
11. Bistro Vatel | *French*
12. Magnolia | *American*
13. Chris Madrid's | *Burgers*
14. Frederick's | *Asian Fusion/French*
15. Las Canarias | *French/Med.*
16. Mi Tierra Café | *Tex-Mex*
17. Grey Moss Inn | *American*
18. Chesters | *Burgers*
19. Chuy's | *Tex-Mex*
20. Rosario's | *Mexican*
21. Silo 1604* | *American*
22. El Jarro de Arturo | *Mexican*
23. Ciao | *Italian*
24. Little Rhein* | *Steak*
25. Bin 555 | *American*
26. County Line* | *BBQ*
27. Landry's | *Seafood*
28. La Frite | *Belgian*
29. P.F. Chang's* | *Chinese*
30. Ácenar | *Tex-Mex*
31. Aldo's | *Italian*
32. Citrus* | *American*
33. Francesca's* | *Southwestern*
34. Cappyccino's | *American*
35. Guenther House* | *American*
36. Sushi Zushi* | *Japanese*
37. Azúca | *Nuevo Latino*
38. Godai | *Japanese*
39. Ruth's Chris* | *Steak*
40. La Hacienda/Los Barrios | *Tex-Mex*

It's obvious that many of the above restaurants are among the San Antonio area's most expensive, but if popularity were calibrated to price, we suspect that a number of other restaurants would join their ranks. Thus, we have added two lists comprising 40 Best Buys on page 300.

KEY NEWCOMERS

Our editors' take on the year's top arrivals. See page 340 for a full list.

Achiote River | *Pan-Latin*

Brasserie Pavil | *French*

Chama Gaucha | *Brazilian*

Ciel | *French*

Coco Chocolate | *Dessert/French*

Oloroso | *Mediterranean*

Roaring Fork | *Southwestern*

Tre Trattoria | *Italian*

Valentino's | *Italian*

Wildfish | *Amer./Seafood*

* Indicates a tie with restaurant above

Top Food Ratings

Excludes places with low votes, unless indicated by a ▽.

29 Le Rêve | French

28 Sandbar Fish | Seafood

27 Magnolia | American
    Biga on the Banks | American
    Godai Sushi | Japanese

26 Francesca's | Southwestern
    Lodge of Castle Hills | American
    Frederick's | Asian Fusion/
      French
    L'Etoile | French/Seafood
    Silo | American
    Bistro Vatel | French
    Bin 555 | American
    Silo 1604 | American
    La Frite | Belgian
    Las Canarias | French/Med.

25 Citrus | American
    Ruth's Chris | Steak
    Chris Madrid's | Burgers
    Fig Tree | Continental
    Sushihana* | Japanese

Morton's Steak | Steak

24 Texas Farm to Table | American
    Boudro's | Seafood/Steak
    Piatti | Italian
    Little Rhein | Steak
    Palm | Steak
    India Palace | Indian
    Da Vinci Gelato | Italian
    Pesca on the River* | Seafood
    Grey Moss Inn | American
    Fleming's | Steak
    Liberty Bar | Eclectic
    Sawasdee | Thai
    Azúca | Nuevo Latino

23 El Mirador | Mexican
    Pappadeaux | Seafood
    Cappy's | American
    Korean BBQ House* | Korean
    La Scala | European
    Rosario's | Mexican

BY CUISINE

AMERICAN (NEW)

27 Biga on the Banks
26 Lodge of Castle Hills
    Silo
    Bin 555
    Silo 1604

AMERICAN (TRAD.)

27 Magnolia
24 Texas Farm to Table
    Grey Moss Inn
23 Guenther House
    Chesters

CHINESE

22 P.F. Chang's
    Wah Kee
    Golden Wok
21 Mencius Gourmet
    Formosa Garden

ECLECTIC

24 Liberty Bar
23 Cappy's
22 Grill at Leon Springs
    La Tuna Grill▽

FRENCH

29 Le Rêve
26 Frederick's
    L'Etoile
    Bistro Vatel
    Las Canarias

ITALIAN

24 Piatti
    Da Vinci Gelato
23 Sorrento Ristorante
    Ciao
    Paesanos*

MEXICAN

23 El Mirador
    Rosario's
22 Paloma Blanca
    Picante Grill*
    Tiago's Cabo Grill

SEAFOOD

28 Sandbar Fish
26 L'Etoile
24 Boudro's
    Pesca on the River
23 Pappadeaux

STEAKHOUSES

- **25** Ruth's Chris
- Morton's Steak
- **24** Boudro's
- Little Rhein
- Palm

TEX-MEX

- **22** Ácenar
- **21** Mi Tierra Café
- Chuy's
- La Hacienda/Los Barrios
- La Margarita

BY SPECIAL FEATURE

BREAKFAST

- **27** Magnolia
- **23** Guenther House
- **21** Mimi's Cafe
- **23** El Mirador
- **21** Mi Tierra Café

BRUNCH

- **26** Las Canarias
- **24** Liberty Bar
- **23** Cappy's
- **22** Guenther House
- Paloma Blanca

BUSINESS DINING

- **29** Le Rêve
- **27** Biga on the Banks
- **26** Frederick's
- Lodge of Castle Hills
- Citrus

CHILD-FRIENDLY

- **25** Chris Madrid's
- **24** Da Vinci Gelato
- **23** Paesanos
- **22** Big'z
- Ácenar

DINING ALONE

- **28** Sandbar Fish
- **26** Koi Kawa
- **23** El Mirador
- Cappy's
- Ciao

MEET FOR A DRINK

- **26** Silo
- **25** Citrus
- **24** Piatti
- Liberty Bar
- **22** Grill at Leon Springs

PEOPLE-WATCHING

- **28** Sandbar Fish
- **24** Boudro's

Piatti
Pesca on the River
Texas Farm to Table

POWER SCENES

- **28** Sandbar Fish
- **27** Biga on the Banks
- **24** Piatti
- Liberty Bar
- **23** Paesanos

QUICK BITES

- **28** Sandbar Fish
- **26** Bin 555
- **25** Chris Madrid's
- **24** Da Vinci Gelato
- Texas Farm to Table

QUIET CONVERSATION

- **29** Le Rêve
- **27** Biga on the Banks
- **26** Francesca's
- Lodge of Castle Hills
- Bistro Vatel

SINGLES SCENES

- **24** Azúca
- **23** Rosario's
- Paesanos
- **22** Paloma Blanca
- Grill at Leon Springs

TRENDY

- **27** Biga on the Banks
- **26** Frederick's
- La Frite
- **24** Texas Farm to Table
- Liberty Bar

WINNING WINE LISTS

- **29** Le Rêve
- **27** Biga on the Banks
- **26** Francesca's
- Lodge of Castle Hills
- L'Etoile

BY LOCATION

ALAMO HEIGHTS

26 Frederick's
    L'Etoile
23 Cappy's
    Sorrento
22 Paloma Blanca

CASTLE HILLS/NORTH

26 Lodge of Castle Hills
25 Sushihana
23 La Scala
22 Chesters
    El Jarro de Arturo

DOWNTOWN

29 Le Rêve
28 Sandbar Fish
25 Citrus
    Morton's Steak
24 Palm

MEDICAL CENTER

24 India Palace
22 Golden Wok
21 Mencius Gourmet
    Aldo's

NORTH CENTRAL

27 Magnolia
27 Godai Sushi
26 Bin 555
25 Ruth's Chris
24 India Palace

QUARRY

24 Piatti
    Fleming's
22 P.F. Chang's
    Paesanos
18 Canyon Café

RIVER WALK

27 Biga on the Banks
26 Las Canarias
25 Fig Tree
24 Boudro's
    Little Rhein

SOUTHTOWN

26 La Frite
24 Azúca
23 El Mirador
    Rosario's
    Guenther House

Top Decor Ratings

27	Francesca's	23	Paloma Blanca
26	Lodge of Castle Hills		Silo
25	Silo 1604		Las Canarias
	Biga on the Banks		Bin 555
	Le Rêve		La Scala
24	Ácenar	22	Fig Tree
	Grey Moss Inn		Grill at Leon Springs*
	Citrus		Ruth's Chris
	Fleming's		Piatti
	Antlers Lodge		Pesca on the River

OUTDOORS

Ácenar
Bin 555
Boudro's
Cappy's
La Hacienda/Los Barrios

Las Ramblas
Paesanos
Pam's Kitchen
Pesca on the River
Scenic Loop Café

ROMANCE

Biga on the Banks
Bistro Vatel
Bohanan's
Citrus
Francesca's

Las Canarias
Le Rêve
Lodge of Castle Hills
Oro
Silo 1604

ROOMS

Biga on the Banks
Bin 555
Bistro Vatel
Bohanan's
Brasserie Pavil

Citrus
Francesca's
Liberty Bar
Lodge of Castle Hills
Silo 1604

VIEWS

Ácenar
Biga on the Banks
Bohanan's
Boudro's
Fig Tree

Grey Moss Inn
Las Ramblas
Little Rhein
Mi Tierra Café
Scenic Loop Café

Top Service

27	Le Rêve
26	Frederick's
	Francesca's
25	Biga on the Banks
	Ruth's Chris
24	Silo 1604
	Palm
	Lodge of Castle Hills
	Antlers Lodge
	Bistro Vatel

	Las Canarias
	Silo
23	Fleming's
	La Scala
	Morton's Steak
	L'Etoile
	Fig Tree
	Sandbar Fish
	Little Rhein
	Bin 555

Best Buys

In order of Bang for the Buck rating.

1. Da Vinci Gelato
2. Magnolia
3. Texas Farm to Table
4. Cheesy Jane's
5. Chris Madrid's
6. Chesters
7. Schilo's Deli
8. Taco Cabana
9. Picante Grill
10. Guenther House
11. Beto's Comida
12. Mama's Café
13. Clear Springs Café
14. Formosa Garden
15. Big'z Burger
16. Madhatters Tea
17. India Palace
18. Golden Wok
19. Mi Tierra Café
20. La Hacienda/Los Barrios

OTHER GOOD VALUES

Cascabel
County Line
Cove
Demo's
Jospehine St. Cafe
La Marginal
La Tuna Grill
Little Red Barn
Mimi's Café
Pam's Patio Kitchen

Phoenix Chinese Café
Sarovar
Sea Island
Smokehouse
Sorrento
Taco Taco
Thai Taste
Tiago's Cabo Grill
Tip Top Cafe
Torres Taco Haven

San Antonio

Ácenar *Tex-Mex*   22 | 24 | 18 | $27

River Walk | 146 E. Houston St. (St. Mary's St.) | 210-222-2362 | www.acenar.com

Locals "love the atmosphere" at this "hip", "noisy" River Walk Tex-Mex set in colorful digs with stellar "people-watching" and a shaded balcony that affords "great views" of the water; the "modern" dishes (and "excellent duck chalupas") win raves, though a few find fault with tabs that are "on the pricier side" and sometimes "inconsistent" service.

NEW Achiote River Café *Pan-Latin*   - | - | - | M

River Walk | Grand Hyatt San Antonio | 600 E. Market St. (Convention Way) | 210-224-1234 | www.achioterivercafe.com

The fiery decor provides a fitting backdrop for the zippy Pan-Latin fare at this stylish newcomer in the Grand Hyatt with terrace seating overlooking the River Walk; the wide-ranging and affordable menu features both modern fusion dishes and regional classics, all with a focus on fresh seafood, including several ceviches and Bahia-style mussels.

Alamo Café *Tex-Mex*   - | - | - | I

North | 14250 Hwy. 281 N. (Bitters Rd.) | 210-495-2233
Northwest | 10060 I-10 W. (Wurzbach Rd.) | 210-691-8827
www.alamocafe.com

Mainstream Tex-Mex cooking with handmade flour tortillas and mild-mannered sauces have made this longtime duo a popular destination for Northside residents; while the easy-on-the-budget tabs appeal to families, the well-made margaritas and convivial atmosphere mean it's also a low-key happy-hour option.

Aldaco's Mexican Cuisine *Mexican*   ∇ 22 | 19 | 19 | $20

San Antonio East | 100 Hoefgen Ave. (bet. Center & Commerce Sts.) | 210-222-0561 | www.aldacos.net ⑤
NEW Stone Oak | 20079 Stone Oak Pkwy. (Hardy Oak St.) | 210-494-0561

"A treasure" laud loyalists of Blanca Aldaco's "slightly upscale" Mexican at Sunset Station in St. Paul Square offering cuisine with "an emphasis on fresh ingredients" and "irresistible drinks"; it's a "fun place" with patio seating and solid service making it "great for kids", though a few lament the location can be a problem when beer-infused crowds descend on the nearby Alamodome for concerts and sporting events; N.B. the Stone Oak branch is new.

Aldino at the Vineyard *Italian*   21 | 22 | 20 | $29

Loop 1604 | Vineyard Ctr. | 1203 N. Loop 1604 W. (Blanco Rd.) | 210-340-0000 | www.aldinos.com

Outstripping its "strip-mall" setting, this Loop 1604 bastion of "imaginative", "fresh" Italian fare is a "pleasant" place to dine thanks to its spacious faux-Roman interior and "excellent patio for lingering after the meal"; in general it's considered a "great neighborhood place", though some sigh servers are "earnest" but "not well versed."

	FOOD	DECOR	SERVICE	COST

Aldo's Ristorante Italiano *Italian* | 21 | 21 | 22 | $33 |

Medical Center | 8539 Fredericksburg Rd. (Wurzbach Rd.) | 210-696-2536
"Semi-formal" yet "homey" (it's inside a ranch house), this mid-priced Medical Center "standby" serves up "extremely consistent" "high-end" Italian fare that's "just short of great"; service can be "uneven", but the "cordial", "quiet" vibe still makes it a "solid" choice for "business meetings" and "special-occasion dinners."

Antlers Lodge ⊠ *Southwestern* | 23 | 24 | 24 | $56 |

San Antonio West | Hyatt Regency Hill Country Resort & Spa | 9800 Hyatt Resort Dr. (Rogers Rd.) | 210-520-4001 | www.hillcountry.hyatt.com
"Beautiful" rustic lodge environs – complete with antlers on the wall – and "outstanding" service draw locals and Sea World visitors to this Southwestern spot at the Hyatt Regency Hill Country Resort; some say the "waiters who do magic tricks" outshine its sometimes "disappointing" and "overpriced" "hotel food", but fans insist the fare is "consistently good."

Asia Kitchen ⊠ *Asian*   ▽ | 25 | 15 | 19 | $16 |

San Antonio West | 1739 SW Loop 410 (Marbach Rd.) | 210-673-0662 | www.asia-kitchen.com
An American military man and his Far Eastern wife run this "friendly" foodery in the far West offering some of "the best Asian" fare in town (i.e. "extremely spicy" Thai plus some Chinese dishes); budget-conscious types, such as "Air Force folks" from nearby bases, appreciate the "very reasonable" prices as well, though aesthetes argue the "homey-feeling" rooms "could use an overhaul."

Azúca Nuevo Latino *Nuevo Latino* | 24 | 22 | 18 | $29 |

Southtown | 713 S. Alamo St. (bet. Durango Blvd. & Presa St.) | 210-225-5550 | www.azuca.net
Southtown partyers who "want good food and music but don't want to spend big bucks" begin and end the night at this Nuevo Latino standout, enjoying "very exciting" specialties and "the best mojitos in town" amid "lovely" "art glass" pieces from the studio next door; the "hopping" bar heats up on weekends as salsa fans shake it to live acts "ranging from the bizarre to the sublime."

Bangkok Cuisine ⊠ *Thai* | - | - | - | I |

Northeast | 8214 Pat Booker Rd. (Village Oak Dr.) | 210-599-8884
Lunch lovers say it's "worth the trip" for a "tempting" Thai buffet at this affordable far Northeast "joint", also favored for its "awesome pad Thai" and seemingly bottomless "pot of tom yum" soup; an "always friendly" staff serves the goods, "and boy, can they spice it up!"

Barn Door, The *Steak* | 19 | 16 | 19 | $25 |

Alamo Heights | 8400 N. New Braunfels Ave. (bet. Crownhill Blvd. & Edgehill Dr.) | 210-824-0116 | www.sawhost.com/barndoor/
Carnivores call this half-century-old steakhouse in Alamo Heights an "SA institution" because it serves up mesquite-grilled chops from its own butcher shop and "great housemade desserts" with the help

of a "solid staff" that "never changes"; the same could be said of the "right-in-the-barn" decor, which fans fondly dub "down-home retro" but up-to-daters undercut as "old and tired."

Beto's Comida Latina *S American* | 21 | 11 | 15 | $13 |

North | 8142 Broadway St. (Flamingo Dr.) | 210-930-9393 | www.betoscomidalatina.com

Hungry hombres are "hooked" on the "delicious" fish tacos and "tasty" house-specialty empanadas at this "fun", quirky Northside South American, where informal, colorful decor and a breezy backyard patio generate a casual vibe; an underwhelmed minority maintains that the food is "decent" but "never makes the grade."

☑ Biga on the Banks *American* | 27 | 25 | 25 | $54 |

River Walk | 203 S. St. Mary's St. (Market St.) | 210-225-0722 | www.biga.com

"Big, bold and beautiful" from decor to dessert, chef-owner Bruce Auden's "consistently top-notch" "jewel" makes "inspiring" use of "local and regional ingredients" to create "original" "but not complicated" New American plates that please "the eye and palate"; with "exemplary" service and "urban modern" rooms overlooking a quiet stretch of the River Walk, it's a "premier" pick for business, romance or impressing "out-of-town guests" that's "unique in the state."

Big'z Burger Joint Ⓜ *Burgers* | 21 | 14 | 14 | $14 |

Loop 1604 | 2303 N. Loop 1604 W. (Huebner Rd.) | 210-408-2029

"Make it dirty for a dollar" by having your "juicy" half-pounder topped with a fried egg at this Loop 1604 yearling, where Le Rêve chef Andrew Weissman plies "tasty burgers with attitude" accompanied by handmade chips, "flavored" mayos and "first-class" shakes; the "family-oriented" setup sports a backyard where "kiddos can run around", but fussier sorts find the "red barn" digs "loud" and the service "slow."

Bin 555 Ⓩ *American* | 26 | 23 | 23 | $35 |

North Central | Shops at Artisans Alley | 555 W. Bitters Rd. (bet. Blanco Rd. & West Ave.) | 210-496-0555 | www.bin555.com

For an "adult evening", this North Central gem is "the chic place to be seen in SA" binging on a "diverse" seasonal assortment of New American "small plates" (courtesy of Lodge chef Jason Dady) and a "novel" wine list; equipped with an "inviting" deck and fire pit, it's a "relaxing" place to "go with a group" and "try different things" "without feeling like you have to roll out."

Bistro Thyme II *Continental* | - | - | - | M |
(fka Bistro Thyme)

Loop 1604 | 1321 N. Loop 1604 E., Ste. 105 (bet. Hwy. 281 & Stone Oak Pkwy.) | 210-495-0244

Inhabiting an artfully decorated strip-mall space in Loop 1604 is this business-lunch standby, where the updated menu reflects a modern approach to Continental cuisine; although the original chef-owner departed in 2008, his signature crab cakes remain on

the menu, sharing time with prime steaks, pastas and a well-priced lineup of wines.

☑ Bistro Vatel Ⓜ *French*　　　26 | 20 | 24 | $46

Olmos Park | 218 E. Olmos Dr. (McCullough Ave.) | 210-828-3141 | www.bistrovatel.com

Damien Watel brings "Paris to San Antonio" as he "performs his magic" at his "cut-above bistro" "tucked away" in Olmos Park, serving "divine" "French soul food" with "easygoing elegance"; with its "sophisticated wine list" and "top-notch" staff, it "reaches to higher planes" with "no hype, no fuss"; N.B. the chef's table offers access to an even more intimate *expérience*.

Boardwalk Bistro Ⓢ *Mediterranean*　　▽ 21 | 14 | 19 | $28

Near North | The Boardwalk | 4011 Broadway St. (Thorman Pl.) | 210-824-0100 | www.boardwalkbistro.net

Locals laud this "neighborhood bistro" on an eclectic stretch of Broadway for "surprisingly tasty" Mediterranean bites like paella and "unusual fresh soups"; those lulled by the waterfall and peaceful patio appreciate that the pace "is not rushed"; N.B. the dinner prix fixe features optional wine pairings from the well-stocked cellar.

Bohanan's Prime Steak &　　　23 | 22 | 21 | $55
Seafood *Seafood/Steak*

Downtown | 219 E. Houston St. (Navarro St.) | 210-472-2600 | www.bohanans.com

"Be ready to pay" for the "quality beef" at this "high-end" steakhouse/ seafooder, which "distinguishes itself" from the chains with "excellent service and an intriguing menu" presented in a "beautiful" Victorian venue overlooking Downtown's historic section; to heighten the "lovely dining experience", insiders request a window seat in early evenings to catch the sunset.

☑ Boudro's on the　　　24 | 20 | 21 | $38
Riverwalk *Seafood/Steak*

River Walk | 421 E. Commerce St. (Presa St.) | 210-224-8484 | www.boudros.com

"Great people-watching" on the River Walk makes it "worth the wait" for an outside table at this "casual" steak-and-seafood favorite, known for its "enjoyable" "amalgamation of Southwest border" fare including "must-have" "guacamole made tableside" and "prickly pear margaritas"; though its rep keeps the "tight" interior "crowded" and "loud", it's always a "best bet" "if you only have one night" in town.

NEW Brasserie Pavil *French*　　　- | - | - | M

Loop 1604 | Plaza Las Campanas | 1818 N. Loop 1604 W. (Huebner Rd.) | 210-479-5000 | www.brasseriepavil.com

This long-anticipated Loop 1604 arrival from chef Scott Cohen (ex Las Canarias) is charmingly Parisian in every detail, from the hand-painted tile floors and zinc bar to the butcher-paper topped tables laden with buttery pastries and savory French dishes like coq au vin; its crowd-pleasing brasserie menu comes with wallet-pleasing prices and all-around professional service.

	FOOD	DECOR	SERVICE	COST

Canyon Café   *Southwestern* — 18 | 20 | 18 | $22

Quarry | Alamo Quarry Mkt. | 255 E. Basse Rd. (bet. Hwy. 281 & Jones Maltsberger Rd.) | 210-821-3738 | www.canyoncafe.com
This Southwestern chain has "discovered the missing link" according to fans who connect with the "Santa Fe flair" of its Quarry Market outpost; the "creative menu" measures up "better than your average Tex-Mex", especially since "each meal is topped off" with a complimentary chocolate nut tamale ("mmmm").

Cappyccino's ☒ *American* — 20 | 20 | 20 | $20

Alamo Heights | 5003 Broadway St. (Mary D. Ave.) | 210-828-6860 | www.cappyccinos.com
"Comfort food of the yuppie sort" captures a "neighborhood" crowd at this Alamo Heights American bistro, which shares a patio with its bigger sib, Cappy's; the "cheerful service", "short menu" of standards "prepared with a gourmet touch" and "well-stocked bar" boasting "more single-malts than a man can drink" combine into a "great place to hang out."

☒ Cappy's Restaurant *American* — 23 | 20 | 22 | $29

Alamo Heights | 5011 Broadway St. (Mary D. Ave.) | 210-828-9669 | www.cappysrestaurant.com
"Imaginative creations and constant favorites" divide the wide-ranging repertoire at this rustic patch of "America, my America" in "tony" Alamo Heights, an "institution that remains fresh" for its local loyalists; capped with "unexpected pleasures" like "on-time" service and "reliably special lunch specials", it's a "quintessential" spot "to see and be seen" "in the 'hood."

Carrabba's Italian Grill *Italian* — 22 | 19 | 22 | $28

Northwest | 12507 I-10 W. (De Zavala Rd.) | 210-694-4191 | www.carrabbas.com
See review in Houston Directory.

Cascabel Mexican Patio ☒ *Mexican* — - | - | - | I

Southtown | 1000 S. St. Mary's St. (Alamo St.) | 210-212-6456
Colorful and *muy* "authentic", this indoor-outdoor "tortilla kitchen" in Southtown plies bargain bites that offer "a true expression" of interior Mexican "home cooking" (like the cup of savory chicken soup preceding every order); even amigos acknowledge "the service is slow, but maybe we need to slow down."

NEW Chama Gaucha *Brazilian* — - | - | - | E

Loop 1604 | Sonterra Place | 18318 Sonterra Pl. (Loop 1604) | 210-564-9400 | www.chamagaucha.com
Even die-hard carnivores might feel overwhelmed by the 14 choices of skewered beef, lamb, pork and chicken arriving nonstop to their plates at this refined Brazilian steakhouse near Loop 1604; the deftly cut meats are brought to the table by gaucho-garbed servers while diners counter with their own walks around the Pampas-sized salad bar, a welcome respite from the bonanza of beef; N.B. lunch offers the same menu at almost half the price.

Chart House *Seafood*

–	–	–	M

Downtown | Tower of the Americas | 600 Hemisfair Plaza Way (bet. Durango Blvd. & Market St.) | 210-223-3101 | www.chart-house.com
This link of the nautically themed seafood chain is docked atop Downtown's iconic Tower of the Americas, offering rotating views of the cityscape from 750-feet up in the air; the moderately priced surf 'n' turf selections sate many an out-of-towner's appetite, though some may prefer to soak in the setting with a cocktail at the attached Bar 601.

Cheesecake Factory *American*

20	20	18	$26

Loop 410 | North Star Mall | 7400 San Pedro Ave. (Loop 410) | 210-798-2222 | www.thecheesecakefactory.com
See review in Houston Directory.

Cheesy Jane's *Burgers*

19	16	18	$11

Alamo Heights | 4200 Broadway St. (Groveland Pl.) | 210-826-0800
Northwest | HEB Ctr. | 11650 Bandera Rd. (Quincy Lee Dr.) | 210-767-9090
www.cheesyjanes.com
"Retro" types turn to this "burger joint" duo for "char-broiled" beef "any way you want it", "tater tots to die for" and creamy shakes; the "'50s diner decor" and "kid-friendly" atmo add a side of "funky fun", though a few skeptics sniff "cheesy is right."

Chesters Hamburger Company *Burgers*

22	13	16	$11

Loop 410 | 1006 NE Loop 410 (New Braunfels Ave.) | 210-805-8600
North | 16609 San Pedro Ave. (Thousand Oaks) | 210-494-3333
Northwest | 9980 I-10 W. (Wurzbach Rd.) | 210-669-1222
"Come hungry" for "burgers so big you can't get your mouth around 'em" at this "rustic" mini-chain, where the "juicy" patties are washed down with an "impressive" array of "beer from all over the world"; sure, you're obliged to "belly up to the counter" to order, but for a "consistent" chowdown "this place rocks."

Chris Madrid's Nachos & Burgers ⊠ *Burgers*

25	13	17	$12

Near North | 1900 Blanco Rd. (Hollywood Ave.) | 210-735-3552 | www.chrismadrids.com
Chris Madrid himself still oversees this Near Northside 1977-vintage beef-and-beer barn, an "institution" for "sublime", "delectably greasy" burgers sized "enormous" enough to "guarantee nobody leaves the property hungry"; with "picnic tables" inside and out, the "laid-back", "self-serve" setup is "the perfect environment", though regulars note "you'll have to take a nap" afterward.

Chuy's *Tex-Mex*

21	19	19	$18

North | 18008 San Pedro Ave. (Loop 1604) | 210-545-0300 | www.chuys.com
See review in Austin and the Hill Country Directory.

Ciao Lavanderia ⊠ *Italian*

23	18	20	$26

Olmos Park | 226 E. Olmos Dr. (El Prado Dr.) | 210-822-3990

(continued)

Ciao2 Ⓜ *Italian*

NEW **Stone Oak** | 20626 Stone Oak Pkwy. (Hwy. 281 N.) | 210-481-7031
www.bistrovatel.com

Sited in a "quirky" "former Laundromat", Damien Watel's "charm-ing" Olmos Park Italian appeals to ciao hounds with a "yummy" (if "limited") lineup of "fresh homemade pasta" and pizzas; the "value and unpretentious service" make it "great for date night" or "a quick bite" at lunch; N.B. the Stone Oak offshoot offers the same menu and casual atmosphere, and both are nestled alongside French sibs Bistro Vatel and Ciel.

NEW **Ciel** Ⓜ *French*　　　　　　　　－ ｜ － ｜ － ｜ E

Stone Oak | 20626 Stone Oak Pkwy. (Hwy. 281 N.) | 210-481-7001 |
www.bistrovatel.com

A bright, open space filled with modern art creates an upbeat mood at this Stone Oak newcomer from Damien Watel, who created a chic, European-style enclave as a counterpoint to the surrounding suburban sprawl; expect French fare like foie gras and Dover sole and appro-priately upper-end service and pricing; N.B. the restaurant shares a banquet room and outdoor space with its Italian sister, Ciao2.

Citrus *American*　　　　　　　　25 ｜ 24 ｜ 21 ｜ $46

Downtown | Hotel Valencia | 150 E. Houston St. (Soledad St.) |
210-230-8412 | www.hotelvalencia.com

There's "no need to leave the hotel" for "inventive" eating thanks to this Downtown showcase for "culinary genius" Jeffrey Balfour's "top-notch" seasonal American fare, matched with "excellent ser-vice" and the "classiest" of contemporary settings; with "romantic" vibes and a River Walk view, it's suitable for "a special occasion" or when "the boss is buying."

Clear Springs Café *Seafood*　　　　19 ｜ 17 ｜ 18 ｜ $15

Stone Oak | 606 W. Afton Oaks Blvd. (N. Loop 1604) | 210-403-3474 |
www.clearspringscafe.com

Country cooking reigns supreme at this "reliable" Stone Oak link of a statewide chain of seafood specialists, "well-known" for "Texas-sized servings" of "simple" dishes like catfish, Baja shrimp and "gotta-get" onion rings; the "outdoorsy decor" is "so tacky it's great", and the child-friendly quarters spring to life on weekends.

NEW **Coco Chocolate**　　　　　　　－ ｜ － ｜ － ｜ M
Lounge & Bistro ◑ *Dessert/French*

North Central | 18402 Hwy. 281 N. (Loop 1604) | 210-491-4480 |
www.sa-coco.com

Sweet-toothed diners are drawn to this decadent French newcomer in far North Central San Antonio where the namesake ingredient is dusted unexpectedly in appetizers, salads and mains (like rack of lamb with white chocolate chutney) and the decadent dessert menu yields a bounty of mousses, molten cakes and fondue; it's also be-come a popular stop for champagne and specialty martinis imbibed amid the red-velvet-draped Moulin Rouge–style surroundings.

SAN ANTONIO

	FOOD	DECOR	SERVICE	COST

County Line, The *BBQ*
20 | 18 | 19 | $23

River Walk | 111 W. Crockett St. (Presa St.) | 210-229-1941
Northwest | 10101 I-10 W. (Wurzbach Rd.) | 210-641-1998
www.countyline.com

BBQ buffs line up behind this regional chain and its "massive", "messy" portions of "decent" 'cue, served in "corny" rough-hewn digs that are "vigorously kid-friendly" and "perfect for out-of-town guests"; the River Walk location is "touristy" and features toe-tapping live music on weekends, while the Northwest outpost lures locals with "family-style" feasts.

Cove, The ⊠ *American*
▽ 20 | 15 | 18 | $15

Downtown | 606 W. Cypress St. (San Pedro Ave.) | 210-227-2683 | www.thecove.us

Nearby colleges and re-gentrified nabes create a niche clientele for this "quirky" Downtown fusion of a "friendly bar/restaurant" with a "carwash, Laundromat and playground"; most covet the eclectic American eats (including "terrific" "grilled fish tacos") chased with a "fantastic beer selection", though "the young and hip" may give them second billing to "some of the best live music in town."

Crumpets Restaurant & Bakery *French*
15 | 20 | 17 | $28

Northeast | 3920 Harry Wurzbach Rd. (Oakwell Ct.) | 210-821-5454 | www.crumpetsa.com

The "peaceful, wooded setting along Salado Creek" in Northeast San Antonio provides a "beautiful" backdrop for this "quaint" "indoor-outdoor" eatery/bakery and chef-owner Francois Maeder's "varied" array of "honest" French fare; longtime supporters salute a menu that "can still surprise", though a minority of grumps grumbles "inconsistent."

Da Vinci Gelato & Caffé *Italian*
24 | 19 | 20 | $12

Stone Oak | Stone Oak Plaza II | 18720 Stone Oak Pkwy. (N. Loop 1604) | 210-545-6686 | www.davincigelati.com

Gelati "like you'd find in Italy" draw dessert lovers to this compact strip-center cafe in Stone Oak for a taste of "authentic" ices that rank with "the best in Florence", not to mention "excellent" panini and crêpes that make it San Antonio's Best Bang for the Buck; with unusual flavors like white chocolate, guiltless fat-free/sugar-free options and the creative combo of espresso over gelato, it's a renais-sance for sweet tooths.

Demo's Greek Food *Greek*
19 | 12 | 14 | $14

Loop 1604 | Vineyard Ctr. | 1205 N. Loop 1604 W. (Blanco Rd.) | 210-798-3840
Near North | 2501 N. St. Mary's St. (Ashby Ave.) | 210-732-7777
North | 7115 Blanco Rd. (Lockhill-Selma Rd.) | 210-342-2772
www.demosgreekfood.com

"You'll want to break a plate" to celebrate the "hearty portions" and "reasonable cost" at this longstanding Northside Greek and its two newer spin-offs, demonstrating for nearly 30 years that Hellenic

eating is "more than gyros"; weekly belly dancing jiggles some sparkle into the no-frills, "no-table-service" setups.

Dough ⊠Ⓜ *Pizza* | - | - | - | I |

North Central | Blanco Junction Shopping Ctr. | 6989 Blanco Rd. (Loop 410) | 210-979-6565 | www.doughpizzeria.com

Pizza lovers flip over this hip trattoria that fashions its pies from hand-thrown dough and fresh toppings all baked together in an authentic wood-burning volcanic stone oven; featuring salads, handmade mozzarella, imported meats and a small but thoughtful wine list, it feels like a slice of Italy, even though you're actually in a North Central shopping center.

El Jarro de Arturo *Mexican* | 22 | 18 | 22 | $21 |

North | 13421 San Pedro Ave. (Bitters Rd.) | 210-494-5084 | www.eljarro.com

Whether for "basic Tex-Mex" or "something more exotic", this Northside pop-spot proffers an "excellent" Mexican selection matched with "professional" service and "upscale family" environs; other attractions include the relaxing patio, live music on Friday and Saturday nights and Sunday brunch ("a must"), though some "followers come for the margaritas alone."

El Mirador *Mexican* | 23 | 17 | 19 | $19 |

Southtown | 722 S. St. Mary's St. (Durango Blvd.) | 210-225-9444 | www.elmiradorsatx.com

The "Saturday homemade soup" specials pack 'em in to Southtown's Mexican crown jewel, which "shines" with "wonderful" "comfort" cuisine that keeps it "full of regulars" (including "local politicos at lunch"); insiders say dinner is "a SA secret" featuring "down-home Tex-Mex done well" alongside "hard-to-find" specialties that justify 40 years of loyalty.

Ernesto's Mexican | 18 | 11 | 21 | $29 |
Specialties & Seafood ⊠ *Mexican/Seafood*

North Central | 2559 Jackson-Keller Rd. (Vance Jackson Rd.) | 210-344-1248

"Not your standard beans-and-tacos" joint, this Mexican seafooder tucked into a North Central strip center specializes in "fresh fish and sauces" that strike some "more as French"; with owner Ernesto overseeing every detail and checking in at each table, the service inspires fealty even if the "bare-bones decor could use some updating."

Fig Tree Restaurant, The *Continental* | 25 | 22 | 23 | $55 |

River Walk | 515 Villita St. (Presa St.) | 210-224-1976 | www.figtreerestaurant.com

"Romantic" sorts gush over the "quaint" ambiance of this "intimate" "gem" overlooking the River Walk, a 19th-century residence in historic La Villita reconfigured for "creative" (if "not very diverse") Continental dining with "superb service"; though it's somewhat "pretentious" and "near tourist" turf, it remains "perfect for that special night out."

	FOOD	DECOR	SERVICE	COST

Fleming's Prime Steakhouse & Wine Bar *Steak*

24 | 24 | 23 | $54

Quarry | Alamo Quarry Mkt. | 255 E. Basse Rd. (bet. Hwy. 281 & Jones Maltsberger Rd.) | 210-824-9463 | www.flemingssteakhouse.com
See review in Houston Directory.

Formosa Garden *Chinese*

21 | 18 | 21 | $17

North Central | 1011 NE Loop 410 (New Braunfels Ave.) | 210-828-9988 | www.formosagarden.com
Thanks to "can't miss" Sino "standards" (plus "decent sushi") and "quick" service, this "modern" Mencius Group Chinese on Loop 410 is "one of the nicer Asians in town"; its North Central location is "convenient for business meals" too, so what with the sizable list of midday specials, it's no surprise this place is "very crowded at lunchtime."

☒ Francesca's at Sunset ☒Ⓜ *Southwestern*

26 | 27 | 26 | $56

La Cantera | Westin La Cantera Resort | 16441 La Cantera Pkwy. (Fiesta Texas Dr.) | 210-558-2442 | www.westinlacantera.com
A "wowza" view of "beautiful sunsets" (and hence the No. 1 Decor rating in San Antonio) would be reason enough for romantics to coo, but it's the "imaginative", "subtly spiced" Southwestern fare that receives "lots of oohs and ahhs" at this "pricey" venue in a La Cantera resort; add "impeccable" service to the "epicurean delight" and natives and visitors alike agree "this place has it all."

☒ Frederick's ☒ *Asian Fusion/French*

26 | 18 | 26 | $47

Alamo Heights | 7701 Broadway St. (Nottingham Pl.) | 210-828-9050 | www.frederickssa.com
NEW Frederick's Bistro *Asian Fusion/French*
North Central | 14439 NW Military Hwy. (Huebner Rd.) | 210-888-1500 | www.fredericksbistro.net
"Well-heeled" types craving a "slight edge of adventure" are in for a "delicious" Asian-French experience at this Alamo Heights hit, where an ex-L'Etoile chef who "knows his business" creates dishes that "open up inventive avenues"; regulars advise "don't let the strip-mall location fool you", the staff "does hospitality right"; N.B. the North Central outpost is new.

Fujiya Japanese Garden *Japanese*

▽ 19 | 19 | 17 | $23

Medical Center | 9030 Wurzbach Rd. (bet. Fredericksburg Rd. & NW Expwy.) | 210-734-3551 | www.fujiyasanantonio.com
"Sushi rules!" at this Japanese in the Medical Center area, whose authentic touches include tatami rooms with cushioned floor seating and a separate bar for livelier times; with its heavy wood doors and trickling stream, the "attractive setting" adds to the warm welcome.

☒ Godai Sushi Bar & Restaurant ☒ *Japanese*

27 | 16 | 20 | $26

North Central | 11203 West Ave. (Blanco Rd.) | 210-348-6781 | www.godaisushi.com
If "inventive", "full-flavored" sushi makes you "want to jump up and slap somebody", this busy Northside Japanese is a godsend thanks

	FOOD	DECOR	SERVICE	COST

to a chef-owner "charmer" who "knows raw fish" and "entertains all night"; many maintain the "large array" of "exotic" rolls is "unquestionably the best" in town, if not "in South Texas, period."

Golden Wok *Chinese*   22 | 19 | 19 | $17

Medical Center | 8822 Wurzbach Rd. (bet. Fredericksburg Rd. & NW Expwy) | 210-615-8282
San Antonio West | 8230 Marbach Rd. (SW Loop 410) | 210-673-2577
www.golden-wok.com

These Sino sibs in Austin and San Antonio serve "authentic" meals ordered from a "large and varied" menu and delivered by servers who are "friendly", if sometimes "a little slow"; conditions can be "crowded", but insiders insist it's "worth the wait", especially for dim sum on Saturdays and Sundays.

Green Vegetarian Cuisine *Vegetarian*   ▽ 18 | 18 | 18 | $14

Downtown | 1017 N. Flores St. (Euclid Ave.) | 210-320-5865 | www.greensanantonio.com

"Finally!" cry crunchy types who consider this "funky" Downtowner the city's "only true vegetarian option" and "a blessing" for its "cheerful" "bistro style" and "yummy" lineup of "basic" "healthy choices" "reminiscent of the '60s–'70s"; but though it's an "inviting oasis", critics cavil about "too much emphasis" on "faux meat."

Grey Moss Inn *American*   24 | 24 | 21 | $45

Helotes | 19010 Scenic Loop Rd. (bet. Babcock & Bandera Rds.) | 210-695-8301 | www.grey-moss-inn.com

"It's a long drive" to Helotes, but "awesome everything" awaits at this "classic" "country steakhouse", where generations continue to trek for a "fantastic" American menu showcasing beef from the "open mesquite grill" and "one of the best wine lists in town"; the "cozy", "Texas eclectic" interior and "romantic" patio are made for "those special occasions."

Grill at Leon Springs *Eclectic*   22 | 22 | 19 | $30

Leon Springs | 24116 I-10 W. (Boerne Stage Rd.) | 210-698-8797 | www.leonspringsgrill.com

This "upscale-casual" Leon Springs eatery from the L'Etoile team offers "interesting", seasonal Eclectic fare that's "delicious and priced well", plus daily specials designed for those out to "try something new"; the Dominion-proximate locale makes it "good for spotting local celebs", even if "service is a little spotty" too.

Guenther House *American*   23 | 22 | 19 | $17

Southtown | 205 E. Guenther St. (Alamo St.) | 210-227-1061 | www.guentherhouse.com

"Carb watchers beware" of the "best breakfast experience" around as the "delectable" "flour-based" "classics" tempt at this "absolutely charming" Southtown American cafe; set in the "lovely historic" home of the Pioneer Flour Mills' founders, its "kitschy museum" and gift shop help "while away the time" during the "forever-long wait" on weekends; N.B. breakfast and lunch only.

	FOOD	DECOR	SERVICE	COST

Houston Street Bistro ☒ *Continental* | 22 | 20 | 23 | $31 |

Downtown | 204 E. Houston St. (St. Mary's St.) | 210-476-8600

A "solid" spot for Downtown business lunch by day, by night this Continental bistro just steps from the Majestic Theater becomes a "convenient" "pre-symphony" lead-in and sets the stage for "after-show cocktails and dessert" "in sophisticated comfort"; admirers applaud the "flavorful" menu, though the service is the star "bravo!"

Hsiu Yu Chinese Restaurant *Chinese* | ▽ 16 | 11 | 16 | $17 |

North | 8338 Broadway St. (Citadell Pl.) | 210-828-2273

Northsiders head to this longtime Sino "oasis" for "great lunch specials" and other "quick", "inexpensive" Chinese served in a friendly neighborhood setting; maybe the atmosphere's "nothing to write home about", but "in a city known for Tex-Mex", supporters shrug "hsiu me, it's good."

Ilsong Garden ☒ *Korean* | ▽ 25 | 19 | 25 | $26 |

North Central | 6905 Blanco Rd. (Loop 410) | 210-366-4508 | www.onewebring.com

Partisans sing the praises of the "intriguing" possibilities at this convenient Northside niche, where "amazing" Korean specialties (including "excellent" barbecue) share the spotlight with "absolutely fabulous" sushi; the "prompt", "lovely service" and "soothing" surroundings add to its "elegant" appeal.

India Oven *Indian* | ▽ 24 | 16 | 18 | $16 |

North Central | 1031 Patricia Dr. (West Ave.) | 210-366-1033 | www.indiaoven.com

"Reliable" and "authentic", this Northside Indian staple heats up at lunchtime owing to a popular buffet whose "quality", "good price" and "vast" array "more than make up for" any shortcomings in decor; dinner is a quieter, candlelit affair that shimmies to life with belly dancing the first Friday of every month.

India Palace *Indian* | 24 | 10 | 17 | $15 |

Medical Center | 8474 Fredericksburg Rd. (Wurzbach Rd.) | 210-692-5262
North Central | 15909 San Pedro Ave. (Paseo Del Norte St.) | 210-403-3688
www.indiapalacesa.com

"Dazzling" lunch-and-dinner buffets that provide "spicy" "variety" at "low prices" qualify this Medical Center–area and Northside duo as hot spots for "outstanding" Indian eats; loyalists label them "a breath of fresh air" despite the rooms' "definitely lacking" looks.

Iron Cactus *Tex-Mex* | 18 | 19 | 18 | $25 |

River Walk | 200 Riverwalk (bet. Commerce & St. Mary's Sts.) | 210-224-9835 | www.ironcactus.com

See review in Austin and the Hill Country Directory.

Josephine St. Cafe ☒ *American* | 20 | 18 | 19 | $19 |

Near North | 400 E. Josephine St. (Ave. A) | 210-224-6169 | www.josephinestcafe.com

"If you haven't been, you're cheating yourself" out of a "real down-home" time at this "funky little" "neighborhood joint" in the Near

North, where the American grub's highlight is "signature steaks and whiskey" at a "reasonable price"; the "diverse menu" means "you can also eat healthy", but its "no-nonsense" style spurs most to "stick with the basics."

Kim Wah Chinese BBQ *Chinese*

_ | _ | _ | I

Northwest | 7080 Bandera Rd. (Huebner Rd.) | 210-520-2200

"Ask for the authentic Chinese menu" or check the handwritten "specials" board at this Northwest real-deal "favorite", where admiwahs "enjoy the adventure into" homestyle dishes like squid, duck feet and sea cucumber; but given the sparse strip-center space, they "go for the food, not the decor."

Koi Kawa Japanese Restaurant & Sushi Bar ⑤ *Japanese*

▽ 26 | 22 | 22 | $23

Near North | 4051 Broadway St. (off Hildebrand Ave.) | 210-805-8111

The "consistently excellent" food makes it safe to "take the Japanese in-laws" to this gem in the Near North, a confirmed "favorite" in the eyes of sushiphiles; besides boosting the "authentic" feel, its quiet setting with a "perfect view of the unspoiled San Antonio River" is "quite a treat."

Kona Grill *American*

20 | 21 | 18 | $27

La Cantera | Shops at La Cantera | 15900 La Cantera Pkwy. (Loop 1604 W.) | 210-877-5355 | www.konagrill.com

See review in Houston Directory.

Korean B.B.Q. House ⑤ *Korean* (aka Go Hyang Jib)

23 | 15 | 18 | $19

San Antonio East | 4400 Rittiman Rd. (Melton Dr.) | 210-822-8846

"Excellent grilled meat" leads the "variety of traditional Korean dishes" that lure seekers far East (fittingly) to this "little" "hole-in-the-wall"; cognoscenti say "ask for scissors" to cut the 'cue "bite-sized."

La Focaccia Italian Grill *Italian*

16 | 13 | 16 | $23

Southtown | 800 S. Alamo St. (Presa St.) | 210-223-5353 | www.lafocaccia-italian-grill.com

"Ask for Luigi, the Roman owner – he'll take care of you" advise regular patrons of this Southtown eatery housed in a onetime service station (remodeled, of course, though still "nothing fancy"); as for the food, it's a split decision: fans find it "consistently good" and "relatively innovative", while foes charge the "uninspired" eats "need work."

La Fogata *Mexican*

_ | _ | _ | M

North | 2427 Vance Jackson Rd. (bet. Addax & Nassau Drs.) | 210-340-1337 | www.lafogata.com

For 30 years loyalists have been heading North to this iconoclastic eatery offering riffs on interior Mexican dishes served up on a sprawling patio warmed by a fire pit and enlivened by mariachi bands; it also features an assortment of potent margaritas imbibed in volume thanks to bottomless bowls of crisp chips and slow, but sincere, service.

	FOOD	DECOR	SERVICE	COST

La Fonda on Main *Mexican*

| - | - | - | I |

Near North | 2415 N. Main Ave. (Woodlawn Ave.) | 210-733-0621 | www.lafondaonmain.com

Situated in a white-adobe converted home with a spacious tree-lined patio, local restaurateur Cappy Lawton's Near Northside centerpiece is frequented by loyal regulars who exhibit a fondness for truly authentic Tex-Mex and interior-Mexico cooking; the circa-1932 digs bolster its claim to being the oldest Mexican eatery in town.

La Frite ⓈⓂ *Belgian*

| 26 | 19 | 21 | $30 |

Southtown | 728 S. Alamo St. (Presa St.) | 210-224-7555

"The best mussels" "since dining in Brussels" and "don't-miss" frites headline the "first-rate" bill of fare at this "real" Belgian bistro in Southtown, which serves as "Bistro Vatel South" for owner Damien Watel; there's "little elbow room", but the "laid-back" "European flair" makes it a "hip" "place to hang out with the locals" ("you feel cooler just being there").

La Hacienda de Los Barrios *Tex-Mex*

| 21 | 19 | 19 | $18 |

North | 18747 Redland Rd. (Gold Canyon Rd.) | 210-497-8000 | www.lhdlb.com

Los Barrios *Tex-Mex*

North | 4223 Blanco Rd. (Basse Rd.) | 210-732-6017

Satisfied surveyors swear by this family-owned Tex-Mex "institution" – the "flagship" Blanco Road location's "outstanding" fajitas "continue to amaze", while the north-of-1604 offshoot draws diners in with a "beautiful patio" and what may be SA's "best margarita menu"; owing to the resulting "crowds", though, it could prove "too noisy to hear your dinner companions."

La Margarita Mexican Restaurant & Oyster Bar *Tex-Mex*

| 21 | 19 | 19 | $20 |

Market Square | Market Sq. | 120 Produce Row (Santa Rosa St.) | 210-227-7140 | www.lamargarita.com

A "must-visit for tourists" and locals alike, this Market Square "staple" owned by the Cortez family (Mi Tierra, Pico de Gallo) dishes out "plentiful portions" of "real SA Tex-Mex" and "potent" eponymous cocktails; staffers who "treat you well" and roving mariachis help foster a "fun, festive atmosphere", though sedater sorts bothered by "rowdy and loud" indoor goings-on may prefer sitting on the patio.

La Marginal *Caribbean/Puerto Rican*

| - | - | - | I |

North Central | 2447 Nacogdoches Rd. (NE Loop 410) | 210-804-2242 | www.lamarginal.com

San Juan's expats flock to this North Central canteen for "big" portions of "authentic" "homestyle Puerto Rican" (like plantains and "great Cuban sandwiches") "at great prices"; the lunch buffet's "tremendous value" means "traffic is crazy" come noon, and once the "live music" and dancing are underway, weekend "nights are wild."

SAN Seafood House
iverwalk *Seafood*
alk | 517 N. Presa St. (College St.) | 210-229-1010 |
ndrysseafoodhouse.com

| 19 | 18 | 18 | $40 |

ple-watching is your thing" "get a table by the water" at this
iver Walk pescatorium, a chain link that loyalists like for a "special
night out"; the fin fare is "reliable" if "nothing special" and staffers are
"friendly", but naysayers warn you're "charged too much for too little."

La Scala *European*

| 23 | 23 | 23 | $32 |

Castle Hills | 2177 NW Military Hwy. (West Ave.) | 210-366-1515 |
www.lascala.us

The "consistent quality" is "always a pleasure" at this "popular local"
fixture nestled among shops and salons in a Castle Hills strip center,
where the "wonderful" menu's "Euro-Italian tendencies" promise
"something for every taste"; its "elegant" "pink-tablecloth" surroundings and "top-notch" service are still "special" to longtime regulars.

Las Canarias *French/Mediterranean*

| 26 | 23 | 24 | $51 |

River Walk | Omni La Mansión del Rio Hotel | 112 College St.
(bet. Navarro & St. Mary's Sts.) | 210-518-1063 | www.lamansion.com

This "destination" restaurant lives up to "the charm and legend" of
its "classy" River Walk hotel home, merging seasonal French-Med
accents and an "inventive use of Texas ingredients" into "refined and
delicious" plates; the follow-through includes a "lovely, relaxing"
setting, an "outstanding" "European stagiere" staff that's "attentive
without being overbearing" and the "wow" of a Sunday brunch
flaunting a "vast" spread that's "a must" for visitors and locals alike.

Las Ramblas *Spanish*

| ∇ 21 | 23 | 21 | $34 |

River Walk | Hotel Contessa | 306 W. Market St. (Navarro St.) |
210-298-8040 | www.thehotelcontessa.com

There's a "refreshing" "selection of tapas" on a hidden bend of the
River Walk at this "personable" Spaniard in the Hotel Contessa,
where "generous" servings of asado meats meet traditional faves
like paella Valenciana; ramblers can stake out "pleasant" waterside
seating or settle inside within earshot of the salsa music.

La Tuna Grill 🗷 *Eclectic*

| ∇ 22 | 22 | 20 | $13 |

Southtown | 100 Probandt St. (Cevallos St.) | 210-212-5727 |
www.latunagrill.com

"All types, from bankers to bikers" assemble at this Southtown
standby across the yard from the like-named bar, a "true melting
pot" noted for chef Mark Dortman's "surprisingly" "solid" Eclectic
eats, featuring inventive sandwiches and fish tacos; the art-filled interior is right in tune with the "interesting" clientele.

🗷 Le Rêve 🗷🗹 *French*

| 29 | 25 | 27 | $110 |

Downtown | Historic Exchange Bldg. | 152 E. Pecan St. (St. Mary's St.) |
210-212-2221 | www.restaurantlereve.com

"A three- to four-hour culinary adventure" awaits at this rêvered
Downtown "jewel" (voted San Antonio's No. 1 for Popularity, Food

and Service), a showcase for "stellar" chef Andrew Weissman "peccable technique" via a seasonal New French prix fixe menu "dazzles" diners and "deserves all accolades"; the "exceptiona staff and "intimate", understated room round out "the ultimate in decadence" and fully justify the ultra-"pricey" tabs; N.B. jackets and reservations well in advance are a must.

Ⓩ L'Etoile *French/Seafood* 26 | 20 | 23 | $45
Alamo Heights | 6106 Broadway St. (Albany St.) | 210-826-4551 | www.letoilesa.com
French cuisine "positioned between bistro and haute" leaves "multi-generational" Alamo Heights dwellers "impressed" at this venerable star among "classy places", a haven of "attentive Gallic service" set in an "elegant" "old house" reminiscent of "a bit of Paris (France, not East Texas)"; regulars single out the "always first-rate" seafood and the value-laden early-bird prix fixe.

Ⓩ Liberty Bar *Eclectic* 24 | 22 | 22 | $25
Near North | 328 E. Josephine St. (Ave. A) | 210-227-1187 | www.liberty-bar.com
You may "feel three sheets to the wind before your first drink" given the "trippy tilted floor" at this "popular" Near Northside hangout, where the "funky" circa-1890 structure is part of the "unique" "charm"; "it just gets better" with "unusual and delicious" Eclectic fare served with "no pretense" at a "reasonable price", ensuring that "visitors always ask to go back."

Little Red Barn *Steak* 17 | 18 | 20 | $18
San Antonio South | 1836 S. Hackberry St. (Rigsby Ave.) | 210-532-4235
At this Southside steakhouse, an "oldie but goodie" (since 1963), "cowboys and cowgirls" "amusingly" tricked out with prop-room six-shooters aim to provide "fast and friendly" service, fetching salads that arrive at the table when you do and "decent, cheap" beef; over-all, the "down-home" "Western atmosphere" (including the menu painted on the wall) makes this place "fun for family dining" if you can swallow the "kinda corny" "faux-Texas" folderol.

Little Rhein Steak House *Steak* 24 | 21 | 23 | $52
River Walk | 231 S. Alamo St. (Market St.) | 210-225-2111 | www.littlerheinsteakhouse.com
Meat eaters who tire of "big, boisterous steakhouses" head 'em out to this "quaint" "old-time" option on the River Walk, where the prime cuts are "perfectly cooked and served" in an "attractively his-toric" setting; just beware of "tourists" who "overwhelm" the ter-race, and "don't look at the bill."

Ⓩ Lodge Restaurant of Castle Hills, The Ⓩ *American* 26 | 26 | 24 | $60
Castle Hills | 1746 Lockhill Selma Rd. (West Ave.) | 210-349-8466 | www.thelodgerestaurant.com
"What a lovely setting" sigh sightseers at this "converted mansion" on tree-studded acreage in Castle Hills, "an excellent escape" en-

| | FOOD | DECOR | SERVICE | COST |

hanced by chef-owner Jason Dady's "extraordinary" New American "palate pleasers", which many rank "right up there with the best" in town; "always-on" service sways diners to go "slowly through each course" whether the occasion is a "classy" lunch with clients or an "intimate dinner."

NEW Luca Ristorante Enoteca *Italian*

| - | - | - | M |

Downtown | Fairmount San Antonio | 401 S. Alamo St. (E. Nueva St.) | 210-888-7030 | www.lucaenoteca.com

Occupying the ground-level storefront in Downtown's historic Fairmount hotel, this contemporary Italian from Dan Ward (Piatti) showcases small plates and pizzas alongside heartier entrees cooked in a wood-burning oven; its casual setup includes a busy bar area featuring handcrafted cocktails and more than 20 wines by the glass, while the dining room is more subdued, with a chic yet comfortable atmosphere enhanced by warm wood tables and candlelight.

Luce Ristorante e Enoteca Ⓢ *Italian*

| ▽ 20 | 23 | 20 | $49 |

Northwest | The Strand | 11255 Huebner Rd. (McDermott Frwy.) | 210-561-9700 | www.lucesanantonio.com

"Beautifully appointed" contemporary digs set the scene for "Italian done superbly" at this corner storefront (formerly Luciano at the Strand) in a Northwest shopping center; aficionados appreciate the "wonderful entree variety" and service from a "professional" team – just make "a trip to the bank first."

Madhatters Tea *Tearoom*

| 20 | 20 | 17 | $16 |

Southtown | 320 Beauregard (Alamo St.) | 210-212-4832

Madhatters Cafe Express Ⓢ *Tearoom*

NEW Downtown | 106 Auditorium Circle (4th St.) | 210-227-4832
www.madhatterstea.com

"Save room" for the "deadly desserts" at this "cute" Southtown tearoom, a counter-service spot also known for its "inventive sandwiches" and some 50 varieties of herbal brews; though a few sniff it "tries too hard to be trendy", most are smitten by this "laid-back" wonderland and say it "fits the neighborhood to a tea"; N.B. the new Express branch features a scaled-back menu and weekday hours only.

Madras Pavilion *Indian*

| 22 | 11 | 14 | $17 |

Northwest | Grandview Shopping Ctr. | 8085 Callaghan Rd. (Pinebrook Dr.) | 210-375-7766 | www.madraspavilion.us
See review in Houston Directory.

NEW Maggiano's Little Italy *Italian*

| 20 | 20 | 20 | $30 |

La Cantera | The Rim | 17603 I-10 W. (La Cantera Pkwy.) | 210-451-6000 | www.maggianos.com
See review in Dallas/Ft. Worth Directory.

Z Magnolia Pancake Haus *American*

| 27 | 17 | 22 | $13 |

North Central | 606 Embassy Oaks (West Ave.) | 210-496-0828 | www.magnoliapancakehaus.com

"If you're a breakfast person, this is your place" for all-American feasts of "divine" waffles, "pure magic" pancakes and "spectacular"

omelets generous "enough for two (with leftovers)"; its roomy North Central site sees stack-ups and "long waits" on weekends, but "no one complains because they know what's in store"; N.B. closes at 2 PM daily.

Mama's Café *American*

| 19 | 14 | 18 | $14 |

Downtown | 100 N. Main Ave. (Commerce St.) | 210-354-2233 ◐ ⊠
Universal City | 7929 Pat Booker Rd. (Live Oak Crossing) | 210-653-2002
North | 14424 San Pedro Ave. (Bitters Rd.) | 210-490-1933
Northeast | 2442 Nacogdoches Rd. (NE Loop 410) | 210-826-8303
www.mamascafe.net

"Always a safe bet" from early morning till late night, these nostalgic cafes please patrons with their Traditional American eats, including "terrific" breakfasts and "night-owl comfort food"; thanks to a "fun" staff and "reasonable" prices, they're "kid-friendly", if "not much to look at" – "a typical greasy spoon."

Melting Pot *Fondue*

| 21 | 20 | 21 | $43 |

North Central | 14855 Blanco Rd. (Bitters Rd.) | 210-479-6358 |
www.meltingpot.com

See review in Austin and the Hill Country Directory.

Mencius Gourmet Hunan *Chinese*

| 21 | 17 | 18 | $17 |

Medical Center | 7959 Fredericksburg Rd. (Medical Dr.) | 210-615-1288

"Great lunch specials" mean "there's always a line" midday at this Medical Center Hunan, where the food is "consistently" "delicious" and "everybody knows it"; the "comfortable" if "plain" dining room is satisfactory, and table service is usually "fast" and "pleasant."

Merchants Bistro and Hardware Bar ⊠ *American*

| – | – | – | M |

Alamo Heights | 5939 Broadway St. (Montclair Ave.) | 210-957-4544 |
www.merchantsgrandcafe.com

Set inside a quaintly renovated hardware store, this Alamo Heights yearling offers spruced up Traditional American pub grub utilizing local ingredients; the simple fare like burgers and chops go down well with the bar's fine stock of brews and old-fashioned cocktails.

Meson European Dining *French/Italian*

| ▽ 18 | 13 | 22 | $40 |

Loop 1604 | Waterford Shopping Ctr. | 923 N. Loop 1604 (Hardy Oak) |
210-494-1055 | www.mesoneuropeandining.com

There's "fancy attitude" at this "lesser-known" outpost recently re-located to Loop 1604 digs, where the "classic" French-Italian menu, "very personable host" and tableside prep pay tribute to fine dining; though the new space is brighter than its predecessor and features a cozy patio, the move has not changed the menu or service that regulars have come to expect.

Mimi's Café *American*

| 21 | 20 | 18 | $19 |

La Cantera | The Rim | 17315 I-10 W. (La Cantera Pkwy.) | 210-877-5792 |
www.mimiscafe.com

"Transplanted Californians" welcome this La Cantera link in the Golden State–based "comfort-food chain" as a "sure bet" for "home-

and shakers" ever since with its "enormous" steaks and lobsters plated in "distinguished" settings adorned with celebrity "caricatures"; sure, the tabs are reminiscent of "mortgage payments" and service can career from "top-notch" to "surly", but ultimately they're "consistently good."

☒ Paloma Blanca *Mexican* — 22 | 23 | 20 | $21

Alamo Heights | Cambridge Shopping Ctr. | 5800 Broadway St. (Austin Hwy.) | 210-822-6151 | www.palomablanca.net

"Trendy" Alamo Heights types tout this "upscale" hacienda for its "mouthwatering" mix of "authentic" Tex-Mex faves and "interior Mexico" specialties that flaunt "a bit of added Latino culinary creativity"; given the "helpful" staff and "classy, comfortable" setting (featuring original art and a "great outside patio"), consensus says "this one stands out."

Pam's Patio Kitchen ☒ Ⓜ *American* — ▽ 26 | 19 | 23 | $15

North | 11826 Wurzbach Rd. (Lockhill-Selma Rd.) | 210-492-1359 | www.pamspatio.com

"Basically, everything's wonderful" gush pampered fans of this Northside "neighborhood" nook in a chic shopping strip, where the New American lineup provides "original sandwiches", soups and salads for the lunch rush and "more upscale choices" at dinner (offered Tuesday–Saturday only); added attractions include a "super-friendly staff" and oft-unusual "art on the wall" courtesy of local talents.

Pappadeaux *Seafood* — 23 | 19 | 20 | $29

Loop 410 | 76 NE Loop 410 (Jones Maltsberger Rd.) | 210-340-7143 | www.pappadeaux.com

See review in Houston Directory.

Pappasito's *Tex-Mex* — 23 | 18 | 20 | $24

Northwest | 10501 I-10 W. (Paige Burch) | 210-691-8974 | www.pappasitos.com

See review in Houston Directory.

Pei Wei Asian Diner *Pan-Asian* — 19 | 15 | 16 | $15

North | Northwoods Shopping Ctr. | 1802 N. Loop 1604 E. (Rte. 281) | 210-507-9160

Northwest | The Strand | 11267 Huebner Rd. (McDermott Frwy.) | 210-561-5600

Northwest | 11398 Bandera Rd. (Brae Ridge Dr.) | 210-523-0040 www.peiwei.com

See review in Dallas/Ft. Worth Directory.

Pesca on the River *Seafood* — 24 | 22 | 20 | $47

River Walk | Watermark Hotel & Spa | 212 W. Crockett St. (St. Mary's St.) | 210-396-5817 | www.watermarkhotel.com

Even the "locals are circling" this "casually elegant" River Walk dock in the Watermark Hotel, a source of "excellent fresh seafood" flown in daily from around the world; many are hooked on its "cool atmosphere" and "hard-to-find" cuisine, though "pricey" tabs may dampen enthusiasm.

	FOOD	DECOR	SERVICE	COST

P.F. Chang's China Bistro *Chinese*   22 | 22 | 20 | $27

La Cantera | Shops at La Cantera | 15900 La Cantera Pkwy. (N. Loop 1604) |
210-507-6500
Quarry | Alamo Quarry Mkt. | 255 E. Basse Rd. (bet. Hwy. 281 &
Jones Maltsberger Rd.) | 210-507-1000
www.pfchangs.com
See review in Dallas/Ft. Worth Directory.

Phoenix Chinese Café *Chinese*   - | - | - | I

North Central | 11821 West Ave. (Blanco Rd.) | 210-525-1961
The Chinese menu and "specials on the blackboard" are "surprisingly
authentic" at this Northside strip-center Cantonese, so those who
"decipher the Chenglish" are in for "wonderful" chow from a "personable staff" that's a "bang for your buck" to boot; as for the frill-free
environs, if you're "fussy about decor" it's also "great for takeout."

Piatti Locali *Italian*   24 | 22 | 23 | $27

Quarry | Alamo Quarry Mkt. | 255 E. Basse Rd. (bet. Hwy. 281 &
Jones Maltsberger Rd.) | 210-832-0300 | www.piatti.com
Shoppers show their *amore* for this Italian chain's Quarry locale,
home to "addictive" dishes whose "inventive" touches and "fresh ingredients" bring to mind "a thoughtful lover, not your grandmother";
the "fancy yet familiar" setup with a "cozy bar" is a "convenient"
"place to meet" that's "less crowded" than others nearby.

Picante Grill *Mexican*   22 | 16 | 19 | $15

Near North | 3810 Broadway St. (Pershing Ave.) | 210-822-3797 |
www.picantegrill.com
Specializing in "Mexico City–style" cuisine, this "neighborhood
place" opposite the Witte Museum "thrills" amigos with "wonderful" enchiladas, fajitas, cochinita pibil and chile en nogada; affable
owners and "affordable" prices add to the appeal; P.S. alfresco fans
can savor the flavors while dining on the "great" plant-filled patio.

Piccolo's Italian Restaurant Ⓜ *Italian*   ▽ 25 | 10 | 21 | $28

Northwest | 5703 Evers Rd. (Wurzbach Rd.) | 210-647-5524
The decor may be "cheesy" ("murals of Vesuvio, oil paintings of
Rome and fake grapes") but the compensations at this family-run
Northwest Neapolitan are many; the "carefully prepared" Southern
Italian fare is "wonderful", and "personal recognition" from the chef-
owner – who "never forgets a face" – makes diners "feel special"; if
the usually "efficient" servers happen to be moving "slowly", regu-
lars urge "be patient" – "big-city tastes" await.

Pico de Gallo Restaurant *Tex-Mex*   ▽ 21 | 16 | ·21 | $14

San Antonio West | 111 S. Leona St. (Commerce St.) | 210-225-6060 |
www.picodegallo.com
Another longtimer from the Cortez family (Mi Tierra, La Margarita),
this "bustling" Tex-Mexer west of Market Square fills up "real San
Antonians" with its "fantastic" soups and "tasty" meat platters
(served with "housemade tortillas"); be warned that mariachis who
"seem to think louder is better" may "ruin your conversation."

	FOOD	DECOR	SERVICE	COST

Ristorante Grissini 🖇 *Italian* ▽ 25 | 18 | 17 | $35

Alamo Heights | Lincoln Heights Shopping Ctr. | 999 E. Basse Rd. (B'way) | 210-615-7270

Alamo Heights is now home to some of "the best Italian" in town courtesy of this cozy trattoria; the fireplace-equipped space is overseen by a "husband cook and wife maitre d'" team, and newfound followers only wish they would open for lunch.

🆕 Roaring Fork *Southwestern* 24 | 24 | 23 | $38

Loop 1604 | Plaza Las Campanas | 1806 N. Loop 1604 W. (bet. Blanco & Huebner Rds.) | 210-479-9700 | www.eddiev.com

See review in Austin and the Hill Country Directory.

Rosario's *Mexican* 23 | 19 | 19 | $20

Southtown | 910 S. Alamo St. (St. Mary's St.) | 210-223-1806 | www.rosariossa.com

"Tourists and locals mix" at this "boisterous" Southtown "favorite" for "first-rate Tex-Mex" augmented by "uncommon" specialties "usually found deep in Mexico"; owner Lisa Wong knows how to create "fun, funky" atmospherics with a "fiesta feel every day", so prepare for a "packed" and "noisy" house.

🄯 Ruth's Chris Steak House *Steak* 25 | 22 | 25 | $57

San Antonio East | St. Paul Sq. | 1170 E. Commerce St. (I-37) | 210-227-8847
North Central | The Concord | 7720 Jones Maltsberger Rd. (McAllister Frwy.) | 210-821-5051
www.ruthschris.com

"Nothing beats a steak sizzling in butter" at this "special-occasion" chain where the "melt-in-your-mouth" meats are "cooked to perfection"; sure, reactions to decor vary – from "blah" to "old-fashioned in a good way" – but service is "attentive" and the "off-the-charts" pricing manageable "so long as your boss doesn't care how much you spend."

🄯 Sandbar Fish House & Market 🖇🅜 *Seafood* 28 | 20 | 23 | $34

Downtown | Historic Exchange Bldg. | 152 E. Pecan St. (St. Mary's St.) | 210-222-2426

You can almost "feel the sand between your toes" at this "real seafood bar", Downtown's "island of choice" for an "amazing" extravaganza of "incredibly fresh", "artfully prepared" fin fare courtesy of über-chef Andrew Weissman; the "small", "simple" space is just around the corner but atmospherically worlds apart from his luxe flagship Le Rêve; N.B. dinner only, Tuesday–Saturday.

Sarika's Thai Restaurant *Thai* ▽ 25 | 17 | 23 | $17

Medical Center | 4319 Medical Dr. (Fredericksburg Rd.) | 210-692-3200

Sure, "the strip-mall location is nothing fancy", but this "cozy" local takes the Medical Center by tsunami with its "tasty" "basic Thai" and "lovely staff"; the modest site morphs into a lunchtime hot spot and a romantic possibility after dark, and given the "good value", supporters say you "can't go wrong."

	FOOD	DECOR	SERVICE	COST

Sarovar Indian Cuisine *Indian*
▽ 21 | 12 | 15 | $18

Northwest | 10227 Ironside Dr. (Ticonderoga Dr.) | 210-558-8280 |
www.sarovar.net

"*Exciting flavors*" await at these Northwest San Antonio and North Austin outposts for "homestyle Indian food", which represents "many different regions" of the Raj via a well-stocked lunch buffet and an "extensive menu" at dinner; the low-key decor "isn't the best", so most focus on the "cheap" tabs.

Sawasdee Thai Cuisine *Thai*
24 | 16 | 20 | $18

North Central | Castle Creek Shopping Ctr. | 6407 Blanco Rd. (inside Loop 410) | 210-979-9110

"Drive your taste buds wild" with the "bold flavors" at this "Thai-rific" North Central joint, a "family-run business" where the menu's "excellent variety" is matched with "very accommodating" service; despite an unassuming location in the corner of a strip center, devotees declare "this place will impress you."

Scenic Loop Café *American/Tex-Mex*
19 | 20 | 20 | $28

Leon Springs | 25615 Boerne Stage Rd. (Toutant Beauregard Rd.) | 210-687-1818 | www.scenicloopcafe.com

"The hunter-gatherer in any Texan" should find what they're looking for in the "diverse" American and Tex-Mex selection at this "casual" retreat set high on the Hill Country rise of Leon Springs; besides "dependable" eating and an "awesome patio", it's "worth the ride" for a "relaxing" scene complete with a "play area" for kids and "live music" on weekends.

Schilo's Delicatessen 🗷 *Deli*
21 | 15 | 19 | $14

Downtown | 424 E. Commerce St. (Presa St.) | 210-223-6692

One of the few remaining reminders of SA's influx of German immigrants, this Downtown deli founded in 1917 is as famous for its "authentic" and "homey" character as it is for its "superb" split pea soup, "killer cheesecake" and "knock-your-boots-off" housemade root beer; the "unpretentious" vibe and "good values" keep this "time warp that works" "popular" (and "overcrowded"); N.B. closes at 8:30 PM.

Sea Island Shrimphouse *Seafood*
19 | 12 | 14 | $15

Selma | The Forum | 8223 Agora Pkwy. (I-35) | 210-658-1100
Loop 410 | 322 W. Rector St. (San Pedro Ave.) | 210-342-7771
Northwest | 11715 Bandera Rd. (N. Loop 1604) | 210-681-7000
Northwest | 4323 Amerisuites Dr. (McDeroitt Frwy.) | 210-558-8989
Northwest | 5959 NW Loop 410 (Ingram Rd.) | 210-520-3033
San Antonio South | 2119 SW Military Dr. (I-35) | 210-921-9700
www.shrimphouse.com

Locals on the lookout for "quick-fix seafood" wash up at this busy chain, a "go-to" for "fried and grilled" fish of "consistent quality", including Gulf shrimp; aye, they're "short on decor" and patrons "stand in line" to order, but "bargain" prices make them "a family favorite."

	FOOD	DECOR	SERVICE	COST

Shiraz ☒ *Persian*
21 | 17 | 18 | $32

Olmos Park | 4230 McCullough Ave. (Olmos Dr.) | 210-829-5050 |
www.dineatshiraz.com

Iranian cuisine isn't exactly common in Alamo City, but you can get
it at this "small, inviting" Olmos Park Persian proffering "delicious"
dishes in an "intimate", "quiet atmosphere"; service is "personal" if
sometimes "slow", and a few take a dim view of the ambient "dark-
ness" ("you need a flashlight"); N.B. though the place was named
for Persia's ancient capital and not the wine, the cellar also contains
many boutique bottles of the eponymous varietal.

☑ Silo *American*
26 | 23 | 24 | $43

Terrell Heights | 1133 Austin Hwy. (Mt. Calvary Dr.) | 210-824-8686 |
www.siloelevatedcuisine.com

"Elevate your taste buds" at this bi-level bistro in Terrell Heights,
where the "superb" New American fare comes with a local twist
(check out the "succulent" chicken-fried oysters) along with
"prompt" service and "modern" surroundings; it also stores up a
"festive bar" scene, and "though a bit pricey", its plates are por-
tioned for "Texas-sized appetites."

☑ Silo 1604 *American*
26 | 25 | 24 | $43

Loop 1604 | Ventura Plaza | 434 NW Loop 1604 (Voigt Dr.) |
210-483-8989 | www.siloelevatedcuisine.com

Boosters boast this "drop-dead gorgeous" Silo spin-off on North
Central's 1604 is "even better than the original" for "swanky" but
"welcoming" vibes, "gourmet" New American cuisine and "attentive" service; like its forerunner, it's "costly but well worth the
money", and the "bar downstairs" is likewise a "welcome addition"
hosting "great live music" and "the latest singles scene."

Simi's India Cuisine *Indian*
▽ 24 | 14 | 21 | $21

Northwest | 4535 Fredericksburg Rd. (Hillcrest Dr.) | 210-737-3166

"Dependable" and "good", this Northwest Indian is known for its
"delicious" subcontinental specialties ("tender lamb curry") and a
lunch buffet that's a "popular" "place for friends to meet" midday;
the owner "greets you with a warm smile" and his staff is "attentive
and respectful", so the only demerit is the unremarkable decor.

Smokehouse, The Ⓜ *BBQ*
- | - | - | I

San Antonio East | 3306 Roland Ave. (Rigsby Ave.) | 210-333-9548

Smoked meat mavens hungry for true "old-school" 'cue drift over to
this East Side pit stop, where the "solid BBQ" is served up "like it
should be" in "an often-smoky dining area with extremely basic
utensils"; "despite its humble surroundings", menu standouts like
homemade sausage, brisket and lamb ribs are an "undeniable" draw.

Sompong's Thai & Chinese Cuisine ☒ *Chinese/Thai*
▽ 18 | 8 | 19 | $15

Medical Center | 8110 Fredericksburg Rd. (Datapoint Dr.) | 210-614-0845

"If you're nearby", Medical Center regulars report this longstanding
Chinese-Thai hybrid is "perfect for a fast lunch" thanks to its "effi-

cient service", "cheap" prices and ample menu of both American-ized and more authentic options; just focus on the food since the strip-center storefront is "not much on decor."

Sorrento Ristorante ☒ *Italian* · 23 | 11 | 18 | $19

Alamo Heights | 5146 Broadway St. (Grove Pl.) | 210-824-0055 | www.sorrentoristorante.com

The "Sorrento scenes on the walls" at this Alamo Heights "neigh-borhood joint" may be "pure Italian kitsch", but "homemade" faves like the "well-crafted" pastas and pizzas make it a "popular" pick; plus the "jammed", "no-frills" space creates a dining experience cognoscenti call "close to the real deal back East."

Stonewerks Big Rock Grill *American* · 18 | 19 | 17 | $21

Loop 1604 | Vineyard Ctr. | 1201 N. Loop 1604 W. (Blanco Rd.) | 210-764-0400

Stonewerks Caffe *American*

Quarry | 7300 Jones Maltsberger Rd. (Basse Rd.) | 210-828-3508
www.stonewerks.com

It's "casual" American food "but they dress it up nice" at this "pop-ular" pair, where the youngish "party/bar crowd" can count on a "ro-bust beverage menu", "great patio", "big-screen" sports and "moderate prices"; both the Quarry original and its roomier 1604 spin-off werk fine for "lively (noisy)" times.

Sushihana *Japanese* · 25 | 21 | 22 | $27

Castle Hills | 1810 NW Military Hwy. (Moss Dr.) | 210-340-7808 | www.sushihanasan.com

Maybe "sushi places are popping up all over town", but this "best-kept secret" in Castle Hills "could start a revolution" ac-cording to enthusiasts who bow to the "excellent selection and presentation" of its Japanese specialties; the "thoughtful" wine list, "great service" and "very Zen" ambiance round out a repast fit for an emperor.

Sushi Zushi *Japanese* · 21 | 20 | 17 | $29

Downtown | 203 S. St. Mary's St. (Market St.) | 210-472-2900
Alamo Heights | 999 E. Basse Rd. (B'way) | 210-826-8500
Northwest | The Colonnade | 9867 I-10 W. (Wurzbach Rd.) | 210-691-3332
Stone Oak | Stone Oak Plaza II | 18720 Stone Oak Pkwy. (N. Loop 1604) | 210-545-6100
www.sushizushi.com

Even "non-sushi lovers" have a "top-notch" "variety of choices" at this "modern" chain, which augments its "huge assortment" of "fresh", "innovative" rolls with a "wide-ranging" lineup of other Japanese "favorites"; but while many hail the menu's "exciting twists", purists pan the occasionally "weird" combos as "not au-thentic" and "not cheap."

Taco Cabana ● *Tex-Mex* · 16 | 11 | 11 | $10

La Cantera | 2347 E. Southcross Blvd. (I-37) | 210-532-2422

(continued)

Taco Cabana

North Central | 2908 Broadway St. (Humphrey Ave.) |
210-829-1616
North Central | 3310 San Pedro Ave. (Hildebrand Ave.) |
210-733-9332
South Central | 543 W. Malone Ave. (bet. Cottomwood & Theo Aves.) |
210-534-8533
San Antonio West | 4723 W. Commerce St. (San Augustine Ave.) |
210-436-4464
www.tacocabana.com

The "cheap eats" will cure "late-night hunger pains" "in a hurry" at
this local eatery turned regional chain, home to "*puro*" Mexican
served up "fast-food"–style; but choosier chowhounds lament "inconsistent service" and grub that's "nothing special."

Taco Taco *Tex-Mex*   - | - | - | I

Olmos Park | 145 E. Hildebrand Ave. (bet. Howard St. & McCullough Ave.) |
210-822-9533 | www.tacotacosa.com

The line trails out the door and into the parking lot at this Olmos
Park Tex-Mex mainstay where it takes two hands to hoist up one
of the huge homemade breakfast tortillas loaded with eggs, potatoes and cheese; plate lunches are equally satisfying, inexpensive and delivered with the same friendly service; N.B. they close
at 2 PM daily.

Taipei Gourmet *Chinese*   20 | 17 | 19 | $18

Castle Hills | 2211 NW Military Hwy. (West Ave.) | 210-366-3012
Stone Oak | 18802 Stone Oak Pkwy. (N. Loop 1604) | 210-403-3316
www.sotaipei.com

Backers boast these "standbys" are "some of the better" "neighborhood" Chinese options, citing "great value" on a "tasty" selection
that extends to a sideline in sushi; and type B's appreciate "rarely
crowded" conditions that make for a less hectic lunch rush.

Texas Farm to Table Cafe *American*   24 | 16 | 19 | $13

Near North | 312 Pearl Pkwy. (Ave. A) | 210-444-1404 |
www.texasfarmtotable.com

"You can't get any fresher" than the "local (and often organic) ingredients" "straight from the farm" at this "friendly, casual" Near
Northside American "niche" in the revitalized Pearl Brewing complex; the "husband-and-wife chef duo" turns out "excellent", "creative" sandwiches, salads and more during daylight hours,
guaranteeing "a healthy lunch" break.

Thai-Lao Orchid 🗷 *Thai*   - | - | - | M

Alamo Heights | 7959 Broadway St. (Sunset Rd.) | 210-832-9889 |
www.thailaoorchid.com

Regulars rely on the "seamless service, quality food and quiet" at
this Alamo Heights "neighborhood" nook, where the lineup is "pre-
dominantly Thai" but takes in Vietnamese and a sushi bar too; the
range of "classic dishes" helps it blossom into a "benchmark for all"
in the area.

	FOOD	DECOR	SERVICE	COST

Thai Pikul *Thai*
| - | - | - | I |

Northwest | Magic Center Plaza | 5136 Fredericksburg Rd. (Callaghan Rd.) | 210-524-9440 | www.thaipikul.com

Admittedly it's a "spare setting", but "the food speaks for itself" at this Northwest strip-center Siamese, a prime pik for Thai buffs drawn to the "great selection" of traditional tastes; for extra incentive, the free-corkage BYO policy keeps it more than affordable.

Thai Spice *Thai*
| ▽ 22 | 14 | 21 | $16 |

Northeast | The Forum | 8327 Agora Pkwy. (bet. I-35 & Loop 1604) | 210-658-1665

The spice is right at this far Northeast outpost, where "they adjust the heat" in the "amazing" Thai specialties "according to your desire"; "impeccable" service and "terrific value" elevate it among the "best in town" – "not at all what you'd expect to find in a strip mall."

Thai Taste ⊠ *Thai*
| - | - | - | I |

Northwest | Crestview Plaza | 5520 Evers Rd. (Loop 410) | 210-520-6800

Look for minimal decor and maximum flavor at this "cheap, cheap, cheap" BYO neighborhood Thai, a popular stop for the Northwest lunch crowd; taste-testers appreciate that the dishes are scaled "from mild to very spicy", as is the clientele.

Tiago's Cabo Grill *Mexican/Tex-Mex*
| 22 | 20 | 21 | $21 |

La Cantera | The Rim | 17711 I-10 W. (La Cantera Pkwy.) | 210-881-2700
Northwest | Shops at Westpointe | 8403 Hwy. 151 (I-410) | 210-647-3600
www.tiagoscabogrille.com

This duo of family-friendly cantinas concocts a "delicious" "blend of Tex-Mex and true Mex" featuring grilled meats, "lots of seafood choices", "unbelievable margaritas" and "awesome" chocolate cake; besides the "dependable" eating, well-wishers warm to the midrange tabs and agreeably upscale decor.

Tip Top Cafe ⓜ ⊄ *American*
| ▽ 25 | 15 | 23 | $13 |

Northwest | 2814 Fredericksburg Rd. (Santa Anna St.) | 210-732-0191 | www.tiptopcafe.com

"Talk about Texas!" exclaim fans of this "classic" '30s-era Northwest "diner", now in its third generation of family ownership and still a "top-notch" source of "delightful" American "comfort food" à la "homemade" chicken-fried steak, onion rings and pie; if the service ("love the waitresses!") and surroundings seem stuck in time, so do the prices.

Tong's Thai Restaurant *Thai*
| 21 | 15 | 19 | $17 |

Terrell Hills | 1146 Austin Hwy. (Mt. Calvary Dr.) | 210-829-7345 | www.tongsthai.com

Addicts who "crave the taste" of Thai turn to this "casual" Terrell Hills entry for "very fresh" dishes and "friendly" service in "cool, dark, Zen" digs; Chinese choices supplement the main menu, "and then there's the bubble tea" to tickle your tong.

Tony Roma's *BBQ*
| | - | - | - | M |

Downtown | Rivercenter Mall | 849 E. Commerce St. (Alamo Plaza) | 210-225-7662 | www.tonyromas.com

"Ribs are the specialty" of this longtime BBQ chain Downtown (that also serves seafood and steaks), though "decent prices" seem to be its strongest suit; still, many say this "dated" franchise is "past its prime", citing "tacky" decor and just "ordinary" cooking.

Torres Taco Haven *Mexican*
| ▽ 23 | 14 | 18 | $13 |

Southtown | 3119 S. Gevers St. (Greer St.) | 210-532-3049
San Antonio South | 1032 S. Presa St. (bet. Claudia & Vance Sts.) | 210-533-2171

"Pick up a coupla breakfast tacos" and "you'll never want any other" at this "cheap and fabulous" Mexican twosome that'll "knock your socks off" with their "down-home" chow; they're a "popular" "go-to" even for "local luminaries" (especially for Sunday breakfast), and visitors can count on the Torres family to "make you feel like a San Antonian."

NEW Tresca *Italian*
| - | - | - | M |

Stone Oak | Plaza at Concord Park | 700 E. Sonterra Blvd., Ste. 1117 (Sigma Rd.) | 210-545-0077 | www.trescaristorante.com

Another entry from Dan Ward (Piatti), this Stone Oak arrival inhabits a tricked-out strip-mall space built around a piazza with a number of warmly appointed dining rooms and a large patio; its midpriced Italian menu showcases modern takes on classic dishes (think fig and prosciutto pizza), making it an appealing stop for both midpriced business lunches and family dinners.

NEW Tre Trattoria 🖫 *Italian*
| - | - | - | M |

Near North | The Boardwalk | 4003 Broadway St. (bet. Allensworth St. & Thorman Pl.) | 210-805-0333 | www.tretrattoria.com

In this Near North space that has seen its share of restaurants come and go, chef-owner Jason Dady (Bin 555) sends out family-style servings of rustic Italian dishes like braised wild boar ragu meant to be shared with housemade salumi and his signature cast-iron griddled pizzas; the spacious room offers comfy booths for conversation or community tables for conviviality, all set amid colorful art, while a parkside patio is a seductive respite on sunny days.

Turquoise Turkish Grill *Turkish*
| - | - | - | M |

Loop 410 | 3720 NW Loop 410 (Fredericksburg Rd.) | 210-736-2887 | www.turquoisegrill.com

As the only true Turk in town, this Loop 410 eatery is a rare supplier of "spicy kebabs", a "selection of Turkish meats" and fresh-baked breads; its impressive selection of Levantine wines and Friday night belly dancing are also impossible to ignore.

NEW 29 Brix 🖫 *Californian*
| - | - | - | M |

Stone Oak | Village at Stone Oak | 22506 Hwy. 281 N., Ste. 106 (Stone Oak Pkwy.) | 210-496-2749 | www.20ninewine.com

A spin-off of 20nine in the Quarry, this Stone Oak wine bar/restaurant serves similarly Napa-inspired New American cooking in a sleek,

bright space with an open kitchen and a plant-lined patio; by day, young moms and ladies-who-lunch linger over salads and sandwiches, but come night, it's filled with twentysomethings who come to drink in the atmosphere and selections from the deep vino list.

20nine Restaurant & Wine Bar *Californian*

`18` `22` `20` `$35`

Quarry | Alamo Quarry Mkt. | 255 E. Basse Rd. (bet. Hwy. 281 & Jones Maltsberger Rd.) | 210-798-9463 | www.20ninewine.com

"It's all about the wine" at this "dark, intimate" Quarry destination that takes Napa Valley's Route 29 for inspiration, offering sips from an "extensive" list plus "creative flights" and artisan beers as well; though a few find the "high-end" Californian "finger food" takes a backseat to the drink selection, the "superfriendly staff" and outdoor seating area make it a "great addition" to the neighborhood nonetheless.

NEW Valentino's di Olmos *Italian*

`-` `-` `-` `M`

Olmos Park | 4331 McCullough Ave. (bet. Earl St. & Olmos Ln.) | 210-832-0600 | www.valentinosdiolmos.com

Occupying an ornate castlelike space modeled on Rudolph Valentino's Hollywood mansion, this Olmos Park newcomer specializes in a broad range of moderately priced Northern Italian dishes, from antipasti and pizzas to veal saltimbocca; a doting staff and a rambling, dimly lit interior cultivate a romantic vibe that's perfect for silent screen–style close-ups.

Van's Chinese Seafood Restaurant *Pan-Asian/Seafood*

▽ `21` `10` `17` `$21`

Near North | 3214 Broadway St. (Mulberry St.) | 210-828-8449 | www.vansrestaurantonline.com

"Shhh, it's a well-kept secret" that "one of the largest wine cellars" in the city is hidden away at this "eclectic" Pan-Asian seafooder just north of Downtown, which is likewise advantaged with "wonderful" cooking at a "great value"; as for the decor, regulars shrug "all their taste is in their food."

Viet-Nam Restaurant *Vietnamese*

`-` `-` `-` `I`

Near North | 3244 Broadway St. (Mulberry St.) | 210-822-7461

"If you didn't know the place", you might overlook this tiny storefront north of Downtown and its "enjoyable and refreshing" mix of authentic Vietnamese eats; while longtime followers feel it's "a little uneven of late", they also agree it's always "worth a try."

Wah Kee Chinese Seafood Cuisine *Chinese*

`22` `16` `20` `$18`

Sonterra | 18360 Blanco Rd. (N. Loop 1604) | 210-497-6669

With an "extensive menu" of "real Chinese" "at its best", this Sonterra seafood specialist qualifies as a "neighborhood" keeper; throw in "value prices" and "quick", "friendly" service, and few fret if "there isn't much in the way of decor"; N.B. the Northwest branch has closed.

	FOOD	DECOR	SERVICE	COST

Water Street Oyster Bar *Seafood*
| 18 | 15 | 16 | $23 |

Alamo Heights | Lincoln Heights Shopping Ctr. | 7500 Broadway St. (Basse Rd.) | 210-829-4853 | www.waterstreetco.com

SA may be "landlocked" but boosters report you can get "great Texas Gulf oysters" at this Alamo Heights seafood specialist with a "nice" bi-level interior and "relaxed" feel; however, surveyors are split on service ("wonderful" vs. "slow and sloppy"), and even admirers admit acoustics can be "way too noisy."

W.D. Deli ⊠ *Deli*
∇ | 21 | 18 | 18 | $11 |

Near North | 3123 Broadway St. (Mulberry St.) | 210-828-2322 | www.wddeli.com

Although the "funky" indoor/outdoor setup signals it's not your bubbe's deli, this "busy" Near Northside "lunch spot" raises "soups and sandwiches to a higher level" with its "wonderful" homemade goods; it's also budget-friendly, so insiders never neglect to check "the bakery case" for "a slice of heaven."

NEW Wildfish
Seafood Grille *American/Seafood*
| - | - | - | E |

Loop 1604 | Plaza Las Campanas | 1834 N. Loop 1604 W. (Huebner Rd.) | 210-493-1600 | www.wildfishseafoodgrille.com

Lines of fans are already hooked on this Loop 1604 newcomer with a New American menu that nets the freshest in-season seafood, fine cuts of Midwestern beef and a global assortment of raw bar items; an exhibition kitchen forms the centerpiece of the flashy room, while the bar teems with trendy professionals enjoying their own catch of the day.

Zuni Grill *Southwestern*
| 19 | 18 | 16 | $29 |

River Walk | 223 Losoya St. (Commerce St.) | 210-227-0864 | www.joesfood.com

"Southwestern food has not gone out of style" on the River Walk, especially since this airy eatery pairs it with "a great view" and "people-watching on the patio"; the menu's "creative" combinations make it a "well-liked" spot for locals and a comparatively "interesting" option for out-of-towners.

SAN ANTONIO
INDEXES

Cuisines

Includes restaurant names, locations and Food ratings.

AMERICAN (NEW)

Z Biga on Banks | **River Walk**	27
Bin 555 | **N Central**	26
Cappyccino's | **Alamo Hts**	20
Z Cappy's | **Alamo Hts**	23
Citrus | **Downtown**	25
Kona Grill | **La Cantera**	20
Z Lodge/Castle Hills | **Castle Hills**	26
Oro | **Downtown**	24
Pam's Kitchen | **North**	26
Scenic Loop | **Leon Springs**	19
Z Silo | **Terrell Hts**	26
Z Silo 1604 | **Loop 1604**	26
Stonewerks | **multi.**	18
NEW 29 Brix | **Stone Oak**	–
NEW Wildfish | **Loop 1604**	–

AMERICAN (TRADITIONAL)

Cheesecake Factory | **Loop 410**	20
Cheesy Jane's | **multi.**	19
Chesters | **multi.**	22
Cove, The | **Downtown**	20
Grey Moss Inn | **Helotes**	24
Guenther Hse. | **Southtown**	23
Josephine St. | **Near North**	20
Madhatters | **Downtown**	20
Z Magnolia Pancake | **N Central**	27
Mama's Café | **multi.**	19
Merchants Bistro | **Alamo Hts**	–
Mimi's Cafe | **La Cantera**	21
Texas Farm/Table | **Near North**	24
Tip Top Cafe | **NW**	25

ASIAN

Asia Kitchen | **San Antonio W**	25

ASIAN FUSION

Z Frederick's | **multi.**	26

BARBECUE

County Line | **multi.**	20
Smokehouse | **San Antonio E**	–
Tony Roma's | **Downtown**	–

BELGIAN

La Frite | **Southtown**	26

BRAZILIAN

NEW Chama Gaucha | **Loop 1604**	–

BURGERS

Big'z Burger | **Loop 1604**	21
Cheesy Jane's | **multi.**	19
Chesters | **multi.**	22
Chris Madrid's | **Near North**	25

CAJUN

Pappadeaux | **Loop 410**	23

CALIFORNIAN

NEW 29 Brix | **Stone Oak**	–
20nine | **Quarry**	18

CHINESE

(* dim sum specialist)

Formosa Gdn. | **N Central**	21
Golden Wok* | **multi.**	22
Hsiu Yu | **North**	16
Kim Wah* | **NW**	21
Mencius Gourmet | **Medical Ctr**	21
P.F. Chang's | **multi.**	22
Phoenix Chinese* | **N Central**	–
Sompong's | **Medical Ctr**	18
Taipei Gourmet | **multi.**	20
Wah Kee | **Sonterra**	22

CONTINENTAL

Bistro Thyme II | **Loop 1604**	–
Fig Tree | **River Walk**	25
Houston St. | **Downtown**	22

DELIS

Schilo's D | **Downtown**	21
W.D. Deli | **Near North**	21

DESSERT

NEW Coco Chocolate | **N Central**	–
Crumpets | **NE**	15
Da Vinci Gelato | **Stone Oak**	24
Madhatters | **Southtown**	20

ECLECTIC

Z Cappy's | **Alamo Hts**	23
Grill/Leon Springs | **Leon Springs**	22
La Tuna Grill | **Southtown**	22
Z Liberty Bar | **Near North**	24

EUROPEAN

La Scala | **Castle Hills**	23

FONDUE

Melting Pot | **N Central**	21

Menus, photos, voting and more – free at ZAGAT.com

FRENCH

⚡ Bistro Vatel	**Olmos Pk**	26
NEW Brass. Pavil	**Loop 1604**	–
NEW Ciel	**Stone Oak**	–
NEW Coco Chocolate	**N Central**	–
Crumpets	**NE**	15
⚡ Frederick's	**multi.**	26
Las Canarias	**River Walk**	26
⚡ Le Rêve	**Downtown**	29
⚡ L'Etoile	**Alamo Hts**	26
Meson	**Loop 1604**	18

GREEK

Demo's Greek	**multi.**	19
Mina & Dimi's	**San Antonio W**	24

HAWAIIAN

Kona Grill	**La Cantera**	20

INDIAN

India Oven	**N Central**	24
India Palace	**multi.**	24
Madras Pavilion	**NW**	22
Sarovar Indian	**NW**	21
Simi's India	**NW**	24

ITALIAN

(N=Northern; S=Southern)

Aldino	**Loop 1604**	21
Aldo's	N	**Medical Ctr**	21
Carrabba's	**NW**	22
Ciao	**multi.**	23
Da Vinci Gelato	**Stone Oak**	24
Dough	**N Central**	–
La Focaccia	**Southtown**	16
NEW Luca	**Downtown**	–
Luce Rist.	**NW**	20
NEW Maggiano's	**La Cantera**	20
Meson	**Loop 1604**	18
⚡ Paesanos	**multi.**	22
Piatti	**Quarry**	24
Piccolo's Italian	S	**NW**	25
Rist. Grissini	**Alamo Hts**	25
Sorrento Rist.	**Alamo Hts**	23
NEW Tresca	**Stone Oak**	–
NEW Tre Trattoria	**Near North**	–
NEW Valentino's	N	**Olmos Pk**	–

JAPANESE

(* sushi specialist)

Fujiya*	**Medical Ctr**	19
⚡ Godai Sushi*	**N Central**	27
Koi Kawa*	**Near North**	26
Mon Thai*	**Alamo Hts**	17
Sushihana*	**Castle Hills**	25
Sushi Zushi*	**multi.**	21

KOREAN

(* barbecue specialist)

Ilsong Gdn.	**N Central**	25
Korean BBQ Hse.*	**San Antonio E**	23

MEDITERRANEAN

Boardwalk Bistro	**Near North**	21
Las Canarias	**River Walk**	26
NEW Oloroso	**Southtown**	–

MEXICAN

Aldaco's	**multi.**	22
Cascabel	**Southtown**	–
El Jarro de Arturo	**North**	22
El Mirador	**Southtown**	23
Ernesto's	**N Central**	18
La Fogata	**North**	–
La Fonda	**Near North**	–
⚡ Paloma Blanca	**Alamo Hts**	22
Picante Grill	**Near North**	22
Rosario's	**Southtown**	23
Taco Cabana	**multi.**	16
Tiago's	**multi.**	22
Torres Taco	**multi.**	23

NUEVO LATINO

Azúca	**Southtown**	24

PACIFIC RIM

Pacific Moon	**North**	18

PAN-ASIAN

Pei Wei	**multi.**	19
Van's	**Near North**	21

PAN-LATIN

NEW Achiote River	**River Walk**	–

PERSIAN

Shiraz	**Olmos Pk**	21

PUERTO RICAN

La Marginal	**N Central**	–

SEAFOOD

Bohanan's	**Downtown**	23
⚡ Boudro's	**River Walk**	24
Chart House	**Downtown**	–
Ernesto's	**N Central**	18
Landry's	**River Walk**	19
⚡ L'Etoile	**Alamo Hts**	26
Pappadeaux	**Loop 410**	23
Pesca/River	**River Walk**	24
⚡ Sandbar	**Downtown**	28
Sea Island	**multi.**	19
Van's	**Near North**	21
Wah Kee	**Sonterra**	22

Water St. Oyster | **Alamo Hts** | 18
NEW Wildfish | **Loop 1604** | -

SMALL PLATES

(See also Spanish tapas specialist)
Bin 555 | **Amer.** | **N Central** | 26
NEW Luca | **Italian** | **Downtown** | -

SOUTH AMERICAN

Beto's Comida | **North** | 21

SOUTHWESTERN

Antlers Lodge | **San Antonio W** | 23
Canyon Café | **Quarry** | 18
Z Francesca's | **La Cantera** | 26
NEW Roaring Fork | **Loop 1604** | 24
Zuni Grill | **River Walk** | 19

SPANISH

(* tapas specialist)
Las Ramblas* | **River Walk** | 21

STEAKHOUSES

Barn Door | **Alamo Hts** | 19
Bohanan's | **Downtown** | 23
Z Boudro's | **River Walk** | 24
NEW Chama Gaucha | **Loop 1604** | -
Fleming's Prime | **Quarry** | 24
Little Red Barn | **San Antonio S** | 17
Little Rhein | **River Walk** | 24
Morton's Steak | **Downtown** | 25
Old San Francisco | **North** | 19
NEW Ounce | **Loop 1604** | -
Palm | **Downtown** | 24
Z Ruth's Chris | **multi.** | 25

TEAROOMS

Madhatters | **multi.** | 20

TEX-MEX

Ácenar | **River Walk** | 22
Alamo Café | **multi.** | -
Chuy's | **North** | 21
Iron Cactus | **River Walk** | 18
La Hacienda/Los Barrios | **North** | 21
La Margarita | **Market Sq** | 21
Mi Tierra | **Market Sq** | 21
Pappasito's Cantina | **NW** | 23
Pico de Gallo | **San Antonio W** | 21
Scenic Loop | **Leon Springs** | 19
Taco Taco | **Olmos Pk** | -
Tiago's | **multi.** | 22

THAI

Bangkok | **NE** | -
Mon Thai | **Alamo Hts** | 17
Sarika's | **Medical Ctr** | 25
Sawasdee | **N Central** | 24
Sompong's | **Medical Ctr** | 18
Thai-Lao Orchid | **Alamo Hts** | -
Thai Pikul | **NW** | -
Thai Spice | **NE** | 22
Thai Taste | **NW** | -
Tong's Thai | **Terrell Hills** | 21

TURKISH

Turquoise Turkish | **Loop 410** | -

VEGETARIAN

Green Veg. | **Downtown** | 18

VIETNAMESE

Viet-Nam | **Near North** | -

Locations

Includes restaurant names, cuisines and Food ratings.

San Antonio Central

DOWNTOWN

Bohanan's | *Seafood/Steak* — 23
Chart House | *Seafood* — -
Citrus | *Amer.* — 25
Cove, The | *Amer.* — 20
Green Veg. | *Veg.* — 18
Houston St. | *Continental* — 22
Z Le Rêve | *French* — 29
NEW Luca | *Italian* — -
Madhatters | *Tea* — 20
Mama's Café | *Amer.* — 19
Morton's Steak | *Steak* — 25
Oro | *Amer.* — 24
Palm | *Steak* — 24
Z Sandbar | *Seafood* — 28
Schilo's D | *Deli* — 21
Sushi Zushi | *Japanese* — 21
Tony Roma's | *BBQ* — -

MARKET SQUARE

La Margarita | *Tex-Mex* — 21
Mi Tierra | *Tex-Mex* — 21

RIVER WALK

Ácenar | *Tex-Mex* — 22
NEW Achiote River | *Pan-Latin* — -
Z Biga on Banks | *Amer.* — 27
Z Boudro's | *Seafood/Steak* — 24
County Line | *BBQ* — 20
Fig Tree | *Continental* — 25
Iron Cactus | *Tex-Mex* — 18
Landry's | *Seafood* — 19
Las Canarias | *French/Med.* — 26
Las Ramblas | *Spanish* — 21
Little Rhein | *Steak* — 24
Z Paesanos | *Italian* — 22
Pesca/River | *Seafood* — 24
Zuni Grill | *SW* — 19

SOUTHTOWN

Azúca | *Nuevo Latino* — 24
Cascabel | *Mex.* — -
El Mirador | *Mex.* — 23
Guenther Hse. | *Amer.* — 23
La Focaccia | *Italian* — 16
La Frite | *Belgian* — 26
La Tuna Grill | *Eclectic* — 22
Madhatters | *Tea* — 20
NEW Oloroso | *Med.* — -

Rosario's | *Mex.* — 23
Torres Taco | *Mex.* — 23

San Antonio East

SAN ANTONIO EAST

Aldaco's | *Mex.* — 22
Korean BBQ Hse. | *Korean* — 23
Z Ruth's Chris | *Steak* — 25
Smokehouse | *BBQ* — -

SELMA

Sea Island | *Seafood* — 19

UNIVERSAL CITY

Mama's Café | *Amer.* — 19

San Antonio North

ALAMO HEIGHTS

Barn Door | *Steak* — 19
Cappyccino's | *Amer.* — 20
Z Cappy's | *Amer.* — 23
Cheesy Jane's | *Burgers* — 19
Z Frederick's | *Asian Fusion/French* — 26
Z L'Etoile | *French/Seafood* — 26
Merchants Bistro | *Amer.* — -
Mon Thai | *Thai* — 17
Z Paloma Blanca | *Mex.* — 22
Rist. Grissini | *Italian* — 25
Sorrento Rist. | *Italian* — 23
Sushi Zushi | *Japanese* — 21
Thai-Lao Orchid | *Thai* — -
Water St. Oyster | *Seafood* — 18

CASTLE HILLS

La Scala | *Euro.* — 23
Z Lodge/Castle Hills | *Amer.* — 26
Sushihana | *Japanese* — 25
Taipei Gourmet | *Chinese* — 20

HELOTES

Grey Moss Inn | *Amer.* — 24

LA CANTERA

Z Francesca's | *SW* — 26
Kona Grill | *Amer.* — 20
NEW Maggiano's | *Italian* — 20
Mimi's Cafe | *Amer.* — 21
P.F. Chang's | *Chinese* — 22
Taco Cabana | *Mex.* — 16
Tiago's | *Mex./Tex-Mex* — 22

LOOP 1604

- Aldino | *Italian* 21
- Big'z Burger | *Burgers* 21
- Bistro Thyme II | *Continental* -
- NEW Brass. Pavil | *French* -
- NEW Chama Gaucha | *Brazilian* -
- Demo's Greek | *Greek* 19
- Meson | *French/Italian* 18
- NEW Ounce | *Steak* -
- Z Paesanos | *Italian* 22
- NEW Roaring Fork | *SW* 24
- Z Silo 1604 | *Amer.* 26
- Stonewerks | *Amer.* 18
- NEW Wildfish | *Amer./Seafood* -

LOOP 410

- Cheesecake Factory | *Amer.* 20
- Chesters | *Burgers* 22
- Pappadeaux | *Seafood* 23
- Sea Island | *Seafood* 19
- Turquoise Turkish | *Turkish* -

MEDICAL CENTER

- Aldo's | *Italian* 21
- Fujiya | *Japanese* 19
- Golden Wok | *Chinese* 22
- India Palace | *Indian* 24
- Mencius Gourmet | *Chinese* 21
- Sarika's | *Thai* 25
- Sompong's | *Chinese/Thai* 18

NEAR NORTH

- Boardwalk Bistro | *Med.* 21
- Chris Madrid's | *Burgers* 25
- Demo's Greek | *Greek* 19
- Josephine St. | *Amer.* 20
- Koi Kawa | *Japanese* 26
- La Fonda | *Mex.* -
- Z Liberty Bar | *Eclectic* 24
- Picante Grill | *Mex.* 22
- Texas Farm/Table | *Amer.* 24
- NEW Tre Trattoria | *Italian* -
- Van's | *Pan-Asian/Seafood* 21
- Viet-Nam | *Viet.* -
- W.D. Deli | *Deli* 21

NORTH

- Alamo Café | *Tex-Mex* -
- Beto's Comida | *S Amer.* 21
- Chesters | *Burgers* 22
- Chuy's | *Tex-Mex* 21
- Demo's Greek | *Greek* 19
- El Jarro de Arturo | *Mex.* 22
- Hsiu Yu | *Chinese* 16
- La Fogata | *Mex.* -
- La Hacienda/Los Barrios | *Tex-Mex* 21
- Mama's Café | *Amer.* 19
- Old San Francisco | *Steak* 19
- Pacific Moon | *Pac. Rim* 18
- Pam's Kitchen | *Amer.* 26
- Pei Wei | *Pan-Asian* 19

NORTH CENTRAL

- Bin 555 | *Amer.* 26
- NEW Coco Chocolate | *Dessert/French* -
- Dough | *Pizza* -
- Ernesto's | *Mex./Seafood* 18
- Formosa Gdn. | *Chinese* 21
- Z Frederick's | *Asian Fusion/French* 26
- Z Godai Sushi | *Japanese* 27
- Ilsong Gdn. | *Korean* 25
- India Oven | *Indian* 24
- India Palace | *Indian* 24
- La Marginal | *Carib./Puerto Rican* -
- Z Magnolia Pancake | *Amer.* 27
- Melting Pot | *Fondue* 21
- Phoenix Chinese | *Chinese* -
- Z Ruth's Chris | *Steak* 25
- Sawasdee | *Thai* 24
- Taco Cabana | *Mex.* 16

NORTHEAST

- Bangkok | *Thai* -
- Crumpets | *French* 15
- Mama's Café | *Amer.* 19
- Thai Spice | *Thai* 22

NORTHWEST

- Alamo Café | *Tex-Mex* -
- Carrabba's | *Italian* 22
- Cheesy Jane's | *Burgers* 19
- Chesters | *Burgers* 22
- County Line | *BBQ* 20
- Kim Wah | *Chinese* -
- Luce Rist. | *Italian* 20
- Madras Pavilion | *Indian* 22
- Pappasito's Cantina | *Tex-Mex* 23
- Pei Wei | *Pan-Asian* 19
- Piccolo's Italian | *Italian* 25
- Sarovar Indian | *Indian* 21
- Sea Island | *Seafood* 19
- Simi's India | *Indian* 24
- Sushi Zushi | *Japanese* 21
- Thai Pikul | *Thai* -
- Thai Taste | *Thai* -
- Tiago's | *Mex./Tex-Mex* 22
- Tip Top Cafe | *Amer.* 25

OLMOS PARK

Z Bistro Vatel	*French*	26
Ciao	*Italian*	23
Shiraz	*Persian*	21
Taco Taco	*Tex-Mex*	–
NEW Valentino's	*Italian*	–

QUARRY

Canyon Café	*SW*	18
Fleming's Prime	*Steak*	24
Z Paesanos	*Italian*	22
P.F. Chang's	*Chinese*	22
Piatti	*Italian*	24
Stonewerks	*Amer.*	18
20nine	*Calif.*	18

SONTERRA

Wah Kee	*Chinese*	22

STONE OAK

Aldaco's	*Mex.*	22
Ciao	*Italian*	23
NEW Ciel	*French*	–
Clear Springs	*Seafood*	19
Da Vinci Gelato	*Italian*	24
Sushi Zushi	*Japanese*	21
Taipei Gourmet	*Chinese*	20
NEW Tresca	*Italian*	–
NEW 29 Brix	*Cal.*	–

TERRILL HEIGHTS/ TERRILL HILLS

Z Silo	*Amer.*	26
Tong's Thai	*Thai*	21

San Antonio South

SAN ANTONIO SOUTH

Little Red Barn	*Steak*	17
Sea Island	*Seafood*	19
Torres Taco	*Mex.*	23

SOUTH CENTRAL

Taco Cabana	*Mex.*	16

San Antonio West

LEON SPRINGS

Grill/Leon Springs	*Eclectic*	22
Scenic Loop	*Amer./Tex-Mex*	19

SAN ANTONIO WEST

Antlers Lodge	*SW*	23
Asia Kitchen	*Asian*	25
Golden Wok	*Chinese*	22
Mina & Dimi's	*Greek*	24
Pico de Gallo	*Tex-Mex*	21
Taco Cabana	*Mex.*	16

Special Features

Listings cover the best in each category and include names, locations and Food ratings. Multi-location restaurants' features may vary by branch.

ADDITIONS

(Properties added since the last edition of the book)

Achiote River | **River Walk**	-
Alamo Café | **multi.**	-
Brass. Pavil | **Loop 1604**	-
Chama Gaucha | **Loop 1604**	-
Ciel | **Stone Oak**	-
Coco Chocolate | **N Central**	-
La Fogata | **North**	-
Luca | **Downtown**	-
Maggiano's | **La Cantera**	20
Oloroso | **Southtown**	-
Ounce | **Loop 1604**	-
Pappasito's Cantina | **NW**	23
Roaring Fork | **Loop 1604**	24
Taco Taco | **Olmos Pk**	-
Tresca | **Stone Oak**	-
Tre Trattoria | **Near North**	-
29 Brix | **Stone Oak**	-
Valentino's | **Olmos Pk**	-
Wildfish | **Loop 1604**	-

BREAKFAST

(See also Hotel Dining)

El Mirador | **Southtown**	23
Guenther Hse. | **Southtown**	23
La Hacienda/Los Barrios | **North**	21
Z Magnolia Pancake | **N Central**	27
Mimi's Cafe | **La Cantera**	21
Mi Tierra | **Market Sq**	21
Pico de Gallo | **San Antonio W**	21
Schilo's D | **Downtown**	21
Torres Taco | **multi.**	23
Zuni Grill | **River Walk**	19

BRUNCH

Aldino | **Loop 1604**	21
Beto's Comida | **North**	21
NEW Brass. Pavil | **Loop 1604**	-
Z Cappy's | **Alamo Hts**	23
Crumpets | **NE**	15
Guenther Hse. | **Southtown**	23
Las Canarias | **River Walk**	26
Z Liberty Bar | **Near North**	24
Madhatters | **Southtown**	20
Z Paloma Blanca | **Alamo Hts**	22
NEW Valentino's | **Olmos Pk**	-

BUFFET SERVED

(Check availability)

NEW Achiote River | **River Walk**	-
India Oven | **N Central**	24
India Palace | **multi.**	24
Las Canarias | **River Walk**	26
Las Ramblas | **River Walk**	21
Madras Pavilion | **NW**	22
Sarovar Indian | **NW**	21
Simi's India | **NW**	24

BUSINESS DINING

NEW Achiote River | **River Walk**	-
Aldo's | **Medical Ctr**	21
Z Biga on Banks | **River Walk**	27
Bistro Thyme II | **Loop 1604**	-
Z Bistro Vatel | **Olmos Pk**	26
Bohanan's | **Downtown**	23
NEW Brass. Pavil | **Loop 1604**	-
Canyon Café | **Quarry**	18
Z Cappy's | **Alamo Hts**	23
NEW Chama Gaucha | **Loop 1604**	-
Ciao | **Stone Oak**	23
NEW Ciel | **Stone Oak**	-
Citrus | **Downtown**	25
Fig Tree | **River Walk**	25
Z Francesca's | **La Cantera**	26
Z Frederick's | **multi.**	26
Houston St. | **Downtown**	22
La Fogata | **North**	-
La Fonda | **Near North**	-
Landry's | **River Walk**	19
La Scala | **Castle Hills**	23
Las Canarias | **River Walk**	26
Las Ramblas | **River Walk**	21
Z Le Rêve | **Downtown**	29
Z L'Etoile | **Alamo Hts**	26
Little Rhein | **River Walk**	24
Z Lodge/Castle Hills | **Castle Hills**	26
NEW Luca | **Downtown**	-
Luce Rist. | **NW**	20
NEW Maggiano's | **La Cantera**	20
Merchants Bistro | **Alamo Hts**	-
Morton's Steak | **Downtown**	25
NEW Oloroso | **Southtown**	-
Oro | **Downtown**	24
NEW Ounce | **Loop 1604**	-
Z Paesanos | **Quarry**	22
Palm | **Downtown**	24

Pappasito's Cantina | **NW**	23
Pesca/River | **River Walk**	24
NEW Roaring Fork | **Loop 1604**	24
Z Ruth's Chris | **multi.**	25
Z Silo | **Terrell Hts**	26
Sushihana | **Castle Hills**	25
NEW Tresca | **Stone Oak**	-
NEW Tre Trattoria | **Near North**	-
NEW 29 Brix | **Stone Oak**	-
NEW Valentino's | **Olmos Pk**	-
NEW Wildfish | **Loop 1604**	-

CELEBRITY CHEFS

Z Biga on Banks | *Bruce Auden* | **River Walk**	27
Bin 555 | *Jason Dady* | **N Central**	26
NEW Brass. Pavil | *Scott Cohen* | **Loop 1604**	-
Z Le Rêve | *Andrew Weissman* | **Downtown**	29
Z Lodge/Castle Hills | *Jason Dady* | **Castle Hills**	26
Z Sandbar | *Andrew Weissman* | **Downtown**	28
NEW Tre Trattoria | *Jason Dady* | **Near North**	-

CHEF'S TABLE

Z Biga on Banks | **River Walk**	27
Z Bistro Vatel | **Olmos Pk**	26
NEW Luca | **Downtown**	-

CHILD-FRIENDLY

(Alternatives to the usual fast-food places; * children's menu available)

Ácenar | **River Walk**	22
Antlers Lodge* | **San Antonio W**	23
Azúca* | **Southtown**	24
Barn Door* | **Alamo Hts**	19
Beto's Comida* | **North**	21
Big'z Burger* | **Loop 1604**	21
Bin 555 | **N Central**	26
Boardwalk Bistro* | **Near North**	21
Z Boudro's* | **River Walk**	24
Z Cappy's* | **Alamo Hts**	23
Chris Madrid's | **Near North**	25
Ciao | **Olmos Pk**	23
Clear Springs* | **Stone Oak**	19
County Line* | **multi.**	20
Cove, The* | **Downtown**	20
Da Vinci Gelato | **Stone Oak**	24
Demo's Greek* | **multi.**	19
El Jarro de Arturo* | **North**	22
El Mirador | **Southtown**	23
Grey Moss Inn* | **Helotes**	24
Josephine St.* | **Near North**	20
Koi Kawa | **Near North**	26

La Focaccia | **Southtown**	16
La Hacienda/Los Barrios* | **North**	21
La Margarita* | **Market Sq**	21
Z Liberty Bar | **Near North**	24
Little Red Barn* | **San Antonio S**	17
Madhatters | **Southtown**	20
Mama's Café* | **multi.**	19
Mina & Dimi's | **San Antonio W**	24
Mi Tierra* | **Market Sq**	22
Z Paesanos | **Loop 1604**	22
Z Paloma Blanca* | **Alamo Hts**	22
Pam's Kitchen | **North**	26
Pei Wei* | **multi.**	19
Piatti* | **Quarry**	24
Picante Grill* | **Near North**	22
Pico de Gallo* | **San Antonio W**	21
Rosario's* | **Southtown**	23
Schilo's D* | **Downtown**	21
Tip Top Cafe* | **NW**	25
Torres Taco | **multi.**	23
Water St. Oyster | **Alamo Hts**	18
W.D. Deli | **Near North**	21
Zuni Grill | **River Walk**	19

DELIVERY/TAKEOUT

(D=delivery, T=takeout)

Ácenar | T | **River Walk**	22
Aldino | T | **Loop 1604**	22
Aldo's | T | **Medical Ctr**	21
Asia Kitchen | T | **San Antonio W**	25
Azúca | T | **Southtown**	24
Bangkok | T | **NE**	-
Barn Door | T | **Alamo Hts**	19
Beto's Comida | T | **North**	21
Bin 555 | T | **N Central**	26
Boardwalk Bistro | T | **Near North**	21
Cappyccino's | T | **Alamo Hts**	20
Z Cappy's | T | **Alamo Hts**	23
Chuy's | D | **North**	21
Ciao | T | **Olmos Pk**	23
County Line | T | **multi.**	20
Crumpets | T | **NE**	15
Da Vinci Gelato | T | **Stone Oak**	24
Demo's Greek | D, T | **multi.**	19
El Jarro de Arturo | T | **North**	22
El Mirador | T | **Southtown**	23
Formosa Gdn. | T | **N Central**	21
Fujiya | D, T | **Medical Ctr**	19
Z Godai Sushi | T | **N Central**	27
Houston St. | T | **Downtown**	22
Hsiu Yu | T | **North**	16
Ilsong Gdn. | T | **N Central**	25
India Oven | T | **N Central**	24
India Palace | D, T | **multi.**	24

Koi Kawa | T | **Near North**	26
Korean BBQ Hse. | T | **San Antonio E**	23
La Focaccia | T | **Southtown**	16
La Hacienda/Los Barrios | T | **North**	21
La Margarita | T | **Market Sq**	21
☑ Liberty Bar | T | **Near North**	24
Madhatters | T | **Southtown**	20
Mencius Gourmet | T | **Medical Ctr**	21
Mina & Dimi's | T | **San Antonio W**	24
Mi Tierra | T | **Market Sq**	21
Mon Thai | T | **Alamo Hts**	17
Pacific Moon | T | **North**	18
☑ Paloma Blanca | T | **Alamo Hts**	22
Pam's Kitchen | T | **North**	26
Pei Wei | T | **multi.**	19
P.F. Chang's | T | **Quarry**	22
Picante Grill | T | **Near North**	22
Piccolo's Italian | T | **NW**	25
Rosario's | T | **Southtown**	23
Sarovar Indian | T | **NW**	21
Sawasdee | T | **N Central**	24
Schilo's D | T | **Downtown**	21
Simi's India | T | **NW**	24
Sompong's | T | **Medical Ctr**	18
Sushi Zushi | D, T | **multi.**	21
Thai Pikul | D, T | **NW**	–
Thai Spice | D, T | **NE**	22
Thai Taste | T | **NW**	–
Tip Top Cafe | T | **NW**	25
Tong's Thai | D, T | **Terrell Hills**	21
Torres Taco | D, T | **multi.**	23
Van's | T | **Near North**	21
Viet-Nam | T | **Near North**	–
Wah Kee | T | **Sonterra**	22
Water St. Oyster | T | **Alamo Hts**	18
W.D. Deli | T | **Near North**	21
Zuni Grill | T | **River Walk**	19

DESSERT

☑ Biga on Banks | **River Walk**	27
NEW Coco Chocolate | **N Central**	–
Crumpets | **NE**	15
Da Vinci Gelato | **Stone Oak**	24
Grey Moss Inn | **Helotes**	24
Las Canarias | **River Walk**	26
☑ L'Etoile | **Alamo Hts**	26
Madhatters | **Southtown**	20
Pam's Kitchen | **North**	26
Pesca/River | **River Walk**	24
☑ Ruth's Chris | **San Antonio E**	25
Tip Top Cafe | **NW**	25

DINING ALONE

(Other than hotels and places with counter service)

☑ Bistro Vatel | **Olmos Pk**	26
Canyon Café | **Quarry**	18
Cappyccino's | **Alamo Hts**	20
☑ Cappy's | **Alamo Hts**	23
Cheesy Jane's | **multi.**	19
Chesters | **multi.**	22
Ciao | **Olmos Pk**	23
Crumpets | **NE**	15
El Jarro de Arturo | **North**	22
El Mirador | **Southtown**	23
Ernesto's | **N Central**	18
Koi Kawa | **Near North**	26
☑ Le Rêve | **Downtown**	29
☑ L'Etoile | **Alamo Hts**	26
☑ Liberty Bar | **Near North**	24
☑ Lodge/Castle Hills | **Castle Hills**	26
Madhatters | **Southtown**	20
Mon Thai | **Alamo Hts**	17
Pei Wei | **multi.**	19
☑ Sandbar | **Downtown**	28
Sushi Zushi | **multi.**	21
Taco Cabana | **multi.**	16
NEW Tre Trattoria | **Near North**	–
Water St. Oyster | **Alamo Hts**	18
Zuni Grill | **River Walk**	19

ENTERTAINMENT

(Call for days and times of performances)

Ácenar | DJ | **River Walk**	22
Azúca | bands | **Southtown**	24
Beto's Comida | varies | **North**	21
Boardwalk Bistro | live jazz | **Near North**	21
County Line | acoustic | **NW**	20
Crumpets | bands | **NE**	15
Demo's Greek | belly dancers | **multi.**	19
El Jarro de Arturo | bands | **North**	22
India Oven | belly dancers | **N Central**	24
La Hacienda/Los Barrios | guitar/piano | **North**	21
La Margarita | mariachi | **Market Sq**	21
Landry's | jazz | **River Walk**	19
Las Canarias | guitar | **River Walk**	26
Madhatters | contemp./folk/jazz | **Southtown**	20
Mina & Dimi's | dancers | **San Antonio W**	24

Mi Tierra | mariachi | **Market Sq**	21
Old San Francisco | piano | **North**	19
Z Paloma Blanca | guitar/vocals | **Alamo Hts**	22
Picante Grill | guitar | **Near North**	22
Pico de Gallo | keyboard/vocals | **San Antonio W**	21
Rosario's | varies | **Southtown**	23
Z Silo | bands | **Terrell Hts**	26
Water St. Oyster | blues/jazz/vocals | **Alamo Hts**	18

GAME IN SEASON

Antlers Lodge | **San Antonio W**	23
Z Biga on Banks | **River Walk**	27
Z Bistro Vatel | **Olmos Pk**	26
Citrus | **Downtown**	25
Crumpets | **NE**	15
Fig Tree | **River Walk**	25
Z Francesca's | **La Cantera**	26
Z Frederick's | **multi.**	26
Grey Moss Inn | **Helotes**	24
Las Canarias | **River Walk**	26
Z Le Rêve | **Downtown**	29
Z L'Etoile | **Alamo Hts**	26
Z Liberty Bar | **Near North**	24
Z Lodge/Castle Hills | **Castle Hills**	26
Oro | **Downtown**	24
20nine | **Quarry**	18

HISTORIC PLACES

(Year opened; * building)

1847 | Little Rhein* | **River Walk**	24
1853 | Fig Tree* | **River Walk**	25
1880 | Oloroso* | **Southtown**	–
1890 | Liberty Bar* | **Near North**	24
1902 | Guenther Hse.* | **Southtown**	23
1906 | Luca* | **Downtown**	–
1907 | Canyon Café* | **Quarry**	18
1910 | Josephine St.* | **Near North**	20
1917 | Schilo's D | **Downtown**	21
1920 | W.D. Deli* | **Near North**	21
1927 | Oro* | **Downtown**	24
1929 | Grey Moss Inn | **Helotes**	24
1930 | Le Rêve* | **Downtown**	29
1930 | Texas Farm/Table* | **Near North**	24
1932 | La Fonda | **Near North**	–
1938 | Tip Top Cafe | **NW**	25
1941 | Mi Tierra | **Market Sq**	21
1952 | Barn Door | **Alamo Hts**	19
1955 | El Jarro de Arturo | **North**	22

HOTEL DINING

Contessa Hotel	
Las Ramblas | **River Walk**	21
Emily Morgan Hotel	
Oro | **Downtown**	24
Fairmount San Antonio, The	
NEW Luca | **Downtown**	–
Grand Hyatt San Antonio	
NEW Achiote River | **River Walk**	–
Hyatt Regency Hill Country	
Antlers Lodge | **San Antonio W**	23
Omni La Mansión del Rio Hotel	
Las Canarias | **River Walk**	26
Valencia Hotel	
Citrus | **Downtown**	25
Watermark Hotel & Spa	
Pesca/River | **River Walk**	24
Westin La Cantera Resort	
Z Francesca's | **La Cantera**	26

JACKET REQUIRED

Z Le Rêve | **Downtown**	29

LATE DINING

(Weekday closing hour)

NEW Coco Chocolate | varies | **N Central**	–
Mama's Café | 12 AM | **Downtown**	19
Mi Tierra | 24 hrs. | **Market Sq**	21
Taco Cabana | varies | **multi.**	16

MEET FOR A DRINK

Ácenar | **River Walk**	22
NEW Achiote River | **River Walk**	–
Alamo Café | **multi.**	–
Azúca | **Southtown**	24
Z Biga on Banks | **River Walk**	27
Bistro Thyme II | **Loop 1604**	–
NEW Brass. Pavil | **Loop 1604**	–
Cappyccino's | **Alamo Hts**	20
Chuy's | **North**	21
Ciao | **Stone Oak**	23
NEW Ciel | **Stone Oak**	–
Citrus | **Downtown**	25
NEW Coco Chocolate | **N Central**	–
Z Frederick's | **multi.**	26
Grill/Leon Springs | **Leon Springs**	22
La Fogata | **North**	–
La Fonda | **Near North**	–
La Hacienda/Los Barrios | **North**	21
Las Ramblas | **River Walk**	21
Z Liberty Bar | **Near North**	24
NEW Luca | **Downtown**	–
Merchants Bistro | **Alamo Hts**	–

SAN ANTONIO

SPECIAL FEATURES

Morton's Steak | **Downtown**		25
Oro | **Downtown**		24
NEW Ounce | **Loop 1604**		-
Z Paesanos | **Quarry**		22
Z Paloma Blanca | **Alamo Hts**		22
Pappasito's Cantina | **NW**		23
Piatti | **Quarry**		24
NEW Roaring Fork | **Loop 1604**		24
Z Silo | **Terrell Hts**		26
Sushi Zushi | **NW**		21
Taipei Gourmet | **Stone Oak**		20
NEW Tresca | **Stone Oak**		-
NEW Tre Trattoria | **Near North**		-
NEW 29 Brix | **Stone Oak**		-
20nine | **Quarry**		18
NEW Valentino's | **Olmos Pk**		-
NEW Wildfish | **Loop 1604**		-
Zuni Grill | **River Walk**		19

OUTDOOR DINING

(G=garden; P=patio; S=sidewalk;
T=terrace; W=waterside)

Ácenar | P, W | **River Walk**		22
NEW Achiote River | P, W | **River Walk**		-
Aldino | P | **Loop 1604**		21
Aldo's | G, P | **Medical Ctr**		21
Azúca | P | **Southtown**		24
Beto's Comida | P | **North**		21
Z Biga on Banks | T, W | **River Walk**		27
Big'z Burger | T | **Loop 1604**		21
Bin 555 | P | **N Central**		26
Z Bistro Vatel | S | **Olmos Pk**		26
Boardwalk Bistro | P | **Near North**		21
Z Boudro's | P, W | **River Walk**		24
Z Cappy's | P | **Alamo Hts**		23
Chuy's | P | **North**		21
Ciao | S | **Olmos Pk**		23
NEW Ciel | P | **Stone Oak**		-
Citrus | T, W | **Downtown**		25
NEW Coco Chocolate | P | **N Central**		-
County Line | P | **River Walk**		20
Crumpets | P, W | **NE**		15
Da Vinci Gelato | S | **Stone Oak**		24
Demo's Greek | P, S | **multi.**		19
El Jarro de Arturo | P | **North**		22
El Mirador | P | **Southtown**		23
Fig Tree | P, T, W | **River Walk**		25
Z Francesca's | T | **La Cantera**		26
Z Godai Sushi | P | **N Central**		27
Grey Moss Inn | P | **Helotes**		24
Houston St. | S | **Downtown**		22
Josephine St. | P | **Near North**		20
La Focaccia | P | **Southtown**		16

La Frite | S | **Southtown**		26
La Hacienda/Los Barrios | P | **North**		21
La Margarita | P | **Market Sq**		21
Landry's | P, W | **River Walk**		19
Las Canarias | T | **River Walk**		26
Las Ramblas | P, W | **River Walk**		21
Little Rhein | G, T, W | **River Walk**		24
Luce Rist. | P | **NW**		20
Madhatters | P | **Southtown**		20
Mon Thai | P | **Alamo Hts**		17
NEW Oloroso | P | **Southtown**		-
Z Paesanos | G | **multi.**		22
Z Paloma Blanca | P | **Alamo Hts**		22
Pam's Kitchen | P | **North**		26
Pei Wei | P, S | **multi.**		19
Pesca/River | P, W | **River Walk**		24
Piatti | S | **Quarry**		24
Picante Grill | P | **Near North**		22
Rist. Grissini | P | **Alamo Hts**		25
NEW Roaring Fork | P | **Loop 1604**		24
Scenic Loop | P | **Leon Springs**		19
Shiraz | P | **Olmos Pk**		21
Tong's Thai | P | **Terrell Hills**		21
NEW Tresca | P | **Stone Oak**		-
NEW Tre Trattoria | P | **Near North**		-
NEW 29 Brix | P | **Stone Oak**		-
20nine | P | **Quarry**		18
NEW Valentino's | P | **Olmos Pk**		-
Water St. Oyster | P | **Alamo Hts**		18
W.D. Deli | P | **Near North**		21
NEW Wildfish | P | **Loop 1604**		-
Zuni Grill | P, W | **River Walk**		19

POWER SCENES

Z Biga on Banks | **River Walk**		27
NEW Brass. Pavil | **Loop 1604**		-
NEW Ciel | **Stone Oak**		-
NEW Coco Chocolate | **N Central**		-
Grill/Leon Springs | **Leon Springs**		22
Z Liberty Bar | **Near North**		24
NEW Luca | **Downtown**		-
Morton's Steak | **Downtown**		25
NEW Ounce | **Loop 1604**		-
Z Paesanos | **multi.**		22
Piatti | **Quarry**		24
Z Ruth's Chris | **San Antonio E**		25
Z Sandbar | **Downtown**		28
NEW Tresca | **Stone Oak**		-
NEW Tre Trattoria | **Near North**		-
NEW Wildfish | **Loop 1604**		-

Menus, photos, voting and more - free at ZAGAT.com

PRIX FIXE MENUS

(Call for prices and times)

Z Biga on Banks	**River Walk**	27
Z Bistro Vatel	**Olmos Pk**	26
Boardwalk Bistro	**Near North**	21
NEW Ciel	**Stone Oak**	-
Crumpets	**NE**	15
Grill/Leon Springs	**Leon Springs**	22
Las Canarias	**River Walk**	26
Z Le Rêve	**Downtown**	29
Z Lodge/Castle Hills	**Castle Hills**	26
Simi's India	**NW**	24

QUIET CONVERSATION

Aldo's	**Medical Ctr**	21
Z Biga on Banks	**River Walk**	27
Z Bistro Vatel	**Olmos Pk**	26
Bohanan's	**Downtown**	23
NEW Brass. Pavil	**Loop 1604**	-
Cappyccino's	**Alamo Hts**	20
Z Cappy's	**Alamo Hts**	23
Citrus	**Downtown**	25
NEW Coco Chocolate	**N Central**	-
Crumpets	**NE**	15
Ernesto's	**N Central**	18
Z Francesca's	**La Cantera**	26
Z Frederick's	**multi.**	26
Fujiya	**Medical Ctr**	19
Grey Moss Inn	**Helotes**	24
Grill/Leon Springs	**Leon Springs**	22
India Oven	**N Central**	24
La Scala	**Castle Hills**	23
Las Canarias	**River Walk**	26
Las Ramblas	**River Walk**	21
Z Le Rêve	**Downtown**	29
Little Rhein	**River Walk**	24
Z Lodge/Castle Hills	**Castle Hills**	26
Meson	**Loop 1604**	18
NEW Oloroso	**Southtown**	-
Oro	**Downtown**	24
NEW Ounce	**Loop 1604**	-
Palm	**Downtown**	24
Pesca/River	**River Walk**	24
Rist. Grissini	**Alamo Hts**	25
Sawasdee	**N Central**	24
Shiraz	**Olmos Pk**	21
Sushihana	**Castle Hills**	25
20nine	**Quarry**	18
NEW Valentino's	**Olmos Pk**	-

ROMANTIC PLACES

Aldo's	**Medical Ctr**	21
Z Biga on Banks	**River Walk**	27

Z Bistro Vatel	**Olmos Pk**	26
Bohanan's	**Downtown**	23
NEW Brass. Pavil	**Loop 1604**	-
Citrus	**Downtown**	25
NEW Coco Chocolate	**N Central**	-
Fig Tree	**River Walk**	25
Z Francesca's	**La Cantera**	26
Grey Moss Inn	**Helotes**	24
Grill/Leon Springs	**Leon Springs**	22
La Fogata	**North**	-
La Scala	**Castle Hills**	23
Las Canarias	**River Walk**	26
Z Le Rêve	**Downtown**	29
Little Rhein	**River Walk**	24
Z Lodge/Castle Hills	**Castle Hills**	26
NEW Luca	**Downtown**	-
Meson	**Loop 1604**	18
NEW Oloroso	**Southtown**	-
Oro	**Downtown**	24
NEW Ounce	**Loop 1604**	-
Shiraz	**Olmos Pk**	21
Z Silo 1604	**Loop 1604**	26
Sushihana	**Castle Hills**	25
20nine	**Quarry**	18
NEW Valentino's	**Olmos Pk**	-
NEW Wildfish	**Loop 1604**	-

SENIOR APPEAL

Alamo Café	**multi.**	-
Barn Door	**Alamo Hts**	19
Z Bistro Vatel	**Olmos Pk**	26
Boardwalk Bistro	**Near North**	21
Bohanan's	**Downtown**	23
NEW Brass. Pavil	**Loop 1604**	-
Z Cappy's	**Alamo Hts**	23
NEW Ciel	**Stone Oak**	-
Crumpets	**NE**	15
El Jarro de Arturo	**North**	22
El Mirador	**Southtown**	23
Fig Tree	**River Walk**	25
Z Frederick's	**multi.**	26
Grey Moss Inn	**Helotes**	24
Grill/Leon Springs	**Leon Springs**	22
La Scala	**Castle Hills**	23
Las Canarias	**River Walk**	26
Z L'Etoile	**Alamo Hts**	26
Little Red Barn	**San Antonio S**	17
Z Lodge/Castle Hills	**Castle Hills**	26
NEW Maggiano's	**La Cantera**	20
Melting Pot	**N Central**	21
Meson	**Loop 1604**	18
Old San Francisco	**North**	19
Z Paloma Blanca	**Alamo Hts**	22

Schilo's D | **Downtown**	21
Sea Island | **Loop 410**	19
☑ Silo | **Terrell Hts**	26
Sushihana | **Castle Hills**	25
Taco Taco | **Olmos Pk**	-
Taipei Gourmet | **Stone Oak**	20
Tip Top Cafe | **NW**	25
NEW Valentino's | **Olmos Pk**	-
Water St. Oyster | **Alamo Hts**	18

SINGLES SCENES

Aldino | **Loop 1604**	21
Azúca | **Southtown**	24
Ciao | **Stone Oak**	23
NEW Coco Chocolate | **N Central**	-
Fleming's Prime | **Quarry**	24
☑ Frederick's | **multi.**	26
Grill/Leon Springs | **Leon Springs**	22
Kona Grill | **La Cantera**	20
NEW Luca | **Downtown**	-
Merchants Bistro | **Alamo Hts**	-
☑ Paesanos | **Loop 1604**	22
☑ Paloma Blanca | **Alamo Hts**	22
Pappasito's Cantina | **NW**	23
NEW Roaring Fork | **Loop 1604**	24
Rosario's | **Southtown**	23
NEW Tresca | **Stone Oak**	-
NEW 29 Brix | **Stone Oak**	-
NEW Wildfish | **Loop 1604**	-

SLEEPERS

(Good to excellent food,
but little known)

Aldaco's | **multi.**	22
Antlers Lodge | **San Antonio W**	23
Asia Kitchen | **San Antonio W**	25
Azúca | **Southtown**	24
Bohanan's | **Downtown**	23
Citrus | **Downtown**	25
Da Vinci Gelato | **Stone Oak**	24
Fig Tree | **River Walk**	25
Golden Wok | **multi.**	22
Grill/Leon Springs | **Leon Springs**	22
Guenther Hse. | **Southtown**	23
Ilsong Gdn. | **N Central**	25
India Oven | **N Central**	24
India Palace | **multi.**	24
Koi Kawa | **Near North**	26
Korean BBQ Hse. | **San Antonio E**	23
La Scala | **Castle Hills**	23
La Tuna Grill | **Southtown**	22
Mina & Dimi's | **San Antonio W**	24
Oro | **Downtown**	24
Pam's Kitchen | **North**	26
Pesca/River | **River Walk**	24

Picante Grill | **Near North**	22
Piccolo's Italian | **NW**	25
Rist. Grissini | **Alamo Hts**	25
Sarika's | **Medical Ctr**	25
Sawasdee | **N Central**	24
Simi's India | **NW**	24
Sushihana | **Castle Hills**	25
Texas Farm/Table | **Near North**	24
Thai Spice | **NE**	22
Tiago's | **multi.**	22
Torres Taco | **multi.**	23
Wah Kee | **Sonterra**	22

TRENDY

Ácenar | **River Walk**	22
Azúca | **Southtown**	24
☑ Biga on Banks | **River Walk**	27
Big'z Burger | **Loop 1604**	21
Ciao | **Stone Oak**	23
NEW Ciel | **Stone Oak**	-
NEW Coco Chocolate | **N Central**	-
Dough | **N Central**	-
☑ Frederick's | **N Central**	26
Kona Grill | **La Cantera**	20
La Frite | **Southtown**	26
☑ Liberty Bar | **Near North**	24
NEW Luca | **Downtown**	-
NEW Oloroso | **Southtown**	-
NEW Ounce | **Loop 1604**	-
Piatti | **Quarry**	24
NEW Roaring Fork | **Loop 1604**	24
Texas Farm/Table | **Near North**	24
NEW Tresca | **Stone Oak**	-
NEW Tre Trattoria | **Near North**	-
NEW 29 Brix | **Stone Oak**	-
20nine | **Quarry**	18
NEW Wildfish | **Loop 1604**	-

VIEWS

Ácenar | **River Walk**	22
NEW Achiote River | **River Walk**	-
Aldaco's | **Stone Oak**	22
Antlers Lodge | **San Antonio W**	23
☑ Biga on Banks | **River Walk**	27
Bohanan's | **Downtown**	23
☑ Boudro's | **River Walk**	24
Fig Tree | **River Walk**	25
☑ Francesca's | **La Cantera**	26
Grey Moss Inn | **Helotes**	24
Las Canarias | **River Walk**	26
Las Ramblas | **River Walk**	21
Little Rhein | **River Walk**	24
Mi Tierra | **Market Sq**	21
Oro | **Downtown**	24
☑ Paesanos | **River Walk**	22

Menus, photos, voting and more – free at ZAGAT.com

Pesca/River | **River Walk** 24
Scenic Loop | **Leon Springs** 19
Zuni Grill | **River Walk** 19

VISITORS ON EXPENSE ACCOUNT

Antlers Lodge | **San Antonio W** 23
Z Biga on Banks | **River Walk** 27
Bistro Thyme II | **Loop 1604** -
NEW Ciel | **Stone Oak** -
Citrus | **Downtown** 25
NEW Coco Chocolate | **N Central** -
Fig Tree | **River Walk** 25
Z Francesca's | **La Cantera** 26
Las Canarias | **River Walk** 26
Las Ramblas | **River Walk** 21
Z Le Rêve | **Downtown** 29
Little Rhein | **River Walk** 24
Morton's Steak | **Downtown** 25
Oro | **Downtown** 24
NEW Ounce | **Loop 1604** -
Palm | **Downtown** 24
Pesca/River | **River Walk** 24
Z Ruth's Chris | **multi.** 25
NEW Valentino's | **Olmos Pk** -
NEW Wildfish | **Loop 1604** -

WINNING WINE LISTS

Aldo's | **Medical Ctr** 21
Z Biga on Banks | **River Walk** 27

Bin 555 | **N Central** 26
Bistro Thyme II | **Loop 1604** -
Bohanan's | **Downtown** 23
Z Boudro's | **River Walk** 24
NEW Brass. Pavil | **Loop 1604** -
NEW Ciel | **Stone Oak** -
NEW Coco Chocolate | **N Central** -
Dough | **N Central** -
Fig Tree | **River Walk** 25
Z Francesca's | **La Cantera** 26
Z Frederick's | **multi.** 26
Grey Moss Inn | **Helotes** 24
Las Canarias | **River Walk** 26
Z Le Rêve | **Downtown** 29
Z L'Etoile | **Alamo Hts** 26
Little Rhein | **River Walk** 24
Z Lodge/Castle Hills | **Castle Hills** 26
NEW Luca | **Downtown** -
Luce Rist. | **NW** 20
Morton's Steak | **Downtown** 25
NEW Ounce | **Loop 1604** -
Z Paesanos | **Loop 1604** 22
Palm | **Downtown** 24
Pesca/River | **River Walk** 24
Z Ruth's Chris | **multi.** 25
Z Silo | **Terrell Hts** 26
Sushihana | **Castle Hills** 25
NEW 29 Brix | **Stone Oak** -
20nine | **Quarry** 18
Van's | **Near North** 21

Wine Vintage Chart

This chart, based on our 0 to 30 scale, is designed to help you select wine. The ratings (by **Howard Stravitz**, a law professor at the University of South Carolina) reflect the vintage quality and the wine's readiness to drink. We exclude the 1991–1993 vintages because they are not that good. A dash indicates the wine is either past its peak or too young to rate. Loire ratings are for dry white wines.

Whites	89	90	94	95	96	97	98	99	00	01	02	03	04	05	06	07
French:																
Alsace	24	25	24	23	23	22	25	23	25	26	22	21	24	25	24	–
Burgundy	23	22	–	27	26	23	21	25	25	24	27	23	26	27	25	23
Loire Valley	–	–	–	–	–	–	–	–	24	25	26	22	23	27	24	–
Champagne	26	29	–	26	27	24	23	24	24	22	26	21	–	–	–	–
Sauternes	25	28	–	21	23	25	23	24	24	29	25	24	21	26	23	27
California:																
Chardonnay	–	–	–	–	–	–	–	24	23	26	26	25	26	29	25	–
Sauvignon Blanc	–	–	–	–	–	–	–	–	–	–	–	26	27	26	27	26
Austrian:																
Grüner Velt./Riesling	–	–	–	25	21	26	26	25	22	23	25	26	26	25	24	–
German:	26	27	24	23	26	25	26	23	21	29	27	24	26	28	24	–

Reds	89	90	94	95	96	97	98	99	00	01	02	03	04	05	06	07
French:																
Bordeaux	25	29	21	26	25	23	25	24	29	26	24	26	24	28	25	23
Burgundy	24	26	–	26	27	25	22	27	22	24	27	25	24	27	25	–
Rhône	28	28	23	26	22	24	27	26	27	26	–	26	24	27	25	–
Beaujolais	–	–	–	–	–	–	–	–	–	–	22	24	21	27	25	23
California:																
Cab./Merlot	–	28	29	27	25	28	23	26	–	27	26	25	24	26	23	–
Pinot Noir	–	–	–	–	–	–	–	24	23	25	28	26	27	25	24	–
Zinfandel	–	–	–	–	–	–	–	–	–	25	23	27	22	23	23	–
Oregon:																
Pinot Noir	–	–	–	–	–	–	–	–	–	–	27	25	26	27	26	–
Italian:																
Tuscany	–	25	23	24	20	29	24	27	24	27	–	25	27	25	24	–
Piedmont	27	27	–	–	26	27	26	25	28	27	–	24	23	26	25	24
Spanish:																
Rioja	–	–	26	26	24	25	–	25	24	27	–	24	25	26	24	–
Ribera del Duero/Priorat	–	–	26	26	27	25	24	25	24	27	20	24	27	26	24	–
Australian:																
Shiraz/Cab.	–	–	24	26	23	26	28	24	24	27	27	25	26	26	24	–
Chilean:	–	–	–	–	–	24	–	25	23	26	24	25	24	26	25	24

ON THE GO.
IN THE KNOW.

ZAGAT TO GO℠

Unlimited access
to Zagat dining &
travel content
in hundreds of
major cities.

Search by name,
location, ratings,
cuisine, special
features & Top Lists.

BlackBerry,® Palm,®
Windows Mobile®
and mobile phones.

Get it now at **mobile.zagat.com**
or text* **ZAGAT** to **78247**

Zagat Products

RESTAURANTS & MAPS

America's Best Dining Deals
America's Top Restaurants
Atlanta
Beijing
Boston
Brooklyn
California Wine Country
Cape Cod & The Islands
Chicago
Chicago Dining Deals
Connecticut
Europe's Top Restaurants
Hamptons (incl. wineries)
Hawaii
Hong Kong
Las Vegas
London
Long Island (incl. wineries)
Los Angeles I So. California
(guide & map)
Miami Beach
Miami I So. Florida
Montréal
New Jersey
New Jersey Shore
New Orleans
New York City (guide & map)
New York City Dining Deals
Palm Beach
Paris
Philadelphia
San Diego
San Francisco (guide & map)
San Francisco Dining Deals
Seattle
Shanghai
Texas
Tokyo
Toronto
Vancouver
Washington, DC I Baltimore
Washington, DC Dining Deals
Westchester I Hudson Valley
World's Top Restaurants

LIFESTYLE GUIDES

America's Top Golf Courses
Movie Guide
Music Guide
NYC Gourmet Shop./Entertaining
NYC Shopping

NIGHTLIFE GUIDES

Los Angeles
New York City
San Francisco

HOTEL & TRAVEL GUIDES

Beijing
Disneyland Resort Insider's Guide
Hawaii
Hong Kong
Las Vegas
London
Montréal
New Orleans
Shanghai
Top U.S. Hotels, Resorts & Spas
Toronto
Vancouver
Walt Disney World Insider's Guide
World's Top Hotels, Resorts & Spas

WEB & WIRELESS SERVICES

ZAGAT TO GO℠ for handhelds
ZAGAT.com℠ • ZAGAT.mobi℠

You shouldn't have to look too hard for nutrition information, because the FDA regulates the size of the labels. They also provide strict guidelines regarding the information that's contained in these labels, which means that we can count on them being large, and clear enough to be easily read and understood.

As always, if you'd like further information on how to better understand how these nutrition labels impact your dietary intake or how to shape your own meal plan, the best place to start is with your physician, a registered dietitian, or a health care professional.

When calculating nutrition in this book, we used the following guidelines:

Pasta:

- When cooking pasta, we don't add salt to the water.

- We use regular pasta when testing the recipes, unless otherwise specified. We do this to ensure that they meet nutritional guidelines. However, you can substitute whole-grain pasta if you're looking to reduce carbs and increase fiber, or even try a combo of the two.

Fruits and Veggies:

- We used medium-sized fruits and vegetables, unless otherwise specified.

Meat:

- We use 95% extra-lean ground beef, unless otherwise specified.

- We use well-trimmed meat.

Poultry:

- We always remove the skin whenever possible.

- We use boneless, skinless chicken breasts whenever possible.

Margarine:

- We use light, trans-fat-free, tub-style margarine, unless otherwise specified.

Breading/Marinades:

- We discard any unused breading or marinade, and these amounts are not figured in our nutritional calculations.

Serving Sizes:

- Nutritional information is based on the serving size shown. Make sure you keep this in mind when you're dishing up a recipe.

Sugar: Good or Bad?

There seem to be a lot of questions about the role that sugar plays in diabetes, so we decided to dig a little deeper and get the facts.

Some folks insist that if you eat too much sugar, you'll get type 1 diabetes, but consuming sugar has nothing to do with developing that form of the disease. While no one knows for sure what causes type 1 diabetes, it's said that genetics play a role. However, it is generally considered that being overweight and inactive are two of the leading causes for developing type 2 diabetes.

In the past, it was thought that if you had diabetes, you couldn't eat sugar at all. Years of research have shown that even though sugar will raise your blood glucose levels, it's more important to watch the total amount of carbohydrate you consume. These days, experts agree that you can include sugar and other carbohydrate-containing foods in your meal plan, as long as you do so in moderation and keep your blood glucose levels in your target range.

It's important to focus on eating a healthy, well-balanced diet. And if you struggle with controlling your sweet tooth, we've got a few tricks to help you out!

Satisfy Your Sweet Tooth

Foods and drinks that use low-calorie sweeteners are an option that may help curb your cravings for something sweet; just remember to use these in moderation.

Sometimes low-calorie sweeteners are also called artificial sweeteners, sugar substitutes, or nonnutritive sweeteners. They can be used to sweeten food and drinks and contain fewer calories and less carbohydrate than regular sugar.

How do these compare with sugar?

The sweetening power of most low-calorie sweeteners varies from brand to brand, which is why it's important to read the instructions on the package, so that you use the right amount.

Brown Sugar Substitutes

For brown sugar substitutes, the general rule is to use half the amount as you would for real brown sugar. We always recommend checking the package of the brand you're using.

Granulated Sugar Substitutes Conversion Chart

Equivalent to granulated sugar	1 cup	1 TBL	1 tsp
• Stevia, powdered extract	1 tsp	1/4 tsp	pinch
• Stevia, liquid extract	1 tsp	6-9 drops	2-4 drops
(Such as Truvia®. Stevia is stable when used in cooking. It won't take the place of sugar in baking without changing the texture. You can substitute part of the sugar, however, and use sugar, xylitol, or erythritol for the rest of the sugar. Stevia has a slightly bitter aftertaste in many foods.)			
• Saccharine, liquid	2 TBL	1/3 tsp	1/8 tsp
• Saccharine, powder	8 tsp	1/2 tsp	1/8 tsp
(Such as Sweet 'n Low®. It keeps its sweetness when heated. It won't take the place of sugar in baking without changing the texture.)			
• Aspartame, granulated	1 cup	1 TBL	1 tsp
(Such as Equal®. It can be used in cooking, but tends to lose some of its sweetness the longer it's heated. If possible, add at or near the end of cooking. It won't take the place of sugar in baking without changing the texture.)			
• Sucralose, granulated	1 cup	1 TBL	1 tsp
(Such as Splenda®. It changes the texture of many baked goods.)			
• Xylitol, granulated	1 cup	1 TBL	1 tsp
• Erythritol, granulated	1 cup	1 TBL	1 tsp
(Such as Swerve®. Erythritol is somewhat less sweet than sugar, and adds stability and shelf life to baked goods, usually without changing the texture too much.)			
• Agave, nectar	2/3 cup	2 tsp	1/2 tsp
(In a recipe calling for white sugar, for each cup of sugar substituted by agave syrup, remove 1/4 to 1/3 cup of liquid.)			

Also, with the exception of aspartame, all of the sweeteners listed cannot be broken down by the body. They pass through our systems without being digested, so they provide no extra calories.

Still, many foods containing low-calorie sweeteners will provide some calories and carbohydrate from other ingredients. That means that foods that carry claims like "sugar-free," "reduced sugar," or "no sugar added" aren't necessarily carbohydrate-free or lower in carbohydrate than the original version of the food. Always check the nutrition facts label, even for foods that carry these claims.

FDA Approved

There are six artificial sweeteners that have been tested and approved by the U.S. Food and Drug Administration (FDA):

- acesulfame potassium (also called ace-K)
- aspartame
- saccharin
- sucralose
- neotame
- advantame

These sweeteners are used by food companies to make diet drinks, baked goods, frozen desserts, candy, light yogurt, and chewing gum. You can buy them to use as tabletop sweeteners, add them to coffee and tea, or sprinkle them on top of fruit. Some are also available in "granular" versions, which can be used in cooking and baking.

For more information, visit the Food and Drug Administration website at www.fda.gov.

Welcome to the Mr. Food Test Kitchen Family!

Whether you've been a fan of the Mr. Food Test Kitchen for years or were just recently introduced to us, we want to welcome you into our kitchen . . . and our family. Even though we've grown in many ways over the years, the one thing that hasn't changed is our philosophy for quick & easy cooking.

Over 40 years ago, we began by sharing our recipes with you through the television screen. Today, not only is the Mr. Food Test Kitchen TV segment syndicated all over the country, but we've also proudly published over 50 best-selling cookbooks. That's not to mention the hugely popular MrFood.com and EverydayDiabeticRecipes.com. And for those of you who love to get social, we do too! You can find us online on Facebook, Twitter, Pinterest, and Instagram—boy, do we love connecting with you!

If you've got a passion for cooking (like we do!), then you know that the only thing better than curling up with a cookbook and drooling over the pictures is actually getting to taste the finished recipes. That's why we give you simple, step-by-step instructions that make it feel like we're in your kitchen guiding you along the way. Your taste buds will be celebrating in no time!

So whether you're new to the family or you've been a part of it from the beginning, we want to thank you. You can bet there's always room at our table for you, because there's nothing better than sharing in all of the . . . "OOH IT'S SO GOOD!!®"

Kelly   Howard   Patty

Other titles you may enjoy from the Mr. Food Test Kitchen:

Christmas Made Easy

Quick & Easy Comfort Cookbook

Sinful Sweets & Tasty Treats

Just One More Bite!

Hello Taste, Goodbye Guilt! (Diabetes Friendly)

Guilt-Free Weeknight Favorites (Diabetes Friendly)

Cook it Slow, Cook it Fast

Wheel of Fortune Collectible Cookbook

The Ultimate Cooking for Two Cookbook

The Ultimate Cake Mix & More Cookbook

The Ultimate 30 Minutes or Less Cookbook

The Ultimate Recipes Across America Cookbook

As always, we fondly remember our company's founder, Art Ginsburg, who taught us the importance of quick & easy cooking with results that are "OOH IT'S SO GOOD!!®". We thank you for empowering us to carry on this philosophy.

Breakfast in Bed Favorites

Family-Sized Breakfast Nachos

SERVES 6, 1 cup per serving

PREP TIME: 10 minutes
COOK TIME: 5 minutes

6	egg whites
1/4	cup fat-free milk
2	teaspoons hot sauce
1/2	teaspoon salt substitute
1/4	teaspoon black pepper
1	tablespoon light, trans-fat-free margarine
4	ounces (4 cups) oven-baked tortilla chips (see Tip)
1/2	cup reduced-sodium black beans, drained and rinsed well
1/2	cup fresh salsa
1/2	cup shredded reduced-fat Colby Jack cheese
1	avocado, diced
1	tablespoon chopped fresh cilantro

1 In a medium bowl, combine egg whites, milk, hot sauce, salt substitute, and pepper; mix well.

2 In a medium skillet over medium-low heat, melt margarine. Add egg mixture and scramble until firm, but not browned.

3 Place chips on platter. Spoon eggs evenly over chips. Top evenly with beans, salsa, cheese, and avocado. Sprinkle with cilantro before serving.

 *Test Kitchen Mr. Food Hints & Tips*

We tested these with the baked tortilla chips that are shaped like a scoop. These make it easy to carry all the goodness from plate to mouth!

NUTRITION INFORMATION   **Choices/Exchanges,** 1 Starch, 1/2 Carbohydrate, 1 Lean Protein, 1 Fat

Calories 200, Calories from Fat 70, **Total Fat** 8.0g, Saturated Fat 2.3g, Trans Fat 0.0g, **Cholesterol** 5mg, **Sodium** 400mg, **Potassium** 570mg, **Total Carbohydrate** 22g, Dietary Fiber 5g, Sugars 2g, **Protein** 10g, **Phosphorus** 135mg

Lighter Brighter Eggs Benedict

SERVES 4, 1 muffin half and 2 tablespoons Hollandaise sauce per serving

PREP TIME: 10 minutes
COOK TIME: 15 minutes

Hollandaise Sauce

1/2	cup fat-free plain Greek yogurt
1	teaspoon lemon juice
1	egg yolk
1/2	teaspoon Dijon mustard
1/4	teaspoon salt substitute
1/8	teaspoon black pepper
4	eggs
2	whole-wheat English muffins
4	slices Canadian bacon
4	tomato slices
1	teaspoon chopped fresh chives
	Paprika for garnish

1 To make Hollandaise Sauce, in a double boiler, beat yogurt, lemon juice, egg yolk, mustard, salt substitute, and pepper. Heat over simmering water about 8 minutes or until sauce has thickened, stirring frequently. Remove from heat and keep warm.

2 Fill a medium skillet halfway with water and bring to a boil. Crack eggs, one at a time, and gently drop into boiling water. Cook 5 to 7 minutes or until yolks and whites are firm.

3 Meanwhile, toast English muffins. At the same time, coat a medium skillet with cooking spray and heat Canadian bacon 2 minutes per side.

4 Place English muffin halves on a plate and top each half with a slice of Canadian bacon and tomato. Using a slotted spoon, remove eggs from water and place one over each slice of tomato. Top each egg with 2 tablespoons Hollandaise Sauce. Garnish with chives and paprika, and serve immediately.

Good for You!

We replaced our traditional Hollandaise sauce recipe with a lighter and brighter version that starts with Greek yogurt. This lets us enjoy lots of great taste, but with a lot fewer calories and less fat!

NUTRITION INFORMATION   Choices/Exchanges, 1 Starch, 2 Lean Protein, 1/2 Fat

Calories 190, Calories from Fat 60, **Total Fat** 7.0g, Saturated Fat 2.2g, Trans Fat 0.0g, **Cholesterol** 240mg, **Sodium** 370mg, **Potassium** 510mg, **Total Carbohydrate** 16g, Dietary Fiber 3g, Sugars 5g. **Protein** 16g, **Phosphorus** 290mg

Mamma Rosa's Breakfast Frittata

SERVES 4, 1 slice per serving

PREP TIME: 10 minutes
COOK TIME: 25 minutes

3	teaspoons olive oil, divided
1	potato, peeled and cut into 1/2-inch cubes
1/2	cup chopped onion
1/4	pound lean turkey sausage
1	cup sliced mushrooms
2	cloves garlic, minced
2	cups fresh spinach
1/2	cup diced tomato
1-1/2	cups liquid egg whites
1	teaspoon salt-free Italian seasoning blend
1/4	teaspoon black pepper

1. In a skillet over medium heat, heat 2 teaspoons oil until hot; cook potato and onion 10 to 12 minutes or until tender, stirring occasionally. Remove potato mixture to a plate; set aside.

2. Add remaining 1 teaspoon oil to skillet and brown sausage 4 to 5 minutes, stirring until sausage crumbles and is no longer pink. Add mushrooms, garlic, and spinach and sauté 3 to 4 minutes or until spinach is wilted. Add potato mixture back to skillet with sausage mixture; add tomatoes and mix well.

3. Meanwhile, in a medium bowl, whisk egg whites, seasoning blend, and pepper. Pour egg mixture over sausage mixture in skillet. Cover, reduce heat to low, and cook 8 to 10 minutes or until center is set. Cut into quarters and serve.

Test Kitchen. Mr. Food Hints & Tips

We tested this in several skillets and found that a 9-inch skillet is ideal. If it's too small, the outside browns too quickly before the center is set, and if it's too large, you end up with an egg pancake.

NUTRITION INFORMATION Choices/Exchanges, 1/2 Starch, 1 Nonstarchy Vegetable, 2 Lean Protein, 1/2 Fat

Calories 170, Calories from Fat 50, **Total Fat** 6.0g, Saturated Fat 1.1g, Trans Fat 0.1g, **Cholesterol** 15mg, **Sodium** 310mg, **Potassium** 550mg, **Total Carbohydrate** 12g, Dietary Fiber 2g, Sugars 3g, **Protein** 18g, **Phosphorus** 105mg

Huevos Rancheros

SERVES 4, 1 egg and 1 tortilla per serving

PREP TIME: 10 minutes
COOK TIME: 10 minutes

1	teaspoon canola oil
1-1/2	cups diced tomatoes
1/2	cup diced onion
1	seeded and chopped jalapeño pepper
2	tablespoons chopped cilantro
2	teaspoons lime juice
1/2	teaspoon ground cumin
1/4	teaspoon salt
4	eggs
4	corn tortillas

1 In a medium skillet over medium-high heat, heat oil until hot. Add tomato, onion, jalapeño, cilantro, lime juice, cumin, and salt. Cover and cook 4 to 5 minutes or until vegetables soften, stirring occasionally.

2 Lightly coat a large skillet with cooking spray. Heat skillet over medium-high heat; add 4 eggs and cook until desired doneness.

3 Meanwhile, warm tortillas according to package directions. Place tortillas on 4 plates, and top each with tomato mixture and 1 egg. Serve immediately.

Serving Suggestion
We like to top these with some fresh chopped cilantro. It adds an authentic South-of-the-Border taste!

NUTRITION INFORMATION Choices/Exchanges, 1 Starch, 1 Nonstarchy Vegetable, 1 Medium-Fat Protein

Calories 170, Calories from Fat 60, **Total Fat** 7.0g, Saturated Fat 1.8g, Trans Fat 0.0g, **Cholesterol** 185mg, **Sodium** 230mg, **Potassium** 350mg, **Total Carbohydrate** 18g, Dietary Fiber 3g, Sugars 4g, **Protein** 9g, **Phosphorus** 210mg

Baked Egg 'n' Tomato Cups

SERVES 4, 1 tomato with 1 egg per serving

PREP TIME: 10 minutes
COOK TIME: 30 minutes

4	beefsteak or heirloom tomatoes
1/2	teaspoon black pepper, divided
1/2	teaspoon salt-free garlic and herb seasoning blend
4	eggs
2	teaspoons reduced-fat grated Parmesan cheese
2	slices bacon, cooked and crumbled

1 Preheat oven to 350°F. Coat a 9- × 13-inch baking dish with cooking spray.

2 Cut 1/4 inch off top of each tomato. Scoop out pulp and seeds, leaving about a 1/2-inch-thick shell. (Reserve tomato pulp for another use or discard.) Place cut-side-up in baking dish. Evenly sprinkle tomatoes with 1/4 teaspoon pepper and the seasoning blend.

3 Break an egg into each tomato. Sprinkle each egg with 1/2 teaspoon cheese and the remaining 1/4 teaspoon pepper. Bake 30 to 35 minutes or until eggs are set. Sprinkle with bacon and serve.

Note: If you're looking for a salt-free garlic and herb seasoning blend in your supermarket, check the spice aisle. There are several brands to choose from; we tested ours with Mrs. Dash®.

Your farmers market is a wonderful place to purchase heirloom tomatoes. Those are the tomatoes that come in a variety of colors. While they may not be as perfectly round as the tomatoes you find in the supermarket, they're very tasty and add a whimsical touch to breakfast.

NUTRITION INFORMATION   **Choices/Exchanges,** 1 Nonstarchy Vegetable, 1 Lean Protein, 1 Fat

Calories 130, Calories from Fat 60, **Total Fat** 7.0g, Saturated Fat 2.4g, Trans Fat 0.0g, **Cholesterol** 195mg, **Sodium** 200mg, **Potassium** 440mg, **Total Carbohydrate** 7g, Dietary Fiber 2g, Sugars 4g, **Protein** 10g, **Phosphorus** 165mg

Spinach & Cheese Brunch Roll

SERVES 8, 1 slice per serving

PREP TIME: 15 minutes
COOK TIME: 20 minutes

2	cups egg substitute
4	eggs
1/2	teaspoon salt
1/8	teaspoon hot pepper sauce
1	(9-ounce) package frozen chopped spinach, thawed and squeezed dry
1/4	cup chopped red onion
1	teaspoon Italian seasoning
2	teaspoons canola oil
8	ounces fresh mushrooms, thinly sliced
1	cup (4 ounces) shredded part-skim mozzarella cheese, divided
1/2	cup diced roasted red pepper

1 Preheat oven to 375°F. Line a 10- × 15-inch rimmed baking sheet with aluminum foil; coat foil with cooking spray and set aside.

2 In a large bowl, whisk egg substitute, eggs, salt, and hot pepper sauce. Stir in spinach, onion, and Italian seasoning. Pour mixture onto baking sheet. Bake 15 to 20 minutes or until set.

3 Meanwhile, in a large skillet over medium heat, heat oil until hot. Sauté mushrooms 5 to 7 minutes or until tender; drain.

4 Place a large cutting board over baking sheet, and carefully invert; remove baking sheet and foil. Spoon mushrooms over baked egg and sprinkle with 3/4 cup cheese.

5 Roll up jelly roll–style, starting with a short side. Place on a serving platter; sprinkle with remaining 1/4 cup cheese and diced red pepper. Serve immediately.

NUTRITION INFORMATION   **Choices/Exchanges,** 1 Nonstarchy Vegetable, 2 Lean Protein, 1/2 Fat

Calories 130, Calories from Fat 50, **Total Fat** 6.0g, Saturated Fat 2.4g, Trans Fat 0.0g, **Cholesterol** 100mg, **Sodium** 440mg, **Potassium** 330mg, **Total Carbohydrate** 5g, Dietary Fiber 1g, Sugars 2g, **Protein** 15g, **Phosphorus** 165mg

Smoked Salmon Breakfast Pizza

SERVES 8, 1 slice per serving

PREP TIME: 15 minutes
COOK TIME: 15 minutes

1	(10-ounce) package prebaked whole-wheat pizza crust
2	teaspoons canola oil
2	tablespoons chopped fresh dill, divided
1	tablespoon light, trans-fat-free margarine
1/2	red bell pepper, diced
1/2	cup diced onion
2	cups liquid egg substitute
1/4	teaspoon salt substitute
1/4	teaspoon black pepper
3	ounces smoked salmon, cut into strips

1 Preheat oven to 425°F. Coat a 12-inch round pizza pan with cooking spray. Place pizza crust on pan.

2 In a small bowl, combine oil and 1 tablespoon dill; mix well. Brush evenly over crust. Bake crust 6 to 8 minutes or until golden.

3 Meanwhile, in a large skillet over medium heat, melt margarine; add red bell pepper and onion and sauté 4 to 5 minutes or until tender. Remove to a plate.

4 In a medium bowl, combine egg substitute, salt substitute, and black pepper; mix well. Coat same skillet with cooking spray, and over medium heat, cook egg mixture, stirring occasionally, until set.

5 Spoon eggs over crust, top evenly with salmon, and remaining dill, cut into 8 slices, and serve immediately.

Good for You!

By adding smoked salmon rather than the typical smoked breakfast meats, we've made sure that each bite is packed with omega-3 fatty acids.

NUTRITION INFORMATION   **Choices/Exchanges,** 1 Starch, 1 Lean Protein, 1/2 Fat

Calories 160, Calories from Fat 35, **Total Fat** 4.0g, Saturated Fat 1.1g, Trans Fat 0.0g, **Cholesterol** 4mg, **Sodium** 370mg, **Potassium** 320mg, **Total Carbohydrate** 19g, Dietary Fiber 3g, Sugars 3g, **Protein** 12g, **Phosphorus** 110mg

Crustless Spinach Quiche

SERVES 8, 1 wedge per serving

PREP TIME: 10 minutes
COOK TIME: 35 minutes

1	(9-ounce) package frozen chopped spinach, thawed and squeezed dry
1	cup shredded reduced-fat Swiss cheese
1	cup shredded fat-free cheddar cheese
1-1/2	cups fat-free milk
4	eggs
1/2	cup reduced-fat biscuit baking mix
1	teaspoon onion powder
1/2	teaspoon ground nutmeg
1/4	teaspoon salt
1/8	teaspoon black pepper

1 Preheat oven to 350°F. Lightly coat a 9-inch pie plate with cooking spray. Evenly spread spinach and cheeses in bottom of pie plate.

2 In a blender, place remaining ingredients; blend on high 1 minute or until smooth. Pour mixture evenly into pie plate.

3 Bake 35 to 40 minutes or until golden and a knife inserted in center comes out clean. Let stand 5 minutes, then cut into 8 wedges and serve.

Good for You!
Adding spinach to this adds a ton of fiber, which can help control your blood glucose and keeps you feeling full longer.

NUTRITION INFORMATION   **Choices/Exchanges,** 1/2 Carbohydrate, 2 Lean Protein, 1/2 Fat

Calories 150, Calories from Fat 50, **Total Fat** 6.0g, Saturated Fat 2.2g, Trans Fat 0.0g, **Cholesterol** 105mg, **Sodium** 390mg, **Potassium** 220mg, **Total Carbohydrate** 10g, Dietary Fiber 1g, Sugars 3g, **Protein** 15g, **Phosphorus** 305mg

Mini Fruity Dutch Pancakes

SERVES 8, 3 per serving

PREP TIME: 10 minutes
COOK TIME: 10 minutes

1	kiwi, diced
1/2	cup blueberries
1/2	cup diced strawberries
2	eggs
1/2	cup fat-free milk
2	tablespoons light, trans-fat-free margarine, melted
1	teaspoon vanilla extract
1/2	cup all-purpose flour
1/4	teaspoon salt

1 Preheat oven to 400°F. Coat 24 mini muffin cups with cooking spray. In a small bowl, combine kiwi, blueberries, and strawberries; set aside.

2 In a blender, combine all ingredients except reserved fruit; blend on high 30 seconds or until smooth. Pour batter into muffin cups, filling halfway full.

3 Bake 10 to 12 minutes or until puffed up. Remove from oven and let sit 2 minutes. Then remove from muffin cups and divide fruit mixture evenly on top of each; serve immediately.

Portion Size Matters

Not only are mini foods fun to eat, but they make it easy to control portion size. With these, we can enjoy a small serving of nutrient-rich fruit at breakfast, without going overboard.

NUTRITION INFORMATION   Choices/Exchanges, 1/2 Starch, 1/2 Fat

Calories 80, Calories from Fat 20, **Total Fat** 2.5g, Saturated Fat 0.8g, Trans Fat 0.0g, **Cholesterol** 45mg, **Sodium** 120mg, **Potassium** 100mg, **Total Carbohydrate** 10g, Dietary Fiber 1g, Sugars 3g, **Protein** 3g, **Phosphorus** 55mg

PB & J French Toast Sticks

SERVES 2, 4 sticks per serving

PREP TIME: 10 minutes
COOK TIME: 5 minutes

1/2	cup liquid egg substitute
1	teaspoon vanilla extract
1/2	teaspoon ground cinnamon
4	slices multigrain bread
2	tablespoons reduced-fat peanut butter
2	tablespoons sugar-free strawberry preserves
2	teaspoons light, trans-fat-free margarine
1/2	cup sliced strawberries

1 In a large bowl, combine egg substitute, vanilla, and cinnamon; mix well.

2 Spread half the bread slices evenly with peanut butter, and the remaining bread with preserves. Make 2 sandwiches; cut each into 4 sticks.

3 In a large skillet over medium-high heat, melt margarine. Coat sticks evenly on all sides with egg mixture. Cook sticks 3 to 4 minutes or until golden brown on all sides, turning occasionally. Top with strawberries and serve.

Out of the Box

You can find lots of different flavor varieties of sugar-free jams, jellies, and preserves in your supermarket, so feel free to experiment! Just don't forget to look at the nutrition labels to find the best fit for your dietary goals.

NUTRITION INFORMATION   **Choices/Exchanges,** 1-1/2 Starch, 1/2 Fruit, 1/2 Carbohydrate, 2 Medium-Fat Protein

Calories 310, Calories from Fat 90, **Total Fat** 10.0g, Saturated Fat 1.9g, Trans Fat 0.0g, **Cholesterol** 0mg, **Sodium** 460mg, **Potassium** 430mg, **Total Carbohydrate** 37g, Dietary Fiber 7g, Sugars 7g, **Protein** 17g, **Phosphorus** 205mg

Banana Nut Pancakes

SERVES 7, 2 per serving

PREP TIME: 10 minutes
COOK TIME: 10 minutes

2	large ripe bananas, divided
1	egg
2	teaspoons canola oil
3/4	cup vanilla soy milk
1	cup whole-wheat pancake mix
2	tablespoons chopped walnuts

1 In a large bowl, mash 1 banana. Stir in egg, oil, and soy milk. Add pancake mix and stir until combined. Let stand 3 minutes.

2 Lightly coat a large skillet or griddle with cooking spray, and place over medium heat. Spoon about 3 tablespoons batter per pancake onto hot skillet. (If you want, you can make smaller pancakes and have 3. This way you'll feel like you're eating more while staying within your daily requirements.)

3 Cook pancakes in batches 1 to 2 minutes per side or until lightly browned. Keep cooked pancakes warm on a plate; cover loosely with aluminum foil. Slice remaining banana. Evenly top pancakes with banana and walnuts, and serve.

Serving Suggestion

Since the bananas add just the right amount of sweetness, you can probably get by without pouring on the table syrup. But just in case you're craving that extra-sticky touch, make sure you use just a tablespoon or so of sugar-free syrup. After all, it's all about making smart choices.

NUTRITION INFORMATION   **Choices/Exchanges,** 1 Starch, 1/2 Fruit, 1 Fat

Calories 150, Calories from Fat 35, **Total Fat** 4.0g, Saturated Fat 0.6g, Trans Fat 0.0g, **Cholesterol** 25mg, **Sodium** 310mg, **Potassium** 270mg, **Total Carbohydrate** 24g, Dietary Fiber 4g, Sugars 5g, **Protein** 5g, **Phosphorus** 215mg

On-the-Go Energy Bites

SERVES 12, 2 per serving

PREP TIME: 10 minutes
COOK TIME: 10 minutes

1/2	cup peanut butter, heated in microwave 20 seconds
1	ripe banana, mashed
1	egg
1	teaspoon vanilla extract
	Brown sugar substitute equal to 2 tablespoons brown sugar (see page x)
2	cups rolled oats
1/4	cup ground flaxseed
1	teaspoon baking soda
1/2	teaspoon salt

1 Preheat oven to 350°F. Coat a baking sheet with cooking spray.

2 In a medium bowl, whisk peanut butter, banana, egg, vanilla, and brown sugar substitute.

3 In another bowl, combine oats, flaxseed, baking soda, and salt. Add oat mixture to peanut butter mixture; mix well. Roll dough into 24 balls, each about 1 tablespoon in size, and place on baking sheet.

4 Bake 10 to 12 minutes or until golden. Let cool on a wire rack.

Good for You!

These will help you add a little more pep to your step in the mornings! Flaxseed is high in vitamins, minerals, and omega-3 fatty acids. It's said to help with everything from brain function and digestive issues to weight loss, cholesterol, and more.

NUTRITION INFORMATION   Choices/Exchanges, 1 Starch, 1-1/2 Fat

Calories 150, Calories from Fat 60, **Total Fat** 7.0g, Saturated Fat 1.5g, Trans Fat 0.0g, **Cholesterol** 15mg, **Sodium** 260mg, **Potassium** 180mg, **Total Carbohydrate** 15g, Dietary Fiber 3g, Sugars 3g, **Protein** 6g, **Phosphorus** 115mg

Pumpkin Patch Oatmeal Bake

SERVES 5, 1/2 cup per serving

PREP TIME: 5 minutes
COOK TIME: 20 minutes

1-1/2	cups old-fashioned oats
	Brown sugar substitute equal to 2 tablespoons brown sugar (see page x)
1	teaspoon pumpkin pie spice
1	teaspoon baking powder
1	cup fat-free milk
1	teaspoon vanilla extract
3/4	cup pure pumpkin
1	egg, beaten

1 Preheat oven to 375°F. Coat a 1-1/2-quart baking dish with cooking spray.

2 In a large bowl, combine oats, brown sugar substitute, pumpkin pie spice, and baking powder.

3 In a medium bowl, combine milk, vanilla, pumpkin, and egg. Add pumpkin mixture to oat mixture; stir well. Pour into baking dish.

4 Bake 18 to 20 minutes or until heated through and top is set. Serve piping hot.

Going Gluten-Free

To make this recipe gluten-free, simply use gluten-free oats instead of traditional ones. Also, make sure to check the nutrition labels of your other ingredients, to confirm that they are also gluten-free. Then dig in!

NUTRITION INFORMATION **Choices/Exchanges,** 1-1/2 Starch, 1/2 Fat

Calories 150, Calories from Fat 20, **Total Fat** 2.5g, Saturated Fat 0.7g, Trans Fat 0.0g, **Cholesterol** 40mg, **Sodium** 110mg, **Potassium** 260mg, **Total Carbohydrate** 25g, Dietary Fiber 4g, Sugars 5g, **Protein** 7g, **Phosphorus** 275mg

Bed & Breakfast Blueberry Muffins

SERVES 12, 1 per serving

PREP TIME: 10 minutes
COOK TIME: 15 minutes

1-1/4	cups low-fat granola
1	cup all-purpose flour
1-1/2	teaspoons ground cinnamon
1	teaspoon baking powder
3/4	teaspoon baking soda
1/2	teaspoon salt
3/4	cup unsweetened applesauce
1/4	cup honey
1/2	cup canola oil
1	egg
1	teaspoon vanilla extract
1	cup blueberries

1 Preheat oven to 375°F. Line a 12-cup muffin tin with paper liners.

2 In a large bowl, combine granola, flour, cinnamon, baking powder, baking soda, and salt; mix well.

3 In another bowl, combine applesauce, honey, oil, egg, and vanilla. Stir in blueberries. Add applesauce mixture to granola mixture, stirring gently to combine. Evenly spoon mixture into muffin cups.

4 Bake 15 to 20 minutes or until a toothpick comes out clean.

Did You Know?

You'll be surprised at how well these measure up when compared to the average blueberry muffin you can buy at a donut shop or coffee house. With only 0.9g of saturated fat, 26g of carbs, and 255 fewer calories, every bite will be even more satisfying!

NUTRITION INFORMATION   **Choices/Exchanges,** 2 Carbohydrate, 1-1/2 Fat

Calories 200, Calories from Fat 90, **Total Fat** 10.0g, Saturated Fat 0.9g, Trans Fat 0.0g, **Cholesterol** 15mg, **Sodium** 240mg, **Potassium** 65mg, **Total Carbohydrate** 26g, Dietary Fiber 2g, Sugars 11g, **Protein** 3g, **Phosphorus** 85mg

Guilt-Free Breakfast Sausage Patties

SERVES 14, 2 per serving

PREP TIME: 10 minutes
COOK TIME: 10 minutes

2	pounds lean ground turkey
1	teaspoon poultry seasoning
1	teaspoon fennel seed
1/2	teaspoon onion powder
1	tablespoon chopped fresh parsley
1/4	teaspoon crushed red pepper flakes (optional)
1/2	teaspoon salt
1/4	teaspoon black pepper
1	tablespoon real maple syrup

1 In a large bowl, combine turkey, poultry seasoning, fennel, onion powder, parsley, red pepper flakes, if desired, salt, pepper, and syrup. Shape mixture into 28 (2-inch) patties.

2 In a large skillet over medium-low heat, cook patties 3 to 5 minutes per side, or until no longer pink in center. Serve immediately.

Good for You!

Gone are the days of giving up some of our favorite foods! This breakfast sausage is full-flavored, thanks to the ground turkey and lots of spices. Breakfast can, once again, become your favorite meal of the day.

NUTRITION INFORMATION

Choices/Exchanges, 2 Lean Protein

Calories 100, Calories from Fat 40, **Total Fat** 4.5g, Saturated Fat 1.4g, Trans Fat 0.1g, **Cholesterol** 50mg, **Sodium** 130mg, **Potassium** 150mg, **Total Carbohydrate** 1g, Dietary Fiber 0g, Sugars 1g, **Protein** 12g, **Phosphorus** 125mg

Snacks & Munchies

10-Minute Greek Isle Dip

SERVES 24, 2 tablespoons per serving

PREP TIME: 10 minutes
COOK TIME: None

1	(8-ounce) container plain hummus
8	ounces plain nonfat Greek yogurt
1/4	cup diced cucumber
2	cloves garlic, minced
1	tablespoon finely chopped red onion
1	teaspoon chopped fresh mint
1/2	cup chopped tomato
1/2	cup fat-free feta cheese crumbles
1/4	cup pitted Kalamata olives, chopped

1 Spread hummus over the bottom of a 9-inch pie plate.

2 In a medium bowl, combine yogurt, cucumber, garlic, onion, and mint; mix well, then spread over hummus. Sprinkle with tomato, cheese, and olives. Serve immediately or cover and chill until ready to serve.

Serving Suggestion

Chopped fresh parsley and coarse black pepper make for the perfect finishing touches! Oh, and don't forget to serve these with a platter of cut-up veggies, so that your guests can dip away. What a healthy start to any get-together!

NUTRITION INFORMATION   Choices/Exchanges, 1/2 Fat

Calories 30, Calories from Fat 15, **Total Fat** 1.5g, Saturated Fat 0.2g, Trans Fat 0.0g, **Cholesterol** 0mg, **Sodium** 85mg, **Potassium** 50mg, **Total Carbohydrate** 2g, Dietary Fiber 1g, Sugars 1g, **Protein** 2g, **Phosphorus** 40mg

Not-Your-Everyday Guacamole

SERVES 8, 1/4 cup per serving

PREP TIME: 10 minutes
COOK TIME: None

1/2	cup coarsely chopped onion
1/2	jalapeño pepper, seeded
1/2	cup fresh cilantro leaves
3	cloves garlic
3	tablespoons lime juice
3	cups torn kale leaves
3	large avocados, pitted, peeled, and cut into chunks
1/2	teaspoon salt
1/4	teaspoon black pepper

1 In a food processor or blender, combine onion, jalapeño, cilantro, garlic, lime juice, and kale; pulse until chopped into small pieces.

2 Add avocados, salt, and pepper; pulse until desired consistency is reached. Serve immediately.

Good for You!

This is an easy and tasty way to eat your veggies! Not only do you get the healthy goodness of avocados, but the kale adds lots of vitamins and fiber too. Serve this with fresh-cut veggies for dipping to make your taste buds and your doctor happy!

NUTRITION INFORMATION

Choices/Exchanges, 1/2 Carbohydrate, 2 Fat

Calories 120, Calories from Fat 90, **Total Fat** 10.0g, Saturated Fat 1.4g, Trans Fat 0.0g, **Cholesterol** 0mg, **Sodium** 160mg, **Potassium** 410mg, **Total Carbohydrate** 9g, Dietary Fiber 5g, Sugars 1g, **Protein** 2g, **Phosphorus** 50mg

Blushing Beet Hummus

SERVES 20, 2-1/2 tablespoons per serving

PREP TIME: 5 minutes
COOK TIME: None

2	(15-1/2-ounce) cans chickpeas, rinsed and drained
1	(14-1/2-ounce) can sliced beets, rinsed and drained
3	cloves garlic, minced
1/3	cup water
3	tablespoons fresh lemon juice
3	tablespoons olive oil
3/4	teaspoon salt substitute

1 Combine all ingredients in a food processor or blender. Process until mixture is smooth and creamy, scraping down sides of bowl as needed.

2 Serve immediately or cover and refrigerate until ready to serve.

Did You Know?

Beets are full of healthy antioxidants. Studies have suggested that the color pigment in beets, which are called betalains, may help reduce inflammation and heart disease.

NUTRITION INFORMATION   Choices/Exchanges, 1/2 Starch, 1/2 Fat

Calories 70, Calories from Fat 20, **Total Fat** 2.5g, Saturated Fat 0.4g, Trans Fat 0.0g, **Cholesterol** 0mg, **Sodium** 70mg, **Potassium** 190mg, **Total Carbohydrate** 8g, Dietary Fiber 2g, Sugars 2g, **Protein** 2g, **Phosphorus** 45mg

Crab Cake Pepper Poppers

SERVES 12, 3 per serving

PREP TIME: 15 minutes
COOK TIME: 20 minutes

1/2	cup Italian-flavored bread crumbs
1/4	cup liquid egg substitute
1/4	cup finely chopped red onion
1/2	cup finely chopped celery
3	tablespoons light mayonnaise
2	teaspoons fresh lemon juice
3/4	teaspoon seafood seasoning (like Old Bay®)
1/4	teaspoon black pepper
2	(6-1/2-ounce) cans lump crabmeat, drained
18	mini sweet peppers, halved and seeded
	Paprika for sprinkling

1 Preheat oven to 350°F. Coat a baking sheet with cooking spray.

2 In a medium bowl, combine bread crumbs, egg substitute, onion, celery, mayonnaise, lemon juice, seafood seasoning, and black pepper; mix well. Gently fold in crabmeat, being careful not to break up the chunks.

3 Spoon the crabmeat mixture evenly among pepper halves and place on baking sheet.

4 Bake 20 to 25 minutes or until tops are golden and the peppers are tender. Sprinkle with paprika before serving.

Note: If you'd like you can bake these in an air fryer, in batches, right in the basket. Just make sure you reduce the cooking time by about 25%.

Serving Suggestion
We like to serve these with wedges of fresh lemon. A little squeeze is all it takes to bring out an ocean of flavor.

NUTRITION INFORMATION

Choices/Exchanges, 1/2 Carbohydrate, 1/2 Fat

Calories 60, Calories from Fat 15, **Total Fat** 1.5g, Saturated Fat 0.2g, Trans Fat 0.0g, **Cholesterol** 20mg, **Sodium** 250mg, **Potassium** 190mg, **Total Carbohydrate** 7g, Dietary Fiber 1g, Sugars 2g, **Protein** 4g, **Phosphorus** 75mg

East-Meets-West Turkey Meatballs

SERVES 8, 3 per serving

PREP TIME: 15 minutes
COOK TIME: 20 minutes

1-1/4	pounds ground turkey breast
3/4	cup rolled oats, ground (see Tip)
1	egg
1/2	teaspoon garlic powder
1/4	teaspoon ground ginger
2	scallions, thinly sliced
2	tablespoons reduced-sodium soy sauce, divided
1/4	cup hoisin sauce
2	tablespoons rice vinegar

1 Preheat oven to 375°F. Coat a baking sheet with cooking spray.

2 In a large bowl, combine turkey, oats, egg, garlic, ginger, scallions, and 1 tablespoon soy sauce. Form into 24 (1-inch) meatballs and place on baking sheet.

3 Bake 12 to 15 minutes or until meatballs are no longer pink in center.

4 Meanwhile, in a medium saucepan over low heat, combine hoisin sauce, vinegar, and the remaining 1 tablespoon soy sauce; mix well and heat until hot. Add meatballs to the sauce and stir until evenly coated. Serve warm.

It's easy to turn rolled oats into ground oats. Simply place them in a food processor with a cutting blade and pulse until they're the consistency of bread crumbs.

NUTRITION INFORMATION

Choices/Exchanges, 1/2 Carbohydrate, 2 Lean Protein

Calories 140, Calories from Fat 20, **Total Fat** 2.0g, Saturated Fat 0.5g, Trans Fat 0.0g, **Cholesterol** 70mg, **Sodium** 310mg, **Potassium** 230mg, **Total Carbohydrate** 10g, Dietary Fiber 1g, Sugars 3g, **Protein** 19g, **Phosphorus** 180mg

NY Deli-Style Reuben Cups

SERVES 24, 1 per serving

PREP TIME: 15 minutes
COOK TIME: 20 minutes

24	wonton wrappers
1	cup sauerkraut, drained, patted dry, and coarsely chopped
4	ounces deli corned beef, chopped
3	tablespoons reduced-fat Thousand Island dressing
1/2	cup shredded Swiss cheese

1 Preheat oven to 350°F. Coat 24 mini muffin cups with cooking spray. Place a wonton wrapper in each muffin cup with edges of wrappers extending over top of cups. Bake 5 minutes.

2 Meanwhile, in a medium bowl, combine sauerkraut, corned beef, and dressing; mix well. Evenly fill each wonton cup with sauerkraut mixture and sprinkle with cheese.

3 Bake 12 to 14 minutes or until filling is heated through and edges of cups are golden.

Serving Suggestion

Since no one likes scrambling at the last minute when it comes to entertaining, you can fill the cups a few hours before serving them. Then all you have to do is pop them in the oven right before your guests arrive!

NUTRITION INFORMATION

Choices/Exchanges, 1/2 Starch

Calories 40, Calories from Fat 10, **Total Fat** 1.0g, Saturated Fat 0.4g, Trans Fat 0.0g, **Cholesterol** 5mg, **Sodium** 150mg, **Potassium** 30mg, **Total Carbohydrate** 5g, Dietary Fiber 0g, Sugars 1g, **Protein** 3g, **Phosphorus** 25mg

Oven-Fried Mozzarella Sticks

SERVES 12, 2 per serving

PREP TIME: 15 minutes
FREEZE TIME: 1-1/2 hours
COOK TIME: 10 minutes

12	reduced-fat mozzarella string cheese sticks
1	egg
2	tablespoons all-purpose flour
5	tablespoons whole-wheat bread crumbs
5	tablespoons whole-wheat panko bread crumbs
2	teaspoons grated Parmesan cheese
1	tablespoon chopped fresh parsley
	Cooking spray

1 Line a baking sheet with wax paper. Cut each cheese stick in half. Place in freezer 30 minutes or until frozen.

2 In a small bowl, whisk egg. Place flour in a medium bowl. In another medium bowl, combine bread crumbs, panko, Parmesan cheese, and parsley. Dip frozen cheese sticks in flour, shaking off excess, then in egg, then in seasoned bread crumbs, coating completely. Place on baking sheet. Place back in freezer at least 1 hour or until ready to bake.

3 When ready to bake, preheat oven to 400°F. Line a baking sheet with aluminum foil and lightly coat with cooking spray. Place frozen cheese sticks on baking sheet and spray lightly with cooking spray.

4 Bake 5 to 6 minutes or until crisp; turn over and bake another 5 minutes or until light golden. (Do not overbake.)

Note: If you have an air fryer, you can make these right in the basket. Just shave a minute or so off the cooking time.

Serving Suggestion

These are great as-is, as they deliver lots of the ooey-gooey cheesiness that you love. But if you want to take these over the top, serve them with a low-sodium marinara sauce for dipping. Now that's doubly good!

NUTRITION INFORMATION

Choices/Exchanges, 1 Lean Protein, 1/2 Fat

Calories 70, Calories from Fat 25, **Total Fat** 3.0g, Saturated Fat 1.2g, Trans Fat 0.0g, **Cholesterol** 20mg, **Sodium** 160mg, **Potassium** 35mg, **Total Carbohydrate** 4g, Dietary Fiber 0g, Sugars 0g, **Protein** 7g, **Phosphorus** 140mg

Easy Broccoli & Cheddar Balls

SERVES 6, 5 per serving

PREP TIME: 15 minutes
COOK TIME: 20 minutes

2	(12-ounce) packages frozen broccoli florets
1	egg
1/3	cup shredded reduced-fat cheddar cheese
1/3	cup plain bread crumbs
1/4	cup chopped onion
1/2	teaspoon garlic powder
1/4	teaspoon salt
1/4	teaspoon black pepper
	Cooking spray

1 Preheat oven to 400°F. Coat baking sheet(s) with cooking spray.

2 In a large microwave-safe bowl, microwave broccoli until thawed; drain liquid. (This will take about 2 minutes.)

3 In a blender or food processor with a cutting blade, combine broccoli, egg, cheese, bread crumbs, onion, garlic powder, salt, and pepper; pulse until mixture is coarsely chopped. (Do not overmix.) Drop 30 rounded teaspoonfuls onto baking sheet(s). Lightly spray tops with cooking spray.

4 Bake 20 to 25 minutes or until golden brown.

These can be made a day or two before you plan on serving them. Just warm them up when you need them. Talk about easy and delicious!

NUTRITION INFORMATION

Choices/Exchanges, 1/2 Starch, 1 Nonstarchy Vegetable, 1/2 Fat

Calories 100, Calories from Fat 25, **Total Fat** 3.0g, Saturated Fat 1.2g, Trans Fat 0.0g, **Cholesterol** 35mg, **Sodium** 230mg, **Potassium** 330mg, **Total Carbohydrate** 11g, Dietary Fiber 3g, Sugars 3g, **Protein** 5g, **Phosphorus** 130mg

Southwestern Mini Egg Rolls

SERVES 12, 2 pieces and 1 teaspoon dipping sauce per serving

PREP TIME: 20 minutes
COOK TIME: 15 minutes

1/2	cup black beans, rinsed and drained
1/2	cup frozen corn, thawed
1/2	cup shredded reduced-fat Colby Jack cheese
1/4	cup taco sauce
2	(4-ounce) cooked chicken breasts, shredded
24	wonton wrappers
2	tablespoons water
	Cooking spray

Cilantro Dipping Sauce

1/4	cup fat-free sour cream
1	tablespoon chopped fresh cilantro
1	teaspoon lime juice

1 Preheat oven to 425°F. Coat a baking sheet with cooking spray.

2 In a medium bowl, combine black beans, corn, cheese, and taco sauce; mix in chicken.

3 Spoon about 1 heaping teaspoon of chicken mixture onto center of each wonton wrapper. Lightly brush edges with water. Fold 1 corner of each wrapper over mixture, then fold both sides in, envelope-style; roll up tightly. Place seam side down on baking sheet. Coat lightly with cooking spray.

4 Bake 15 to 18 minutes or until crispy.

5 Meanwhile, in a small bowl, make Cilantro Dipping Sauce by combining sour cream, cilantro, and lime juice; mix well. Serve egg rolls immediately with dipping sauce.

Note: These can bake up perfectly in an air fryer. Just place them in the basket, in batches, and cook until crispy. It should take about 3 or 4 minutes less than in a conventional oven.

Good for You!
By making these ourselves, rather than ordering them in a restaurant, we cut down the saturated fat and sodium by more than half!

NUTRITION INFORMATION   Choices/Exchanges, 1 Starch, 1 Lean Protein

Calories 110, Calories from Fat 20, **Total Fat** 2.0g, Saturated Fat 0.8g, Trans Fat 0.0g, **Cholesterol** 20mg, **Sodium** 200mg, **Potassium** 115mg, **Total Carbohydrate** 12g, Dietary Fiber 1g, Sugars 1g, **Protein** 10g, **Phosphorus** 95mg

Bacon-Wrapped Fiesta Shrimp

SERVES 6, 2 per serving

PREP TIME: 10 minutes
COOK TIME: 10 minutes

2	tablespoons olive oil
2	tablespoons lime juice
1	teaspoon lime zest
1/2	teaspoon chili powder
12	large shrimp, peeled and deveined, with tails on*
6	slices bacon, cut in half
1	tablespoon honey

1 Preheat oven to 450°F. Line a baking sheet with aluminum foil.

2 In a large bowl, combine olive oil, lime juice, lime zest, and chili powder; mix well. Add shrimp and toss until evenly coated (reserve lime juice mixture).

3 Place bacon on paper towels on a microwave-safe plate and cover with paper towels. Microwave on high 2 minutes or until bacon is still soft; let cool slightly. Wrap each shrimp with a piece of bacon, securing with a toothpick (reserve lime juice mixture). Place shrimp on baking sheet. Brush remaining lime juice mixture over bacon-wrapped shrimp.

4 Bake 8 to 10 minutes or until bacon is browned and shrimp turn pink. Brush with honey and serve immediately.

Did You Know?

Honey tastes sweeter than white sugar because it contains a higher percentage of fructose to glucose. That means a little goes a long way!

If possible, use fresh (never frozen) shrimp, or shrimp that are free of preservatives (for example shrimp that have not been treated with salt or STPP [sodium tripolyphosphate]).

NUTRITION INFORMATION   **Choices/Exchanges,** 1 Lean Protein, 1-1/2 Fat

Calories 120, Calories from Fat 80, **Total Fat** 9.0g, Saturated Fat 2.0g, Trans Fat 0.0g, **Cholesterol** 35mg, **Sodium** 210mg, **Potassium** 100mg, **Total Carbohydrate** 4g, Dietary Fiber 0g, Sugars 3g, **Protein** 7g, **Phosphorus** 75mg

Artichoke Dip Potato Skins

SERVES 10, 2 per serving

PREP TIME: 20 minutes
COOK TIME: 50 minutes

10	baby red potatoes
1	(9-ounce) package frozen chopped spinach, thawed and well drained
1-1/2	cups artichoke hearts, chopped
1/2	cup shredded part-skim mozzarella cheese
1/3	cup whipped cream cheese
1	tablespoon grated Parmesan cheese
1	tablespoon finely chopped onion
1/4	teaspoon garlic powder

1 Preheat oven to 375°F. Coat a rimmed baking sheet with cooking spray. Place potatoes on baking sheet and pierce all over with a fork.

2 Bake 40 to 45 minutes or until tender. Let stand until cool enough to handle, then cut potatoes in half lengthwise. Carefully scoop out pulp, leaving thin shells. Save pulp for another use or discard.

3 Meanwhile, in a medium bowl, combine remaining ingredients.

4 Right before serving, turn oven temperature to broil. Broil potato skins 4 to 6 minutes or until edges brown. Spoon spinach mixture evenly into skins. Broil an additional 3 to 4 minutes or until warmed through and the tops are golden. Serve warm.

Portion Size Matters

Instead of setting out a big bowl of spinach-artichoke dip for your guests to dig into, why not make these? Not only do they look fancy, but by portioning the dip on baby potato skins, it reduces the chances of overindulging.

NUTRITION INFORMATION   **Choices/Exchanges,** 1/2 Carbohydrate, 1/2 Fat

Calories 60, Calories from Fat 20, **Total Fat** 2.5g, Saturated Fat 1.5g, Trans Fat 0.0g, **Cholesterol** 10mg, **Sodium** 105mg, **Potassium** 190mg, **Total Carbohydrate** 6g, Dietary Fiber 2g, Sugars 1g, **Protein** 3g, **Phosphorus** 70mg

One-Bite Spaghetti Squash Cups

SERVES 12, 2 per serving

PREP TIME: 15 minutes
COOK TIME: 50 minutes

1	spaghetti squash (about 3 pounds)
2	tablespoons olive oil
1/2	cup finely chopped onion
2	cloves garlic, minced
1/2	(8-ounce) package cream cheese, cut into 1/2-inch chunks, softened
1	egg
1/2	teaspoon poultry seasoning
1/8	teaspoon black pepper
1/2	cup dried cranberries for garnish

1 Fill a soup pot with 1 inch water; place squash in water. Bring to a boil over high heat, cover, and cook 25 to 30 minutes or until tender when pierced with a knife. Remove squash to a cutting board and allow to cool slightly. Cut squash in half, lengthwise. Remove and discard seeds with a spoon. With a fork, scrape the inside of one half, shredding it into noodle-like strands. Place shredded squash in a large bowl. Reserve remaining half for a later use.

2 Meanwhile, in a small skillet over medium-low heat, heat oil until hot. Cook onion and garlic 3 to 4 minutes or until softened, stirring occasionally; add to squash.

3 Add cream cheese to squash mixture and mix until thoroughly combined. Stir in egg, poultry seasoning, and pepper.

4 Preheat oven to 400°F. Coat 1 (24-cup) mini muffin tin with cooking spray. Spoon equal amounts of squash mixture into each muffin cup and lightly press 2 to 3 dried cranberries on top of each. Bake 25 to 30 minutes or until lightly browned. Let cool slightly, then remove from muffin tin and serve.

Since this recipe only uses half of the cooked spaghetti squash, use the other half for another tasty recipe. An easy idea is to scrape out the squash and sauté it with a little pesto sauce. This makes for a two-ingredient side dish that's packed with flavor!

NUTRITION INFORMATION

Choices/Exchanges, 1/2 Carbohydrate, 1 Fat

Calories 90, Calories from Fat 50, **Total Fat** 6.0g, Saturated Fat 2.3g, Trans Fat 0.0g, **Cholesterol** 25mg, **Sodium** 40mg, **Potassium** 70mg, **Total Carbohydrate** 7g, Dietary Fiber 1g, Sugars 5g, **Protein** 1g, **Phosphorus** 25mg

Almond-Crusted Chicken Skewers

SERVES 10, 1 per serving

PREP TIME: 15 minutes
COOK TIME: 15 minutes

10	chicken tenders
10	(6-inch) skewers (see Tip)
1/8	teaspoon garlic powder
1/8	teaspoon black pepper
1/2	cup reduced-sugar raspberry preserves
1	teaspoon Thai chili sauce
1	tablespoon lime juice
2	cloves garlic, minced
2	tablespoons chopped almonds

1 Preheat oven to 400°F. Coat a baking sheet with cooking spray.

2 Thread chicken on skewers; place on baking sheet. Sprinkle chicken evenly with garlic powder and pepper.

3 Meanwhile, whisk raspberry preserves, chili sauce, lime juice, and garlic. Set aside half the mixture; brush remaining half on chicken. (See Tip.)

4 Bake 15 minutes or until no longer pink in center. Sprinkle with nuts and serve with remaining raspberry mixture.

If using wooden skewers, be sure to soak them in water for at least 15 minutes to prevent them from burning while they bake. Also, make sure to set aside half of the raspberry mixture before you start brushing the chicken. That way you don't have any cross contamination when you serve the remaining mixture.

NUTRITION INFORMATION

Choices/Exchanges, 1/2 Carbohydrate, 1 Lean Protein

Calories 90, Calories from Fat 20, **Total Fat** 2.0g, Saturated Fat 0.4g, Trans Fat 0.0g, **Cholesterol** 30mg, **Sodium** 40mg, **Potassium** 150mg, **Total Carbohydrate** 6g, Dietary Fiber 0g, Sugars 4g, **Protein** 12g, **Phosphorus** 95mg

Buffalo-Style Chicken Pizza

SERVES 10, 1 slice per serving

PREP TIME: 10 minutes
COOK TIME: 10 minutes

3	tablespoons hot cayenne pepper sauce
1	teaspoon light, trans-fat-free margarine, melted
2	cups diced cooked chicken breast (about 1/2 pound)
1	celery stalk, diced (about 1/2 cup)
1	(10-ounce) package prebaked whole-wheat pizza crust
2	tablespoons blue cheese crumbles
1/3	cup shredded reduced-fat mozzarella cheese

1 Preheat oven to 400°F.

2 In a medium bowl, combine cayenne pepper sauce and margarine; mix well. Add chicken and celery; toss to coat well. Place pizza crust on pizza pan. Top evenly with chicken mixture and sprinkle with blue cheese and mozzarella cheese.

3 Bake 8 to 10 minutes or until crust is crispy and cheese is melted. Cut into 10 slices and serve immediately.

Make sure you don't mix up hot cayenne pepper sauce with regular hot sauce. Hot cayenne pepper sauce is chicken wing sauce and is not as fiery hot as many of the other hot sauces on the market.

NUTRITION INFORMATION

Choices/Exchanges, 1 Starch, 1 Lean Protein

Calories 130, Calories from Fat 30, **Total Fat** 3.5g, Saturated Fat 1.6g, Trans Fat 0.0g, **Cholesterol** 25mg, **Sodium** 320mg, **Potassium** 160mg, **Total Carbohydrate** 14g, Dietary Fiber 3g, Sugars 1g, **Protein** 11g, **Phosphorus** 140mg

Balsamic & Feta Watermelon Wedges

SERVES 15, 2 per serving

PREP TIME: 10 minutes
COOK TIME: None

1	watermelon (about 5 pounds)
1/4	teaspoon sea salt
1/4	cup thinly sliced red onion
1/3	cup crumbled feta cheese
2	tablespoons balsamic glaze
1	cup pistachio nuts, coarsely chopped

1 Cut watermelon in half lengthwise, then cut each half into 3/4-inch-thick slices. Cut slices into 30 wedges total. Place in a single layer on serving platters, and sprinkle with salt.

2 Evenly top each wedge with onion and feta. Drizzle with balsamic glaze, sprinkle with pistachio nuts, and serve.

Out of the Box

If you think this combo sounds strange, think again! The touch of sea salt brings out the sweetness in the melon, while the onion and feta adds a welcome Mediterranean flavor, and the balsamic glaze brings everything together. One bite and it'll all make sense.

NUTRITION INFORMATION   Choices/Exchanges, 1/2 Fruit, 1 Fat

Calories 80, Calories from Fat 40, **Total Fat** 4.5g, Saturated Fat 1.0g, Trans Fat 0.0g, **Cholesterol** 5mg, **Sodium** 75mg, **Potassium** 180mg, **Total Carbohydrate** 10g, Dietary Fiber 1g, Sugars 6g, **Protein** 3g, **Phosphorus** 60mg

Salads & Sandwiches

Better-for-You Caesar Salad

SERVES 6, 1 cup per serving

PREP TIME: 10 minutes
COOK TIME: None

Caesar Dressing

1/2	cup light mayonnaise
3	tablespoons grated reduced-fat Parmesan cheese, divided
2	cloves garlic, minced
3	tablespoon lemon juice
1/8	teaspoon salt substitute
1/4	teaspoon black pepper
6	cups chopped kale
1/4	cup coarsely crushed croutons

1. To make the Caesar Dressing, in a small bowl, combine mayonnaise, 2 tablespoons Parmesan cheese, the garlic, lemon juice, salt substitute, and pepper; mix well.

2. Place kale in a large bowl. Pour dressing over kale and toss to combine. Sprinkle with croutons and remaining 1 tablespoon Parmesan cheese and serve.

Good for You!

By now you've probably heard how good kale is for you. In case you haven't—it's a great source of fiber, potassium, and vitamins C and B6, which have all been found to support a healthy diet. We almost forgot to mention how tasty it is too!

NUTRITION INFORMATION   **Choices/Exchanges,** 1/2 Carbohydrate, 1 Nonstarchy Vegetable, 1 Fat

Calories 110, Calories from Fat 50, **Total Fat** 6.0g, Saturated Fat 0.9g, Trans Fat 0.0g, **Cholesterol** 5mg, **Sodium** 250mg, **Potassium** 410mg, **Total Carbohydrate** 12g, Dietary Fiber 3g, Sugars 2g, **Protein** 4g, **Phosphorus** 95mg

Harvest Brussels Sprouts Salad

SERVES 6, 1 cup per serving

PREP TIME: 15 minutes
COOK TIME: None

Honey-Dijon Vinaigrette
1/4	cup canola oil
3	tablespoons cider vinegar
1	tablespoon fresh lemon juice
1	tablespoon honey
1-1/2	teaspoons Dijon mustard
1/2	teaspoon garlic powder
1/4	teaspoon black pepper
1	pound fresh Brussels sprouts, thinly sliced (see Tip)
1	Granny Smith apple, diced
1	teaspoon lemon juice
1/3	cup pomegranate arils
1/4	cup chopped walnuts

1 To make Honey-Dijon Vinaigrette, in a small bowl, whisk together all dressing ingredients; set aside.

2 Place Brussels sprouts in a large bowl.

3 In a small bowl, toss apple with lemon juice. Add to Brussels sprouts along with pomegranate arils and walnuts. Pour dressing over salad and toss until evenly coated. Serve immediately or chill until ready to serve.

Test Kitchen. Mr. Food Hints & Tips

The best way to slice the Brussels sprouts is to trim off the stem end and place the cut side down (to prevent it from rolling around while cutting). Then with a chef's knife, slice away!

NUTRITION INFORMATION

Choices/Exchanges, 1/2 Fruit, 1 Nonstarchy Vegetable, 2-1/2 Fat

Calories 180, Calories from Fat 120, **Total Fat** 13.0g Saturated Fat 1.0g, Trans Fat 0.0g, **Cholesterol** 0mg, **Sodium** 50mg, **Potassium** 350mg, **Total Carbohydrate** 16g, Dietary Fiber 4g, Sugars 9g, **Protein** 3g, **Phosphorus** 75mg

Summer's Best Salad

SERVES 6, 1/2 cup per serving

PREP TIME: 15 minutes
COOK TIME: None

3	cups cubed watermelon
1	cucumber, seeded and diced
1/4	cup thinly slivered red onion
2	tablespoons chopped fresh mint

Lime Dressing

1/4	cup lime juice
1	teaspoon agave
1/4	cup canola oil

1 In a large bowl, combine watermelon, cucumber, onion, and mint.

2 To make the Lime Dressing, in a small bowl, whisk lime juice, agave, and oil. Pour dressing over watermelon mixture, toss gently to coat, and serve.

Good for You!

When it comes to adding cucumber to a salad, do you typically peel it or not? Well, here's something to consider: The peel of the cucumber is a great source of insoluble fiber, which is important for healthy digestion. Plus, it's loaded with beta carotene, an antioxidant that can help prevent cancer, as well as keep your skin and eyes healthy.

NUTRITION INFORMATION

Choices/Exchanges, 1/2 Fruit, 2 Fat

Calories 120, Calories from Fat 80, **Total Fat** 9.0g, Saturated Fat 0.7g, Trans Fat 0.0g, **Cholesterol** 0mg, **Sodium** 0mg, **Potassium** 150mg, **Total Carbohydrate** 9g, Dietary Fiber 1g, Sugars 6g, **Protein** 1g, **Phosphorus** 20mg

Sun-Kissed Health Salad

SERVES 6, 1-1/2 cups per serving

PREP TIME: 30 minutes
COOK TIME: 20 minutes

Citrus Dressing

2	tablespoons olive oil
2	tablespoons lemon juice
2	tablespoons fresh orange juice
1/4	of an avocado, pitted, peeled, and diced
1/4	cup loosely packed fresh parsley, stems removed
1/4	teaspoon salt
1	clove garlic
1	large head Boston or Bibb lettuce, cut into 1-inch pieces
1	cup cherry or grape tomatoes, cut in half
1/2	cup quinoa, cooked according to package directions, cooled
1	cup frozen shelled edamame, cooked according to package directions
3/4	of an avocado, pitted, peeled and diced
2	tablespoons unsalted pepitas (see note)

1 In a blender or food processor, blend Citrus Dressing ingredients until smooth; set aside.

2 In a large bowl, combine lettuce, tomato, quinoa, edamame, avocado, and pepitas. Pour dressing over salad and toss gently. Serve immediately or chill until ready to serve.

Did You Know?

If you're not familiar with pepitas, you can find them in most markets alongside all of the other seeds and nuts. In case you're wondering whether they're the same as pumpkin seeds, the answer is . . . sort of. Pepitas are pumpkin seeds that come from specific varieties of pumpkins, like oilseed pumpkins. These pumpkin seeds don't have outer shells and are green, rather than white.

NUTRITION INFORMATION   Choices/Exchanges, 1 Starch, 1 Lean Protein, 1-1/2 Fat

Calories 190, Calories from Fat 110, **Total Fat** 12.0g, Saturated Fat 1.6g, Trans Fat 0.0g, **Cholesterol** 0mg, **Sodium** 105mg, **Potassium** 490mg, **Total Carbohydrate** 17g, Dietary Fiber 5g, Sugars 3g, **Protein** 7g, **Phosphorus** 170mg

Un-Beet-Able Citrus Salad

SERVES 5, 2 cups per serving

PREP TIME: 15 minutes
COOK TIME: 15 minutes

3	fresh beets, trimmed (see Tip)

Fresh Orange Dressing

2	tablespoons canola oil
2	tablespoons fresh orange juice
1	tablespoon balsamic vinegar
1	teaspoon agave
1	teaspoon Dijon mustard
1	teaspoon minced onion
1/4	teaspoon black pepper
1	(10-ounce) package mixed baby salad greens
1	orange, peeled and sliced
1	pound boneless, skinless cooked chicken breasts, thinly sliced
2	tablespoons goat cheese crumbles

1 Place beets in a saucepan with enough water to cover. Bring to a boil over medium heat; cook 15 to 20 minutes or until tender. Drain and let cool, then peel and cut into 1/4-inch-thick slices.

2 Meanwhile, to make Fresh Orange Dressing, in a small bowl, whisk together oil, orange juice, balsamic vinegar, agave, mustard, onion, and black pepper; set aside.

3 Divide salad greens evenly onto 5 plates. Arrange beets, orange slices, and chicken evenly over greens. Sprinkle with goat cheese, drizzle with dressing, and serve.

When handling the beets, make sure you wear gloves so that your hands don't get stained red. If they do, cut a lemon in half, squeeze the lemon over your hands, and vigorously rub them together. Rinse and repeat until your hands are stain free.

NUTRITION INFORMATION   **Choices/Exchanges,** 1/2 Fruit, 1 Nonstarchy Vegetable, 4 Lean Protein, 1/2 Fat

Calories 260, Calories from Fat 90, **Total Fat** 10.0g, Saturated Fat 1.8g, Trans Fat 0.0g, **Cholesterol** 80mg, **Sodium** 160mg, **Potassium** 560mg, **Total Carbohydrate** 11g, Dietary Fiber 2g, Sugars 7g, **Protein** 31g, **Phosphorus** 250mg

Make-Your-Own Taco Salad

SERVES 8, 1 cup per serving

PREP TIME: 20 minutes
COOK TIME: 20 minutes

1	(8-ounce) package mini sweet peppers
2	teaspoons canola oil
1	pound lean ground turkey breast
2	teaspoons no-salt-added taco seasoning
1/3	cup water
2/3	cup fresh salsa
1/2	cup fat-free sour cream
1	tablespoon chopped fresh cilantro
1/2	head romaine lettuce, shredded
2	tomatoes, diced
1	(15-ounce) can no-salt-added black beans, rinsed and drained
1/2	cup shredded fat-free cheddar cheese

1 Preheat oven to broil.

2 In a medium bowl, toss sweet peppers with oil and place on baking sheet. Broil 8 to 10 minutes or until peppers are tender and skin starts to blister.

3 In a medium skillet over medium-high heat, cook turkey 6 to 8 minutes, stirring until turkey crumbles and is no longer pink. Stir in taco seasoning and water, reduce heat to low, and simmer 5 minutes; set aside.

4 Meanwhile, in a small bowl, combine salsa, sour cream, and cilantro; mix well and set aside.

5 Arrange lettuce on a large serving platter. Place turkey across center of lettuce. Place tomatoes, beans, cheese, and peppers in rows on both sides of turkey, as shown. Serve with salsa mixture.

NUTRITION INFORMATION   Choices/Exchanges, 1/2 Starch, 1 Nonstarchy Vegetable, 2 Lean Protein

Calories 170, Calories from Fat 25, **Total Fat** 3.0g, Saturated Fat 0.6g, Trans Fat 0.0g, **Cholesterol** 35mg, **Sodium** 270mg, **Potassium** 610mg, **Total Carbohydrate** 17g, Dietary Fiber 4g, Sugars 5g, **Protein** 21g, **Phosphorus** 295mg

Bistro Tuna Lettuce Wraps

SERVES 4, 2 per serving

PREP TIME: 15 minutes
COOK TIME: None

1	(12-ounce) can tuna in water, drained well
3	tablespoons nonfat plain Greek yogurt
2	tablespoons light mayonnaise
1/2	cup chopped celery
1/4	cup chopped red bell pepper
2	teaspoons chopped fresh dill
1/2	teaspoon onion powder
1/8	teaspoon black pepper
8	leaves butter or Bibb lettuce

1 Place tuna in a medium bowl and break it up so there are no chunks. Add all the ingredients, except lettuce. Toss well until evenly mixed.

2 Place lettuce leaves on a flat surface and top each leaf with a 1/4 cup of the tuna mixture. Gently roll each leaf around the tuna creating a wrap. Chill slightly before serving.

Did You Know?
Tuna packed in water has less than half of the calories than tuna packed in oil. It's being aware of these little things that helps us stay on track.

NUTRITION INFORMATION

Choices/Exchanges, 2 Lean Protein

Calories 90, Calories from Fat 30, **Total Fat** 3.5g, Saturated Fat 0.3g, Trans Fat 0.0g, **Cholesterol** 25mg, **Sodium** 300mg, **Potassium** 240mg, **Total Carbohydrate** 3g, Dietary Fiber 1g, Sugars 1g, **Protein** 14g, **Phosphorus** 145mg

Chicken Salad Avocado Toast

SERVES 4, 1 per serving

PREP TIME: 10 minutes
COOK TIME: None

1	tablespoon olive oil
1	tablespoon plus 1 teaspoon lemon juice, divided
1	tablespoon honey
1/2	tablespoon Dijon mustard
1	clove garlic, minced
1/4	teaspoon black pepper
2	cups shredded cooked chicken breast
1/4	cup finely diced apple
1	avocado, seeded, peeled, and cut into chunks
4	slices light multigrain bread
2	cups arugula
1	tablespoon unsalted pepitas (see note on page 74)

1 In a medium bowl, combine oil, 1 tablespoon lemon juice, the honey, mustard, garlic, and pepper; mix well. Stir in chicken and apples, and toss until evenly coated; set aside.

2 In a small bowl, combine avocado and remaining 1 teaspoon lemon juice; mash with a fork, leaving a little chunky.

3 Toast bread. Evenly spread avocado mixture on toast and top with arugula. Top with chicken mixture and sprinkle with pepitas. Serve immediately.

Portion Size Matters

Rather than putting out a platter of chicken salad, a bowl of mixed greens, and a stack of bread, we think it's a good idea to pre-make sandwiches like this. This way, everyone gets just the right portion size to fill them up!

NUTRITION INFORMATION   **Choices/Exchanges,** 1/2 Starch, 1/2 Carbohydrate, 3 Lean Protein, 1-1/2 Fat

Calories 290, Calories from Fat 120, **Total Fat** 13.0g, Saturated Fat 2.3g, Trans Fat 0.0g, **Cholesterol** 60mg, **Sodium** 170mg, **Potassium** 470mg, **Total Carbohydrate** 19g, Dietary Fiber 5g, Sugars 7g, **Protein** 26g, **Phosphorus** 240mg

Spruced-Up BLT Sandwiches

SERVES 4, 1 per serving

PREP TIME: 10 minutes
COOK TIME: 5 minutes

8	slices reduced-sodium turkey bacon
4	slices multigrain bread
1/4	cup reduced-fat mayonnaise
1	clove garlic, minced
1/4	teaspoon black pepper
4	pieces leaf lettuce
8	slices tomato
1	avocado, pitted, peeled, and thinly sliced

1 Coat a large skillet with cooking spray. Heat over medium-high heat; cook bacon 5 to 7 minutes or until crisp. Remove to a paper towel–lined plate.

2 Meanwhile, toast bread; set aside. In a small bowl, combine mayonnaise, garlic, and pepper; mix well.

3 Spread equal amounts of mayo mixture on each slice of toast and evenly top with lettuce, tomato, bacon, and avocado.

Did You Know?

A slice of turkey bacon is leaner than traditional pork bacon. Per serving, it has about 25 fewer calories and about a third of the saturated fat. It's also lower in sodium.

NUTRITION INFORMATION **Choices/Exchanges,** 1 Starch, 1 Nonstarchy Vegetable, 1 Lean Protein, 2 Fat

Calories 240, Calories from Fat 140, **Total Fat** 15.0g, Saturated Fat 2.3g, Trans Fat 0.1g, **Cholesterol** 20mg, **Sodium** 450mg, **Potassium** 480mg, **Total Carbohydrate** 20g, Dietary Fiber 5g, Sugars 4g, **Protein** 10g, **Phosphorus** 160mg

Piled-High Veggie Stack Sandwiches

SERVES 4, 1 sandwich per serving

PREP TIME: 10 minutes
COOK TIME: 10 minutes

1	small zucchini, cut into 1/4-inch strips lengthwise
1	large red bell pepper, cut into eighths
1	sweet onion, cut into 1/4-inch rounds
3	tablespoons light balsamic vinaigrette dressing, divided
1	small eggplant, cut into 1/4-inch rounds
2	portobello mushrooms, sliced into eighths
1/4	teaspoon garlic powder
1/8	teaspoon black pepper
1/4	cup garlic-herb cheese spread
4	whole-wheat sandwich thin rolls

1 Preheat oven to broil. Coat a baking sheet with cooking spray.

2 In a large bowl, combine zucchini, red bell pepper, onion, and 1-1/2 tablespoons of the dressing; toss until vegetables are evenly coated and place on baking sheet. Add eggplant, mushrooms, and remaining dressing to bowl and toss until evenly coated; place on baking sheet with other vegetables. Arrange in a single layer and sprinkle with garlic powder and black pepper.

3 Broil 8 to 10 minutes or until lightly browned and tender; let cool slightly.

4 Evenly spread cheese on cut sides of each roll. On the bottom half of each roll, layer evenly with eggplant, red bell pepper, zucchini, mushroom, and onion. Place top of roll over onion and serve.

Good for You!

When you cook portobello mushrooms, like we did here, their taste and texture is very similar to beef. What a great way to satisfy your cravings for meat!

NUTRITION INFORMATION   **Choices/Exchanges,** 1-1/2 Starch, 4 Nonstarchy Vegetable, 1/2 Fat

Calories 240, Calories from Fat 50, **Total Fat** 6.0g, Saturated Fat 2.4g, Trans Fat 0.0g, **Cholesterol** 10mg, **Sodium** 410mg, **Potassium** 750mg, **Total Carbohydrate** 41g, Dietary Fiber 10g, Sugars 13g, **Protein** 9g, **Phosphorus** 220mg

Round-'Em-Up Cowboy Flatbread

SERVES 4, 1 per serving

PREP TIME: 20 minutes
COOK TIME: 25 minutes

4	ounces fat-free cream cheese, softened
1	teaspoon garlic powder, divided
2	tablespoons chopped fresh cilantro, divided
4	(7-inch) high-fiber, low-carb whole-wheat tortillas
	Cooking spray
2	tablespoons canola oil
1/2	onion, cut into matchstick pieces
1/2	green bell pepper, cut into matchstick pieces
1/2	yellow bell pepper, cut into matchstick pieces
1/2	red bell pepper, cut into matchstick pieces
1/4	teaspoon black pepper
1	(8-ounce) sirloin steak, well trimmed
1/2	cup black beans, drained and rinsed
1/4	cup shredded Colby Jack cheese

1 In a small bowl, combine cream cheese, 1/2 teaspoon garlic powder, and 1 tablespoon cilantro; mix well and set aside.

2 Preheat oven to 400°F. Place tortillas on an ungreased baking sheet and lightly spray with cooking spray. Bake 4 to 5 minutes or until tortillas begin to brown. Remove from oven and set aside.

3 Meanwhile, in a large skillet over medium heat, heat oil until hot. Add onion and cook 6 to 8 minutes or until it begins to brown, stirring occasionally. Add bell peppers, the remaining 1/2 teaspoon garlic powder, and the black pepper and cook 5 minutes or until soft. Remove vegetables to a plate.

4 Thinly slice steak. Add to skillet and cook 2 to 3 minutes or until no longer pink, stirring occasionally; drain excess liquid. Add vegetables back into skillet with steak; mix well and set aside.

5 Spread cream cheese mixture over tortillas. Top evenly with beef and vegetable mixture, the beans, and cheese. Place back in oven and cook 5 to 6 minutes or until cheese has melted. Sprinkle with remaining 1 tablespoon cilantro and serve.

These are also great to finish off on the grill. Just place the fully assembled flatbreads over low heat on the racks of the grill. While the cheese is melting, the bottom of the flatbread will get crispy and the edges will get all toasty. Yum!

NUTRITION INFORMATION   Choices/Exchanges, 1 Starch, 1 Nonstarchy Vegetable, 3 Lean Protein, 1-1/2 Fat

Calories 280, Calories from Fat 130, **Total Fat** 14.0g, Saturated Fat 2.6g, Trans Fat 0.1g, **Cholesterol** 35mg, **Sodium** 490mg, **Potassium** 480mg, **Total Carbohydrate** 24g, Dietary Fiber 11g, Sugars 4g, **Protein** 24g, **Phosphorus** 360mg

Family-Favorite Veggie Burgers

SERVES 5, 1 per serving

PREP TIME: 15 minutes
COOK TIME: 10 minutes

1	(15-ounce) can black beans, rinsed and drained, divided
2	cups chopped portobello mushrooms
1	cup chopped fresh broccoli florets
3/4	cup frozen corn, thawed
1/4	cup chopped onion
1	teaspoon garlic powder
1/4	teaspoon black pepper
2	eggs, beaten
1	tablespoon Worcestershire sauce
1	cup panko bread crumbs
1/4	cup grated Parmesan cheese
1	tablespoon canola oil
2-1/2	whole-wheat hamburger buns

1 In a large bowl, mash 1 cup of the black beans. Add remaining whole black beans, the mushrooms, broccoli, corn, onion, garlic powder, and pepper; mix well. Add eggs, Worcestershire sauce, bread crumbs, and Parmesan cheese; mix just until combined.

2 Form mixture into 5 equal-sized patties. In a large skillet over medium heat, heat oil until hot. Cook burgers 4 to 5 minutes per side or until golden brown and heated through.

3 Meanwhile, toast buns. Place each burger on a half of a bun and serve.

Save the rest of the package of hamburger buns in the freezer, so you can have them on hand down the road. Not only are they good for burgers, but they also make great French toast and are the perfect start to homemade croutons and bread crumbs.

NUTRITION INFORMATION

Choices/Exchanges, 3 Starch, 1 Lean Protein, 1/2 Fat

Calories 280, Calories from Fat 60, **Total Fat** 7.0g, Saturated Fat 1.7g, Trans Fat 0.0g, **Cholesterol** 75mg, **Sodium** 320mg, **Potassium** 570mg, **Total Carbohydrate** 43g, Dietary Fiber 8g, Sugars 6g, **Protein** 13g, **Phosphorus** 275mg

5-Napkin Pulled Beef Sandwiches

SERVES 6, 1 per serving

PREP TIME: 10 minutes
COOK TIME: 2-3/4 hours

2-1/2	pounds boneless beef chuck roast, well trimmed
1/2	teaspoon salt substitute
1/2	teaspoon black pepper
3	cloves garlic, minced
1	large onion, sliced
1-1/2	cups fat-free, low-sodium beef broth
6	(2-ounce) mini hard rolls
1/2	cup giardiniera (marinated vegetables), drained

1 Preheat oven to 350°F.

2 Place roast in a roasting pan and evenly sprinkle top with salt substitute, pepper, and garlic. Place onions on top and around the roast. Pour broth over roast. Cover with aluminum foil.

3 Roast 2-3/4 to 3 hours or until pull-apart, fork-tender. Remove roast to a cutting board; let rest 10 minutes.

4 Meanwhile, cut rolls in half, removing center from each half. Discard this and set aside crusty shells. Shred the meat with 2 forks, then place meat back in pan with juices.

5 When ready to serve, remove the meat mixture from pan with a slotted spoon and place evenly in rolls. Top with giardiniera and drizzle with pan juices. Serve immediately.

Did You Know?

Giardiniera is an Italian-style relish made from pickled veggies. It can be found in the same aisle as the pickles in your supermarket.

NUTRITION INFORMATION

Choices/Exchanges, 1-1/2 Starch, 1 Nonstarchy Vegetable, 5 Lean Protein

Calories 380, Calories from Fat 100, **Total Fat** 11.0g, Saturated Fat 3.4g, Trans Fat 0.4g, **Cholesterol** 120mg, **Sodium** 480mg, **Potassium** 810mg, **Total Carbohydrate** 27g, Dietary Fiber 2g, Sugars 3g, **Protein** 43g, **Phosphorus** 350mg

Warm-Ya-Up Soups, Stews, & Chilis

Mom's Veggie Barley Soup

SERVES 6, 1-1/2 cups per serving

PREP TIME: 15 minutes
COOK TIME: 35 minutes

2	teaspoons canola oil
2	medium carrots, thinly sliced
1	cup chopped onion
1/2	cup chopped celery
1	zucchini, cut into 1/2-inch chunks
2	cups reduced-sodium beef broth
3	cups water
1	(14-1/2-ounce) can no-salt-added diced tomatoes, undrained
1	teaspoon garlic powder
1/2	teaspoon Italian seasoning
1/2	teaspoon black pepper
1/2	cup quick-cooking pearl barley
1/2	pound sliced fresh mushrooms

1 In a soup pot over high heat, heat oil until hot. Add the carrots, onion, celery, and zucchini, and sauté 5 minutes.

2 Add beef broth, water, tomatoes with their juice, garlic powder, Italian seasoning, and pepper; bring to a boil. Reduce heat to low, cover and simmer 15 minutes, stirring occasionally.

3 Add barley and mushrooms and simmer, covered, for an additional 10 to 15 minutes, or until barley is tender.

Good for You!

Barley is great for helping you feel fuller longer. This whole grain is high in fiber, which not only aids with digestion, but also slows it down. It's loaded with vitamins and minerals, and is a low–glycemic index food. It doesn't get much better than that!

NUTRITION INFORMATION   Choices/Exchanges, 1/2 Starch, 2 Nonstarchy Vegetable, 1/2 Fat

Calories 110, Calories from Fat 20, **Total Fat** 2.0g, Saturated Fat 0.2g, Trans Fat 0.0g, **Cholesterol** 0mg, **Sodium** 200mg, **Potassium** 540mg, **Total Carbohydrate** 20g, Dietary Fiber 4g, Sugars 6g, **Protein** 5g, **Phosphorus** 115mg

Unstuffed Stuffed Cabbage Soup

SERVES 6, 1-1/3 cups liquid and 3 meatballs per serving

PREP TIME: 15 minutes
COOK TIME: 40 minutes

1/2	pound lean ground turkey breast
1/4	cup plain bread crumbs
1	egg
1/2	teaspoon garlic powder
1/2	teaspoon onion powder
1/2	teaspoon black pepper, divided
1/2	head cabbage, shredded (5 cups)
4	cups fat-free, low-sodium chicken broth
2	cups no-salt-added crushed tomatoes
2	tablespoons lemon juice
3	tablespoons brown sugar
1/2	teaspoon salt

1 In a medium bowl, combine ground turkey, bread crumbs, egg, garlic powder, onion powder, and 1/4 teaspoon pepper; mix well. Form mixture into 18 (1-inch) meatballs.

2 Coat a soup pot with cooking spray and cook meatballs over medium heat 5 to 7 minutes or until browned.

3 Add remaining ingredients including remaining 1/4 teaspoon pepper; mix gently and bring to a boil. Reduce heat to low and simmer 25 minutes or until cabbage is tender. Serve piping hot.

Good for You!

We've greatly reduced all of the work that it takes to make stuffed cabbage since there's no need to separate and roll cabbage leaves. We've also cut down on the calories and sodium by replacing traditional ground chuck with lean ground turkey breast and using low-sodium broth and tomatoes. It's so easy and so guilt-free!

NUTRITION INFORMATION   Choices/Exchanges, 1/2 Carbohydrate, 2 Nonstarchy Vegetable, 2 Lean Protein

Calories 150, Calories from Fat 20, **Total Fat** 2.0g, Saturated Fat 0.6g, Trans Fat 0.0g, **Cholesterol** 50mg, **Sodium** 360mg, **Potassium** 610mg, **Total Carbohydrate** 16g, Dietary Fiber 3g, Sugars 9g, **Protein** 17g, **Phosphorus** 205mg

Worth-the-Wait Chicken Soup

SERVES 8, 1 cup per serving

PREP TIME: 15 minutes
COOK TIME: 3-1/2 hours

1	(3-pound) whole chicken, cut into 8 pieces
1	large onion, cut into 1-inch chunks
3	large carrots, cut into 1-inch chunks
2	celery stalks, cut into 1/2-inch chunks
3	sprigs parsley
1/4	teaspoon salt
1/4	teaspoon black pepper
4	cups fat-free, low-sodium chicken broth
2	cups water
8	ounces fresh spinach, washed, and large stems removed
6	ounces medium-wide whole-grain egg noodles

1 Place chicken in a 5-quart or larger slow cooker. Place onion, carrots, celery, and parsley around chicken and sprinkle with salt and pepper. Add broth and water, and cover.

2 Cook on high 3-1/2 to 4 hours or low 7 to 8 hours or until the chicken is fall-apart tender.

3 Carefully remove chicken from broth. (It's going to be hot.) Let it sit until it's cool enough to handle. Remove and discard chicken skin and bones, and shred chicken.

4 Stir chicken and spinach into the slow cooker and simmer 10 minutes or until spinach is wilted.

5 Meanwhile, cook noodles according to package directions. Just before serving, add noodles to soup and serve.

If you're planning on making this ahead of time and serving it in the next couple of days, we suggest you don't add the noodles until right before serving. Also, when you remove it from the refrigerator, before reheating it, make sure you remove any of the fat on top of the soup.

NUTRITION INFORMATION   **Choices/Exchanges,** 1 Starch, 1 Nonstarchy Vegetable, 3 Lean Protein

Calories 220, Calories from Fat 45, **Total Fat** 5.0g, Saturated Fat 1.4g, Trans Fat 0.0g, **Cholesterol** 55mg, **Sodium** 470mg, **Potassium** 620mg, **Total Carbohydrate** 23g, Dietary Fiber 4g, Sugars 4g, **Protein** 23g, **Phosphorus** 225mg

Boston Clam Chowda

SERVES 6, 1 cup per serving

PREP TIME: 15 minutes
COOK TIME: 30 minutes

2	(6-1/2-ounce) cans chopped clams, undrained
2-3/4	cups low-sodium vegetable broth
3	red potatoes, diced
1/3	cup chopped onion
1	stalk celery, chopped
1/4	teaspoon salt-free seasoning
1/4	teaspoon black pepper
1/4	cup cornstarch
1	(12-ounce) can fat-free evaporated milk, divided
1	tablespoon chopped fresh parsley
1/2	teaspoon dried thyme

1 In a soup pot over medium-high heat, combine clams with their liquid, vegetable broth, potatoes, onion, celery, salt-free seasoning, and pepper; cover and bring to a boil. Reduce heat to low and simmer 12 to 15 minutes or until potatoes are fork-tender.

2 In a small bowl, dissolve cornstarch in 1/2 cup of evaporated milk; slowly stir into soup.

3 Add remaining evaporated milk, the parsley, and thyme. Cook an additional 5 minutes or until thickened, stirring frequently. Serve immediately.

NUTRITION INFORMATION   Choices/Exchanges, 1-1/2 Starch, 1/2 Fat-Free Milk, 1 Lean Protein

Calories 190, Calories from Fat 0, **Total Fat** 0.0g, Saturated Fat 0.0g, Trans Fat 0.0g, **Cholesterol** 15mg, **Sodium** 480mg, **Potassium** 660mg, **Total Carbohydrate** 32g, Dietary Fiber 2g, Sugars 9g, **Protein** 12g, **Phosphorus** 220mg

Chinatown Hot 'n' Sour Soup

SERVES 5, 1 cup per serving

PREP TIME: 10 minutes
COOK TIME: 15 minutes

3-1/2	cups fat-free, low-sodium chicken broth, divided
2	tablespoons cornstarch
3/4	pound firm tofu, cut into small chunks
1/4	pound sliced fresh mushrooms
3	tablespoons reduced-sodium soy sauce
3	tablespoons white vinegar
1	teaspoon ground ginger
1/2	teaspoon black pepper
1	egg, lightly beaten
1/2	cup canned bean sprouts, drained
1/2	teaspoon sesame oil

1 In a small bowl, combine 1/4 cup chicken broth and the cornstarch; mix well and set aside.

2 In a soup pot, combine the remaining 3-1/4 cups chicken broth, the tofu, mushrooms, soy sauce, vinegar, ginger, and pepper; mix well and bring to a boil over high heat. Reduce heat to low; slowly add in the cornstarch mixture, stirring until thickened.

3 Gently stir the beaten egg into the hot soup, creating strands of egg. Simmer 1 to 2 minutes or until heated through, stirring occasionally.

4 Add bean sprouts and sesame oil; mix well and serve.

Serving Suggestion
To add a splash of color, top each bowl with some sliced scallions or shredded carrots.

NUTRITION INFORMATION   Choices/Exchanges, 1/2 Carbohydrate, 2 Lean Protein

Calories 110, Calories from Fat 40, **Total Fat** 4.5g, Saturated Fat 1.0g, Trans Fat 0.0g, **Cholesterol** 35mg, **Sodium** 450mg, **Potassium** 360mg, **Total Carbohydrate** 7g, Dietary Fiber 1g, Sugars 1g, **Protein** 13g, **Phosphorus** 190mg

Tomato & Shrimp Bisque

SERVES 8, 1 cup per serving

PREP TIME: 5 minutes
COOK TIME: 15 minutes

2	(28-ounce) cans no-salt-added crushed tomatoes, undrained
1	tablespoon sugar
1	teaspoon garlic powder
1/2	teaspoon black pepper
1/4	teaspoon seafood seasoning (like Old Bay®)
1	(12-ounce) can fat-free evaporated milk
1/2	pound cooked small shrimp, peeled*
2	tablespoons chopped fresh basil, divided

1 In a soup pot over medium-high heat, combine tomatoes with their juice, sugar, garlic powder, pepper, and seafood seasoning; bring to a boil, stirring occasionally.

2 Reduce heat to low and slowly stir in evaporated milk. Add shrimp and 1 tablespoon basil and simmer an additional 4 to 5 minutes or until heated through.

3 Top each bowl with additional basil, before serving.

Did You Know?

We like using evaporated milk in this recipe because it adds creaminess to the soup without all the extra fat and calories that come from half-and-half or heavy cream. Evaporated milk is simply regular milk with about 60% of the water removed before the canning process.

*If possible, use fresh (never frozen) shrimp, or shrimp that are free of preservatives (for example, shrimp that have not been treated with salt or TPP [sodium tripolyphosphate]).

NUTRITION INFORMATION   Choices/Exchanges, 1/2 Fat-Free Milk, 2 Nonstarchy Vegetable, 1 Lean Protein

Calories 140, Calories from Fat 5, **Total Fat** 0.5g, Saturated Fat 0.2g, Trans Fat 0.0g, **Cholesterol** 55mg, **Sodium** 115mg, **Potassium** 790mg, **Total Carbohydrate** 17g, Dietary Fiber 3g, Sugars 14g, **Protein** 14g, **Phosphorus** 225mg

Roasted Carrot Soup

SERVES 8, 3/4 cup per serving

PREP TIME: 10 minutes
COOK TIME: 45 minutes

2	pounds carrots, cut in half
1	onion, cut into 1-inch chunks
2	tablespoons olive oil
4	cups water
2	teaspoons fresh minced ginger
1/2	teaspoon salt
1/8	teaspoon black pepper
	Fresh dill for garnish

1 Preheat oven to 425°F. In a large bowl, combine carrots, onion, and oil; toss until evenly coated. Place on a baking sheet. Roast 30 minutes or until tender and beginning to brown.

2 Working in batches, if necessary, place roasted carrot mixture in a blender with water. Process until smooth, then pour into a soup pot. Add ginger, salt, and pepper.

3 Over medium heat, bring to a boil, then reduce heat to low. Simmer 5 minutes or until heated through. Garnish each serving with fresh dill.

Did You Know?
Roasting vegetables in the oven caramelizes the natural sugars in them, and in this case, adds an amazing depth of flavor to the soup.

NUTRITION INFORMATION

Choices/Exchanges, 3 Nonstarchy Vegetable, 1/2 Fat

Calories 80, Calories from Fat 30, **Total Fat** 3.5g, Saturated Fat 0.5g, Trans Fat 0.0g, **Cholesterol** 0mg, **Sodium** 220mg, **Potassium** 390mg, **Total Carbohydrate** 13g, Dietary Fiber 4g, Sugars 6g, **Protein** 1g, **Phosphorus** 45mg

Sunday Beef Stew

SERVES 6, 1 cup per serving

PREP TIME: 15 minutes
COOK TIME: 85 minutes

1-1/2	pounds boneless lean beef chuck steak, cut into 1-inch chunks
2	tablespoons all-purpose flour, divided
1	tablespoon canola oil
1	cup chopped onion
2	carrots, cut into 1-inch slices
3	small red potatoes, cut into 1-inch cubes
2	cups low-fat, reduced-sodium beef broth
1-1/4	cups water, divided
1	teaspoon garlic powder
1/2	teaspoon dried thyme
1/4	teaspoon black pepper
3	portobello mushrooms, cut into 1-1/2-inch pieces

1 In a medium bowl, toss beef with 1 tablespoon flour until evenly coated. In a soup pot over medium-high heat, heat oil until hot; sauté beef 5 to 7 minutes or until browned.

2 Add onion, carrots, potatoes, broth, 1 cup water, the garlic powder, thyme, and pepper; bring to a boil. Reduce heat to low, cover, and simmer 45 minutes. Add mushrooms and cook 15 more minutes or until beef is tender.

3 In a small bowl, whisk remaining 1 tablespoon flour in remaining 1/4 cup water. Slowly stir flour mixture into stew and cook 5 minutes or until thickened. Enjoy.

Good for You!

We cut the amount of beef in half and added chunks of portobello mushrooms to the stew in its place. You see, when the mushrooms are cooked, they have a similar texture and taste to beef. It's little tricks like this that allow us to eat what we crave, without having all the guilt.

NUTRITION INFORMATION

Choices/Exchanges, 1-1/2 Starch, 1 Nonstarchy Vegetable, 3 Lean Protein

Calories 270, Calories from Fat 60, **Total Fat** 7.0g, Saturated Fat 2.1g, Trans Fat 0.3g, **Cholesterol** 60mg, **Sodium** 220mg, **Potassium** 880mg, **Total Carbohydrate** 25g, Dietary Fiber 3g, Sugars 4g, **Protein** 26g, **Phosphorus** 290mg

Fisherman's Stew

SERVES 6, 2 cups per serving

PREP TIME: 10 minutes
COOK TIME: 25 minutes

2	tablespoons olive oil
1/2	cup chopped onion
1/2	cup chopped celery
1	cup low-sodium spaghetti sauce
1/2	cup water
4	sprigs fresh thyme (or 1/2 teaspoon dried thyme)
1/4	teaspoon black pepper
1/2	pound large raw shrimp, unpeeled
1	pound littleneck clams, washed
1	pound mussels, washed

1 In a deep skillet or soup pot over medium-high heat, heat oil until hot. Add onion and celery and sauté 5 minutes or until tender, stirring occasionally. Add spaghetti sauce, water, thyme, and pepper; bring to a boil.

2 Reduce heat to medium, stir in shrimp, clams, and mussels. Cover and cook 8 to 10 minutes or until shrimp are pink and clams and mussels are open. Discard any unopened clams or mussels, and serve stew immediately.

Good for You!
Since we're serving the clams and mussels in their shells, each serving of this looks huge! But really, they're filling up the bowl with flavor and not with lots of calories or fat. We eat with our eyes, so this is extra appealing!

NUTRITION INFORMATION

Choices/Exchanges, 1/2 Carbohydrate, 2 Lean Protein

Calories 140, Calories from Fat 50, **Total Fat** 6.0g, Saturated Fat 0.9g, Trans Fat 0.0g, **Cholesterol** 55mg, **Sodium** 240mg, **Potassium** 350mg, **Total Carbohydrate** 7g, Dietary Fiber 1g, Sugars 5g, **Protein** 13g, **Phosphorus** 155mg

Game Day Chili Pot

SERVES 4, 1-1/4 cups per serving

PREP TIME: 10 minutes
COOK TIME: 50 minutes

1	pound 95% extra-lean ground beef
1	cup chopped onion
1	green bell pepper, cut into 1-inch chunks
2	cups no-salt-added crushed tomatoes
1	(14-1/2-ounce) can no-salt-added pinto beans, undrained
1-1/2	cups water
2	cloves garlic, minced
1	teaspoon hot sauce
1-1/2	tablespoons chili powder
1/2	teaspoon ground cumin
1/4	teaspoon salt
1/2	teaspoon black pepper

1 Coat a soup pot with cooking spray and cook ground beef, onion, and bell pepper over medium-high heat 6 to 8 minutes or until meat is browned. Add remaining ingredients; mix well.

2 After bringing to a boil, reduce heat to low and simmer 30 minutes or until chili is thickened, stirring occasionally. Serve piping hot.

Serving Suggestion

Rather than serving this with calorie-laden toppings, like sour cream and shredded cheese, how about putting out bowls of sliced scallions, chopped jalapeños, and avocado to add fun and extra good-for-you veggies?

NUTRITION INFORMATION   **Choices/Exchanges,** 1 Starch, 3 Nonstarchy Vegetable, 4 Lean Protein

Calories 300, Calories from Fat 50, **Total Fat** 6.0g, Saturated Fat 2.4g, Trans Fat 0.3g, **Cholesterol** 65mg, **Sodium** 300mg, **Potassium** 1210mg, **Total Carbohydrate** 28g, Dietary Fiber 9g, Sugars 8g, **Protein** 34g, **Phosphorus** 395mg

Blonde Turkey Chili

SERVES 6, 1 cup per serving

PREP TIME: 10 minutes
COOK TIME: 45 minutes

1	tablespoon canola oil
1	pound extra-lean turkey breast tenderloins, cut into 1-inch chunks
1	cup chopped onion
3	cups fat-free, low-sodium chicken broth
2	(15-ounce) cans Great Northern beans, rinsed and drained
1	jalapeño pepper, seeded and diced
4	cloves garlic, minced
2	teaspoons ground cumin
1-1/2	teaspoons dried oregano
6	tablespoons shredded reduced-fat cheddar cheese

1 In a soup pot over medium-high heat, heat oil until hot; cook turkey and onion 6 to 8 minutes or until browned, stirring occasionally.

2 Add remaining ingredients except cheese. Bring to a boil, then reduce heat to low and simmer 25 minutes or until slightly thickened, stirring often.

3 Ladle chili into soup bowls. Top evenly with cheese and serve immediately.

Out of the Box

If you only think of turkey around Thanksgiving—you're missing out! Turkey tenders add a rich flavor to this chili, while helping us stay within recommended nutritional guidelines.

NUTRITION INFORMATION   **Choices/Exchanges,** 1 Starch, 1 Nonstarchy Vegetable, 4 Lean Protein

Calories 270, Calories from Fat 50, **Total Fat** 6.0g, Saturated Fat 1.6g, Trans Fat 0.0g, **Cholesterol** 50mg, **Sodium** 380mg, **Potassium** 690mg, **Total Carbohydrate** 23g, Dietary Fiber 7g, Sugars 4g, **Protein** 31g, **Phosphorus** 380mg

Feel-Good Poultry

Chicken & Bean One-Pot

SERVES 6, 1 cup per serving

PREP TIME: 10 minutes
COOK TIME: 20 minutes

1-1/2	pounds boneless, skinless chicken thighs, each cut into quarters
1/2	teaspoon garlic powder
1/4	teaspoon black pepper
1	teaspoon canola oil
1/2	cup chopped onion
1	carrot, diced
2	cloves garlic, minced
1	cup fat-free, low-sodium chicken broth
2	tablespoons tomato paste
3	sprigs fresh thyme
2	tomatoes, cut into chunks
1	(15-ounce) can navy beans, drained and rinsed

1 Sprinkle chicken on both sides with garlic powder and pepper.

2 In a deep skillet over medium-high heat, heat oil until hot. Cook chicken 5 to 6 minutes or until brown on both sides. Add onion, carrot, and garlic, reduce heat to medium, and sauté 3 minutes, stirring occasionally.

3 Add broth, tomato paste, and thyme; mix well. Cook 5 minutes. Add tomatoes and beans and simmer 5 to 7 minutes or until slightly thickened and heated through. Serve immediately.

We found that boneless, skinless chicken thighs work best in this recipe. Not only are they budget-friendly, but because they're a fattier cut, they retain their juiciness and flavor in recipes like this. However, if you prefer chicken breasts, go ahead and substitute!

NUTRITION INFORMATION   **Choices/Exchanges,** 1/2 Starch, 1 Nonstarchy Vegetable, 3 Lean Protein, 1/2 Fat

Calories 230, Calories from Fat 60, **Total Fat** 7.0g, Saturated Fat 1.9g, Trans Fat 0.0g, **Cholesterol** 105mg, **Sodium** 230mg, **Potassium** 630mg, **Total Carbohydrate** 16g, Dietary Fiber 6g, Sugars 3g, **Protein** 23g, **Phosphorus** 260mg

Farm-Stand Stuffed Chicken

SERVES 4, 1 per serving

PREP TIME: 15 minutes
COOK TIME: 25 minutes

1	tablespoon canola oil
1	small zucchini, shredded
1	medium carrot, shredded
1/2	red bell pepper, finely diced
1/2	cup chopped onion
2	cloves garlic, minced
1/2	teaspoon Italian seasoning
4	(4-ounce) boneless, skinless chicken breasts

Sundried Tomato Topping

1/4	cup sundried tomatoes
2	tablespoons canola oil
1	clove garlic
1	tablespoon fresh parsley, stems removed

1 Preheat oven to 350°F. Coat a 9- × 13-inch baking dish with cooking spray.

2 In a medium skillet over medium heat, heat 1 tablespoon oil until hot. Add zucchini, carrot, bell pepper, onion, garlic, and Italian seasoning; sauté 5 to 7 minutes or until tender, then set aside.

3 With a sharp knife, butterfly each chicken breast, cutting horizontally, 3/4 of the way through. Open each like a book. Place equal amounts of vegetable mixture (about 1/2 cup) on half of each breast. Fold tops over and place in baking dish.

4 To make Sundried Tomato Topping, in a mini-food processor or blender, pulse ingredients until finely chopped. Spoon equal amounts over each chicken breast.

5 Bake 20 to 25 minutes or until chicken is no longer pink in center. Serve immediately.

To learn how to best butterfly a chicken breast, you may want to check out our "How To" video on www.mrfood.com. Just type **how to butterfly a chicken breast** *in the search box.*

NUTRITION INFORMATION   **Choices/Exchanges,** 2 Nonstarchy Vegetable, 3 Lean Protein, 1-1/2 Fat

Calories 270, Calories from Fat 130, **Total Fat** 14.0g, Saturated Fat 1.6g, Trans Fat 0.0g, **Cholesterol** 65mg, **Sodium** 220mg, **Potassium** 670mg, **Total Carbohydrate** 11g, Dietary Fiber 3g, Sugars 6g, **Protein** 26g, **Phosphorus** 230mg

Naked Sweet 'n' Sour Chicken

SERVES 5, 1 cup per serving

PREP TIME: 15 minutes
COOK TIME: 15 minutes

1	tablespoon canola oil
1-1/4	pounds boneless, skinless chicken breasts, cut into thin strips
1	cup broccoli florets
1	red bell pepper, cut into 3/4-inch chunks
3/4	cup snow peas, trimmed
1	(8-ounce) can sliced water chestnuts, drained
1	(8-ounce) can pineapple chunks, drained, with liquid reserved
1/4	cup water
2	tablespoons reduced-sodium soy sauce
1	tablespoon white vinegar
2	tablespoons ketchup
1-1/2	tablespoons cornstarch
2	tablespoons sugar

1 In a large skillet or wok over medium-high heat, heat oil until hot. Add chicken and stir-fry 4 to 5 minutes or until no pink remains.

2 Add broccoli, bell pepper, and snow peas. Stir-fry 4 minutes, then stir in water chestnuts and pineapple, and continue to cook 4 to 5 minutes or until vegetables are crisp-tender.

3 Meanwhile, in a small bowl, whisk reserved pineapple liquid, water, soy sauce, vinegar, ketchup, cornstarch, and sugar; mix well. Stir into skillet and cook 2 minutes or until sauce thickens. Serve immediately.

Good for You!
Traditionally, Sweet and Sour Chicken is battered and deep-fried, but we save calories, carbs, and fat by keeping this chicken "naked" and stir-frying it.

NUTRITION INFORMATION   Choices/Exchanges, 1/2 Fruit, 1 Carbohydrate, 1 Nonstarchy Vegetable, 3 Lean Protein

Calories 250, Calories from Fat 50, **Total Fat** 6.0g, Saturated Fat 1.0g, Trans Fat 0.0g, **Cholesterol** 65mg, **Sodium** 360mg, **Potassium** 460mg, **Total Carbohydrate** 24g, Dietary Fiber 3g, Sugars 16g, **Protein** 26g, **Phosphorus** 215mg

Bacon Cheddar Chicken Breasts

SERVES 4, 1 per serving

PREP TIME: 5 minutes
COOK TIME: 20 minutes

28	gluten-free "everything" baked crackers, crushed (see note)
1/4	cup reduced-fat ranch dressing
4	(4-ounce) boneless, skinless chicken breasts
1/2	teaspoon garlic powder
1/4	teaspoon black pepper
1/4	cup shredded reduced-fat cheddar cheese
1	tablespoon turkey bacon bits

1 Preheat oven to 375°F. Coat a baking sheet with cooking spray.

2 Place crackers in a shallow dish. Place ranch dressing in another shallow dish. Evenly sprinkle chicken with garlic powder and pepper. Dip chicken in ranch dressing, then in cracker crumbs, coating evenly on both sides.

3 Bake 15 minutes, then sprinkle evenly with cheese and bacon bits and cook an additional 5 to 10 minutes or until no longer pink in center and the coating is crispy. Serve immediately.

Going Gluten-Free

These days there are so many great gluten-free products available in our markets. We found several versions of gluten-free crackers that are coated with "everything." When we crush these up, they give us the crunch we like, as well as lots of flavor.

NUTRITION INFORMATION   **Choices/Exchanges,** 1 Starch, 3 Lean Protein, 1/2 Fat

Calories 250, Calories from Fat 80, **Total Fat** 9.0g, Saturated Fat 2.3g, Trans Fat 0.0g, **Cholesterol** 70mg, **Sodium** 360mg, **Potassium** 270mg, **Total Carbohydrate** 13g, Dietary Fiber 2g, Sugars 2g, **Protein** 27g, **Phosphorus** 295mg

Cheesy Crusted Chicken Tenders

SERVES 4, 2 per serving

PREP TIME: 10 minutes
COOK TIME: 15 minutes

8	chicken tenders (about 1-1/4 pounds)
1/2	teaspoon onion powder
1	cup finely crushed reduced-fat cheese crackers
1/4	cup sesame seeds
1	teaspoon chopped fresh parsley
1/4	teaspoon salt
1/8	teaspoon cayenne pepper
1	egg
1	tablespoon water
	Cooking spray

1 Preheat oven to 400°F. Coat a rimmed baking sheet with cooking spray. Sprinkle tenders evenly with onion powder.

2 In a shallow bowl, combine crushed crackers, sesame seeds, parsley, salt, and cayenne pepper; mix well. In another shallow bowl, beat egg and water.

3 Dip each chicken tender into egg mixture, then the cracker mixture, coating well. Place chicken on baking sheet and lightly spray with cooking spray.

4 Bake 15 to 20 minutes or until chicken is no longer pink in center. Serve hot or cold.

Did You Know?

By spraying the chicken with cooking spray, we're basically covering it with a light coating of vegetable oil. That way, after it's baked, we end up with super-crispy, oven-fried chicken that's much better for us!

NUTRITION INFORMATION   **Choices/Exchanges,** 1 Starch, 5 Lean Protein, 1/2 Fat

Calories 310, Calories from Fat 110, **Total Fat** 12.0g, Saturated Fat 2.3g, Trans Fat 0.0g, **Cholesterol** 125mg, **Sodium** 430mg, **Potassium** 340mg, **Total Carbohydrate** 15g, Dietary Fiber 2g, Sugars 0g, **Protein** 35g, **Phosphorus** 330mg

Wrapped-Up Roasted Chicken

SERVES 5, About 9.5 ounces per serving

PREP TIME: 5 minutes
COOK TIME: 65 minutes

1	(3-pound) whole chicken, skin removed
4	large iceberg lettuce leaves, washed and patted dry
1/2	teaspoon paprika
1/2	teaspoon garlic powder
1/2	teaspoon onion powder
1/8	teaspoon black pepper
2	tablespoons fat-free Italian dressing

1 Preheat oven to 350°F. Place chicken, breast-side-up, on a lettuce leaf and place in a 9- × 13-inch baking dish.

2 In a small bowl, combine paprika, garlic powder, onion powder, and pepper; mix well. Rub chicken evenly with spice mixture and drizzle with dressing. Lay remaining lettuce leaves over the chicken, curving them around and completely covering the chicken.

3 Roast 65 to 70 minutes or until juices run clear and no pink remains. Discard lettuce leaves before serving.

Did You Know?
Since we remove the skin from the chicken, we use lettuce leaves to help keep it moist and flavorful while it roasts. It may sound crazy, but it really works!

NUTRITION INFORMATION

Choices/Exchanges, 4 Lean Protein

Calories 190, Calories from Fat 60, **Total Fat** 7.0g, Saturated Fat 2.0g, Trans Fat 0.0g, **Cholesterol** 85mg, **Sodium** 150mg, **Potassium** 250mg, **Total Carbohydrate** 1g, Dietary Fiber 0g, Sugars 0g, **Protein** 28g, **Phosphorus** 195mg

Chicken Bundles Florentine

SERVES 4, 1 per serving

PREP TIME: 10 minutes
COOK TIME: 25 minutes

1	tablespoon olive oil
1	cup frozen chopped spinach, thawed, drained (see Tip)
1/2	cup finely chopped fresh mushrooms
1	clove garlic, minced
1/4	teaspoon black pepper
4	(4-ounce) boneless, skinless chicken breasts, lightly pounded to 1/4-inch thickness
4	light spreadable Swiss cheese wedges (see Note)
1/4	cup crushed reduced-fat butter crackers
1/4	teaspoon paprika
2	teaspoons light, trans-fat-free margarine, melted

1 Preheat oven to 350°F. Coat a 6-cup muffin tin with cooking spray.

2 In a medium skillet over medium heat, heat oil until hot; sauté spinach, mushrooms, garlic, and pepper 5 minutes. Place equal amounts of vegetable mixture in center of each chicken breast. Place a cheese wedge in center of spinach mixture and tightly roll chicken breasts up, tucking in sides as you roll. Place bundles seam-side-down in muffin cups.

3 In a small bowl, combine crackers, paprika, and margarine; mix well. Sprinkle evenly over each chicken bundle.

4 Bake 20 to 25 minutes or until chicken is no longer pink and filling is heated through. Serve immediately.

Note: We tested this recipe using Laughing Cow® Light Swiss Cheese.

To drain frozen spinach, be sure to let it thaw completely (either in the fridge or microwave), and then, using your hands, form it into a ball and squeeze out the moisture. After that, it's ready for cooking!

NUTRITION INFORMATION   **Choices/Exchanges,** 1/2 Carbohydrate, 4 Lean Protein, 1/2 Fat

Calories 240, Calories from Fat 80, **Total Fat** 9.0g, Saturated Fat 2.4g, Trans Fat 0.0g, **Cholesterol** 70mg, **Sodium** 330mg, **Potassium** 390mg, **Total Carbohydrate** 7g, Dietary Fiber 1g, Sugars 2g, **Protein** 28g, **Phosphorus** 345mg

Easy Chicken & Broccoli Casserole

SERVES 6, 1 cup per serving

PREP TIME: 10 minutes
COOK TIME: 40 minutes

1	tablespoon canola oil
1/2	cup chopped onion
1/2	cup diced celery
1-1/4	pounds boneless, skinless chicken breasts, cut into 1-inch pieces
2	cups chopped fresh broccoli, or frozen and thawed
2	cups sliced mushrooms
4	tablespoons light, trans-fat-free margarine
3	tablespoons all-purpose flour
3	cups fat-free, low-sodium chicken broth
2/3	cup shredded reduced-fat cheddar cheese
1	tablespoon chopped roasted red peppers, drained
1	cup coarsely crushed corn flake cereal

1 Preheat oven to 400°F. Lightly coat a 2-quart baking dish with cooking spray.

2 In a large skillet over medium heat, heat oil until hot. Add onion and celery and sauté 3 minutes. Add chicken and cook 5 to 6 minutes or until chicken is no longer pink. Add broccoli and mushrooms and continue to cook 3 to 5 minutes or until vegetables are tender.

3 In a medium saucepan over medium heat, melt margarine, then whisk in flour; cook 1 minute. Slowly stir in chicken broth and cook until thickened. Stir in cheese until melted. Pour sauce over chicken mixture, add red peppers, and mix well. Pour mixture into baking dish. Sprinkle the top with crushed cereal.

4 Bake 25 to 30 minutes or until bubbly hot and golden.

We think it's best to shred a block of reduced-fat cheddar cheese for this sauce, rather than using pre-shredded. The sauce will be creamier and will taste cheesier.

NUTRITION INFORMATION   **Choices/Exchanges,** 1/2 Starch, 1 Nonstarchy Vegetable, 3 Lean Protein, 1-1/2 Fat

Calories 260, Calories from Fat 100, **Total Fat** 11.0g, Saturated Fat 3.2g, Trans Fat 0.0g, **Cholesterol** 60mg, **Sodium** 350mg, **Potassium** 510mg, **Total Carbohydrate** 14g, Dietary Fiber 2g, Sugars 3g, **Protein** 27g, **Phosphorus** 315mg

Fiesta Chicken Fajitas

SERVES 5, 1 per serving

PREP TIME: 10 minutes
MARINATE TIME: 60 minutes
COOK TIME: 15 minutes

Fajita Marinade

1/4	cup lime juice
	Zest from 1 lime
1	tablespoon honey
2	tablespoons chopped fresh cilantro
2	cloves garlic, minced
1	teaspoon chili powder
1/2	teaspoon ground cumin
1/4	teaspoon black pepper
1	pound boneless, skinless chicken breasts, cut into thin strips
1	tablespoon canola oil
2	red bell peppers, sliced
1	onion, sliced into 1/2-inch half-moon pieces
5	(7-inch) low-carb whole-wheat flour tortillas

1 To make Fajita Marinade, in a medium bowl, combine lime juice, lime zest, honey, cilantro, garlic, chili powder, cumin, and black pepper; mix well. Add chicken and toss to evenly coat. Cover and marinate in refrigerator 1 hour.

2 In a large skillet over medium-high heat, heat oil until hot; sauté bell peppers and onion 8 to 10 minutes or until tender, stirring occasionally. Remove to a plate.

3 Drain chicken and discard excess marinade. Add chicken to pan, and cook 6 to 8 minutes or until no longer pink, stirring occasionally. Return vegetables to skillet, mix well, and cook 1 to 2 minutes or until heated through.

4 Meanwhile, heat tortillas according to package directions. Divide chicken mixture evenly down center of tortillas, roll up, and serve.

Serving Suggestion

Cut up a few extra limes into wedges and let everyone squeeze on! With all of this flavor, you won't be tempted to pile on high-fat toppings like sour cream and shredded cheese.

NUTRITION INFORMATION   **Choices/Exchanges,** 1 Starch, 1 Nonstarchy Vegetable, 3 Lean Protein

Calories 210, Calories from Fat 60, **Total Fat** 7.0g, Saturated Fat 0.9g, Trans Fat 0.0g, **Cholesterol** 50mg, **Sodium** 260mg, **Potassium** 360mg, **Total Carbohydrate** 20g, Dietary Fiber 10g, Sugars 5g, **Protein** 25g, **Phosphorus** 205mg

Old-Fashioned Chicken & Dumplings

SERVES 6, 1 cup and 1 dumpling per serving

PREP TIME: 15 minutes
COOK TIME: 30 minutes

2	celery stalks, sliced
2	carrots, sliced
8	cups fat-free, low-sodium chicken broth
1/2	teaspoon poultry seasoning
1/4	teaspoon black pepper
3	cups shredded cooked chicken

Dumplings

1	cup heart-healthy, reduced-fat biscuit baking mix
5	tablespoons fat-free milk
2	teaspoons chopped fresh dill

1 Coat a soup pot with cooking spray and heat over medium-high heat. Add celery and carrots; sauté 5 to 6 minutes or until tender. Stir in broth, poultry seasoning, and pepper; bring to a boil. Stir in chicken.

2 Meanwhile, in a medium bowl, make dumpling batter by mixing together biscuit mix, milk, and dill until well combined. Drop 6 spoonfuls of dumpling batter into boiling broth. Reduce heat to low and simmer 5 minutes; cover and cook an additional 8 minutes or until dumplings are cooked through. Serve immediately.

The key to plump dumplings is covering them for the second half of their cooking time. This allows the dumpling to be infused with the flavor-packed steam, so that every bite is full of flavor.

NUTRITION INFORMATION   **Choices/Exchanges,** 1 Starch, 1 Nonstarchy Vegetable, 3 Lean Protein

Calories 230, Calories from Fat 35, **Total Fat** 4.0g, Saturated Fat 0.9g, Trans Fat 0.0g, **Cholesterol** 60mg, **Sodium** 480mg, **Potassium** 630mg, **Total Carbohydrate** 19g, Dietary Fiber 2g, Sugars 5g, **Protein** 29g, **Phosphorus** 400mg

Maple Mustard Chicken Thighs

SERVES 4, 2 per serving

PREP TIME: 5 minutes
COOK TIME: 35 minutes

2	tablespoons grainy brown mustard
2	tablespoons real maple syrup
1	clove garlic, minced
8	boneless, skinless chicken thighs (about 1-1/2 pounds)
1/2	teaspoon salt substitute
1/4	teaspoon black pepper

1 Preheat oven to 375°F. Coat a 9- × 13-inch baking dish with cooking spray.

2 In a small bowl, combine mustard, syrup, and garlic; mix well. Evenly sprinkle both sides of chicken with salt substitute and pepper.

3 Dip chicken lightly into mustard mixture and place in baking dish. Spoon remaining mustard mixture over top of each chicken thigh.

4 Bake 35 to 40 minutes or until juices run clear and no pink remains in center of chicken. Serve immediately.

Serving Suggestion

This bold and flavorful chicken goes great with a side of veggies or a small green salad. Dinner is going to be delicious!

NUTRITION INFORMATION

Choices/Exchanges, 1/2 Carbohydrate, 4 Lean Protein, 1/2 Fat

Calories 240, Calories from Fat 90, **Total Fat** 10.0g, Saturated Fat 2.6g, Trans Fat 0.0g, **Cholesterol** 155mg, **Sodium** 210mg, **Potassium** 680mg, **Total Carbohydrate** 7g, Dietary Fiber 0g, Sugars 6g, **Protein** 28g, **Phosphorus** 255mg

Garden Chicken Kabobs

SERVES 4, 1 per serving

PREP TIME: 15 minutes
COOK TIME: 15 minutes

4	large metal or wooden skewers

Pesto Sauce

1	cup basil leaves
2	tablespoons pine nuts, toasted
2	cloves garlic, minced
2	tablespoons olive oil
2	tablespoons grated Parmesan cheese
1/2	teaspoon salt
1/4	teaspoon black pepper
2	small zucchini, cut into 12 (1-inch) rounds
12	cherry tomatoes
1	pound boneless, skinless chicken breasts, cut into 12 (1-1/2-inch) chunks
1/2	red onion, cut into 8 chunks

1 Coat a baking sheet with cooking spray. (If you're using wooden skewers, soak them in water for 15 minutes before skewering.)

2 To make the Pesto Sauce, in a blender or food processor, combine basil, pine nuts, garlic, oil, Parmesan cheese, salt, and pepper; pulse until finely chopped.

3 On each skewer, alternately thread 3 pieces of zucchini, 3 tomatoes, 3 chicken chunks, and 2 onion chunks. Place skewers on a baking sheet. Preheat broiler to high and broil 3 minutes per side.

4 Remove from oven and brush evenly with half the pesto sauce. Return to oven and broil 8 to 10 more minutes or until no pink remains in center of chicken, turning halfway through cooking and brushing with remaining pesto when turning.

Since we used skewers with wooden handles, we covered the handles with layers of aluminum foil while cooking to protect them. We also kept the handles in the front part of the oven, so that they were not directly under the heat source.

NUTRITION INFORMATION

Choices/Exchanges, 1 Nonstarchy Vegetable, 4 Lean Protein, 1/2 Fat

Calories 220, Calories from Fat 90, **Total Fat** 10.0g, Saturated Fat 1.7g, Trans Fat 0.0g, **Cholesterol** 65mg, **Sodium** 370mg, **Potassium** 580mg, **Total Carbohydrate** 7g, Dietary Fiber 2g, Sugars 4g, **Protein** 26g, **Phosphorus** 260mg

Sheet Pan Roasted Turkey and Veggies

SERVES 6, 3 ounces turkey and 1 cup vegetables per serving

PREP TIME: 15 minutes
COOK TIME: 25 minutes

3	tablespoons olive oil
1	fresh lemon, cut in half, divided
3	sprigs fresh rosemary, stems removed, chopped
1	teaspoon garlic powder
1	teaspoon paprika
1/2	teaspoon salt
1/4	teaspoon black pepper
1-1/4	pounds lean, boneless turkey tenderloins, each cut in half
2	bell peppers (1 red, 1 yellow), cut into 2-inch chunks
1	zucchini, cut into 1-inch chunks
1	cup mushrooms, cut in half
1/2	red onion, cut into 1-inch chunks

1 Preheat oven to 400°F.

2 In a large bowl, combine oil, juice from 1/2 lemon, rosemary, garlic powder, paprika, salt, and black pepper; mix well. Add turkey and toss until evenly coated. Place on a baking sheet. Add bell peppers, zucchini, mushrooms, and onion to oil mixture and toss until evenly coated. Place vegetables and lemon halves on baking sheet.

3 Roast 25 to 30 minutes or until no pink remains in turkey and vegetables are tender. With a pair of tongs, squeeze roasted lemon halves over turkey and vegetables, and serve immediately.

If you like your vegetables roasted a little longer, remove turkey to a plate, cover to keep warm, and cook vegetables an additional 10 minutes or so.

NUTRITION INFORMATION   **Choices/Exchanges,** 1 Nonstarchy Vegetable, 3 Lean Protein, 1/2 Fat

Calories 200, Calories from Fat 80, **Total Fat** 9.0g, Saturated Fat 1.4g, Trans Fat 0.0g, **Cholesterol** 60mg, **Sodium** 270mg, **Potassium** 450mg, **Total Carbohydrate** 7g, Dietary Fiber 2g, Sugars 3g, **Protein** 24g, **Phosphorus** 210mg

Saucy BBQ Drumsticks

SERVES 4, 2 per serving

PREP TIME: 10 minutes
COOK TIME: 50 minutes

1/4	cup light, trans-fat-free margarine
1/2	cup chopped onion
3	cloves garlic, minced
8	drumsticks, skin removed
1/2	teaspoon onion powder
1/2	teaspoon black pepper

BBQ Sauce

1	(8-ounce) can no-salt-added tomato sauce
	Brown sugar substitute equal to 1/2 cup firmly packed brown sugar (see page x)
2	tablespoons Worcestershire sauce
1	tablespoon yellow mustard
1	teaspoon hot pepper sauce
1	teaspoon lemon juice
1/4	cup water

1 In a deep skillet over medium heat, melt margarine; sauté onion and garlic 5 minutes.

2 Evenly sprinkle chicken with onion powder and pepper, and add to skillet. Cook 8 to 10 minutes or until browned on all sides.

3 Meanwhile, to make BBQ Sauce, in a medium bowl, combine remaining ingredients; mix well, then pour over chicken. Reduce heat to low and cook 35 to 40 minutes or until no pink remains in chicken, turning occasionally.

Good for You!
Many off-the-shelf BBQ sauces are loaded with sugar and sodium, which aren't great for people with diabetes. By making our own sauce, we can control what's in it.

NUTRITION INFORMATION   Choices/Exchanges, 1/2 Carbohydrate, 1 Nonstarchy Vegetable, 3 Lean Protein, 1 Fat

Calories 240, Calories from Fat 100, **Total Fat** 11.0g, Saturated Fat 2.5g, Trans Fat 0.0g, **Cholesterol** 80mg, **Sodium** 320mg, **Potassium** 510mg, **Total Carbohydrate** 10g, Dietary Fiber 1g, Sugars 5g, **Protein** 26g, **Phosphorus** 200mg

Southern (Not-Fried) Fried Chicken

SERVES 5, 2 pieces per serving

PREP TIME: 10 minutes
COOK TIME: 50 minutes

1	(3-pound) chicken, cut into 10 pieces, skin removed (see Tip)
1-1/2	tablespoons sriracha sauce
3	tablespoons all-purpose flour
1/4	teaspoon salt
1/4	teaspoon black pepper
3	egg whites
2-1/4	cups oven-toasted wheat cereal, crushed
1/2	teaspoon poultry seasoning
	Cooking spray

1 Preheat oven to 350°F. Coat a rimmed baking sheet with cooking spray. In a large bowl, toss chicken with sriracha sauce until evenly coated; set aside.

2 In a shallow dish, combine flour, salt, and pepper. In another shallow dish, lightly beat egg whites. Combine cereal crumbs and poultry seasoning in a third shallow dish.

3 Dip chicken pieces in flour mixture, then in egg whites, then in cereal crumbs, coating completely with each. Place on baking sheet and lightly spray top of chicken with cooking spray.

4 Bake 50 to 55 minutes or until no pink remains and juices run clear.

When it comes to the chicken, you can either buy it already cut up or you can pick up a whole chicken and cut it yourself. Cutting it yourself will often save you a few cents per pound. Either way, we suggest that you cut both breasts in half as they are often very large. That way, they'll take the same amount of time to cook as the rest of the bird.

NUTRITION INFORMATION

Choices/Exchanges, 1 Starch, 4 Lean Protein

Calories 270, Calories from Fat 70, **Total Fat** 8.0g, Saturated Fat 2.1g, Trans Fat 0.0g, **Cholesterol** 85mg, **Sodium** 440mg, **Potassium** 330mg, **Total Carbohydrate** 18g, Dietary Fiber 2g, Sugars 4g, **Protein** 33g, **Phosphorus** 245mg

Louisiana Chicken Gumbo

SERVES 8, 3/4 cup gumbo and 1/2 cup rice per serving

PREP TIME: 10 minutes
COOK TIME: 30 minutes

2	tablespoons light, trans-fat-free margarine
1	pound boneless, skinless chicken breasts, cut into 1-inch chunks
1	pound boneless, skinless chicken thighs, cut into 1-inch chunks
1/2	cup chopped onion
1	cup sliced celery
1	medium green bell pepper, chopped
3	cloves garlic, minced
2	tablespoons all-purpose flour
1	teaspoon chili powder
1/4	teaspoon salt
1/4	teaspoon cayenne pepper
2	(14-1/2-ounce) cans no-salt-added diced tomatoes, undrained
1	cup frozen okra, thawed
1	cup water
4	cups cooked brown rice

1 In a soup pot over medium heat, melt margarine; add chicken breasts and thighs and brown 5 minutes, stirring often. Add onion, celery, bell pepper, and garlic, and cook 5 more minutes or until vegetables are tender, stirring occasionally.

2 Stir in flour, chili powder, salt, and cayenne pepper; cook 1 minute. Add tomatoes with their juice, okra, and water, and bring to a boil. Reduce heat to low and simmer 10 to 15 minutes or until thickened, stirring occasionally. Serve with brown rice.

Since we're always looking for ways to cut down on carbs, we've reduced the amount of flour used to thicken up our gumbo and added okra, which is a natural thickener. It also adds a nice traditional touch.

NUTRITION INFORMATION   **Choices/Exchanges,** 2 Starch, 1 Nonstarchy Vegetable, 3 Lean Protein

Calories 300, Calories from Fat 60, **Total Fat** 7.0g, Saturated Fat 1.8g, Trans Fat 0.0g, **Cholesterol** 85mg, **Sodium** 220mg, **Potassium** 600mg, **Total Carbohydrate** 34g, Dietary Fiber 4g, Sugars 4g, **Protein** 25g, **Phosphorus** 310mg

Turkey 'n' Stuffing Rollups

SERVES 6, 1 per serving

PREP TIME: 15 minutes
COOK TIME: 35 minutes

2	tablespoons light, trans-fat-free margarine
1/2	cup chopped celery
1/2	cup chopped carrot
1/4	cup finely chopped onion
1	cup crushed herb stuffing
1/2	cup fat-free, low-sodium chicken broth, warmed
6	(4-ounce) boneless, skinless turkey breast cutlets
1	teaspoon poultry seasoning
1/2	teaspoon black pepper
1	(12-ounce) jar fat-free turkey gravy
	Paprika for sprinkling

1 Preheat oven to 350°F. Coat a 9- × 13-inch baking dish with cooking spray.

2 In a medium skillet over medium heat, melt margarine; sauté celery, carrot, and onion 4 to 5 minutes or until tender, stirring occasionally.

3 In a medium bowl, combine stuffing, sautéed vegetables, and broth; mix well. Evenly sprinkle turkey cutlets on both sides with poultry seasoning and pepper. Place equal amounts of stuffing mixture (about 1/3 cup) on top of each cutlet and roll up. Place rolls seam-side-down in baking dish, pour gravy evenly over top, and sprinkle with paprika. Cover with aluminum foil.

4 Bake 30 to 35 minutes or until no pink remains in turkey. Serve immediately.

Portion Size Matters

If you're planning on having a more intimate holiday celebration, then our Turkey 'n' Stuffing Rollups are perfect for you. They feature a taste of Thanksgiving, without having to prepare the whole bird. Actually, these are great year-round, for any time you crave those Turkey Day flavors!

NUTRITION INFORMATION **Choices/Exchanges,** 1 Starch, 3 Lean Protein

Calories 220, Calories from Fat 35, **Total Fat** 4.0g, Saturated Fat 0.9g, Trans Fat 0.0g, **Cholesterol** 75mg, **Sodium** 570mg, **Potassium** 400mg, **Total Carbohydrate** 15g, Dietary Fiber 1g, Sugars 2g, **Protein** 30g, **Phosphorus** 255mg

Powerhouse Turkey Burgers

SERVES 4, 1 per serving

PREP TIME: 10 minutes
COOK TIME: 10 minutes

1	pound lean ground turkey breast
1/2	cup cooked quinoa
1/2	cup kale, chopped
2	scallions, thinly sliced
1	teaspoon garlic powder
1/2	teaspoon salt
1/4	teaspoon black pepper

Apricot Sauce

1/2	cup sugar-free apricot preserves
1/4	cup light mayonnaise
1/8	teaspoon cayenne pepper

1 In a large bowl, combine ground turkey, quinoa, kale, scallions, garlic powder, salt, and pepper; mix well. Form mixture into 4 patties.

2 Coat a grill pan or large skillet with cooking spray; cook burgers over medium heat 5 to 6 minutes per side or until no longer pink in center.

3 Meanwhile, to make Apricot Sauce, in a small bowl, combine preserves, mayonnaise, and cayenne pepper; mix well. Top burgers with a dollop of sauce and serve.

Good for You!
Between the protein in the turkey and the quinoa, and the vitamins in the kale, it's easy to see why we've nicknamed these our "powerhouse" burgers. Plus, they're not just good for you, they're good to eat too (especially with our apricot sauce)!

NUTRITION INFORMATION

Choices/Exchanges, 1 Carbohydrate, 4 Lean Protein

Calories 220, Calories from Fat 50, **Total Fat** 6.0g, Saturated Fat 1.0g, Trans Fat 0.0g, **Cholesterol** 65mg, **Sodium** 460mg, **Potassium** 440mg, **Total Carbohydrate** 13g, Dietary Fiber 5g, Sugars 2g, **Protein** 30g, **Phosphorus** 310mg

Cozy Beef & Pork

Balsamic Steak with Blistered Peppers

SERVES 4, 4 ounces steak with 2 peppers per serving

PREP TIME: 10 minutes
COOK TIME: 40 minutes

Balsamic Glaze

1	teaspoon olive oil
2	cloves garlic, minced
1/4	cup balsamic vinegar
	Brown sugar substitute equal to 1 tablespoon brown sugar (see page x)
2	sprigs fresh rosemary
1/4	cup fat-free, reduced-sodium beef broth
1	teaspoon olive oil
1	pound flank steak, well trimmed
1/4	teaspoon salt
1/4	teaspoon black pepper
1	sprig fresh rosemary, stem removed, chopped
8	ounces mini sweet peppers

1 To make the Balsamic Glaze, in a small saucepan over medium heat, heat 1 teaspoon oil until hot; add garlic and cook 1 minute. Add vinegar, brown sugar substitute, and 2 sprigs rosemary; bring to a boil. Reduce heat to low and simmer 5 minutes. Add broth, bring to a boil, then reduce heat to low and simmer 10 minutes or until thickened. Set aside.

2 Rub 1 teaspoon oil over entire steak, then sprinkle evenly with salt, pepper, and chopped rosemary.

3 In a grill pan over medium-high heat, cook steak 5 to 6 minutes per side for medium-rare (145°F), or to desired doneness. Remove to a cutting board and let rest at least 5 minutes.

4 Meanwhile, in a medium bowl, toss peppers in 1 tablespoon of Balsamic Glaze. In the same grill pan over medium-high heat, cook peppers 8 to 10 minutes or until the skins start to blister, turning once halfway through cooking.

5 Slice steak on the diagonal and drizzle with remaining Balsamic Glaze. Serve with blistered peppers.

Did You Know?

Letting a cooked steak or roast rest for 5 to 10 minutes after cooking keeps the meat juicier. That way, when you carve it, the juices stay in each piece rather than flowing out all over the cutting board.

NUTRITION INFORMATION   Choices/Exchanges, 1/2 Carbohydrate, 3 Lean Protein, 1/2 Fat

Calories 200, Calories from Fat 70, **Total Fat** 8.0g, Saturated Fat 2.8g, Trans Fat 0.0g, **Cholesterol** 60mg, **Sodium** 230mg, **Potassium** 440mg, **Total Carbohydrate** 7g, Dietary Fiber 1g, Sugars 5g, **Protein** 23g, **Phosphorus** 195mg

Take-Out Beef Fried Rice

SERVES 5, 1 cup per serving

PREP TIME: 10 minutes
COOK TIME: 10 minutes

1	tablespoon sesame oil
1/2	red bell pepper, cut into 1/2-inch chunks
1/4	pound snow peas
1	pound bottom round thin sliced steak, well trimmed and cut into 1/4-inch strips
2	cloves garlic, minced
3	cups cooked brown rice, chilled (see Tip)
3	tablespoons reduced-sodium soy sauce
1/2	teaspoon ground ginger
1/4	teaspoon black pepper
2	scallions, thinly sliced

1 In a large skillet over medium-high heat, heat oil until hot. Add bell pepper and snow peas; cook 3 to 4 minutes or until vegetables are crisp-tender.

2 Add steak and garlic and cook 2 to 3 minutes or until steak is browned. Stir in rice, soy sauce, ginger, and black pepper, and continue to cook 4 to 5 minutes or until heated through. Stir in scallions just before serving.

Test Kitchen. Mr. Food Hints & Tips

The trick to making a really good stir-fry is to use a large pan, so that your ingredients don't get overcrowded. This will allow everything to cook evenly and prevent it from getting soggy. And if you're wondering why we use chilled rice, it's because it helps keep the rice from getting sticky.

NUTRITION INFORMATION　　**Choices/Exchanges,** 2 Starch, 1 Nonstarchy Vegetable, 2 Lean Protein, 1/2 Fat

Calories 300, Calories from Fat 70, **Total Fat** 8.0g, Saturated Fat 2.1g, Trans Fat 0.0g, **Cholesterol** 50mg, **Sodium** 360mg, **Potassium** 390mg, **Total Carbohydrate** 34g, Dietary Fiber 3g, Sugars 2g, **Protein** 22g, **Phosphorus** 295mg

Rancher's Meat Loaf

SERVES 8, 1 slice per serving

PREP TIME: 10 minutes
COOK TIME: 60 minutes

1-1/2	pounds 95% extra-lean ground beef
8	ounces mushrooms, finely chopped
1/2	cup chopped onion
1	egg
1	cup rolled oats
1	cup barbecue sauce,* divided
1-1/2	teaspoons garlic powder
1/4	teaspoon salt
1/2	teaspoon black pepper

1. Preheat oven to 350°F. Coat a 9- × 13-inch baking dish with cooking spray.

2. In a large bowl, combine ground beef, mushrooms, onion, egg, oats, 3/4 cup barbecue sauce, the garlic powder, salt, and pepper. Using your hands, gently mix ground beef mixture just until combined. (Do not overmix or the meat loaf will be tough.) Form into a loaf and place in baking dish.

3. Bake 55 minutes. Brush with remaining 1/4 cup barbecue sauce and bake an additional 5 to 10 minutes or until no pink remains. Drain off excess liquid, then let cool 5 minutes before cutting into 8 slices and serving.

Good for You!

We use rolled oats instead of traditional bread crumbs in this recipe because oats are much higher in fiber, which can help in maintaining blood glucose and aids in digestion.

Look for barbecue sauce that has less than 11g of carbohydrate and less than 300mg of sodium per 2-tablespoon serving.

NUTRITION INFORMATION

Choices/Exchanges, 1-1/2 Carbohydrate, 3 Lean Protein

Calories 220, Calories from Fat 50, **Total Fat** 6.0g, Saturated Fat 2.3g, Trans Fat 0.1g, **Cholesterol** 75mg, **Sodium** 480mg, **Potassium** 490mg, **Total Carbohydrate** 21g, Dietary Fiber 2g, Sugars 9g, **Protein** 20g, **Phosphorus** 240mg

Skinny Skillet Shepherd's Pie

SERVES 6, 3/4 cup beef and vegetables plus 1/3 cup potatoes per serving

PREP TIME: 15 minutes
COOK TIME: 35 minutes

4	potatoes, peeled and cut into chunks
2	tablespoons light, trans-fat-free margarine
3/4	cup plus 2 tablespoons low-fat milk, divided
1/2	teaspoon garlic powder
1/2	teaspoon black pepper, divided
1-1/2	pounds 95% extra-lean ground beef
2	cups frozen mixed vegetables, thawed
1	(10-1/2-ounce) can fat-free, reduced-sodium, condensed cream of mushroom soup
1/2	teaspoon onion powder
	Paprika for sprinkling

1. Place potatoes in a medium saucepan and cover with water. Bring to a boil over medium-high heat and cook 15 minutes or until fork-tender; drain well. Add margarine, 2 tablespoons milk, garlic powder, and 1/4 teaspoon pepper; beat until smooth, cover with aluminum foil to keep warm, and set aside.

2. Meanwhile, in a large skillet over medium-high heat, sauté ground beef 6 to 8 minutes or until browned; drain off excess liquid. Add mixed vegetables, soup, the remaining 3/4 cup milk, onion powder, and remaining 1/4 teaspoon pepper. Mix well and cook 5 to 8 minutes or until heated through, stirring occasionally.

3. Dollop skillet mixture evenly with mashed potatoes, sprinkle with paprika, and serve.

If you make this in an oven-safe skillet, you could pop it into a 400°F oven after topping it with the potatoes. This will allow the potatoes to get a nice golden crust to them.

NUTRITION INFORMATION

Choices/Exchanges, 2 Starch, 1/2 Carbohydrate, 3 Lean Protein, 1/2 Fat

Calories 340, Calories from Fat 80, **Total Fat** 9.0g, Saturated Fat 3.5g, Trans Fat 0.1g, **Cholesterol** 75mg, **Sodium** 300mg, **Potassium** 1180mg, **Total Carbohydrate** 35g, Dietary Fiber 5g, Sugars 5g, **Protein** 28g, **Phosphorus** 325mg

Grilled Pub-Style Sirloin

SERVES 6, 4 ounces per serving

PREP TIME: 5 minutes
MARINATE TIME: 2 hours
COOK TIME: 10 minutes

Marinade

1	(12-ounce) bottle dark beer
1/4	cup reduced-sodium soy sauce
	Brown sugar substitute equal to 1/4 cup brown sugar (see page x)
3	cloves garlic, minced
1-1/2	pounds top sirloin steak, well trimmed
1/4	teaspoon sea salt
1/4	teaspoon black pepper

1 To make Marinade, in a large resealable plastic bag or glass baking dish, combine beer, soy sauce, brown sugar substitute, and garlic; mix well.

2 Place steak in marinade and refrigerate 2 to 4 hours, turning meat occasionally.

3 Preheat grill or grill pan to medium-high heat. Remove steak from marinade and discard excess marinade.

4 Grill steak 4 to 5 minutes per side or until center is cooked to medium-rare (135°F) or until desired doneness. Sprinkle steak with salt and pepper, then slice on an angle across the grain, and serve.

To infuse the steak with the most flavor, before placing it in the marinade, poke both sides with a fork several times. This allows the marinade to penetrate the steak faster and deeper.

NUTRITION INFORMATION　　　　　　　　　　**Choices/Exchanges,** 3 Lean Protein

Calories 150, Calories from Fat 35, **Total Fat** 4.0g, Saturated Fat 1.6g, Trans Fat 0.1g, **Cholesterol** 40mg, **Sodium** 290mg, **Potassium** 300mg, **Total Carbohydrate** 2g, Dietary Fiber 0g, Sugars 0g, **Protein** 23g, **Phosphorus** 185mg

Swiss Steak Italiano

SERVES 4, 1 steak with 1/3 cup sauce per serving

PREP TIME: 10 minutes
COOK TIME: 55 minutes

4	beef cube steaks (about 5 ounces each)
1/4	teaspoon salt
1/2	teaspoon black pepper
1/2	tablespoon canola oil
1/2	cup chopped onion
1/2	cup diced celery
1	(14-ounce) can no-salt-added diced tomatoes, undrained
1	cup reduced-sodium beef broth
1	teaspoon Italian seasoning
1	teaspoon cornstarch
1	tablespoon water

1 Season steaks with salt and pepper. In a large skillet over medium-high heat, heat oil until hot. Cook steaks in batches, 2 to 3 minutes per side or until browned. Remove to a platter.

2 In the same skillet over medium heat, sauté onion and celery 5 minutes. Add tomatoes with their juice, the broth, and Italian seasoning; mix well. Return steaks to skillet, cover, reduce heat to low, and cook 40 to 45 minutes, or until meat is tender.

3 In a small bowl, mix cornstarch and water, and stir into skillet. Cook 5 more minutes or until sauce is thickened. Spoon sauce over steaks and enjoy.

Did You Know?

By mixing cornstarch with water we create what is known as a slurry. A slurry is simply a quick and easy way to thicken up sauces. Just make sure you cook the sauce for a minimum of 5 minutes after adding it, so that your sauce doesn't taste like cornstarch.

NUTRITION INFORMATION   Choices/Exchanges, 1 Nonstarchy Vegetable, 4 Lean Protein

Calories 230, Calories from Fat 70, **Total Fat** 8.0g, Saturated Fat 2.4g, Trans Fat 0.0g, **Cholesterol** 80mg, **Sodium** 310mg, **Potassium** 520mg, **Total Carbohydrate** 8g, Dietary Fiber 2g, Sugars 4g, **Protein** 30g, **Phosphorus** 215mg

Skillet Stuffed Peppers

SERVES 6, 1 (1/2 pepper) per serving

PREP TIME: 10 minutes
COOK TIME: 25 minutes

1-1/4	pounds 95% extra-lean ground beef
1/2	cup chopped onion
1-1/2	cups cooked brown rice
1	teaspoon garlic powder
1/2	teaspoon salt
1/4	teaspoon black pepper
3	bell peppers, split lengthwise and cleaned
2-1/2	cups low-sodium spaghetti sauce
1/2	cup water

1 In a large skillet over medium-high heat, brown ground beef and onion 4 to 5 minutes, stirring until meat crumbles and is no longer pink. Drain excess liquid, then add rice, garlic powder, salt, and black pepper; mix well. Evenly spoon mixture into bell pepper halves.

2 In the same skillet over medium-low heat, add spaghetti sauce and water; place stuffed pepper halves in skillet. Cover and cook 20 to 25 minutes or until peppers are tender and heated through. Spoon sauce over peppers and serve.

Out of the Box
Here's a chance to add some color to your table—just mix and match red, yellow, green, and orange peppers. You can even use poblano peppers, which are a mild south-of-the border favorite that taste amazing when stuffed and roasted.

NUTRITION INFORMATION Choices/Exchanges, 1-1/2 Starch, 1 Nonstarchy Vegetable, 2 Lean Protein, 1/2 Fat

Calories 260, Calories from Fat 70, **Total Fat** 8.0g, Saturated Fat 2.6g, Trans Fat 0.1g, **Cholesterol** 60mg, **Sodium** 270mg, **Potassium** 830mg, **Total Carbohydrate** 26g, Dietary Fiber 4g, Sugars 7g, **Protein** 23g, **Phosphorus** 275mg

Greek Kofta Skewers

SERVES 4, 2 skewers and 1-1/2 tablespoons sauce per serving

PREP TIME: 15 minutes
COOK TIME: 15 minutes

3/4	pound 95% extra-lean ground beef
1	cup cooked brown rice
1/4	cup fat-free feta cheese crumbles
1	teaspoon oregano
1/2	teaspoon onion powder
1/2	teaspoon garlic powder
1/4	teaspoon salt substitute
1/4	teaspoon black pepper
8	(6-inch) wooden skewers (see Note)

Tzatziki Sauce

1/2	cup fat-free sour cream
1/2	cup finely diced cucumber
1	tablespoon chopped fresh mint
1	clove garlic, minced
1	teaspoon lemon juice
1/4	teaspoon salt substitute
1/8	teaspoon black pepper

1 Preheat oven to 350°F. Coat a baking sheet with cooking spray.

2 In a medium bowl, combine ground beef, rice, feta, oregano, onion powder, garlic powder, salt substitute, and pepper; mix well. Roll mixture into 8 sausage-like shapes. Place a skewer into the end of each and place on baking sheet.

3 Bake 15 to 18 minutes or until no pink remains.

4 Meanwhile, to make Tzatziki Sauce, in a small bowl, combine ingredients. Serve skewers with sauce (about 2-1/2 teaspoons per skewer).

Note: Be sure to soak wooden skewers 20 minutes before using, so that they don't burn.

Out of the Box

To make these meat skewers (kofta) even more authentic, try replacing half of the beef with extra-lean ground lamb. And for those who like a smoother sauce versus a chunkier one, grate the cucumber instead of dicing it.

NUTRITION INFORMATION **Choices/Exchanges,** 1 Starch, 1/2 Carbohydrate, 2 Lean Protein

Calories 210, Calories from Fat 45, **Total Fat** 5.0g, Saturated Fat 2.3g, Trans Fat 0.1g, **Cholesterol** 55mg, **Sodium** 150mg, **Potassium** 710mg, **Total Carbohydrate** 20g, Dietary Fiber 1g, Sugars 2g, **Protein** 22g, **Phosphorus** 265mg

"Spaghetti" and Meatballs

SERVES 4, 2 meatballs, 1 cup spaghetti squash, and 1/2 cup sauce per serving

PREP TIME: 25 minutes
COOK TIME: 50 minutes

1	small spaghetti squash
1	pound 95% extra-lean ground beef
1/4	cup plain bread crumbs
3	tablespoons grated, reduced-fat Parmesan cheese, divided
3/4	cup water plus extra for cooking squash, divided
2	tablespoons chopped fresh parsley
1	egg
1	teaspoon garlic powder
1/2	teaspoon black pepper
2	cups low-sodium spaghetti sauce

1 Fill a soup pot with 1 inch water and place whole squash in water. Bring to a boil over high heat, cover, and cook 25 to 30 minutes, or until tender when pierced with a knife. Remove squash to a cutting board and allow to cool slightly. Cut squash in half lengthwise; remove and discard seeds with a spoon. Scrape inside of squash with a fork, shredding into noodle-like strands. Cover to keep warm.

2 Meanwhile, in a large bowl, combine ground beef, bread crumbs, 2 tablespoons Parmesan cheese, 1/4 cup water, the parsley, egg, garlic powder, and pepper; gently mix until well combined. Form mixture into 8 equal-sized meatballs.

3 Coat a large skillet with cooking spray. Cook meatballs over medium heat 8 to 10 minutes or until browned, turning them occasionally. Add spaghetti sauce and remaining 1/2 cup water. Cover and cook 10 to 15 minutes or until meatballs are no longer pink in center.

4 Serve the spaghetti squash topped with sauce and meatballs. Sprinkle with remaining 1 tablespoon Parmesan cheese just before serving.

Did You Know?

One cup of spaghetti squash only has 42 calories and 10g of carbs. Compare that to the spaghetti we all grew up with, which has 220 calories and 42g of carbs. It's no wonder everyone is going crazy for this low-carb veggie!

NUTRITION INFORMATION **Choices/Exchanges,** 1 Starch, 2 Nonstarchy Vegetable, 3 Lean Protein, 1 Fat

Calories 320, Calories from Fat 100, **Total Fat** 11.0g, Saturated Fat 4.0g, Trans Fat 0.2g, **Cholesterol** 125mg, **Sodium** 270mg, **Potassium** 930mg, **Total Carbohydrate** 25g, Dietary Fiber 4g, Sugars 9g, **Protein** 29g, **Phosphorus** 340mg

Autumn Pork Chops

SERVES 4, 1 pork chop with 1/4 cup sauce per serving

PREP TIME: 10 minutes
COOK TIME: 20 minutes

1	tablespoon canola oil
4	(4-ounce) boneless center-cut loin pork chops, well trimmed
1/2	teaspoon salt
1/2	teaspoon black pepper
1/2	cup pitted prunes, sliced
1/2	cup dried apricots, sliced
1	onion, thinly sliced
1/2	cup water
	Brown sugar substitute equal to 2 tablespoons brown sugar (see page x)
2	tablespoons apple cider vinegar

1 In a large skillet over medium-high heat, heat oil until hot. Sprinkle pork chops with salt and pepper, then cook 4 to 5 minutes per side or until browned.

2 Add remaining ingredients to skillet. Cover, reduce heat to low, and simmer 8 to 10 minutes or until pork is cooked to medium (145°F) or until desired doneness. Serve each topped with sauce (about 1/4 cup).

Did You Know?

We add apple cider vinegar to this dish for two reasons. The first is that the acid in the vinegar reacts with the brown sugar substitute, creating a pungent, sweet, and tangy sauce. The second is that it also helps break down the fibers in the pork, allowing the sauce to penetrate it and giving it more flavor.

NUTRITION INFORMATION

Choices/Exchanges, 2 Fruit, 3 Lean Protein, 1 Fat

Calories 300, Calories from Fat 100, **Total Fat** 11.0g, Saturated Fat 2.8g, Trans Fat 0.0g, **Cholesterol** 60mg, **Sodium** 340mg, **Potassium** 740mg, **Total Carbohydrate** 29g, Dietary Fiber 4g, Sugars 20g, **Protein** 23g, **Phosphorus** 215mg

Skewered Pork over Red Cabbage

SERVES 4, 1 skewer with 4 ounces meat and 3/4 cup cabbage per serving

PREP TIME: 10 minutes
MARINATE TIME: 60 minutes
COOK TIME: 55 minutes

2	tablespoons canola oil
1	tablespoon apple cider vinegar
1/4	teaspoon ground cloves
1/4	teaspoon black pepper
1	pound pork tenderloin, cut into 1/2-inch slices

Tangy Cabbage

1	tablespoon canola oil
1/2	cup chopped onion
1	Granny Smith apple, peeled, cored, and chopped
1/4	cup apple cider vinegar
1/2	red cabbage, cut into 1-inch pieces
1/4	teaspoon ground cloves
1/4	teaspoon salt
1/4	teaspoon black pepper
4	(6-inch) wooden skewers (see Note)

1. In a small bowl, whisk 2 tablespoons oil, 1 tablespoon vinegar, 1/4 teaspoon ground cloves, and 1/4 teaspoon pepper; pour mixture into a large resealable plastic bag. With a meat mallet or soup can, slightly flatten each piece of pork. (See photo for desired thickness.) Add pork to bag; seal and toss pork until evenly coated. Refrigerate at least 1 hour.

2. Meanwhile, to make the Tangy Cabbage, in a large deep skillet over medium heat, heat 1 tablespoon oil until hot. Add onion and cook 3 minutes. Stir in apple and 1/4 cup vinegar, and cook 5 minutes. Add cabbage, 1/4 teaspoon cloves, salt, and 1/4 teaspoon pepper; mix well. Cover, reduce heat to low, and cook 45 to 50 minutes or until tender, stirring occasionally.

3. Preheat oven to 450°F. Place 3 pieces of pork on each skewer and place skewers on rimmed baking sheet. Discard marinade. Bake 8 to 10 minutes or to desired doneness, turning halfway through cooking. Serve pork skewers over cabbage.

Note: Be sure to soak wooden skewers 20 minutes before using, so that they don't burn.

NUTRITION INFORMATION **Choices/Exchanges,** 1/2 Fruit, 2 Nonstarchy Vegetable, 3 Lean Protein, 1/2 Fat

Calories 240, Calories from Fat 80, **Total Fat** 9.0g, Saturated Fat 1.5g, Trans Fat 0.0g, **Cholesterol** 60mg, **Sodium** 220mg, **Potassium** 690mg, **Total Carbohydrate** 15g, Dietary Fiber 3g, Sugars 9g, **Protein** 24g, **Phosphorus** 240mg

Countryside Pork Chops

SERVES 4, 1 pork chop with 1/3 cup sauce per serving

PREP TIME: 10 minutes
COOK TIME: 20 minutes

4	(4-ounce) boneless center-cut pork chops, well trimmed
1/2	teaspoon salt, divided
1/2	teaspoon black pepper, divided
2	tablespoons canola oil
2	onions, cut into 1/2-inch slices
3	cloves garlic, slivered
1	(14-ounce) can no-salt-added stewed tomatoes, undrained
1/2	cup dry white wine
1	tablespoon capers
1/2	teaspoon dried thyme leaves

1 Evenly sprinkle pork chops with 1/4 teaspoon salt and 1/4 teaspoon pepper.

2 In a large skillet over medium-high heat, heat oil until hot; add pork chops. Brown pork chops, 2 to 3 minutes per side; remove to a plate. Add onions and garlic and cook 3 minutes, stirring occasionally.

3 Add remaining ingredients including the remaining 1/4 teaspoon salt and 1/4 teaspoon pepper; mix well. Return pork chops to skillet and simmer over low heat 10 to 15 minutes or until no pink remains.

Serving Suggestion

As the saying goes, we eat with our eyes. That's why we decided to slice each pork chop on the diagonal before serving it. Not only does this make it look great, but it also allows the flavor-packed sauce to soak between every piece.

NUTRITION INFORMATION   **Choices/Exchanges,** 3 Nonstarchy Vegetable, 3 Lean Protein, 2 Fat

Calories 290, Calories from Fat 130, **Total Fat** 14.0g, Saturated Fat 3.1g, Trans Fat 0.0g, **Cholesterol** 60mg, **Sodium** 410mg, **Potassium** 640mg, **Total Carbohydrate** 16g, Dietary Fiber 2g, Sugars 8g, **Protein** 23g, **Phosphorus** 220mg

7-Spice Rubbed Pork Tenderloin

SERVES 4, 4 ounces per serving

PREP TIME: 5 minutes
COOK TIME: 20 minutes

1/2	teaspoon paprika
1/4	teaspoon dried thyme
1/4	teaspoon ground cumin
1/4	teaspoon garlic powder
1/8	teaspoon ground cinnamon
1/4	teaspoon salt
1/4	teaspoon black pepper
1	(1-pound) pork tenderloin
2	teaspoons olive oil

1 Preheat oven to 375°F. Coat a baking sheet with cooking spray.

2 In a small bowl, combine paprika, thyme, cumin, garlic powder, cinnamon, salt, and pepper; mix well. Rub pork with olive oil, then sprinkle spice mixture evenly over entire pork and rub again until evenly coated.

3 Roast 20 to 25 minutes or to desired doneness. Let rest 5 minutes, then slice and serve.

Did You Know?

The days of cooking pork until it's well done are long gone. According to the USDA, pork roasts should be cooked to a minimum internal temperature of 145°F, which is 15° less than previously recommended. This ensures that every bite will be juicy and delicious!

NUTRITION INFORMATION   Choices/Exchanges, 3 Lean Protein

Calories 140, Calories from Fat 45, **Total Fat** 5.0g, Saturated Fat 1.3g, Trans Fat 0.0g, **Cholesterol** 60mg, **Sodium** 190mg, **Potassium** 360mg, **Total Carbohydrate** 1g, Dietary Fiber 0g, Sugars 0g, **Protein** 22g, **Phosphorus** 200mg

Seafood, Pasta, & More

Pan-Seared Salmon with Avocado Salsa

SERVES 4, 1 fish fillet and 1/4 cup salsa per serving

PREP TIME: 15 minutes
COOK TIME: 10 minutes

1/2	teaspoon chili powder
1/2	teaspoon ground cumin
1/2	teaspoon paprika
1/2	teaspoon onion powder
1/4	teaspoon salt
1/4	teaspoon black pepper
4	(4-ounce) salmon fillets
2	teaspoons canola oil

Avocado Salsa

1	avocado, cut into 1/4-inch chunks
1/2	cup canned low-sodium black beans, rinsed and drained
1/4	cup diced red onion
2	tablespoons fresh lime juice
2	tablespoons chopped cilantro
1/4	teaspoon salt

1 In a small bowl, combine chili powder, cumin, paprika, onion powder, 1/4 teaspoon salt, and the pepper; mix well. Rub both sides of salmon fillets with oil, then sprinkle evenly with seasoning mixture.

2 In a medium bowl, combine Avocado Salsa ingredients; mix well. Keep refrigerated until ready to serve.

3 Coat a grill pan or skillet with cooking spray and over medium heat, cook fillets 4 to 5 minutes per side or until fish flakes easily with a fork. Top with Avocado Salsa and serve.

Good for You!

Avocados have a good amount of potassium in them, which can help control blood pressure. And because they're high in monounsaturated fats (the "good" fats), they can help lower cholesterol too!

NUTRITION INFORMATION   Choices/Exchanges, 1 Carbohydrate, 3 Lean Protein, 2 Fat

Calories 290, Calories from Fat 140, **Total Fat** 16.0g, Saturated Fat 2.8g, Trans Fat 0.0g, **Cholesterol** 60mg, **Sodium** 370mg, **Potassium** 720mg, **Total Carbohydrate** 11g, Dietary Fiber 4g, Sugars 1g, **Protein** 25g, **Phosphorus** 350mg

Greek Isles Cod "Under Wraps"

SERVES 4, 1 fillet per serving

PREP TIME: 15 minutes
COOK TIME: 25 minutes

1	tablespoon canola oil
2	tablespoons chopped red bell pepper
2	cloves garlic, minced
4	cups baby spinach
2/3	cup reduced-fat crumbled feta cheese
2	tablespoons grated Parmesan cheese
8	(9- × 14-inch) sheets frozen phyllo pastry, thawed Cooking spray
4	(4-ounce) cod fillets

1 Preheat oven to 425°F. Coat a baking sheet with cooking spray.

2 In a medium skillet over medium heat, heat oil until hot; sauté bell pepper 3 to 4 minutes or until tender. Add garlic and spinach and cook 1 to 2 minutes or until spinach is wilted. Remove from heat and stir in feta cheese and Parmesan cheese; set aside.

3 On a cutting board or your counter, place one sheet of phyllo and lightly coat with cooking spray. Top with another sheet of phyllo and lightly coat with cooking spray. Repeat 2 more times, ending up with 4 phyllo sheets together. Cut layered phyllo sheets in half widthwise and set aside. Repeat with remaining 4 phyllo sheets.

4 Divide spinach mixture equally in the center of phyllo sheets. Place a cod fillet on top of spinach mixture and wrap the phyllo dough around the fish envelope-style. Place seam-side-down on baking sheet.

5 Bake 20 to 25 minutes or until golden brown and fish flakes easily with a fork.

Serving Suggestion

This goes great with our homemade Dill Sauce. To make it, in a small bowl, combine 1/4 cup reduced-fat sour cream, 1 teaspoon lemon juice, 2 teaspoons chopped fresh dill, 1/2 teaspoon garlic powder, and 1/4 teaspoon black pepper; mix well. This sauce can be made ahead and stored in an airtight container in your refrigerator until ready to serve.

NUTRITION INFORMATION

Choices/Exchanges, 1 Starch, 4 Lean Protein

Calories 260, Calories from Fat 80, **Total Fat** 9.0g, Saturated Fat 2.5g, Trans Fat 0.0g, **Cholesterol** 60mg, **Sodium** 440mg, **Potassium** 430mg, **Total Carbohydrate** 17g, Dietary Fiber 2g, Sugars 1g, **Protein** 28g, **Phosphorus** 250mg

Sizzlin' Cajun Catfish

SERVES 4, 1 fillet per serving

PREP TIME: 5 minutes
COOK TIME: 10 minutes

4	(6-ounce) U.S. Farm-Raised Catfish fillets
1-1/2	teaspoons Cajun seasoning, divided
1/2	cup yellow cornmeal
3	tablespoons self-rising flour
1	tablespoon light, trans-fat-free margarine
2	tablespoons olive oil

1 Sprinkle catfish with 1 teaspoon Cajun seasoning. In a small bowl, combine remaining 1/2 teaspoon Cajun seasoning, the cornmeal, and flour. Dredge fillets in mixture, shaking off excess.

2 In a large skillet over medium heat, melt margarine with oil. Add fillets and cook 4 to 5 minutes per side or until fish is golden and flakes easily with a fork. You may have to cook these in batches, depending on how big your skillet is. Serve immediately.

Good for You!

If you haven't tried U.S. Farm-Raised Catfish, then you're missing out! We love this mild-tasting and versatile fish. Plus, it's good for a diabetes meal plan because it's a great protein choice.

NUTRITION INFORMATION Choices/Exchanges, 1 Starch, 4 Lean Protein, 2 Fat

Calories 360, Calories from Fat 170, **Total Fat** 19.0g, Saturated Fat 3.6g, Trans Fat 0.1g, **Cholesterol** 100mg, **Sodium** 350mg, **Potassium** 610mg, **Total Carbohydrate** 14g, Dietary Fiber 1g, Sugars 0g, **Protein** 30g, **Phosphorus** 420mg

New England Fish Casserole

SERVES 2, 1 cup per serving

PREP TIME: 15 minutes
COOK TIME: 45 minutes

2	small baking potatoes, peeled and cut into 1-inch chunks
2	teaspoons reduced-fat sour cream
1/2	teaspoon garlic powder
2	tablespoons light, trans-fat-free margarine
1/4	cup finely chopped onion
2	tablespoons all-purpose flour
1-1/4	cups low-sodium vegetable broth
8	ounces fresh cod, cut into 1-inch chunks
1/2	cup frozen peas and carrots, thawed
1/2	teaspoon dried thyme leaves
1/4	teaspoon seafood seasoning (like Old Bay®)
1/4	teaspoon black pepper

1 In a medium saucepan, place potatoes in enough water to cover; bring to a boil. Cook 15 to 20 minutes or until fork-tender; drain well.

2 Return potatoes to saucepan. Add sour cream and garlic powder. Mash well; cover to keep warm.

3 Meanwhile, in another saucepan over medium heat, melt margarine; sauté onion 5 minutes. Whisk in flour and cook 1 minute. Whisk in broth and cook until slightly thickened. Add cod, peas and carrots, thyme, seafood seasoning, and pepper, and cook 10 minutes or until fish flakes easily with a fork.

4 Spoon fish mixture into individual dishes and dollop evenly with mashed potatoes Serve immediately.

Serving Suggestion

*If you want to brown the tops of the potatoes, spoon the filling into individual **ovenproof** casserole dishes and top them with the potatoes. Then, pop them into a 450°F oven, on the top shelf, for a couple of minutes.*

NUTRITION INFORMATION   **Choices/Exchanges,** 2 Starch, 2 Nonstarchy Vegetable, 2 Lean Protein, 1/2 Fat

Calories 330, Calories from Fat 60, **Total Fat** 7.0g, Saturated Fat 1.7g, Trans Fat 0.0g, **Cholesterol** 50mg, **Sodium** 360mg, **Potassium** 860mg, **Total Carbohydrate** 41g, Dietary Fiber 5g, Sugars 6g, **Protein** 25g, **Phosphorus** 270mg

Lemon Herb Tilapia Bundles

SERVES 4, 1 per serving

PREP TIME: 10 minutes
COOK TIME: 20 minutes

1	teaspoon garlic powder
4	sprigs fresh thyme leaves, removed from stems
1/8	teaspoon salt
1/4	teaspoon black pepper
4	(6-ounce) tilapia fillets
2	teaspoons canola oil
4	(12-inch) squares aluminum foil
4	slices lemon
2	cups broccoli florets
8	cherry tomatoes, cut in half

1 Preheat oven to 375°F.

2 In a small bowl, combine garlic powder, thyme, salt, and pepper. Brush both sides of tilapia evenly with canola oil, then sprinkle both sides with seasoning mixture.

3 Lay one fillet on each piece of foil, then place 1 lemon slice on each and top evenly with broccoli and cherry tomato halves. Loosely fold foil over fillets and seal edges.

4 Place foil packets on a rimmed baking sheet and roast 18 to 20 minutes or until fish flakes easily with a fork. (Be careful when opening the foil packets as the steam will be very hot.)

Did You Know?

Foil packet dinners like this can be prepped in advance and kept ready in the fridge for up to a day before cooking them. When you're ready to cook, just pop them in the oven or air fryer and, before you know it, dinner is on the table!

NUTRITION INFORMATION

Choices/Exchanges, 1 Nonstarchy Vegetable, 4 Lean Protein

Calories 200, Calories from Fat 50, **Total Fat** 6.0g, Saturated Fat 1.4g, Trans Fat 0.0g, **Cholesterol** 75mg, **Sodium** 160mg, **Potassium** 690mg, **Total Carbohydrate** 5g, Dietary Fiber 2g, Sugars 2g, **Protein** 35g, **Phosphorus** 295mg

Fresh Catch Salmon Cakes

SERVES 4, 2 per serving

PREP TIME: 10 minutes
COOK TIME: 30 minutes

1	pound fresh salmon fillets, skin removed
1/4	cup water
1	cup fresh spinach, chopped
1/2	cup plain bread crumbs
3	tablespoons light mayonnaise
1/4	cup liquid egg substitute
1/4	cup finely chopped celery
2	tablespoons finely chopped onion
2	teaspoons fresh lemon juice
1	teaspoon seafood seasoning (like Old Bay®)
1/2	teaspoon black pepper
2	teaspoons canola oil, divided

1 Preheat oven to 350°F.

2 Place salmon in an 8-inch square baking dish and add water. Cover with foil and bake 22 to 25 minutes or until fish flakes easily with a fork. Drain excess liquid and allow fish to cool.

3 Meanwhile, in a medium bowl, combine remaining ingredients except oil; mix well.

4 Once salmon is cool, flake it with your hands. Fold salmon into the spinach mixture until thoroughly combined. Form mixture into 8 equal patties.

5 In a large skillet over medium-low heat, heat 1 teaspoon oil until hot. Add patties and cook in batches, 3 to 4 minutes per side or until golden brown, adding remaining oil as needed. Serve immediately.

Serving Suggestion

These go great with our creamy Dijon Dipping Sauce! To make it, in a small bowl, combine 1/4 cup nonfat Greek yogurt, 1 teaspoon Dijon mustard, 1/4 teaspoon onion powder, and 1/8 teaspoon black pepper; mix well. This dipping sauce can be made ahead and stored in an airtight container in your refrigerator until ready to serve.

NUTRITION INFORMATION   Choices/Exchanges, 1 Starch, 4 Lean Protein, 1 Fat

Calories 280, Calories from Fat 110, **Total Fat** 12.0g, Saturated Fat 2.0g, Trans Fat 0.0g, **Cholesterol** 50mg, **Sodium** 430mg, **Potassium** 530mg, **Total Carbohydrate** 12g, Dietary Fiber 1g, Sugars 2g, **Protein** 28g, **Phosphorus** 300mg

Sensational Shrimp Fried "Rice"

SERVES 5, about 5 shrimp and 1 cup cauliflower mixture per serving

PREP TIME: 10 minutes
COOK TIME: 10 minutes

1	small head cauliflower, cut into florets
3	tablespoons sesame oil, divided
1	cup frozen peas and carrots, thawed
2	tablespoons reduced-sodium soy sauce
1	teaspoon garlic powder
1/2	teaspoon black pepper
8	ounces peeled and deveined medium shrimp*
2	tablespoons chopped scallions

1 To turn the cauliflower into "rice," place cauliflower in a food processor with a cutting blade attached. Pulse until it's the consistency of rice.

2 In a large skillet over medium heat, heat 2 tablespoons oil until hot. Add cauliflower and peas and carrots; cook 5 minutes, stirring often. Add soy sauce, garlic powder, and pepper; mix well. Transfer to a bowl; cover to keep warm.

3 In the same skillet, heat remaining 1 tablespoon oil; cook shrimp 3 to 5 minutes or until shrimp are pink and cooked through. Return cauliflower mixture to skillet, along with scallions; mix well. Cook 1 to 2 minutes or until heated through, and serve.

Riced veggies are becoming more common. In fact, you can find already-riced cauliflower in many markets. Just look in the produce section or in the freezer aisle. That means one less step for you to do!

*If possible, use fresh (never frozen) shrimp, or shrimp that are free of preservatives (for example, shrimp that have not been treated with salt or TPP [sodium tripolyphosphate]).

NUTRITION INFORMATION

Choices/Exchanges, 2 Nonstarchy Vegetable, 1 Lean Protein, 1-1/2 Fat

Calories 160, Calories from Fat 80, **Total Fat** 9.0g, Saturated Fat 1.3g, Trans Fat 0.0g, **Cholesterol** 75mg, **Sodium** 310mg, **Potassium** 430mg, **Total Carbohydrate** 8g, Dietary Fiber 3g, Sugars 3g, **Protein** 13g, **Phosphorus** 155mg

Asian-Style Scallops with Veggies

SERVES 4, 3 to 4 scallops and 1 cup vegetables per serving

PREP TIME: 15 minutes
COOK TIME: 15 minutes

3	teaspoons sesame oil, divided
2	carrots, sliced diagonally
1	celery stalk, sliced diagonally
1	small onion, cut into 1/2-inch half-moon pieces
4	ounces mushrooms, quartered
2	tablespoons reduced-sodium soy sauce
3	cloves garlic, minced
1/2	teaspoon ground ginger
1	pound sea scallops,* patted dry

1 In a large skillet over medium-high heat, heat 2 teaspoons oil until hot. Sauté carrots, celery, onion, and mushrooms 3 to 5 minutes or until just tender. Stir in soy sauce, garlic, and ginger, and heat 2 minutes.

2 Meanwhile, in another large skillet over medium-high heat, heat remaining 1 teaspoon oil until hot. Sauté scallops 3 to 4 minutes per side or until browned and firm in center. Serve scallops over vegetables.

*For perfectly cooked scallops, start with a heavy pan that's **not** nonstick. While the pan heats up on the stovetop, pat the scallops dry with a paper towel. Add the oil and once it's hot, add the scallops to the hot pan. You'll know when they're ready to flip when they develop a crust on the bottom and easily release from the pan.*

*If possible, use fresh (never frozen) scallops, or scallops that are free of preservatives (for example, scallops that have not been treated with salt or TPP [sodium tripolyphosphate]).

NUTRITION INFORMATION   **Choices/Exchanges,** 2 Nonstarchy Vegetable, 2 Lean Protein

Calories 150, Calories from Fat 40, **Total Fat** 4.5g, Saturated Fat 0.7g, Trans Fat 0.0g, **Cholesterol** 30mg, **Sodium** 500mg, **Potassium** 510mg, **Total Carbohydrate** 12g, Dietary Fiber 2g, Sugars 4g, **Protein** 17g, **Phosphorus** 365mg

Garlic Scampi over Angel Hair

SERVES 4, about 5 shrimp and 1 cup pasta per serving

PREP TIME: 15 minutes
COOK TIME: 20 minutes

1/2	pound whole-wheat angel hair pasta
4	tablespoons light, trans-fat-free margarine
4	cloves garlic, minced
1/4	teaspoon salt substitute
1/4	teaspoon black pepper
12	ounces peeled and deveined extra-large shrimp*
1/2	cup low-sodium vegetable broth
2	tablespoons fresh lemon juice
1	tablespoon chopped fresh parsley

1 Cook pasta according to package directions, omitting salt; drain and keep warm.

2 Meanwhile, in a large skillet over medium heat, melt margarine. Add garlic, salt substitute, and pepper, and sauté 1 minute. (Do not brown.) Stir in shrimp and cook 2 to 3 minutes or until just pink. Stir in broth, lemon juice, and parsley, and heat 2 minutes or until hot.

3 Pour shrimp mixture over pasta and toss until evenly coated. Serve immediately.

Shrimp is sold by the number of shrimp per pound. The smaller the number, the larger the shrimp. Although we prefer extra-large shrimp (26–30) for this dish (since it gives you more to bite into), if medium shrimp (36–40) are on sale, go ahead and make the swap.

*If possible, use fresh (never frozen) shrimp, or shrimp that are free of preservatives (for example, shrimp that have not been treated with salt or TPP [sodium tripolyphosphate]).

NUTRITION INFORMATION

Choices/Exchanges, 3 Starch, 2 Lean Protein

Calories 330, Calories from Fat 50, **Total Fat** 6.0g, Saturated Fat 1.3g, Trans Fat 0.0g, **Cholesterol** 140mg, **Sodium** 190mg, **Potassium** 530mg, **Total Carbohydrate** 45g, Dietary Fiber 6g, Sugars 3g, **Protein** 27g, **Phosphorus** 345mg

Veggie Pasta Toss with Chicken

SERVES 6, 2 cups per serving

PREP TIME: 15 minutes
COOK TIME: 25 minutes

3	tablespoons olive oil, divided
1	pound boneless, skinless chicken breasts, cut into 1-inch pieces
1/2	cup chopped onion
5	large tomatoes, cut into 1-inch chunks
4	cloves garlic, minced
1/4	teaspoon salt
1/4	teaspoon black pepper
8	ounces bow tie pasta
1	(14-ounce) can quartered artichoke hearts, drained
1/4	cup sliced fresh basil

1 In a large skillet over medium-high heat, heat 1 tablespoon oil until hot. Cook chicken 6 to 8 minutes or until no longer pink in center. Remove to a bowl; set aside.

2 In the same skillet, heat remaining 2 tablespoons oil until hot. Cook onion 5 minutes; add tomatoes, garlic, salt, and pepper, and cook 8 to 10 minutes or until tomatoes begin to break down, stirring occasionally.

3 Meanwhile, cook pasta according to package directions; drain.

4 Add artichokes and cooked chicken to the skillet; cook an additional 3 to 5 minutes or until heated through. Place pasta in a large bowl, add chicken mixture and basil, toss, and serve.

We are big fans of fresh basil. Whenever we want to add the freshness of basil to a dish like this, we toss it in right before serving. This way the flavor-packed oils in each leaf are released right before you take your first bite.

NUTRITION INFORMATION   **Choices/Exchanges,** 2 Starch, 2 Nonstarchy Vegetable, 2 Lean Protein, 1 Fat

Calories 350, Calories from Fat 90, **Total Fat** 10.0g, Saturated Fat 1.6g, Trans Fat 0.0g, **Cholesterol** 45mg, **Sodium** 260mg, **Potassium** 700mg, **Total Carbohydrate** 41g, Dietary Fiber 6g, Sugars 7g, **Protein** 24g, **Phosphorus** 245mg

Lightened-Up Lasagna Rollups

SERVES 8, 1 per serving

PREP TIME: 15 minutes
COOK TIME: 35 minutes

2	cups low-sodium spaghetti sauce, divided
1	(15-ounce) container fat-free ricotta cheese
1	cup shredded reduced-fat mozzarella cheese, divided
1/4	cup grated Parmesan cheese
1	(9-ounce) package frozen chopped spinach, thawed and squeezed dry
1	egg
1	teaspoon garlic powder
1/4	teaspoon salt
8	lasagna noodles, prepared according to package directions

1 Preheat oven to 375°F. Pour 1 cup spaghetti sauce over the bottom of a 9- × 13-inch baking dish.

2 In a large bowl, combine ricotta cheese, 1/2 cup mozzarella cheese, the Parmesan cheese, spinach, egg, garlic powder, and salt; mix until well blended.

3 Spoon cheese mixture over lasagna noodles, distributing evenly, and roll up tightly. Place rollups seam-side-down in baking dish; top with remaining sauce and sprinkle with remaining mozzarella cheese.

4 Bake 35 to 40 minutes or until heated through; serve.

Did You Know?

The curly edges on lasagna noodles were added as a way to help trap the sauce on top of the noodles. What a fun and practical way to ensure that every bite is mouthwateringly delicious!

NUTRITION INFORMATION   **Choices/Exchanges,** 1-1/2 Starch, 1/2 Fat-Free Milk, 1 Lean Protein, 1/2 Fat

Calories 220, Calories from Fat 50, **Total Fat** 6.0g, Saturated Fat 2.3g, Trans Fat 0.0g, **Cholesterol** 50mg, **Sodium** 280mg, **Potassium** 420mg, **Total Carbohydrate** 27g, Dietary Fiber 3g, Sugars 6g, **Protein** 17g, **Phosphorus** 260mg

Mediterranean Stuffed Portobellos

SERVES 4, 1 per serving

PREP TIME: 20 minutes
COOK TIME: 40 minutes

1/4	cup uncooked quinoa, (i.e., not cleaning stems) rinsed and drained
2/3	cup water
4	large portobello mushrooms, stems removed, and cleaned with damp paper towel
1	tablespoon olive oil
2	tablespoons balsamic vinegar
1	cup diced tomatoes
1/2	cup whole-wheat bread crumbs
1/2	cup fat-free crumbled feta cheese
1/4	cup chopped fresh basil
1	teaspoon garlic powder
1/4	teaspoon black pepper

1 Preheat oven to 375°F.

2 Place quinoa and water in a medium saucepan and bring to a boil over high heat. Reduce heat to low and simmer 15 to 18 minutes or until quinoa absorbs all the water.

3 Meanwhile, place mushrooms stem-side-up on an ungreased baking sheet. Brush with olive oil and evenly drizzle with vinegar.

4 In a medium bowl, combine cooked quinoa, tomatoes, bread crumbs, feta cheese, basil, garlic powder, and pepper; mix well. Evenly divide quinoa mixture (about 2/3 cup) between mushrooms and mound with a spoon.

5 Bake 15 to 20 minutes or until mushrooms are tender and filling is heated through. Serve immediately.

One of the things we learned early on about quinoa is that it needs to be rinsed and drained before it's cooked. To do this, simply place the quinoa in a fine-mesh strainer and run cold water over it for about 2 minutes. This removes the quinoa's natural coating, called saponin, which tends to make it taste bitter and soapy.

NUTRITION INFORMATION   **Choices/Exchanges,** 1 Starch, 1 Nonstarchy Vegetable, 1 Lean Protein, 1/2 Fat

Calories 160, Calories from Fat 40, **Total Fat** 4.5g, Saturated Fat 0.6g, Trans Fat 0.0g, **Cholesterol** 5mg, **Sodium** 150mg, **Potassium** 480mg, **Total Carbohydrate** 23g, Dietary Fiber 3g, Sugars 5g, **Protein** 9g, **Phosphorus** 200mg

Just-the-Right-Size Pepperoni "Pizza"

SERVES 2, 1/2 pizza per serving

PREP TIME: 5 minutes
COOK TIME: 10 minutes

1	(10-inch) spinach tortilla
2	tablespoons low-sodium marinara sauce
3	tablespoons shredded part-skim mozzarella cheese, divided
10	slices turkey pepperoni
1	tablespoon chopped green bell pepper
1	tablespoon chopped yellow bell pepper
1	tablespoon chopped red onion
1/2	teaspoon dried oregano
1/2	teaspoon garlic powder

1 Preheat oven to 425°F. Coat a rimmed baking sheet with cooking spray.

2 Place tortilla on baking sheet. Spread evenly with marinara sauce and sprinkle with 2 tablespoons cheese. Layer evenly with pepperoni slices, then sprinkle green and yellow bell peppers, red onion, oregano, garlic powder, and remaining 1 tablespoon cheese.

3 Bake 7 to 9 minutes or until cheese is melted and tortilla is crispy around the edges. Cut into wedges and enjoy.

Did You Know?

The American Diabetes Association recommends a minimum of 3 to 5 servings of nonstarchy vegetables a day. That's why we topped this fabulous favorite with a nutritious and colorful mix of peppers and onion!

NUTRITION INFORMATION   Choices/Exchanges, 1-1/2 Starch, 1 Lean Protein, 1/2 Fat

Calories 170, Calories from Fat 50, **Total Fat** 6.0g, Saturated Fat 2.2g, Trans Fat 0.3g, **Cholesterol** 20mg, **Sodium** 480mg, **Potassium** 190mg, **Total Carbohydrate** 22g, Dietary Fiber 2g, Sugars 2g, **Protein** 9g, **Phosphorus** 160mg

Baked Eggplant Planks

SERVES 8, 1 per serving

PREP TIME: 15 minutes
COOK TIME: 35 minutes

1	cup panko bread crumbs
2	tablespoons grated Parmesan cheese
1	teaspoon Italian seasoning
1	teaspoon garlic powder
1	tablespoon chopped fresh parsley
1/4	cup all-purpose flour
2	eggs, lightly beaten
1	tablespoon water
1	large eggplant, trimmed and cut lengthwise into 8 (1/2-inch) slices
	Cooking spray
1	cup low-sodium spaghetti sauce
1/2	cup (2 ounces) finely shredded part-skim mozzarella cheese

1 Preheat oven to 375°F. Coat 2 rimmed baking sheets with cooking spray.

2 In a shallow dish, combine bread crumbs, Parmesan cheese, Italian seasoning, garlic powder, and parsley; mix well. In another shallow dish, place flour. In a third shallow dish, whisk eggs and water.

3 Dip eggplant slices in flour, then egg, then bread crumb mixture, coating completely. Arrange slices in a single layer on baking sheets. Lightly spray tops of slices with cooking spray.

4 Bake 17 to 20 minutes, flip each slice, and bake an additional 10 minutes or until golden. Spoon spaghetti sauce evenly over each slice, then sprinkle with mozzarella cheese. Bake 3 to 5 minutes or until cheese is melted. Serve immediately.

Good for You!

We cut down on calories and fat in our version of eggplant parmesan. By baking it, rather than frying it, and using part-skim cheese and low-sodium sauce, we can still enjoy one of our favorite Italian dishes without feeling guilty! You can even make this in your air fryer, in batches. And since air fryers cook quickly, reduce the cooking time to about 14 to 16 minutes before adding the cheese.

NUTRITION INFORMATION   **Choices/Exchanges,** 1 Starch, 1 Nonstarchy Vegetable, 1/2 Fat

Calories 120, Calories from Fat 30, **Total Fat** 3.5g, Saturated Fat 1.4g, Trans Fat 0.0g, **Cholesterol** 50mg, **Sodium** 95mg, **Potassium** 310mg, **Total Carbohydrate** 17g, Dietary Fiber 3g, Sugars 5g, **Protein** 6g, **Phosphorus** 110mg

Sin-Sational Side Dishes

Fool 'Em Mashed Potatoes

SERVES 10, 1/2 cup per serving

PREP TIME: 10 minutes
COOK TIME: 30 minutes

1-1/2	pounds yellow gold potatoes, cut into chunks
1	(15-ounce) package frozen cauliflower florets
4	tablespoons light, trans-fat-free margarine
1/4	cup fat-free milk
1/2	teaspoon garlic powder
1/2	teaspoon salt
1/4	teaspoon black pepper

1 Place potatoes in a large pot with enough water to cover; bring to a boil. Cook 15 minutes. Add cauliflower, return to a boil, and cook 5 more minutes. Drain potatoes and cauliflower really well and return to pot.

2 Add margarine, milk, garlic powder, salt, and pepper; beat with an electric mixer until smooth and creamy. Serve piping hot.

Out of the Box
These mashed potatoes taste so rich and creamy, they'll never know there's cauliflower mixed in. (That's right, you're going to "fool 'em!") We suggest leaving the skins on the potatoes to give these more fiber, but that's up to you. And if you'd like to load these potatoes up with even more goodness, try stirring in a cup of fresh baby spinach, chopped cooked broccoli, or slivered scallions.

NUTRITION INFORMATION   Choices/Exchanges, 1 Starch

Calories 90, Calories from Fat 20, **Total Fat** 2.0g, Saturated Fat 0.5g, Trans Fat 0.0g, **Cholesterol** 0mg, **Sodium** 160mg, **Potassium** 320mg, **Total Carbohydrate** 15g, Dietary Fiber 2g, Sugars 1g, **Protein** 2g, **Phosphorus** 45mg

Pepperoni Pizza Tots

SERVES 4, 6 tots per serving

PREP TIME: 20 minutes
COOK TIME: 15 minutes

1/2	head cauliflower
2	egg whites
1/4	cup panko bread crumbs
1	tablespoon grated Parmesan cheese
1/2	teaspoon onion powder
1/2	teaspoon garlic powder
1/8	teaspoon salt
1/8	teaspoon black pepper
1/2	ounce (8 slices) turkey pepperoni, finely chopped
1/4	cup shredded part-skim mozzarella cheese

1 Preheat oven to 400°F. Coat a baking sheet with cooking spray.

2 Place cauliflower in a food processor with a cutting blade and pulse until it looks like rice. Place in a microwave-safe bowl, cover, and microwave 3 to 4 minutes or until tender. Let cool 10 minutes, stirring occasionally.

3 Add egg whites, bread crumbs, Parmesan cheese, onion powder, garlic powder, salt, and pepper; mix well. Stir in pepperoni and mozzarella cheese.

4 Form mixture into about 24 tot shapes (see photo). Place on baking sheet. Bake 10 minutes, turn tots over, and bake 6 to 8 more minutes or until golden and crispy.

Serving Suggestion

These can be a great side dish or a fun appetizer. Either way, serve these up with some low-sodium marinara sauce, and dip away! (And, if you'd rather buy already-riced cauliflower, just use 1-1/2 cups.)

NUTRITION INFORMATION   **Choices/Exchanges,** 1/2 Carbohydrate, 1 Lean Protein

Calories 80, Calories from Fat 20, **Total Fat** 2.0g, Saturated Fat 1.2g, Trans Fat 0.0g, **Cholesterol** 10mg, **Sodium** 260mg, **Potassium** 270mg, **Total Carbohydrate** 8g, Dietary Fiber 2g, Sugars 2g, **Protein** 7g, **Phosphorus** 105mg

Always-the-Best Potato Salad

SERVES 10, 1/2 cup per serving

PREP TIME: 15 minutes
COOK TIME: 30 minutes
CHILL TIME: 60 minutes

2	pounds red baby potatoes
1/2	cup reduced-fat mayonnaise
1/4	cup reduced-fat sour cream
1/2	teaspoon salt
1/4	teaspoon black pepper
2	hard-boiled eggs, chopped
1	cup chopped celery
1/2	cup finely diced red bell pepper
1/4	cup finely chopped red onion

1 Place potatoes in a large pot with enough water to cover. Bring to a boil and cook about 20 minutes or until fork-tender. Drain, let cool, then cut into 1-inch chunks.

2 In a large bowl, combine mayonnaise, sour cream, salt, and pepper; mix well.

3 Add potatoes, eggs, celery, bell pepper, and onion; mix well. Chill 1 to 2 hours before serving.

Good for You!

Put down the potato peeler! That's right, we suggest keeping the skins on your potatoes. The skin of the potato is full of nutrients, including fiber, iron, vitamin C, and more!

NUTRITION INFORMATION   **Choices/Exchanges,** 1 Starch, 1/2 Carbohydrate, 1/2 Fat

Calories 130, Calories from Fat 35, **Total Fat** 4.0g, Saturated Fat 1.0g, Trans Fat 0.0g, **Cholesterol** 40mg, **Sodium** 240mg, **Potassium** 410mg, **Total Carbohydrate** 20g, Dietary Fiber 2g, Sugars 2g, **Protein** 4g, **Phosphorus** 75mg

Potato & Squash Au Gratin

SERVES 6, 1/2 cup per serving

PREP TIME: 15 minutes
COOK TIME: 55 minutes

2	tablespoons light, trans-fat-free margarine
1	onion, thinly sliced
3	russet potatoes, thinly sliced
1/4	cup water
1	yellow squash, thinly sliced
1/4	teaspoon salt
1/4	teaspoon black pepper
1	cup fat-free half-and-half
1/2	cup shredded reduced-fat sharp cheddar cheese

1 Preheat oven to 425°F. Coat a 1-1/2-quart casserole dish with cooking spray.

2 In a large skillet over medium heat, melt margarine; sauté onion 10 minutes or until slightly browned.

3 Meanwhile, place potatoes in a microwave-safe bowl, add water, cover, and microwave 2 to 3 minutes or until slightly tender; drain.

4 Layer half the potatoes, squash, and onion in the casserole dish. Sprinkle with 1/8 teaspoon each salt and pepper. Pour 1/2 cup half-and-half over mixture and sprinkle with 1/4 cup cheese. Repeat.

5 Cover and bake 30 minutes, then uncover and bake an additional 12 to 15 more minutes or until fork-tender and the top is golden.

Test Kitchen. Mr. Food Hints & Tips

Now would be a good time to dig out that mandolin that you bought years ago. It's the ideal tool to cut all these veggies into perfectly even and thin slices. Don't forget to use the guard that comes with it, just to play it safe!

NUTRITION INFORMATION

Choices/Exchanges, 1-1/2 Starch, 1 Nonstarchy Vegetable, 1/2 Fat

Calories 160, Calories from Fat 35, **Total Fat** 4.0g, Saturated Fat 1.7g, Trans Fat 0.0g, **Cholesterol** 5mg, **Sodium** 230mg, **Potassium** 660mg, **Total Carbohydrate** 26g, Dietary Fiber 2g, Sugars 4g, **Protein** 7g, **Phosphorus** 185mg

Roasted Balsamic Sweet Potatoes

SERVES 6, 1/2 cup per serving

PREP TIME: 10 minutes
COOK TIME: 25 minutes

2	pounds sweet potatoes, peeled and cut into 1-inch cubes
1	small onion, cut into half-moon pieces
2	tablespoons canola oil
1/4	teaspoon salt
1/4	teaspoon black pepper
2	tablespoons balsamic vinegar
2	tablespoons real maple syrup

1 Preheat oven to 400°F.

2 In a medium bowl, toss sweet potatoes and onion with oil, salt, and pepper until evenly coated. Place sweet potato mixture in a single layer on a rimmed baking sheet. Roast 25 to 30 minutes or until fork-tender, tossing halfway through cooking.

3 Meanwhile, in a saucepan over low heat, combine vinegar and maple syrup; simmer about 5 minutes or until sauce is slightly reduced and thickened.

4 Place roasted potatoes in a bowl, drizzle with sauce, and toss to coat evenly. Serve immediately.

Did You Know?

Sweet potatoes are often considered a good choice for a person with diabetes because they are higher in dietary fiber, vitamins, and minerals than regular white potatoes.

NUTRITION INFORMATION   **Choices/Exchanges,** 1 Starch, 1/2 Carbohydrate, 1 Fat

Calories 150, Calories from Fat 45, **Total Fat** 5.0g, Saturated Fat 0.4g, Trans Fat 0.0g, **Cholesterol** 0mg, **Sodium** 135mg, **Potassium** 490mg, **Total Carbohydrate** 27g, Dietary Fiber 3g, Sugars 12g, **Protein** 2g, **Phosphorus** 55mg

Maple Sweet Potato Pancakes

SERVES 6, 2 per serving

PREP TIME: 10 minutes
COOK TIME: 10 minutes

1/2	cup rolled oats
1/3	cup whole-wheat flour
1	teaspoon baking powder
1/2	teaspoon ground cinnamon
1/4	teaspoon salt
1-1/2	cups cooked mashed sweet potato (see Tip)
1	egg, beaten
1	tablespoon real maple syrup (see Tip)

1 In a blender or food processor with a cutting blade, pulse oats until fine. In a medium bowl, combine oats, flour, baking powder, cinnamon, and salt; mix well. Stir in sweet potato, egg, and syrup until combined.

2 Coat a griddle or skillet with cooking spray and heat over medium heat. Spoon 1/4 cup of batter for each pancake and cook 2 to 3 minutes or until golden and some bubbles begin to form on top. Turn pancakes over and cook 1 to 2 minutes or until golden and center is firm. Repeat with remaining batter.

You can use leftover baked sweet potatoes for this recipe— just remove the skin and mash them. You can also peel 2 large sweet potatoes, cut them into chunks, and boil them until tender. After they're drained, mash them, and let them cool slightly. And by the way, we suggest real maple syrup here versus pancake syrup since the flavor is more intense and a little goes a long way.

NUTRITION INFORMATION   Choices/Exchanges, 2 Starch

Calories 130, Calories from Fat 15, **Total Fat** 1.5g, Saturated Fat 0.4g, Trans Fat 0.0g, **Cholesterol** 30mg, **Sodium** 190mg, **Potassium** 260mg, **Total Carbohydrate** 27g, Dietary Fiber 4g, Sugars 7g, **Protein** 4g, **Phosphorus** 170mg

Buttery Smooth Mac 'n' Cheese

SERVES 8, 1/2 cup per serving

PREP TIME: 20 minutes
COOK TIME: 40 minutes

2	tablespoons light, trans-fat-free margarine
1	tablespoon all-purpose flour
2	cups fat-free milk
2	cups shredded fat-free cheddar cheese
1	teaspoon dry mustard
1/4	teaspoon black pepper
1/2	(12-ounce) package frozen mashed butternut squash, thawed
8	ounces whole-grain elbow macaroni, cooked according to package directions
1	tablespoon grated Parmesan cheese

1 Preheat oven to 375°F. Coat a 1-1/2-quart baking dish with cooking spray.

2 In a large saucepan over medium heat, melt margarine. Whisk in flour and cook 1 minute. Add milk, whisking until smooth and mixture begins to thicken. Stir in cheddar cheese, dry mustard, and pepper, and cook until cheese is melted. Stir in squash and pasta; mix well.

3 Place mixture in baking dish and sprinkle with Parmesan cheese. Bake 25 to 30 minutes or until heated through and the top is golden.

Good for You!

By adding the mashed butternut squash, we can enjoy a rich and creamy consistency without adding lots of extra cheese or cream. And the best part is, it's so good, no one will ever know what you used to make it!

NUTRITION INFORMATION

Choices/Exchanges, 2 Starch, 1 Lean Protein

Calories 190, Calories from Fat 20, **Total Fat** 2.0g, Saturated Fat 0.5g, Trans Fat 0.0g, **Cholesterol** 5mg, **Sodium** 340mg, **Potassium** 210mg, **Total Carbohydrate** 28g, Dietary Fiber 3g, Sugars 5g, **Protein** 16g, **Phosphorus** 280mg

Spaghetti Squash & Mushroom Toss

SERVES 8, 1/2 cup per serving

PREP TIME: 15 minutes
COOK TIME: 45 minutes

1-1/2	pounds spaghetti squash
2	tablespoons olive oil
1/2	cup chopped onion
8	ounces sliced mushrooms
3	cloves garlic, minced
2	teaspoons chopped fresh parsley
2	tablespoons grated Parmesan cheese
1/4	teaspoon salt
1/4	teaspoon black pepper

1 Fill a soup pot with 1 inch water and place the whole squash in water. Bring to a boil over high heat, cover, and cook 25 to 30 minutes or until tender when pierced with a knife. Remove squash to a cutting board and allow to cool slightly.

2 Cut squash in half lengthwise, then use a spoon to remove and discard seeds. Scrape inside of squash with a fork, shredding into noodle-like strands; set aside.

3 In a large skillet over medium-high heat, heat oil until hot. Sauté onion 3 minutes, stirring occasionally. Add mushrooms and garlic and sauté 5 minutes, stirring occasionally. Stir in squash, parsley, Parmesan cheese, salt, and pepper; cook 5 minutes or until heated through. Serve immediately.

The easiest way to cook a spaghetti squash is to steam it like we do in this recipe. It's a lot easier than trying to cut the very hard, raw squash in half and then baking it. Keep this in mind if you have other recipes that require you to cook a spaghetti squash.

NUTRITION INFORMATION   Choices/Exchanges, 1 Nonstarchy Vegetable, 1 Fat

Calories 60, Calories from Fat 35, **Total Fat** 4.0g, Saturated Fat 0.7g, Trans Fat 0.0g, **Cholesterol** 0mg, **Sodium** 100mg, **Potassium** 170mg, **Total Carbohydrate** 5g, Dietary Fiber 1g, Sugars 2g, **Protein** 2g, **Phosphorus** 45mg

Toasted Almond Asparagus

SERVES 6, 1/2 cup per serving

PREP TIME: 5 minutes
COOK TIME: 15 minutes

1	pound fresh asparagus, trimmed and cut into 2-inch pieces
3	tablespoons light, trans-fat-free margarine
3	tablespoons sliced almonds
2	tablespoons thinly sliced roasted red bell pepper, drained
1/4	teaspoon black pepper

1 Place asparagus in a large skillet with enough water to cover; bring to a boil. Reduce heat to low and simmer about 3 minutes or until asparagus is crisp-tender; drain and set aside.

2 In the same skillet over medium heat, melt margarine; add almonds, and sauté 2 to 3 minutes or until golden. Add asparagus back to skillet along with the red bell pepper and black pepper. Cook 3 to 5 minutes or until heated through.

Toasting the almonds brings out their natural oils and adds lots of flavor to this dish. Just make sure you keep an eye on these while they're cooking because once they start browning they go very quickly.

NUTRITION INFORMATION　　　　　　　　　**Choices/Exchanges,** 1 Nonstarchy Vegetable, 1 Fat

Calories 60, Calories from Fat 40, **Total Fat** 4.5g, Saturated Fat 0.7g, Trans Fat 0.0g, **Cholesterol** 0mg, **Sodium** 60mg, **Potassium** 170mg, **Total Carbohydrate** 4g, Dietary Fiber 2g, Sugars 1g, **Protein** 2g, **Phosphorus** 50mg

Italian-Style Blistered Tomatoes

SERVES 4, 1/4 cup per serving

PREP TIME: 5 minutes
COOK TIME: 10 minutes

1	tablespoon olive oil
1	(12-ounce) container grape or cherry tomatoes
2	cloves garlic, slivered
2	tablespoons balsamic vinegar
	Sugar substitute equal to 2 teaspoons sugar

1 In a large skillet over high heat, heat oil until hot. Sauté tomatoes 4 to 5 minutes or until skins begin to brown and blister.

2 Stir in garlic and cook 1 minute. Add balsamic vinegar and sugar substitute and continue to cook 1 to 2 minutes or until mixture begins to thicken. Serve hot or at room temperature.

Serving Suggestion

Make this your new weeknight, go-to side dish. It's super-fast, super-cheap, and can turn any meal into an extra-special one. Just spoon them over some brown rice, make them the crowning touch over grilled chicken, or serve them alongside a fresh green salad. What an easy way to go from basic to restaurant-fancy!

NUTRITION INFORMATION

Choices/Exchanges, 1 Nonstarchy Vegetable, 1 Fat

Calories 50, Calories from Fat 30, **Total Fat** 3.5g, Saturated Fat 0.5g, Trans Fat 0.0g, **Cholesterol** 0mg, **Sodium** 5mg, **Potassium** 220mg, **Total Carbohydrate** 5g, Dietary Fiber 1g, Sugars 4g, **Protein** 1g, **Phosphorus** 25mg

Hawaiian Shaved Brussels Sprouts

SERVES 6, 1/2 cup per serving

PREP TIME: 10 minutes
COOK TIME: 10 minutes

1	tablespoon canola oil
1	(16-ounce) package Brussels sprouts, shaved (see Tip)
1	tablespoon brown sugar
1/2	teaspoon salt
1/4	teaspoon black pepper
1	(8-ounce) can pineapple tidbits, drained well
1	tablespoon chopped macadamia nuts

1 In a large skillet over medium heat, heat oil until hot. Sauté Brussels sprouts 5 to 7 minutes or until they begin to brown, stirring occasionally. (If you prefer your Brussels sprouts a little crispier, feel free to add a couple of extra minutes.)

2 Stir in brown sugar, salt, pepper, and drained pineapple; cook 3 to 5 minutes or until heated through. Sprinkle with macadamia nuts and serve.

There are a couple of ways to shave Brussels sprouts. One way to do it is by hand—just trim the stem-end of each sprout so that it sits flat on a cutting board. Then using a chef's knife, cut it into very thin slices. (Trimming the end prevents it from rolling around.) Another way is to use a food processor. Simply place the sprouts in the chute and let the slicing attachment do the work!

NUTRITION INFORMATION   **Choices/Exchanges,** 1/2 Carbohydrate, 1 Nonstarchy Vegetable, 1/2 Fat

Calories 80, Calories from Fat 30, **Total Fat** 3.5g, Saturated Fat 0.4g, Trans Fat 0.0g, **Cholesterol** 0mg, **Sodium** 210mg, **Potassium** 300mg, **Total Carbohydrate** 12g, Dietary Fiber 3g, Sugars 6g, **Protein** 3g, **Phosphorus** 50mg

Crispy Baked Bunny Fries

SERVES 6, 4 sticks per serving

PREP TIME: 10 minutes
COOK TIME: 25 minutes

3	carrots, peeled
2	tablespoons all-purpose flour
3/4	cup Italian-flavored bread crumbs
1	egg
1	tablespoon low-fat milk
	Cooking spray

1 Preheat oven to 400°F. Coat a baking sheet with cooking spray.

2 Cut each carrot in half widthwise, then cut each in half lengthwise, and then cut each piece so that they look like French fries.

3 Place flour in a shallow dish and bread crumbs in another shallow dish. In a third shallow dish, whisk egg with milk. Coat each carrot stick with flour, then dip in egg mixture, then coat completely with bread crumbs. Place on baking sheet and spray the carrots with cooking spray.

4 Bake 25 to 30 minutes or until crispy and golden, turning halfway through cooking.

Get the kids involved! After the carrots are cut, invite the kids to help bread them. When breading, remember to show them to use one hand for the wet ingredients and the other for the dry stuff. This will prevent them from breading their fingers, rather than the carrots.

NUTRITION INFORMATION   **Choices/Exchanges,** 1 Starch, 1/2 Fat

Calories 90, Calories from Fat 20, **Total Fat** 2.0g, Saturated Fat 0.5g, Trans Fat 0.0g, **Cholesterol** 30mg, **Sodium** 250mg, **Potassium** 150mg, **Total Carbohydrate** 15g, Dietary Fiber 1g, Sugars 2g, **Protein** 4g, **Phosphorus** 50mg

Orchard-Kissed Coleslaw

SERVES 7, 3/4 cup per serving

PREP TIME: 10 minutes
COOK TIME: None

1/2   cup plain fat-free Greek yogurt
1   tablespoon canola oil
    Sugar substitute equal to
    1 cup sugar (see page xi)
1   tablespoon yellow mustard
2   tablespoons apple cider vinegar
1/2   teaspoon salt
1/2   teaspoon black pepper
1   (16-ounce) package shredded
    coleslaw mix (4 cups; see Tip)
1   apple, cored and finely diced

1 In a large bowl, combine yogurt, oil, sugar substitute, mustard, cider vinegar, salt, and pepper; mix well.

2 Add coleslaw mix and apple; toss to mix well. Serve immediately or cover and chill until ready to serve.

If you prefer to shred your own cabbage instead of buying the pre-shredded mix from the store, go ahead! You'll get about 4 cups of shredded cabbage out of half a head of cabbage. Add some shredded carrot for color and you're good to go!

NUTRITION INFORMATION   **Choices/Exchanges,** 1/2 Carbohydrate, 1 Nonstarchy Vegetable, 1/2 Fat

Calories 70, Calories from Fat 20, **Total Fat** 2.5g, Saturated Fat 0.2g, Trans Fat 0.0g, **Cholesterol** 0mg, **Sodium** 210mg, **Potassium** 210mg, **Total Carbohydrate** 11g, Dietary Fiber 2g, Sugars 7g, **Protein** 2g, **Phosphorus** 40mg

Mediterranean Zucchini Casserole

SERVES 8, 1/2 cup per serving

PREP TIME: 15 minutes
COOK TIME: 40 minutes

4	cups shredded zucchini (about 3 to 4 zucchini)
1	egg, beaten
1/4	cup grated Parmesan cheese
2	tablespoons all-purpose flour
1	teaspoon onion powder
1/4	teaspoon salt
1/4	teaspoon black pepper
1/2	cup crumbled goat cheese, divided
1	tablespoon prepared pesto sauce, warmed

1 Preheat oven to 375°F. Coat a 1-1/2-quart baking dish with cooking spray.

2 In a large bowl, combine zucchini, beaten egg, Parmesan cheese, flour, onion powder, salt, and pepper; mix well. Stir in 1/4 cup goat cheese. Spoon mixture into casserole dish and top with remaining 1/4 cup goat cheese.

3 Bake 40 to 45 minutes or until center is heated through. Drizzle with pesto sauce right before serving.

Good for You!

When adding cheese to your dishes, keep in mind that it's best to use stronger, bolder cheeses. That way, you get lots of the taste you love while being able to cut back on the amount you use. More goodness, less guilt!

NUTRITION INFORMATION

Choices/Exchanges, 1/2 Carbohydrate, 1/2 Fat

Calories 60, Calories from Fat 30, **Total Fat** 3.5g, Saturated Fat 1.8g, Trans Fat 0.0g, **Cholesterol** 30mg, **Sodium** 160mg, **Potassium** 170mg, **Total Carbohydrate** 4g, Dietary Fiber 1g, Sugars 2g, **Protein** 4g, **Phosphorus** 70mg

Shortcut Butternut Risotto

SERVES 8, 1/2 cup per serving

PREP TIME: 10 minutes
COOK TIME: 20 minutes

1	tablespoon olive oil
1/4	cup finely chopped onion
1	cup uncooked arborio rice
1-1/2	cups (1/2-inch) butternut squash cubes
1/3	cup white wine
3	cups low-sodium vegetable broth, divided
2	tablespoons low-fat plain yogurt
2	tablespoons grated Parmesan cheese

1 In a large saucepan over medium-high heat, heat oil until hot; sauté onion 3 minutes or until golden. Add rice, squash, and wine, and cook until all the wine is absorbed. Add 1 cup broth, stirring constantly until liquid is nearly absorbed. Repeat process, adding remaining broth 1 cup at a time, stirring until each addition of broth is absorbed before adding next portion. Remove from heat.

2 Stir in yogurt and Parmesan cheese until thoroughly combined. Serve immediately

Did You Know?

The reason that we specifically call for arborio rice in this recipe is because it's a starchier rice that's perfect for risotto. As it cooks, the starch gives the dish its creamy, smooth texture.

NUTRITION INFORMATION   Choices/Exchanges, 1-1/2 Starch

Calories 120, Calories from Fat 20, **Total Fat** 2.0g, Saturated Fat 0.5g, Trans Fat 0.0g, **Cholesterol** 0mg, **Sodium** 70mg, **Potassium** 190mg, **Total Carbohydrate** 21g, Dietary Fiber 2g, Sugars 2g, **Protein** 2g, **Phosphorus** 70mg

Desserts That Make You Smile

Oh-My-Goodness Chocolate Cake

SERVES 24, 1 piece per serving

PREP TIME: 15 minutes
BAKE TIME: 25 minutes
CHILL/COOL TIME: 5-1/2 hours

1	(16-ounce) package sugar-free devil's food cake mix
1-1/4	cups water
1/3	cup canola oil
3/4	cup liquid egg substitute
1	(4-serving-size) package instant sugar-free chocolate pudding mix
2	cups fat-free milk
1	(8-ounce) container sugar-free frozen whipped topping, thawed

1 Preheat oven to 350°F. Coat a 9- × 13-inch baking dish with cooking spray.

2 In a large bowl with an electric mixer, beat cake mix, water, oil, and egg substitute until thoroughly combined. Pour batter into baking dish. Bake 25 to 30 minutes or until toothpick inserted in center comes out clean. Let cool 1 hour.

3 Using a wooden spoon handle, poke holes all over top of cake.

4 In a medium bowl, whisk pudding mix and milk until slightly thickened, but still pourable. Reserve 1/2 cup pudding and place in another bowl. Pour remaining pudding into holes, spreading any excess over cake. Refrigerate 30 minutes.

5 Fold whipped topping into reserved pudding and spread evenly over cake. Refrigerate at least 4 hours or overnight. Cut into 24 pieces when ready to serve.

NUTRITION INFORMATION

Choices/Exchanges, 1 Carbohydrate, 1 Fat

Calories 120, Calories from Fat 45, **Total Fat** 5.0g, Saturated Fat 1.5g, Trans Fat 0.0g, **Cholesterol** 0mg, **Sodium** 210mg, **Potassium** 120mg, **Total Carbohydrate** 19g, Dietary Fiber 1g, Sugars 9g, **Protein** 3g, **Phosphorus** 95mg

Apple Lover's Coffee Cake

SERVES 10, 1 slice per serving

PREP TIME: 10 minutes
BAKE TIME: 30 minutes

1-1/2	cups all-purpose flour
	Sugar substitute equal to 1/2 cup sugar (see page xi)
1-1/2	teaspoons baking powder
1/2	teaspoon ground cinnamon
1/4	teaspoon salt
4	tablespoons (1/4 cup) light, trans-fat-free margarine, melted
2	eggs
3	tablespoons fat-free milk
2	tart apples, peeled, cored, and chopped (about 2-1/2 cups)

Cinnamon Pecan Topping

	Brown sugar substitute equal to 1 tablespoon brown sugar (see page x)
1/4	cup chopped pecans
1/2	teaspoon ground cinnamon
2	tablespoons light, trans-fat-free margarine, melted

1 Preheat oven to 350°F. Coat a 9-inch round cake pan with cooking spray.

2 In a large bowl, beat flour, sugar substitute, baking powder, 1/2 teaspoon cinnamon, the salt, 1/4 cup margarine, and eggs until thoroughly combined. Stir in milk and apples, then spread batter into cake pan.

3 To make Cinnamon Pecan Topping, in a small bowl, combine ingredients; mix well and sprinkle evenly over batter.

4 Bake 30 to 35 minutes or until toothpick inserted in center comes out clean. Serve warm or allow to cool, then cover until ready to serve.

Did You Know?

Cinnamon contains a large number of antioxidants, which can help keep you healthy. Studies have also shown that this spice may aid in lowering blood pressure and blood glucose.

NUTRITION INFORMATION

Choices/Exchanges, 1-1/2 Carbohydrate, 1 Fat

Calories 160, Calories from Fat 50, **Total Fat** 6.0g, Saturated Fat 1.4g, Trans Fat 0.0g, **Cholesterol** 35mg, **Sodium** 180mg, **Potassium** 85mg, **Total Carbohydrate** 21g, Dietary Fiber 1g, Sugars 5g, **Protein** 4g, **Phosphorus** 125mg

Triple-Berry Cheesecake

SERVES 16, 1 slice and 2 tablespoons fruit mixture per serving

PREP TIME: 20 minutes
BAKE/COOK TIME: 50 minutes
CHILL/COOL TIME: 2 hours

1-1/2	cup quick-cooking oats
1/2	cup walnuts
	Brown sugar substitute equal to 1/2 cup brown sugar (see page x)
4	tablespoons (1/4 cup) light, trans-fat-free margarine
2	(8-ounce) packages fat-free cream cheese, softened
	Sugar substitute equal to 1/2 cup granulated sugar (see page xi)
1	tablespoon all-purpose flour
1-1/2	teaspoons vanilla extract
3	eggs
1/4	cup reduced-fat milk
1	cup reduced-fat sour cream

Berry Sauce

2	cups strawberry halves
3/4	cup blueberries
1	cup raspberries
1/3	cup water
	Sugar substitute equal to 2 tablespoons granulated sugar (see page xi)

1 Preheat oven to 350°F.

2 In a food processor, pulse oats and walnuts until finely chopped. In a medium bowl, combine oat mixture, brown sugar substitute, and margarine. Press mixture firmly into bottom of an 8-inch springform pan. Bake 10 minutes.

3 Meanwhile, in a large bowl with an electric mixer, beat cream cheese and sugar substitute until creamy. Beat in flour and vanilla until well combined. Add eggs, one at a time, beating well after each addition. Beat in milk and sour cream, just until blended. Pour batter into crust.

4 Bake 40 to 45 minutes or until center is just set and slightly jiggly. Turn oven off and leave in oven for 30 minutes. Remove from oven and let cool at room temperature. When cool, refrigerate 4 hours or overnight.

5 Meanwhile, to make Berry Sauce, in a saucepan over medium heat, combine strawberries, blueberries, raspberries, water, and sugar substitute. Cook 10 to 15 minutes or until fruits start to break down and sauce starts to thicken up.

6 Before serving, gently remove side of springform pan. Place cake on serving platter, cut into slices, and serve with Berry Sauce.

BASIC NUTRITIONAL VALUES

Choices/Exchanges, 1 Carbohydrate, 1 Lean Protein, 1 Fat

Calories 160, Calories from Fat 60, **Total Fat** 7.0g, Saturated Fat 2.0g, Trans Fat 0.0g, **Cholesterol** 45mg, **Sodium** 230mg, **Potassium** 210mg, **Total Carbohydrate** 16g, Dietary Fiber 2g, Sugars 7g, **Protein** 8g, **Phosphorus** 235mg

Chocolate Raspberry Cream Roll

SERVES 15, 1/2-inch slice per serving

PREP TIME: 20 minutes
BAKE TIME: 7 minutes
CHILL/COOL TIME: 2 hours

1/2	cup all-purpose flour
1/4	cup plus 2 teaspoons unsweetened cocoa, divided
3/4	teaspoon baking powder
1/4	teaspoon salt
4	eggs
1/3	cup granulated sugar
1/4	cup water
2	teaspoons vanilla extract

Cream Cheese Filling

6	ounces fat-free cream cheese, softened
2	tablespoons confectioners' sugar
1-1/2	cups frozen reduced-fat whipped topping, thawed
1	cup raspberries

1. Preheat oven to 375°F. Line a 10- × 15-inch rimmed baking sheet with wax paper and coat with cooking spray. In a small bowl, combine flour, 1/4 cup cocoa, the baking powder, and salt; set aside.

2. In a large bowl with an electric mixer on high speed, beat eggs 3 to 4 minutes or until very thick. Gradually beat in sugar. Beat in water and vanilla until well blended. Reduce speed to low and beat in flour mixture just until smooth. Pour into baking sheet. Bake 7 to 9 minutes or until a toothpick inserted in center comes out clean.

3. Sprinkle a clean kitchen towel with remaining 2 teaspoons cocoa and invert cake onto towel. While still hot, peel off wax paper and roll up cake and towel jelly roll–style, starting from a narrow end. Allow to cool on a wire rack.

4. Meanwhile to make the Cream Cheese Filling, in a medium bowl, beat cream cheese and confectioners' sugar until smooth. Fold in whipped topping and raspberries.

5. Unroll cake and remove towel. Spread raspberry filling over cake and roll it up again. Place on a serving platter, seam-side-down. Cover loosely and chill at least 1 hour or until ready to serve.

NUTRITION INFORMATION   **Choices/Exchanges,** 1 Carbohydrate, 1/2 Fat

Calories 100, Calories from Fat 25, **Total Fat** 3.0g, Saturated Fat 1.6g, Trans Fat 0.0g, **Cholesterol** 50mg, **Sodium** 160mg, **Potassium** 105mg, **Total Carbohydrate** 15g, Dietary Fiber 1g, Sugars 7g, **Protein** 4g, **Phosphorus** 135mg

Pumpkin Spice Bars

SERVES 24, 1 piece per serving

PREP TIME: 15 minutes
BAKE TIME: 25 minutes
COOL TIME: 30 minutes

1	cup all-purpose flour
1-1/2	cups whole-wheat flour
1/3	cup sugar
2	teaspoons ground cinnamon
1	teaspoon ground cloves
1/2	teaspoon ground nutmeg
1-1/2	teaspoons baking soda
1/2	cup molasses
2	egg whites
1	cup water
1/2	cup canned pure pumpkin
1/2	cup raisins
1/4	cup walnuts
1/2	teaspoon confectioners' sugar for sprinkling

1 Preheat oven to 350°F. Coat a 9- × 13-inch baking dish with cooking spray.

2 In a large bowl, combine all-purpose flour, whole-wheat flour, sugar, cinnamon, cloves, nutmeg, and baking soda; mix well. Add molasses, egg whites, water, and pumpkin; stir until thoroughly mixed. Stir in raisins and walnuts. Spread evenly in baking dish.

3 Bake 25 to 30 minutes or until toothpick inserted in center comes out clean. Let cool completely, then cut into pieces. Sprinkle with confectioners' sugar before serving.

Out of the Box

This makes a great change-of-pace dessert for your fall holiday spread or potluck. It's easy to make and take, and it's full of the flavors of the season!

NUTRITION INFORMATION

Choices/Exchanges, 1-1/2 Carbohydrate

Calories 100, Calories from Fat 10, **Total Fat** 1.0g, Saturated Fat 0.1g, Trans Fat 0.0g, **Cholesterol** 0mg, **Sodium** 85mg, **Potassium** 180mg, **Total Carbohydrate** 21g, Dietary Fiber 2g, Sugars 10g, **Protein** 2g, **Phosphorus** 45mg

Orange Dream Poke Cake

SERVES 21, 1 piece per serving

PREP TIME: 15 minutes
BAKE TIME: 25 minutes
COOL/CHILL TIME: 6 hours

1	(16-ounce) package sugar-free white cake mix
1	cup water
1/3	cup canola oil
3/4	cup liquid egg substitute
1	(4-serving-size) package sugar-free orange gelatin
1	cup boiling water
1/2	cup cold water
1	(4-serving-size) package instant sugar-free vanilla pudding mix
1	cup fat-free milk
1	(8-ounce) container sugar-free whipped topping, thawed

1 Preheat oven to 350°F. Coat a 9- x 13-inch baking dish with cooking spray.

2 In a large bowl with an electric mixer, beat cake mix, water, oil, and egg substitute until thoroughly combined. Pour batter into baking dish. Bake 25 to 30 minutes or until toothpick inserted in center comes out clean. Let cool 1 hour.

3 Using a serving fork, poke holes (20–25) all over top of cake. In a medium bowl, dissolve gelatin in boiling water, then stir in cold water. Slowly pour this mixture over cake so that it fills the holes. Refrigerate 1 hour.

4 In a large bowl, whisk pudding mix and milk until thickened. Fold in whipped topping until thoroughly combined. Spread mixture evenly over cake. Refrigerate 4 hours or overnight. Cut into 21 pieces when ready to serve.

Most of the time we use the handle of a wooden spoon to make the holes for our poke cakes, but for this recipe we suggest you use a large serving fork, since you're infusing the cake with a flavored gelatin rather than a thicker pudding. Not only is this cake creative, but it's super-moist too!

NUTRITION INFORMATION

Choices/Exchanges, 1 Carbohydrate, 1 Fat

Calories 140, Calories from Fat 60, **Total Fat** 7.0g, Saturated Fat 2.1g, Trans Fat 0.0g, **Cholesterol** 0mg, **Sodium** 260mg, **Potassium** 55mg, **Total Carbohydrate** 19g, Dietary Fiber 0g, Sugars 1g, **Protein** 2g, **Phosphorus** 130mg

Almond Blackout Cake

SERVES 16, 1 slice per serving

PREP TIME: 30 minutes
BAKE TIME: 25 minutes
COOL/CHILL TIME: 45 minutes

1-1/2	cups all-purpose flour
	Sugar substitute equal to 3/4 cup sugar (see page xi)
1/4	cup unsweetened cocoa powder
1	teaspoon baking soda
1/4	teaspoon salt
1	cup water
3/4	cup fat-free sour cream
1	egg
1	teaspoon vanilla extract

Chocolate Ganache

1/2	cup sugar-free chocolate chips
1/4	cup fat-free evaporated milk
1	teaspoon almond extract
2	teaspoons sliced almonds

1 Preheat oven to 350°F. Coat a 9-inch cake pan with cooking spray.

2 In a large bowl, whisk flour, sugar substitute, cocoa powder, baking soda, and salt. Add water, sour cream, egg, and vanilla and beat with an electric mixer until smooth. Pour batter into cake pan.

3 Bake 25 to 30 minutes or until toothpick inserted in center comes out clean. Let cool 10 minutes, then remove from pan and finish cooling on wire rack.

4 To make Chocolate Ganache, place chocolate chips in a small bowl. In a small microwave-safe bowl, heat evaporated milk in microwave 30 to 45 seconds or until hot. Pour over chocolate chips and let sit 3 minutes. Add almond extract, then stir until smooth.

5 Pour ganache over cake and let drip down sides. Sprinkle with almonds. Let sit until ganache hardens or refrigerate 15 minutes. Serve or store in refrigerator until ready to enjoy.

Good for You!

Traditionally, ganache is made by pouring hot, heavy cream over chocolate chips and whisking it together until the chocolate melts. We've lightened things up by replacing the heavy cream with fat-free evaporated milk and swapping out regular chocolate chips with sugar-free ones. Even though we've lightened this one up, it still tastes decadently delicious!

NUTRITION INFORMATION

Choices/Exchanges, 1 Carbohydrate, 1/2 Fat

Calories 100, Calories from Fat 20, **Total Fat** 2.5g, Saturated Fat 1.2g, Trans Fat 0.0g, **Cholesterol** 15mg, **Sodium** 140mg, **Potassium** 90mg, **Total Carbohydrate** 16g, Dietary Fiber 1g, Sugars 2g, **Protein** 3g, **Phosphorus** 55mg

Frosted Carrot Cake Cupcakes

SERVES 10, 1 per serving

PREP TIME: 10 minutes
BAKE TIME: 20 minutes
COOL TIME: 30 minutes

1-1/2	cups all-purpose flour
	Brown sugar substitute equal to 1/2 cup brown sugar (see page x)
1	teaspoon ground cinnamon
1/2	teaspoon baking soda
1/4	teaspoon salt
1/2	cup unsweetened applesauce
1/3	cup canola oil
2	teaspoons white vinegar
1-1/2	teaspoons vanilla extract
1	cup shredded carrot

Vanilla Frosting

1	(4-serving size) package sugar-free instant vanilla pudding mix
1	cup fat-free milk
2	cups reduced-fat frozen whipped topping, thawed

1 Preheat oven to 350°F. Place 10 cupcake liners in muffin tins.

2 In a large bowl, combine flour, brown sugar substitute, cinnamon, baking soda, and salt; mix well. In a medium bowl, combine applesauce, oil, vinegar, vanilla, and carrots; mix well. Stir carrot mixture into flour mixture until thoroughly combined. Divide batter evenly into cupcake liners.

3 Bake 18 to 22 minutes or until toothpick comes out clean. Let cool.

4 Meanwhile, to make Vanilla Frosting, in a medium bowl, whisk pudding mix and milk; refrigerate 5 minutes. Remove from refrigerator and fold in whipped topping. Spread about 1 tablespoon of frosting over each cupcake and serve.

Portion Size Matters

Rather than tempt ourselves with a big slice of mile-high carrot cake layered with lots of rich, cream cheese frosting, we like to bake these perfectly sized and lightened-up carrot cake cupcakes. They're sweet, satisfying, and guilt-free!

NUTRITION INFORMATION

Choices/Exchanges, 2 Carbohydrate, 1-1/2 Fat

Calories 210, Calories from Fat 80, **Total Fat** 9.0g, Saturated Fat 2.2g, Trans Fat 0.0g, **Cholesterol** 0mg, **Sodium** 270mg, **Potassium** 125mg, **Total Carbohydrate** 29g, Dietary Fiber 1g, Sugars 7g, **Protein** 3g, **Phosphorus** 130mg

Portion-Perfect Nutty Chocolate Cakes

SERVES 8, 1 per serving

PREP TIME: 15 minutes
BAKE TIME: 30 minutes
COOL TIME: 30 minutes

1	(15-ounce) can reduced-sodium black beans, rinsed and drained
1/3	cup canned pure pumpkin
1/3	cup unsweetened applesauce
1/2	cup liquid egg substitute
1/3	cup unsweetened cocoa powder
	Sugar substitute equal to 1/2 cup sugar (see page xi)
1-1/2	teaspoons baking powder
1/4	teaspoon salt
1	teaspoon vanilla extract
3	tablespoons peanut butter baking chips, chopped
2	tablespoons chopped dry roasted peanuts

1 Preheat oven to 350°F. Coat 8 muffin tin cups with cooking spray.

2 In a blender or a food processor with a cutting blade, combine black beans, pumpkin, applesauce, egg substitute, cocoa powder, sugar substitute, baking powder, salt, and vanilla; process until smooth. Stir baking chips into batter. Pour batter evenly into muffin cups. Evenly sprinkle tops of each with peanuts.

3 Bake 30 to 35 minutes or until toothpick comes out clean. Let cool 10 minutes, then remove to a wire rack to cool completely.

Did You Know?

What keeps these so moist is the combo of black beans, pumpkin, and applesauce. These ingredients also help lighten up this dessert, since they replace the butter and oil. Just wait till you taste how good these are!

NUTRITION INFORMATION

Choices/Exchanges, 1/2 Starch, 1/2 Carbohydrate, 1/2 Fat

Calories 120, Calories from Fat 30, **Total Fat** 3.5g, Saturated Fat 2.0g, Trans Fat 0.0g, **Cholesterol** 0mg, **Sodium** 260mg, **Potassium** 250mg, **Total Carbohydrate** 16g, Dietary Fiber 4g, Sugars 5g, **Protein** 7g, **Phosphorus** 180mg

Chocolate Chip Meringue Cookies

SERVES 5, 3 per serving

PREP TIME: 5 minutes
BAKE TIME: 75 minutes
COOL TIME: 15 minutes

2	egg whites, at room temperature
1/2	teaspoon cream of tartar
1	tablespoon sugar
1/2	teaspoon vanilla extract
1/4	cup mini chocolate chips

1 Preheat oven to 250°F. Coat a baking sheet with cooking spray.

2 In a large bowl with an electric mixer, beat egg whites with cream of tartar until soft peaks form. Add sugar and vanilla, and beat until sugar is dissolved and stiff peaks form. Fold in chocolate chips.

3 Drop 15 tablespoonfuls of mixture onto baking sheet, each about 1 inch in diameter.

4 Bake 30 minutes. Turn off oven and allow cookies to stay in oven for an additional 45 minutes. Remove from oven and place on a wire rack to cool completely. Serve or store in an airtight container until ready to serve.

The key to great meringue cookies is to make sure that the sugar is totally dissolved, so that they're not gritty. The cookies should also be about the same size, so that they bake evenly. Finally, it's important to keep them in the oven until they're fully dried as this is what makes them light and crisp.

NUTRITION INFORMATION

Choices/Exchanges, 1/2 Carbohydrate, 1 Fat

Calories 70, Calories from Fat 30, **Total Fat** 3.5g, Saturated Fat 2.0g, Trans Fat 0.0g, **Cholesterol** 0mg, **Sodium** 25mg, **Potassium** 115mg, **Total Carbohydrate** 10g, Dietary Fiber 1g, Sugars 9g, **Protein** 2g, **Phosphorus** 15mg

Double-Chocolate Chippers

SERVES 15, 2 per serving

PREP TIME: 10 minutes
BAKE TIME: 10 minutes
COOL TIME: 10 minutes

1-1/3	cups all-purpose flour
3	tablespoons unsweetened cocoa powder
1/2	teaspoon baking soda
1/8	teaspoon salt
8	tablespoons (1/2 cup) light, trans-fat-free margarine, softened
	Brown sugar substitute equal to 1 cup brown sugar (see page x)
1	large egg
1	teaspoon vanilla extract
1	tablespoon fat-free milk
1/3	cup sugar-free chocolate chips

1 Preheat oven to 375°F. Coat baking sheets with cooking spray.

2 In a medium bowl, whisk flour, cocoa powder, baking soda, and salt; set aside.

3 In a large bowl with an electric mixer, beat margarine, brown sugar substitute, egg, and vanilla until light and fluffy. Slowly add flour mixture and milk to margarine mixture until thoroughly combined. Stir in chocolate chips. Drop by teaspoonfuls onto baking sheets.

4 Bake 9 to 11 minutes or until set around edges. Let cool 2 minutes then remove to wire racks to cool completely.

NUTRITION INFORMATION

Choices/Exchanges, 1 Carbohydrate, 1 Fat

Calories 120, Calories from Fat 40, **Total Fat** 4.5g, Saturated Fat 1.7g, Trans Fat 0.0g, **Cholesterol** 10mg, **Sodium** 115mg, **Potassium** 60mg, **Total Carbohydrate** 17g, Dietary Fiber 1g, Sugars 3g, **Protein** 2g, **Phosphorus** 35mg

Cranberry Lemon Drops

SERVES 18, 2 per serving

PREP TIME: 10 minutes
BAKE TIME: 10 minutes
COOL TIME: 10 minutes

1	(16-ounce) package sugar-free yellow cake mix
1/3	cup canola oil
2	eggs
2	teaspoons lemon extract
1	teaspoon lemon zest
1/4	cup reduced-sugar, dried cranberries

1 Preheat oven to 350°F. Coat baking sheets with cooking spray.

2 In a large bowl with an electric mixer, beat cake mix, oil, and eggs until well blended. Add lemon extract, lemon zest, and cranberries; mix well. Drop by teaspoonfuls onto baking sheets.

3 Bake 10 to 14 minutes or until cookies are firm. Remove cookies to a wire rack to cool completely. Serve or store in an airtight container until ready to serve.

Lemon zest adds a fresh burst of flavor to this dessert! To zest a lemon, you can either use a zester or a fine grater. Just make sure you don't go too deep or you'll get to the white, bitter part, also known as the pith.

NUTRITION INFORMATION
Choices/Exchanges, 1-1/2 Carbohydrate, 1 Fat

Calories 130, Calories from Fat 60, **Total Fat** 7.0g, Saturated Fat 1.3g, Trans Fat 0.0g, **Cholesterol** 20mg, **Sodium** 200mg, **Potassium** 25mg, **Total Carbohydrate** 21g, Dietary Fiber 1g, Sugars 1g, **Protein** 2g, **Phosphorus** 95mg

Friendship is a
sheltering tree.
-Samuel Taylor Coleridge

Mini Peach Pies

SERVES 8, 1 per serving

PREP TIME: 15 minutes
BAKE TIME: 15 minutes
COOL TIME: 10 minutes

8	wonton wrappers
	Cooking spray
1	tablespoon light, trans-fat-free margarine
2-1/2	cups fresh finely chopped peeled peaches (5 to 6 peaches)
2	tablespoons brown sugar
1/2	teaspoon ground cinnamon
1/4	cup water
1	teaspoon cornstarch
1/4	cup sugar-free frozen whipped topping, thawed

1 Preheat oven to 350°F. Coat 8 muffin tin cups with cooking spray. Place a wonton wrapper in sprayed muffin cups, and press into bottom and up sides. Lightly spray wrappers with cooking spray. Bake 6 minutes or until golden. Allow to cool slightly, then remove.

2 Meanwhile, in a skillet over medium heat, melt margarine; add peaches, brown sugar, and cinnamon and cook 6 to 8 minutes or until softened.

3 In a small bowl, whisk water and cornstarch. Stir mixture into peaches and heat 1 to 2 minutes or until thickened. Spoon peach mixture evenly into wonton cups and allow to cool. Dollop with whipped topping and serve.

If your peaches are really sweet, then you may be able to cut down on the brown sugar. We usually find that the sweetest peaches are available in late summer, which is peak season for this juicy fruit.

NUTRITION INFORMATION   Choices/Exchanges, 1/2 Fruit, 1/2 Carbohydrate

Calories 80, Calories from Fat 10, **Total Fat** 1.0g, Saturated Fat 0.5g, Trans Fat 0.0g, **Cholesterol** 0mg, **Sodium** 60mg, **Potassium** 190mg, **Total Carbohydrate** 16g, Dietary Fiber 2g, Sugars 10g, **Protein** 2g, **Phosphorus** 25mg

Bubblin' Strawberry Rhubarb Cobbler

SERVES 5, 1 per serving

PREP TIME: 10 minutes
BAKE TIME: 30 minutes

2	cups sliced fresh strawberries
2	cups chopped fresh or frozen and thawed rhubarb
1	tablespoon honey
1/3	cup rolled oats
2	tablespoons brown sugar
1/4	teaspoon ground cinnamon
1	tablespoon light, trans-fat-free margarine

1 Preheat oven to 350°F.

2 In a medium bowl, combine strawberries, rhubarb, and honey; mix well. Spoon mixture evenly into 5 (8-ounce) ramekins or oven-proof serving dishes.

3 In a small bowl, stir oats, brown sugar, cinnamon, and margarine until crumbly. Sprinkle evenly over fruit. Place ramekins on baking sheet.

4 Bake 30 to 35 minutes or until bubblin' hot and tops are golden. Serve warm.

Did You Know?
Fruit can be eaten in exchange for other sources of carbohydrates in your meal plan, such as starches, grains, or dairy. Keep that in mind when you're craving something sweet!

NUTRITION INFORMATION **Choices/Exchanges,** 1/2 Fruit, 1/2 Carbohydrate, 1/2 Fat

Calories 90, Calories from Fat 15, **Total Fat** 1.5g, Saturated Fat 0.4g, Trans Fat 0.0g, **Cholesterol** 0mg, **Sodium** 20mg, **Potassium** 270mg, **Total Carbohydrate** 18g, Dietary Fiber 3g, Sugars 11g, **Protein** 2g, **Phosphorus** 45mg

Caramel Poached Pears

SERVES 6, 1 (1/2 pear) per serving

PREP TIME: 10 minutes
COOK TIME: 20 minutes

1	cup no-sugar-added apple juice
2	cups water
3	pears, peeled and cut in half
1/4	cup sugar-free caramel sauce

1 In a large skillet over medium heat, bring apple juice and water to a boil. Add pear halves, then cover and cook 20 to 25 minutes or until tender, turning occasionally and basting with liquid.

2 Remove from liquid and serve warm with caramel sauce (about 2 teaspoons each).

Good for You!

Pears are high in fiber and vitamins C, K, B2, and more. They're a great choice for people with diabetes and they taste amazing too!

NUTRITION INFORMATION

Choices/Exchanges, 1 Fruit, 1/2 Carbohydrate

Calories 80, Calories from Fat 0, **Total Fat** 0.0g, Saturated Fat 0.0g, Trans Fat 0.0g, **Cholesterol** 0mg, **Sodium** 25mg, **Potassium** 115mg, **Total Carbohydrate** 22g, Dietary Fiber 3g, Sugars 9g, **Protein** 0g, **Phosphorus** 15mg

Ice Cream Sundae Cake

SERVES 16, 1/2-inch slice per serving

PREP TIME: 10 minutes
FREEZE TIME: 6 hours

1	quart no-sugar-added vanilla ice cream, softened
10	sugar-free fudge-dipped vanilla wafers, coarsely chopped
8	maraschino cherries, chopped
1/4	cup sugar-free hot fudge
1/2	cup sugar-free frozen whipped topping, thawed

1 Line an 8- × 4-inch loaf pan with plastic wrap.

2 In a large bowl, combine ice cream, chopped wafers, and cherries; mix well. Spoon into loaf pan, pressing down to mold to pan. Cover with plastic wrap and freeze 6 hours or until firm.

3 Right before serving, invert ice cream loaf onto serving platter and remove plastic wrap. Drizzle with hot fudge and top with whipped cream. Serve immediately.

If, for some strange reason, you have any leftovers, cut this cake into slices and freeze them on a baking sheet. Once they're firm, wrap each slice in plastic wrap. That way you can easily grab a slice whenever you get the hankering for something sinfully delicious.

NUTRITION INFORMATION   **Choices/Exchanges,** 1 Carbohydrate, 1 Fat

Calories 100, Calories from Fat 40, **Total Fat** 4.5g, Saturated Fat 2.5g, Trans Fat 0.0g, **Cholesterol** 5mg, **Sodium** 55mg, **Potassium** 90mg, **Total Carbohydrate** 14g, Dietary Fiber 2g, Sugars 3g, **Protein** 2g, **Phosphorus** 35mg

Coffee Shop Granita

SERVES 10, 1/4 cup per serving

PREP TIME: 10 minutes
FREEZE TIME: 6 hours

2 cups strong brewed hot coffee
Sugar substitute equal to
1/4 cup sugar (see page xi)
1 cup sugar-free frozen whipped
topping, thawed, divided

1 In a large bowl, stir coffee and sugar substitute until sugar substitute is dissolved. Let cool. Add 1/2 cup whipped topping and stir until thoroughly combined. Pour mixture evenly into ice cube trays and freeze 6 hours or until solid.

2 Place ice cubes in a blender or food processor and pulse until ice is shaved. Spoon evenly into serving dishes and serve immediately or freeze until ready to serve. When ready to serve, top each with a teaspoon-sized dollop of whipped topping.

If you're worried about the caffeine keeping you up at night, we recommend making this sweet treat with a decaffeinated brew. You'll get the same tasty results without the caffeine buzz!

NUTRITION INFORMATION   Choices/Exchanges, Free food

Calories 20, Calories from Fat 10, **Total Fat** 1.0g, Saturated Fat 0.8g, Trans Fat 0.0g, **Cholesterol** 0mg, **Sodium** 5mg, **Potassium** 30mg, **Total Carbohydrate** 1g, Dietary Fiber 0g, Sugars 1g, **Protein** 0g, **Phosphorus** 5mg

Index

Note: Page numbers followed by *ph* refer to photographs.

My Favorite Recipes

Recipe Name   **Page Number**

_____

_____

_____

_____

_____

_____

_____

_____

_____

_____

_____

_____

_____

_____

_____

_____

_____

_____

_____

_____